Adding Sense

In recent years, with the rise of new media, the phenomenon of "multimodality" (communication via a number of modes simultaneously) has become central to our everyday interaction. This has given rise to a new kind of literacy that is rapidly gaining ground as an area of research. A companion to *Making Sense*, which explored the functions of reference, agency, and structure in meaning, *Adding Sense* extends this analysis with two more surrounding functions. It addresses the ways in which "context" and "interest" add necessary sense to immediate objects of meaning, proposing a "transpositional grammar" to account for movement across these different forms of meaning. *Adding Sense* weaves its way through philosophy, semiotics, social theory, and the history of ideas. Its examples cross a range of social contexts, from the meaning universes of the First Peoples, to the new forms of meaning that have emerged in the era of digitally-mediated communication.

MARY KALANTZIS was from 2006 to 2016 Dean of the College of Education at the University of Illinois, Urbana-Champaign.

BILL COPE is a Professor in the College of Education at the University of Illinois, Urbana-Champaign. His research interests include theories and practices of pedagogy, and new technologies of representation and communication.

MARY KALANTZIS AND BILL COPE have co-authored *Making Sense: Reference, Agency, and Structure in a Grammar of Multimodal Meaning* (2020).

Adding Sense

Context and Interest in a Grammar
of Multimodal Meaning

Mary Kalantzis
University of Illinois at Urbana-Champaign

Bill Cope
University of Illinois at Urbana-Champaign

CAMBRIDGE
UNIVERSITY PRESS

University Printing House, Cambridge CB2 8BS, United Kingdom

One Liberty Plaza, 20th Floor, New York, NY 10006, USA

477 Williamstown Road, Port Melbourne, VIC 3207, Australia

314–321, 3rd Floor, Plot 3, Splendor Forum, Jasola District Centre,
New Delhi – 110025, India

79 Anson Road, #06–04/06, Singapore 079906

Cambridge University Press is part of the University of Cambridge.

It furthers the University's mission by disseminating knowledge in the pursuit of
education, learning, and research at the highest international levels of excellence.

www.cambridge.org
Information on this title: www.cambridge.org/9781108495349
DOI: 10.1017/9781108862059

First published 2020

Printed in the United Kingdom by TJ International Ltd, Padstow Cornwall

A catalogue record for this publication is available from the British Library.

ISBN 978-1-108-49534-9 Hardback

Gunther Kress, *in memoriam*.

Contents

Figures

Key to In-text Markers

Footnote to a source[123]
Cross-reference to ideas discussed or lives described in another section of this book[§1.2.3] or its companion volume, *Making Sense*[§MS1.2.3]
Related media to be found online at meaningpatterns.net*

Part 0 Meaning

> A grammar is a resource for meaning, the critical functioning semiotic by means of which we pursue our everyday life. It therefore embodies a theory of everyday life; otherwise it cannot function in this way ... A grammar is a theory of human experience.   M.A.K. Halliday.[1]

We started the companion volume to this book, *Making Sense*, with this quote from Michael Halliday. We start again with this quote because, for grammar to be a theory of human experience and to embody a theory of everyday life, it needs to go beyond the conventional frames of linguistics and language-centered theories of meaning. We want to agree with Halliday. We also want to create an account of meaning that is as good as his word.

Making Sense addressed three meaning functions – reference, agency, and structure – in terms roughly parallel to Halliday's three "metafunctions," ideational, interpersonal, and textual.[§MS0.3a] This volume "adds sense" by exploring two additional functions that we call "context" and "interest."

Halliday speaks to "situation" and "purpose," which might be considered roughly parallel to our context and interest. However, although they are an important part of his account of language, for him they sit outside of the meaning of a written text or a spoken utterance. They are around his system, helping to explain it, but not in it. In this book we elevate context and interest to full meaning functions – always present, always integral to meaning, always multimodal.

---

[1] M.A.K Halliday, 2000 [2002], "Grammar and Daily Life: Concurrence and Complementarity," pp. 369–83 in *On Grammar*, The Collected Works of M.A.K. Halliday, Volume 1, edited by J.J. Webster, London: Continuum, pp. 369–70. A note on the dates of references: we're incidentally interested in the history of ideas, so when there are two dates, the older is the date when the edition we are referencing was first published and, if not in English, in its original language. The newer is the date of the edition we have at hand, for the purposes of page referencing.

In the "transpositional grammar" that we develop in these two volumes, the following five functions can always be found in any meaning. *Making Sense* addressed the first three. Now *Adding Sense* addresses the last two.

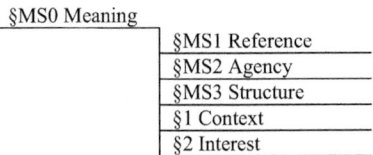

Fig. 0: Meaning and its functions

The concepts we develop for each function are at a sufficient level of generality to be applied across all forms of meaning, not just text and speech.

As for "transposition," we refer to two vectors of changeability, differences that can be made in the ways meanings are expressed. The first is meaning form. The same things can be meant in the forms of text, image, space, object, body, sound, and speech. But whenever they are meant in a different form, the meaning is never quite the same. This is why we refer to multimodality, one meaning form supplementing another.

The second dimension of transposition is meaning function. All five are always present, but we can for moments turn the focus of our attention to meaning in terms of one of the five functions or another. These are always-possible, alternative orientations to meaning. Then, within each function, meanings are constantly on the move. There is no categorical fixity to meaning. There are no stable structures. This, however, does not prevent us from creating an account of the patterning. Rather, the account must explain movability. Function is process.

A note on who this book is for. Theoretically, this book and its companion volume aim to create a framework with which to account for meaning that crosses the disciplinary paradigms of semiotics, linguistics (mainly pragmatics), the sociology of action, cultural and media studies, philosophy (ontology), and computer science (ontology again, or data structures). We hope that it will provide a framework by means of which a range of practitioners can work together, sharing a common conceptual framework across education, communications, media, architecture, the arts, design, computing, and more.

These disciplines and their related work practices have their own distinctive but mostly separate frameworks for understanding their respective domains of action. But all deal in their daily practices with meanings in their profound multimodality. The challenge we have set ourselves in this pair of books is to develop a more widely encompassing framework, able to extend, even in modest ways, these repertoires of theory and practice – to "add sense," if you will.

Along the way, we bring into the conversation key thinkers across these disciplines, so addressing the patterning of meaning in a cross-disciplinary way. Our perspective traverses a range of cultures and historical moments. Casting the intellectual net widely, we contend, can generate new insights. We also analyze the affordances of digital as well as legacy media in representation and communication, and their peculiar scope for meaning and action. In these respects, this book has a somewhat encyclopedic quality.

Some practical notes about the reading of this book: when an idea or person is discussed in more detail elsewhere in this or the companion volume, we include a cross-reference marker like this.[§0.0] We hope this will support the different interests of readers, and non-linear readings. Also, it wasn't practical to include in a book format the kinds of media and number of images we wanted, so these have been put on the web at meaningpatterns.net and links to these marked in the text like this.[*] The text can be read without reference to these media.

§0.1   Meaning Form

> **Meaning Form.** *Possibilities for meaning, the patterning of which is shaped by their material media: text, image, space, object, body, sound, and speech.*

This book and its companion volume outline a theory of multimodal meaning. Rather than using "mode" to name its manifestations, we choose to describe the different patterning of text, image, space, object, body, sound, and speech as "forms."

Meaning forms	Text	Image	Space	Object	Body	Sound	Speech

Fig. 0.1: Meaning forms

Multimodality is a useful term for us, because it captures processes of interaction and overlay between and across forms. Multimodality also names a rich, emerging literature, the shape of which has been defined in large part by the work of our long-time friend and colleague, Gunther Kress.[2] Multimodality has emerged as well from educational concerns, in particular by the widely-felt

---

[*] http://meaningpatterns.net

[2] Gunther Kress, 2009, *Multimodality: A Social Semiotic Approach to Contemporary Communication*, London: Routledge.

need to extend the old canons of literacy to embrace the "multiliteracies" of contemporary representation and communication.[*] This is work we have undertaken at times with Kress, or in parallel with his work.[3]

In this grammar, we stay with Michael Halliday's notion of metafunction, as does Kress,[4] though we simply name its components "functions," modifying and extending the theory somewhat. In our exploration of multimodality, we also want to stay faithful to the new tradition Kress has established, pushing Halliday's approach beyond speech and text. However, at various points we find ourselves revising the terminology of multimodality and reconsidering details in its ways of thinking and seeing.

So why describe the constituent components of multimodality as "meaning forms" rather than modes? While there is wide agreement in the literature that multimodality is an important focus for analysis, particularly in the era of digital media, there is little agreement about the conceptualization of modes. In Kress, modes are what you will have them to be: photography or layout; image or language.[5] Hartmut Stöckl says mode is a "rather heterogenous concept," with at least three strands of meaning: organized code systems such as music, image, and language; channels of sensory perception defined by visual, auditive, tactile, olfactory, and gustative signs; and media determinations, of which printed poster, podcast, or recorded music might be examples.[6] Jay Lemke says we "ought to question whether the division of meaning-making into language, gesture, drawing, action etc. is not mostly artificial."[7]

However, delineation of what we now call forms of meaning is for us an important task. For instance, a central question: Is language a meaning form with a unitary character, or are text (closely allied with image and space) and speech (closely allied with sound and body) different meaning forms – as different from each other as text is from image or space and speech is from sound or body? The multimodality literature points us towards this question, but the blurry elisions that come with the word "mode" do not allow the kinds of conceptual distinction that we need to make before we can attempt an answer.

---

[*] http://meaningpatterns.net/kress

[3] Bill Cope and Mary Kalantzis, eds. 2000, *Multiliteracies: Literacy Learning and the Design of Social Futures*, London: Routledge; Mary Kalantzis, Bill Cope, Eveline Chan, and Leanne Dalley-Trim, 2016, *Literacies* (Edn 2), Cambridge: Cambridge University Press.

[4] Gunther Kress, 2009, *Multimodality: A Social Semiotic Approach to Contemporary Communication*, London: Routledge.

[5] Gunther Kress, 2014. "What Is Mode?" pp. 60–75 in *The Routledge Handbook of Multimodal Analysis*, edited by C. Jewitt, London: Routledge, p. 65.

[6] Hartmut Stöckl, 2014, "Semiotic Paradigms and Multimodality," pp. 274–86 in ibid., pp. 276–77.

[7] Jay Lemke, 2014, "Multimodality, Identity, Time," pp. 165–75 in ibid., p. 166.

"Mode," moreover, means something rather different in Halliday's scheme from the new literature on multimodality – it is an again rather vaguely and inconsistently specified "role ... being played by language and other semiotic systems in a situation." It includes a peculiar mix of things such as rhetorical orientation and turn-taking, for instance monologue or dialogue.[8]

"Mode" in ordinary language also tends to mean quite different things. It can mean media, process, or method – three more, distinct meanings. This lack of conceptual clarity is the reason we prefer to call the different aspects of multimodality meaning forms, rather than modes.

In support of "form," there is a neat contrast of form with function. This is occasionally taken up in linguistics. Canale and Swain and then Calderon and Cummins distinguish between language teaching that focuses on the forms of language (learning the rules of phonology, morphology, syntax, and lexis) and the communicative or functional approaches to language-in-use that they advocate in their applied linguistics.[9] We extend this distinction to other forms of meaning, but not to favor one side of the dichotomy over the other.

Besides, the term "form" has a long and storied history in philosophy and the social sciences, evolving through series of distinctions that we believe are helpful in the work of tracing patterns in meaning. This history is without doubt fraught, but the ways in which it is fraught are themselves revelatory. If we work through the contentious alternatives the term raises, we can reach a point where we have a useful tool for analyzing this dimension of meaning.

Plato was first. We inhabit an imperfect and unreliably varied and uncertain material world, he said, and the task of philosophy is to determine essential and eternal meanings – ideas or forms – "that which essentially is: ... the Beautiful, Good ..., Bigness, Health, Strength."

Says Plato's interlocutor, Socrates, "he who will do this most perfectly, who approaches the object with thought alone, ... tries to track down reality pure and by itself ... because the body confuses the soul and does not allow it to acquire truth." For "the soul reasons best when none of the ... senses troubles it, neither hearing, nor pain, nor sight nor pleasure, but when it is most by itself, taking leave of the body and as far as possible having no contact with it in its search for reality ... Philosophy ... persuades the soul to withdraw from the senses."[10]

[8] M.A.K. Halliday and Christian M.I.M. Matthiessen, 2014, *Halliday's Introduction to Functional Grammar* (Edn 4), Milton Park: Routledge, pp. 33–34.

[9] Michael Canale and Merrill Swain, 1980, "Theoretical Bases of Communicative Approaches to Second Language Teaching and Testing," *Applied Linguistics* 1:1–47; Margarita Calderon and Jim Cummins, 1982, "Communicative Competence in Bilingual Education, Theory and Research, Packet I: Language Proficiency Acquisition, Assessment, and Communicative Behavior, Series B, Teacher Edition," Bilingual Education Teacher Training Packets, Dallas, TX: Evaluation, Dissemination and Assessment Center, Dallas Independent School District.

[10] Plato, *c*.399–347 BCE [1997], "Phaedo," in *Complete Works*, edited by J.M. Cooper, Indianapolis, IN: Hackett, pp. 57, 72.

When it comes to writing, it is the very materiality of its form that dooms it to inadequacy. Those who "put trust in writing" fall prey to "forgetfulness into the soul" because it is "external and depends on signs that belong to others, instead of trying to remember from the inside, completely on their own."[11] Unmediated, pure thought works from mind, not media. It is wholly cognitive, without material distraction.

In the philosophical split between idealism and materialism,[§MS3.1] Plato is unabashedly an idealist. However, to achieve his idealism he needs a dualistic conception of the world that recognizes the pervasive – albeit, in his conception, corrupting – presence of the materialized meanings. He needs to be a dualist in order to be able to favor one side over the other, to prioritize the ideal form over its material manifestations and sensible apprehensions.

Vilém Flusser calls this kind of contempt for the raw, resistant world, the "Platonic prejudice."[12] Gilles Deleuze[§MS3.1.1b] criticizes the "Platonic motivation: to distinguish essence from appearance, intelligible from sensible, Idea from image, original from copy, and model from simulacrum. Copies are ... well-founded pretenders, guaranteed by resemblance; simulacra are like false pretenders, built upon a dissimilarity, implying an essential perversion or a deviation."[13]

Later and still in the idealist mold, Immanuel Kant[§MS3.3e] follows Plato's notion of idea or form, where pure intellectual intuition represents "maximum perfection" in an elevated place of philosophical thinking, and where "the principle of cognition" is "exempt from the laws of the senses."[14] Kant makes a distinction here between empirical and pure concepts. "The pure concept, in so far as it has its origin in the understanding alone (not in the pure image of sensibility), is called a notion. A concept formed from notions and transcending the possibility of experience is an idea or concept of reason."[15] So, form is the categorical ideal, and Kant places this at the center of his system of reason.

Flusser and Deleuze are just two in a long line of the materialist critics of Platonic forms and their derivatives. Of course, we must join them. The ideal and the sensuously material are immanent in each other. They are not opposites where one side is to be prioritized over the other as a site of essential meaning.

---

[11] Ibid., pp. 551–52.
[12] Vilém Flusser, 1991 [2014], *Gestures*, translated by N.A. Roth, Minneapolis: University of Minnesota Press, pp. 47, 43.
[13] Gilles Deleuze, 1969 [1990], *The Logic of Sense*, translated by M. Lester, New York: Columbia University Press, p. 256.
[14] Immanuel Kant, 1770 [1894], *Kant's Inaugural Dissertation*, translated by W.J. Eckoff, New York: Columbia College, pp. 55, 77.
[15] Immanuel Kant, 1787 [1933], *Critique of Pure Reason*, translated by N.K. Smith, London: Macmillan, p. 314.

However, in the millennia-long discussion of form, some distinctions emerge that are worth maintaining in a theory of meaning. This grammar contains many refractions of the form/sensuous matter distinction, principally in contrast of form with medium[§1.4] made in our theory of context, where form is the shaping and patterning of meaning offered by their material realizability in textual, imaged, spaced, objectified, embodied, sounded, and spoken artifacts of meaning – the affordances of these media. Form is the meaning that can be made. Medium is the stuff from which the meaning has been made. Medium determines the scope for meanability that is form.

Another refraction of form in this grammar is the play of the ideal (now close to Plato's sense of form, but without his one-sided favoring) and the material that in tandem constitutes structure.[§MS3.1] Another: between meanings-in (systemic patterning as forms) and meanings-for (meanings put to work in their messy variability).[§MS0.3.3] And another: designs (the forms of patterning, conventional by virtue of their repeatability) and designing (their uniquely voiced and never-repeatable reconstruction).[§MS3.2] Still another: concepts in their criterial generality and instances in their unique specificity.[§MS1.1]

If the first half of these theoretical contrasts resonates with form and the second part with matter, these remain Platonic distinctions. But for us, these contrasts must be accompanied by foundational disagreements with their originator: neither can be prior, either in terms of process or in its explanatory power. Nor can they be these dualisms. They are immanences, the one impossible to mean without the other.

§0.1a M.M. Bakhtin's Formal Method of Literary Scholarship

M.M. Bakhtin (and, or, co-author or pseudonym P.N. Medvedev)[§2.1.2b] addresses the question of form in his critique of the formalist school of literary criticism.[*] As his counterpoint he quotes Roman Jakobson,[§1.4.1a] then a prominent Russian formalist poet and literary critic, who says that poetry is in the form of its expression "indifferent to the object of the utterance."[16] Literary form is isolated from its socially functional content.

Bakhtin is not unsympathetic to an agenda that analyzes form. But he does criticize the formalists for their one-sided attentions to form. The formalists made a distinction between literary forms such as poetry, characterized by a catalogue of "devices," and practical, communicative language without such formalisms. Formalist analysis focuses on the question of "literariness" – how

---

[*] http://meaningpatterns.net/bakhtin

[16] P.N. Medvedev, 1928 [1985], *The Formal Method in Literary Scholarship: A Critical Introduction to Sociological Poetics*, Cambridge, MA: Harvard University Press, p. 87.

a literary work is different from the vernacular, the everyday. But what about the "exceptionally complicated" patterning of practical language itself? Bakhtin asks.[17] Why should form be just a question for literary and other high arts?

The formalists, Bakhtin goes on to say, neglect "the material presence of the work." Material media and literary or artistic form work together in a process of mutual generation. "[O]nly by being realized in words, actions, clothing, and organizations of people and things – in a word, in some definite semiotic material."[18]

Bakhtin also criticizes the formalists for their failure to attend to social content. Of formal devices: "Whatever plot or motif we choose, we always reveal the purely ideological values which shape its structure." Analyzing an image, for instance, the question is not just of its form, but its capacity "to generalize, typify, symbolically widen its significance" with its "ideological meaning" – or what we would term its interest. "Every concrete utterance is a social act. At the same time that it is an individual material complex, a phonetic, articulatory, visual act, the utterance is also part of a social reality." If we "tear the utterance out of social intercourse and ... we lose the organic unity of all its elements. ... Social evaluation always establishes an organic tie between the presence of the utterance and the generality of its meaning."[19]

Bakhtin's conclusion: in formalism, "[a]rt is reduced to empty combinations of forms."[20] So, we must do analysis of form, but never separated from its materialization. Nor can form be separated from its social content.

Jakobson went on to be a founder of structuralist linguistics. When he moved from literary analysis to analysis of speech, his focus was on phonemic form rather than its social content or meaning. We might mount critiques of this and other structuralisms along the same lines as Bakhtin's, including Saussure's favoring of system over socio-historical expression,[§MS3d] and Chomsky's favoring a universal grammar over the social pragmatics of language.[§MS3.1.2f] All of these systems require both sides of a form/content distinction, or what Halliday calls system/realization.[21] The problem for formalisms and structuralisms, we would say in sympathy with Bakhtin, is to prioritize one side over the other.

In this grammar, our version of Bakhtin's literary form/social content distinction is located in the contrast meaning-form/meaning-function. Form and function are integral to each other. Neither is prior.

---

[17] Ibid., pp. 110, 93.   [18] Ibid., pp. 95, 7.   [19] Ibid., pp. 17, 119, 118, 120, 121, 126.

[20] Ibid., p. 90.

[21] David G. Butt, 2008, "The Robustness of Realizational Systems," pp. 59–83 in *Meaning in Context: Strategies for Implementing Intelligent Applications of Language Studies*, edited by J.A. Webster, London: Continuum.

§0.2   Meaning Function

> **Meaning Function.** *What meanings do: they refer to things and action; they relate agents; they hang together in coherent relationships; they connect to their surroundings; and they express purposes.*

Halliday comes to a theory of context in part through the influence of his doctoral supervisor, J.R. Firth, who in turn drew inspiration from renowned anthropologist Bronisław Malinowski.[§1.1.3b] Firth took a junior position at London School of Economics while Malinowski was a professor there. Malinowski had drawn a large part of his inspiration from the Trobriand Islanders, but some as well from the nineteenth century German linguist Philipp Wegener, for whom language only has meaning to the extent that it has been invested with meaning by context, where inferences are necessarily made from situation.[22]

Taking Malinowski's notion of "context of situation," Firth defined meaning as "a property of the mutually relevant people, things, events in the situation. Some of the events are the noises made by the speakers." The relevant features of a situation are participants present in their embodied persons, their verbal and non-verbal actions, relevant objects, and the effects of verbal actions.[23] These, Halliday systematized into three metafunctions of lexicogrammar: ideational, interpersonal, and textual.

But Halliday then did something that Firth had not. On another dimension, he created a system of planes or strata. Danish linguist Louis Hjelmslev had already introduced planes when he created a two-plane system, distinguishing the expression plane from the content plane. In Hjelmslev, the expression plane has two inseparable aspects: the expression substance, which in the case of speech he calls a sound chain; and the form of its expression in a system of sounding. The content plane has two aspects as well: the substance of thought, and the form of its expression in the meaning-system that is language.[24] In the terminology we are

---

[22] Philipp Wegener, 1885 [1971], "The Life of Speech," pp. 111–294 in *Speech and Reason: Language Disorder and Mental Disease*, edited by D.W. Abse, Charlottesville: University Press of Virgina, p. 270; Brigitte Nerlich, 1990, *Change in Language: Whitney, Bréal, and Wegener*, London: Routledge, pp. 162, 181; J.R. Firth, 1968, *Selected Papers of J.R. Firth, 1952–1959*, Bloomington: Indiana University Press, p. 139; David Butt and Rebekah Wegener, 2008, "The Work of Concepts: Context and Metafunction in the Systemic Functional Model," pp. 590–618 in *Continuing Discourse on Language: A Functional Perspective*, Volume 2, edited by R. Hasan, C.M.I.M. Matthiessen and J.J. Webster, London: Equinox.

[23] J.R. Firth, 1937 [1986], *The Tongues of Men*, Westport, CT: Greenwood Press, pp. 110–13; J.R. Firth, 1968, *Selected Papers of J.R. Firth, 1952–1959*, Bloomington: Indiana University Press, pp. 138, 14, 147–48.

[24] Louis Hjelmslev, 1963 [1970], *Language: An Introduction*, translated by F.J. Whitfield, Madison: University of Wisconsin Press, pp. 99, 106; Louis Hjelmslev, 1943 [1961],

adopting in this grammar, Hjelmslev's expression plane is what we call form, and the content plane we would call function. We agree with Hjelmslev that any such planes are inseparably co-creating; neither is to be prioritized.

Halliday created five strata, each one realizing the next: phonetics > phonology > lexicogrammar > semantics > context of situation.[25] Sometimes he adds a sixth, context of culture, so establishing a top-level stratum of situation types.[26] Halliday's lexicogrammar, semantics, situation, and culture might be taken more or less to align with Hjelmslev's content plane, and phonetics and phonology with Hjelmslev's expression plane.[27]

Just as the planes are inseparable for Hjelmslev, so are strata for Halliday. Ruqaiya Hasan puts it this way: the strata are layered into a series of "bidirectional relations, ... a dialectic between content and form on the one hand and between system and instance, on the other." This means that the stratum of "context must be taken as integral to all linguistic theory."

The strata of expression and lexicogrammar in Halliday's system are crosscut by ideational, interpersonal, and textual functions.[*] The commensurate functional realities in the semantic and context strata are accounted for in a theory of register where they are named field, tenor, and mode respectively.[28] "By functional," says Halliday, "we simply mean that language is doing something in a context."[29]

In the Hallidayan tradition, the overall framework comes in many permutations. J.R. Martin's strata are phonology > grammar > semantics > register > genre > ideology.[30] Sometimes there are more metafunctions, four perhaps if

---

[*] http://meaningpatterns.net/hh-strata

Prolegomena to a Theory of Language, translated by F.J. Whitfield, Madison: University of Wisconsin Press, pp. 48–57.

[25] M.A.K. Halliday and Christian M.I.M. Matthiessen, 2014, *Halliday's Introduction to Functional Grammar* (Edn 4), Milton Park: Routledge, p. 31.

[26] M.A.K. Halliday, 1999, "The Notion of 'Context' in Language Education," pp. 1–24 in *Text and Context in Functional Linguistics*, edited by M. Ghadessy, Amsterdam: John Benjamins, p. 16.

[27] M.A.K. Halliday and Christian M.I.M. Matthiessen, 2014, *Halliday's Introduction to Functional Grammar* (Edn 4), Milton Park: Routledge, p. 26; Rebekah Wegener, 2016, "Studying Language in Society and Society through Language: Context and Multimodal Communication," pp. 227–48 in *Society in Language, Language in Society: Essays in Honour of Ruqaiya Hasan*, edited by W.L. Bowcher and J.Y. Liang, Berlin: Springer, pp. 235–36.

[28] M.A.K. Halliday and Christian M.I.M. Matthiessen, 2014, *Halliday's Introduction to Functional Grammar* (Edn 4), Milton Park: Routledge, p. 33; Annabelle Lukin, Alison Moore, Maria Herke, Rebekah Wegener, and Canzhong Wu, 2008, "Halliday's Model of Register Revisited and Explored," *Linguistics and the Human Sciences* 4(2):187–213, pp. 192–93.

[29] M.A.K. Halliday and Ruqaiya Hasan, 1985, *Language, Context, and Text: Aspects of Language in a Social-Semiotic Perspective*, Geelong, Australia: Deakin University Press, p. 10.

[30] J.R. Martin, 1992, *English Text: System and Structure*, Philadelphia: John Benjamins, p. 496; J.R. Martin, 1999, "Modelling Context: A Crooked Path of Progress in Contextual

ideational is split into two and renamed as experiential-relational, and logical.[31] Jay Lemke renames the original three: presentational, orientational, and organizational.[32]

What persists through these reconfigurations is the idea that, however much context is needed for the purposes of social explanation, it is a stratum on the outside of the expression forms of the meaning system. And in the delineation of strata, written text and speech are frequently conflated, mostly just by ignoring writing. Phonology is the canonical form of expression in language.

The consequences of this conflation are serious, as an analysis of context and interest will show. Take "is" or "here" – the meaning of time (e.g. tense) or place (e.g. case). These are radically different between in-person speech and written text, and this difference is determined by context. In text, "is" and "here" are "was" and "there," whereas in speech they more or less are what they say they are. Or for the function of interest, the "I" of speaking, versus the "I" of the text of a novel – the dynamics of empathy,[§2.5b] in which I feel for you, are fundamentally different – the one an embodied, visceral co-presence of a corporeal "you," where the textual "you" is a distanced "other" in time and space.[§MS2.2] In the analysis of interest and context we come across more of the many reasons why we need to abandon the idea of language in a multimodal grammar, collapsing as it does forms of meaning that should, for their quite basic differences, be kept analytically separate.

These are some of the reasons why, in this grammar, context is not a stratum, across which functions traverse. It is itself a meaning function, an orientation within meaning as distinctive, significant, universal, and cross-cutting as the other functions. So is interest.

Meaning Functions
Reference
Agency
Structure
Context
Interest

Fig. 0.2(i): Meaning functions

In this grammar, we locate medium as an aspect of context because it consists of the material stuff that gets pulled from the world, the available raw materials with which to make meaning and their practical scope for

Linguistics," pp. 25–62 in *Text and Context in Functional Linguistics*, edited by M. Ghadessy, Amsterdam: John Benjamins, pp. 38–39.

[31] M.A.K. Halliday and Christian M.I.M. Matthiessen, 2014, *Halliday's Introduction to Functional Grammar* (Edn 4), Milton Park: Routledge, p. 85.

[32] Jay Lemke, 2009, "Multimodal Genres and Transmedia Traversals: Social Semiotics and the Political Economy of the Sign," *Semiotica* 173(1):283–97, pp. 284–85.

meaning. These raw materials are phonemics as the medium of expression for speech,[§1.4.1] and graphemics as the medium of expression for text.[§1.4.7] Their affordances are profoundly different, and this helps us to account for the differences of their form.

Or, in John Bateman's terms, the forms of meaning, or the technical features of a semiotic mode, are realized in a "material substrate."[33] Form is designable meaning, and medium the raw materials for meaning, available to be pulled from context in sensuous human reality and affording each form its meaning-potentials. Here is a rough map with examples of media and their characteristic affordances as forms of meaning:

		Text	Image	Space	Meaning Forms Object	Body	Sound	Speech
Strata in Context	*Form (meaning affordance)*	Phonemic or ideographic graphemes, unspeakable names, number, calculation	Two-dimensional spatial array	Barriers, divisions, openings, flows	Three-dimensionality, tangibility	Gesticulation, appearance, enactment	Noise, alerts, music	Temporal sequence, voice
	Medium (material manifestation)	Scribing, typography	Diagram, picture	Architecture, landscape	Physical things	Body form, clothing, gesture, kinesthetic activity	Audible sounds	Monologue, conversation

Fig. 0.2(ii): Form and media

Connecting form to function, we can create a matrix. By filling out its empty cells, we are able to raise foundational questions about meaning.

		Text	Image	Space	Meaning Forms Object	Body	Sound	Speech
Meaning Functions	Reference							
	Agency							
	Structure							
	Context							
	Interest							

Fig. 0.2(iii): Matrix for a transpositional grammar

On one axis, we can raise a series of questions about the function of some meaning, any meaning, every meaning, that may for the moment have become

---

[33] John A. Bateman, 2016, "Methodological and Theoretical Issues in Multimodality," pp. 36–74 in *Handbuch Sprache Im Multimodalen Kontext*, edited by N. Klug and H. Stöckl, Berlin: Walter de Gruyter, pp. 46–47; John A. Bateman, 2011, "The Decomposability of Semiotic Modes," pp. 17–38 in *Multimodal Studies: Exploring Issues and Domains*, edited by K. O'Halloran and B.A. Smith, London: Routledge, p. 19; ibid., p. 21.

an object of our concern. Reference: What is this about? Agency: Who or what is doing this? Structure: What holds this together? Context: How does this fit with its surroundings? Interest: What is this for?

Then, on the other axis, questions about its form: How is this meaning made, in text, image, space, object, body, sound, or speech, or combinations of these? How do the material media of these acts of representation and communication shape the form of their meaning?

Meaning form and meaning function in this conception are not bipolar opposites. They are not a dualism. The one is immanent in the other. They are an inseparable unity. No meaning form without meaning function. Meaning form is how meaning manifests itself – in text, image, space, object, body, sound, and speech. Meaning function is what it does, to refer, to establish agency, to structure, to set in context, to express or realize an interest.

Nor is one dimension to be prioritized over the other. Form does not (just) follow function. Function does not (just) determine form. Meaning is the tension that integrates form and function.

§0.3   Multimodality

> **Multimodality.** *Meaning forms in their monosensorial or multisensorial combination: text, image, space, object, body, sound, and speech.*

The materiality of meaning is mediated by the human body through its senses: sight, smell/taste, touch, and hearing. (In our account of forms of meaning, we define body narrowly, as gesticulation, appearance, and enactment.)

Some forms of meaning are able to work exclusively through one sense – notably text and image through sight, and speech through hearing. This potential for sensorial isolation lends text and speech their archetypical features as forms of meaning – their affordances, as well as their constraints, begging multimodality even when that is at the expense of some redundancy in meaning.

Fig. 0.3 is a rough accounting for meaning forms in terms of their requirements for the human senses, with some examples. On the measure of the human sensorium,[*] some meaning forms are intrinsically multisensorial – notably meanings in object and body. However, for their monosensorial possibilities, text and speech could not be more different. This is is another of the reasons we have arranged the array of meaning forms in the way that we have, maximally separating text and speech.

---

[*] http://meaningpatterns.net/sensorium

Senses \ Forms	Text	Image	Space	Object	Body	Sound	Speech
Sight	Scribing, typography, unicode	Picture, diagram	Proxemics, architectonics	Shape, color, luminescence	Gesture, kinesics, appearance		
Smell and Taste			Atmospherics	Smells, tastes	Body odors, scents		
Touch				Haptics	Intimacy, violence	Vibration	
Hearing				Ambient sound	Involuntary or semi-voluntary sounds (e.g. panting, crying, belching), conversation, speech performance	Music, alerts	Radio, voice recording, voice synthesis, telephonics

Fig. 0.3: Meaning forms and human senses

This is also the reason why, in this grammar, we have found it necessary to abandon the notion of "language," replacing it with two fundamentally different forms of meaning – written text closely aligned in its form to image and space, and speech, closely aligned in its form to sound and body. There are connections between text and speech, to be sure, because the graphemes in some languages are phonemic as well as ideographic. However, phonemic reading is impractical – most reading in alphabetically represented languages captures morphemes as units.[§MS0.2.1b] Then there are primarily ideographic languages, notably Chinese. In the era of digital text, most graphemes in Unicode are ideographic, rather than phonemic.[§MS0.2.1a] The syntax of text and speech are fundamentally different.[§MS0.2.7a] And much "vocabulary" in digital text is practically unspeakable – for instance, the linked names of webpages,[§MS1.1.1d] finely differentiated colors named by number,[§MS1.3.1h] or abstract mathematical or algorithmic relations.[§MS1.3.2] From the point of view of a multimodal grammar, the connections between text and speech are no stronger than those between text-image-space or speech-sound-body. In the digital era, the separations between the forms of text and speech have become greater than ever.

However, by technological sleight of hand, digital media also bring together these most disparate of forms, text-image and speech-sound. Digital media are unlike the analogue media that preceded them in the degree to which they can record and render both text-image[§MS1.2.2e] and sound-speech[§1.4.2d] by the same underlying mechanism, decomposing them into quantities (naming by number, quantification, calculation) and recomposing them at the point of rendering.

This contradictory pulling-away of text from speech as meaning forms, at the same time as their material coming together in digital media, is one of the main reasons why there is a certain urgency for a grammar of multimodality. Any such grammar must show a commitment to classifying forms in order to analyze their distinctive affordances, and the changes in our capacities to mean that are under way in the era of digital media, when these diverging meaning forms are brought together onto the same platforms for their representation and communication. Paradoxically, it is the very media that bring them together that also tear them apart.

One of the few things in the history of media that has come close to digital media in bringing together a range of meaning forms was sound film, but this it did awkwardly, in juxtaposed channels, literally sticking side-by-side fundamentally different recording technologies. Now the technologies for creation and distribution are the same, the technologies of binary calculability.

As well as the digital convergence of text-image and sound-speech, there are many other such conjunctions. Space and object can be represented in computer aided design, and recomposed as assembly instructions and 3D printing. Body can be recorded and represented in video and holographic representations. So-called 4D cinema even adds gimmicky haptics to cinema, and virtual and augmented reality a sense of bodily movement.[§1.3.2a] Of the human sensorium, only smell and taste cannot (yet) be digitized, either as recording or rendering. Nor can the sensorial roots of emotion – feelings of fear, anger, disgust, pleasure, or happiness, for instance.

§0.4   Transposition

> **Transposition.** *Movements across the meaning forms of text, image, space, object, body, sound, and speech, changes of attention to the always-present meaning functions of reference, agency, structure, context, and interest, and always-movability within these meaning functions.*

The principal innovation we are attempting in this grammar is to develop and apply a notion of transposition to account for movement across meaning forms and meaning functions.[*]

In much of the literature, multimodality is evidenced in things, artifacts of meaning that can be parsed for their amalgam of modes – text and image in a captioned picture, a web page as it appears on a screen, a gesture that accompanies speech, and any number of such found objects in the museum of human meanings. Mode is a state, presented in an analysis of how objects are ordered, and frozen for the moment of their analysis. Transposition, by contrast, is a process, how a meaning came to be and what it could soon become.

---

* http://meaningpatterns.net/transposition

Rarely in the multimodality literature do we find accounts of movement, how one meaning has become another and why, at any moment, it could move again. Helpfully, Gunther Kress has a concept for movement that he calls "transduction."[34] Denise Newfield speaks of "transmodal translation."[35] Hartmut Stöckl speaks to the "transcription" of meaning from one mode to another.[36] Jay Lemke analyzes "transmedia transversals."[37] We use the concept of synesthesia,[§MS0.2.9] as does Kress, in order to align multimodality with movement of meanings across senses. But such acknowledgments of movement are the exception rather than the rule.

Refining and extending these nascent ideas, we develop a notion of "transposition" that works across dimensions of form and function, albeit differently along each dimension. Across the form dimension, meaning functions are parallel. Anything and everything can be represented or communicated in every meaning form according to the functions reference, agency, structure, context, and interest. Function is a way to track parallels across forms. Such tracking will find that meanings can be more or less the same, but never quite. Different forms of meaning offer specific opportunities to mean, as well as constraints, and these can be traced back to the materiality of their media. Moving form-to-form entails gains as well as losses in meaning. This is why we are every-ready to transpose a meaning across different forms, even if that brings with it some redundancy. The purpose of transposition is to supplement meaning across forms.

Transposition across the function dimension has a somewhat different dynamic. Traversing the five functions, transposition becomes a matter of shifting attention because all are always present. We can focus on each function as an alternative orientation to a meaning. In one moment we may attend to the function of a meaning as reference to things or happenings, in another to the play of agency, in another to the relations by means of which it coheres, in another to its meaning in relation to its surrounds, and in another to its reason as an expression of interest.

But then, within a function, a meaning is only where it is momentarily because it has moved to be there, and it is always ready to move again. Movement is imminent because movability is immanent. Here are just a few of the functional

---

[34] Gunther Kress, 2003, *Literacy in the New Media Age*, London: Routledge, p. 151; Katharine Cowan and Gunther Kress, 2019, "Documenting and Transferring Meaning in the Multimodal World: Reconsidering 'Transcription'," pp. 66–77 in *Remixing Multiliteracies: Theory and Practice from New London to New Times*, edited by F. Serfini and E. Gee, New York: Teachers College Press.

[35] Denise Newfield, 2014, "Transformation, Transduction and the Transmodal Moment," pp. 100–13 in *The Routledge Handbook of Multimodal Analysis*, edited by C. Jewitt, London: Routledge, p. 103.

[36] Hartmut Stöckl, 2009, "The Language-Image-Text: Theoretical and Analytical Inroads into Semiotic Complexity," *Arbeiten aus Anglistik und Amerikanistik* 34(2):203–26, p. 205.

[37] Jay Lemke, 2009, "Multimodal Genres and Transmedia Traversals: Social Semiotics and the Political Economy of the Sign," *Semiotica* 173(1):283–97.

transpositions that we explore across this grammar: between single instance and its countable concept;[MS1.1] between actions and entities;[MS1.2] between qualities and their quantitative measurement and alphanumeric naming;[MS1.3] between self and other;[MS2.2] between representation and communication;[1.2] and between reified meaning[2.3] and its rhetorical expression.[2.1]

So, we reject static or deterministic functionalisms that are the basis of studies of language stretching from Saussure to Chomsky – and now also, we fear, extending into a good deal of the newer literature on multimodality. We do not want to formalize structures of meaning into categorical objects, frozen for the moment of analysis. Rather, we are interested in the patterns of their becoming, what they have been and what they are begging yet to become.

Transposition is a likelihood, an impatience, a risk, a danger, a possibility, an opportunity, an impossibility, a shock, a hell, a utopia. Hence: design is a process of meaning; and meaning is a matter of social history at both a micro level (us, now, in this moment) and a macro level (natural and species history). To the extent that transposition is patterning, it is itself a structuralism but of a different kind, driven by social process and history across many scales.

The primary organizing principle for this pair of books is meaning function and its transposabilities. Secondarily, we look at transpositions across meaning form. Here, by way of retrospect and anticipation, is our map of meaning functions, the first three of which we analyzed in *Making Sense*. The remaining two of which we now explore in *Adding Sense*.

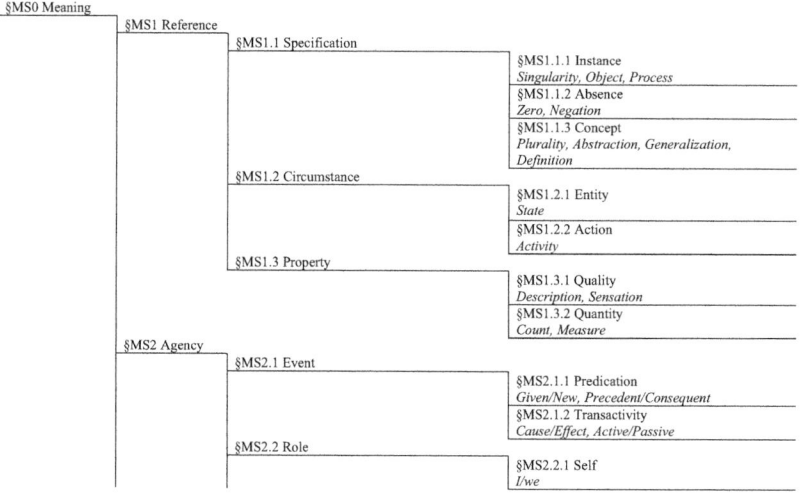

Fig. 0.4: A transpositional grammar

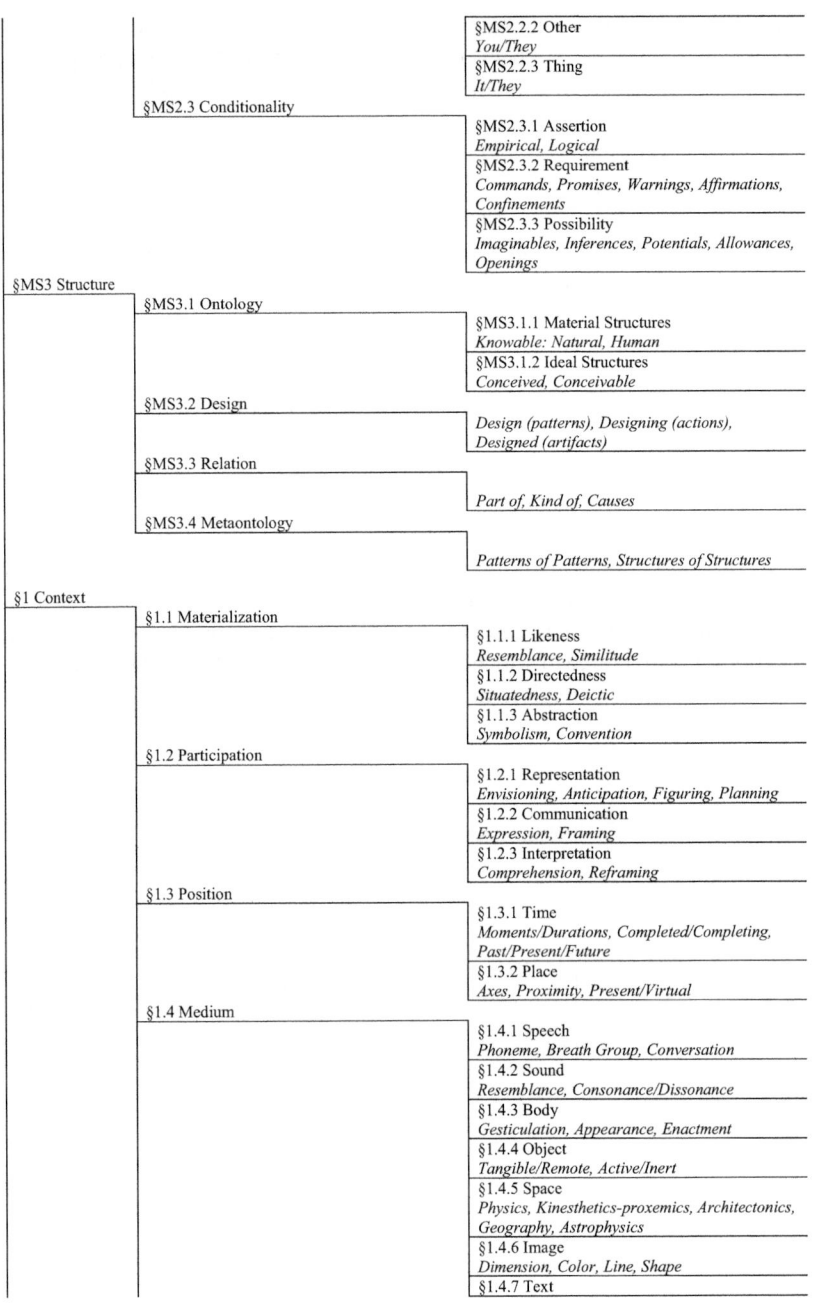

Fig. 0.4: (cont.)

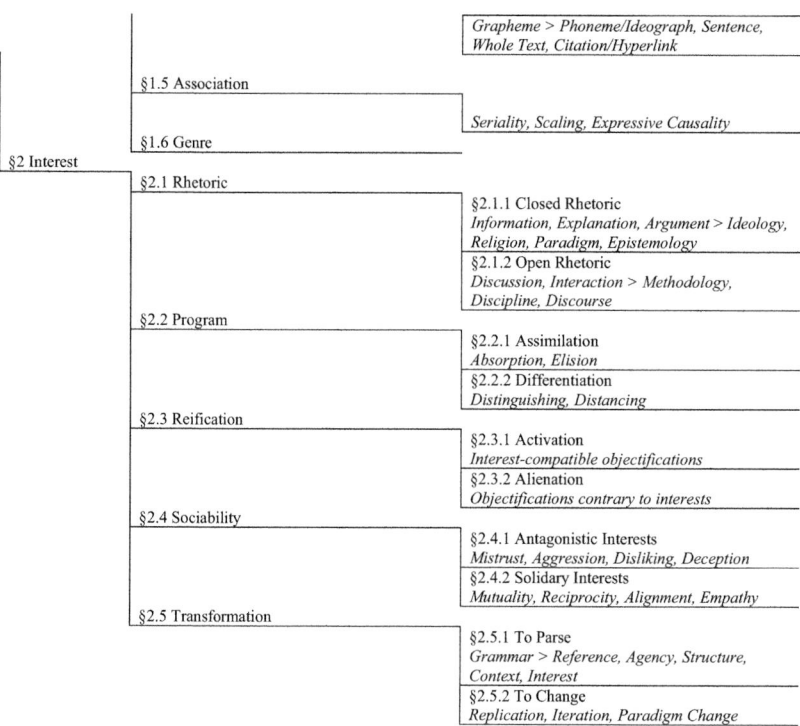

Fig. 0.4: (cont.)

Part 1 Context

§1.0   Overview of Part 1

Meanings sit in contexts, and contexts become part of meanings. This part of the book focuses on the ways in which context informs meaning.

Meanings are connected to context in the manner of their materialization; some are by likeness (for instance a spoken word that sounds like something, an image that looks like something), by directedness (for instance, a gesture that points to something, or the design of a space that directs wayfinders), or by abstraction (for instance, the arbitrary relation of written word to its referent, or a symbolic object).

Meanings also occur in social context, where the context is connected as a function of participation, whether this a connection to social meanings by representation (meaning for oneself), communication (meaning for others), or interpretation (making sense of others' meanings).

Meanings are positioned in the context of time and place. They can be nested inside each other such that their meaning shifts according to timescale or geolocation. Or they can be placed serially beside each other in time and space.

Meanings are affected by the affordances of their media, material resources for meaning pulled from context in speech-sound, body, object, space, and image-text. We hyphenate speech-sound and image-text because for each pair the affordances of medium are the same, and speech and text are as different as possible across the range of media available for representation and communication of meanings.

In viewing medium as a function, we are for the moment turning our attention to one aspect of the forms of meaning, and that is the materiality of their expression. Media are material things that are pulled from context to support the work of meaning. This very materiality affects what can be meant, the scope of their meaning function.

Media offer both openings for meaning and constraints. The constraints of function in media prompt us to supplement each medium with others. This is the reason we have multimodality, essentially and in our species' nature.

Meanings are associated by the ways in which they are placed near other meanings, be that contiguity and its effects of juxtaposition and seriality, or nesting, where one meaning fits inside another and meaning is a matter of scale. Meanings can also be associated by what we call expressive causality, where region, ecosystem, social structure, culture, or era find expression in a particular meaning.

Then, within and across forms of meaning and their corresponding media, there are genres, or kinds of meaning where conventionally patterned meaning forms are explicable in terms of their peculiar meaning functions.

Here is a map of the functions of context, and of this part of the book:

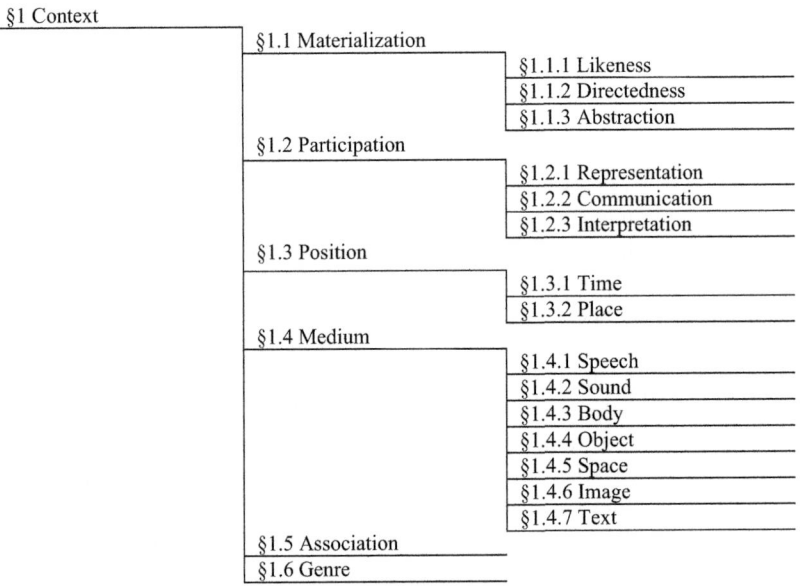

Fig. 1.0: Functions of context

§1.0a   V. Welby's What is Meaning?

> In the world of Symbol – the only one that signifies – Sign and Speech in grand array, with Talk, Scribble, and a crowd of little Letters and Syllables arranged in groups, a few Colons and Commas curling and dotting gaily about, and a pompous Full Stop, sat holding a Meeting. They had called it to consult as to what fresh orders they should issue to their Slave of all work, Man. … [The meeting soon falls into disarray, the participants in meaning arguing about relative importance of their roles, then Man arrives, hears their bickering and says,] "If you treat me as a slave and abuse my powers, you will

lose me and I shall leave you Meaningless. For Meaning goes with me; and well you know what *that* is in your life."[1]

V. Welby was a pioneer philosopher of meaning, or in more modern terms, a theorist in the discipline of semiotics, the study of meaning.[*] In several books and numerous articles published in the last decades of the nineteenth century and the first of the twentieth, Welby makes the case that language itself is by no means the exclusive seat of meaning. Indeed, if we stop our analysis at language, as if to assume that it captures the full scope of human meaning, we would miss some of language's inadequacies, deceptions even. "The form of expression called linguistic, our phrase and our word spoken or written, betrays us daily more disastrously, and atrophies alike action and thought."[2]

So Welby creates a three-cornered semiotic, a triad of: sense ⇔ meaning ⇔ significance.

Sense. A better word, says Welby, is "sensal." Not only in language, "realities, verities, actual facts may be set forth pictorially . . . Or they may be given in action, being lived or acted in outward conduct, thus impressing present spectators, hearers, touchers, with the sensuous conviction of their reality." For "our organism is a plexus of energies, intimately related to that 'environment' which we call the material or physical world . . . [or] what is usually called experience. We are fully 'in touch' . . . with the world we live on . . . 'Sense' . . . becomes the fitting term for that which makes the value of 'experience' in this life on this planet.'" Nor is this an exclusively human ground of meaning. "The whole 'animal kingdom' (if not the plant order) shares the sense-world."[3] Or, in the terms we have been developing in this grammar, the ground of meaning is multimodal experience.

Meaning. This is the expression of the immediate "intention of the user," and such "Expression [may come in the form of] action or sound, symbol or picture." Here Welby wants to emphasize "the power of symbol not only in Word, as in legend, narrative, parable, name, and all social speech and all intellectual discussions; but also, in act, as in ritual, ceremony, performance, posture, dance." This is to rectify an absence in hitherto existing analyses and theories of meaning. "There has been as yet no adequate, no thorough, no logical and scientific attempt on the widest basis to deal with this central interest of man's expression and realisation of himself and the world through Symbol."[4]

---

[*] http://meaningpatterns.net/welby

[1] V. Welby, 1897, "A Royal Slave," *Fortnightly Review* 62:432–34.
[2] V. Welby, 1911, *Significs and Language: The Articulate Form of Our Expressive and Interpretative Resources*, London: Macmillan, p. 6.
[3] V. Welby, 1903, *What Is Meaning? Studies in the Development of Meaning*, London: Macmillan, pp. 12–13, 120, 27–28.
[4] V. Welby, 1911, *Significs and Language: The Articulate Form of Our Expressive and Interpretative Resources*, London: Macmillan, pp. 11, 9, 41.

Significance. If meaning is localized, significance is broader and deeper meaning – meaning in a wider context. "For a thing is significant ... in proportion as it is expressible through bare sign or pictorial symbol or representative action ... It is [also] significant in proportion as it is capable of expressing itself in, or being translated into, more and more phases of thought or branches of science. The more varied and richer our employment of signs, the greater our power of ... inter-translating ... and coming closer to the nature of things ..., for the acquisition of fresh knowledge, new truth."[5] As a consequence, "Significance is always manifold, and intensifies its sense as well as its meaning, by expressing ... its universal or at least social range ... Why do we value experience? ... Because we are the Expression of the world, as it were 'expressed from' it by the commanding or insistent pressure of natural stimulae."

Welby called this new science of meaning, "significs," claiming for it "a new departure in philosophy and psychology."[6] Significs demands we put an end to "the old antithesis, 'matter and mind'."[7]

Man ... must learn to signify ... He must discover, observe, analyse, appraise first the sense of all that he senses through touch, hearing, sight, and to realize its interest, what it practically signifies for him ... Thus at last he will see the Significance, the ultimate bearing, the central value, the vital implication – of what? of all experience, all fact, and all thought.[8]

Live in Me; learn and know Me, saith all that is Real.[9]

In the terms we have been developing in this grammar, Welby's "sense" is more or less our reference; "meaning," more or less our agency and structure; "significance," more or less our context and interest; and "inter-translation," more or less our notion of transposition.

§1.0b   Charles Sanders Peirce's "Three Kinds of Interpretant"

C.S. Peirce to V. Welby, March 14, 1909: "I find now that my division ... [into] the three kind[s] of Interpretant ... nearly coincides with yours, as it ought to exactly, if both are correct. I am not in the least conscious of having been at all influenced by your book in setting my trichotomy ... and I don't believe there was any such influence ... But as far as the public goes, I can only point out the agreement, and confess to having read your book."[10]

---

[5] V. Welby, 1903, *What Is Meaning? Studies in the Development of Meaning*, London: Macmillan, pp. 5–6, 150.

[6] Ibid., pp. 23, 251.   [7] Ibid., pp. 50, 95–6, 110.   [8] Ibid., p. 6.

[9] V. Welby, 1911, *Significs and Language: The Articulate Form of Our Expressive and Interpretative Resources*, London: Macmillan, p. 93.

[10] Charles S. Hardwick, ed., 1977, *Semiotics and Significs: The Correspondence between Charles S. Peirce and Victoria Lady Welby*, Bloomington: Indiana University Press, p. 109.

Peirce is today recognized as a founder of the philosophical school of "pragmatism," friend of philosopher William James, and teacher of John Dewey.[§1.1] But he was barely known in his lifetime. Peirce's work had come to Welby's attention when she read his entry, "Laws of Thought," in Baldwin's *Dictionary of Philosophy and Psychology.*

Welby's correspondence with Peirce began in 1903 when, at Welby's request, the publisher sent Peirce a copy of *What is Meaning?* Peirce wrote a review, published in *The Nation* in November 1903, and sent it to Welby. In fact, it was a review of two books. The other was the first volume of Russell's *Principles of Mathematics*, a precursor to Russell and Whitehead's *Principia Mathematica.*[§MS1a]

"Two really important works of logic are these; or at any rate, they deserve to become so ... [As for] Mr Russell's book ... [t]hat he should continue these most severe and scholastic labors for so long, bespeaks of grit and industry ... Lady Victoria Welby's ... is a feminine book ... free from the slightest shade of pedantry or pretension ... The greatest service the book can render is that of bringing home the question that forms its title, a very fundamental question which has received superficial, forma-listic replies."[11]

Lady Victoria Alexandrina Maria Louisa Welby, born into the English aristocracy. She had been named after Queen Victoria, who christened the baby Victoria just five days before she ascended the throne in 1837. After her parents died, Lady Victoria became a maid of honor in the court of the Queen. A prolific writer, and in Peirce's view a thinker of considerable importance, she was to be a founding member of the British Sociological Society and the Royal School of Art Needlework.[12]

Welby to Peirce: "Before I say more, may I confess that in signing my book 'V. Welby,' I hoped to get rid as far as possible of the irrelevant associations with my unlucky title? ... You will understand my desire to be known as simply as possible, though I cannot altogether ignore the 'Hon' conferred upon me as Maid of Honour to the late Queen. But the only honor I value is that of being treated ... as a serious worker."[13]

Peirce to Welby: "My Dear Lady Victoria, I receive today your deeply interesting letter of Nov. 18, being here delivering some lectures of which I enclose a list." Peirce was at Harvard University, delivering his Lowell

---

[11] Ibid., p. 157.

[12] William Andrew Myers, 1995, "Victoria, Lady Welby (1837–1912)," pp. 1–24 in *A History of Women Philosophers*, Volume 4, edited by M.E. Waithe, Dordrecht: Kluwer Academic Publishers; Susan Petrilli, 2015, "Sign, Meaning, and Understanding in Victoria Welby and Charles S. Peirce," *Signs and Society* 3(1):71–102.

[13] Charles S. Hardwick, ed., 1977, *Semiotics and Significs: The Correspondence between Charles S. Peirce and Victoria Lady Welby*, Bloomington: Indiana University Press, p. 13.

Lectures. "As soon as I get back to Pike County" – Peirce had built a house in rural Pennsylvania – "I mean to hunt up the solitary copy of ... my original paper on the three categories ... So you shall have my last copy ... As to Bertrand Russell's book ... whatever merit it may have as a digest of what others have done, it is pretentious and pedantic, attributing to the author merit that cannot be accorded to him."[14]

Welby to Peirce: "My dear Dr. Peirce, I have been much hindered lately but have now been able to read ... your generously appreciative Notice of my little book." At 321 pages, Welby's book could only be considered little beside the 534 pages of Russell's book, and the 1,233 pages of Whitehead and Russell's three-volume sequel.

"I ... can but express my warm gratitude ... I am now engaged in reading for the fourth time and analyzing from my own point of view ... 'Principles of Mathematics' ... [and] propose to write some Notes on those parts or passages which more especially concern my work and aims. This I shall hope to send to him ... [on] the importance of that – may I call it practical extension – of ... Logic proper, which I have called Significs ... the very attribute which may be said to give human value to life, – that is (1) its 'Sense' and sense-power in every sense from the biological to the logical, (2) its intention, conscious and increasingly definite and rational, which we call 'Meaning' and ... (3) its Significance, its bearing upon, its place among, its interpretation of, all other cosmical facts."[15]

Peirce to Welby: "My dear Lady Welby: Not a day has passed since I received your last letter that I have not lamented the circumstances that prevented me from writing that very day." Peirce spent the last decade of his life struggling to manage a country property, personal financial crisis, and his own and his wife's ill-health.[16]

"But I wanted to write to you about signs, which in your opinion and mine are matters of so much concern ... I think today I will explain the outlines of my classification of signs ... to throw all ideas into three classes of Firstness, of Secondness, and of Thirdness ... The typical ideas of Firstness are qualities of feeling, or mere appearances ... The ... idea of Secondness is the experience of effort ... one thing acting upon another ... I now come to Thirdness ... the interpreting thought ... something which brings a First into relation to a Second."

Peirce builds a system of meaning where trichotomy layers over trichotomy. Firstness ⇔ Secondness ⇔ Thirdness; icon ⇔ index ⇔ symbol;[§1.1.3]

---

[14] Ibid., pp. 8–9.   [15] Ibid., pp. 5–6.
[16] Joseph Brent, 1993, *Charles Sanders Peirce: A Life*, Bloomington: Indiana University Press.

qualisign ⇔ sinsign ⇔ legism, and others, reaching twenty-six sign triads by the time he had come to the end of his letter.[17]

Peirce to Welby: "My dear Lady Welby: Please excuse me for writing on this paper, as I find to my surprise that I have run out of everything else except such as is still less fit for writing to you; and it is 3½ A.M. and I am 5 or 6 miles from a stationer's. I cannot tell you how delighted I was on Saturday last to see your hand-writing on an envelope."[18]

Peirce to Welby: "[The] threefold Definition of a Sign ... [might generate] six trichotomies, instead of determining 729 classes of signs, as they would if they were independent, only yield 28 classes; and if, as I strongly opine (not to say almost prove) there are four other trichotomies of the same order of importance, instead of making 59049 classes, these will only come to 66."[19]

Peirce also built visualizations of his system in the form of "Existential Graphs," which he sent to Welby, by means of which "I desire to aid you ... furnishing an icon of thought which in formal respects is of the highest exactitude."[20] When words were only able to represent the system with imprecision, visualization was needed.[*]

Peirce to Welby: "My Dear Lady Victoria: No letter from you, I beg you to believe, could be too long, especially if it has in view the more forcible presentations of our recommendations ... I brought along an old number of [the journal] the *Monist* in order to read an article of yours it contains ... I don't believe I shall ever cross the water again, & shall not have the pleasure of seeing you; but it would be a great delight if I could have a photograph of your ladyship."[21] In one of Peirce's triads, a photograph would be classified as an icon.

Peirce to Welby: "I received your ladyship's photograph last night & put it on my study mantelpiece among the very small number of those friends I love to look at, and I am sure there will be none that will do more solid good than your bright and good face. The reason I have not written is that my dear wife has been very ill & for five weeks hardly left her bedside & even now that she is up, I am continually worried about her too great energy, besides being myself in a state of nervous fatigue."[22]

The Welby–Peirce correspondence continued until 1911. Welby died in 1912, and Peirce in 1914.

---

[*] http://meaningpatterns.net/peirce-welby

[17] Charles S. Hardwick, ed., 1977, *Semiotics and Significs: The Correspondence between Charles S. Peirce and Victoria Lady Welby*, Bloomington: Indiana University Press, pp. 22–31.

[18] Ibid., p. 66.   [19] Ibid., p. 84.   [20] Ibid., p. 96   [21] Ibid., pp. 10–11.   [22] Ibid., pp. 16–17.

§1   CONTEXT

> ***Context.*** *The ways in which surroundings inform acts and artifacts of meaning.*
> *The relation of meaning to context varies according to the dynamics of its*
> *materialization in likeness (resemblance), directedness (pointing), and*
> *abstraction (symbolism). Context is determined in part by kinds of participation*
> *in meaning, according to the uses to which meanings are put in acts of*
> *representation, communication, or interpretation. Context can be specified as*
> *position: time and place. Context also supplies media of particular kinds, the*
> *means of the materialization of meaning, affording shape to meaning in speech,*
> *sound, body, object, space, image and text. Meanings may connect with each*
> *other by association: serially, by scaling, or through expressive causality. And*
> *meanings can, by the conventions of genre, be patterned in similar ways.*

Meaning does not just subsist in artifacts of communication – sounded speech, written text, or meaningful object. It lives as much in the relationships of these artifacts to their contexts. Welby and Peirce both begin to offer accounts of these relationships in their notion of the sign. The sign is not just a thing-in-itself. It has meaning in a practical, material relationship with the world and in the world.

Grammars of language mostly focus on structures isolated within the form of their meaning – take Saussure's structuralism,[§MS3d] for instance – and, at that, a single form of meaning in artificial isolation. Or even more narrowly, they focus on one aspect of one form – the syntax of speech in the case of Chomsky.[§MS3.1.2f]

There is a subdiscipline within linguistics which uses the same word to describe its practices as Peirce[§1.0b] and his successors did for their philosophy, "pragmatics."[23] Pragmatists spread their wings more widely, analyzing not only speech as a product, but the context in which this product is put to use. Where Chomsky finds ambiguity in speech isolated from context, pragmatics finds clarity in meaning by accounting for its context. Austin's speech act theory[§MS2.3.1a] is one of the founding texts of pragmatics, uncovering the meanings in speech that are discoverable not from the sounded words alone, but in the meanings of these words articulated in the context of their use.

Pragmatics brings us closer to a grammar of multimodality, but not close enough. For a start, it purports to deal with language, but in practice almost only addresses speech, neglecting writing once again by conflating it into the word "language." Once again, we respond, writing is radically different from speech, closer in many respects to image. Much actionable text today – the ontologies that drive dynamic digital text for instance,[§MS3.3a] or the arrangement of words and numbers in

---

[23] Stephen C. Levinson, 1983, *Pragmatics*, Cambridge: Cambridge University Press; Jacob L. Mey, 2001, *Pragmatics: An Introduction*, Oxford: Blackwell Publishing; Yan Huang, 2014, *Pragmatics*, Oxford: Oxford University Press.

databases[§1.4.6a] – can only make sense as visualized array. Peirce found it necessary to create "existential graphs" to represent his elaborate thoughts on the meaning of meaning. Pragmatics, however, centers its analysis on one focal form – speech – whose meanings can be supplemented by an account of externalities – context. It is nevertheless a speech-centric view of meaning.

For a grammar of multimodality there are no internalities with which externalities need to be aligned. There are no central, prior, or privileged sites of meaning. Nor do we want to prioritize speech as the center-point to which context is aligned. There is meaning in all of text, image, space, object, body, sound, and speech, simultaneously, in parallel, and always in combination. The purpose of a grammar of multimodality is to create an account of the shared functions of meaning across these forms of meaning and the traffic between them, a traffic we have called transposition. Context is not peripheral. It is also the meaning, and just as much.

The context of a piece of writing of whatever size – a word, a paragraph, a book – is the form of participation of the user, the place and time it is found, and its relations to other pieces of writing. The context of an image is: its means of materialization as a likeness, a directed sign or an abstraction; the form of participation as maker or viewer; its placement, its associations in the visual field; and its similarities and differences with other images. The context of a space is a widening series of spaces – in a room, a building, a city, a landscape; the forms of participation in these spaces; and their distinctiveness as determined by similar or different spaces. Objects may be found, made, or understood; they may have meanings manifest in themselves, or they may be symbolic; they may be aspects of other objects; and they may be similar to or differentiable from other objects. Bodies are felt, enacted, or experienced; they are similar to, or notably different from, other bodies in presence by expression in gesture or style. Sounds repeat other sounds, warn, or symbolize; they are recalled, made, or heard; they are patterns of contrast, and sequences of sounds are distinctive or similar to others. Speech, as the pragmatists describe in rich detail, makes sense in the surrounds of its performance, and the dynamics of speaking and hearing. These are some of the practical manifestations of context.

§1a   C.K. Ogden and I.A. Richards' "Sign-Situatedness"

Dear Ogden,

"The Meaning of Meaning" reached me a few days ago . . . I have . . . read it and I ought to confess to you frankly that I believe you have not quite caught the problems which . . . I was at in my book (whether or not I have given the correct solution) . . .

Yours Sincerely,
L. Wittgenstein[24]

---

[24] Ludwig Wittgenstein, 1973, *Letters to C.K. Ogden*, Oxford: Basil Blackwell, p. 69.

Ludwig Wittgenstein[§MS2.1.1a] was writing in 1923 to C.K. Ogden, his commissioning editor at the publisher, Kegan Paul. Ogden, then a student, had been taking tea with Russell at Cambridge in 1911 when Wittgenstein first appeared, wanting to study with Russell, too. In 1922–3, Ogden and Wittgenstein were engaged in extensive correspondence, finalizing the text for the first, bilingual German/English edition of the *Tractatus.* With co-author I.A. Richards, Ogden had just finished The *Meaning of Meaning,* a book that was to run to eight editions between 1923 and 1946.

Welby to Peirce, 2 May 1911: "Meanwhile, the news I was anxious to impart . . . is that I have found you, I think, a disciple at Cambridge. He has been studying with care all I could show him of your writing . . . The name of the recruit is C.K. Ogden, and he is at Magdalene College."[25]

The *Meaning of Meaning* includes an appendix that is a masterful eleven-page summary of Peirce's letters to Welby.[26] These, Welby had shared with Ogden, though they were not to be published in full for another fifty years. This appendix is one of the main ways Peirce's work came to be better known after his death.

Welby also wrote to Russell recommending that he read Peirce.

Russell to Welby: "to those of us who do not know him, the little he has published is tantalizing. Still, I admit, the number of readers who will profit by work such as his, without benefits of his personal explanations, is necessarily small."[27]

In their book, Ogden and Richards advance the idea of "sign-situatedness," or the processes of attribution of meaning in context. "A context is a set of entities (things or events) related in a certain way." Interpretation is a process of seeing patterns in meaning based on experience.

Theorizing the sign, they offer yet another three-cornered diagram of meaning in its context,[*] after Welby's sense ⇔ meaning ⇔ significance,[28] and Peirce's many triads. Theirs is: referent ⇔ thought or reference ⇔ symbol. Referent: Napoleon, the person. Reference, a long chain of sign-situations: the word – historian – contemporary record – eyewitness – referent. Symbol: the word

---

[*] http://meaningpatterns.net/triads

[25] Charles S. Hardwick, ed., 1977, *Semiotics and Significs: The Correspondence between Charles S. Peirce and Victoria Lady Welby,* Bloomington: Indiana University Press, pp. 138–39.

[26] C.K. Ogden and I.A. Richards, 1923 [1989], *The Meaning of Meaning,* San Diego, CA: Harcourt Brace Jovanovich, pp. 279–90.

[27] Mrs Henry Cust, 1931, *Other Dimensions: A Selection from the Later Correspondence of Victoria Lady Welby, Edited by Her Daughter,* London: Jonathan Cape, p. 160.

[28] W. Terrence Gordon, 1990, "Significs and C.K. Ogden: The Influence of Lady Welby," pp. 179–96 in *Essays on Significs: Papers Presented on the Occasion of the 150th Anniversary of the Birth of Lady Victoria Welby, 1837–1912,* edited by H.W. Schmitz, Amsterdam: John Benjamins.

"Napoleon."[29] Each of these triads is an attempt to situate moments and artifacts of meaning in their contexts, such that the context is an integral part of the meaning.

§1.1 Materialization

> **Materialization.** The traffic of meaning between the material and the ideal, where the manner of its manifestation, and the situating of meaning in its context, may vary according to likeness, directedness, or abstraction.

Says Peirce's student from their Johns Hopkins University days, John Dewey,

Of all affairs, communication is the most wonderful. That things should be able to pass from the plane of external pushing and pulling to that of revealing themselves to man, and thereby to themselves; and that the fruit of communication should be participation, sharing, is a wonder by the side of which transubstantiation pales.[30]

Or, to rephrase Dewey, the great philosophical successor to Peirce and popularizer of the philosophy of pragmatism, meaning travels, between the material and the ideal, where the meaning-filled material, through its pushing and pulling on us, reveals itself to us.* There is always more that might be revealed, the excess of the material. But there is more in the play of the ideal than what simply presents itself in the material.

Events turn into objects, things with a meaning ... Events when once they are named lead an independent and double life. In addition to their original existence, they are subject to ideal experimentation: their meanings may be infinitely combined and rearranged in imagination, and the outcome of this inner experimentation – which is thought – may issue forth in interaction with crude or raw events.[31]

The meanings in the material may spread in their scope indefinitely across context, known to unknown. The meanings in the ideal may spread their scope indefinitely across context, real to imagined.§MS3.1 Then the ideal may return to the material; it can be materialized.

Meaning travels between the material and the ideal in several ways. Peirce classified these in one of his triads as icon/index-indication/symbol-token. Icons are "likenesses ... which serve to convey the ideas of things they represent by simply imitating them."[32] "An index ... asserts nothing, it only says 'There!' It

* http://meaningpatterns.net/dewey

[29] C.K. Ogden and I.A. Richards, 1923 [1989], *The Meaning of Meaning*, San Diego, CA: Harcourt Brace Jovanovich, pp. 58, 57, 11.

[30] John Dewey, 1925, *Experience and Nature*, Chicago, IL: Open Court, p. 166.   [31] Ibid.

[32] Charles Sanders Peirce, 1998, *The Essential Peirce: Selected Philosophical Writings,* Volume 2: *1893–1913*, Bloomington: Indiana University Press, p. 5.

takes hold of our eyes, as it were, and forcibly directs them to a particular object . . . a pointing finger being the type of the class."[33] A symbol or token is a convention that "cannot indicate any particular thing; it denotes a kind of thing."[34]

We rename and slightly redefine these ways of traveling between the ideal and the material as likeness, directedness, and abstraction. With materialization, the ideal is manifest as likeness, direction, or abstraction. Materialization is a process of situating meaning in context.

Here is a rough map of some processes of materialization:

Form / Function: / Materialization	Text	Image	Space	Object	Body	Sound	Speech
Likeness	Onomatopoeia, ideographs of likeness	Realism	Similarity of form and use	Object resemblance	Mimicry, mime	Sounds of imitation	Phonemes of imitation
Directedness	Proper nouns, pronouns, deictics	Sign, in the sense of visual direction	Space directing flow	Object use determined by form	Pointing	Sounds of direction	Phonics of direction
Abstraction	Common nouns, verbs, adjectives, arbitrary ideographs	Abstract imagery	Conventional uses of space	Symbolic objects	Gestures with conventional meanings	Conventional sound meanings	Prosody of a conventional kind

Fig. 1.1: Materialization

Each of likeness, directedness, and abstraction in its own characteristic way directs the traffic of meaning between the ideal and the material, a traffic that attributes meaning by connecting meaning in contexts, and recontextualizing it in the act of meaning.

These processes of the materialization of meaning can occur at the same time in the combination of likeness, and/or directedness, and/or symbolization. Or one kind of materialization can become one or more of the others. Such are the slippery dynamics of functional transposition, where meanings are ever ready to move, and move all the time they do.

§1.1.1   Likeness

> *Likeness.* *The materialization of a meaning in its context by visual, sounded, tangible, gestural similitude – never the same, because the time, place, and available resources for materialization are inevitably different in some respect, though similar enough to spark recognition.*

[33] Charles Sanders Peirce, 1992, *The Essential Peirce: Selected Philosophical Writings*, Volume 1: *1867–1893*, Bloomington: Indiana University Press, p. 225.
[34] Ibid., p. 9.

Crossing the gamut of multimodality, likeness includes photographs, imitative gestures, onomatopoeia, and objects and spaces whose functions are self-evident. With "that which can be represented in Unicode" as our definition of text, Unicode has many iconic ideographs that are likenesses, now including 3,053 emojis.[§1.1.1a]

§1.1.1a Emojis

A smiling face and a heart were among the first emojis to be included in the Unicode character set,[§MS0.2.1a] added to version 1.1 for its release in 1993.[35] Subsequent releases of Unicode have added more, bringing the total to 3,053 in version 12.0.[36] The word "emoji" is Japanese for pictograph, and an "emoticon" is a kind of emoji that expresses feeling, a contraction of the words emotion + icon.[37] The modern origins of pictographic imagery can be traced to Otto Neurath and Marie Reidemeister's groundbreaking work in the 1920s at the Vienna Museum of Society and Economy.[§MS1.1.3h]

The first digital emojis* were created by Bruce Parello, a student working on PLATO IV at the University of Illinois in 1972.[38] (PLATO was the world's first e-learning system, and incidental to its invention were other firsts – digitally mediated text, visual rendering of text to a plasma screen, synthesized sound, and games.[39])

Scott Fahlman, a young professor at Carnegie Mellon University created the smiley face :-) and unhappy face :-(, first sending them in a message at 11.44pm on September 19, 1982.[40]

One hundred and seventy-six emojis designed by Shigetaka Kurita were made available on mobile phones by the Japanese telephone company NTT in 1999. For this history-making contribution to human practices of visualization, in 2016 they were acquired for the collection of the Museum of Modern Art in New York. In its announcement, the museum called them "humble masterpieces of design [that] planted the seeds for

---

* http://meaningpatterns.net/emojis

[35] https://emojipedia.org/unicode-1.1/   [36] https://unicode.org/emoji/charts/full-emoji-list.html
[37] Richard Kern, 2015, *Language, Literacy, and Technology*, Cambridge: Cambridge University Press, pp. 261–67.
[38] Brian Dear, 2017, *The Friendly Orange Glow: The Untold Story of the Plato System and the Dawn of Cyberculture*, New York: Pantheon Books, pp. 338–42.
[39] Bill Cope and Mary Kalantzis, 2017, "Conceptualizing E-Learning," pp. 1–45 in *E-Learning Ecologies*, edited by B. Cope and M. Kalantzis, New York: Routledge.
[40] www.cs.cmu.edu/~sef/sefSmiley.htm

the explosive growth of a new visual language."[41] Emojis were added to Microsoft Windows in 2008, the Apple OS in 2011, Google Android in 2013. Facebook launched its "Like" emoji on 9 February 2009,[42] and added other so-called "reactions" in 2016.[43]

Different tech companies each render emojis in their own ways, but through Unicode share their underlying meanings. The importance of likeness in so many emojis became the focal point of a crisis at Google in 2017, when it was discovered that its hamburger emoji had cheese underneath the meat patty, instead of on top. This was a failure of similitude that had to be rectified urgently.[44]

Text today – defined by this grammar as that which is represented in Unicode – includes materializations of meaning that cross icon (such as emojis and dentistry symbols), directedness (such as arrows, warning signs), and abstractions (including the letters of phonic alphabets that only conventionally and arbitrarily mean the sounds they reference). Some emojis are directed signs or abstract symbols, but most are like-nesses. Today, people use likeness emojis more and more. As we begin to type a word on a phone, suggestive text prompts us to use an emoji instead.

Moving beyond the constraints of abstract and arbitrary phonemes and graphemes, in the era of total globalization, emojis of likeness have burgeoned to become a universal, translingual semantics. Here is another place where text is diverging still further from speech, using more likenesses and fewer abstractions. Though of course, even if more universal for their divergence from speech, they are not without cross-cultural weirdnesses[45] and divergent interpretations.[46]

Emojis expressed in Unicode have become useful to marketeers wanting to know how people feel in the global marketplace. The universal semantics standardized in Unicode helps them to do this – in aggregate, not to mention the finely grained knowing of us all individually.

Brandwatch Analytics styles itself "the world's leading social listening platform." For its 2017 report, Brandwatch analyzed six billion emojis generated in Twitter over a two-year period. "This report from Brandwatch . . . quite possibly . . . gives us the richest look at social media and brand sentiment to date," gushed Dennis Wakabayashi, VP, Digital Marketing and Commerce

[41] https://news.artnet.com/exhibitions/emoji-museum-of-modern-art-collection-722330
[42] www.facebook.com/notes/facebook/i-like-this/53024537130
[43] www.wired.com/2016/02/facebook-reactions-totally-redesigned-like-button/
[44] https://blog.emojipedia.org/google-fixes-burger-emoji/
[45] https://hackernoon.com/samsungs-bizarre-emojis-6be568a3b7d9
[46] Jaram Park, Vladimir Barash, Clay Fink, and Meeyoung Cha, 2013, "Emoticon Style: Interpreting Differences in Emoticons across Cultures," paper presented at the Proceedings of the Seventh International AAAI Conference on Weblogs and Social Media.

Integration @The Integer Group. Brandwatch's "technologies help us ... understand how mindset and emotional state affects brands. This means richer insights, smarter engagement, and more relevance. You might even think of it as the dawning of Internet Emotional Intelligence."[47]

§1.1.2 Directedness

> **Directedness.** *The materialization of a meaning in its context by pointing to referents in context, in the coincident time and place, or across time and place.*

Directedness points to context: materializing meaning in a pronoun, a proper noun, a vocative exclamation, an arrow, a diagram, a map, a gesture of pointing, or a warning sound.

§1.1.2a John Wyclif's De Eucharista Tractatus

We'll return to Dewey's discussion of communication as participation,[§1.2] but for the moment we want to consider his mention of transubstantiation.[§1.1] It is as if for Dewey the communion of shared human meanings were as mysterious and profound as the moment of the ringing of the priest's bell, when the bread and wine of the eucharist become the body and blood of Christ.

Transubstantiation is a nice example with which to illustrate alternative processes for the materialization of meaning. In different interpretations, the eucharist is a matter of likeness, directedness, or abstraction. In each interpretation, the mystery of the meaning is in the (un)believable relations of material and ideal. Indeed, precisely this question of the manner of materialization in and of meaning became the basis for the best part of a thousand years of argument.

Likeness: Pope Innocent III convened the Fourth Lateran Council to meet in Rome in 1215. This is the conclusion to which the congregation of 404 bishops and numerous other representatives of church and state came in Canon I: "There is indeed one universal church of the faithful, outside of which nobody at all is saved, in which Jesus Christ is both priest and sacrifice. His body and blood are truly contained in the sacrament of the altar under the forms of bread and wine, the bread and wine having been changed in substance, by God's power, into his body and blood."[48]

---

[47] www.brandwatch.com/reports/the-emoji-report/view/
[48] Norman P. Tanner, ed. 1990, *Decrees of the Ecumenical Councils,* Volume 1: *Nicea I to Lateran V,* London: Sheed and Ward, p. 230.

The bread and wine have here become so thoroughly like the body and blood of Christ that they are always this again in every sanctioned re-enactment of the eucharist. They are not the same, of course, because the repetitions happen in different times and places, but they are construed to be as substantively alike as things in different times and places can be. We can consider a likeness this strong to be as "the same" as the same ever will be, because the same repeated can never be totally the same.

Directedness: John Wyclif (*c.*1330 to 1385) was a philosopher, early translator of the English Bible, and professor at Oxford University.[*] Of transubstantiation, he wrote, "I believe that, of all the heresies by which the Church has ever been infected, none ... deceives the people in such various ways ... [I]t renders them idolaters ... and ... subverts Grammar, Logic, all natural science, and even (which is still worse) ... completely destroys the sense of the Gospel."[49]

Wyclif's argument turned on the word "hoc," the "this" in the Latin source text from which he translated the Bible. "This is my body," said Christ, breaking bread for his disciples at the original eucharist. "This" is a sign of directedness. It points to the meaning of the sacrament, the moment of Christ's promise to sacrifice himself. Only *cutlores signorum*, said Wyclif, sign worshipers or idolaters, could think that a mortal priest could effect such a material change. "When writers write letters, words and sentences, the paper and ink remain beneath the symbols. But through custom and skill those who can read pay much more attention to the significance of the symbols than the natural characteristics of the signs ... Much more so the habit of faith brings the faithful to grasp through the consecrated bread the true body of Christ."[50] Wyclif issues an early warning of the coming epistemology of the protestant reformation, a new rationalism that sought to reconcile meanings manifest in the material with the ideal of faith. For his heretical views, Wyclif was expelled from Oxford University.[51]

Symbolism: Now we come to uncompromisingly Protestant meaning, in the founding canons of the Church of England, pronounced at the time of its split from Rome. Here is article XXVIII of the Thirty-nine Articles of 1571:

Transubstantiation (or the change of the substance of Bread and Wine) in the Supper of the Lord, cannot be proved by Holy Writ, but is repugnant to the plain words of Scripture, overthroweth the nature of a Sacrament, and hath given occasion to many

---

[*] http://meaningpatterns.net/wyclif

[49] John Wyclif, *c.*1382 [1892], *De Eucharista Tractatus*, edited by I. Loserth, London: Trubner & Co, pp. iii, xx–xxi, xliii–xliv.

[50] Anthony Kenny, 1985, *Wyclif*, Oxford: Oxford University Press, p. 89.

[51] Maurice Keen, 1986, "Wyclif, the Bible, and Transubstantiation," pp. 1–16 in *Wyclif in His Times*, edited by A. Kenny, Oxford: Oxford University Press.

superstitions. The body of Christ is given, taken, and eaten in the Supper, only after an heavenly and spiritual manner. And the means whereby the body of Christ is received and eaten in the Supper is Faith.[52]

Now, the sacrament of the eucharist is a symbol, an abstraction.

In all three mysteries of meaning, the context is a traffic between the feeding bodies of priests and the eating and drinking bodies of supplicants. These are transpositions of form between spoken words, human gestures, and objects. Meanings are thus materialized, but the manner of their materialization is in each case different.§MS3.1

Beyond each and every meaning-ritual of the communion table is a fraught history of sense making. The different versions of the sacrament of eucharist only make sense as alternatives offered by disputants in the larger histories of Catholicism and Protestantism, and for that matter the ongoing dialogue between materialist (Wyclif) and idealist (Lateran Council) ontologies.

In these contexts, the senses that are made through these three materializations of meaning indicate profoundly different ways of conducting the traffic between the material and the ideal. These are confounding differences, as between likeness, directedness, and abstraction. The intricacies of argumentation are bewilderingly endless. Just one of Wyclif's texts, his *de Eucharista Tractatus*, perhaps his most important on this subject, runs to 348 pages.

The source of the confounding is the always-possible functional transposition of meaning, the fluid movement between likeness, directedness, and abstraction. The mystery of materialization is its ever-ready transposability. Even within his own lifetime, Wyclif had changed his mind. The Protestant Reformation tried to change the minds of congregants. And surely many a committed supplicant's mind must still at times stray across the imminent possibilities of meaning as they partake in the bread and the wine.

§1.1.3 Abstraction

> **Abstraction.** *The materialization of a meaning in its context by conventional agreement and arbitrary connection between ideal and material, neither denoting a thing in a way that would be obvious to those not party to social agreement as to its meaning, nor pointing directly to a referent.*

Abstractions are conventionally agreed meanings where meaning is materialized in a form that neither bears resemblance to its referent, nor points directly to it: a

---

[52] www.churchofengland.org/prayer-and-worship/worship-texts-and-resources/book-common-pr ayer/articles-religion#XXVIII

common noun, a ritual object, a sound that evokes feeling, abstract imagery, or symbolic colors, for instance.

§1.1.3a Terrence Deacon's Symbolic Species

"The symbolic species," Terrence Deacon calls *homo sapiens*, an animal, but like no other. His erudite book of this title moves between neuroscience, linguistics, philosophy, physical anthropology, and evolutionary biology.

Deacon's central argument puts to work Peirce's triad, icon ⇔ index ⇔ symbol.[§1.0b] Other animals can communicate with icons and indexes, he says – "vervet monkey alarm calls or honeybee dances, and the socially transmitted sequences that make humpback whale songs." But only humans can use symbols, and language is the main conduit for symbolism. "Biologically, we are just another ape. Mentally, we are a new phylum of organisms."[53] Language makes the difference.

Deacon presents the edge case of Kanzi, a young bonobo who learned to symbolize to a remarkable degree, incidental to the efforts to train his mother by researchers at the Language Research Center of Georgia State University.[*] Sue Savage-Rumbaugh and Duane Rumbaugh taught Kanzi to communicate symbolically using a "lexigram keyboard" they had developed. Kanzi's capacity forces Deacon to draw another line. Although undoubtedly Kanzi could symbolize, he could not teach what he had learned to other bonobos, which means he did not develop the characteristically human capacity to participate in a replicable culture of symbolism or abstraction.[54]

Deacon's thesis is that the human brain and language co-evolved. "The changes in this organ responsible for this miracle were a direct consequence of the use of words ... [T]he physical changes that make us human are the incarnations, so to speak, of the process of using words." Or, more narrowly than this, leaving writing out of language, symbolic cognition is a derivative speech: "Spoken language is the vehicle that first introduces the power of symbols to children."[55]

Others in the neuroscience business don't agree with Deacon that human brains are so very different from the brains of other animals. Merlin Donald, for

---

[*] http://meaningpatterns.net/kanzi

[53] Terrence W. Deacon, 1997, *The Symbolic Species: The Co-Evolution of Language and the Brain*, New York: W.W. Norton, pp. 70, 31, 23.

[54] Ibid., pp. 84–86, 124–25; Pär Segerdahl, William Fields, and Sue Savage-Rumbaugh, 2005, *Kanzi's Primal Language: The Cultural Initiation of Primates into Language*, London: Palgrave Macmillan; Duane M. Rumbaugh, ed. 1977, *Language Learning by a Chimpanzee: The Lana Project*, New York: Academic Press.

[55] Terrence W. Deacon, 1997, *The Symbolic Species: The Co-Evolution of Language and the Brain*, New York: W.W. Norton, pp. 322, 352–53.

instance, says that primate brains have essentially the same structure as human brains. But this doesn't stop him from coming to a conclusion similar to Deacon's, this time naming our species-virtue "consciousness," a phenomenon "made dependent upon our human capacity for symbolization ... [where] becoming aware of something is synonymous with capturing its symbolic form ... This rigorous standard of awareness invariably excludes animals from true consciousness, primarily because we have language and they don't."[56] Further: "Ideas that are not within the purview of one's language are not accessible."[57]

A grammar of multimodality shifts the balance away from language, and narrowly on the virtues of language as a symbolic system. We want to put a different interpretation on Peirce's icon ⇔ index ⇔ symbol[§1.0b] – our version of which is likeness ⇔ directedness ⇔ abstraction. Likeness, directedness and abstraction are integrally related processes; none is cognitively or practically superior. Nor should we attribute to language alone human mental capacities to abstract, or even more narrowly, to speech as its proxy.

Humans do abstraction in other forms. The most advanced science and medicine cannot be done without diagrams, and spatialized data presentations, and specialized instruments in dedicated lab spaces. These direct the both-ways traffic of meaning between the ideal – abstractions in these varied forms – and the material universe of things and bodies. In high science, there is a lot of talking around its practices,[58] but the most systematic application of the combinatorial powers of abstraction can't be done in speech.

The quintessential artifacts of abstract knowledge are things like journal articles, medical records, databases, and engineering drawings. Not only are the affordances of speech for abstraction limited; in the most complex and generalizing of abstractions, text is pushed further and further away from speech, and closer to image, in for instance the essentially visual arrangement of ontologies,[§MS3.3a] datasets,[§1.4.6a] and mathematical notation.

Nor is abstraction the highest form of meaning. High science and advanced medicine, to stay with these examples, are necessarily full of likeness (for instance, images) and directedness (for instance, plans). Meanings can be profound without having to be abstract. Indeed, to be effective, abstraction must be supported by sense-making that shunts backwards and forwards across the functions of materialization – likeness, directedness, abstraction. The power of the meaning is in the functional transposition – a kind of "transubstantiation,"[§1.1.2a] if you like.

---

[56] Merlin Donald, 2001, *A Mind So Rare: The Evolution of Human Consciousness*, New York: W.W. Norton, pp. 111–12, 119.
[57] Merlin Donald, 1991, *Origins of the Modern Mind*, Cambridge, MA: Harvard University Press, p. 235.
[58] Bruno Latour and Steve Woolgar, 1986, *Laboratory Life: The Construction of Scientific Facts*, Princeton, NJ: Princeton University Press.

Humans make abstract sense, though as B.F. Skinner[§MS3.1.2d] and other behaviorists have shown, other sentient creatures can make sense in directed ways that at the very least verge on abstraction. Without needing to argue about the borderline of our specially human smarts, we can agree that we share with other creatures the capacity to make sense in likeness and directedness. We stay a natural species to the extent that there is a traffic between mind and matter that we have called materialization. Skinner was not wrong; this traffic means that all sentient creatures can learn, and the processes of learning in all animal species are not fundamentally, existentially, different. In our sense-making, we remain a natural species, and the mystery of meaning is not species-specific. Other creatures live by shared meanings as well. If there is mystery, it is sentience itself.

Just how smart is this species, anyhow? For all our abstraction, for our "consciousness," for our "language," what have we as a species achieved?

We live in a remnant of prairie forest in Central Illinois, and in 2016 the Emerald Ash Borer arrived. Before larvae emerge as brilliant green beetles, they feed on the inner bark and kill the tree. Now the borer/beetle has destroyed the conditions of its living. The ash trees in our forest have all died. Nobody knows, but wood packing for imports from Asia, where the borer is a native, may have brought it to North America. But self-harming change agents like these appear in nature from time to time, and humans are one such creature of nature. Nature is a state of perpetual unbalance, and humans, natural creatures, are just another manifestation of that unbalance.

As sentient creatures, we have proven ourselves no smarter than the Emerald Ash Borer, destroying on a global scale the natural conditions of our own living. We kill each other in wars, and treat each other to cruel inequalities, in fact more so than any other species. If we are different in any respect, we are uniquely hypocritical for our boastful self-congratulation about how smart we are to have language.

We are not that different, and to the extent that we can mean by systems of abstraction as well as by likeness and directedness, our meaning capacities demand more of our species. Our extended powers of materialization and the sociability of our meaning ideally afford us the capacity to care for each other and the earth.

Humans' only difference then is an ethical one, a species responsibility that lies in our unrealized capacities. We have from time to time made ourselves political and economic promises to reach for such ideals beyond the immediate materialities of history. But so far, we have failed to materialize these ideals.

Until some day in a future that is as-yet only ideal, we cannot congratulate ourselves for our capacities to make better sense in the world than other creatures. Before then, we cannot with any justification call ourselves, by virtue of our sense-making capacities, a different kind of species.

In the meantime we remain, just like other creatures, multimodal meaning-makers with limited capacities for meaning and learning. We have yet to honor the fully conscious potentials that we suppose to be the promise of our species.

§1.1.3b Bronisław Malinowski's "Context of Situation"

After the C.S. Peirce appendix in *Meaning of Meaning*,[1a] Ogden and Richards included a forty-page supplement by Bronisław Malinowski.[*] A professor at the London School of Economics, Malinowski became one of the twentieth century's best-known anthropologists, initially for the publication of his doctoral study, *The Family Among the Australian Aborigines*,[59] and later his study of the Trobriand Islanders of Melanesia, *Argonauts of the Western Pacific*.[60]

Ogden and Richards had given Malinowski the proofs of their book, and in the supplement, he heaped praise on their thinking. He takes a fragment from a conversation between Trobrianders about a canoe – "We run front-wood ourselves, we paddle in place, we turn we see companion ours, he runs rear-wood" – and shows that it can't make sense "without reference to the broader context of verbal utterance," the meanings of things and social relationships, both practical and magical, that make the totality of Trobriand culture. For Ogden and Richards' phrase "sign-situatedness," Malinowski substitutes "context of situation." Malinowski is interested in "speech as mode of action rather than as a countersign of thought ."[61] This approach to meaning he characterizes as "functionalist."[62]

M.A.K. Halliday draws inspiration from this idea in Malinowski. "The context of situation is a generalized semiotic construct deriving from the culture – something that is recognized by the members as a form of social activity that they can engage in. Now, any given instance of a situation-type can be defined in terms of three factors that we call field, tenor and mode: what's going on, who's taking part, and what part the particular semiotic system (in this case language) is playing."[63] The meaning is in the function of language in

---

[*] http://meaningpatterns.net/malinowski

[59] Bronislaw Malinowski, 1913 [1963], *The Family Among the Aborigines*, New York: Schocken Books.
[60] Bronislaw Malinowski, 1922 [1984], *Argonauts of the Western Pacific*, Prospect Heights, IL: Waveland Press.
[61] C.K. Ogden and I.A. Richards, 1923 [1989], *The Meaning of Meaning*, San Diego, CA: Harcourt Brace Jovanovich, pp. 300–02, 304, 306, 326; Bronislaw Malinowski, 1948, *Magic, Science and Religion, and Other Essays*, Glencoe, IL: The Free Press, pp. 228–76.
[62] Bronislaw Malinowski, 1962, *Sex, Culture, and Myth*, New York: Harcourt, Brace & World, pp. 223–25.
[63] J.R. Martin, ed. 2013, *Interviews with M.A.K. Halliday: Language Turned Back on Himself*, London: Bloomsbury, p. 80.

the context of situation, hence the name for Halliday's theory, "systemic-functional grammar."§MS0.3a

Halliday's field creates a function in language he calls "ideational" – roughly our "reference." Tenor creates an "interpersonal" function, roughly our "agency." And mode creates a "textual" function, roughly our "structure." But Halliday's system starts and ends with language. His three kinds of function point out from language to situation; the contextual meanings he finds and analyzes are only those to be found in language, meanings on its outside.

For a multimodal grammar, we want to argue, meaning is just as much out there, in and with the context itself. The traffic of meaning goes both ways, between artifacts that are evidence of meaning (speech, writing, objects, and the rest), and the contexts in which they are found. This is why we extend the functions of meaning into context itself. Malinowski, we think, would likely agree.

§1.1.3c Anindilyakwa Kin Classification

As a young student studying for a master's degree in anthropology at Cambridge University, Frederick G.G. Rose was, like M.A.K. Halliday, also inspired by Bronisław Malinowski.§1.1.3b After graduating, he headed for Australia in 1937, and without funding for his work, decided to train as a meteorologist in the hope of being posted somewhere in the remote, tropical north of the continent.

That opportunity came in 1938 when a meteorologist was needed at Umbakumba Bay on Groote Elyandt in the Gulf of Carpentaria. A weather man was needed there because the flying boats on the Sydney to Southampton route of Qantas Empire Airways were about to start landing in the lagoon. It was halfway between Townsville and Darwin, one of many refueling stops in a nine-day flight from Australia to England. Modernity was coming to Groote Eylandt, and Rose wanted to analyze the lives of the indigenous Anindilyakwa people before it was too late.[64]

Rose set himself the task of documenting Anindilyakwa kinship structures.[*] Of the 325 people who lived on the island, he photographed 219, then used the photographs to ask them how they were related to others. He made 25,000 kinship identifications, at which point he had only scratched the surface of a bewilderingly intricate classificatory system.[65]

---

[*] http://meaningpatterns.net/anindilyakwa

[64] Peter Monteath and Valerie Munt, 2015, *Red Professor: The Cold War Life of Fred Rose*, Mile End, Australia: Wakefield Press, pp. 19–20, 40–42; Frederick G.G. Rose, 1968, *Australia Revisited: The Aborigine Story from the Stone Age to the Space Age*, Berlin: Seven Seas Publishers, pp. 50, 119–59.

[65] Frederick G.G. Rose, 1960, *Classification of Kin, Age Structure and Marriage Amongst the Groote Eylandt Aborigines: A Study in Method and a Theory of Australian Kinship*, Berlin: Academie-Verlag.

It was not until he moved to the other side of the continent, to the meteorological station in Broome, that Rose started to make sense of his data. In Broome, he made friends with a young resident medical practitioner, Alec Jolly, newly arrived from the south. Jolly had already scandalized the locals by refusing to have different surgery hours for Aborigines.[66]

Had Rose read Friedrich Engels' *Origin of the Family, Private Property and the State?* asked Jolly. No, he hadn't.[67] Jolly explained that late in his life, Engels' long-time friend and colleague, Karl Marx, had taken an interest in the foundational writings of the American anthropologist Lewis H. Morgan. Marx honored the relative absence of inequalities of the first human societies by naming them "primitive communism."

After Marx died, Engels took Marx's notes and wrote the *Origin of the Family*. Engels' focus was on the material conditions of life in these first societies. These were matrilineal, he argued, as a consequence of the role women played in the reproduction of life itself. These forms of family life came to an end with the arrival of private property and the state. "The overthrow of mother-right was the world historical defeat of the female sex. The man seized the reins in the house also, the woman was degraded, enslaved, the slave of the man's lust, a mere instrument for breeding children."[68]

Using Rose's data from Groote Island, Rose and Jolly wrote an article that was published in 1942 in *Man*, the prestigious journal of the Royal Anthropological Institute in London. There, they concluded that although Anindilyakwa women and men were able to marry multiple husbands and wives and have other sexual relations without sanction, a complex system of kin classification created an intricate pattern of sexual taboos that limited the possibilities of consanguinity in a small population, and thus the emergence of recessive genes. In Australia, some tribes were matrilineal, and even when others appeared to be patrilineal, these, they argued, must originally have been matrilineal. In any event, they at least remained indirectly matrilineal.[69]

Rose and Jolly followed this up with a long article in the *Annals of Eugenics* analyzing with help of elaborate diagrams the major kinship systems in Australia, quite different in their schematic forms, but to the same genetic effect and with underlying matrilineal architectures.[70] In presenting this thesis, they were

---

[66] Peter Monteath and Valerie Munt, 2015, *Red Professor: The Cold War Life of Fred Rose*, Mile End, Australia: Wakefield Press, p. 53.

[67] Ibid., p. 55.

[68] Friedrich Engels, 1892, *The Origin of the Family, Private Property and the State*, New York: International Publishers, p. 47.

[69] Frederick G.G. Rose and A.T.H. Jolly, 1942, "An Interpretation of the Taboo between Mother-in-Law and Son-in-Law," *Man* 42:15–16; Frederick G.G. Rose, 1987, *The Traditional Mode of Production of the Australian Aborigines*, Sydney, Australia: Angus and Robertson, p. 205.

[70] A.T.H. Jolly and Frederick G.G. Rose, 1943, "The Place of the Australian Aboriginal in the Evolution of Society," *Annals of Eugenics* 12:44–87.

following Engels, though they didn't cite him – presumably that wouldn't have helped them to get their paper published in prestigious scholarly journals.

Jolly was a member of the Communist Party of Australia, and Rose's experience of the shocking conditions of life of Aboriginal people on the margins of colonial society prompted him to join as well. The Communist Party published a 64-page booklet they had written together, under the pseudonym "Jagara," *Frederick Engels, Lewis Morgan and the Australian Aborigine.*

"Throughout the Capitalist world today the diplomaed flunkies of the Capitalist State unite in chorus against Morgan and his work and there is hardly an anthropologist of any official standing outside of the Soviet Union, who is not anti-Morgan." In the booklet, they outlined for the benefit of comrades and fellow travelers the elaborate systems of Aboriginal kinship, manifest in "a continual fitting of everybody he meets into his own classificatory system."[71]

After leaving Broome, Rose became a public servant in the Department of Territories in Canberra. Here he was regarded with suspicion and continuously followed by the secret state police, ASIO. In an official government inquiry, he was accused of being a spy for the Soviet Union. Unable to keep his public service job and blocked from getting an academic job, Rose fled Australia.

In 1956, Rose managed to secure a university position in East Berlin. In order to become a professor there, he wrote up his Groote Elyandt research and submitted it for the postdoctoral degree of *Habilitationsschrift* to the Faculty of Philosophy, Humboldt University – "in the democratic sector of Berlin," he said in the introduction. It was published as a 572-page book in 1960, *Classification of Kin, Age Structure and Marriage Amongst the Groote Eylandt Aborigines: A Study in Method and a Theory of Australian Kinship.* Rose dedicated the book "To the Australian working class who alone can ensure the full emancipation of Australian Aborigines."[72]

Meanwhile, in the Soviet Union, Marxist intellectual orthodoxy was on the move. Engels came under fire for regarding the conditions of reproduction of the family as foundational, rather than the means of material production or economic life in so-called "primitive communism," which for Engels – also in retrospective error from a newly minted Soviet point of view – was a subject of "romantic idealization."[73] By his 1960 book, Rose had been forced to toe the party line and Engels, once again, barely gets a mention.[74]

---

[71] Jagara (pseudonym), 1946(?), *Frederick Engels, Lewis Morgan and the Australian Aborigine*, Sydney, Australia: Current Book Distributors, pp. 7, 25.

[72] Frederick G.G. Rose, 1960, *Classification of Kin, Age Structure and Marriage Amongst the Groote Eylandt Aborigines: A Study in Method and a Theory of Australian Kinship*, Berlin: Academie-Verlag, p. v.

[73] L.A. Leontiev, 1944, "Political Economy in the Soviet Union," *Science & Society* 8(2):115–25, pp. 115–16.

[74] Peter Monteath and Valerie Munt, 2015, *Red Professor: The Cold War Life of Fred Rose*, Mile End, Australia: Wakefield Press, p. 88.

When we visited Groote Eylandt to do our literacy work,[§MS0.0a] a missionary linguist, Julie Waddy, was translating the Bible into Anindilyakwa. An Anglican Mission had been set up on Groote in 1943, and one of its first agendas was to build dormitories for girls to prevent what was considered "promiscuity." Christian ideas of monogamy were based on a different and far simpler kin classificatory system than the Anindilyakwa. The notion of promiscuity itself failed to recognize the presence of an elaborate and strictly rule-governed Anindilyakwa system of kin.

Rose called these rules of kin polygyny and gerontocracy, where both men and women who lived their whole lifespan would have at least four marriages, and where the age differences were vast in both directions, older/younger men and women marrying younger/older men and women. All of this was regulated by elaborate marriage promises and incest taboos, as well as an economic logic related to the work of men and women, and the reproductive age of women.[75]

If the missionaries failed to see this, they did nevertheless find a bewilderingly complex system in the language – which also expressed, unbeknown to them, evidence of pre-dormitory kinship practices.

"Anindilyakwa is the world's hardest language," Julie Waddy's missionary assistant told us when we were doing our research there. "There are five noun classes for non-human things, eighteen personal pronoun prefixes, including distinctions such as between first-person inclusive and first-person exclusive … There is lots of redundancy. For example, both pronouns and verbs indicate person. In writing the Bible down, a lot of the redundancy is removed, edited out." The "editing out" was not just linguistic. The dormitories and the Bible translation together were editing out a way of life.[76]

This brings us back to our multimodal grammar. Rose showed, in the case of the Anindilyakwa, Aboriginal kinship systems were extraordinarily complex, and for a systematic purpose. This is the "context of situation" of a complicated set of relationship classifiers. Rose found thirty-three Anindilyakwa relationship words during his research, including *dadidja* or mother's mother's brother's daughter, and *nabura*, father's sister's son. This was the contextual basis for the plethora of pronouns encountered by the Bible translators and the elaborate redundancy through syntactic inflection. These were not mere

---

[75] Frederick G.G. Rose, 1965, *The Winds of Change in Central Australia: The Aborigines at Angus Downs, 1962*, Berlin: Academie-Verlag, pp. 1–2, 100; Frederick G.G. Rose, 1987, *The Traditional Mode of Production of the Australian Aborigines*, Sydney, Australia: Angus and Robertson, pp. xiii–xiv.

[76] Bill Cope, 1998, "The Language of Forgetting: A Short History of the Word," pp. 192–223 in *Seams of Light: Best Antipodean Essays*, edited by M. Fraser, Sydney, Australia: Allen and Unwin; Velma J. Leeding, 1996, "Body Parts and Possession in Anindilyakwa," pp. 193–249 in *The Grammar of Inalienability: A Typological Perspective on Body Part Terms and the Part–Whole Relation*, edited by H. Chappel and W. McGregor, Berlin: Mouton de Gruyter; R.M.W. Dixon, 1980, *The Languages of Australia*, Cambridge: Cambridge University Press, p. 84.

figments of language, nor singularly conceptual. They were deeply written into
the material experience of life – the meanings in bodies and words were at one.

And even more in the Anindilyakwa grammar of multimodality: the structures of lineage that governed marriage and taboos – clans, moieties, sections,
and subsections – were marked by totems. By transposition, groups and persons
in those groups are the wind, a bird, the central hill on the island. People live at
the classificatory intersection of their co-presence as totemic animals, as
representatives of place. These meanings are tied together into "Dreamtime"
accounts of the genesis of the universe, pasts that are also manifest as destinies
eternally to be re-enacted in every present.

Still more complicated, the names are fluid – different people known and
named according to the namer's relation to them. And when someone dies, the
world must be renamed. Not only exceedingly complex, these meanings were
far more fluid than static systems of meaning in the modern world where
signifier–signified relations are relatively stable, stable enough to afford, as
Saussure did,[§MS3d] priority to structure over history in meaning.

In terms of our typology of materialization, Anindilyakwa kin is a system of
abstraction. Kin and totemic meanings are not formed on the basis of resemblance or direct pointing; they are as purely arbitrary as Peirce's and Deacon's
"symbols."[§1.1.3a] The difference between these and modern abstractions is their
integrated multimodality, the essential synesthesia of their materialization.
Abstractions like Bertrand Russell's [§MS1a] or Ludwig Wittgenstein's[§MS2.1.1a]
are isolated in text, idealizations with tenuous connections to the material world
that they might be expected to encompass. Aboriginal kinship classifications,
no less abstract, subsist in a continuous dialogue between the ideal and the
material.

Not that some of the most famous anthropologists have been able to notice
this complexity in the ways Rose did. Emile Durkheim and Marcel Mauss
conceded that Aboriginal kin was indeed a classificatory system, albeit
"simple."[77] Lucien Lévy-Bruhl was impressed enough by so-called "primitive
mentality" to write about it extensively, but still considered it "pre-logical."[78]
Perhaps the twentieth century's most famous anthropologist, Claude Lévi-
Strauss,[§1.4.7a] drew a distinction between the "savage mind" and the modern
mind, the former like the "bricoleur" cobbling together "the oddments left over
from human endeavors," the latter like an engineer with abstract projects and
conceptual plans that transcend immediate experience. He invokes Saussure to
say how the savage mind conflates image/signifier and concept/signified, and

---

[77] Emile Durkheim and Marcel Mauss, 1903 [1963], *Primitive Classification*, translated by R.
Needham, Chicago, IL: University of Chicago Press.

[78] Lucien Lévy-Bruhl, 1910 [1985], *How Natives Think*, translated by L.A. Clare, Princeton, NJ:
Princeton University Press; Lucien Lévy-Bruhl, 1921 [1923], *Primitive Mentality*, translated by
L.A. Clare, New York: Macmillan.

Peirce to indicate its serial directedness.[79] But when Rose's *Classification of Kin* book came out, Lévi-Strauss did write him a nice note: "As far as I know your inquiry into age structure, associated with a series of marriage rule and kinship systems is something quite new."[80]

Notwithstanding the ideological pressure, Rose never fully recanted his support for Engels. In a book published in Australia near the end of his life, he quoted him again, this time to restate his case "that regularities were certain to be found in Australian kinship systems, these regularities were the concrete expression – or the philosophical necessity – of the reciprocity and cooperative nature of Aboriginal society."[81] In Aboriginal society work, sex, and philosophy were a unitary system. The differences between First Peoples and modern people is not their degrees of abstraction, but the kinds of multimodal transposition they practice.

The Australian working class proved unable, and also likely unwilling, to emancipate Aboriginal people. The German Democratic Republic[§2.3d] imploded the year Rose died. However, recent thinking in anthropology has vindicated Morgan's, Engels', and Rose's proposition that the societies of First Peoples were matrilineal.[82]

The missionaries are gone from Groote now. When we were working there, random gunshots rang out through the night. The policeman told us that it had the highest rate of crime per capita in the world. Police wouldn't even go to Umbakumba, he said, nor the ambulance, it was too dangerous. The ambulance people say that if you can't get yourself out to the medical center in white settlement near the manganese mine, you're not going to survive anyway.[83]

§1.2   Participation

> ***Participation.*** *The making of meaning in the context of the social relations of its sharing – whether it is representation (making meanings for oneself); communication (making meanings that are accessible to others); or interpretation (making sense of meanings in the found objects of multimodal communication).*

---

[79] Claude Lévi-Strauss, 1962 [1966], *The Savage Mind*, Chicago, IL: University of Chicago Press, pp. 16–22.

[80] Peter Monteath and Valerie Munt, 2015, *Red Professor: The Cold War Life of Fred Rose*, Mile End, Australia: Wakefield Press, p. 183.

[81] Frederick G.G. Rose, 1987, *The Traditional Mode of Production of the Australian Aborigines*, Sydney, Australia: Angus and Robertson, p. 203.

[82] Chris Knight, 2008, "Early Human Kinship Was Matrilineal," pp. 61–82 in *Early Human Kinship*, edited by N.J. Allen, H. Callan, R. Dunbar, and W. James, Oxford: Blackwell.

[83] Bill Cope, 1998, "The Language of Forgetting: A Short History of the Word," pp. 192–223 in *Seams of Light: Best Antipodean Essays*, edited by M. Fraser, Sydney, Australia: Allen and Unwin. Also at: http://newlearningonline.com/literacies/chapter-1/cope-on-indigenous-austra lian-language-change

The fruit of communication is participation, says John Dewey.[1.1] And more: "there is a natural bridge that joins the gap between existence and essence; namely communication, language, discourse."[84]

We want to formulate this differently. Participation in meaning is not (just) an outcome of communication. This is to position communication too centrally in human meaning, to make communication the causal center of meaning at the expense of other kinds of participation. In Dewey we once again encounter the pervasive bias towards language as the pre-eminent human meaning system, and within language, speech-as-communication at the expense of writing.

We begin with Dewey's term "participation," but we want to turn his formulation around the other way. Participation, or the sociability of shared human meanings, is the remarkable thing. Communication is just one way to situate the functions of a meaning in the context of their use.

Participation functions in three, quite different ways: representation, communication, and interpretation. These may be different moments and places of meaning-action, or they may happen together in real time and shared space. They are integrally related to each other because the one is always ready to become the other, by transposition. But they are qualitatively different. And the meanings always shift in the transposition from the one to the other.

Participation is as miraculous as the transubstantiation of the bread and wine of the eucharist into the body and blood of Christ.[1.1.2a] That we can share meanings is miraculous, and we do this through functional transpositions between representation, communication, and interpretation. Each time, this a creative act where although the patternings are recognizable in their sources, the world never stays quite the same. Rather, it is redesigned in some way.

Here is a rough map of sense-making participation as the relation of meaning to context:

Form / Function: Participation	Text	Image	Space	Object	Body	Sound	Speech
Representation	Figuring things out by writing, notes to self	Visualizing, mental images	Envisioning space or in space, the architect	Envisioning an object or with an object, the designer	Envisioning embodied action, or by acting out	Anticipating a sound, or sounding to oneself	Inner speech
Communication	Writing for others	Image making	Making space	Creating or placing objects	Embodied action	Making a sound	Audible speech
Interpretation	Reading	Viewing	Navigating space, inhabiting	Making use or sense of objects, consumer	Encountering or observing other bodies	Listening to a sound	Hearing

Fig. 1.2: Participation

[84] John Dewey, 1925, *Experience and Nature*, Chicago, IL: Open Court, p. 167.

§1.2.1 Representation

> ***Representation.*** *Doing things to make sense for oneself, in thought and action –*
> *where individual bodies and minds re-enact the social in order to make personal*
> *meaning.*

Raymond Williams locates in the writings of John Wyclif the first use in
English of "representation" to mean "standing for" – "ymagis that representen
pomp and glorie of tho worlde" (*c.*1380).[85] Wyclif would have needed a
distinction between representation and communication in order to make his
case about transubstantiation – the bread and wine of the eucharist means to the
communicant the body and blood of Christ (by representation), though it is also
not that (in the materiality of communication).[§1.1.2a]

In recent social theory, a distinction between "representation" and "communication" is often lost. Here is Stuart Hall: "Meanings can only be shared through our
common access to language ... Language is the privileged medium in which we
'make sense' of things, in which meaning is produced and exchanged. Language is
able to do this because it operates as a representational system ... In language, we
use signs and symbols ... to stand for or to represent to other people our concepts,
ideas, and feelings."[*] Apart from this language-centrism, Hall's "circuit of culture"
leaves out communication because it has been displaced by representation – but by
"representation," he seems to mean what we would call communication.[86]

Gunther Kress[§2c] has been one of the few to make a distinction that we need
as much today as Wyclif did in his day: "Representation and communication
are distinct social practices. Representation focuses on my interest in my
engagement with the world and on my wish to give material realization to
my meanings about that world. Communication focuses on my wish or need to
make that representation available to others, in my interaction with them."[87]

Representation and communication are both social, but differently so.
Communication is manifestly social: to encounter a meaning that has been
made by another, this kind of participation in meaning. Representation is a
completely different kind of participation because it is only secondarily
social. It is making meaning for myself, perhaps just in my thinking and so
in a way that is not immediately visible to others, or in material objects of

---

[*] http://meaningpatterns.net/hall

[85] Raymond Williams, 1976, *Keywords: A Vocabulary of Culture and Society*, Glasgow: Fontana/
Croom Helm, p. 233.

[86] Stuart Hall, Jessica Evans, and Sean Nixon, 2013, *Representation*, London: Sage, pp. xvii–xviii.

[87] Gunther Kress, 2009, *Multimodality: A Social Semiotic Approach to Contemporary
Communication*, London: Routledge, p. 49.

meaning that I make to support my thinking. I speak silently to myself, I create mental images, I envision a gesture, I plan in my mind's eye how I might navigate a space.

We experience these ways of making sense in our personal selves, but these kinds of mental work are grounded in our life-specific and materially grounded experiences of speech, sight, embodiment, and space. We can anticipate, expect, plan, and hope meanings based on our social-historical experiences of meaning. We can also – ideally – exceed these meanings, but always building on the ground of their figuring.

Representation, however, is not just a cognitive thing. Some meanings are too hard to figure just in the head, only mentally. They require cognitive prostheses, thinking extensions for the mind and body. So, to help us think, we may need to write, or draw, or practice a sounding, or rehearse a gesture, or hold an object, or make a model, or conduct an experiment. We need to work at our representations not just in mental effort, but using media. So, we may materialize our meanings without necessary intent to communicate. We may mutter under our breath, hum, sketch, make notes, enact, walk through, and a myriad of other such acts of representation.

More than just thinking, we represent meanings to ourselves as creatures whose experience of the material world is perennially immersive. The sources of our meanings are in the materiality of our meaning practices. As much as they are in our heads, they are in the things around us, our available resources for meaning, pulled down from our contexts.

The story of participation may end with representation. Something can be thought and enacted to make meaning for oneself, then never communicated – unless, of course, another person chances to overhear your muttering, come across your sketch, or notice you walking through. Nevertheless, the resources for representation are previously communicated meanings and learned capacities to use media. These are the found objects on which our representational designs are based – so in this sense, there is no priority of representation over communication, only simultaneity.

§1.2.1a Lev Vygotsky's "Inner Speech"

"Inner speech is speech for oneself; external speech is for others,"[88] says Lev Vygotsky,[§MS1.1.3a] and though these are connected, they are fundamentally different in their forms and functions.[*]

---

[*] http://meaningpatterns.net/inner-speech

[88] Lev Semyonovich Vygostky, 1934 [1986], *Thought and Language*, Cambridge, MA: MIT Press, p. 225.

In our terminology, inner speech is representation, and external speech is communication. Communication is not a straightforward replication of representation, as if we could simply say what we thought. Nor is thinking simply a product of what is sayable, as if the development of our meanings were singularly speech-centered. There is always a grammatical transposition, whether one chooses to use the word "grammar" in its narrower sense, as the syntax of speech, or in the broader sense of patterns in meaning that we use in this book.

Vygotsky's starting point is an argument he has with the work of child psychologist Jean Piaget, his contemporary. Piaget documents the "egocentric speech" of the young child, a stage of development where the child speaks to themself, oblivious of communication. As the child gets older, egocentric speech disappears. Egocentric speech is a moment in the transition from the asocial baby to the social child. It appears as a stage in the assimilation of speech, until a point where it is internalized as self-speaking thought. Then, speaking to oneself becomes like speaking to others. Speech has come to mind.[89]

At every point, Vygotsky, and in later reiterations, Luria, turn this narrative of life history and meaning formation around the other way. The child starts social, connected to the breast of its mother, acquiescing to the orders of its elders. Egocentric speech is social too. Vygotsky's empirical research shows that children mostly speak to themselves when there are others around. He calls this "collective monologue," requiring that the child is "with comprehending others to maintain the illusion of being understood."

In a final stage, the vocalization stops, and becomes what Vygotsky terms "inner speech" – social meaning again, but in a different way. The social has become individual, and so the individual is socialized. Where Piaget's primal individual becomes social by assimilation and speech becomes a conduit for thought, Vygotsky's primal social being becomes individual by transposing social meanings into their representations.

And here is another fundamental difference between Piaget and Vygotsky – the grammar of representations in inner speech does not during the course of development converge with speech; rather it diverges from the grammar of vocalized speech. The divergence can be traced in the processes of development of egocentric speech in the small child, which with time becomes less scrutable compared to vocalized speech. Inner speech becomes less and less intelligible to an accidental listener; it becomes less and less like speech in its form and less communicative in its function.

If speech requires action structures of predication,[§MS2.1.1] where there is a subject, late egocentric speech is a precursor to inner speech, where there are only predicates. As it moves toward inner speech, egocentric speech becomes more

---

[89] Ibid., pp. 226, 231; Jean Piaget, 1923 [2002], *Language and Thought of the Child*, London: Routledge.

abbreviated and less coherent to people who may happen to be overhearing.[90] In the terms of our grammar, inner speech (representation) is maximally context-dependent. We don't need an explicitly referenced subject because we are the subject or the subject is just obvious. Overt speech (communication) needs a subject if the predicate is to have meaning intelligible to another person. These are fundamental differences – differences we must navigate in the transposition of meanings-in-representation to meanings-in-communication.

Sometimes representation may come closer to communication, when for instance we rehearse something that we plan to say, or when we envisage a photograph in our mind's eye before we take it, or where we foreshadow a gesture – pointing in each case to the imminent movability of meanings in transposition. These are the kinds of meaning-work we do in order to move between representation and communication. In any case, anticipatory representation is by no means straightforward prefiguring of the communication that may follow.

We also suggest that these representations are intrinsically synesthetic, more so than communication which is always constrained by the practicalities of its materiality. A word in inner speech is overlaid in simultaneous multimodal hieroglyph of image, embodied feeling, senses of space, sound, and more. The further inner speech is from vocalized speech in its grammatical structures, the more tightly bound it will be with other forms of meaning.

Representation, then, is a primary site of synesthesia. The practicalities of communication, and the materiality of its media – the affordances of communication – tend to separate the forms of meaning to a greater degree than happens in the mind. Representation is more fluidly synesthetic because its media are virtual, immaterial envisionings of practices of meaning that were in the first instance social and material, but which in the moment of representation are no longer that.

In thought, we can exceed the material and plan to transform the social. This is why the mind becomes a fertile site for the hopes and dreams of what Jean-Paul Sartre calls "the Imaginary."§MS3.1.2b

§1.2.2   Communication

> **Communication.** *Encounters with the material traces of meanings made by others – texts, images, spaces, objects, bodies, sounds, speech. The forms of these traces that can be received by others as meaningful.*

---

[90] Lev Semyonovich Vygostky, 1934 [1986], *Thought and Language*, Cambridge, MA: MIT Press, pp. 226–38; Aleksandr Romanovich Luria, 1981, *Language and Cognition*, New York: John Wiley and Sons, pp. 104–07; James V. Wertsch, 1991, *Voices of the Mind*, Cambridge, MA: Harvard University Press, pp. 40–43.

Although participation may end with representation – meaning can be made without communication – there can be no communication without prior representation. Communication, however, is not a straightforward re-enactment of representation. It involves functional transposition, and with transposition, design and transformation of meaning. Inner speech[§1.2.1a] is quite different from vocalized speech in the form of its meaning. Mental images are quite different from perception and pictures.[§MS3.1.2b] The grammars of representation are fundamentally different from those of communication, and meaning-work needs to be done for transposition to occur. Material as well as mental work is required to turn representation into communication.

Some representation may already come close to communication, where for instance meaning for oneself begins to take material forms. In order to think, a meaning-maker may re-enact multimodal experience of their learning to mean, purely in their mind's eye or using media supports as cognitive prostheses. The meaning in representation is made by moving backwards and forwards between the ideal and the material media of would-be communication. Representation is a dialectical movement between the ideal and the material, where the possible shape of the ideal has been prefigured in a life-historical relation to available designs of meaning – in text, images, spaces, objects, body, sound, speech.

When such representations come closer to communication, when they use its artifacts, communication may happen that was not necessarily intended. An artifact of representation may be communicated if sufficiently materialized and then found – a diary read that had been meant for no other eyes, a demeanor noticed, whispering to oneself that is overheard. Such forms of representation come close to communication even before they are encountered by others. These are hybrid, intermediate meanings, caught halfway through the transposition from representation to communication.

A musician in practice (representation) prefigures as best they can a performance (communication), and the practice might incidentally be overheard. A teacher marking a student essay does so, not because they need to know its communicated contents; it is more like they are listening in to the student's thinking aloud, the exercise of writing that gives shape to their thoughts. Such transpositions are fluid, always works-in-progress. On the journey from representation to communication, in this work of meaning, there are many such halfway forms. Representation and communication, like all moments of meaning, are never even for a moment stable functions. They are always moving, the one always ready to become the other, indeed begging that becoming.

And communicated meanings need not be intentional in another way. Natural things also communicate meaning. The meanings of a lake, a star in the sky, or a zebra are what they are because, manifestly, they exist in meaningful form. They are meanings encountered, meanings-in. We also re-mean them in each new encounter because they have been meant before, by us or by others, in image, word, and embodied experience. Natural things mean themselves, and then their meanings are mediated through our human experiences of nature. As well, there are no human-made meanings that don't have a natural-material substrate, in media and the entities and actions referenced.

Aleksandr Luria:[§MS1.1.3a] "One must seek the origins of human consciousness activity and 'categorical' behavior not in the recesses of the human brain or in the depths of the spirit, but in the external conditions of life . . ., the social and historical forms of human existence."[91]

Here now is our response to Chomsky's late "weirdness,"[§MS3.1.2j] the mystery of human speech, a core of meaning that he thinks must be located somewhere in the depths of biological evolution, but that he concedes may never be found. Our account of the sources of meaning suggests a prosaic alternative. In a multimodal grammar, individuals are immersed in the meanings-in the world that surrounds them – their contexts – not just in speech but in bodies, objects, spaces, images, texts, sounds. Some of these are natural, meanings-in, and when they are, human meanings are overlaid, meanings-for. Others of these are human, but even human meanings have been shaped with tools made of and in nature.

The world is meaning-full, and learning is a process of becoming that meaning for oneself. A life of sense-making is a life of continuous reinvention of the world through the work of participation through transposition: representation ⇔ communication ⇔ interpretation. Learning comes through participation.

§1.2.2a The Rule of St Benedict

Appalled by the vices and hypocrisies of the Church in Rome, St Benedict of Nursia (c.480–543) devised *The Rule of St Benedict*, laying out an ideal form of institutional life.[*] This writing becomes the foundational text of Western Monasticism.[92]

"There are four kinds of monks," Benedict says in the first of the seventy-three chapters in his *Rule*. There are hermits, who strive alone to find the meaning of God. There are societies of cohabiting monks with no rules. There are monks who are wanderers. But a fourth kind of monk lives under the rule of an abbot.[93] It is this kind of institutional sociability – of participation – that the *Rule* prescribes.

---

* http://meaningpatterns.net/benedict

[91] Aleksandr Romanovich Luria, 1981, *Language and Cognition*, New York: John Wiley and Sons, p. 25.
[92] F.A. Forbes, 1921, *Saint Benedict*, New York: P.J. Kennedy and Sons, p. 71.
[93] St Benedict, c.530 [1949], *The Holy Rule of St. Benedict*, translated by Rev. Boniface Verheyen, Grand Rapids, MI: Christian Classics Ethereal Library, Chapter 1.

"To thee, therefore, my speech is now directed, who, giving up thine own will, takest up the strong and most excellent arms of obedience, to do battle for Christ the Lord, the true King."[94]

The *Rule* is presented as speech transcribed into text. It is definitively communication, the traces of representation erased in abstract commands. The commandant – the ultimate speaker – is Christ-God, and the abbot an interlocutor. In the constitution of social meanings, the authority of God is communicated through the authority of the abbot. The abbot commands, however these commands are God's, not his. Nowhere is there an account of God the dialogical deliberator. God just commands. God communicates without knowable representation. The communication comes down the line, and when the abbot communicates God's commands, no scope is allowed for divergent re-representation, for interpretation.

"For it belongeth to the master to speak and to teach; it becometh the disciple to be silent and to listen. If, therefore, anything must be asked of the Superior, let it be asked with all humility and respectful submission."[95]

These are habits we have developed in unequal societies with their bias towards communication, erasing deliberative agency in prior representation, and then, with communication, dialogue, and subsequent interpretation. This is how our theories of meaning have come to focus on communication as if that were the focal form of participation in meaning, at the expense of representation and interpretation.

Sometimes, this communication-as-command presents itself as gentle power, only exposing its more fundamental social conditions of participation in moments of potential or actual transgression. In Benedict's *Rule*, the relation of master and disciple was made to seem perfectly reasonable, expressing hierarchy in ways that were also at times delicately cajoling. But when in other moments command is its fundamental purpose, the commandant must be direct in their communication and severe in their enforcement.

"For in his teaching the Abbot should . . . show the severity of the master and the loving affection of a father. He must sternly rebuke the undisciplined and restless; but he must exhort the obedient, meek, and patient to advance in virtue." The monk, for his part, should adopt a demeanor of humility, so "if hard and distasteful things are commanded, nay, even though injuries are inflicted, he accept them with patience and even temper, and not grow weary or give up, but hold out."[96]

The *Rule* is the stuff of text, whose injunctions communicants must heed. It also prescribes certain forms of speech: listen silently to the speech of the master, and if speech is required, it must be submissive. These rules of text and speech are also framed by context, or what Giorgio Agamben calls, after

---

[94] Ibid., Prologue.   [95] Ibid., Chapter 6.   [96] Ibid., Chapters 2, 7.

Wittgenstein, [§MS2.3.2a] a form-of-life. This includes the architectonics of the monastery, its "total mobilization of existence" through the strict timing of prayers and work. The monk's affectedly modest habit with its leather belt constitutes the monk as a "soldier of Christ." The speaking master and the listening disciple cannot assume these positions except in embodied social behavior, in collocated space and simultaneous time. The meaning of the *Rule* is in the reciprocal relations of text and speech to its form-of-life. These are "constitutive norms."[97]

One such configuration of objects and bodies in time and space is the *lectio* – when the abbot speaks or reads aloud the *Rule* or the Gospel. This is a peculiar halfway practice, somewhere between reading and speaking. Functionally, it is an artifact of meaning where participation is reduced to communication, at the expense of representation and interpretation.

In the parallel development of global modernity, this is not just a Western form – Islam in its first centuries invents the same hierarchical relations of meaning: the "Qur'an" or Koran means recitation,[§MS3a] from the Arabic verb *qara'a*; *lectio* derives from the Latin verb *legere*, to read out, read aloud, or recite.[98]

In human history, this is a new configuration of meaning, where speech and action are constitutionally regulated by textual rule. It becomes not just the social relations of the "lecture," but later becomes a central practice in the modern form of life that is institutionalized education. Or at least this is the case in its most didactic forms, where transmission via communication is emphasized at the expense of participation through representation and interpretation, where command is at the expense of agency, where epistemic replication is at the expense of creative thinking and rethinking, where repetition is at the expense of creative divergence, and where reproduction of meaning is at the expense of generative (re)design.

§1.2.2b Daphne Koller on MOOCs

In 2012 MOOCs (Massive Open Online Courses) were new, and Coursera only six months old.[*] Already, said its co-founder, Daphne Koller, in a TED talk, Coursera had offered courses to "640,000 students from 190 countries. We have 1.5 million enrollments, 6 million quizzes in the 15 classes that have launched so far have been submitted, and 14 million videos have been

---

[*] http://meaningpatterns.net/koller

[97] Giorgio Agamben, 2011 [2013], *The Highest Poverty: Monastic Rules and Form-of-Life*, translated by A. Kotsko, Stanford, CA: Stanford University Press, pp. 23, 15, 61, 71–72.

[98] George Makdisi, 1981, *The Rise of Colleges: Institutions of Learning in Islam and the West*, Edinburgh: Edinburgh University Press, pp. 242–43.

viewed."[99] These numbers seem small by web standards, but were impressive for a start-up company.

The difference in communication was not in the manner of participation. That was still fundamentally that of *lectio* or the *qara'a*.[§1.2.2a] MOOCs are essentially video recordings of lectures, assembled into "courses," and where it still becometh the disciple of knowledge to be silent and listen. The difference is only a minor recalibration of the terms of participation.

In MOOCs you can view the lectures in your own time and place, and they are free or affordably cheap, depending on the level of recognition the learner wants for their participation. They are conveniently broken into 8–12 minute pieces. A viewer can replay something they didn't understand the first time. They skip the parts they already think they know, or they can play them at double speed, and the lecture is still intelligible. For these recalibrations in the lecture as a medium of communication, MOOCs soon had millions, then tens of millions of enrollments.

Koller continues, and you can hear echoes of St Benedict's cajoling:

Of course, we all know as educators that students don't learn by sitting and passively watching videos. Perhaps one of the biggest components of this effort is that we need to have students who practice with the material in order to really understand it ... even simple retrieval practice, where students are just supposed to repeat what they already learned gives considerably improved results on various achievement tests down the line than many other educational interventions. We've tried to build in retrieval practice into the platform ... For example, even our videos are not just videos. Every few minutes, the video pauses and the students get asked a question.[100]

This is a minor refinement of St Benedict's relations of communication. The spread of digitally recorded, internet-delivered lectures has been rapid, in ordinary classrooms too, where in the wake of MOOCs, the craze of the "flipped classroom" has taken off.[101] Instead of lecturing in real time and collocated space, the teacher records their lecture on video. With a camera today on every computer and phone, recording is easy and cheap. But, fundamentally, this is still

[99] www.ted.com/talks/daphne_koller_what_we_re_learning_from_online_education   [100] Ibid.
[101] Jacob Bishop and Matthew Verleger, 2013, "The Flipped Classroom: A Survey of the Research," paper presented at the American Society for Engineering Education, 23–26 June, Atlanta, GA; Mary Kalantzis and Bill Cope, 2015, "Learning and New Media," pp. 373–87 in *The Sage Handbook of Learning*, edited by D. Scott and E. Hargreaves, Thousand Oaks, CA: Sage; Bill Cope and Mary Kalantzis, 2015, "Assessment and Pedagogy in the Era of Machine-Mediated Learning," pp. 350–74 in *Education as Social Construction: Contributions to Theory, Research, and Practice*, edited by T. Dragonas, K.J. Gergen, S. McNamee and E. Tseliou, Chagrin Falls, OH: Worldshare Books; Bill Cope and Mary Kalantzis, 2017, "Conceptualizing E-Learning," pp. 1–45 in *E-Learning Ecologies*, edited by B. Cope and M. Kalantzis, New York: Routledge.

the *lectio* or *qara'a*. New life has been breathed into a communicative form that is a millennium and a half old.

When we went back to Daphne Koller's TED Talk, two and a half million people already had viewed it, itself a *lectio* or *qara'a*. We work in e-learning too. We know Daphne Koller and have ourselves been creating MOOC courses since Coursera's early days. But we only feel we know MOOCs because we have participated in these things, not just as the objects of communication, but as subjects, turning our representations into these recalibrated forms of communication. This is how we have learned the meaning of the MOOC, by mastering this transposition from representation to communication, not just by being its disciples. As for the interpretation of our meanings, apart from star-ratings and short reviews, that is as lost on us as it is in any communication-centered medium.

§1.2.3   Interpretation

> ***Interpretation.*** *Making sense of found objects of communicated meaning, an act of re-representation where the communicated meaning is never a matter of unmediated transmission; rather the meaning is in what we make of the object of communication, a relation between that object and the interpreter's making of it.*

To interpret is to make a meaning of something communicated, whether that meaning is communicated intentionally, or a found artifact of representation, or a naturally occurring meaning-in. Interpretations are not what things are, or what is communicated, but what we make of them. Interpretations are re-representations, and not just cognitively so. They are the simultaneously mental-material work of reading, viewing, inhabiting, using, observing, and listening. Interpretation is the job we do to reframe communicated meaning to serve our interests.

Participation requires transposition: representations are always ready to be communicated; communications are always ready to be interpreted; and interpretations are at the same time new representations. Representation, communication, and interpretation are quite different kinds of meaning work, but participation requires all three kinds of work and the ever-ready transposability of one kind of work for another.

This makes for the continuity and sociability in meaning, its reiterated patterning. But it also makes for change as agents of meaning continuously transform the work by never-before-created recombinations and the excesses of their imagination.

Participation, to put it another way, is a design activity; if representation works with available designs, and communication is designing that leaves traces encountered by others, then interpretation is the re-design of these traces to make sense for ourselves.[§MS0.4.1]

§1.2.3a Roland Barthes' "Death of the Author"

Following Charles Sanders Peirce,[§1.0b] Umberto Eco[§2.1] defines the "interpretant" as new representation that refers to an object of communication.[102] It is a new meaning by virtue of a process of re-representation where the experiences of the meaning-maker are always uniquely configured to the circumstances of their life history – James Paul Gee calls these "networks of association."[103] Meanings in interpretation are never the same as meanings communicated.

However, the meaning made is not arbitrary. It is a product of what Eco calls social "habit," of meaning convention. It is not that the representation, or the communication, or the interpretation, ever transparently means the object of its attention – such an ontological realism is not possible. Rather, what is possible is a "pragmatic realism," the truth of human meaning that is created habitually in the "continual circularity" of "accepted correlations" and "public agreement."[104]

So, says Roland Barthes,[§MS1.2.2d] don't fall into the modern trap where we privilege communication by inquiring into the author's intention, as if that could transparently convey their meaning.[*] Don't think for a moment that meaning could be singularly the author's, because their representational resources are themselves social – never truly representative of their individually sensible selves because the meanings they make are always re-representational, products of an earlier moment of interpretation. "The text is a tissue of quotations drawn from the innumerable centres of culture."[105]

We can track meanings back as far as we may wish through the infinite regress of the participatory chain. Then, when the reader comes to make sense of the text, they work not just with an author and the artifact of their communication. They work with the polyphony of text, the multifariousness of its antecedent meanings. The reader "is simply that someone who holds together in a single field all the traces by which the written text is constituted." So,

---

* http://meaningpatterns.net/barthes

102 Umberto Eco, 1976, *A Theory of Semiotics*, Bloomington: Indiana University Press, pp. 15–17, 68–69; Umberto Eco, 1979, *The Role of the Reader: Explorations in the Semiotics of Texts*, Bloomington: Indiana University Press, pp. 180–89.

103 James Paul Gee, 1992 [2013], *The Social Mind: Language, Ideology, and Social Practice*, Champaign, IL: Common Ground, pp. 42–44.

104 Umberto Eco, 1979, *The Role of the Reader: Explorations in the Semiotics of Texts*, Bloomington: Indiana University Press, pp. 192–93, 197–98.

105 Roland Barthes, 1976, *Image-Music-Text*, translated by S. Heath, London: Fontana, p. 146.

Barthes concludes with a celebrated rhetorical flourish, "the birth of the reader must be at the cost of the death of the author."[106]

Or to reframe this for a transpositional grammar, the birth of the interpreter must be at the cost of the death of the communicator – or at least the communicator as the paragon of participatory meaning.

§1.2.3b Hans-Georg Gadamer's Truth and Method

" . . . and so we will start by following Heidegger," says Hans-Georg Gadamer at the end of a long introductory section in his magnum opus, *Truth and Method*.[107] Here we encounter another of the famed modern texts on the function of language in the creation of meaning.*

Gadamer starts within Heidegger's hermeneutical circle, a circle of interpretation where "fore-having, fore-sight, and fore-conception" are integral to our meaning. Meanings are not simply to be found in the artifacts of speech, text, art. We bring our prior experiences of meaning to bear as we make sense of the meanings we encounter. "What Heidegger is working out here is not primarily a prescription for the practice of understanding, but a description of the way interpretive understanding is achieved."[108]

Gadamer develops his own terms to describe what an interpreter brings to meaning: horizon, tradition, and prejudice.

Horizon: "We define the concept of 'situation' by saying that it represents a standpoint that limits the possibility of vision. Hence essential to the concept of situation is the concept of 'horizon.' The horizon is the range of vision that includes everything that can be seen from a particular vantage point."[109]

Tradition: "The anticipation of meaning that governs our understanding of a text is not an act of subjectivity, but proceeds from the commonality that binds us to the tradition."[110]

Prejudice: "The prejudices of the individual . . . constitute the historical reality of his being." Our prejudices are the starting point for interpretation. We make meaning from within the horizons of our life experience, on the basis of tradition, in ways that are peculiar to ourselves and our histories. "Thus the meaning of 'belonging' – i.e., the element of tradition in our historical-hermeneutical activity – is fulfilled in the commonality of fundamental, enabling prejudices." Then, in defense of this seemingly heretical idea: "The fundamental prejudice of the

---

* http://meaningpatterns.net/gadamer

[106] Ibid., p. 148.
[107] Hans-Georg Gadamer, 1960 [2004], *Truth and Method*, translated by J. Weinsheimer and D.G. Marshall, London: Continuum, p. 254.
[108] Ibid., p. 269.   [109] Ibid., p. 301.   [110] Ibid., p. 293.

Enlightenment is the prejudice against prejudice itself, which denies tradition its power."[111]

Gadamer's system nevertheless leaves scope for openness and change, albeit limited. It allows that the meaning-maker's horizons can expand, that traditions can evolve in history, and that prejudices can be incrementally revised. This is because the meanings one encounters are never from the same time and place. They must always be to some degree strange to us. So, we find ourselves in a conversational relationship with them. However, the effect is always within horizon, and tradition. Our prejudices can be deepened, but we can't escape them.

"It is in the play between the traditionary text's strangeness and familiarity to us, between being a historically intended, distanced object and belonging to a tradition. The true locus of hermeneutics is this in-between." A strange meaning encountered gives us reason to be aware of our prejudices, perhaps to revise them. "Thus it is quite right for the interpreter not to approach the text directly, relying solely on the fore-meaning already available to him, but rather explicitly to examine the legitimacy – i.e., the origin and validity – of the fore-meanings dwelling within him." So: "The important thing is to be aware of one's own bias, so that the text can present itself in all its otherness and thus assert its own truth against one's own fore-meanings."[112] However, to the extent that revision is always within horizon and tradition, to revise means to refine.

"Wittgenstein's concept of 'language games' seemed quite natural to me when I came across it," Gadamer remarks casually in a footnote.[113] Like the late Wittgenstein,[§MS2.3.2a] Gadamer locates language in the context of forms of life. And like Wittgenstein, language remains the center of human meaning.

"All understanding is interpretation, and all interpretation takes place in the medium of a language that allows the object to come into words and yet is at the same time the interpreter's own language ... [L]anguage is the universal medium in which understanding occurs." It is "this universal mystery of language that is prior to everything else."[114]

Gadamer uses enough metaphor and so many examples that go beyond language (vision in image, horizons in space, the architecture of object-in-space), to suggest there is more to meaning than language alone. But he does not distinguish, as we would want, between the characteristic forms of speech which are indeed dialogical in form, and writing, which is not. Or at least writing is dialogical in a very different way from speech. Instead of reducing participation in meaning to language, the concept of interpretation will work equally well for all forms of meaning. The broader canvas of life and historical

---

[111] Ibid., pp. 278, 295, 273.   [112] Ibid., pp. 295, 270, 271–72.   [113] Ibid., p. xxxvi.
[114] Ibid., pp. 390, 370.

experience influences new meaning. Interpretation is a play between prior and newly encountered meanings.

And what of Heidegger's historical situation, then Gadamer's? If context is so important to both of their philosophies, what was their context?

Heidegger, Gadamer's teacher, joined the Nazi Party in 1933 and remained a member until the party was dissolved in 1945. When he died in 1976, he asked his son to be sure that thirty-four "Black Notebooks" remain sealed for one hundred years. However, when publication began in 2014, further evidence was revealed to show that his Nazi affiliation was complemented by explicit anti-Semitism and racism.[115]

Gadamer did not become a member of the Nazi Party, however he did voluntarily attend a political camp run by the National Socialist University Lecturers Association, during which he glimpsed the figure of the visiting Führer. He did also benefit in 1934 from the dismissal for his race of his Jewish friend and philosopher, Richard Kroner – Gadamer willingly took his position as professor. When Gadamer visited Paris in 1941, the year after the Nazi invasion, he lectured French prisoners of war, explaining that Germany's battlefield successes were an expression of superior culture, the "genetic spirit and character of a Volk," distinguished by the "depth and breadth of historical self-consciousness." This was for that time his "horizon," his "tradition," his "prejudice." The text of this lecture has been omitted from Gadamer's collected works.[116]

But, by and large, his defenders say, Gadamer remained neutral, quietly doing his arcane philosophical work while the world around him convulsed.[117] "To be sure, the secret police also came to my courses ... but the only result was that they didn't understand a word."[118]

What of the situation? Should not the pre-eminent philosopher of interpretation have scanned horizons, interrogated tradition, and questioned its prejudices? Even if there was avoidance of context on Gadamer's part, what does that context tell of its avoidance?

In modernity, we have lived for the past centuries in a succession of cycles of catastrophe. We have also nurtured in this context imaginations of dreamworld,[119] a persistence of hope that things might be made different.

---

[115] Jesús Adrián Escuder, 2015, "Heidegger's 'Black Notebooks' and the Question of Anti-Semitism," *Gatherings: The Heidegger Circle Annual* 5:21–49.

[116] Richard Wolin, 2000, "Untruth and Method: Nazism and the Complicities of Hans-Georg Gadamer," *New Republic* (May 15):36–45, pp. 38, 43.

[117] Richard E. Palmer, 2002, "A Response to Richard Wolin on Gadamer and the Nazis," *International Journal of Philosophical Studies* 10(4):467–82.

[118] Jacques Derrida, Hans-Georg Gadamer, and Philippe Lacque-Labarthe, 1988 [2016], *Heidegger, Philosophy, and Politics: The Heidelberg Conference*, translated by J. Fort, New York: Fordham University Press, p. 71; Jean Grondin, 2003, *Hans-Georg Gadamer: A Biography*, translated by J. Weinsheimer, New Haven, CT: Yale University Press.

[119] Susan Buck-Morss, 2000, *Dreamworld and Catastrophe: The Passing of Mass Utopia in East and West*, Cambridge, MA: MIT Press.

In the case of Gadamer, the catastrophe of context itself becomes the meaning of a philosophy that silently stays within the horizons of tradition, whose only mark of progress is incremental evolution or deeper personal immersion in that tradition, catastrophic though it has been.

The situation is the meaning, the context wider than any interpretations. But the situation does not necessarily have to be. This is why in this book we have gone out of our way, not just to interpret meanings but, as part of our interpretation, to set them in the context of their making. Then, to our situation: as we pass by thinkers and actors in this book, we do this to acknowledge the way they have touched our thinking and acting. They are our context.

To return to the pejorative meaning of "prejudice," interpretation can indeed be this, but of a kind that is self-confirming. In the midst of catastrophe, prejudice produces not transformative dialogue, but unhearing, unseeing, unfeeling. Not just refinement of more-of-the-same, interpretation must have the capacity for disruption. Interpretation is not only to internalize the world, but to change the world.

§1.3 Position

> **Position.** *Meanings in the context of their time and place.*

The meaning of an entity or action can be parsed as a process of action involving entities – we have called this predication, the stuff of an event in itself.[§MS2.1] However, an event's meaning is determined as well by its position in time and place. Position is an aspect of context that may also help us account for the meaning of an event in terms of cause and outcome, emergence and history. The context of time and place not only surrounds every meaning; by transposition time and place become immanent within meaning.

Sometimes, but not always, proximity is most powerful in shaping this meaning – recent or nearby entities or actions may be particularly telling, or at least a starting point for the analysis of position. But oftentimes, meaning is also powerfully established in widening circles of context, where the meaning of an event should also be set in contexts that could be as long as the time of human or natural history, or as wide as the earth or the cosmos.

The view that we will develop here is that position – in time and place – is experientially real, grounded materially in our everyday experiences. In this, we dare to defy the revered Immanuel Kant.[§MS3.3e]

Kant on time: "we deny to time all claim to be absolute reality; that is to say, we deny that it belongs to things absolutely ... independently of any reference to the form of our sensible intuition. ... [I]f we abstract from the conditions of sensible intuition, time is nothing, and cannot be ascribed to the objects themselves."[120]

Kant on space: "Space does not represent any property of things in themselves, nor does it represent them in relation to one another . . . It is . . . solely from the human standpoint that we can speak of space. If we depart from the subjective condition under which we alone can have outer intuition, namely, liability to be affected by objects, the representation of space stands for nothing whatsoever."[121] Space and time are for Kant mere figments of the human mind. Otherwise, they don't exist.

Not only do we contend that time and space are experientially real, but the historically located practices of time and space can vary, though within limits set by experiential reality. These limits define the scope of human diversity, and that scope is broad. Here arises our second problem with Kant: his conception of a priori ideas such as time and space is unable to account for human diversity. Chomsky's idealist universalism has the same problem.[§MS3.1.2j]

§1.3.1   Time

> **Time.** Events positioned for moments and durations in past, present, and future.

By its fourth edition, the minutiae in M.A.K. Halliday's big grammar had become bewilderingly complicated. If tenses are in speech classical markers of time, there were now thirty-six, including theoretical possibilities but practical improbabilities such as this variation of the verb "to take": "will have been going to have been taken," a permutation of a future that was anticipated in the past.[122]

Hans Reichenbach comes up with a more straightforward scheme.[*] There are two kinds of time, points in time and extended times. Every point of time or extended time needs to be addressed from three time perspectives: the time of the event, the time of reference, and the time of speech. This produces twelve perspectives on time that are reflected for points of time in English tenses as past perfect, simple past, present perfect, present, simple future, future perfect, and for durations in extended versions of each of these. For instance, where the future perfect is "I shall have seen John," the extended version of this referring

---

[*] http://meaningpatterns.net/reichenbach-time

[120] Immanuel Kant, 1787 [1933], *Critique of Pure Reason*, translated by N.K. Smith, London: Macmillan, A36/B52.
[121] Ibid., A26/B42.
[122] M.A.K. Halliday and Christian Matthiessen, 2004, *An Introduction to Functional Grammar*, London: Routledge, pp. 401–03.

to a duration is "I shall have been seeing John."[123] Things don't need to get more complicated than this.

We rename and reframe Reichenbach's schema as follows, where M is a moment, D is duration, R is the point of reference, P is the point of participation, > is sequence, and = are things happening together. Our example is the verb "to see," expressed in English tenses.

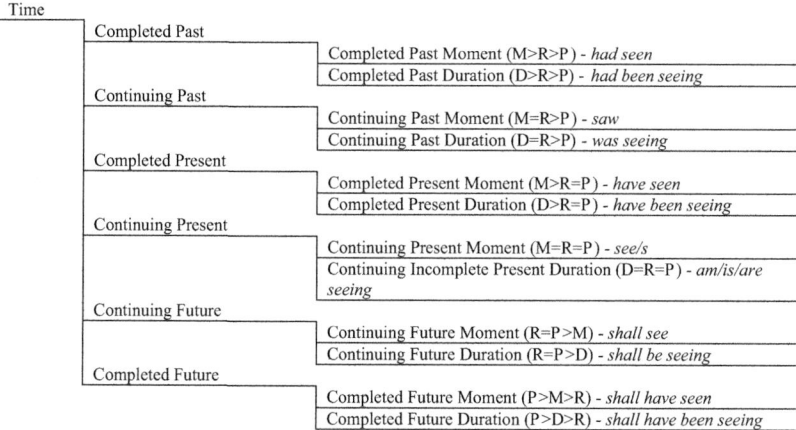

Fig. 1.3.1(i): Past, present, and future time

Beyond tense, there are of course other markers of time in speech, such as prepositions – ubiquitously, "before," "after," "when," "later," "then," "now," "during," "at," and "in" – and most of these, terribly ambiguously, can also refer to things not related to time.

Here we find yet another point where the grammar of speaking is radically different from the grammar of text, because although words written and words spoken may seem the same, their point of participation in speech is different – always "now" in speech, but inevitably "then" in writing. This is also the case for recorded speech, when this hybrid form becomes more like text than speech. Again in this respect, text is more like image than speech.

If speech and text in their own ways have elaborate ways for representing time, what of image? For its primary spatiality and according to conventional wisdom, image seems to capture a static moment, frozen in time.

No, says E.H. Gombrich, there is never a fraction of time when movement can be absolutely stilled. Time is integral to image, but in different ways. From a logical point of view, he says, time is not made of static moments; there is continuous movement. And from a psychological point of view, "we are not

[123] Hans Reichenbach, 1947, *Elements of Symbolic Logic*, New York: Macmillan, pp. 287–98.

cameras but rather slow registering instruments which cannot take in much at a time." Viewing takes time.[124] Eadweard Muybridge used photography to show how artists who had been attempting to still moving objects had got time and movement wrong. His photographs revealed realities in the galloping of a horse and a man running that had not been noticed before.[§MS2.2.3a]

Even in stillest image, there are always traces of movement, and so traces of time – if not in the form of explicit references such as blurring and vectors of action, then imagined positioning essential to make sense of the image – the freshness and impermanence of cut flowers in a vase, for instance, or the journey of the train in Turner's *Rain, Steam and Speed*.[§MS2a] Which also means of course that even when an event is conceived as a moment, it is part of a duration – another transposition, always imminent, ever immanent.

If time is not directly marked in image, we cannot help ourselves but to add time-meaning in, because it is not possible to mean outside of time. Then there are objects, images, and texts that are explicitly designed to show time, often with greater clarity than speech – clocks, timelines, and timetables, for instance. And there are visual practices that explicitly represent time with particular precision, such as comic sequences, cinema, and video.[125]

Here, then, is a rough map of time across the forms of meaning:

Form / Function: Time	Text	Image	Space	Object	Body	Sound	Speech
Moment	Tenses, prepositions expressing moment; the moment of text communication is "then"	The moment, with references to movement such as vectors, blurring; explicit visual representations of moment	Spatial co-ordinates stabilized at a point in time	Presence of an object	Instants of bodily experience; chronological age	Pitch, volume	The point of communication is "now"
Duration	Tenses, prepositions expressing duration in relation; the point of text communication is "while"	Implications in antecedence, consequences; explicit visual representations of duration	Continuity and change in space represented over time	Continuity or change and change in the life of an object; causes and effects	Felt and lived episodes; sensuous living as narrative; stage in life	Tempo	The point of communication is "during"

Fig. 1.3.1(ii): Moment and duration

---

[124] E.H. Gombrich, 1964, "Moment and Movement in Art," *Journal of the Warburg and Courtauld Institutes* 27:293–306, pp. 297, 301, 295–96.

[125] Robin Le Poidevin, 2007, *The Images of Time: An Essay on Temporal Representation*, Oxford: Oxford University Press, pp. 133–34.

We are referring here not only to events bound to time, because timelessness is another variant of time, outside of time but not escaping it. Logic is timeless, unless we can take logic to speak for all of time, that most expansive of durations.[126]

§1.3.1a Albert Einstein's "Illusion of Time"

Hans Reichenbach was one of only five students who signed up for Albert Einstein's course on relativity when he first offered it at the University of Berlin in 1919. Reichenbach and Einstein lived in the same suburb and they would take the streetcar home together. Later, after Einstein purchased a tiny car and Reichenbach had also become a professor, Einstein would give him a ride home. Talking abstractedly about theories of physics and meanings of life, the policeman at the Brandenburg Gate would wave them on, "Get going with your baby-buggy."[127]

One side of Reichenbach's thinking was reflected in his alignment with the logical-positivist ideas of the Vienna Circle.[§MS1.1.3i] He had a lifelong friendship with one of its leading lights, Rudolf Carnap, and enlisted Moritz Schlick to start a new journal with him, *Knowledge*. It was in this spirit that Reichenbach analyzed straightforward meanings of time as reflected in the tenses of verbs[§1.3.1] – "such an analysis of language ... makes thought processes clear."[128]

Reichenbach remained a lifelong friend of Einstein and an exponent of the theory of relativity in a succession of widely read books of "scientific philosophy."[129] Here, time meant something else. Mathematically, said Reichenbach, time is a uniform flow, but when we seek a reference point for this uniformity in the universe we can only reach a conclusion that time exists only by definition, not in observable reality. Time is relative. Here, Reichenbach returns to the spirit of Kant.[§1.3]

Then comes the question of simultaneity, raising the problem of the same time at two different points. Lightning flashes, then thunder claps. We are captives of the signal that transmits the message to us that an event has occurred. Even in the case of light, the fastest of all message transmitters, the message takes time to reach us. Simultaneity can never be in scientific reality what it seems in ordinary experience.

---

[126] Ronnie Cann, 1993, *Formal Semantics*, Cambridge: Cambridge University Press, p. 233.

[127] Hans Reichenbach, 1920 [1965], *The Theory of Relativity and a Priori Knowledge*, translated by M. Reichenbach, Berkeley: University of California Press, p. xv.

[128] Hans Reichenbach, 1947, *Elements of Symbolic Logic*, New York: Macmillan, p. 3.

[129] Hans Reichenbach, 1930 [1957], *Atom and Cosmos: The World of Modern Physics*, translated by E.S. Allen, New York: George Braziller Inc.; Hans Reichenbach, 1942, *From Copernicus to Einstein*, New York: Philosophical Library.

Now comes Einstein's thesis of time dilation. If one of a pair of hypothetical twins takes a cosmic trip at speeds approaching the speed of light, "he would be younger than the other after his return ... This conclusion follows with unquestionable logic from within Einstein's well-confirmed theory," says Reichenbach. Time is relative, a fourth dimension in a time-space continuum where time and space can be bent against each other. For the Logical Positivist who had elsewhere so neatly identified the flow of time from pasts into presents and futures,[§1.3.1] this was a paradox. "Scientific analysis has led to an interpretation of time very different from the experience of time in everyday life."[130]

Time is an illusion, Einstein famously concluded.[*] Einstein had traveled from Berlin to Paris in 1922 to debate philosopher of time Henri Bergson[§MS1.2.2b] on just this point. The philosopher was famous and Einstein by then a celebrity, so the evening of 6 April was "a sensation that the intellectual snobbery of the capital could not pass up." After listening to Bergson's half-hour speech, Einstein spoke for less than a minute: "The time of philosophers does not exist," he said.[131]

Later that year, Bergson published an extended version of his argument in a book, *Duration and Simultaneity*. He wanted to agree with Einstein on many things, but time for him remained real and time dilation was too much. One of the two time-traveling twins was "real," Bergson says, and the other "fictional."[132] Einstein's method, he argues, "consists essentially in finding a mathematical representation of things which will be independent of the observer's point of view, (or, more precisely, of the system of reference)." To supplement Einstein's mathematized time, Bergson proposed "a metaphysics which has as its basis the experience of duration." Not that the physicist could ever be exempted from metaphysics, because he, "whether relativist or no, takes his measurements in the Time here-now, which is our time and everybody else's."[133]

Einstein's time consisted of quantifiable unities, mathematically expressible consistencies, and shockingly counter-intuitive theoretical possibilities that

---

* http://meaningpatterns.net/einstein-time

130 Hans Reichenbach, 1953, *The Rise of Scientific Philosophy*, Berkeley: University of California Press, pp. 146–47, 152, 155; Hans Reichenbach, 1927 [1957], *The Philosophy of Space and Time*, translated by M. Reichenbach and J. Freund, New York: Dover Publications, pp. 124–28, 285.

131 Jimena Canales, 2015, *The Physicist and the Philosopher: Einstein, Bergson, and the Debate That Changed Our Understanding of Time*, Princeton, NJ: Princeton University Press, p. 5.

132 Henri Bergson, 1922 [1965], *Duration and Simultaneity, with Reference to Einstein's Theory*, translated by L. Jacobson, Indianapolis: Bobbs-Merrill, pp. 74–79, 151–52, 163–64.

133 Henri Bergson, 1934 [1946], *The Creative Mind*, translated by M.L. Andison, New York: The Philosophical Library, p. 301.

could be proved by calculation. Bergson's time was grounded in the ordinary human experience of duration, with its open-ended change, complexities, indeterminacies, and inconsistencies.

If the relativity of time was hard to believe, Einstein himself found it hard to believe the next main theory of the material universe, quantum mechanics.[§1.4.4b] Einstein wanted there to be a definite material reality, but quantum mechanics came to say that in the realm of subatomic particles the act of observation determines what is observed – this sounds very Kantian – and that there are no certainties, only probabilities. But improbably: a subatomic particle can be in several places at the same time; particles can become each other; particles can know each other or even be each other at enormous distances across the universe; and they can go back in time.[134] "Nature is absurd from the point of view of common sense," said Nobel prize-winning quantum physicist Richard Feynman.[135] Subatomic nature is a place of "inescapable strangeness," say two of his latter-day followers.[136] And even in the latest quantum mechanics, some quite basic things still don't have explanations, absurd or otherwise – empty space and gravity, for instance.

"I fucking love science," says the eponymous website and Facebook page, and of course, along with its 25 million other followers, we do too – but science still has a lot of explaining to do.

When a new English language translation of *Duration and Simultaneity* was issued in 1965, the publisher recruited English philosopher of science, Herbert Dingle, to write an introduction. Here he quoted Einstein as having said in his lectures at Princeton University in 1921 that speed of light was chosen as a reference point because it is one of the few "processes concerning which we know something for certain." If this reference point is an accident of available knowledge, other speeds are conceivable, Dingle said, and the asymmetrical aging of the twins, "is almost inexplicable." Einstein was "mistaking ideas for experience, symbols for observations."[137]

Besides, a whole lot of science speaks to times that are not reversible or so readily transformable into space by mathematical fiat. Nor do the main narratives of science give any impression that time could be mere illusion. Some examples:

---

[134] Hans Reichenbach, 1944, *Philosophic Foundations of Quantum Mechanics*, Berkeley: University of California Press; Philip Ball, 2017, "Quantum Teleportation Is Even Weirder Than You Think," *Nature*, doi:10.1038/nature.2017.22321.

[135] Richard P. Feynman, 1985, *QED: The Strange Theory of Light and Matter*, Princeton, NJ: Princeton University Press, p. 10.

[136] Brian Cox and Jeff Forshaw, 2011, *The Quantum Universe: Everything That Can Happen Does Happen*, London: Allen Lane, p. 1.

[137] Henri Bergson, 1922 [1965], *Duration and Simultaneity, with Reference to Einstein's Theory*, translated by L. Jacobson, Indianapolis: Bobbs-Merrill, pp. xxiii, xxv, xli.

A "big bang" may have happened 13.8 billion years ago, and the universe continues to expand in space measurable by time. On 6 October 2013, astronomers looking through an observatory on Palomar Mountain near San Diego, California, detected the explosion of a star in Galaxy NGC7610 within 3 hours of the start of the process, 160 million light years away in space-time, or quite recently in the billions of years of cosmic time.[138] The explosion, we might reasonably assume, happened in the irreversible past.

Then there is the second law of thermodynamics, where events occur over durations that are not reversible: the burning log, the digestion of food, or the bursting of a bubble.[139] Events inexorably flow, and time is the direction of that flow. These things can only be reversed in imaginative reconstruction, like running the video of nature backwards. At this point, the ideal must exceed the material in the structure of meaning.[§MS3.1]

And another widely agreed narrative of science: natural selection. Life is on the move all the time, where biology throws up random mutations and some prove themselves to make more environmental sense than others. Natural history is a crooked path. Nature is in part creature of happenstance, or happenstance is a part of its biophysical design. Only accountable retrospectively, biohistory mercilessly happens in time.[140] In its narrative form, evolution feels more like Bergson's account of duration than Einstein's calculations. The narrative of natural selection is akin to our account of design,[§MS0.4.1] where there are historical patternings of meaning, but every moment of meaning design is a moment of redesign. The complex contingencies of the moment lead us to make meaning in a way that is necessarily new as well as derivative. We make sense of design by parsing its patterns and contingencies over time.

In the debate between Bergson and Einstein, we may want to sympathize with Einstein to the extent that calculation has become in our modernity a matter of ubiquitous utility. Its reference point is arbitrary, and that point might as well be light as one of the several regular things in the universe.

So, finally concluded the Bureau International des Poids et Mesures in 1983, "The metre is the length of the path travelled by light in vacuum during a time interval of 1/299,792,458 of a second."[141] We live according to such numbering and calculation in modernity, and it works for us.

However we also want to revive Bergson, whose work has fallen out of fashion in an era that has elevated algorithmic thinking as a proxy for empirical

[138] www.theguardian.com/science/2017/feb/13/massive-supernova-visible-millions-of-light-years-from-earth

[139] Hans Reichenbach, 1957, *The Direction of Time*, Berkeley: University of California Press, pp. 49–56.

[140] Elizabeth Grosz, 2004, *The Nick of Time: Politics, Evolution, and the Untimely*, Durham, NC: Duke University Press, pp. 7–10, 200.

[141] www.bipm.org/en/CGPM/db/17/1/

science and history.[142] Bergson called our deep-rooted senses of time "intuitions," which feels too Kantian for us. We reframe Bergson to say that these deep-rooted senses are grounded in our practices of meaning and the materiality of their media. Time is inarguably real, in science and everyday life.

Here, then, is time – experientially, materially:

In the present, we perceive. We experience moments in the present, and they are often to be understood in terms of their intrinsic directionality and flow. Simultaneity we experience as "while." Spacings may be experienced in the moment as tardiness or haste.

If perception is of the moment, memory is of the past. Many of the artifacts of meaning in the present are from the past: reminders in the form of objects, spaces, texts, recordings. Things of the present are ordered in reference to the past. The designs of meaning are available to us in the form of residues and retained meanings.

And now, we await futures. Feelings for the future may be experienced as foretastes, presages, expectations, intimations, suggestions, or hints. We also know that the past can be repeated, though in the nature of redesign, it can never be quite the same. We know that some things are not seeable, reachable, or doable right now. But they might possibly be so, in time. Or they may be impossibly unmaterializable. Things seen-as in one moment might be re-seen differently later on, a process of reinterpretation. The future can be imagined in the present by redesigning meanings from the past. And for that matter, the past can also be changed by reinterpretation, though of course the traces of the past (its "facts") resist our imposition of any-old meaning.

The mathematics of Einstein's time dilations may seem improbable, but time dilations of meaning in the form of memory and anticipation – pasts-in-presents and futures-in-presents – are as real as meanings get. Time travel is deeply written into narrative, a primal element of lived experience.[143] There is a metaphysics to time in natural language with its constant indexical and anaphorical references to time.[144] There may even be neural correlates of temporality.[145]

The transpositions of meaning that we make across time are continuous and persistent: presents into pasts and futures as our attentions dart backwards and forwards across time, the one meaning function impossible without the others.

Then there are also transpositions of position from time into space, where time and space only make sense in relation to each other, hence stasis,

[142] Sabine Hossenfelder, 2018, *Lost in Math: How Beauty Leads Physics Astray*, New York: Basic Books.

[143] David Wittenberg, 2013, *Time Travel: The Popular Philosophy of Narrative*, New York: Fordham University Press.

[144] Peter Ludlow, 1999, *Semantics, Tense, and Time: An Essay on the Metaphysics of Natural Language*, Cambridge, MA: MIT Press.

[145] Dan Lloyd, 2012, "Neural Correlates of Temporality: Default Mode Variability and Temporal Awareness," *Consciousness and Cognition* 21:695–703.

coincidence, speed, acceleration. Meanings of time and space can slip over into each other, though they are never the same, least of all by fiat of calculation. Meanings of time and space are not relative. They are transposable, which is to say that they do not stay the same in the transposition. Rather the meaning is both in their continuities and circumstantial differing.

As much as we want to have our Bergson – the self-evident existential reality of time – we want to have our Einstein too, in the form of the relativity of our historical practices of time calculation in modernity. We want our metaphysics, and our physics as well.

As for the difference between a moment and a duration, this is a matter of orientation, whether one sees an event more from the perspective of its diachronic cohesion than its synchronic, positional context.

Though of course, historical time is often still to be experienced as a crooked path. Fascist time caught up with Einstein and Reichenbach in 1933 when they were both excluded from their professorships at the University of Berlin for their Jewish "race." Both were exiled, forced to move their academic careers to the United States.

§1.3.1b Network Time Protocol and iCalendar

In global modernity, measures of time are, from the point of view of strict calculation, rough and ready, a hodge-podge of conventionalities. Some are grounded in things that are ubiquitously material. In our modernity we have: year lengths determined by the orbit of the earth but which periodically have to be adjusted as 365 or 366 days because the earth's orbit doesn't neatly coincide with days; months are very roughly determined by the phases of the moon; and days coincide with the rotation of the earth on its axis.

Somewhat more arbitrarily, year numbers are determined by the nominal date of birth of the religious leader of modern colonizers. This is nevertheless real to the extent that the historical imagination is a part of our lives. The whole world, in one way or another, now marches to this number.

But the 7 days in a week, 24 hours in a day, 60 minutes in an hour, and 60 seconds in a minute – these are numbers whose reference is to nothing in particular, and in awkwardly non-decimal denominations.

Since 1985, we've been keeping these numbers in sync on networked computers with the Network Time Protocol, maintaining a margin of error of no more than a few milliseconds.[146] The measure of time is a cesium atomic clock that won't gain or lose more than a second in 1.4 million years.

---

[146] www.ntp.org; Barbara Liskov, 1993, "Practical Uses of Synchronized Clocks in Distributed Systems," *Distributed Computing* 6(4):211–19.

The simultaneity this establishes is numbered by Coordinated Universal Time (UTC). First adopted in 1967, its reference point is the time at the Greenwich Observatory in London, defined as such in 1884 at the International Meridian Conference in Washington DC. Other times around the world are offset by plus or minus a number of hours according to slices of space called time zones. The reference point for counting backwards and forwards, strangely in 24s, 60s, and 60s, is zero hour (midnight) at zero meridian. The International Telecommunications Union today solemnly keeps count, every now and then having to add or delete a leap second to keep things in sync with the vagaries of earth's movement.

The ordering of sequential events and coordinating of simultaneous events is now defined in the universal language of iCalendar, first created by the Calendaring and Scheduling Working Group of the Internet Engineering Task Force, another one of those not-for-profit but corporate-dominated entities[§MS3.4a] that today govern our meanings.[*] Its meanings for time are full of events, starts, ends, recurrences, alarms, reminders, action items ("to-dos"), free/busy times, and a whole host of other numerable and calculable temporalities – namable moments or durations.[147] This is how calendars talk to each other across different software products and devices, in a universal digital ontology of numbered time.

An odd thing about this digital modernity is that the relativity of time is receding in the practicalities of our lives and our conscious self-understanding. Once we would periodically set our clocks and watches, knowing they were fallible machines. Now that our computers, phones, and digital watches are synced, time is definitive and leap-second adjustments are added without our noticing. The "correct" time is no longer even a question; the smart phone, the computer screen or the web-connected timepiece speaks to us today in universal, univocal, unequivocal time. Numbered and calculated time is for practical purposes infallible.

The numbers, of course, are all relative to a ramshackle array of natural phenomena, religious leaders, colonial pasts, and in the case of weeks, hours, minutes, and seconds, little more than human precociousness. We have nevertheless done everything to stabilize and universalize time that our human wits and modern counting technologies will allow.

In defiance of Einstein, in an ordinary experiential sense, this numbered, computer-generated, global time is less illusory than ever. Because this time is now nearly everybody's, non-negotiable time, any underlying relativity has slipped from our field of vision. Contrary to Kant, time is experienced less and less as a figment of our a priori intuitions.

---

[*] http://meaningpatterns.net/iCalendar

[147] https://tools.ietf.org/html/rfc5545

So, when we feel pressed for time in our modernity,[148] the feeling is real.[149] However, in a longer frame, the experience is historical and peculiar to modernity. When we are racing to catch a train, we can track this back to the railway timetable,[§1.4.6a] a foundational modern textual artifact governing space-time relations.[150] When our work productivity is measured as output over time, we can track this back to the origins of industrial capitalism,[151] and the mechanics of its calculation to Frederick Winslow Taylor's[§1.4.3e] time and motion studies.[152]

§1.3.1c Hopi Time: Benjamin Lee Whorf's "Linguistic Relativity"

Since Albert Einstein's idea of relativity[§1.3.1a] was such an intellectual buzz for much of the twentieth century, it comes as no surprise that linguists should also have discovered "linguistic relativity."[*] Though, it was not a professional linguist who first and most clearly articulated this idea, but a fire prevention inspector from the Hartford Fire Insurance Company.

Benjamin Lee Whorf had studied chemical engineering at the Massachusetts Institute of Technology, and for the rest of his life he had only one paying job, inspecting fire sprinkler systems at industrial buildings and chemical plants. The job gave him opportunities to travel, and a good deal of flexibility with his uncharacteristically not-quite-modern time.

Whorf developed an interest in language, including the language of the Hopi, a First People whose ancestral lands are in today's Arizona. He visited there just once, in 1938, but from 1932 he began documenting the language of a Hopi speaker, Ernest Naquayouma, at the time living in New York City.[153]

Whorf's focus became the differences between Hopi and English languages, illustrated powerfully in the comparison of concepts of time. Hopi verbs have nine aspects, he concluded, all implicating time in delicately graduated ways not explicitly marked in English tenses: punctual, durative, segmentative, punctual-segmentative, inceptive, progressional, spatial (often a metaphor[§1.4.4a] for time),

---

[*] http://meaningpatterns.net/whorf

[148] Judy Wajcman, 2015, *Pressed for Time: The Acceleration of Life in Digital Capitalism*, Chicago, IL: University of Chicago Press.

[149] Norbert Elias, 1987 [1992], *Time: An Essay*, translated by E. Jephcott, Oxford: Blackwell, pp. 21–23.

[150] Wolfgang Schivelbusch, 1977 [2014], *The Railway Journey: The Industrialization of Time and Space in the Nineteenth Century*, Berkeley: University of California Press, pp. 33–34.

[151] E.P. Thompson, 1976, "Time, Work-Discipline, and Industrial Capitalism," *Past & Present* 38:56–97.

[152] Frederick Winslow Taylor, 1911, *The Principles of Scientific Management*, New York: Harper & Brothers.

[153] Benjamin Lee Whorf, 1956, *Language, Thought and Reality: Selected Writings of Benjamin Lee Whorf*, Cambridge, MA: MIT Press, p. 17.

projective, and continuative.[154] There are three tenses – factual or present-past, future, and generalized or usitative – and these do not align with the big three of English.[155]

The Hopi present-past is that which is "accessible to the senses, the historical physical universe," material traces that have a degree of objectivity. The Hopi future is that which is manifesting, processes of eventuation captured in anticipations that must in their nature be subjective, expectancies in the form of necessarily mental figments. At the edge of the present-past and the future, is the inceptive.[156]

Not only do Hopi tenses frame time differently from English; time is commonly expressed as unfolding action, in verbs. In English, time is a sequence of repeating events, objectified as nouns homogenized by the property of number: repetitively as hours, days, and years. In this way, English and other languages that Whorf calls "standard average European" objectify time. By quantification of lengths of time, "artificially ... expressed by a linear relation of past-present-future," we "lose contact with the subjective experience of 'becoming later'," or what might be considered in Hopi to be "durating," or "eventing – the ceaseless 'latering' of events."[157]

After Whorf's death, an unpublished article was found among his papers in which he concludes that, in Hopi, there is "no general notation or intuition of time as a smooth flowing continuum in which everything in the universe proceeds at an equal rate ... [T]he Hopi language is seen to contain no words, grammatical forms, constructions that refer directly to what we call time."[158]

Critics have seized upon this sentence. Of course, the Hopi language has notions of time, and linguist Ekkehart Malotki finds enough examples to fill 677 pages of his book with anti-Whorf invective.[159] But Whorf's point was not that Hopi had no notions of time. Rather, they were different from "what we call time" in languages like English. Whorf is at meticulous pains to document those differences. Perhaps if he brought this article to publication he might have

---

[154] Ibid., p. 103.

[155] Benjamin Lee Whorf, 1936, "The Punctual and Segmentative Aspects of Verbs in Hopi," *Language* 12(2):127–31, p. 127.

[156] Benjamin Lee Whorf, 1950, "An American Indian Model of the Universe," *International Journal of American Linguistics* 16(2):67–72, pp. 68–69; Benjamin Lee Whorf, 1938, "Some Verbal Categories of Hopi," *Language* 14(4):275–86.

[157] Benjamin Lee Whorf, 1956, *Language, Thought and Reality: Selected Writings of Benjamin Lee Whorf*, Cambridge, MA: MIT Press, pp. 140, 144, 146, 151.

[158] Benjamin Lee Whorf, 1950, "An American Indian Model of the Universe," *International Journal of American Linguistics* 16(2):67–72, p. 67.

[159] Ekkehart Malotki, 1983, *Hopi Time: A Linguistic Analysis of the Temporal Categories in the Hopi Language*, Berlin: Mouton; David W. Dinwoodie, 2006, "Time and the Individual in Native North America," pp. 327–48 in *New Perspectives on Native North America*, edited by S.A. Kan and P.T. Strong, Lincoln: University of Nebraska Press.

reworded these sentences in a more circumspect way, though in the larger context of his work, his meaning should have been obvious even to the most insistently unsympathetic reader.

Perhaps more remarkable than the details of his linguistics was that Whorf was prepared to countenance an until-then barely thinkable idea. This was that people who had hitherto been considered primitive not only thought in ways that were different from the inhabitants of the science-drenched West, but might think in ways that were in some respects more perspicacious.[160]

The Hopi language, Whorf said, "is capable of accounting for and describing correctly ... all observable phenomena in the universe." This shows that "it is possible to have descriptions of the universe, all equally valid, that do not contain our familiar contrasts of time and space. The relativity viewpoint of modern physics is one such view, conceived in mathematical terms, and the Hopi Weltanschauung [worldview] is another quite different one."

More than this, in contrast to understandings of homogenous time and space in Newtonian mechanics, Hopi contains "abstractions for which our language lacks adequate terms."[161] Hopi, says Whorf, also comes closer to Bergson's notion of "duration"[§1.3.1a] than the mathematical time of modern physics. So, "the linguistic relativity principle: ... each language is not merely a reproducing instrument for voicing ideas but rather is itself a shaper of ideas."[162] "Language first of all is a classification and arrangement of the stream of sensory experience which results in a certain world-order."[163] And some languages, in some respects, may do this better than others.

Whorf met academic linguist Edward Sapir at a conference in 1928, but did not form a close association with him until 1931 when Sapir took up a post as Professor of Anthropology at Yale University, not far from Whorf's insurance company's office in Hartford. He began attending Sapir's classes, and this steered his linguistic interests in the direction of American languages.[164]

This is how linguistic relativity has come to be called "the Sapir-Whorf hypothesis." Languages, said Sapir, are "arbitrary systems of symbolism," each of which is "the outward facet of thought." In this perspective, so-called "primitive languages have a formal richness, a latent luxuriance of expression, that eclipses anything known to the languages of modern civilization."[165]

---

[160] Benjamin Lee Whorf, 1956, *Language, Thought and Reality: Selected Writings of Benjamin Lee Whorf*, Cambridge, MA: MIT Press, p. 81.

[161] Ibid., p. 58.   [162] Ibid., pp. 216, 221, 212.

[163] Benjamin Lee Whorf, 1936, "The Punctual and Segmentative Aspects of Verbs in Hopi," *Language* 12(2):127–31, p. 130.

[164] Benjamin Lee Whorf, 1956, *Language, Thought and Reality: Selected Writings of Benjamin Lee Whorf*, Cambridge, MA: MIT Press, p. 16.

[165] Edward Sapir, 1921, *Language: An Introduction to the Study of Speech*, New York: Harcourt Brace, pp. 11, 15, 22.

Sapir's was an outsider's perspective. Never comfortable at Yale, he was one of only four Jews among 569 faculty. For this, he was denied membership of the Graduate Club, a crucial place for academic networking.[166]

Not to favor "the parochial point of view of the favored parties" of history, Whorf suggests that, more than merely relative, the Hopi view might in some respects be closer to Einstein's relativity than our conventional Newtonian understandings. "Certain ideas born of our own time-concept, such as that of absolute simultaneity, would ... be devoid of meaning under the Hopi concept."[167] Einstein would agree with the Hopi about this, although of course they reach their respective conclusions by different paths.

Albert Einstein had been a mediocre student. After he failed the entrance examination to the Federal Institute of Technology in Zurich, he attended instead the liberal cantonal school in Aarau, Switzerland. Here he was taught by linguist Jost Winteler. Einstein was taken in by him as a boarder, becoming an adopted family member. Winteler was a founder of the field of dialectology, where he developed and applied the notion of "configurational relativity" to speech. This was a lucky moment for Einstein, and his biographers agree, an academic turning point. Forty years later, Einstein would call his intellectual mentor his inspiration, "the clairvoyant Papa Winteler."[168]

§1.3.2 Place

> **Place.** *Events positioned in proximity or distance, according to the place-defining coordinates of length, breadth, and depth.*

Space, we are going to propose, is a meaning form, and place is a meaning function. Senses of space can be made in every meaning function (reference, agency, structure, context, and interest), and senses of place can be made in every meaning form (text, image, space, object, body, sound, and speech).

Place, like time, positions meaning in context. Place represents meaning in the context of the proximate or the distant, and on three dimensions or axes.

By measurement: distance of lengths (along an x axis), areas of lengths and breadths (x and y axes); and volumes of lengths, breadths, and depths (x, y, and

---

[166] Gelya Frank, 1997, "Jews, Multiculturalism, and Boasian Anthropology," *American Anthropologist* 99(4):731–45, p. 736.

[167] Benjamin Lee Whorf, 1956, *Language, Thought and Reality: Selected Writings of Benjamin Lee Whorf*, Cambridge, MA: MIT Press, pp. 218, 153, 158.

[168] Frank Heynick, 1983, "From Einstein to Whorf: Space, Time, Matter, and Reference Frames in Physical and Linguistic Relativity," *Semiotica* 45(1/2):35–64, pp. 53–54; Roman Jakobson, 1972, "Verbal Communication," *Scientific American* 227(3):72–81, p. 75.

z axes). Image has just x and y axes; space and objects extend along all of x, y, and z axes.

By transposition: lengths can be considered as breadths, either in terms of the orientation of the viewer, or the convention that, when there are two dimensions, length is longer than breadth. Lengths can be conceived partially in areas, and both lengths and areas within volumes. These are not just stable qualities; by another transposition, they can be actions: lengthening/shortening, widening/narrowing; growing/shrinking; making bigger/smaller. And the qualities of movement in place can be determined as a relationship with time: velocity and acceleration.

By relation, relative to the embodied ego or materialized object: right/left; above/below; front/behind; beside/against; near (one)/between (two)/among (a few)/amidst (many); arrive/depart, enter/leave.

By relation, according to fixed coordinates: cardinal directions, orientation, motion and directionality, fixedness/mobility, containment/open-ness, paths across, apertures/barriers.[169]

Here is a rough map of senses of place:

Form / Function: Place	Text	Image	Space	Object	Body	Sound	Speech
Proximate	Prepositions, the writer's "here"	Visible figure in the image, contrasted with ground	Here and near, as experienced and measurable from spatial co-ordinates	Immediate objects	Bodies here: the present self or other	Heard, present sounds	Listening, here
Distant	Prepositions, place names, the writer's "there"	Visble ground in the image, contrasted with figure; surrounds not immediately visible in the image	Far and directionality, travel, as experienced and measurable from spatial co-ordinates	Possible, potentially experienceable objects	Bodies away: the non-present other	Sound projections, recordings	Speech there: the unheard, quotation, recording, radio, telephone

Fig. 1.3.2: Place

Once again, speech and text are radically different – listening is here (as are present bodies and sound), while the writer's here is actually there (as is the picturer's image).

---

[169] Michel Aurnague, Maya Hickmann and Laure Vieu, eds. 2007, *The Categorization of Spatial Entities in Language and Cognition*, Amsterdam: John Benjamins; Maya Hickmann and Stéphane Robert, eds. 2006, *Space in Languages: Linguistic Systems and Cognitive Categories*, Amsterdam: John Benjamins.

Then, if not a sense of place, we have its absence in the form of disorientation, or the placelessness of universal things and relations that could be anywhere (like logic's relation to time[§1.3.1]).

§1.3.2a The Place of the "Virtual"

The impression of striking here-ness of somewhere else is today offered by renderings on digital devices. This creates an effect that those enamored with new media like to call "virtual reality."[170] As if by miracle of the machine, the distant seems proximate.

We might narrowly define the virtual as two-dimensional imaging, sometimes enhanced to give the impression of three-dimensionality through binocular rendering. Wagering on the future, the two-year-old company that had created the Oculus virtual reality headset was bought by Facebook for $2.4 billion in 2014.[171] This and similar headsets work by shutting off contextual viewing and hearing.[*]

Not that there is anything particularly new about this, or not enough one would think to warrant such billions. Binocular still imaging is as old as photographic techniques themselves, using double-lens cameras, dual images, and viewers.[172] The first 3-D cinema images were created in 1903.[173] The idea of closing off immediate context to enhance the effect of the virtual was captured in Morton L. Helig's US Patent of 1962 for the "Sensorama Simulator": an "apparatus ... to stimulate the senses of an individual to simulate an actual experience realistically ... by developing sensations in a plurality of the senses."[174]

In a longer view, the effect of proximity despite distance is as old as drawing and painting (tens of thousands of years), writing (thousands),[§1.4.7a] printing (a millennium),[§1.4.7b] linear perspective (half a millennium),[§MS2.2b] photography (a century and a half),[§MS2.2.2a] cinema (a century),[§MS1.1.3f] television (half a century), and the internet (decades).[§1.4.7e] The "virtual" has been part of our experience of meaning for as long as our species' practices of recorded and transmitted meaning.

---

[*] http://meaningpatterns.net/virtual

[170] Howard Rheingold, 1991, *Virtual Reality*, New York: Summit Books; Brian Massumi, 2002, *Parables for the Virtual: Movement, Affect, Sensation*, Durham, NC: Duke University Press.
[171] www.fastcompany.com/3028244/facebook-acquires-oculus-vr-for-2-billion
[172] Helmut Gernsheim and Alison Gernsheim, 1969, *The History of Photography, from the Camera Obscura to the Beginning of the Modern Era*, New York: McGraw-Hill, pp. 253–62.
[173] R.M. Hayes, 1989, *3-D Movies: A History and Filmography of Stereoscopic Cinema*, Jefferson, NC: McFarland and Company, p. 3.
[174] Morton L. Heilig, 1962, "Sensorama Simulator," edited by U.S. Patent Office.

McKenzie Wark calls this telesthesia, or "perception at a distance," where "we bring what is distant near, and make what is distant a site of action."[175] Functionally, telesthesia occurs by transposition, where, by fiat of meaning, the far is always ready to be made near, the distant made proximate.

People who work with place as their line of trade – geographers for instance – tend to prioritize proximity. Here is Tobler's famed first law of geography: "everything is related to everything else, but near things are more related than distant things."[176] He had come to this conclusion while working on a computer simulation of urban growth in Detroit. When we looked on Google Scholar his original article had been cited 6,146 times, and to establish this degree of academic fame the spatial proximity of his referencers did not seem to have mattered.

In our reading of proximity versus distance in senses of place, this has been a nonsense for tens of thousands of years. There is no reason why the distant should not be just as related as the near, and at times even more related. By transposition, we can make the distant as meaningful as the nearby, or more. Indeed, texts and images transposed across greater distance in space and time may for that very reason acquire an unusual power over us. Religious texts and icons are a case in point.

As for the virtual, there is nothing terribly new in the phenomenology of its transpositions. A 1958 Bell Telephone System advertisement shows a wife sitting on a comfortable chair, apron on, vacuum cleaner behind her, and a small table beside her with a framed picture of her husband. She's on the phone.

The Telephone Way to a Happier Day
Try it today when the dishes are done, beds made, clothes in the washer. You've earned a break.

So relax a little and pick up the telephone. Enjoy a cheerful visit with a friend or loved one.

It's so easy to do, whatever the miles may be. For no one is ever far away by telephone.

It helps to make any day a happier day at both ends of the line.[177]

The husband, and the friend, are virtual, and perhaps happiness too. It's the same husband, friend, happiness, here or there. But in the nature of transposition, the meanings are not (quite) the same.

---

[175] McKenzie Wark, 2012, *Telesthesia: Communication, Culture and Class*, Cambridge: Polity, pp. 15, 207.

[176] W.R. Tobler, 1970, "A Computer Movie Simulating Urban Growth in the Detroit Region," *Economic Geography* 46 (Supplement: Proceedings of the International Geographical Union, Commission on Quantitative Methods):234–40, p. 236; W.R. Tobler, 2004, "On the First Law of Geography: A Reply," *Annals of the Association of American Geographers* 94(2):304–10.

[177] http://blog.modernmechanix.com/the-telephone-way-to-a-happier-day/

§1.3.2b   Gladys B. West's Global Positioning System

> He had brought a large map representing the sea,
>   Without the least vestige of land:
> And the crew were much pleased when they found it to be
>   A map they could understand.
> "What's the good of Mercator's North Poles and Equators.
>   Tropics, Zones, and Meridian Lines?
> So the Bellman would cry: and the crew would reply
>   "They are merely conventional signs!"[178]

The map in Lewis Carroll's *Hunting of the Snark* is blank, as featureless as the middle of an ocean.* These sailors' coordinates may have been merely conventional signs, but today, in quantified modernity, such signs have attained a universality that grounds them in new ways. Here is the backstory.

Much to the shock of the Americans, who did not see it coming, the Soviet Union launched Sputnik on October 4, 1957. This was the earth's first artificial satellite, a mere 58 centimeters in diameter with two pairs of antennae communicating radio signals back to earth. In the three months before it crashed out of orbit, Sputnik traversed the entire inhabited earth.[179]

Sputnik was launched on a Friday, and when William Guier and George Weiffenbach came to work at the Applied Physics Laboratory at Johns Hopkins University on Monday, they were surprised to find that nobody had yet attempted to track its signal. Guier had created computer simulations of hydrogen bomb explosions, and Weiffenbach was at the time finishing his Ph.D. in microwave spectroscopy.

Soon they detected the signal and calculated the satellite's trajectory. By dint of Cold War necessity, they were mere eavesdroppers. On the prompting of Frank McClure, the Laboratory's director, they realized that not only could they determine the location of the radio transmitter, but the location of the receiver when tracked against the trajectory of the satellite. Geographical position could be determined in a passive communication system – just by receiving a signal, without having to send one.[180] It was this insight that was became the basis for the subsequent development of the Global Positioning System (GPS).

For forty-two years, Gladys B. West worked for the US Naval Surface Warfare Center where she was one of the key creators of GPS. "The primary

---

* http://meaningpatterns.net/gps

[178] Lewis Carroll, 1876 [1981], *The Hunting of the Snark*, Los Altos, CA: William Kaufmann, pp. 15–16.
[179] Yanek Mieczkowski, 2013, *Eisenhower's Sputnik Moment: The Race for Space and World Prestige*, Ithaca, NY: Cornell University Press.
[180] George Weiffenbach and William Guier, 1998, "Genesis of Satellite Navigation," *Johns Hopkins APL Technical Digest* 19(1):14–17, p. 16.

mission," she wrote in a now-declassified document, "meets the geodesy requirement to provide the Department of the Navy with a global data base of 10cm precision radar altimeter measurements. This data will allow for improvements in the gravitational models required by advanced Submarine Launched Ballistic Missile systems."[181]

At the US Air Force Base, GPS project leader Brad Parkinson had posted on the wall of his office this guiding slogan: "The mission of this Program Office is to drop 5 bombs into the same hole." Parkinson's word was turned into practice for the first time in the 1991 Gulf War.

Billions of dollars later, by 1995 the US had a complete satellite system in place, with thirty-eight satellites circling the globe at a distance of approximately 20,000 kilometers. The GPS signal was opened to full civilian use in 2000. The Soviets started launching their own system in 1982, followed by partial and still incomplete European, Chinese, and Indian systems.[182] It's irrelevant how many systems there are, because the numbers driving them all are the same – the three-dimensional geocoordinate system of latitude, longitude, and elevation that was established at the 1884 International Meridian Conference in Washington DC.

Today, there are billions of GPS receivers, mostly mobile phones, and an unthinkable number of daily calculations of place. To work, a receiver needs a line of sight to at least four satellites. Every satellite has an accurately synchronized atomic clock, and the time it takes for the signal to reach your device tells how far the receiver is from each satellite. In a calculation transposing these times into space, the machine can determine where you are with a margin of error of 30 centimeters. Combining the Russian signals with the US signals, a beet farmer can achieve accuracy of less than an inch, at which point the position of every seed is recorded and then each beet dug up without damage.[183]

Here we encounter another significant difference between speech and text. Speech can only refer to place awkwardly or ambiguously – "near/far," "before/after," "in front of/behind." The numbered coordinates that are named in text and drive geolocation are for practical purposes unspeakable.

An incidental effect of the time-space basis of GPS technology is that, as well as determining locations, GPS satellites today also drive most of the world's clocks. GPS time commenced at midnight on 5 January, 1980.[184]

Returning to Einstein[§1.3.1a] for a moment, in material and experiential terms, time and space are profoundly not the same. To make time a fourth dimension in a continuum is to ignore an irreducible difference between the three

---

[181] Gladys B. West, 1986, *Data Processing System Specifications for the Geosat Satellite Radar Altimeter*, Report NSWC TR 86-149, Dahlgren, VA: Naval Surface Weapons Center, p. 1.

[182] Greg Milner, 2016, *Pinpoint: How GPS Is Changing Technology, Culture, and Our Minds*, New York: W.W. Norton, pp. 56–58, 88, 100, 144.

[183] Ibid., pp. 101–05.   [184] Ibid., p. 154.

dimensions of space on the one hand, and the trajectory of time on the other. Time and space do not need to be jammed into the same frame of dimensionality for their meanings to be transposable. The power of GPS is not its conflation of space-time into a unified continuum, but in the mechanics of its transposition, its cross-calibrations between meanings that are fundamentally different, and whose efficacy is in the difference.

Then, another transposition is required, from numbered geocoordinates that are unspeakable when it gets down to meters and centimeters, to the instantiation of place represented by speakable names – though these too are so many that they can't be remembered for spontaneous speech. We need to read them off our devices for the purposes of navigating directions.

The transposition from numbered to named place is achieved by Geographic Information Systems (GIS), a phrase used for the first time in a 1965 report by Michael Dacey and Duane Marble for the US Office of Naval Research.[185] GeoNames contains an all-but definitive list of more than 25 million place names on earth, with 645 feature codes, including "anchorage," "automatic teller machine," "asylum," "arch," and "abandoned police post."[186] Since its launch in 2005, Google Maps has become the most definitive GIS software, layered into Google Street View and Google Earth – covering just about every street in the world. OpenStreetMap is an open data, collaborative mapping project hosted by the not-for-profit OpenStreet Map Foundation.[187]

Connecting GPS to GIS, Yelp will find you almost any restaurant. In the United States, Zillow will show you current and historical prices of almost every house, along with pictures inside its bedrooms and bathrooms that may have been posted by realtors at an earlier sale. On Facebook and Instagram, users create place names, and when other users search for nearby places, they find geotags where they can "check in." Cameras with GPS include incidentally recorded geographical metadata in Exchangeable image file format (Exif),[§1.4.6c] and locations are automatically marked in albums that bring GIS to bear on GPS.

Based as they are in a now-singular and universal grammar of place, a hugely detailed, semantically regimented representation of empirical locations has been created by giant companies and millions of information-contributing users. This representation of place is arguable in its minutiae, but definitive in its generality. Its validity can be tested and refined against a myriad of moments of experiences of place, and internal place–place calculations when people and machines corroborate data with data.[188]

---

[185] Michael F. Dacey and Duane F. Marble, 1965, "Some Comments on Certain Technical Aspects of Geographic Information Systems," Office of Naval Research.
[186] www.geonames.org/export/codes.html   [187] www.openstreetmap.org/about
[188] Franz-Benjamin Mocnik, Amin Mobasheri, Luisa Griesbaum, Melanie Eckle, Clemens Jacobs, and Carolin Klonner, 2018, "A Grounding-Based Ontology of Data Quality Measures,"

In the unspeakable numbers that power these transpositions from place to number to text, and back again, we encounter what Félix Guattari calls, in a nice turn of phrase, "asignifying semiotics." He explains: "the systems of logical, topological, algebraic algorithm, the processes of recording, memory storage, and data processing used by mathematicians, sciences, technology, harmonic and polyphonic music, etc., do not have an aim to denote or fill in the morphemes of a fully constituted referent, but to produce them through their own machinics." He calls this a "machinic unconscious," in order "to stress that it is populated not only with images and words, but also with all kinds of machinisms that lead it to produce and reproduce these images and words."[189]

Or in our terms, the transposition from place (context) to its naming (text), picturing (image), and embodied presence (space) is by means of "machinic" mediation where the intermediate texts are unspeakable and unreadable. In the now-universal grammar of digital place, calculable position is always waiting to be turned into meanings-for-us.

Along the way, we've lost track of the fact that place may be relative to historical contingency. Our ontology of place has become now so universal and so definitive in its details that we can lose track of its historicity, its strangeness in the span of human species-life. Notwithstanding its peculiarities, except in the most minor of ways, it has become practically non-negotiable.

Since May 20, 2019, we have grounded universal calculation of place, time, and other measures in the most stable natural phenomena scientists have found, and their cross-calculable transpositions. From that date, Bureau International des Poids et Mesures in France deemed that the kilogram will be measured by the amount of energy it takes to balance its weight using electromagnetic forces.[190] Now, all seven base units of measure (meter, kilogram, second, ampere, kelvin, mole, and candela) are to be calculated against physical constants, and in calculations against each other. These transpositions, so it seems, are now definitive.

A meter had already been determined in 1983 to be the distance covered by light in a vacuum in 1/299,792,458 of a second, and in 1967 a second as the duration of 9,192,631,770 periods of the radiation corresponding to the transition between the two hyperfine levels of the ground state of the cesium-133

Journal of Spatial Information Science (16):1–25; Franz-Benjamin Mocnik, 2018, "The Polynomial Volume Law of Complex Networks in the Context of Local and Global Optimization," *Scientific Reports* 8(11274):1–10.

[189] Félix Guattari, 1979 [2001], *The Machinic Unconscious: Essays in Schizoanalysis*, translated by T. Adkins, Los Angeles: Semiotext(e), pp. 20, 216, 10; Gary Genosko, 2008, "A-Signifying Semiotics," *Public Journal of Semiotics* 11(1):11–21.

[190] www.economist.com/science-and-technology/2018/11/17/the-kilogram-and-three-other-metr ic-units-are-about-to-be-revamped

atom.[191] So, it would seem, we have naturalized place in relation to other measures, and fixed these measures to non-negotiable materiality for all time.

Not that this now-universal grammar of place is, by virtue of its ubiquity, in the slightest neutral. Far from it: the conventions of calculable place reflect the conquest of certain patterns of place-sense over others.

The new cognitive prostheses of place and wayfinding begin their calculations on a universe of fixed coordinates and cardinal directions. This is an objective world, grounded in the historicity of its measures. At the same time, subjectively they position the self at the world's center. "Turn left," says the GPS. "Recenter," you say, and the map puts the little arrowed directional dot of the ego back in the center of the world. Along the road, the map is oriented to the direction of travel, not the north of past mapping convention. The objectified spatiality of the world is recalculated and transposed onto the subjectively self-centered world of the GPS-dependent wayfinder.

There is, for the moment at least, only one other thing of final relevance in the map of the world, the destination icon. In between, there is a line, so the two-dimensionality of printed maps has effectively been reduced to one, a direction. The GPS barks your marching orders, and barely conceals its irritation at your mistakes.

The software does the transposition for you, from two-dimensional place to one-dimensional direction, from context to self, from objective place to subjective wayfinding. This process entails loss as much as gain. The most obvious loss is agency, the relative control of place and path afforded by two-dimensional mental maps. By relieving the wayfinder's burdens, the cognitive prosthesis displaces a wider, contextualizing cognition. The world is narrowed, and maps of self become "maps of ignorance."[192]

§1.3.2c Guugu Yimithirr Place

"My own people," says Australian Indigenous activist Noel Pearson, "first saw Europeans when the Endeavour limped into Gangarr, the site today known as Cooktown, during that now infamous voyage in 1770."[*] The Endeavour was Captain James Cook's ship, and his voyage was in subsequent centuries to be celebrated by colonial and then federated Australia as one of "discovery."

Cook and his crew spent six weeks repairing their ship on the banks of what they named the Endeavour River. Cook recorded a word list of the local

---

[*] http://meaningpatterns.net/gy

[191] https://en.wikipedia.org/wiki/SI_base_unit
[192] Marco D'Eramo, 2017, "Geographies of Ignorance," *New Left Review* (108):43–45.

language, Guugu Yimithirr. "Gangaruu," or grey wallaby in Guugu Yimithirr, became "kangaroo" in English.

Of the people, Cook wrote in his journal:

> They live in tranquility which is not disturbed by the inequality of condition. The earth and sea of their own accord furnishes them with all things necessary for life. They live in a warm and fine climate, and enjoy every wholesome air, so that they have very little need of clothing. In short they seem to set no value upon anything we gave them; nor would they ever part with anything of their own. This in my opinion argues that they think themselves provided with all the necessaries of life.[193]

Nevertheless, the consequences of imperial "discovery" and after that, colonial "settlement" were for Australia's First Peoples devastating – it was an invasion. A mission was established in 1886 fifty kilometers out of Cooktown at a place in Guugu Yimithirr country that the Lutheran missionaries named, without sense of irony, Hope Vale. Here, Guugu Yimithirr language has survived, with an estimated 775 speakers in 2016.[194]

In Guugu Yimithirr experience, place and movement are figured in terms of four cardinal coordinates, *gungga, jiba, naga,* and *guwa.* It is too simple to say these align any more than roughly with (respectively) north, south, east, and west in modern geolocation. The Guugu Yimithirr compass is rotated slightly clockwise to reflect where the sun rises in these tropics, *naga,* and these four cardinal directions represent quadrants of space rather than lines directed at idealized points on the horizon as is the case of today's quantitized N/S/E/W coordinates.[195]

Guugu Yimithirr people express place, not in relative reference to the self, but in terms of these absolute coordinates. Instead of an ego-centered relativity of place where I might say that you are on my left or right, a Guugu Yimithirr will say that you are to my east or my west. Rather than ask someone to "move back from the table," they might say *guwagu-manaayi,* "move a bit to the west."[196] John B. Haviland concludes: Guugu Yimithirr "takes as its primitives global geocentric coordinates . . . fixed, as it were, by the earth (and perhaps the sun) and not subject to the rotation of observers or reference objects."[197]

---

[193] Noel Pearson, 1993, "A Troubling Inheritance," *Race and Class* 35(4):1–9, pp. 1–2.

[194] John B. Haviland, 1985, "The Life History of a Speech Community: Guugu Yimidhirr at Hopevale," *Aboriginal History* 9(1/2):170–204; John B. Haviland, 1996b, "Owners Versus Bubu Gujin: Land Rights and Getting the Language Right in Guugu Yimithirr Country," *Journal of Linguistic Anthropology* 6(2):145–60; http://stat.data.abs.gov.au/Index.aspx?DataSetCode=ABS_C16_T09_SA

[195] John B. Haviland, 1993, "Anchoring, Iconicity, and Orientation in Guugu Yimithirr Pointing Gestures," *Journal of Linguistic Anthropology* 3(1):3–45, pp. 5–6; John B. Haviland, 1998, "Guugu Yimithirr Cardinal Directions," *Ethos* 26(1):25–47, pp. 29–30.

[196] John B. Haviland, 1993, "Anchoring, Iconicity, and Orientation in Guugu Yimithirr Pointing Gestures," *Journal of Linguistic Anthropology* 3(1):3–45, pp. 5–6.

[197] John B. Haviland, 1998, "Guugu Yimithirr Cardinal Directions," *Ethos* 26(1):25–47, p. 25.

On these semantic foundations, Guugu Yimithirr builds an elaborately inflected case system. A myriad of subtle distinctions are made, in the following examples for the quadrant *naga*, east: *naga*, east from a point; *naga-ar*, to a point east; *naga-alu*, east, over some point or obstacle; *naga-nun*, from a given point east to reference point; *naga-nu-nganh*, out of a point east; *naga-almun*, from east toward reference point; *naga-almu-nganh*, out of an easterly direction – to name just a few of many fine distinctions.[198]

Not that agency is elided in a geocentric universe, far from it. Nor is the figuring a matter of speech determining meaning: speech, gesture, and place figure into each other, by multimodal transposition of their forms.

Jack Bambi tells a story in Guugu Yimithirr about when he and a companion were in a mission boat that capsized, and they had to swim to shore through shark-infested waters. Sitting in Hope Vale thirty years later, Haviland recounts, Jack gestures in reference to "the three and a half miles to the beach at Bala, not by pointing in some arbitrary direction," relative to the narrating self, "and not to the northeast where Bala actually lies from where he sits, but southwest, calculating from the narrated perspective of his capsized boat."

Once safely on the shore, Jack Bambi looks back, gesturing to the cardinal north to his companion, then in the story and again now in its reliving in speech. In a narrative transposition of time now/then and place here/there, he sets the action in the context of Guugu Yimithirr coordinates, the black spot of the sinking boat in the distance, and in the same direction, a shark. After their ordeal, the two walked for several hours back to Hope Vale. Exhausted, they knocked on the missionary's door, whose first thought was the fate of the boat. He sent them straight back to recover it, told to be another gesture away.[199]

Agency in the form of heroic survival and conflicting missionary interests – the points of the story – have by no means been drained by a geocentric rather than egocentric orientation to place. However, the orientation to place is profoundly different from the modern, egocentric one. In the case of Guugu Yimithirr and other First Peoples, this involves a highly developed sense of direction, layering over the land intricate mental maps of terrain, scenes, landmarks, and paths. It also reflects the widely held self-characterization of Indigenous peoples of their relationships to land in Australia, that "we belong

---

[198] Ibid., pp. 30–36.
[199] John B. Haviland, 2000, "Pointing, Gesture Spaces, and Mental Maps," pp. 13–46 in *Language and Gesture*, edited by D. McNeil, Cambridge: Cambridge University Press, pp. 15, 19–20; John B. Haviland, 1996a, "Projections, Transpositions, and Relativity," pp. 271–323 in *Rethinking Linguistic Relativity*, edited by J.J. Gumperz and S.C. Levinson, Cambridge: Cambridge University Press, pp. 286–88; John B. Haviland, 1993, "Anchoring, Iconicity, and Orientation in Guugu Yimithirr Pointing Gestures," *Journal of Linguistic Anthropology* 3(1):3–45, pp. 11–16, 19–31.

to country," rather than "country belongs to us." By multimodal transposition, Guugu Yimithirr means at once speech, people, and country.

None of this diminishes agency. It's just that agency is figured in relation to place in very different ways from our calculating modernity. Indeed, the irony of the modern self living in the Global Positioning System, is that although the underlying mechanism is obsessively finely grained cardinality, its transposition into egocentric place creates certain kinds of blindness to the wider context of place, certain kinds of ignorance.[§1.3.2b] Navigating by GPS, although self is centered in place determined by self-centered instrumental ends in the form of the line as a destination point, the self subsequently ends up losing two-dimensional context and becomes captive to instructions transposed into second person imperatives.

In modernity also, we like to think that some place belongs to us, a fantasy of private property, when in fact, at best we own little more than tiny private spaces, and many nothing at all. Beyond this, agency is heavily circumscribed, by the owners of shopping malls,[§2.3c] the edges of streets, and the rules of the road. By comparison, Guugu Yimithirr have a deeper working knowledge of place, a more profound awareness of self-in-context, and more control over their meanings of place.

The larger question here is, how different can humans be? Chomsky says, not very: "The long term aim [of his generative grammar] has been, and remains, to show that, contrary to appearances, human languages are basically cast in the same mold, that they are instantiations of the same fixed endowment, and that they 'grow in the mind' much like other biological systems, triggered and shaped by experience, but only in restricted ways."[200]

Against this stands the linguistic relativity hypothesis, famously initiated by Whorf and Sapir, exploring the breadth of human differences. Profoundly different conceptions of color,[§MS1.3.1a] time,[§1.3.1c] and place[201] are selected as

---

[200] Noam Chomsky, 2002, "Chomsky's Revolution: An Exchange," *New York Review of Books*, 18 July, pp. 64–65.

[201] Stephen C. Levinson, Sotaro Kita, Daniel B.M. Haun, and Björn H. Rasch, 2002, "Returning the Tables: Language Affects Spatial Reasoning," *Cognition* 84(2):155–88; Stephen Levinson, Sérgio Meira, and the Language and Cognition Group, 2003, " 'Natural Concepts' in the Spatial Topological Domain–Adpositional Meanings in Crosslinguistic Perspective: An Exercise in Semantic Typology," *Language* 79(3):485–516; Stephen C. Levinson, 2003, *Space in Language and Cognition: Explorations in Cognitive Diversity*, Cambridge: Cambridge University Press; Stephen C. Levinson, 1996a, "Relativity in Spatial Conception and Description," pp. 177–202 in *Rethinking Linguistic Relativity*, edited by J.J. Gumperz and S.C. Levinson, Cambridge: Cambridge University Press; Stephen C. Levinson, 1996b, "Language and Space," *Annual Review of Anthropology* 25:353–82; Stephen C. Levinson, 1997, "Language and Cognition: The Cognitive Consequences of Spatial Description in Guugu Yimithirr," *Journal of Linguistic Anthropology* 7(1):98–131; Asifa Majid, Melissa Bowerman, Sotaro Kita, Daniel B.M. Haun, and Stephen C. Levinson, 2004, "Can Language Restructure Cognition? The Case for Space," *Trends in Cognitive Sciences* 8(3):108–14; John A. Lucy,

staple examples to illustrate the proposition that different languages realize radically different ways of thinking and being.[202]

In a multimodal grammar, it is not just a matter of saying that language shapes thought, nor even that it reflects thought in some peculiarly prescient way. Meanings are made in forms of life, to return to a phrase of Wittgenstein,[§MS2.3.2a] though here we want to account for radical differences in forms of life in a way that Wittgenstein did not. Nor do we want to follow Wittgenstein, primarily to use forms of life to account for meanings in language. The meaning is in the form of life itself: bodies in relation to space, gesture in relation to place, and topography itself as meaning. Geocentric cosmologies of place are very different forms of life from egocentric cosmologies. The occlusions of egocentric place in the one-dimensional modernity of GPS are different from the bewilderment of Lewis Carroll's sailors when confronted with two-dimensional modernity.[§1.3.2b] The differences are telling.

But we don't just want to posit relativity, leaving things at a neutral this-compared-with-that. There are species universals, but these are to be accounted for in terms of natural history rather than the languaged brain. Whether Guugu Yimithirr time or GPS time, whether Hopi time or atomic clock time, place and time are materially experienced universals in our species-experience in natural history – felt by bodies in space, referenced in text and speech, seen in image and gesture. The reference point should be our shared species characteristics as multimodal meaning-makers. This is also the measure of our differences in meaning form and meaning function.

On the scale of multimodal meaning potentiality, some meaning frames may in some respects be smarter than others. Compared to modernity and notwithstanding all its acquired powers of representation and communication, First Peoples meant their lives in ways that established comparatively stable and harmonious relations to nature, and reciprocal agencies of social equality. We have done a horrible job at both these things in modernity. However, if we as a species can have been this different, the lesson to be learned in a pained modernity is that we can be this different again.

Human nature is variable and plastic, within the affordances offered by nature writ large. We have escaped the bounds of change determined for

1998, "Space in Language and Thought: Commentary and Discussion," *Ethos* 26(1):105–11; Bill Palmer, 2015, "Topography in Language: Absolute Frame of Reference and the Topographic Correspondence Hypothesis," pp. 179–226 in *Language Structure and Environment: Social, Cultural, and Natural Factors*, edited by R.J. LaPolla and Rik De Busser, London: John Benjamins.

[202] John J. Gumperz and Stephen C. Levinson, 1991, "Rethinking Linguistic Relativity," *Current Anthropology* 32(5):613–23; John A. Lucy, 1992, *Language Diversity and Thought: A Reformulation of the Linguistic Relativity Hypothesis*, Cambridge: Cambridge University Press; John A. Lucy, 1997, "Linguistic Relativity," *Annual Review of Anthropology* 26:291–312.

other species primarily by natural selection, to become a species capable of self-transformation through self-ascribed meaning, using the ideal to extend the material.[203] In a grammar of multimodality, our freedom is to design. This, paradoxically, is in our universal human nature, our historical and creative nature.

Within this frame of reference, our human differences point to the scope of human possibility, and offer hope for our self-transformability as a species whose recent history has been a story of tragic self-harm. We can change the world by (re)designing our forms of life. We can change ourselves by changing the conditions of our living.

§1.4   Medium

> **Medium.** *The sensuous materials and practices brought to forms of meaning – text, image, space, object, body, sound, and speech – the potential meaning functions that each offers, and our consequent need for multimodality.*

To become sensible, meaning must be made material. Text, image, space, object, body, sound, and speech are materialized in media and experienced as sensuous activity. In their materiality, media open out certain possibilities for meaning, while constraining meaning as well. Media both shape and limit meaning. We need multimodality as a practical consequence of the functional peculiarities and limits of each of the meaning forms.

Now, for a while in our narrative, we are going to switch axes, arraying text, image, space, object, body, sound, and speech on the functional axis. On the form axis, they can mean the same things. But on the functional axis, when conceived in terms of the affordances of their media, they mean quite differently. Conceived as media, our focus becomes functional: what are the effects of media on the scope of meaning? Why, then, functionally speaking, do we need multimodality for our meaning?

Meaning forms are the meaning patterns, conventions, and systems characteristic of text, image, space, object, body, sound, and speech. Medium is the manner of their materialization which gives shape to those forms. It is what we see, hear, touch, move through, and feel. Forms are the shapes of meanings that are thinkable, imaginable, doable. Media are their material means, using sensuous resources drawn from context. With these media come different functional possibilities or meaning effects.

Here is a rough map:

---

[203] David Christian, 2004, *Maps of Time: An Introduction to Big History*, Berkeley: University of California Press, pp. 139–42.

Form Function: Medium	Text	Image	Space	Object	Body	Sound	Speech
Medium	See-able in scribing and reading, graphemes in Unicode	See-able in two-dimensional picture, diagram, pixelated image	Move-throughable in three-dimensional space	Sensible three-dimensional object	Feelable by the body	Hearable in sound	Listenable in speech

Fig. 1.4: Medium

Medium is the Latin noun for middle, and *mediare* the verb, to occupy a middle position – hence "mediate." In modern English usage, Raymond Williams points out, media and mediation can mean three quite different kinds of between-ness: tools for communication in the sense of transmission of meaning,[§1.2.2] interpretation,[§1.2.3] and rhetorical appeal,[§2.1] directing meaning to the communicator's interest; or when interests obviously diverge, intercession with a view to reconciliation of antagonistic positions.[204] Or another three, this time in Galloway, Thacker, and Wark: media as exegesis (purporting); media as hermeneutics (interpretation); media as symptomatics (what is missing).[205]

Friedrich Kittler says that philosophers since Aristotle have tended to ignore their media, as if they were transparent.[206] To avoid this error, he arrives at a media determinism: "the only thing that can be known about the soul or the human are the technical gadgets with which they have been historically measured at any given time."[207] Or, in the famous formula of Marshall McLuhan, the medium is the message.[208]

Then there is mediation on mediation: "transmediation" (Elleström), when media content is mediated for a second or third time;[209] or "remediation" (Bolter and Grusin), when one medium is represented in another.[210]

---

[204] Raymond Williams, 1976, *Keywords: A Vocabulary of Culture and Society*, Glasgow: Fontana/ Croom Helm, pp. 169–72.

[205] Alexander R. Galloway, Eugene Thacker, and McKenzie Wark, 2014, *Excommunication: Three Inquiries in Media and Mediation*, Chicago, IL: University of Chicago Press, pp. 153–54.

[206] Friedrich A. Kittler, 2009, "Towards an Ontology of Media," *Theory, Culture & Society Message* 26(2–3):23–31.

[207] Friedrich A. Kittler, 1999 [2010], *Optical Media*, translated by A. Enns, Cambridge: Polity, p. 35.

[208] Marshall McLuhan and Quentin Fiore, 1967 [1996], *The Medium Is the Massage: An Inventory of Effects*, Berkeley, CA: Gingko Press; Marshall McLuhan, 1964 [2001], *Understanding Media: The Extensions of Man*, London: Routledge.

[209] Lars Elleström, 2010, "The Modalities of Media: A Model for Understanding Intermedial Relations," pp. 11–50 in *Media Borders, Multimodality and Intermediality*, edited by L. Elleström, London: Palgrave Macmillan, p. 4.

[210] Jay David Bolter and Richard Grusin, 1999, *Remediation: Understanding New Media*, Cambridge, MA: MIT Press, p. 45; Lev Manovich, 2001, *The Language of New Media*, Cambridge, MA: MIT Press.

Ease of mechanical reproducibility of media in the industrial era, says Walter Benjamin,[§MS0b] both reduces the aura of authenticity in art (the presence of a stage actor, versus the film actor, for instance,) while at the same time making its depths accessible to the masses.[211]

The effect of media, says John Peters, is that they have at once "extended and handicapped the human sensorium." Radio, for instance, freed speech, allowing it to span space, but with the deletion of vision. The gramophone freed sound, allowing it to span time, but with the deletion of embodied presence. The extensions are created "by recording media that compress time, and by transmitting media that compress space."[212] The deletions give shape to the arts and sciences of media practice.

Sometimes the lossiness of media are as meaningful as their gains – the poignancy and power of the medium. The constraint can be generative: the metric line of iambic hexameter, for instance, or the two-dimensional oils-on-canvas, stilled to a moment and confined within the edges of the frame. The technique and the art are in the taming of the medium, the domestication of its constraints. The closures and openings of media are their "affordances."

Psychologist James Gibson coined the word "affordance," an idea that is critical to our understanding of the ways in which meaning forms are shaped by the materiality of their media. His work was at an elemental, creaturely level: "The affordances of the environment are what it offers the animal, what it provides or furnishes, either for good or ill."[213] They are the bases of systematic action, for good in the example of objects that afford walking-on or sitting-on, or avoidance of ill in the case of "visual cliffs".[214] Gibson is a radical empiricist in the Lockean mold,[§MS1.3a] perhaps even more radically so. We have become what the world of our affordances has allowed.[215]

However, for all the sway of the material that we must of course acknowledge, we also want to recognize the co-presence of the ideal, as the non-stereotypical Locke would, too.

---

[211] Walter Benjamin, 1936 [2008], "The Work of Art in the Age of Its Technological Reproducibility," in *The Work of Art in the Age of Its Technological Reproducibility and Other Writings on Media*, edited by M.W. Jennings, B. Doherty, and T.Y. Levin, Cambridge, MA: Harvard University Press.

[212] John Durham Peters, 2015, *The Marvelous Clouds: Toward a Philosophy of Elemental Media*, Chicago, IL: University of Chicago Press, pp. 25, 37; John Durham Peters, 1999, *Speaking into the Air: A History of the Idea of Communication*, Chicago, IL: University of Chicago Press.

[213] James J. Gibson, 1979 [2015], *The Ecological Approach to Visual Perception*, New York: Psychology Press, p. 119.

[214] James J. Gibson, 1977, "The Theory of Affordances," pp. 67–82 in *Perceiving, Acting, and Knowing: Toward an Ecological Psychology*, edited by R. Shaw and J. Bransford, London: Routledge, pp. 68, 80.

[215] James J. Gibson, 1966, *The Senses Considered as Perceptual Systems*, Boston, MA: Houghton Mifflin, pp. 47–48.

In this grammar, we propose text, image, space, object, body, sound, and speech as distinct meaning systems, operating simultaneously across all five meaning functions: reference, agency, structure, context, and interest. When it comes to media, we are interested in examining the affordances for meaning offered by the necessarily material manifestations of these forms. Gunther Kress calls these "resources for meaning."[216]

Media are made of raw materials that have been called out, pulled down – grabbed if you will – from context. They are available resources not only in the sense of their meaning forms (say, writing), but the unavoidably materiality of their media (pens and paper; printing presses and books; and iPhones "designed in California," – which must be a country? – but "made in China").

Media are what Roland Barthes calls the "material substance of signifieds."[217] They are found objects, then once found, they demand of us work, with our hands, eyes, ears, and sensuous bodies. We take media out of their context. Refashioning them in our own hands and minds, we make meanings whose precise contextual coordinates and material manifestation has never been made before. Such is design.[§MS0.4.1]

Then, what of the media-shaped differences in forms of meaning? There is nothing that language can't express, any language, every language, says Louis Hjelmslev,[§0.2] conflating, as is the habit of linguists, text with speech.[218] Yes, we can show a mountain in a picture and speak of it as well.[§MS0.0] But we can sometimes do more with a picture, because the picture and speech are not the same. We often do the two at the same time precisely because of their differences in affordance. This is why we mix our media, why we need our multimodality.

Transposition from form to form, using one medium then the next or several media juxtaposed, is how we exceed the constraints to meaning in media. There may be some redundancy, but that may be a good thing to the extent that interpreters' meaning proclivities are different. This grammar does not propose that each form is straightforwardly a creature of its media; it's about meaning as incessant movement and metamorphosis.

Because the functions of reference, agency, structure, context, and interest cross all forms and their media, this may suggest congruence, or the possibility of simply "standing for." Far from it. Transpositions always involve slippage, bending, and refraction. A multimodal grammar must track these processes of reversioning. It will track changes, acknowledging provenance and tracing patterns of transformation through the processes of transposition. In every act

[216] Gunther Kress, 2009, *Multimodality: A Social Semiotic Approach to Contemporary Communication*, London: Routledge, pp. 12–14.
[217] Roland Barthes, 1964 [1977], *Elements of Semiology*, New York: Hill and Wang, p. 47.
[218] Louis Hjelmslev, 1963 [1970], *Language: An Introduction*, translated by F.J. Whitfield, Madison: University of Wisconsin Press, pp. 39–41.

of transposition the result is always something never-before-meant – an artifact of meaning uniquely reconfigured, not only in its form but in its media as well.

This process is a play of the material as well as the ideal.$^{§MS3.1}$ Now transposition creates its own marvels. Something material, in the media of the here and now, can take us across time (the persistence of the material trace), and space (its transportation). By fiat of media, the past and the future become radically simultaneous; and the anywhere and everywhere else become radically here and now. Media are prostheses that can turn material impossibilities into the ideal of imaginary possibility; and paradoxically, they achieve this by means that are nothing but material. The result is every bit as magical as Einsteinian physics$^{§1.3.1a}$ and quantum mechanics.$^{§1.4.4b}$

For Sigmund Freud, such powers are cause for anxiety: "Man has ... become a kind of prosthetic God," whose "auxiliary organs [are] truly magnificent." Still, these same organs "give him much trouble at times ... ; present-day man does not feel happy in his Godlike character."[219]

§1.4.1 Speech

> **Speech.** *Meanings expressed in the medium of voiced sound, bound to the logic of unrecoverable time, in the co-presence of an interlocutor and shared context.*

Speech sits beside sound in our rough map of meaning forms, and now as medium as well. It is a long way from text, which in many respects is more like image. Writing and image are positioned by place. Speech and sound are positioned by time. Unfolding across time, in the very nature of its medium, speech is somewhat better at representing narrative sequence than arrayed space.

However, the logic of meaning is more complicated than either the temporal linearity of speech or the two-dimensional spatiality of text. To mean in either speech or writing is to struggle with their media. The struggle of speech is between the multidimensionality of meaning and the linearity of time. The result is repetition, redundant reiteration, audible recovery from missteps, and "um"s and "ah"s while the mind catches up. If what you want to say is sensitive, better write an email than to phone, because an email can be framed more carefully without the unrecoverable linearity of speech, intrinsic to its medium.

Then there is the grammar in the old-fashioned sense of syntax, made of clauses, not the sentences of text, says Halliday.$^{§MS0.3a}$ The self is manifest in the explicit "I" of the speaker. Conversation entails carefully modulated turn-

---

[219] Sigmund Freud, 1930 [2005], *Civilization and Its Discontents*, translated by J. Strachey, New York: W.W. Norton, p. 76.

taking between multiple I/yous (even the I/you of talking to oneself). Meanings are frequently "unmarked" because they are assumed from the context of co-presence.[220]

Or in the terms we have been developing in this grammar, here are some functional transpositions that are characteristic of the medium: speech prioritizes action ahead of entity in clauses; self ahead of other; context ahead of reference. These patterns of transposition are radically different from the canonical forms of text. Compare: the larger blocks of action in text, where sense is made more meaningfully in sentences, paragraphs, and larger text units; the thingification of self and other; and the anywhere and everywhere context in text requiring explicit reference versus the here and now of speech that does not.

Then there are meanings of great importance and subtlety which are rarely transcribed into text, and when they are, only in the crudest of ways: intonation, dialect, accent, gender/age, at the most elementary level, personal voice – no two voices are the same. We depend on these differences in speech, but by and large we lose them in text, and their meanings.

These are the distinctive features of the grammar of speech, now in our wider understanding of grammar. However, there are intermediate media, crossing between forms of meaning, as is our wont in lives of multimodality. Poetry, songs, readings, and lectures in part bring the grammar of text into speech. Conversely, direct quotation, messaging on phones and social media interactions bring part of the grammar of speech into text. But never completely – these are hybrids, multimodal meanings coming to us as we struggle to overcome the limitations of one form by co-opting another, and putting to work the materiality of the media of each.

Finally, the complex multimodality of modernity is intensified with technologies of transmission of voice across space (telephone, radio), and time (analogue, then digital recording). These technologies give to speech some of the material qualities that were historically the exclusive preserve of text and image. Radio programs can be methodically edited. Recorded conversations can be carefully reviewed and parsed. But as complex and hybrid in their multimodality as these transpositions across forms and media are, they don't change the paradigmatic grammar of speech.

§1.4.1a *Roman Jakobson's* Sound Shape of Language

Roman Jakobson was living in Petrograd when the Bolshevik leader, Vladimir Lenin, returned from exile on April 16, 1917. One of Jakobson's literary

---

[220] Leonard Talmy, 2017, *The Targeting System of Language*, Cambridge, MA: MIT Press, pp. 4–13.

friends, Osja Brik, went to the railway station to hear him speak. "He seems to be crazy, but he's very convincing," he told Jakobson. Then someone said Lenin would be speaking at 8.00pm at the Kshesinskaja Palace. "Let's go listen to him." So they did. But it was Zinoviev, another Bolshevik leader, not Lenin. "We got bored and finally left."[221] By the revolution of October 1917, Lenin had proved himself to be more convincing than crazy.

Jakobson was a contemporary of M.M. Bakhtin.[§2.1.2b] They were just one year apart in age. Their paths crossed at least on paper,[§0.1a] Jakobson a self-described "futurist" poet, a "formalist" literary critic, and one of the founders in 1915 of the Moscow Linguistic Circle. After the revolution, Jakobson worked for a time as assistant to Brik, by now director in the Fine Arts Division of the People's Commissariat of Enlightenment. There, he wrote an article, "The Tasks of Artistic Propaganda." Its conclusion: "the tasks of genuine revolutionary artistic propaganda are to revolutionize cultural, particularly aesthetic, habits ... Those who project the muses into life, who cry out for tolerance in art, are akin to the adherents of 'pure democracy,' who, in Lenin's words, take a formal similarity for a factual one."[222]

In 1920, Jakobson went to Prague to work as a translator in the Soviet diplomatic mission, where he worked until 1927. He enrolled for a Ph.D. at the University of Prague and founded the Prague Linguistic Circle,[223] developing a structuralist account inspired by the theory of Ferdinand de Saussure.[§MS3d] He became a Czech citizen in 1937. Many of Jakobson's poet and formalist friends who stayed in the Soviet Union had perished by the end of the thirties, though not Bakhtin, who managed to survive in internal exile and then provincial obscurity.

After the Nazi invasion of Czechoslovakia in 1939, Jakobson fled. As a Jew and former Bolshevik diplomat, his life was in danger. It was a lucky escape, crossing a remote northern border from Norway into Sweden. A Norwegian socialist was recruited to drive him across the border in a cart. Jakobson lay in the back of the cart in a coffin, speechless of course, his wife sitting with the driver, playing grieving widow.[224]

Finally making it to the United States, Jakobson at first found a place lecturing at the New School for Social Research in New York, where he and fellow Jewish refugee Claude Levi-Strauss[§1.4.7a] attended each other's lectures. This is where, says the famous anthropologist, "the revelation of structural linguistics" came to

---

[221] Roman Jakobson, 1992 [1997], *My Futurist Years*, translated by S. Rudy, New York: Marsilio Publishers, p. 39.

[222] Ibid., pp. xvi, 154.

[223] F.W. Galan, 1985, *Historic Structures: The Prague School Project, 1928–1946*, Austin: University of Texas Press.

[224] Roman Jakobson, 1992 [1997], *My Futurist Years*, translated by S. Rudy, New York: Marsilio Publishers, p. x.

him, "as a result of which I would later be able to crystallize into a body of coherent ideas."[225] This became the school of thought that, across a number of academic disciplines, came to be called "structuralism."[§MS3e] Jakobson went on to a long and distinguished career as a linguist at Harvard University.

Jakobson's version of structuralism started with the "sound-shape of language:"[226] an analysis of the elementary phonemes of speech, characterizing them as a series of contrasts.[*] These finely modulated sound differences would be detectable on a spectrograph once such a thing had been invented.[227] As early as 1923 Jakobson proposed a new science, "phonology," which he defined as "the study of speech sounds with regard to meaning and ... the strictly relational character of the sense-discriminative entities, linked to each other by binary oppositions as components of the ever-hierarchical phonological systems."[228]

Then, "[w]hile phonetics seeks to collect the most exhaustive information on gross sound matter, in its physiological and physical properties, phonemics, and phonology in general, intervenes to apply strictly linguistic criteria to the sorting and classification of the material registered by phonetics."[229] These, he said, were the "fundamentals of language" – a science of system and order in phonemes, syllables, and prosodic features such as tone and force, pitch, loudness, and duration.

To the structuralist point, these features made no sense in isolation: "Saussure rightly emphasised that the important thing as far as phonemes are concerned is not at all each phoneme's individual phonic quality considered in isolation and existing in its own right. What matters is their reciprocal oppositions within a phonological system."[230] Following Saussure, the sound signifiers were arbitrary in relation to the things they signified.[231] After this insight, in 1928, a new organizing concept for the theoretical repertoire of the Prague Linguistics Circle: "structural linguistics."[232]

---

* http://meaningpatterns.net/jakobson

[225] Roman Jakobson. 1976 [1978], *Six Lectures on Sound and Meaning*, translated by J. Mepham, Cambridge, MA: MIT Press, pp. xi–xii.

[226] Roman Jakobson and Linda R. Waugh, 1979 [2002], *The Sound Shape of Language*, Berlin: Mouton de Gruyter.

[227] Roman Jakobson, 1972, "Verbal Communication," *Scientific American* 227(3):72–81, p. 74.

[228] Roman Jakobson, 1980 [1985], *Verbal Art, Verbal Sign, Verbal Time*, Minneapolis: University of Minnesota Press, p. 4.

[229] Roman Jakobson and Morris Halle, 1956, *Fundamentals of Language*, The Hague: Mouton, p. 7.

[230] Roman Jakobson, 1976 [1978], *Six Lectures on Sound and Meaning*, translated by J. Mepham, Cambridge, MA: MIT Press, p. 76.

[231] Roman Jakobson, 1971, *Selected Writings,* Volume 2: *Word and Language*, The Hague: Mouton, p. 345.

[232] Roman Jakobson, 1970, *Main Trends in the Science of Language*, New York: Harper and Row, p. 13.

For Jakobson, the atomic units of language are phonemes, qualified by however many other voiceable overlays. Today, these phonemes are codified in the International Phonetic Alphabet.[233] Supported in Unicode, this is unequivocally text, albeit an attempt at comprehensive transliteration of the speech of any language. In the International Phonetic Alphabet, the Roman alphabet is extended to 107 characters, modified by 31 diacritics, and 19 characters to represent tone, stress, and intonation. The phonetic alphabet is only for linguistic aficionados and even then, it is nowhere near enough to capture the full gamut of variation in speech.

Maintained by the International Phonetic Association (or in its own script, the ɪntəˈnæʃənəl fəˈnɛtɪk əsoʊsiˈeɪʃn), the alphabet was founded in 1886 and is today managed by a private company directed by academics and registered in Britain. Between Unicode and the International Phonetic Alphabet, here is yet another instance of the strangely haphazard governance of our means of production of meanings in the era of digitally-mediated representation and communication.

Not merely a distinct science, Jakobson says, phonemics is the basis of all language. But how so, if text is so different, as we have been arguing? (But half the world is illiterate, Jakobson says.) How so for Chinese? (But its readers still hear the words if they say these to themselves as they read, he says.) How so the sign languages created in deaf communities, which are primarily ideographic?[§1.4.3] (But this is only one person in a thousand, he says.)[234] And what about reading itself, where phonemic sounding, aloud or silently, is too slow for meaningful comprehension? Instead we read in "saccades" where our eye jumps then rests for an instant on syllables or words, and in this way alphabetical text effectively becomes ideographic. None of these counter arguments seems strong enough for Jakobson to undo his conflation of speech and text into language, and then its reduction to phonemics. But they are strong enough for us.

When does phonemics reach its limits? When are the differences in affordance so great that transliteration is impossible and multimodality becomes essential? Here we will rely on an example of Jakobson's. "A former actor of Stanislavskij's Moscow Theater told me how at his audition he was asked by the famous director to make forty different messages from the phrase *Segodnja vecerom*, 'this evening,' by diversifying its expressive tint. He made a list of some forty emotional situations, then emitted the given phrase in accordance with each of these situations, which his audience had to recognize only from the

[233] International Phonetic Association, 1999, *Handbook of the International Phonetic Association*, Cambridge: Cambridge University Press.
[234] Roman Jakobson and Linda R. Waugh, 1979 [2002], *The Sound Shape of Language*, Berlin: Mouton de Gruyter, p. 74.

changes in the sound shape of the same two words."[235] No text could capture this, not even the International Phonetic Alphabet.

Then there is Jakobson's other great love, poetry, as parsed by structural linguistics: "Versification, with its diaphanous dichotomies of downbeat-upbeat, break-bridge, and with its correlation of two fundamental metrical concepts, namely design and instance, offered the self-evident possibility of determining the relational invariance that the verse retains across its fluctuations, and of defining and interpreting the scale of the latter."[236]

However, we would retort, for its premeditation and unavoidably multilinear design processes, poetry is in the first instance and quintessentially a textual product, though anticipating, of course, its sound shape at the point of recitation or reading. Speech finds its canonical expression in spontaneous, unscripted, self-to-other, or self-to-self utterance. Poetry is a hybrid, a creature of multi-modal transposition, a multimedia materialization.

And now to the era of digitized sounds. A first generation of computer scientists and computational linguists attempted to implement voice synthesis with computer on the basis of transposition of text to phonemic units (characters, diphthongs, syllables).[237] This has in most instances today been supplanted by breaking up text into n-grams, words and phrases recorded by voice actors – in other words, contiguous phonemes or syllables that are distinguishable in text as ideographs.

Speech Synthesis Markup Language is a World Wide Web Consortium's standard that ties these processes together across different platforms.[238] This change of approach directly parallels what was in the area of text, the shift from structuralist approaches to machine translation in the Chomskyan mold, to statistical machine translation.[§2.2.1a]

So when GPS[§1.3.2b] today speaks us on our way, the source of its meanings and the units of its rendering are semantically defined synthetic units that have been recorded as whole spoken words, and aligned in another multimodal transposition to the geocoordinates of space. The sounds of synthetic speech are not kept as a small number of phonemes, but in huge databases with very large numbers of whole words and phrases, ready for transposition of digitized representations of space into text or speech. The unit of storage is the sounded equivalent of the ideograph, not the phoneme.

---

[235] Roman Jakobson, 1960, "Closing Statement: Linguistics and Poetics," pp. 350–77 in *Style in Language*, edited by T.A. Sebeok, Cambridge, MA: MIT Press, p. 354.
[236] Roman Jakobson, 1980 [1985], *Verbal Art, Verbal Sign, Verbal Time*, Minneapolis: University of Minnesota Press, p. 3; Richard Bradford, 1994, *Roman Jakobson: Life, Language, Art*, London: Routledge.
[237] Jonathan Allen, M. Sharon Hunnicutt, and Dennis Klatt, 1987, *From Text to Speech: The Mitalk System*, Cambridge: Cambridge University Press.
[238] www.xml.com/pub/a/2004/10/20/ssml.html

Phonemic structures may offer an account for the microdesign of speech in the terms Jakobson described in his structural linguistics, but functionally speaking there is no meaning in these. Or to return to Saussure's terminology, at this level we have things that look like signifiers but without a signified. Today, phonemics have become less relevant or helpful than ever for managing the transpositions of text to speech or other meanings. Or, as Jack Goody has told us,[§MS0.2.1a] we're all turning Chinese.

§1.4.1b Margaret Masterman's "Breath Groups"

If Roman Jakobson mined the sound-shape of speech for its patterning, what is its sense-shape? We address now, not multimodal hybrids such as poetry or recorded speech, but the canonical form of spontaneous speech. Here, thought and speech trip over each other in their simultaneity. Thinking is for speaking and speaking is for thinking in an "evanescent time frame," to use Dan Slobin's nice turn of phrase.[239]

With Michael Halliday,[§MS0.3a] Margaret Masterman[§2.2.1c] was founder of the Cambridge Language Research Unit, and later its director. Masterman rails against Chomsky's "drastic abstractions from the facts of language" and his "grossly artificial unit of the 'sentence'."[240] The sentence, says Halliday, is a unit of writing, whereas the clause is the elementary meaning unit of speech[§MS0.2.7a] – a difference of fundamental importance.

Masterman, however, wanted to go smaller still in her analysis of speech, the "breath group."[*] Here, she took her inspiration from the Yugoslav linguist Petar Guberina whose life's work had been to analyze the processes of speech in order to teach deaf people to speak.[241] Units of meaning in speech are closely aligned with breathing – sounding while breathing out, punctuated by pauses while the speaker breathes in. These elemental units Masterman called "phrasing."[242] Speech is connected with body in a multimodality this primordial, this visceral.

Working now at the level of phrasing, Guberina and now Masterman uncovered the patterning of meaning in phrases which could be illustrated as

---

* http://meaningpatterns.net/masterman

[239] Dan I. Slobin, 1996, "From "Thought and Language" to "Thinking for Speaking," pp. 70–96 in *Rethinking Linguistic Relativity*, edited by J.J. Gumperz and S.C. Levinson, Cambridge: Cambridge University Press, p. 76.

[240] Margaret Masterman, 2005, *Language, Cohesion and Form*, Cambridge: Cambridge University Press, p. 266.

[241] Petar Guberina, 1964 [1971], "Studies in the Verbo-Tonal System," Columbus, OH: Department of Speech, Ohio State University.

[242] Margaret Masterman, 2005, *Language, Cohesion and Form*, Cambridge: Cambridge University Press, pp. 227–53.

"semantic squares." Multidimensionally cross-cutting meanings that might be represented as such, with arrows crossing squares, were in speech turned into linear phrase units. Across the coordinates of a phrase conceived two-dimensionally, and between phrases from square to square, there are patterns of contrast, recapitulation, reiteration, synthesis. and modification. Guberina wanted to understand the underlying logic of these patterns in order to teach deaf people to speak. Anticipating computer applications, these Masterman called "semantic algorithms."[243]

In order to represent the constituent elements of breath groups, Masterman proposed an "ideographic language," a notation for concepts. This was reminiscent of Wittgenstein's "picture language." Masterman had written up the notes of Wittgenstein's 1933–34 lectures for his *Blue Book*. It was also reminiscent of Halliday's early work on Chinese. To the extent that the unit of meaning in a computer is an n-gram – not an isolable grapheme in the case of alphabetic text, or a phoneme in the case of speech – this prediction of hers has come true. She made this proposition in 1953, the only woman in a collection, *British Philosophers in the Mid-Century.*

As for ideography, units of meaning are just as easily represented today as an image (emojis,[§1.1.1a] diagrams, and images, for instance). The elementary n-grams are images of clustered characters in text, and speech is made up of clustered sounds. Almost nothing meaningful is happening at the level of graphemes or phonemes. To this extent, Masterman says, "English is like Chinese, and both are like metaphysics."[244]

Which we would rephrase as: The elementary unit of meaning in English and Chinese are sound collocations, transposable into collocations of graphemes in text (though never with quite the same meaning), transposable into iconic or symbolic image (again never with the same meaning), and so on across forms of meaning. All are tied together for the purposes of mechanical retrieval and transmission in ontologies and metaontologies[§MS3.4] – the metaphysics of our times. This is how speech-to-text transposition works today, mechanically speaking. This is how our world of digital meaning works.

§1.4.1c *Courtney Cazden's* Classroom Discourse

Moving scale beyond the phrase, the next significant chunk of meaning in speech is the turn in conversation. Speech is always speaking-with, others or self. One person speaks at a time, each in their turn.

---

[243] Ibid., pp. 270–74.

[244] Margaret Masterman, 1957, "Metaphysical and Ideographic Language," pp. 283–360 in *British Philosophy in the Mid-Century*, edited by C.A. Mace, London: George Allen and Unwin, pp. 309–10.

Diana Slade and Suzanne Eggins were students of M.A.K. Halliday's at the University of Sydney who in their Ph.D.s and later research took up the challenge to create a grammar of conversation. Conversation, they say, is a play of solidarity and difference whose pivot points are recurring speaker change.[245] The play may involve one kind of dialectic or another: question/answer, complaint/denial, offer/acceptance, request/grant, or their negations, or an absence of response. The players may be doctors/patients, bosses/workers, sellers/buyers, drivers/passengers, teachers/students, experts/laypersons, traversing any number of social differences. Some of these paired differences involve conscionable complementarities, others unconscionable inequalities.[§2.4] In every case, the dynamic of speech is quite different from that of text, where in each domain, parallel repositories of textual meaning are to be found taking quite different grammatical forms – in textbooks, technical manuals, or scientific journal articles, for instance.

Courtney Cazden, like Jakobson a long-time Harvard University professor, parses one of these conversational plays, between teachers and students in the canonical form of "classroom discourse."[*]

T[EACHER] : "Three-quarters of the crayons in Mrs. R.'s box are broken. How many unbroken Crayons are there?"
S[TUDENT] : Sean offers to show his solution. "It would be four." (He draws and talks on the chalkboard.)
T : "Why . . . "

Then later in the conversation there will be confirmation of the answer by the teacher, or if wrong, denial.

This is the beginning of a typical pattern in teacher/student talk: teacher initiates, student responds, then teacher evaluates. This is called "IRE" in the teaching business. These are "display questions," as if the teacher didn't know the answer, and where the student is playing a game of guessing what is in the teacher's head.[246] "Hands up!" after the question, then one student answers at a time, a proxy for the others who must listen in silence if the conversation is not to become chaotic. Here, speech in its canonical turn-taking form is pivotal, though of course not without multi-modal transpositions of bodies ("hands up!"), objects (crayons), and text (on the chalkboard).

---

* http://meaningpatterns.net/ccazden

[245] Suzanne Eggins and Diana Slade, 1997, *Analysing Casual Conversation*, London: Cassell.
[246] Courtney B. Cazden, 2001, *Classroom Discourse: The Language of Teaching and Learning*, Portsmouth, NH: Heinemann, pp. 30, 46; Courtney B. Cazden, 2018, *Communicative Competence, Classroom Interaction, and Educational Equity: The Selected Works of Courtney B. Cazden*, New York: Routledge.

At a time when education is turning towards e-learning, either blended into traditional in-person classrooms or purely at-a-distance, hybrid grammars are emerging in the speech-like text of discussion boards and activity streams. An "update" initiated by the teacher may evoke not just one response, but simultaneous "comments" from many students, if not all. Instead of one right answer, many variants of answer become visible. A productive diversity in the resulting dialogue replaces a discursive architecture oriented to sameness. Oral discourse had by dint of practical pedagogical necessity mostly been directed to one "correct" answer. The sentences and punctuation in online discussion boards show that these are grammatically somewhere between text and speech, and this may not be a bad thing on the route to "academic literacy." The conversational pattern of IRE is still there, but the affordances have also been utterly transformed, and with this the dynamics of meaning and learning.[247]

Inspired by Cazden, we have in our research and development work built out a "social knowledge" app that we have called "Community," and analyzed the subsequent shifts in classroom discourse.[248] Our aim: to explore the affordances of new media for reflexive instead of transmission pedagogy.[249] Spoken classroom discourse, as Cazden points out, involves certain kinds of closure, peculiar forms of inauthenticity, and digital media may in some respects open these out. These concerns have been one of her life projects as a linguist and a pedagogue, and ours too.

With Courtney, we talked our way across the vast expanses of Australian Aboriginal country. We saw schools where the community had written their world across the school walls in powerful paintings. We met teachers bridging the oral and the written in bilingual literacy.§MS0.0a

As our four-wheel-drive rattled across the desert tracks, Courtney talked of the speech closures that had driven her life. Her husband, Norman, had been an ethnomusicologist at the University of Illinois while she was a masters student in the College of Education. Both had been members of the Communist Party of the United States.

[247] Bill Cope and Mary Kalantzis, 2017, "Conceptualizing E-Learning," pp. 1–45 in *E-Learning Ecologies*, edited by B. Cope and M. Kalantzis, New York: Routledge.
[248] US Department of Education, Institute of Education Sciences: "The Assess-as-You-Go Writing Assistant" (R305A090394); "Assessing Complex Performance" (R305B110008); "u-Learn.n et: An Anywhere/Anytime Formative Assessment and Learning Feedback Environment" (ED-IES-10-C-0018); "The Learning Element" (ED-IES-lO-C-0021); and "InfoWriter: A Student Feedback and Formative Assessment Environment" (ED-IES-13-C-0039). Bill and Melinda Gates Foundation: "Scholar Literacy Courseware." National Science Foundation: "Assessing 'Complex Epistemic Performance' in Online Learning Environments" (Award 1629161).
[249] Mary Kalantzis and Bill Cope, 2016a, "New Media and Productive Diversity in Learning," pp. 310–25 in *Diversity in Der Lehrerinnenbildung*, edited by S. Barsch and N. Glutsch, Münster: Waxmann; Bill Cope and Mary Kalantzis, 2017, "Conceptualizing E-Learning," pp. 1–45 in *E-Learning Ecologies*, edited by B. Cope and M. Kalantzis, New York: Routledge.

Against McCarthyism, along with her fellow students and professors, Courtney fought long and hard in those Illinois years.[250] Under investigation by the FBI at the behest of the House Un-American Activities Committee,[251] Norman Cazden,[§1.4.2a] a promising young scholar, lost his job. It took him sixteen years to find another academic position.[252]

§1.4.1d Uber, Controlling the Conversation in the "Sharing Economy"

The world of digitally mediated meanings is today full of conversations, though these are increasingly per medium of text: discussion boards in learning management systems,[§1.4.1c] SMS messages with their left/right side conventions visualizing conversational turns,[253] social media feeds, and conversations that establish person-to-person relations in the so called "sharing economy." In terms of our grammar, tracing the forms of meaning and the characteristic functions of their media, these are hybrids. In their peculiarities, they are creatures of their combination of media. These hybrid forms hover uneasily between the grammars of speech, text, space, time – and body too, when you are holding the conversational device in your hand.

"Where to?" asks the Uber app at the beginning of a conversation that overlays a journey.[*] Uber starts knowing who you are, where you are, and what time you ask the question: these points of reference and position are drawn mechanically from context – "asignifying semiotics" Félix Guattari calls these.[§1.3.2b] But "where to?" is a question that no amount of artificial intelligence can figure, unless, knowing your ways, it's somewhere you have been before, in which case, Uber will suggest that as a possibility.

I can see Uber cars, like little cockroaches crawling over the map of Camden Town on my phone. A driver accepts my request. I guess the Uber algorithm has calculated he was closest and available.

Thirty-nine minutes to the airport, price £38.86, the car four minutes away, now three minutes, now two. I see the little icon inching along a tangle of one-way streets, so phone the driver to say which corner I am on. I have his number plate, the make, model, and color of his car, and a picture of that kind of car. But I call to be sure he knows where I am. It's a personal thing these days, to give a cellphone number, and intrusive to call with voice, but the relationship we are about to have is this personal. Phoning has become all-the-more personal since

---

[*] http://meaningpatterns.net/uber

[250] Walter Feinberg, 2019, *Educational Thought at the University of Illinois at Urbana-Champaign, 1867 to 2017: A Philosophical History*, unpublished manuscript, pp. 123–27.
[251] Victor Navasky, 1980, *Naming Names*, New York: Viking Press.
[252] Stephen Erdely, 1981, "Norman Cazden (1914–1980)," *Ethnomusicology* 25(3):493–96.
[253] David Crystal, 2008, *Txting: The Gr8 Db8*, Oxford: Oxford University Press.

the rise of texting; voice calls have become rarer out of deference for other people's right, as Richard Kern says, to manage the terms of their participation in a conversation.[254]

Abdullahi has been driving with Uber for one and a half years, has a 4.7 rating, and speaks English, Arabic, and Somali – so the app tells me. Thirty people have checked the diamond icon, "Excellent service," six the "Great Chat" icon. But he has only three recommendations for "Great Route Choice," an odd thing because there is no choice – the driver can't take routes other than the one prescribed by Uber. Which incidentally means that he can't pull that old taxi driver dodge, taking a longer route for a bigger fare. Uber micromanages the route, offering at least this peace of mind to the rider, mitigating in this particular way the generalized anxieties that are intrinsic to the differential interests of sellers and buyers.[§2.4.1]

GPS[§1.3.2b] also lowers the barriers to access that were present in the old taxi industry. In London, taxi drivers have to pass a grueling map test, known in the trade as "the Knowledge."[255] GPS has not only made this kind of knowledge redundant; the scale of empirical detail captured in GPS, now that we have it, has made any kinds of memorized spatial knowledge inadequate.

And another nice thing about Uber: If you are in a country where you don't speak the language, no speech is needed, because the driver's textual and visual interface is in one language and yours in another. Conversational turn-taking works because its grammar is multimodal (place, time, map) and multilingual (a translation interface). The mechanics of conversation have shifted from speech in natural language, to a shared ontology[§MS3.3a] of streets, persons, and the scripted universal dialogue of being driven that operates in a semantic architecture that is beyond natural language. If there is text on my screen, its natural language has become circumstantial and arbitrary in a way that it never was when hailing a cab and having to tell the driver in speech where you wanted to go.

Sometimes you even wish that you didn't belong to a shared speech community, when the Uber driver's life situation – their three jobs and their medical bills with no insurance – are just too grueling, or their social opinions too unnerving. But Uber even steps in on the rider's behalf to regulate this, because when the ride is over, "Conversation" is one of the rating buttons.

My conversation with Abdullahi brings our transitory relationship into the context of his wider life. Uber takes 25 percent of the fare, a lot I thought, just

[254] Richard Kern, 2015, *Language, Literacy, and Technology*, Cambridge: Cambridge University Press, p. 248.

[255] Eleanor A. Maguire, David G. Gadian, Ingrid S. Johnsrude, Catriona D. Good, John Ashburner, Richard S.J. Frackowiak, and Christopher D. Frith, 2000, "Navigation-Related Structural Change in the Hippocampi of Taxi Drivers," *Proceedings of the National Academy of Sciences* 97(8):4398–403.

for a piece of software which manages the conversation that coordinates my riding with his driving. Better than being a mini-cab driver, he says. He was this before, but now he's more in control of his own life. No longer a worker, he's a small business person now. In the "gig economy," even the minimal labor rights of traditional employees are cast asunder.

No, it's more complicated, he's with forty other Somali drivers in an "Ayuuto" collective. Each contributes £100 per week, and every couple of weeks the collective buys a new car for one of its participants. "Ayuuto": Somalized version of "help." There's a hashtag for it on Twitter, pointing to moments in a socialism of sorts, albeit with Somalian characteristics. This is how, to use anthropologist David Graeber's formulation,[§2.4.1] two entirely different "systems of moral accounting," Ayuuto and Uber, are held together in uneasy tension, each with its own characteristic patterns of multimodal conversation.[256]

Abdullahi drops me off at the airport. I've been writing with my thumbs, and now I pay with my fingerprint. On a newer phone it would have been face recognition. Or, as we would say in this grammar, this turn in the conversation is a viscerally embodied communication of my personhood, singularly instantiated bodily characteristics that can't be faked.

But before the conversation comes to an end, I have to rate Abdullahi, and he has to rate me. If I get ratings that are bad enough – like, I am drunk and have thrown up in his car – I will get banned from Uber. There is a whole genre of reputation software to keep track of patterns in behavior.[257] And rating the driver: no stars to five stars; and suggested improvements could be "professionalism," "driving," "navigation," "car quality," "music," "pickup." Uber's algorithms are listening, of course, and anticipating possible follow-up conversations where the company may need to arbitrate: "I was involved in an accident >," "I would like a refund >," "I lost an item >," "my driver was unprofessional >." The range of predictable and allowable conversations has been pre-scripted.

But mostly, the experience is at this point reduced to a number, a rating, and in a culture of obsessive and overvalued calculation, this becomes the crux of the conversation. After the rating there is no process for dispute resolution, and if fault is admitted, there is no way to make amends. There is nothing more to discuss. A ride-sharing driver in California tried to educate his passengers by putting up in his car a picture of a four-out-of-five star rating, with the caption, "This driver sucks, fire him slowly; it does not mean 'average' or above 'average.'"[258]

---

[256] David Graeber, 2011, *Debt: The First 5,000 Years*, Brooklyn, NY: Melville House, p. 114.

[257] F. Randall Farmer and Bryce Glass, 2010, *Web Reputation Systems*, Sebastopol, CA: O'Reilly; Phillip J. Windley and Devlin Daley, 2006, "A Framework for Building Reputation Systems" (www.windley.com/essays/2006/dim2006/framework_for_building_reputation_systems).

[258] https://qz.com/1244155/good-luck-leaving-your-uber-driver-less-than-five-stars/

Far from solving "market asymmetries," say a trio of computational economists, mutual rating systems tend to "reputation inflation," motivated by mutual fear grounded precisely in these asymmetries of interest.[259] Mutual reporting is mutual policing; mutual trust is the regulation of mistrust; sharing is an alibi for the generalized antagonisms of the market; and the interpersonal is colonized by coordinating software that serves private profit.

"Sharing" is the way it feels when you are in a private person's car, and you are asked to make life-impinging judgments of each other's demeanor. But "renting" is what this conversation really is, and Uber are the agents, stitching the conversation together. By this conversational framing, Uber is also offloading onto customers what in another setting would have been a corporate responsibility. All this, scripted into the grammar of multimodal conversation.

Ultimately, Uber controls this conversation, and it is a corollary that they who control the conversation stand to profit more.

Jackson Cunningham got into trouble with another of the sharing behemoths, the home-sharing app Airbnb, driven by a conversational structure and business model that is similar to Uber's. He dared to comment on a "host" in a Google listing, outside of the Airbnb rating and commenting framework. Or at least, he guesses this was where he must have overstepped the conversational mark, because Airbnb would provide no explanation why he had been banned.

Dear Jackson,

We regret to inform you that we'll be unable to support your account moving forward, and have exercised our discretion under our Terms of Service to disable your account(s). **This decision is irreversible** and will affect any duplicated or future accounts.

Please understand that **we are not obligated to provide an explanation** for the action taken against your account. Furthermore, we are not liable to you in any way with respect to disabling or canceling your account. Airbnb reserves the right to make the final determination with respect to such matters, and **this decision will not be reversed.**[260]

End of conversation.

This is how Jackson discovered that, behind the dialogism of the sharing economy, there was a new dictatorship of speech, where a handful of software companies dominate driving here and staying there. Airbnb and Uber not only facilitate the conversation; they own the conversation. The only things that

---

[259] Apostolos Filippas, John J. Horton, and Joseph M. Golden, 2018, "Reputation Inflation," in *EC '18: Proceedings of the 2018 ACM Conference on Economics and Computation*, Ithaca, NY.

[260] https://medium.com/@jacksoncunningham/digital-exile-how-i-got-banned-for-life-from-airb nb-615434c6eeba

have changed since the Cazdens' experience of McCarthyism[§1.4.1c] is the grammar of control and the identities of the controllers.

§1.4.2   Sound

> **Sound.** *Meanings that are pulled from the audible context to mean something, varying according to their likeness (resemblance), directedness (pointing), and abstraction (symbolism).*

Text is strictly visual, but we have in this grammar pulled it out as a distinct system. So too, speech is strictly audible, but we have also pulled it out as a distinct system. Roman Jakobson supplies a physiological rationale for the separation: when presented together, speech sounds are better discerned and identified by the right ear; musical and environmental sounds by the left.[261]

In order to parse the affordances of sound as a medium for meaning, we are going to return to the distinctions we made earlier, between different kinds of materialization: likeness, directedness, and abstraction, roughly following Peirce's trichotomy of icon, series, and symbol.[§1.1.3a]

Likeness is achieved in sound by resemblance. A dog barks, and I know from experience that it is a dog that I am hearing. The bark audibly is a dog, even when I cannot see it. We live in the meaningful soundscapes of nature,[262] and of cities.[263] Likeness can also be achieved in music – Rimsky-Korsakov's "Flight of the Bumble Bee" is a case in point.[*]

Directedness is a sound that points to something other than itself: a siren, a bell, a car horn, a train whistle, the start-up sound of a computer, a phone ringing. Then there are the at-times involuntary sounds people make, in their endless variation: crying (by a baby, an adult weeping); laughing (hearty, evil); sighing (in resignation, in despair).[264]

Abstractions are generalized or symbolic meanings. The various kinds of dings that are the alerts and notifications on a computer or a phone have purely conventional or symbolic relations to their meanings. Organ music and hymns

---

[*] http://meaningpatterns.net/sound

[261] Roman Jakobson, 1972, "Verbal Communication," *Scientific American* 227(3):72–81, p. 76; Roman Jakobson and Linda R. Waugh, 1979 [2002], *The Sound Shape of Language*, Berlin: Mouton de Gruyter, pp. 34–36.

[262] Bernie Krause, 2015, *Voices of the Wild: Animal Songs, Human Din, and the Call to Save Natural Soundscapes*, New Haven, CT: Yale University Press.

[263] Emily Thompson, 2002, *The Soundscape of Modernity: Architectural Acoustics and the Culture of Listening in America, 1900–1933*, Cambridge, MA: MIT Press.

[264] Steven Connor, 2014, *Beyond Words: Sobs, Hums, Stutters and Other Vocalizations*, London: Reaktion Books.

call up associations with church, carols Christmas, a movie soundtrack horror or triumph, blues music a certain kind of melancholy. Kinds of ambient music speak to kinds of places. Abstract meanings are so by convention, meanings that have come to be that way through cultural and historical experience. Lyrics can add explicit meaning to musical tunes, so when you hear the music, a voice in your head speaks: "Summertime, and the livin' is easy"; "While my guitar gently weeps"; "God save the Queen/The fascist regime."

These distinctions, between likeness, directedness, and abstraction, are not hard and fast. Transposition from one function to another is always waiting to happen. In iconic sound a likeness can become a directed warning. A warning can become an abstract symbol.

There is meaning also in absence, the silence between movements in a concerto, and between tracks in recorded playback. Or just silence – if there can ever be such a thing, as John Cage brings to the attention of musical audiences.[§MS1.1.2a] And sounds at the borderlands of meaning, sounds that are not noted because they are not notable: background sounds or white noise; or just noise; or dissonance.[§1.4.2b]

As for the foundational differences in medium between sound (and with it speech) and image (and with it text), sound unfolds across time while image is arrayed across place. We have seen how image can nevertheless represent time, if somewhat awkwardly.[§MS2a] And we have seen how speech can represent place, awkwardly too.[§1.3.2b] Despite its favoring of time, recorded sound can represent place, for instance with stereo speakers or headphones, when the sound seems to come from two places though in the recording it is coming from one. Stereophonic sound recordings serve a two-dimensional spatial world, arrayed along an egocentric left–right axis relative to the hearer. This is a smart effect more than a reality, a trope of naturalism akin to the feigned three-dimensional realism of linear perspective in two-dimensional image.[§MS2.2b]

Today, with digital audio recording, further dimensionality can be given to sound by the precedence effect.[265] By adding an identical track some microseconds after the first, although the hearer hears a single sound, they perceive the sound as coming from behind them, so creating the impression in sound of a third dimension in place. Leaving the lag a bit longer, the sound will be heard as an echo, another three-dimensional representation of place in sound. More artifice in the representation–communication–interpretation of sound leads us to think it is more realistic, when in multimodal reality it is less. Such are the marvels of media.

---

[265] Hans Wallach, Edwin B. Newman, and Mark R. Rosenzweig, 1949, "The Precedence Effect in Sound Localization," *The American Journal of Psychology* 62:315–36.

"I thought about killing you," sings Kanye West eerily, then asking his fans to comment on one of his first attempts at what he calls 3D audio: "Turn your volume up pretty high, I think it sounds better that way."

§1.4.2a Norman Cazden's "Theory of Realism in Music"

Norman Cazden was born in 1914 in the Bronx, New York, to Yiddish-speaking immigrants from Belarus. Their family name had been changed from Kazhdan. Norman's talent as pianist became obvious from an early age. He made his debut performance at age twelve in New York's Town Hall.

A composer of over one hundred works and an ethnomusicologist, during summer months from 1945 to 1960, Cazden was musical director at Camp Woodland, an eight-week annual summer camp near Phoenica in the Northern Catskill Mountains. Just two hours out of New York City, the nature of the Catskills was everything that the teeming City was not.

Camp Woodland had been founded during Franklin Delano Roosevelt's New Deal, offering work for artists. Here, applying the "progressive education" ideas of John Dewey, campers would go out into the community with Norman and other camp leaders, listening to songs, writing down lyrics, and notating the music.[266] Then they would sing back to the source singer to check the accuracy of the transcription. Cazden and campers eventually collected more than a thousand traditional ballads and fiddle tunes across upstate New York and New England, much of it the unwritten music of itinerant workers.*

Courtney Cazden recalls of Camp Woodland,

Its curriculum was definitely Dewey-like, but with what might be called a more "political agenda," from the United Nations to more inclusive freedom struggles closer to home. In 1945, my first Woodland summer, with the ending of World War Two I remember marching through Phoenicia in the victory parade, singing the UN hymn with its chorus:

> United Nations on the march, with flags unfurled,
> together fight for victory, a brave new world...

Then in the mid-fifties, the Camp recruited staff from African American activists at lunch counters in the south. Pete Seeger would make an annual visit, teaching us new songs and learning new ones himself which he then made famous – such as "Guantanamera" that he learned from a Cuban staff member.

---

* http://meaningpatterns.net/ncazden

[266] Paul C. Mischler, 1999, *Raising Reds: The Young Pioneers, Radical Summer Camps, and Communist Political Culture in the United States*, New York: Columbia University Press, pp. 99–107.

The Catskills had long been a cultural and musical crossroads. For Norman Cazden and his camp co-workers, this became the base for collecting songs drawing on English, Irish, and African-American traditions, immigrants and emancipated slaves reinventing themselves in the New World. Then, other cross-currents: the Southern Catskills were a favorite holiday destination for Jewish New York, and summer camps for communist youth. The Communist Party of the United States comprised mainly Eastern European immigrants, a significant proportion of whom were Jews.[267]

Cazden and colleagues were eventually to document their work in a massive two-volume compendium.[268]

Cazden had enrolled at Harvard University, receiving his masters degree in 1944, and Ph.D. in 1948, with a dissertation titled *Musical Consonance and Dissonance*. He embarked then on an academic career, teaching at the University of Illinois from 1950 to 1953. He was denied tenure because the FBI was investigating him for his communist connections.[§1.4.1c] Citing his Fifth Amendment rights he refused to testify to the House Un-American Activities Committee in 1954, but these rights were not enough to get him back his academic career. It was sixteen years before he could get another academic job, in 1969 at the University of Maine.[269]

Cazden's theory of music more or less tracks our theory of the materialization of meaning, articulated in two long and densely packed philosophical and technical articles, one published in 1951 while he was still at the University of Illinois, "Towards a Theory of Realism in Music,"[270] and the other in 1980, the year he died, in an obscure Yugoslav music journal, "The Definition of Consonance and Dissonance."[271]

Likeness: Cazden called this "naturalism" or sound imitation. For instance, in Beethoven's Pastoral Symphony, the nightingale, quail, and cuckoo are represented in passages for flute, oboe, and clarinet. This is for music, what onomatopoeia is for speech.[272] The representation is necessarily inexact, limited as it is by the affordances of musical instruments as media – but herein lies the art.

---

[267] Nathan Glazer, 1961, *The Social Basis of American Communism*, New York: Harcourt, Brace & World, pp. 130ff.
[268] Norman Cazden, Herbert Haufrechet, and Norman Studer, 1982, *Folk Songs of the Catskills*, Albany: State University of New York Press; Courtney Cazden, personal communication.
[269] Stephen Erdely, 1981, "Norman Cazden (1914–1980)," *Ethnomusicology* 25(3):493–96; www .normancazden.com/biography/
[270] Norman Cazden, 1951, "Towards a Theory of Realism in Music," *The Journal of Aesthetics and Art Criticism* 10(2):135–51.
[271] Norman Cazden, 1980, "The Definition of Consonance and Dissonance," *International Review of the Aesthetics and Sociology of Music* 11(2):123–68.
[272] Norman Cazden, 1951, "Towards a Theory of Realism in Music," *The Journal of Aesthetics and Art Criticism* 10(2):135–51, pp. 135–36.

Directedness: This, Cazden called "pictorialism." In his *Durch Adams Fall Ist Ganz Verderbt,* says Cazden, "Bach interprets the opening line of the text by means of a series of wide, descending leaps of a chromatic, distorted type in the bass. If this be called to our attention, verbally, we readily accept it as a valid though obvious type of musical commentary, a sort of pictorial illustration of the fall of Adam."[273]

Abstraction: Some would say that music is "a wondersome play of sounding forms, and it signifies nothing." No, says Cazden, lest we fall "victim to the inane mysticisms of the purists who deny that music has any meaning at all."[274]

The word he wants to use for music's less directed meanings is "realism." This works for us in our grammar in the sense that these are abstractions developed in social and culture context. They are conventional meanings that are not obvious in a naturalistic or pictorial way, whose broader meanings are only intelligible to insiders in the culture. Musical meanings are conjured by association in riffs, phrases, songs, movie scores – the sound shapes of feeling that connect with wider patterns of meaning by multimodal transposition.

"Reference to the real world is present in all music," says Cazden. "It is what we derive from music as an aesthetic experience ... [T]he listener is a member of a human social group, and he does not come to music with a blank, innocent, and ignorant mind, but with a deposit of musical experiences, associations, and orientation." So, "music is realistic, in the sense that it is the real practice of real people. Musical experience ... relates primarily to common values and meaning in the human world." Musical composition, he says, is "a translation and adaptation by the composer of the previous musical experience of his audience for the creating of a new revelation."[275] The revelation, in the terms of our grammar, is in the redesign.

And from the Catskills – the mountainous, poor, immigrant, folkish, Jewish, communist Catskills – the revelations flowed. No longer Robert Zimmerman, the Jewish boy from Duluth, Minnesota, Bob Dylan took up residence for a while in the sixties. He recorded his Basement Tapes there, backed by The Band. Janis Joplin recorded there too, in the same studio. Then the Woodstock Festival in 1969, in nearby Bethel.[276] This is the meaning of a whole lot of the music living in our bones, its social abstractions and, for this, its "realism."

§1.4.2b Theodor Adorno's "On Jazz"

Doyen of the Frankfurt School and friend of Walter Benjamin,[MS0b] Theodor W. Adorno wrote a million words on music, today largely ignored compared to

---

[273] Ibid., p. 138.   [274] Ibid., pp. 141–42.   [275] Ibid., pp. 150, 141, 137, 144.
[276] Weston Blelock and Julia Blelock, eds. 2009, *Roots of the 1969 Woodstock Festival: The Backstory of Woodstock,* Woodstock, NY: Woodstock Arts.

his oeuvre of Critical Theory. An émigré by necessity when the Nazis closed the School for Social Research in Frankfurt, Adorno joined fellow Jewish and socialist exiles at the "university in exile" in New York, the New School for Social Research.

Pianist and composer Norman Cazden[§1.4.2a] was at the time studying music at the City College of New York and the Julliard School. Adorno was a composer too, his work a difficult modernism for orchestra.[*]

"Music is similar to language." So Adorno begins a theoretical reflection of 1931, before he left Germany. Well no, we want to clarify, music is similar to speech, sharing as it does the same medium, sound. In music, "[q]uestions, exclamations, subordinate clauses are everywhere, voices rise and fall, and, in all of this, the gesture of music is borrowed from the speaking voice."[277] The comparison is now with speech, and for a moment, we can agree.

But then, a formulation from Adorno that contradicts his earlier one, music is not like language, intentionally referring or unambiguously signifying. For this reason, "[i]t is impossible to determine in any comprehensive way the meaning of music ... [T]here is something enigmatic that is apparent in all music."[278] No, we would say, meanings in speech and text are more complicated than this counterposition suggests; and meanings indeed there are in music, and of a similar range. Cazden calls this range naturalism, pictorialism, and realism. These parallel what we call likeness, directedness, and abstraction.

Then, another formulation of Adorno's that jars: "music has no concepts."[279] And now again, we need to disagree. In our grammar, concepts are things that happen in the plural, sharing a generality.[§MS1.1.3] Concepts are the raw material of Cazden's realism in music, Peirce's symbolism, and in this grammar, our abstraction.[§1.1.3]

With no concepts, Adorno's music slips into a place where analysis is no longer required. "What music says is a proposition at once distinct and concealed. Its idea is the form of the name of God. It is demythologized prayer, freed from the magic of making anything happen, the human attempt, futile as always, to name the name itself, not communicate meanings."[280]

Norman Cazden is of greater help than Adorno in the making of a functional grammar of music, parsing the forms of its meaning in relation to the intricacies of its media. Music is a structure of contrasts between simultaneous or successive tones, he says, experienced as consonance or dissonance, harmony or disharmony, smoothness or roughness. Speech is a structure of sound contrasts, said Ferdinand de Saussure,[§MS3d] then Roman Jakobson.[§1.4.1a] But Cazden

---

[*] http://meaningpatterns.net/adorno

[277] Theodor W. Adorno, 2002, *Essays on Music*, translated by S.H. Gillespie, Berkeley: University of California Press, p. 113.
[278] Ibid., p. 137.   [279] Ibid., p. 113.   [280] Ibid., p. 114.

goes further than de Saussure and Jakobson, because his structures are always in movement and inevitably socio-historical. The meanings are in this movement, and the socio-historical context that gives movement its meaning.

Consonance and dissonance, says Cazden, are integral to larger structures in what he called a "systemic theory" of music: "a diatonic base, against which chromatic inflections may accordingly react; tonality, or gravitation towards a tonal center, which thereby dialectically admits its opposite, modulation; modality, notably reduced from an earlier multiplicity of qualities to the antithesis between major and minor; a predominance of metrical rhythm, as over against free, rhapsodic or prose rhythm; and functional harmony that involves a species of voice-leading rooted in polyphony."[281]

In Cazden's systemic theory, the task is not merely a matter of "identifying consonance with tuning ratio, and hence inadvertently with a supposedly inherent property of intervals considered in isolation."[282] Such an approach "reduces the objective range of the data to sensory elements below the observed level of their function."[283] It treats them as "isolated attributes . . . overlooking . . . the experiential context that inevitably conditions musical perception. That prior context is the cumulative, lifetime experience with music by the perceiver."[284]

In this larger context, "[c]onsonance refers to the stable moment following upon the resolution of dissonance, while dissonance means the unstable moment calling for resolution to consonance. Their inter-relations emerge during the harmonic progressions which characterize the systemic framework of the traditional Western tonal system."[285]

In a systemic theory, dissonance is not merely a place in sound where music shouldn't go, the over-the-border that retrospectively delineates the border. Music always strays edgily towards but not-too-far over that border, and as it does, it demands of itself resolution, a coming-back. Dissonance is a kind of impatience, a complication requiring closure. Cazden's structures are not simply to be discovered in an elemental decomposition of a stable system – an occupational hazard for structural analyses. Consonance and dissonance are in our terms transpositions, structural points in a sounding system that are always begging movement.

---

[281] Norman Cazden, 1980, "The Definition of Consonance and Dissonance," *International Review of the Aesthetics and Sociology of Music* 11(2):123–68, p. 167.

[282] Ibid., p. 124.

[283] Norman Cazden, 1962, "Sensory Theories of Musical Consonance," *The Journal of Aesthetics and Art Criticism* 20(3):301–19, p. 312.

[284] Norman Cazden, 1979, "Can Verbal Meanings Inhere in Fragments of Melody?", *Psychology of Music* 7(1):34–38, pp. 34–36.

[285] Norman Cazden, 1980, "The Definition of Consonance and Dissonance," *International Review of the Aesthetics and Sociology of Music* 11(2):123–68, p. 166.

Nor are Cazden's structures reducible to the technical forms and objectivities of sound. Although the bases of consonance and dissonance are in the materialities of sound as medium, their meanings vary because these are also social and historical. "[L]isteners conditioned to Western music sense a somewhat directionless indecision of harmonic moment when they attend to the heterophonic gamelan music of Bali or to the highly mannered Gagaku music of Japan. Conversely, systemic habits undoubtedly engender bewilderment at the seeming irrelevance of Western harmonic relationships to the classical Karnatic music of India or to the drum ensemble music of Ghana."[286]

Consonance and dissonance are "functional moments akin to grammatical constructions, in that their hallmarks are among the learned responses peculiar to a specific system of music-making ... The expectations involved in recognizing and responding to consonant and dissonant moments thus become embedded in the systemic set, in the built-in complex of familiar forms, normative expectations and habits that are common to members of a given human society during a definable historical period."[287]

And another example: although dissonance is written into and around all music, modernist music is disorientingly overwrought with it. A 2018 "big data" statistical analysis searched for tritone intervals in MIDI files of 9,996 classical music pieces by 76 composers between 1500 and 1900. In Western music, tritones are conventionally understood to be dissonant. The result: tritones became more frequent as music became more modern.[288] On modernism in its highest forms, concludes Cazden, "non-tonal music is not so much the bewildering absence of resolution, but the even more disconcerting absence of criteria for the expectation of resolution."[289] To this we would add a corollary: modernism is only disconcerting to moderns, alert to dissonance, and that is its meaning. To others, it is meaningless.

The music that Adorno revered was the high modernism of Arnold Schönberg and Alban Berg.[290] Adorno moved to Vienna in 1925 – Otto Neurath's Vienna,[§MS1.1.3h] Ludwig Wittgenstein's Vienna,[§MS2.1.1d] Victor Gruen's Vienna[§2.3b] – to study composition with Berg and Schönberg, the so-called Second Viennese School. Schönberg's goal: "the emancipation of dissonance." This was Western classical music at its end point, as dissonant as it would get. When the Nazis came to power, music of this kind was considered

---

[286] Ibid., p. 161.   [287] Ibid., p. 159.

[288] Eita Nakamura and Kunihiko Kaneko, 2018, "Statistical Evolutionary Laws in Music Styles," arXiv:1809.05832 [physics.soc-ph].

[289] Norman Cazden, 1980, "The Definition of Consonance and Dissonance," *International Review of the Aesthetics and Sociology of Music* 11(2):123–68, p. 167.

[290] Theodor W. Adorno, 1949 [2006], *Philosophy of New Music*, translated by R. Hullot-Kentor, Minneapolis: University of Minnesota Press.

"degenerate art." Schönberg fled to the United States, also because he was a Jew.

After this, Adorno's writings strayed well beyond his music of choice. And when he encountered contemporary "popular" music, he violated his own theoretical principle, managing to find plenty of meaning. Now in exile, in 1936 he wrote an article, "On Jazz."

Jazz, said Adorno, has "a tone which is rigid and objective; . . . it ascribes to it subjective emotions without this being allowed to interrupt the fixedness of the basic sound pattern." It has a "quality of mechanical soullessness or licentious decadence" that "does not come up to the standards for the crudest characteristic of rhythmic and tonal interference." It is "technically backward, . . . a rigid system of tricks."[291]

As for social meanings, Adorno's own music was inscrutable. But not jazz.

Race: Jazz was "supposed to perversely subject the over-stimulated Western nerves to the vitality of blacks."

Sex: Jazz evokes "a sense of having been erotically emancipated through that which is dangerously modern or perverse . . . [T]he rhythm of the gait is similar to the rhythm of sexual intercourse; . . . an immediate reference to coitus." However, "it leads nowhere and is arbitrarily withdrawn by an undialectical, mathematical incorporation into the beat. It is plainly a 'coming-too-early.'"

Class: Jazz is "delivered up to loudspeakers and the bands in clubs for the masses." But it is at best "pseudo-democratic . . . The more deeply jazz penetrates society, the more reactionary elements it takes on, the more completely beholden it is to banality . . . The more democratic jazz is, the worse it becomes." And when the upper class takes to jazz, "the mechanism of psychic mutilation upon which the present conditions depend for their survival also holds sway over the mutilators themselves."

Capitalism: "jazz is a commodity in the strict sense: its suitability for use permeates its production in terms none other than its marketability . . . With jazz, a disenfranchised subjectivity plunges from the commodity world into the commodity world." It is an expression of "helplessness (the whimpering vibrato) . . . [A]nxiety in the face of the fatal characteristics of capitalism, seeks a despairing way out."[292]

Adorno did not like jazz. And he never did like America, returning to the ruins of Frankfurt to direct the School for Social Research once the war ended.

---

[291] Theodor W. Adorno, 2002, *Essays on Music*, translated by S.H. Gillespie, Berkeley: University of California Press, pp. 471, 470, 472, 475.
[292] Ibid., pp. 471, 476, 486, 490, 474, 475, 474, 473, 478, 480, 473.

This city of the Rothschilds and Anne Frank had before the Nazis a population of thirty thousand Jews, but only six hundred when Adorno decided to return.

"Adorno wrote some of the most stupid pages ever written about jazz," says Eric Hobsbawm,[293] arguably the greatest world-historian of the twentieth century. Hobsbawm also wrote about jazz, and extensively.[294] For Hobsbawm, this was a music redolent of social critique and resistance, inscribed in its methods of improvisation and spontaneous conversation between musicians. Two Jews, two people who had grown up in Germany, two socialists, and they read such different social meanings into jazz. Our point here not so much their differences, but that, as music, they both found it readable. Both were prepared to parse its meanings.

One of the things Adorno didn't like about jazz was that it was unwritten, the "improvisational elements of disruption" as a consequence of which "all jazz is inconsistent." Some of the variation he put down to mere "[e]rrors in musical orthography."[295] Adorno evidently liked his music to have been written. The dissonances of modernism had to be carefully crafted if they were not to descend into unrecognizable noise.

A score, said Adorno, is a "picture" of the music, postulated in "formal schemata," where practices such as dissonance are a "complex relationship of deviation to schema." Once composed, "the music, as text, is really fixed, and is not actually becoming something as it is already all there."[296]

If music is similar to speech, musical notation is similar to poetry, a fastidiously premeditated design for faithful performance. Musical performance off a script is a hybrid. It is to sound what poetry reading is to speech. Musical notation also bears the same kind of inexact relationship to sound that phonetic transcription has to speech. Performance requires interpretation to add meaning that is inevitably missing from notation, given the affordances of its transposability. This is why no two performances can be the same. No matter how faithful the performer is to the design in the script, performances are inevitably redesigns.

Where Adorno expressed his disdain for jazz, Norman Cazden in his ethnomusicological practice transcribed and notated the as-yet unwritten music of the poor and the marginal. Their meanings, expressed in their peculiar plays of consonance and dissonance, he assumed as his own.

---

[293] Eric Hobsbawm, 1988, *Uncommon People: Resistance, Rebellion, and Jazz*, New York: The New Press, p. 253.

[294] Eric Hobsbawm, 1989 [1993], *The Jazz Scene*, New York: Pantheon Books.

[295] Theodor W. Adorno, 2002, *Essays on Music*, translated by S.H. Gillespie, Berkeley: University of California Press, p. 483.

[296] Ibid., pp. 163, 165, 171.

§1.4.2c *Arseny Avraamov's* Symphony of Factory Sirens

On 7 November 1922, the whole city of Baku came alive to Arseny Avraamov's "Symphony of Factory Sirens."[*] Baku was the capital of Azerbaijan, incorporated into the Soviet Union as a Socialist Republic in 1920. This day was a holiday to celebrate the anniversary of the Revolution. In those heady days five years before, Avraamov had spoken at the first conference on proletarian cultural education in Petrograd. On the panel with him was Osip Brik, Roman Jakobson's friend at the time and later his director at the People's Commissariat of Enlightenment.[§1.4.1a]

Avraamov was principal conductor on this day in 1922 as well as the symphony's composer. Standing at the top of a specially made tower, he sent signals with colored flags and pistol shots to a team of co-conductors around the city. His orchestration called for factories to sound their sirens, navy ships in the harbor to blow their foghorns, field artillery to fire, railway locomotives to whistle, car horns to honk, and machine guns to ring out shots. Massed military bands played and choirs of school children around the city sang *The Internationale:*

> "Stand up . . .
> All the world's starving and enslaved!
> . . . take back what is ours–
> Fire up the furnace and hammer boldly,
> while the iron is still hot! . . .
> All the power to the people of labor! . . .
> We will build our new world.
> He who was nothing will become everything!"

The crowds joined in. No mere audience, the masses were both performers and performance.[297]

Baku was an industrial city of great importance, center of the Soviet oil industry. The city was divided into ethnic enclaves with a recent history of conflict, and the performance embraced all quarters. The city's three main newspapers, *Baku's Worker, Labor,* and *Communist,* published instructions so the people could participate. Singing with the choirs, citizens engaged in a call-and-response between voice and machine across the cityscape. The symphonic narrative: first movement, revolutionary battle where bodies were invisible

---

[*] http://meaningpatterns.net/avraamov

[297] Mel Gordon, 1992, "Songs from the Museum of the Future: Russian Sound Creation, 1910–30," pp. 197–243 in *Wireless Imagination: Sound, Radio and the Avant-Garde,* edited by D. Kahn and G. Whitehead, Cambridge, MA: MIT Press, pp. 240–42; Delia Duong Ba Wendel, 2012, "The 1922 'Symphony of Sirens' in Baku, Azerbaijan," *Journal of Urban Design* 17(4):549–72.

actors hidden by machines; second movement, revolutionary triumph where bodies became visible, animating machines.

In order to capture the full gamut of sound in his orchestrations, Avraamov created a microtonal system based on mathematical modeling, settling eventually on a 48-step "ultrachromatic" octave. He also developed a technique for sampling, analyzing, and synthesizing sounds.[298] He called these musical designs the "Welttonsystem" or "World Tone System," able to encompass all existing musical systems, including not only the twelve-tone Western system, but Java's five-step system and India's twenty-two-step system.[299] This was the kind of music that would be required in performances like the one in Baku, capturing the musical sounds of machines as well as people, and the range of musical forms across the city's ethnic enclaves.

Then, for Avraamov, a revelation pointing to the future of music, "the amazing invention of the young Soviet engineer, L.S. Theremin." Avraamov wrote, "His 'Theremin' is not a simple 'new musical instrument' as our muscritics are thinking, no, it is a solution to the huge social-scientific-art problem; it is the first big step into the future, into our future – it is a social revolution in the art of music, its revival." With its "full freedom of timbral and intonational nuances," said Avraamov, the theremin – as the machine came to be called – could at last forge a connection between the Western tone system and the "grandiose art of the East."[300]

The theremin was the world's first electronic music-making machine, controlled by waving hands over radio antennae. Leon Theremin demonstrated it to Lenin in 1921, playing for him Glinka's "Lark." Impressed, Lenin invited him to tour Russia with the instrument, promoting the project of electrification.[301] Following Lenin's lead, Soviet composers started to write music for the theremin.

Not only a sensation in the Soviet Union, Leon Theremin toured the world with his music machine.[302] Visiting the United States in 1925, he decided to stay, and registered a patent for his invention, "a method of and apparatus for ... producing sounds in musical tones or notes of variable pitch, volume and timbre

---

[298] Andrey Smirnov, 2013, *Sound in Z: Experiments in Sound and Electronic Music in Early 20th Century Russia*, London: Koenig Books, pp. 28–31.

[299] Nikolai Izvolov, 1998, "The History of Drawn Sound in the USSR," *Animation Journal*: 54–59, p. 54.

[300] Andrey Smirnov, 2013, *Sound in Z: Experiments in Sound and Electronic Music in Early 20th Century Russia*, London: Koenig Books, p. 43.

[301] Mel Gordon, 1992, "Songs from the Museum of the Future: Russian Sound Creation, 1910–30," pp. 197–243 in *Wireless Imagination: Sound, Radio and the Avant-Garde*, edited by D. Kahn and G. Whitehead, Cambridge, MA: MIT Press, p. 235; Andrey Smirnov, 2013, *Sound in Z: Experiments in Sound and Electronic Music in Early 20th Century Russia*, London: Koenig Books, p. 45.

[302] Albert Glinsky, 2000, *Theremin: Ether Music and Espionage*, Urbana: University of Illinois Press.

in realistic imitation of the human voice and various known musical instruments."[303] The commercial music giant, RCA, took out a license to manufacture. Robert Moog was later to adapt the theremin's design, adding a keyboard and in 1964 creating the Moog Synthesizer. John Cage[§MS1.1.2a] was an early adopter, and numerous "pop" musicians.

Theremin returned to the Soviet Union in 1938. Under the reign of suspicion during Stalin's "Great Purge," he was sent to Siberia. There his prodigious talents were put to work to create eavesdropping equipment, the most storied of which was in 1945 placed in the Great Seal of the United States in the US embassy building in Moscow, not to be discovered until 1952. Leon Sergeyevich Theremin was awarded the Stalin Prize in 1947, though not for his services to music.[304]

§1.4.2d Hiroshi Yasuda and Leonardo Chiariglione's MP3

Two modern inventions change the frame of contextual reference for performed music from a single, shared position in time and place for performer and listener, to multiple positions across time and place. The phonograph – literally, a "voice writer" – of 1877 transported music across both time and place;[305] and the radio of 1895 transported it across place.[306]

Of course, the repetition of musical compositions across time and place was nothing new – that could already be achieved with musical notation. The radically new affordance of these media was the transportation of the performance, without the inevitable losses of transcription and performer interpretation. Not only were the phonograph and radio immediately more faithful to an original; they allowed audio transcriptions of genres of music whose subtleties resisted notation – the improvisations of jazz for instance.[§1.4.2b]

With these new connections across time and place came new disconnections: of the performance from its hearing; and of its performers from their audiences. This meant that contexts of listening could be more varied and music put to different kinds of use. The meanings-in-the-hearing are quite different for a listener who is jogging to the concentrated beat of headphones, compared to half-heard elevator music. Stereophonic recorded music is spatial in an exaggerated way, more so than is possible in live music. Paradoxically, recorded music is more "accurate" than repeated performance in the sense of being

---

[303] Leo Sergejewitsch Theremin, 1928, "Method of and Apparatus for the Generation of Sounds," edited by U.S. Patent Office.

[304] Andrey Smirnov, 2013, *Sound in Z: Experiments in Sound and Electronic Music in Early 20th Century Russia*, London: Koenig Books, pp. 55, 52.

[305] Michael Chanan, 1995, *Repeated Takes: A Short History of Recording and Its Effects on Music*, London: Verso, pp. 1–3.

[306] Marc Raboy, 2016, *Marconi: The Man Who Networked the World*, Oxford: Oxford University Press.

nearly identical in each rendition subsequent to its recording; but the reception is more varied. And another thing, between the performance and its hearing, the production values of the studio can be added. "Mixing" becomes part of the music. All this was new to these media.

Theodor Adorno[§1.4.2b] worried about the reductions of radio and recorded music.[*] "What characterizes a symphony when experienced in immediate listening ... is a particular intensity and concentration," he says. "The 'surrounding' function of music also disappears ... partly because of the monoaural conditions of radio ... The sound is no longer 'larger' than the individual." These are some of the ways in which "symphonies brought to the overburdened hypothetical farmer in the Middle West are ... deteriorated by radio transmission," – and phonograph.[307] This was before the application of place-dimensionality to music with stereophonic recordings, and its extension with the precedence effect.[§1.4.2]

Then digitized music – the first commercial digital recording was made by Nippon Columbia in 1971, a jazz recording, "Something" by Steve Marcus. Adorno would have been doubly displeased. The Compact Disc, a large-capacity laser disc for digital recordings, was brought to market in 1982.[308] The first commercial release was ABBA's album, *The Visitors*. Then, with the Internet and the need to compress digital sound files without loss of quality, came the MP3 format.

In 1988 Hiroshi Yasuda of the Visual Media Lab at Nippon Telegraph and Telephone in Tokyo and Leonardo Chiariglione of Telecom Italia's research labs, commenced an initiative, the Motion Picture Expert Group (MPEG) under the auspices of the International Standardization Organization. Its brief: to develop an international standard for audio and video encoding. The original group of twenty-five people consisted of representatives of the recording, telecommunications, and media industries. Again, we find corporate interests rising above the competitive fray of the market to create another of the universal frameworks of our contemporary meaning.

MPEG-1 was released in 1993 and MPEG-2 in 1997. Layer I is basic data mapping, Layer II bit allocation, and Layer III audio frequency resolution and file compression, or "MP3" for short. Since its beginnings with the phonograph, sound recording worked by registering the amplitude of sound vibration over time. Digital recording required recording in numbers, encoding, storing, then decoding and converting the numbers back into sound. This is how sound-making

---

[*] http://meaningpatterns.net/recorded-music

[307] Theodor W. Adorno, 2002, *Essays on Music*, translated by S.H. Gillespie, Berkeley: University of California Press, pp. 245, 257, 253.
[308] Thomas Fine, 2008, "The Dawn of Commercial Digital Recording," *ARSC Journal* 39 (1):1–17.

became a domain of calculation, on principles envisaged by Ada Lovelace[§MS1.3.2a] and Alan Turing.[§MS1.3.2b] The transposition runs like this: sound > recording in calculable number (text) > recalculation for the re-rendering as sound.

MP3 recordings sample sound at a rate of 44,100 records per second (44.1 kHz). The human ear can discriminate sound up to about 20 kHz, so the sampling rate is plenty for two-channel sound. The data at this rate of sampling is big – it was too big for home computing devices in the 1980s, hence the invention of the Compact Disc laser reader. Even with the CD's larger storage capacity, part of the trick was to compress files by removing redundant information. Combining the innovation of the disc compression software, a CD could hold about seventy minutes of music. With the rise of larger storage capacities on hard drives or solid state memory, and the data pipeline of the internet rapidly expanding, the CD was a doomed technology. Now the MP3 format and its slightly modified descendants rule supreme.[309]

If the phonograph and radio transformed the cultural practices of music, the medium of digitization adds to these some new social functions of meaning. A logic of mass production and economies of scale had been built into analogue record manufacture and wireless radio. Setting up a record studio for analogue recordings and pressing records only made sense on the economies of scale of mass production. These technologies only worked on an industrial scale. So, the business model for music production became long runs for mass markets. Radio bandwidths were limited and transmission facilities were large and expensive, so in any one geographic area there could be no more than a handful of options. Popular music was reduced to best-selling "hits," and "classical" music to a limited repertoire of old European masters. This massification of culture and the creation of passive audiences was what Adorno and Horkheimer railed against in their critical theory of the "culture industries."[310]

But with music digitization and streaming, by the end of the 2010s, Apple Music offered about 45 million songs, and Spotify 35 million – including pieces by Cazden,[§1.4.2a] Adorno,[§1.4.2b] and Avraamov[§1.4.2c] that could never have made it into the top forty, that would be uneconomical to press as records, and that local stores would never stock. The result: no two music libraries, no two playlists, are quite the same. This affords a radical shift in the social designs of interpretation in late modernity, from homogenizing-massifying of interest, to differentiating-dividing. It's not that this changes the basic

---

[309] Hans Georg Musmann, 2006, "Genesis of the Mp3 Audio Coding Standard," *IEEE Transactions on Consumer Electronics* 52(3):1043–49; Marina Bosi and Richard E. Goldberg, 2003, *Introduction to Digital Audio Coding and Standards*, New York: Springer Science.

[310] Theodor W. Adorno and Max Horkheimer, 1944 [2002], *Dialectic of Enlightenment*, translated by E. Jephcott, Stanford, CA: Stanford University Press, pp. 94–136.

structures of inequality, rather that the dynamics of the maintenance of inequality become quite different.[§2.2.2]

At the same time, and perhaps not so paradoxically, there has been a huge concentration of control in the means of production and distribution of our musical meanings. There are just two comprehensive streaming services, or perhaps four if you add Amazon and YouTube to Apple Music and Spotify. Not only do these providers archive music on a massive scale; they also record the minutiae of every user's listening habits in ways not previously possible. All-knowing megacorporations track our musical proclivities in meticulous detail. We are complicit when their "artificial intelligence" makes a new music suggestion that is uncannily prescient, a piece you should have known about but didn't, or that somehow you have forgotten.

In reality, the intelligence is not so clever as such flashes of recognition might trick us into believing. The smarts are not in the 44,100 digital samples per second, nor their calculation for the purposes of encoding and decoding. Only the simplest of mechanical sense can be made of the math. Most of its genius is simply to name and record a myriad of sequential moments of sound amplitude, an avalanche of detail that is useful for manufacture but mindless for humans in its detail.

The innovation, rather, is to record the range of self-declared human affinities named as the product numbers[§MS1.1.1c] and track these numbers in a database – "recommender systems," they are called.[311] This affords what Norman Cazden called "realism in music,"[§1.4.2a] a social realism when someone whose finely calibrated tastes are calculated to be close to yours. Of the tens of millions of options, another user may have a certain two pieces in their playlist, and you have just one, so the machine offers you their second as a suggestion. Recommendation software works simply by recording data that it was until now impractical to record, in this case, the minutiae of every user's listening. The machine listens to its listeners. The meaning is social. And these megacorporations now know our meanings.

§1.4.3 Body

> **Body.** *Meanings made in the configuration of human bodies: gesticulations, bodily appearances, and enactments.*

Meaning is a full-bodied experience. Body is a material medium for meaning. It is also where all other forms of meaning meet the person, in their materiality.

---

[311] Joseph A. Konstan and John Riedl, 2012, "Recommender Systems: From Algorithms to User Experience," *User Modeling and User-Adapted Interaction* 22(1–2):101–23. doi: 10.1007/s11257-011-9112-x.

Speech is material, and meets the listener's body in its audible materiality. Text is material, meeting the reader's body in its visible materiality. Body meets object in touch. Body meets space in the configuration of self and others in constructed spaces and nature. This is why we place body near the middle in our rough, "supermarket"[§MS0d] ordering of the forms of meaning, and now also in this functional re-ordering of their affordances as media.

However, for now, we are going to focus on body more narrowly, as a medium in its own right, rather than a medium interacting with other media. What meanings, we will ask, do bodies, in themselves, afford?

We want to delineate for bodies three media subsystems: gesticulation, appearance, and enactment.

Gesticulation is a system of hand–arm movements and facial expression that accompany speech. Gesticulation can also serve as a complete substitute for speech. In deaf communities, for instance, "signing" is a dedicated system of gesticulation.[312] Deaf signing is ideographic, more akin to Chinese text than the impossible phonemics of fluent reading in alphabetical languages.[§1.4.1a] Only after a critique of the "phonocentrism" of Western linguistics does it become possible to acknowledge the complete transposability into gesture across the full gamut of human materializations of meaning – likeness, directedness, and abstraction.

Appearance is made at the boundaries of the body, in sheer incorporeality ("race," gender, age, body shape); and cultural accoutrements (the second skins of fashion, jewelry, cosmetics, and hair arrangement).

Enactments depict in posture, demeanor, comportment, and emotion.

Across each of the three kinds of materialization,[§1.1] likeness, directedness, and abstraction, Fig. 1.4.3 is a rough map with some examples.

And of course, following the logic of our transpositional grammar, at no time is any one of these meaning functions stably located. Each one is always begging to slip into another.

§1.4.3a David McNeill's Hand and Mind

Gesticulation is the movement of the hands and arms that accompanies talking, or mental images of talking.

Speaking, says David McNeill, and gesticulation are two sides of a common cognitive process. Gesticulation is a supplement to speech, saying less while adding more. We "conduct" our speech as if our hands were conductor and speech the orchestra.[*] The "preparation" for gesticulation begins with the start

* http://meaningpatterns.net/mcneill

[312] H-Dirksen L. Bauman, 2008, "Listening to Phonocentrism with Deaf Eyes: Derrida's Mute Philosophy of (Sign) Language," *Essays in Philosophy* 9(1):1–14.

Media / Materialization	Gesticulation	Appearance	Enactment
Likeness	Mime, dance, hand pictures, imitation	Fashion that copies or repeats, e.g. as costume or uniform	Repetition of habitual enactments, comportments, role play, theatrical performance
Directedness	Pointing, hand alerts, spontaneous emotion, facial expressions of feeling	Fashion directs to a role e.g. body parts, environment, activity	Comportment: presentation of self, meanings given off
Abstraction	Conventional meanings of hand signs and facial expressions, culturally contingent expressions of emotion	Fashion indicating style or social group, bodily features indicating social categories and meanings ascribed to them, e.g. from "race" to racism, sex to sexism	Ritual moves, demeanor as a kind of person in a particular social context

Fig. 1.4.3: Body as meaning

of a spoken phrase; the "stroke" marks the emphatic point of this momentary meaning structure; and the "retraction" marks its end. These gesticulations are spontaneous and relatively unconscious, in an instant anticipating and then synchronizing with speech. They are assembled with speech into a sequence of idea units. Mind produces meaning with hands and speech, syncopated in real time.[313]

Then, closely linked with both speech and gesture are facial expressions. With twenty-two pairs of facial muscles, thousands of expressions are possible across the range of stretch intensities and muscle combinations. Facial meanings are far more nuanced in their range – their references to the self and its context – than speech ever can be, which is how they also orchestrate speech.[314]

Like speech, gesticulation and facial expression are captive to time, occurring in irreversible sequential segments, overlaying clauses (Halliday[§MS0.2.7a]) or breath groups (Masterman[§1.4.1b]) in real time. Theater, cinema, and now video can overcome a contiguity in time and place normally required in speech. They turn gesticulation into a kind of writing, re-enacting a referenced moment

---

[313] David McNeill, 1992, *Hand and Mind: What Gestures Reveal About Thought*, Chicago, IL: University of Chicago Press, pp. 23–28; David McNeill, 2012, *How Language Began: Gesture and Speech in Human Evolution*, Cambridge: Cambridge University Press; Adam Kendon, 2004, *Gesture: Visible Action as Utterance*, Cambridge: Cambridge University Press; Ellen Fricke, 2013, "Towards a Unified Grammar of Gesture and Speech: A Multimodal Approach," pp. 733–54 in *Body-Language-Communication: An International Handbook on Multimodality in Human Interaction*, edited by C. Müller, A. Cienki, E. Fricke, S.H. Ladewig, D. McNeill, and J. Bressem, Berlin: De Gruyter Mouton.

[314] Daniel McNeill, 1998, *The Face*, Boston, MA: Little, Brown and Company.

of spontaneity in plannable performances and editable recordings of performance.

Other moments of gesticulation are premeditated and highly conscious. This is frequently the case in person-to-person contexts where speech is not viable. The distance may be too far for speech, the context too noisy or too quiet. In such situations some gestures may take the form of likeness (drawing the shape of something in a hand pictures, imitation); others directedness ("stop," or waving someone through); still others abstractions (nodding or shaking one's head are only by convention "yes" and "no"). Gesticulations that materialize meanings by abstraction are more varied by culture and context than those meaning by likeness or directedness. This also means that they are more open to misconstrual. Gestures that are offensive or laughable are so by convention or difference in interpretation.

Gestural signing with the omission of speech can achieve a range of meaning equal to spoken language, as evidenced in deaf sign languages,[§1.4.3] for instance, or the sign languages used by Walpiri women in Australia when they are sworn to silence to mourn the death of a relative.[315] This testifies to the power of multimodality, the possibility of meaning as fully as any human could wish, even in the complete absence of sensorial capacity for one or more media. Such an extraordinary ability to substitute meaning forms shows that, in the sense that we make as a species, always-possible transposability may be the main game.

§1.4.3b Anthony Damasio's Self Comes to Mind

The "material me, the self-as-subject," says Anthony Damasio, is "a dynamic collection of integrated neural processes, centered on the representation of the human living."[*] In the context of the materialized body, "emotion-based signals" serve as "somatic markers" that create "feelings of knowing." So, "[t]here is no dichotomy between self-as-object and self-as-knower."[316] Or, to put this another way, feeling and thinking, emotion and cognition, form an integrated meaning system.

There are "deep-seated bodily sources of human meaning," says Mark Johnson, elaborating upon Damasio. These are the "neuro chemical bases of

---

* http://meaningpatterns.net/damasio

[315] David McNeill, 1992, *Hand and Mind: What Gestures Reveal About Thought*, Chicago, IL: University of Chicago Press, pp. 42–54; Adam Kendon, 1989, *Sign Languages of Aboriginal Australia: Cultural, Semiotic and Communicative Perspectives*, Cambridge: Cambridge University Press.

[316] Antonio Damasio, 2010, *Self Comes to Mind: Constructing the Conscious Brain*, New York: Pantheon, pp. 9–10, 108ff.; Antonio Damasio, 1994, *Descartes' Error: Emotion, Reason and the Human Brain*, New York: Penguin Putnam.

feeling and emotion." We are "creatures of the flesh," whose "visceral connections to life and the bodily conditions of life" are the primordial ground of our meaning. "[E]mbodied meaning ... emerges as structures of organism–environment interactions and transactions."[317] There is a chemistry and neurology of pleasure, pain, and fear. Not only are they felt in the body as medium for their meaning (meaning-as-representation[§1.2.1]); often they are also visibly felt (meaning-as-communication[§1.2.2]).

For this grammar we parse feelings and emotional meanings across the same threefold range of materialization that we have used elsewhere: likeness, directedness, and abstraction.[§1.1]

Likeness we're putting first, because this is where we have shelved it already in our "supermarket"[§MS0d] of meanings. However, now it is not first analytically, because when it comes to feelings and emotions, likeness is secondary, mimicking or acting out embodied expressions of emotion that have been materialized in the first instance as directedness or abstraction.

Directedness indicates the rawest and most spontaneous signs of our emotions, feelings that cause us to laugh, cry, wince, blush, sweat, shiver, recoil, scream, or sigh, and often involuntarily. When we feel these in ourselves or see them in others, the relation to the feeling or the seeing is one of directedness – meaning is a process of pointing in the direction of emotion. Here are some entries for a catalogue of directed emotional meanings: happiness/sadness; safety/fear; consilience/anger; relish/disgust; pleasure/pain; enjoyment/discomfort; mania/depression; and of course there are many more.

Abstraction occurs in more elaborated emotional frames, where the emotional meaning is determined more by context and convention. Abstracted meaning is by functional social agreement, learned by cultural attribution rather than involuntary eruption. Here are some possible entries for a catalogue of conventionally abstracted emotions: admiration/jealousy; love/hate; pride/shame; certainty/doubt; confidence/embarrassment; sympathy/indifference; empathy/apathy; focus/distraction; excitement/complacency; relaxation/stress; surprise/boredom; serenity/anxiety; expectation/shock; contempt/appreciation; drive/laziness; motivation/discouragement; and many more, not to mention intermediate variations between these antinomies, as well as a panoply of ambiguous combinations. Such abstract emotions are historically contingent, though for that, no less felt. Notwithstanding their cultural relativity, such meanings are just as embodied in the human biome, their feeling as deeply embedded in the body. Viscerally, such emotions can be life-affirming or life threatening.

---

[317] Mark Johnson, 2007, *The Meaning of the Body: Aesthetics of Human Understanding*, Chicago, IL: University of Chicago Press, pp. 11, 54, xi, xii.

Of course, the place we have put each of these pairs in the catalogue of emotional directedness or abstractions is rough. Person to person, context to context, an emotion may be more or less directed, more or less abstract. And any can be repeated or imitated, by way of likeness.

Nor do these emotions ever stay the way they are for long. As much as they are immanent, vital bodily experiences, they are always ready to change or be changed. We experience this emotional transposability in the dialectic of mood swings, or emotional games of bait-and-switch. Love-hate, pride-jealousy, drive-laziness – we feel these and other emotions as unities-in-tension, vital immanences always warning or promising the imminence of the alternative, the always-readiness of transposition.

The medium for emotional meanings is the physiological frame of the body. These are meanings whose chemistry and neurology we share with other sentient creatures. And even when we reach the heights of reasoning smarts we have as a species, reason is layered over emotion, cognition over body-as-medium, humanity over our animality. Reason, as Lakoff and Johnson argue, and even our frame of moral reference, are grounded in embodied experience and the sensorimotor system.[318]

And between bodies and other media – speech, sound, object, space, image, and text – the traffic runs both ways. Not only can other media represent emotion-in-body, but other media can evoke these physiological effects – (mere!) words or images can trigger body chemicals and neurons, so we feel with our bodies what is written or pictured.

We have been examining thus far the centered self, the self made bodily aware of its own meanings – Damasio's "self brought to mind." We also want to mention the empathetic self,[§2.5b] when, by transposition from material to ideal,[§MS3.1] self transposes its-self to an-other.[§MS2.2]

Conversely, the absence of emotion as another kind of emotional presence. This is the unaware, unconscious self, meaning without necessary or even adequate knowing. For its failure to read emotions or to speak to them, this kind of self is sent to the school of "emotional intelligence," an antidote for unawareness first named as such in 1964 by Michael Beldoch.[319] Though of course, this kind of self presents itself to everyone at least fleetingly, when embodied meanings happen before you know it, and emotional self-recognition is an after-effect.

---

[318] George Lakoff and Mark Johnson, 1999, *Philosophy in the Flesh: The Embodied Mind and Its Challenge to Western Thought*, New York: Basic Books, pp. 555–58.

[319] Michael Beldoch, 1964, "Sensitivity to Expression of Emotional Meaning in Three Modes of Communication," pp. 31–42 in *The Communication of Emotional Meaning*, edited by J.R. Davitz, New York: McGraw-Hill.

§1.4.3c Toni Morrison's "Black"

"You should always wear white, Bride. Only white and all white all the time."
Jeri, calling himself a "total person" designer, insisted. Looking for a make-
over for my second interview at Sylvia, Inc., I consulted him. "Not only
because of your name," he told me, "but because of what it does to your
licorice skin," he said. "And black is the new black."

In Nobel Prize winner Toni Morrison's eleventh novel, *God Help the Child*,
Bride – "Midnight black, Sudanese black" – wants to work in fashion.[320]

"Race" is the appearance of body, given meaning. It is skin color, and some
more – hair color and texture, height and physique.[*] Technically speaking these
are the phenotypical features into which the old race science subclassified the
human species. With categories such as "Negroid," "Australoid,"
"Mongoloid," and "Caucasoid,"[321] human races, so called, could be ordered
into a hierarchy of intelligence and civilizability.

Race, in the terms we are developing in this grammar, is an abstraction,
a social construction, a bodily reality drenched in meaning, but by convention alone. Signs of emotion, like crying or laughing, point to an
embodied meaning.[§1.4.3b] Race points to a meaning that is nothing but
socially scripted, written onto the color of skin, an excess of the ideal over
the material.[§MS3.1]

Bride's sometime boyfriend explains black skin:

"It's just a color," Booker had said. "A genetic trait – not a flaw, not a curse, not a
blessing nor a sin." "But," she countered, "other people think racial – " Booker cut her
off. "Scientifically there's no such thing as race, Bride, so racism without race is a
choice. Taught, of course, by those who need it, but still a choice. Folks who practice it
would be nothing without it."[322]

Here is the science of race, such as it can be: on biological measures of
difference, there is greater inherited biological variation within phenotypically
marked populations than the average variation between populations.
Reviewing a burst of biometric research in the opening decades of the
twenty-first century, Yudell and his geneticist colleagues conclude, "commonly
defined racial groups are genetically heterogeneous and lack clear-cut genetic
boundaries," and "phylogenetic and population genetic methods do not support
a priori classifications of race, as expected for an interbreeding species like
Homo Sapiens. ... [R]acial classifications do not make sense in terms of

---

[*] http://meaningpatterns.net/race

[320] Toni Morrison, 2015, *God Help the Child*, New York: Knopf Doubleday, pp. 33, 3.
[321] Robert Bennett Bean, 1932, *The Races of Man: Differentiation and Dispersal of Man*, New
York: The University Society.
[322] Toni Morrison, 2015, *God Help the Child*, New York: Knopf Doubleday, p. 143.

genetics."[323] A wide variety of skin colors is to be found in Africa, concludes another group of geneticists, and also the genetic basis for all variations that occur subsequently in the natural history of the human body.[324]

Not that the science needs to be terribly new for the point to be made – W.E.B. Du Bois[§1.4.6b] had said as much, and as early as 1906: "The human species so shade and mingle with each other that not only indeed is it impossible to draw a color line between black and other races, but in all physical characteristics the Negro race cannot be set off by itself as absolutely different."[325]

Bride's boyfriend Booker is black, but he nevertheless

... suspected most of the real answers concerning slavery, lynching, forced labor, share-cropping, racism, Reconstruction, Jim Crow, prison labor, migration, civil rights and black revolution movements were all about money. Money withheld, money stolen, money as power, as war. ... White folks' hatred, their violence, was the gasoline that kept the profit motors running. So as a graduate student he turned to economics – its history, its theories – to learn how money shaped every single oppression in the world.[326]

Only as the handmaiden of racism does race mean anything. It means slavery, imperialism, and grossly unequal educational and economic outcomes. This is how race, the appearance of body, works as abstraction. If racism is an excess of the ideal over the material, the effects of its meanings are material. If race is unreal, racism is as real as real can be, though it can only be experienced and felt as social convention and its embodied extensions in the forms of racist violence and incarceration.[327]

Or, it just feels awkward. Bride recalls,

I remember one date in particular, a medical student who persuaded me to join him on a visit to his parents' house up north. As soon as he introduced me it was clear I was there to terrorize his family, a means of threat to this nice old white couple.

[323] Michael Yudell, Dorothy Roberts, Rob DeSalle, and Sarah Tishkoff, 2016, "Taking Race out of Human Genetics: Engaging a Century-Long Debate About the Role of Race in Science," *Science* 351(6273):564–65, p. 565; Michael Yudell, 2014, *Race Unmasked: Biology and Race in the Twentieth Century*, New York: Columbia University Press.

[324] Brian McEvoy, Sandra Beleza, and Mark D. Shriver, 2006, "The Genetic Architecture of Normal Variation in Human Pigmentation: An Evolutionary Perspective and Model," *Human Molecular Genetics* 15(2):R176–81; Nicholas G. Crawford, et al. 2017, "Loci Associated with Skin Pigmentation Identified in African Populations," *Science* 235(8433):1–14; Sandra Beleza, et al. 2012, "The Timing of Pigmentation Lightening in Europeans," *Molecular Biology and Evolution* 30(1):24–35; Rasmus Nielsen, Joshua M. Akey, Mattias Jakobsson, Jonathan K. Pritchard, Sarah Tishkoff, and Eske Willerslev, 2017, "Tracing the Peopling of the World through Genomics," *Nature* 541:302–10.

[325] W.E.B. Du Bois, 1906, *The Health and Physique of the Negro American: Report of a Social Study Made under the Direction of Atlanta University*, Atlanta, GA: Atlanta University Press, p. 16.

[326] Toni Morrison, 2015, *God Help the Child*, New York: Knopf Doubleday, pp. 110–11.

[327] Robert Miles, 1989, *Racism*, London: Routledge; Dorothy Roberts, 2011, *Fatal Invention: How Science, Politics, and Big Business Re-Create Race in the Twenty-First Century*, New York: Free Press.

"Isn't she beautiful?" he kept repeating. "Look at her, Mother? Dad?" His eyes were gleaming with malice.

But they outclassed him with their warmth – however faked – and charm. His disappointment was obvious, his anger thinly repressed. His parents even drove me to the train stop, probably so I wouldn't have to put up with his failed racist joke on them.[328]

Racism's meanings are rarely straightforward, doubling back on themselves as soon as their worst excesses seem to have been mitigated. Parsing its iniquities is a laborious process, its target deep and meanings ever-shifting.

Nor can skin color be isolated from other aspects of appearance. Bodily appearances come as a whole. Jeri counsels Bride to wear white because she is black.

Walter Benjamin:[§MS0b] "Every fashion couples the living body to the inorganic world . . . Every fashion is to some extent a bitter satire on love; in every fashion, perversities are suggested by the most ruthless means."[329] Clothing is a second skin, hiding skin then revealing skin by its hiding. Its functions: likeness, in costume or uniform; directedness, to body part, environmental function, and activity; and abstraction, in style or fashion.

Jeri, advising me, said, "Listen, Bride baby. If you must have a drop of color limit it to shoes and purses, but I'd keep both black when white simply won't do. And don't forget: no makeup. Not even lipstick or eyeliner. None."

I asked him about jewelry. Gold? Some diamonds? An emerald brooch? "No. No." He threw his hands up. "No jewelry at all. Pearl dot earrings, maybe. No. Not even that. Just you, girl. All sable and ice. A panther in snow. And with your body? And those wolverine eyes? Please!"

I took his advice and it worked. Everywhere I went I got double takes but not like the faintly disgusted ones I used to get as a kid. These were adoring looks, stunned but hungry. Plus, unbeknownst to him, Jeri had given me the name for a product line. YOU, GIRL.[330]

§1.4.3d Iris Marion Young's "Throwing Like a Girl"

Simone de Beauvoir begins her world-changing feminist classic, *The Second Sex,* by stating the dangerously obvious – "the truth is that anyone can clearly see that humanity is split into two categories of individuals with manifestly different clothes, faces, bodies, smiles, movements, interests, and occupations; these differences are perhaps superficial; perhaps they are destined to

---

[328] Toni Morrison, 2015, *God Help the Child*, New York: Knopf Doubleday, p. 37.

[329] Walter Benjamin, 1999b, *The Arcades Project*, translated by H. Eidland and K. McLaughlin, Cambridge, MA: Harvard University Press, p. 79.

[330] Toni Morrison, 2015, *God Help the Child*, New York: Knopf Doubleday, p. 34.

disappear. What is certain is that for the moment they exist in a strikingly obvious way."[331]

In the terms we have been developing for this grammar, these differences are embodied. Women's gesticulations are distinctive, the hand and arm orchestration that go with their speech. Women's appearance is distinctive, from body shape and functions, to hair arrangements and fashion. Women's enactments are distinctive – their bodily movements in the form of body comportment, motility, and bodily relations in space.

In a celebrated article reinterpreting Erwin Straus' observations about the way girls throw a ball,[332] Iris Marion Young writes, "Not only is there a typical style of throwing like a girl, but there is a more or less typical style of running like a girl, climbing like a girl, swinging like a girl, hitting like a girl. They have in common, first, that the whole body is not put into fluid and directed motion, but rather, in swinging and hitting, for example, the motion is concentrated in one body part; and second, that the woman's motion tends not to reach, extend, lean, stretch, and follow through in the direction of her intention."* The consequence: "Feminine existence ... often does not enter bodily relation to possibilities by its own comportment toward its surroundings in an unambiguous and confident 'I can.'"[333]

In our grammar, we are calling this kind of bodily meaning an enactment. For women, as Young continues her reading of the wider meanings of female comportment, there is "a latent and sometimes conscious fear of getting hurt, which we bring to a motion. That is, feminine bodily existence is self-referred in that the woman takes herself as the object of the motion rather than its originator." This, in a larger context where

patriarchal society defines woman as object, as a mere body, and that in sexist society women are in fact frequently regarded by others as objects and mere bodies, ... the ever present possibility that one will be gazed upon as a mere body, as shape and flesh that presents itself as the potential object of another subject's intentions and manipulations, rather than as a living manifestation of action and intention ... The threat of being seen is, however, not the only threat of objectification which the woman lives. She also lives the threat of invasion of her body space; ... feminine spatiality is in part a defense against such invasion.[334]

---

* http://meaningpatterns.net/gender

[331] Simone de Beauvoir, 1949 [2011], *The Second Sex*, translated by C. Borde and S. Malovany-Chevallier, New York. Vintage Books, p 24.

[332] Erwin W. Straus, 1966, *Phenomenological Psychology: The Selected Papers of Erwin W. Straus*, New York: Basic Books, pp. 157–58.

[333] Iris Marion Young, 1980, "Throwing Like a Girl: A Phenomenology of Feminine Body Comportment, Motility, and Spatiality," *Human Studies* 3(1):137–56, pp. 143, 146.

[334] Ibid., pp. 148, 154.

The repetition of this engendered experience is captured in the twenty-first century as #MeToo. From the microdynamics of localized enactments, the whole question of comportment must delve this deep and travel wide into context, parsing the extensive frames reference in social life where bodies-as-media enact meaning.

Notwithstanding the painful repetitions of gender, in the century after de Beauvoir's and Young's insights, the "strikingly obvious" of womanhood has become obviously complicated. Meanwhile, the phenomena that de Beauvoir considered "perhaps superficial" and possibly transient are showing no signs of imminent disappearance.

The signs of gendered difference are today everywhere, but they fit less comfortably the woman/man dualism. In terms of the old dichotomies, a man or a woman might be equally good or not at throwing a ball. Heterosexual man and heterosexual woman can be more or less "effeminate" or "butch," and so can homosexual men or women. Add to these a panoply of other boundaryless sexualities and their attendant comportments: genderqueer, asexual, bisexual, bigender, gender-fluid, gender non-conforming, pansexual, cisgender, trans-gender, transsexual, transvestite, non-binary, androgyne, agender, asexual, aromantic, intersex, and when none of these categories fits or another cannot be found, just "other." The range of differences within a named group is often as great as the average differences between groups. Or the comportments may be misleading.

These differences also defy the old sex/gender dualism, a dualism of biology/culture, embodiment/mindedness. Now the words of classification, apparently clear when the dualisms seemed to work, begin to fail us. Bodily enactments demand of us ever-more nuanced parsing. Elsewhere, we have coined and applied the word "gendre,"[335] pushing the bipolar associations with the word "gender" in the direction of range and complexity captured in the word "genre."[336]

And where words fail us, all may be well, because in their appearances and enactments bodies can speak for themselves. In Peter Gärdenfors' nice turn of phrase, "the obvious goes without saying,"[337] and perhaps today it may be wise to say less. But, we would add, the obvious never goes without meaning.

As much as they are designs in natural and social history, bodies are open to redesign, as media as well as meaning. Deeper than the second skin of fashion

---

[335] Mary Kalantzis and Bill Cope, 2016b, "Learner Differences in Theory and Practice," *Open Review of Educational Research* 3(1):85–132.

[336] Bill Cope and Mary Kalantzis, eds. 1993, *The Powers of Literacy: Genre Approaches to Teaching Writing*, London, UK: Falmer Press and Pittsburgh, PA: University of Pennsylvania Press.

[337] Peter Gärdenfors, 2014, *Geometry of Meaning: Semantics Based on Conceptual Spaces*, Cambridge, MA: MIT Press, p. 93.

are tattoos, body piercing, the sculptable body of plastic surgery, and sex reassignment. Layered over by the subtleties of gesticulation and enactment, the old gender bipolarity is becoming anachronistic, not that it ever worked terribly well. Not even a spectrum will work now, because these differences can't be located along a line.

Nevertheless, de Beauvoir and Young still have much to offer a grammar of the body. They provide a methodology for parsing embodied meanings. The only difference we may find today is that the meanings we uncover in our parsing have changed – though also often, tragically not. "When I use the word 'woman' or 'feminine'," cautioned de Beauvoir, "I obviously refer to no archetype, to no immutable essence; 'in the present state of education and customs' must be understood to follow most of my affirmations."[338]

Maurice Merleau-Ponty was de Beauvoir's contemporary and, with her and Jean-Paul Sartre,[§MS3.1.2b] co-editors of the seminal journal, *Les Temps Moderne*. In his *Phenomenology of Perception*, Merleau-Ponty says, "Consciousness is being-towards-the-thing through the intermediary of the body. A movement is learned when the body has understood it, that is, when it has incorporated it into its 'world' . . . Consciousness is in the first place not a matter of 'I think that' but of 'I can.'" This was the basis for his critique of traditional philosophies of cognition and language-centered theories of meaning: "the corporeal schema presents great difficulties to traditional philosophies, which are always inclined to conceive synthesis as intellectual synthesis."[339]

Where Descartes had said, "I think therefore I am,"[§MS3.1.2g] we suggest this alternative, one that centers embodied meaning in the universe: "I can therefore I am." Then, de Beauvoir's agenda is for everyone, to make "can" a reality for all: "The same drama of flesh and spirit, and of finitude and transcendence, plays itself out in both sexes; both are eaten away by time, stalked by death . . . ; and they can take the same glory from their freedom; if they knew how to savor it, they would no longer be tempted to contend for false privileges."[340]

§1.4.3e *Donna Haraway's* Cyborg Manifesto

"In the traditions of 'Western' science and politics – the tradition of racist, male-dominant capitalism; the tradition of progress; the tradition of the appropriation of nature as resource for the productions of culture; the tradition of

---

[338] Simone de Beauvoir, 1949 [2011], *The Second Sex*, translated by C. Borde and S. Malovany-Chevallier, New York: Vintage Books, p. 328.

[339] Maurice Merleau-Ponty, 1945 [2002], *Phenomenology of Perception*, translated by C. Smith, London: Routledge, pp. 160–61, 159, 164.

[340] Simone de Beauvoir, 1949 [2011], *The Second Sex*, translated by C. Borde and S. Malovany-Chevallier, New York: Vintage Books, p. 859.

reproduction of the self from the reflections of the other – the relation between organism and machine has been a border war." So begins Donna Haraway in her *Cyborg Manifesto*.*

"Late twentieth-century machines have made thoroughly ambiguous the difference between natural and artificial, mind and body, self-developing and externally designed, and many other distinctions that used to apply to organisms and machines. Our machines are disturbingly lively, and we ourselves frighteningly inert."[341]

Truth be known, as Haraway goes on to argue, we are all cyborgs now – part human, part machine in our experience of the world. Even though the machines have become a bigger part of our lives, in some senses as a species we have been cyborgs all along. In our species-nature, we have all along been tool-using animals, *homo faber*, where objects are essential extensions of the self. This is how the impossibly separated body becomes the possible self of inseparably multimodal object–body enactment. To move the body at such speeds was impossible before the railway. To think at such speeds was impossible before the computer.

"The difference between machine and organism is thoroughly blurred; mind, body, and tool are on very intimate terms."[342] However, we have also been at war with the machine because it has been an instrument of our domination as often as it has, by bodily extension, created new affordances for our meaning.

Henry Ford accounted for his life in a best-selling moral tale, *My Life and Work*. Here he disclosed, to those who might aspire to follow in his steps, the secrets of his phenomenal success as an inventor and businessman. The key was to supplement unskilled bodies and untrained minds with bodily and mental extensions of the machine and the factory.

Ford's message was not in support of differently abled access when he said,

The blind man or cripple man can, in the particular place to which he is assigned, perform just as much work and receive exactly the same pay as a wholly able bodied man would . . . To discover what was the real situation, I had all of the different jobs in the factory classified to the kind of machine and work . . . It turned out at the time of the inquiry that there were then 7882 different jobs in the factory. Of these, 949 were classified as heavy work requiring strong, able bodied and practically physically perfect men . . . The lightest jobs were classified to discover how many of them required the use of full faculties and we found that 670 could be filled by legless men, 2637 by one-legged men, 2 by armless men, 715 by one-armed men and 10 by blind men.

* http://meaningpatterns.net/cyborg

[341] Donna Haraway, 1985 [2016], *A Manifesto for Cyborgs: Science, Technology, and Socialist Feminism in the 1980s*, Minneapolis: University of Minnesota Press, pp. 7, 11.
[342] Ibid., p. 36.

Which meant that the machines could do what eyes, arms, and legs might otherwise have been required to do. And of course, the division of labor was so finely differentiated into minimalist tasks, that few workers required much training: "The length of time to become proficient in the various occupations is about as follows: 43 per cent of jobs require not over one day of training; 36 per cent require from one day to one week; 6 per cent require from one to two weeks; 14 per cent require from one month to one year; one per cent required from one to six years."[343]

The celebrated theorist of the modern factory, Frederick Winslow Taylor, laid out the process of parsing the multimodal relation of body and machine in his classic *Principles of Scientific Management*. "Study the exact series of elementary operations or motions which each of these men uses in doing the work which is being investigated, as well as the implements each man uses ... Study with a stop watch the time required to make each of these elementary movements and then select the quickest way of doing each element of the work ... Eliminate all false movements, slow movements and useless movements ... After doing away with all unnecessary movements, collect into one series the quickest and best movements."[344] This was a science of cyborgs, of human–machine integration where bodies themselves could be conceived mechanistically.

"Taylor's system," Vladimir Lenin[§MS0.2.9a] wrote in the Bolshevik Party's newspaper, *Pravda*, "without the knowledge and against the will of its authors, is preparing that time when the proletariat will seize all production into its hands and will assign its own workers' commissions for the proper distribution and regulation of all social labor."[345]

So, in the Central Institute of Labor directed by Aleksei Gastev, a writer and poet of some fame, these preparations were made. The human body was to be an efficient machine, and machines were there at least in part to replace bodies. The human was robot, and the robot was substitute human, and various intermediate permutations. Such machine–body transpositions were for the purpose of liberating labor from its former oppressions.

> Brain machines – high load.
> Cinema eyes – fix.
> Electric nerves – to work.
> Arterial pumps, activate.

---

[343] Henry Ford, 1922, *My Life and Work*, Sydney, Australia: Angus & Robertson, pp. 103–10.

[344] Frederick Winslow Taylor, 1911, *The Principles of Scientific Management*, New York: Harper & Brothers, pp. 117–18; Charles D. Wrege and Ronald G. Greenwood, 1991, *Frederick W. Taylor, the Father of Scientific Management: Myth and Reality*, Homewood, IL: Business One Irwin.

[345] Mark R. Beissinger, 1988, *Scientific Management, Socialist Discipline, and Soviet Power*, Cambridge: Harvard University Press, p. 23.

When writer Maxim Gorky visited the institute, he embraced Gastev: "Now I understand why you have left fiction."[346]

Working at the Scientific and Research Institute for Jet Propulsion in Moscow, in 1931 and then again in 1938 Ary Sternfeld patented an apparatus that he called an "android," which registered the movements of the human body for the purpose of their reproduction in machines.

Sternfeld survived Stalin, but Gastev did not. During Stalin's purges, he was tried and shot in 1939 for being connected with "the conspiratorial organization the Real Trotskyites." Leon Trotsky was Stalin's by-then-banished rival, also soon-to-be-murdered.[347] Bullets are another kind of machine–body engagement, cruel extensions of the shooting body and the interests of its body politic.

At the end of the same century, Donna Haraway's feminist call was "explicitly embracing the possibilities inherent in the breakdown of clean distinctions between organism and machine and similar distinctions structuring the Western self . . . embracing the skillful task of reconstructing the boundaries of daily life . . . [S]cience and technology are possible means of great human satisfaction, as well as a matrix of complex dominations."[348] Her challenge: to embrace the cyborg as a scope for human possibility rather than an instrument of oppression; to make peace with the machine.

Walter Benjamin again: "in technology, body, image and space so interpenetrate that all revolutionary tension becomes bodily collective innervation."[349]

§1.4.3f *James Paul Gee's* Why Video Games are Good for Your Soul

James Paul Gee takes something as apparently uneducational as first-person shooter games, and offers a learning theory to account for why youth might find video games more engaging than school.[350] It's not the shooting but the forms of "conversation," he says.[*] As for conversation, we have learned much in our half-lifetime of working and talking with Jim.

---

[*] http://meaningpatterns.net/gee

[346] Andrey Smirnov, 2013, *Sound in Z: Experiments in Sound and Electronic Music in Early 20th Century Russia*, London: Koenig Books, p. 106.

[347] Ibid., pp. 111, 105–06, 260.

[348] Donna Haraway, 1985 [2016], *A Manifesto for Cyborgs: Science, Technology, and Socialist Feminism in the 1980s*, Minneapolis: University of Minnesota Press, pp. 67, 53, 67.

[349] Walter Benjamin, 1929 [1999], "Surrealism: The Last Snapshot of the European Intelligentsia," pp. 207–21 in *Walter Benjamin: Selected Writings, Volume 2: 1927–1934*, edited by M.W. Jennings, H. Eidland, and G. Smith, Cambridge, MA: Harvard University Press, p. 217.

[350] James Paul Gee, 2004, *Situated Language and Learning: A Critique of Traditional Schooling*, London: Routledge; James Paul Gee, 2013, *The Anti-Education Era: Creating Smarter Students through Digital Learning*, New York: Palgrave Macmillan.

Gee lists thirty-six places (at least) where even the most otherwise unedifying games are based on sounder learning principles than the conventional classroom, including: the "situated meaning principle," where "meanings of signs (words, actions, objects, artifacts, symbols, texts, etc.) are situated in embodied experience," and the "distributed principle," where "meaning/ knowledge is distributed across the learner, objects, tools, symbols, technologies, and the environment."[351] The word we give this traffic of meaning is transposition.

Gee calls avatars in games "projective identity," or "double selves." A player's other-self appears in "dynamic images tied to perceptions of the world and of our own bodies, internal states, and feelings."[352] In our terms this might be phrased a transposition of role when the fictive other (an avatar) becomes an enacting self. And as the self is virtualized, another transposition, across meaningful time and place.

Players stay in the game because the conversation engages them, unlike the traditional texts of the scientific and cultural canon, and the texts of school. "Films, books, and music do not respond turn by turn to the viewer, reader, or listener and thereby co-shape an act of continuous meaning making. Viewers, readers, and listeners can respond in their minds – or to their friends – but their response cannot change the film, book, or music. Books, film, and music are not reciprocal or co-designed" in the way games are.[353] It's not that engagement can't happen in traditional media and schools. It's just that the dynamics of transposition are different.

In games, the conversation is with the (virtual) world, in a "turn-taking system." And "even many sorts of animals can engage in this turn-taking system": probe/world responds/reflect/probe again.[354] By this process, the game is open-ended, as its outcomes are determined in collaboration between the player and the game designer.[355] "[I]n a sense, [the players] design the game with the designers."[356]

Or, to reframe this in some of the other terms we have been developing in this grammar, enacting the transpositions of conditionality, the anxiety of possibility meets the requirements of the game to become assertable experience.[§MS2.3]

---

[351] James Paul Gee, 2003, *What Video Games Have to Teach Us About Learning and Literacy,* New York: Palgrave Macmillan, pp. 203–10.

[352] James Paul Gee, 2015, *Unified Discourse Analysis: Language, Virtual Worlds, and Video Games,* London: Routledge, pp. 176, 206, 25.

[353] Ibid., pp. 9–10.   [354] Ibid., pp. 10–11.

[355] McKenzie Wark, 2007, *Gamer Theory,* Cambridge, MA: Harvard University Press; Ian Bogost, 2006, *Unit Operations: An Approach to Videogame Criticism,* Cambridge, MA: MIT Press; Alexander R. Galloway, 2006, *Gaming: Essays on Algorithmic Culture,* Minneapolis: University of Minnesota Press.

[356] James Paul Gee, 2007, *Good Video Games + Good Learning: Collected Essays on Video Games, Learning and Literacy,* New York: Peter Lang, p. 173.

These are fluid relations, imminent (always about to move) and immanent (the one function meaningless without its impatient transposability into the others).

And the meaning of these meanings? "These pleasures are connected to control, agency, and meaningfulness," says Gee. "If the body feeds on food, the soul feeds on agency and meaningfulness."[357]

§1.4.4 Object

> **Object.** *A three-dimensional meaning, a tangible and perhaps manipulable thing, at times acting for itself or acting with persons.*

We place objects beside bodies in our "supermarket"[§MS0d] ordering of meanings because, although much of our experience of objects comfortably transposes more distantly to text, image, space, sound, and speech, there is also something immediate and viscerally embodied about encounters with objects. More than passive "things," objects can be burning/hot/tepid/cool/cold/freezing, hurting/pleasuring, stinging/itchy/tingling, vibrating/still, sharp/blunt, rough/smooth, soft/hard, light/heavy, movable/immovable, and many other such qualities for a grammar of lively objects. The reappearance of a familiar object is the renewal of its meaning in my life, always new to some degree no matter how minor that difference, if only in context. Such is the dynamic, never completely repeatable process of meaning-as-design.[§MS3.2]

Even the more distant transpositions will include anticipations of the possibility of visceral object–body experience – to see, for instance, something that could be felt as burn, or something that might be heard as hard. For that matter, other bodies may be experienced in part as objects, one of the many possible transpositions that constitute the meaning of persons. This may for instance be experienced as pleasure (sensuous physicality), or oppression (the alienating reifications of the factory[§1.4.3e] or sexism[§1.4.3d]).

Objects work as integral extensions of our body. A car is a spatio-temporal prosthesis; a smart phone is a cognitive and communicative prosthesis. Objects and bodies are more than a traffic of between-ness; they are layered in and with each other for our cyber-persons.[§1.4.3e]

Digital devices today are sensuously alert to our meanings. We participate in their meanings through their haptics[358] – vibrations, feelable buzzes, clicks, mouse-overs, swipes, touches, multifinger gestures, holds, pressable buttons, and such like. This is how objects act on their own immediate initiative, or act

---

[357] James Paul Gee, 2005, *Why Video Games Are Good for Your Soul: Pleasure and Learning*, Melbourne: Common Ground, p. 4.

[358] https://medium.com/iotforall/intro-to-haptic-technology-368340400375

in a chain of human–machine interactions. They are fused to our bodies in the meanings of our lives.

Far from passively inert, animated objects come to life for us. As much as persons, they are sites of agency.[§MS2.3.3] They prompt events (predication and transactivity);[§MS2.1] their roles can be swapped out, where a thing can represent self or other;[§MS2.2] and conditionally, they may assert (a definitive presence), require (the insistence of their presence and use), or offer possibility (any number of potential meanings and uses).[§MS2.3]

However, notwithstanding their close connections to our bodies, the meanings of objects are no more material than any other media – text and speech are equally material in their manifestation, though on the measure of the human sensorium,[§0.3] as different as two media can be. All media are in equal measure material, and objects as much as other media are open to the idealizations of the imagination.

As is the case for all media, the ideal of objects, our imagination of their potentialities and powers, can exceed the material.[§MS3.1] Meanings-in objects also manifest themselves in ways no different from other media, be that alike (a crucifix, for instance), directed (the blood and body of Christ in John Wyclif's eucharist[§1.1.2a]), or abstracted (a Catholic nun's ring, as a bride of the reincarnated Christ).[§1.1]

§1.4.4a George Lakoff and Mark Johnson's Metaphors We Live By

We have needed to do away with "language" for this multimodal grammar, because text and speech are so fundamentally different.[§MS0.2.7a] Now we are going to abandon another frequently used term to describe certain kinds of meaning, "metaphor."

"Meta-phor," to return to the word to its Greek etymology, is to "carry across." A boat can carry across, or a train, or a car. The word itself is a metaphor.[359] In our grammar we use the concept of transposition to account for the traffic across and between forms of meaning and the media in which they are made manifest. This idea addresses a much wider expanse of meaning than metaphor which, in a language-centered view of human meaning, is limited to the transportation of meaning from a thing, to a word or phrase, to a comparable thing.

In the way we have arrayed our forms of meaning, it is a relatively distant journey to text via image and to speech via sound. In their *Metaphors We Live By,*

---

[359] John Durham Peters, 2015, *The Marvelous Clouds: Toward a Philosophy of Elemental Media,* Chicago, IL: University of Chicago Press, p. 101; Zoltán Kövecses, 2002, *Metaphor: A Practical Introduction,* Oxford: Oxford University Press.

George Lakoff and Mark Johnson demonstrate the journey from figures of speech by way of metaphor to object, body, and space.[*]

Object–speech–object: We use "container metaphors" for situations, when for instance "in" or "out" of love or trouble. The mind or body might be considered a machine, where my thinking or running is considered to be "rusty" or "running out of steam."[360] We might "be in touch" with a person or understanding. We might "grasp" a concept, or it might be "out of reach."[361]

Body–speech–body: We might "give birth" to a new idea or "point to" the solution for a problem. Illness may be a metaphor, which directs us to the "pain" of experience.[362] Eating may be metaphorical: to be "hungry" for experience or "gluttonous" in one's excess.

Space–speech–body: Things are heading "up" or "down." Someone is "in the middle" of the action, or "left out." We "face the future," "move forward" with an agenda, and "look forward to an outcome."[363]

Metaphor may be by way of metonymy, where a word or phrase can make one thing stand for another non-congruent meaning – "I drank a bottle," says someone who is reluctant to speak more directly to their drinking or what they drank.[364] Or metaphor may be by way of synecdoche, where a part is called upon to mean for a whole – "I've got a new set of wheels," says someone who has just purchased a car.[365]

But this is more than a matter of words, spoken in these examples as figures of speech. As objects or pictures of them[§2a] the bottle or the wheels can mean this without the words. These are not merely incongruent uses of words; they are multimodal transpositions. Mindsight is transpositional.[§MS3.1.2b] Music is transpositional.[§1.4.2a] The body and blood of Jesus in the Christian eucharist is a multimodal transposition of one kind or another, depending on one's religious conviction.[§1.1.2a] None of these things is merely a metaphor in the sense of words that have incongruent meanings. They are multimodal practices of meaning.

---

[*] http://meaningpatterns.net/metaphors

[360] George Lakoff and Mark Johnson, 1980 [2003], *Metaphors We Live By*, Chicago, IL: University of Chicago Press, pp. 29, 59, 27.

[361] Mark Johnson, 2007, *The Meaning of the Body: Aesthetics of Human Understanding*, Chicago, IL: University of Chicago Press, pp. 20, 66.

[362] Susan Sontag, 1977, *Illness as Metaphor*, New York: Farrar, Straus and Giroux; Susan Sontag, 2003, *Regarding the Pain of Others*, London: Hamish Hamilton.

[363] George Lakoff and Mark Johnson, 1980 [2003], *Metaphors We Live By*, Chicago, IL: University of Chicago Press, pp. 24, 43.

[364] Umberto Eco, 1984, *Semiotics and the Philosophy of Language*, Bloomington: Indiana University Press, p. 114.

[365] George Lakoff and Mark Johnson, 1980 [2003], *Metaphors We Live By*, Chicago, IL: University of Chicago Press, p. 36.

If the idea of metaphor indicates a certain kind of non-literal similarity or symbolic association, we want to say that this is true of all meaning transpositions. Meanings are always the same and forever different, both in transposition and by design.[§MS0.4.1] There is never such a thing as a straightforwardly congruent meaning. And perhaps, as Umberto Eco says, language is itself metaphorical.[366]

As an antonym for metaphor, "literal" is indeed a strange idea, to assume that some meanings can be more congruent than others. Besides, where does metaphor stop and congruence begin? "To stop" might be considered a transposition from space and body to other kinds of experience.[367] But without conscious association in the act of meaning, "stop" has become a new congruence. Or one participant in meaning might make the metaphorical connection, and another not.

For these reasons, congruence is not a practicable concept, as if it can simply be applied to a figure of speech or its multimodal proxy. There is no such thing as literal simply to be contrasted with metaphorical. Metaphors are mappings between domains, says Peter Gärdenfors,[368] or in our terminology, multimodal transpositions, resonances across the forms of meaning.

Sometimes, to complicate matters further, these transpositions may involve certain kinds of meaningful displacement – meaning as pointed absence, as avoidance, as concealment of interest, as dissembling, as obfuscation, as hypocrisy.[§2] An error may be said to be a crime, or a crime an error.[369] The transpositions may selectively illuminate in order to hide.

These processes of transposition are, moreover, in our very natures. They are in the ontogenesis of every infant as a human meaning-maker. This is how, to use Daniel Stern's words, "infants bring together separate sounds, movements, touches, sights and feelings," developing a "sense of self that is a single, distinct, integrated body; an agent of actions, experiencer of feelings, maker of intentions, architect of plans, the transposer of experience into language, the communicator or sharer of personal knowledge." So, even before learning to speak, an infant has developed "senses of the self ... in preverbal forms of agency, physical cohesion, continuity in time, having intentions in mind."[370]

In these ways, multimodal transposition figures objects, bodies, spaces, images, and sounds as prostheses for our thinking, prior to the acquisition of

---

[366] Umberto Eco, 1984, *Semiotics and the Philosophy of Language*, Bloomington: Indiana University Press, p. 88.

[367] Ibid., p. 115.

[368] Peter Gärdenfors, 2014, *Geometry of Meaning: Semantics Based on Conceptual Spaces*, Cambridge, MA: MIT Press, p. 40.

[369] Umberto Eco, 1984, *Semiotics and the Philosophy of Language*, Bloomington: Indiana University Press, p. 103.

[370] Daniel L. Stern, 1985, *The Interpersonal World of the Infant: A View from Psychoanalysis and Developmental Psychology*, New York: Basic Books, pp. 3–6.

speech, and later still in the life of a child, in writing. Text and speech merely extend this process, without changing its basis.

§1.4.4b Karen Barad's Meeting the Universe Halfway

In Niels Bohr's model of elementary particles, says Karen Barad,[*] the atom is a tiny solar system where electrons take "quantum leaps" from one orbit to another, in this way changing state.[371] Bohr won the Nobel Prize for physics for this discovery in 1922. A Dane and a Jew, when the Nazis invaded he fled Denmark for England and the United States to help with the development of the atomic bomb, returning to Denmark after the war.

In quantum theory and experimental practice, elementary objects such as the photons are conceived at the same time as particles and waves. As a wave, the frequency of a photon is its color.[§MS1.3.1c] That objects such as photons can be seen alternately as one kind of entity, then the other, he said was a figment of instrumentation. But both aspects of the phenomenon of light can't be seen at the same time. To this extent, reality is a figment of seeing, in this case the different kinds of apparatus instrumenting different kinds of insight. There is an inseparable relation between "observed object" and "agencies of observation."[372] Also entanglement: one object in one place can be meaningfully and simultaneously connected with another somewhere else. Einstein[§1.3.1a] was not prepared to accept such indeterminacies, nor to conceive of relationships exceeding the limits of the speed of light.[373]

Not only true for the commonsensically weird universe of elementary particles and fundamental waves, "quantum mechanics," says Karen Barad, "is the correct theory of nature on all scales." And the correct theory of human agency in nature. Intentionality is "a complex network of human and non-human agents ... an entangled state of agencies. ... [P]henomena are the ontological inseparability of agentially-interacting components; ... distinct agencies do not precede, but rather emerge through, their intra-action." This accounts for "the world's radical aliveness," on every scale.[374]

This, Barad explains, is the basis for her "agential realist ontology, or what one might call a 'quantum ontology,' based on the existence of phenomena

---

[*] http://meaningpatterns.net/barad

[371] Karen Barad, 2007, *Meeting the Universe Halfway: Quantum Physics and the Entanglement of Matter and Meaning*, Durham, NC: Duke University Press, p. 162.

[372] Karen Barad, 2003, "Posthumanist Performativity: Toward an Understanding of How Matter Comes to Matter," *Signs: Journal of Women in Culture and Society* 28(3):801–31, p. 814.

[373] Karen Barad, 2007, *Meeting the Universe Halfway: Quantum Physics and the Entanglement of Matter and Meaning*, Durham, NC: Duke University Press, pp. 19–20, 82–83, 106–07, 120–21, 173–74.

[374] Ibid., pp. 85, 2e, 33.

rather than of independently existing things, ... performatively materializing entanglements of spacetimemattering."[375] She says, "[o]n my agential realist elaboration, phenomena do not merely mark the epistemological inseparability of 'observer' and 'observed'; rather, phenomena are the ontological insepar-ability of agentially intra-acting 'components.'"[376]

Barad calls her theory "posthumanist performativity." Of performativity, she says this is a necessary antidote to contemporary theories of knowing because "[l]anguage has been granted too much power." Performativity is something that happens in non-human matter and human bodies. It is an account of entities in relation to their actions, where it would be a conceit to privilege the human.[377]

However, perplexingly she also says hers is an account of "discursive practices," to pick up on Derrida, Foucault, and Judith Butler.[378] It's not clear how discursive practices can affect the meaning of atoms any more than, through instrumentation, seeing them as images or feeling them as objects. In much social theory, and here also in physics, it still seems hard to get away from privileging language (Derrida's "text"[§MS2.3.1b]); discourse (Foucault's "discur-sive practice"[§2.5a]); or performative speech (Austin's speech acts[§MS2.3.1a]), no matter how deep its acknowledged inveiglement with objects or bodies.

In a transpositional grammar, we can encompass both text and speech by addressing a wider range of forms of meaning, accounting for shared meaning functions as well as affordances peculiar to the characteristic media of each form. But none is privileged. This is why the proper frame for a theory of meaning, as Barad also so rightly says, is ontology rather than language.

This also means that we don't need to "meet the universe halfway," as if there were two places from which to depart. Humans are in the design of natural history. We are the universe, for our self-importance at the same time as our insignificance.

In this respect, "posthuman" and "posthumanism" may be a false modesty, a symptom of our need to recover from the horrors of "Enlightenment."[379] To mean is eminently human (and animal-like, and natural). Meaning is a matter of participation[§1.2] in the world, where humans recognize that meaning is not just

[375] Karen Barad, 2012, "Nature's Queer Performativity," *Kvinder, Køn og forskning/Women, Gender and Research* 12(1–2):25–53, p. 45.

[376] Karen Barad, 2003, "Posthumanist Performativity: Toward an Understanding of How Matter Comes to Matter," *Signs: Journal of Women in Culture and Society* 28(3):801–31, p. 815.

[377] Ibid., p. 810, 810.

[378] Karen Barad, 2007, *Meeting the Universe Halfway: Quantum Physics and the Entanglement of Matter and Meaning*, Durham, NC: Duke University Press, pp. 34, 45, 62–65, 88, 133, 135, 140, 145–48, 151–52.

[379] Theodor W. Adorno and Max Horkheimer, 1944 [2002], *Dialectic of Enlightenment*, translated by E. Jephcott, Stanford, CA: Stanford University Press.

in themselves (their minds, or somewhat less reductively, their bodies) but in their situation in the world, including the universe itself, and its independently natural history. This is just human, which is just natural.

Earlier, we ventured to suggest that this might be a quantum grammar.[§MS1.2.2b] What we learn from Barad is that quantum mechanics is no mere metaphor for the world. It is all of the world as intra-action of dynamic objects where nature and humans, even if they could be separated, are equally agentive. Matter and meaning are indeed entangled, and this is not merely discursive. It is meaning in matter, or ontology.

So, for this grammar, each function is like an observational apparatus, a moment to stop and to see a meaning one way rather than another, each time making quantum leaps across and between reference, or agency, or structure, or context, or interest. Paradoxically, stopping to look closely is not to freeze-frame. It is how we can trace and anticipate meanings manifest in what Barad calls "lively potentiality."[380]

§1.4.5 Space

> **Space.** Three-dimensional meanings, arrangements between objects and bodies, and the movement or flow of objects and bodies.

Space is that which is found between objects and the relations established by their placement. Objects can enclose spaces, and spaces can be defined by objects. In an architectural space, a wall and a window are objects, in the grammar of space creating different kinds of separation between the inside and the outside.

Traversing different scales, the sciences and professions of space include physics, kinesthetics-proxemics, architecture,[§1.4.5b] geography, and astronomy. All are concerned with the key dimensions of spatiality: presence/absence, placement, orientation, verticality/horizontality/depth, distance, speed, and trajectory.

Though every one of these sciences is also concerned with objects, their greater interest is space and the flow of objects or bodies across space. Bodies have a specialized grammar of spatiality:[§1.4.5a] proxemics or the spacing of bodies, itself often a rationale for or an effect of an architectonic program; and kinesthetics, or the flow of bodies in space, the experience of bodily motion.

---

[380] Karen Barad, 2007, *Meeting the Universe Halfway: Quantum Physics and the Entanglement of Matter and Meaning*, Durham, NC: Duke University Press, p. 92.

§1.4.5a *Erving Goffman's* Presentation of Self in Everyday Life

Erving Goffman, son of a Ukrainian-Canadian Jewish shopkeeper who escaped a pogrom by the Russian army, in his scholarly analyses retained a shopkeeper's instinct for ordinary things.[381] A shop is a "frame" for performance: an inside for selling and an outside for things that have been sold, with "front spaces" for display and "back spaces" for warehousing, and then all the selective revelations and concealments that are the performative tricks and tropes of retail.[§2.3f]

In his parsing of the theater of everyday life, Goffman was less interested in the messages given in speech than the impressions "given off" in the configuration of persons in space.[*] Meaning in this latter sense was a "dramaturgical problem," a matter of "stage-craft and stage management." In the performance, "interaction constraints . . . play upon the individual and transform his activities into performances."[382]

In an architectonic sense, front spaces and back spaces might be the restaurant/kitchen, reception/office, shop/storeroom, living room/bedroom, or stage/backstage.[383] In image, a rough parallel might be figure/ground; in speech, theme/rheme.[§MS2.1.1] Then, there is the outside, or that which is on the other side of a borderline, though juxtaposed meaningfully because it is a space of already-having-been performed or ready-to-be performed by way of anticipation or expectation.

Frames are distinctive patterns of spatialized social performance: seller/buyer (market frame); performer/audience (theatrical frame); teacher/student (educational frame); doctor/patient (medical frame).[384] Frames, Goffman says, are "definitions of situation . . . built up in accordance with principles of organization which govern events . . . and our subjective involvement in them."[385]

Frames are repeated by design,[§MS0.4.1] but also by design they are never (quite) the same. Frames are designed into spaces in a premediated way by architects, town planners, and other social designers. They become a semi-

---

* http://meaningpatterns.net/goffman

[381] Gary Alan Fine and Philip Manning, 2000, "Erving Goffman," pp. 457–85 in *The Blackwell Companion to Major Contemporary Social Theorists*, edited by G. Ritzer, Oxford: Blackwell.

[382] Erving Goffman, 1959, *The Presentation of Self in Everyday Life*, New York: Doubleday Anchor, pp. 2, 15, 65; Dean MacCannell, 2000, "Erving Goffman (1922–1982)," pp. 8–36 in *Sage Masters of Modern Social Thought: Erving Goffman*, edited by G.A. Fine and G.W.H. Smith, London: Sage.

[383] Erving Goffman, 1959, *The Presentation of Self in Everyday Life*, New York: Doubleday Anchor, pp. 106ff.

[384] Daniel Miller, 2010, *Stuff*, Cambridge: Polity, p. 49.

[385] Erving Goffman, 1974, *Frame Analysis: An Essay on the Organization of Experience*, Cambridge, MA: Harvard University Press, pp. 10–11.

conscious medium for our meaning in the habituated materiality of spaces. Frames can also be "keyed"[386] – this is a function for space akin to quoting in text. Hence: dramatic scripts, rehearsals, simulations, or training practice. They can indicate a certain kind of meaningful absence of frame, for instance, the "civil inattention" that is anonymity in a crowd.

Nor are the meanings necessarily congruent. In the creation of impressions, they entail certain kinds of concealment, obfuscation or deception in selectivity: decorum, politeness, or social front; or fabrication and duping. If to tell a lie in speech is deceit, to feign is a spatial lie. Or hypocrisy: certain things being said, while other things are being "given off" by the situation. Or self-delusion: to believe the lie.

The "information game," says Goffman, is "a potentially infinite cycle of concealment, discovery, false revelation, and rediscovery." Though the cycle does not necessarily reach rediscovery, for as he says wryly, "he who would combat false consciousness and awaken people to their true interests has much to do, because the sleep is very deep."[387]

If Wittgenstein's focus was on "language games,"[§MS2.3.2a] Goffman's was not the script, but the stage setting and action for such games in the drama of everyday life. An inveterate gamer himself, in his spare time Goffman worked as blackjack dealer at the Station Plaza Casino in Las Vegas. There, this aficionado of everyday spatial configurations was promoted to a pit boss, dedicated to managing the relationship between front and back spaces of the gaming floor, where the name of the game was to align the hopes for good fortune of players with the guaranteed fortune of the casino proprietor, whose interest it is to have their patrons, on average, lose.[388]

§1.4.5b *Denise Scott-Brown and Robert Venturi's* Learning from Las Vegas

If proxemics/kinesethetics[§1.4.5a] addresses at a micro level the relations of bodies in space, architecture addresses in a more expansive way the home that humans make for themselves in the built environment.

Here are four architectural practitioner-theorists. Christopher Alexander was born in Vienna, and his family fled the Nazis for England and then the United States. Alexander created the idea of a "pattern language" that would account for meaning in the constructed environment. Charles-Édouard Jeanneret, better known by his professional name, Le Corbusier, was a French-Swiss architect,

---

[386] Ibid., p. 44, 58–62.

[387] Ibid., pp. 83, 70–71, 14; Erving Goffman, 1959, *The Presentation of Self in Everyday Life*, New York: Doubleday Anchor, pp. 107, 29, 43–46, 2, 8.

[388] Gary Alan Fine and Philip Manning, 2000, "Erving Goffman," pp. 457–85 in *The Blackwell Companion to Major Contemporary Social Theorists*, edited by G. Ritzer, Oxford: Blackwell, p. 459.

doyen of modernism. Denise Scott-Brown, born in South Africa to Jewish parents, and Robert Venturi, a child of Italian-American Philadelphia, were to become doyens of postmodernism.[*]

We'll start with Alexander's idea of pattern, then look at two canonical patterns, modernism and postmodernism, each in its particular way configuring our meanings in the spaces of modernity. A "pattern language," says Alexander, "gives each person who uses it the power to create an infinite variety of new and unique buildings, just as his ordinary language gives him the power to create an infinite variety of sentences."[389] Constructing the environment is based on a program, a word commonly used in architecture, which we would rephrase as the attempt to realize interest[§2] scenarios in building. Hence: houses, schools, parks; these are different kinds of building serving different kinds of interest.

Alexander and his co-workers offer 253 patterns, each finely parsed: neighborhoods with "28. Eccentric Nucleus," "29. Density Rings," and "30. Activity Nodes"; path networks including "49. Looped Local Roads," "55. Raised Walks," and "56. Bike Paths"; buildings including "76. Houses for a Small Family," "85. Schools," and "87. Shops"; rooms including "139. Kitchens," "143. Bedrooms," and "145. Bathrooms"; then spaces that "fine tune" rooms, "192. Windows Overlooking Life," "198. Closets," and "200. Open Shelves," and, now nearing the end of the taxonomy, "249. Ornament," "251. Chairs," and finally, 1165 pages after this exhaustive journey began, "253, Things from Your Life" – an awkwardly classified, omnibus other, the realm of "décor" or "interior design" which may in a house be subclassified as the placement of objects and pictures in "collections, family remembrances, and old adventures."[390]

No pattern, says Alexander, "is an isolated entity. Each pattern can exist in the world only to the extent that it is supported by other patterns . . . [W]hen you build a thing you cannot merely build that thing in isolation, but must also repair the world around it."[391] With this, Alexander promises "a timeless way of building," though as we read his books, it is hard to escape the sense that his patterns refer more to a suburban modernity with its cars and parks, than a petrochemical plant, or a railway yard, or an office-ridden city, or the sacred sense of place held by the Guugu Yimithirr in their country.[§1.3.2c]

Nevertheless, the idea of a pattern language fits nicely with our notion of multimodality, transposing as it does meanings between text and space. This is our project too, writing this text, although the scope of our transposition is

---

[*] http://meaningpatterns.net/architecture

[389] Christopher Alexander, 1979, *The Timeless Way of Building*, New York: Oxford University Press, p. xi.

[390] Christopher Alexander, Sara Ishikawa, and Murray Silverstein, 1977, *A Pattern Language: Towns, Buildings, Construction*, New York: Oxford University Press.

[391] Ibid., p. xiii.

wider, from text to all other modes, and to trace patterns in the meanings of meanings.

Alexander's "pattern language" served as inspiration for Ward Cunningham, inventor of the wiki. He received a copy of Alexander's *Timeless Way of Building*. Moved by this idea, in 1995 he created a program in both the architectural and a software sense. The wiki is a patterned textual space where people share the writing of text, their own texts, different texts. As medium, the wiki is not unlike the general patterning of houses, where notwithstanding the generalizable pattern, people in particular houses could live their lives in different ways. Waiting for a shuttle bus in Hawai'i, he lighted upon the name. The bus was called the WikiWiki, in the indigenous language of Hawai'i, the word for "quick."[392]

Our next architect: Le Corbusier's modernist building projects ranged from the Soviet Union in the 1920s and 1930s, to the United Nations building in New York at the end of the 1940s, to the design and the principal public buildings of Chandigarh, capital city of the Indian states of Haryana and Punjab, constructed in the 1950s.[393] "Architecture or Revolution!" he promised, advocating an emphatic pattern language for modernity. "The incredible industrial activity of today ... puts before our eyes every hour, either directly or through newspapers and magazines, objects of arresting novelty whose whys and wherefores interest, delight and disconcert us ... If we set ourselves against the past, we see that new formulas have been found that only need to be exploited and that, if we can break with routine, will bring real liberation from the constraints hitherto endured."[394]

Hence, some maxims for modernism. "Form follows function" (after Adolf Loos).[§MS2.1.1b] "Less is more" (after Ludwig Mies van der Rohe). So, said Le Corbusier, "The house is a machine for living in."[395] In his book, *Toward an Architecture*, he celebrated the utilitarian aesthetics of factories, grain elevators, airplanes, and automobiles. His houses were straight-lined and white. He said the claustrophobic city of slums of old Paris should be torn down, and replaced with towers in parks – a formula that was to be repeated in the socialist east[§2.3d] and the capitalist west. The program was not the solution because poverty was still poverty, and the towers became the new slums.

---

[392] http://c2.com/doc/etymology.html

[393] Jean-Louis Cohen and Tim Benton, 2014, *Le Corbusier Le Grand*, New York: Phaidon.

[394] Le Corbusier, 1928 [2007], *Toward an Architecture*, translated by J. Goodman, Los Angeles: Getty Publications, pp. 297, 304.

[395] Ibid., p. 87.

"Less is a bore," was the retort from Denise Scott-Brown and Robert Venturi. In 1968 they took the students in their Yale University architecture studio to Las Vegas, where more was never enough. Together, they parsed "the Strip," the focal axis in a cityscape of excess. "Learning from the existing landscape is a way of being revolutionary for an architect. Not in the obvious way, which is to tear down Paris and begin again, as Le Corbusier suggested in the 1920s, but another, more tolerant way; that is, to question the way we look at things."[396]

Tolerant, in the case of the Las Vegas Strip, meant reconciling oneself to the screaming commercialism of signs, the huge parking lots behind the signs, and beyond the cars, barely visible from the street, the "decorated sheds" that were the casinos or the shops. This is representative of the now-ubiquitous strip mall architecture. This was also to be eviscerated, as it transpires, by another kind of modernism, the modernism of the shopping mall.[§2.3c]

"The emerging Strip is a complex order. It is not the easy, rigid order of the urban renewal project or the fashionable 'total design' of the megastructure," say Scott-Brown and Venturi. So, they celebrated the "honky tonk improvisations" and things that might be regarded as "commercial vulgarities – Las Vegas's values are not questioned here."[397] Signs and ornament – these were to become two defining motifs of postmodernism, in social theory[398] as well as architecture.[399]

"I like boring things"[400] – Scott-Brown and Venturi quote Andy Wahol, and so do we.[§MS0a] But we know they didn't like what they found to be boring about modernism.

And another boring thing for Denise Scott-Brown. Venturi was named winner of the 1991 Pritzker Prize, the equivalent of a Nobel Prize in architecture, but not Scott-Brown. "Room at the Top?" she asked in a celebrated article, "Sexism and the Star System in Architecture."[401] To no avail, people petitioned Pritzker. "20,000 people wrote from all over the world," she said in an interview, "and every one of them called me Denise."[402]

[396] Robert Venturi, Denise Scott Brown, and Steven Izenour, 1977, *Learning from Las Vegas: The Forgotten Symbolism of Architectural Form*, Cambridge, MA: MIT Press, p. 3.

[397] Ibid., pp. 87, 52, 72, 6.

[398] Hal Foster, ed. 1983, *Postmodern Culture*, London: Pluto Press; Jean-François Lyotard, 1979, *The Postmodern Condition: A Report on Knowledge*, Manchester: Manchester University Press.

[399] Fredric Jameson, 1991, *Postmodernism, or, the Cultural Logic of Late Capitalism*, Durham, NC: Duke University Press; Heinrich Klotz, 1984 [1988], *The History of Postmodern Architecture*, Cambridge, MA: MIT Press.

[400] Robert Venturi, Denise Scott Brown, and Steven Izenour, 1977, *Learning from Las Vegas: The Forgotten Symbolism of Architectural Form*, Cambridge, MA: MIT Press, p. 87.

[401] Denise Scott-Brown, 1989 [2015], "Room at the Top? Sexism and the Star System in Architecture," *MAS Context* 27:25–39.

[402] www.architectsjournal.co.uk/news/denise-scott-brown-recognised-with-2017-jane-drew-priz e/10017080.article

§1.4.6 Image

> **Image.** *Bodies, objects, and spaces rendered onto a two-dimensional plane.*

By transposition – in fact much of the time by means of *trompe d'oeuil* and clever illusion[§MS2.2c] – three-dimensional spaces, objects, and bodies can be represented in two-dimensional digital image.

There are the enormous differences between speech and text, the one prioritizing time (the ineluctable linear temporality of sounded words), the other space (the two-dimensional array of textual and picture elements).[§MS1.2.2e] Image is action stilled in entities; speech is a sequenced narrative of action. Cinema and video bring image and speech together, entities and actions.

Text relies on image. Indeed, some of its meaning is purely visual – those parts not representable in Unicode (our definition of text[§1.4.7]), the spaces and lines around and between text. Text is an inevitably multimodal amalgam with image, even if some theorists might like to have thought that language was a discrete and unified speech–text system. It is neither.

Meaning-makers strategically bring together text and image in the visual design of text. In white space, paragraphing, tables, or mathematical notation the meaning is not (just) in the text – the concatenation of Unicode graphemes – but in the spatial composition of the page. These spatial aspects of text are for most practical purposes unspeakable, or at least with the conciseness and clarity of the multimodal text–image alliance.

Speech is by contrast temporal and thus linear, and relentlessly so in a way that text, for its alliance with image, is not. Spoken word must follow spoken word. Noam Chomsky[§MS3.1.2f] uncovers meaning structures underlying speech which are necessarily non-linear, because the representable world is not always linear and straightforwardly sequential. His grammar points to the convolutions that we need to endure to turn recursive meanings into speech, and the affordances of speech as constraint.

By dint of its medium we have to speak in a linear way, but our meanings are non-linear. To make our meanings in speech, we must struggle with its affordances as a medium, as a material practice constrained by time.

With its orientation to space and the multilinear materiality of its practice, text can render meanings of far more elaborated complexity than any of Chomsky's sentence-level tree diagrams. The spatiality of the text can be as complex as the spatiality of the world – hence, science, math, social theory, and the other insights of the modern textual universe. First Peoples also needed text-image to supplement speech in their equally complex and profound cosmologies.

As for the supposed cognitive superiority of language afforded by recursion (Chomsky's "Merge"[§MS3.1.2j]), in debate with Fitch, Hauser, and Chomsky,

Jackendoff and Pinker point out that recursion happens in imaging too. There it is "a domain of 'discrete infinity' in visual perception, with hierarchical structure of unlimited depth, its organization in this case governed by gestalt principles," or seeing things as wholes.[403]

In other words, things are nested within things in the visual world, and we can see these nestings in different ways and levels depending, in any moment, on our attentional interests. This happens for other animals as much as for humans, as they go about their daily spatio-temporal and social existences. Among the sentient creatures of the earth, visual meaning and its correlates in embodied sensation are near universal, deeply embedded in what Bernard Crick then Christof Koch call the "neurological correlates of consciousness."[404] And another argument against language as a defining feature of our humanity: in the life of a child, visual perception comes before speech.

Even when it comes, speech is never enough. Sometimes we humans may choose to use image allied with text to represent recursion (diagram, table, mathematical notation, or computer code – all of which are practically unspeakable), because such image–text hybrids can represent recursion more easily and effectively than speech. It's a nice irony that Chomsky himself had to use image in the form of tree diagrams and quasi-mathematical visually/spatially arranged notation to re-represent underlying meanings that were difficult to see in speech itself, given its affordances as a medium.[§MS3.1.2f]

§1.4.6a Newman's Indian Bradshaw

George Bradshaw, English Quaker, cartographer and printer, published the first railway timetable in 1839.[405] Thenceforth, railway timetables in England came to be called "Bradshaws," and in India too, where modernity was forced to follow the colonial template.[*]

January 30, 1981. We want to travel (let's say), from Bakhtiyarpur to Patna, and we have in our hand the December 1980 edition of Newman's *Indian Bradshaw*. These stations are on the main line from Howrah to Mughal Saria. Many of the express trains have started their journey at Howrah station in Calcutta, including our train, Number 167 Up, T-W Bombay Janata Express. "Up" means in the direction of Delhi, nodal center of Indian Railways. "Janata"

---

[*] http://meaningpatterns.net/tables

[403] Ray Jackendoff and Steven Pinker, 2005, "The Nature of the Language Faculty and Its Implications for Evolution of Language (Reply to Fitch, Hauser, and Chomsky)," *Cognition* 97(2):211–25, p. 217.

[404] Christof Koch, 2004, *The Quest for Consciousness: A Neurobiological Approach*, Engelwood, CO: Roberts and Company.

[405] Percy Fitzgerald, 1890, *The Story of "Bradshaw's Guide,"* London: The Leadenhall Press.

is Hindi for "people's," and the train is 2nd Class only, though of course, this being India, there are many classes within 2nd Class (two-tier sleeper, three-tier sleeper, hard, soft). The train departs Mondays, Wednesdays, and Fridays, leaving Bakhtiyarpur Junction at 21.35, arriving Patna Junction at 23.10.

Newman's *Indian Bradshaw* lays out in the tabular form of a railway time-table an infinite number of possibilities for travel and several millions of assertable actualities[§MS2.3] for the travelers on this day in 1981. And a require-ment: be there then, or you will miss the train. It's all text (numbers, letters, and a fine array of different kinds of asterisk), but the complex requirements, actualities, possibilities of meaning are visual, in two-dimensional, tabular array. The table represents the essential torsion of event:[§MS2.1] entities (bodies and places) and action (moving trains moving bodies). And positions:[§1.3] place named and ordered by location along a line; times by number according to the speed of the train. And pointed absences:[§MS1.1.2] the " . . . " ellipses to indicate that the train will not stop at stations so marked in the grid.

In the configuration of a table, columns and rows might represent relations between concepts (field names), and the content in the cells are instances (data). Or they may represent relations between instances or concepts in the rows or columns and their calculable quantities or namable qualities in the cells. And for that matter, the data in the cells may be repeating, and so a concept. When we arrive in Patna at 23.10 on that day in January 1981, this is a singular instance of arrival, the kind that someone planning to meet us would want to know. We might have sent ahead an itinerary, or recorded this after the event in a travel diary.

But timetables are about many such arrivals, in both possibility and actuality. In the always-transposability of instances with concepts, what might be an instance in our traveling becomes a concept in the timetable. The number in the cell of the table is about many arrivals on Mondays, Wednesdays, and Fridays; the train runs three times per week, although Patna is clearly instantiated.

And, if these transpositions are not complicated enough, tables are linked to tables – you need to go to another table to see a journey to Bombay, or to change trains at a junction. The whole Bradshaw, hundreds of pages of it, is an integrated mesh of tables connected to each other, concepts awaiting our instantiation. The visual frame of the timetable represents dynamic meaning as movement across place in time, always repeatable and never the same.

When Alan Turing started to consider the computability of numbers,[§MS1.3.2b] he conceived a machine whose memory and thinking was recorded on a paper tape. Like writing when materialized in medium, by affordance the tape was inevitably linear, one instruction laboriously executed after another. Though like both writing and Chomsky's grammar, in the struggle to overcome linear-ity, later instructions could refer back to earlier ones.

In 1970, E.F. Codd, an English computer scientist working in the US at IBM, brought computing back to the visual design of a table. He developed what came to be called the "relational model" of data. Data was arrayed in tables with columns and rows. Each contained an atomic value (datum). Tables were accessible by table name and could connect with each other. Codd had extended the written lines of programming with the two-dimensional relationality of tables.[406]

The only difference between this and our Bradshaw was this: if this was a computerized timetable and our train was running ten minutes late, the arrival time at subsequent stations could be updated. With relations expressed in algorithms, relevant atomic values could be recalculated by the machine. To Codd's dismay, his employer did not understand the significance of his invention. But a company called Oracle did, and today most of the world's data is stored in relational databases.

The thinking and culture of computable visual-textual array first reached the consciousness of the masses with VisiCalc. This was the first spreadsheet, created by Dan Bricklin and Bob Frankston and released in 1979. Like Noam Chomsky, Bricklin was a son of Jewish Philadelphia. Frankston was Brooklyn-born. After completing an engineering degree at MIT, Bricklin enrolled in an MBA at Harvard Business School. There, legend has it, he saw a professor calculating business variables on the blackboard, erasing and revising columns or rows. This inspired him to invent the now-ubiquitous spreadsheet.

In the *Whole Earth Software Catalog,* computing luminary Ted Nelson waxed lyrical. VisiCalc, he said, "represented a new idea of a way to use a computer and a new way of thinking about the world. Where conventional programming was thought of as a sequence of steps, this new thing was no longer sequential in effect: When you made a change in one place, all other things changed instantly and automatically."[407] In truth, this was to repeat in more accessible visual form the underlying logic of the relational database, or, to track back further, to automate the Bradshaw with dynamically re-renderable text.

Notwithstanding his Harvard Business degree, Bricklin was unable to become rich from his invention, not in the way that Microsoft would subsequently make Bill Gates rich with Multiplan of 1982, renamed Excel in 1985.[408]

In 2014, Reddit and then other social media sprang aflame with an Excel spreadsheet created by a husband and emailed to a wife documenting rejections of his sexual advances over the previous seven weeks. This was a transposition

[406] E.F. Codd, 1970, "Relational Model of Data for Large Shared Data Banks," *Communications of the ACM* 13(6):377–87; Bill Cope, Mary Kalantzis, and Liam Magee, 2011, *Towards a Semantic Web: Connecting Knowledge in Academic Research*, Cambridge: Elsevier, p. 217.

[407] Stewart Brand, ed. 1986, *The Whole Earth Software Catalog*, Garden City, NY: Quantum Press, p. 66.

[408] Burton Grad, 2007, "The Creation and the Demise of Visicalc," *IEEE Annals of the History of Computing* 29(3):20–31.

into the now-ubiquitous tabular format that the thousands of commenters said was clumsy, awful, and much more.[409]

§1.4.6b W.E.B. Du Bois' Exhibit of American Negroes

Microsoft Excel[§1.4.6a] will turn any table into a visualization. Number and labels that have been arrayed across the two dimensions of a table can be transformed by the software into column charts, line charts, pie charts, and any number of other images for the purposes of reconceptualization.

Civil rights leader, scholar, and polymath W.E.B Du Bois[§1.4.3c] made himself a master, not only of sociological data, but its visualization.[*] The first African-American to earn a doctorate, he was appointed professor of Sociology at Atlanta University in 1897. In this same year, he published in *The Atlantic* his first general appeal, "The Strivings of Negro People." Connecting his singular person with the many African-Americans, he spoke to his own experience of being marked "black" in a world bifurcated by the racism of "white."

Not color, the roots of the division were "slavery . . ., the sum of all villainies, the cause of all sorrow, the root of all prejudice." Not color, but "being a problem is a strange experience, – peculiar even for one who has never been anything else . . . like, mayhap, in heart and life and longing, but shut out from their world by a vast veil."

Racism created for Du Bois, sociologist and activist, "a peculiar sensation, this double-consciousness, this sense of always looking at one's self through the eyes of others, of measuring one's soul by the tape of a world that looks on in amused contempt and pity. One feels his two-ness, – an American, a Negro; two souls, two thoughts, two unreconciled strivings; two warring ideals in one dark body, whose dogged strength alone keeps it from being torn asunder."[410]

In 1900, du Bois was invited to design and present his *Exhibit of American Negroes* in the Pavilion of Social Economy at the Universal Exposition in Paris. For this, he created a beautiful series of tableaux of a kind that might today be called infographics, transposing the data that he had captured in tabular form in his sociological research,[411] into visual form.

Here, the reality of Negro life was complicated by all manner of lines, and not just the "color line." In accompanying photographs, the exhibition depicted African-Americans in the multidimensionality of their strivings. In a

---

[*] http://meaningpatterns.net/dubois

[409] https://theconcourse.deadspin.com/pouty-husband-sends-wife-spreadsheet-detailing-sex-life-1607350830/+tcberman

[410] W.E.B. Du Bois, 1897, "Strivings of the Negro People," *The Atlantic* (August).

[411] W.E.B. Du Bois, 1906, *The Health and Physique of the Negro American: Report of a Social Study Made under the Direction of Atlanta University*, Atlanta, GA: Atlanta University Press.

connection that could not be accidental for someone so knowledgeable about imaging, Du Bois had his picture taken by Paul Nadar, son of one of the greats of photography, Félix Nadar. The father was still alive and working with his son in their Paris studio.[§MS2.2.2c]

"I have stepped within the Veil," said Du Bois three years later in his *Souls of Black People,* "raising it that you may view faintly its deeper recesses," and so revealing "the strange meaning of being black here at the dawning of the Twentieth Century."[412] Strange meant more complicated than a single dividing line, and this is what he showed visually in the tableaux he had made for the Universal Exposition.

§1.4.6c Digital Images and "Artificial Intelligence"

Charge Coupled Devices (CCD sensors), and now more commonly, Complementary Metal Oxide Semiconductors (CMOS sensors) capture light across a framed lattice of pixels, registering color and luminosity.[§MS1.2.2e] As two-dimensional arrays, digital photographs are another variation of the ubiquitously modern, two-dimensional table or spreadsheet.[§1.4.6a]

New Yorker George E. Smith and Canadian Willard Boyle invented the CCD image sensor in AT&T Bell Labs in 1969,[413] winning the Nobel Prize in Physics for their achievement in 2009. Smith's doctoral thesis was awarded by the University of Chicago on the surface characteristics of the element bismuth. He was a man of few words but dense algorithms: it was just eight pages long.[414]

Using a CCD censor, the first digital photograph was taken in December 1975 by Steven Sasson,[*] with a makeshift camera he had created while working in the Eastman Kodak labs.[415] The failure of the Kodak company to recognize the significance of this invention became the failure of this image manufacturing giant, which after a long and painful decline fell into bankruptcy in 2012. The first commercially released digital camera was the Fuji DS-1P of 1988.[416]

Digital cameras have developed over the decades, not because there has been any change in the principles of digital image capture since 1969, but as a consequence of increases in the sheer recording and calculating capacities of computer chips. According to Moore's law, every two years, twice as many transistors can be

---

[*] http://meaningpatterns.net/digital-imaging

[412] W.E.B. Du Bois, 1903, *The Souls of Black Folk: Essays and Sketches,* Chicago, IL: A.A. McClurg & Co, pp. viii, vii.
[413] W.S. Boyle and G.E. Smith, 1970, "Charge Coupled Semiconductor Devices," *The Bell System Technical Journal* 49(4):587–93.
[414] www.revolvy.com/page/George-E.-Smith   [415] www.megapixel.co.il/english/archive/35884
[416] www.fujifilm.com/innovation/achievements/ds-1p/

"crammed into" an integrated circuit.[417] This prognostication has proved to be more or less correct in the half century after he wrote his 1965 article.

There are millions of pixels[§MS1.2.2e] (megapixels) in each image taken on a phone, tens of millions in higher-end digital cameras. Considering that each pixel is represented by up to 24 bits of information about the light at a particular coordinate, a typical digital image may be decomposed into hundreds of millions of elemental zeros and ones before it is recomposed. Much of this is just alphanumeric naming of the quality of one pixel after another, column by column, row by row, in order to reproduce the same name as a color in another place. The algorithms in the first instance are simply to record and then reconstruct the array.

Then comes compression, where the algorithms that drive the near-universal file JPEG format remove up to 90 percent of the data because it is minimally useful to the reconstruction of the image. Several hundred pixels close together that are more or less the same color do not have to be named in their 24-bit specificity several hundred times. Instead, there can just be a command, "repeat however-many hundred times," which will be mostly good enough even though in the capture they are likely slightly different.

Developed in 1986 and since then maintained by the Joint Photographic Experts Group,[418] we encounter here yet another place for the establishment of the universalizing frame of meaning that is digital modernity. The group's members are nominated by government standards bodies, but they mostly come from businesses that have an interest in digital imaging. Attached to digital image files are Exif data – Exchangeable image file format, another international standard[419] – adding metadata about geolocation, date, device, and camera settings. Since 2015, JPEG has been complemented by the tighter compression of the High Efficiency Image File format (HEIF or HEIC) developed by the Moving Pictures Expert Group, interoperable with JPEG.

Cameras have always in some ways and to varying extents lied,[§MS2.2.2a] but algorithmic readjustment of the light entering the lens in digital cameras helps them to lie more. High dynamic range (HDR) creates an evened-out luminosity across the image, reducing contrasts to bring some things out of the shadow and to make visible other things that would otherwise have been blinded in comparative brightness. Eyes do not work this way, taking time to adjust to significant variations in the intensity of light. In film photography these are areas of under- and over-exposure. Actually, a more accurate name for HDR would be unrealistically flattened dynamic range. As a consequence, the digital image becomes more rigorously space-bound in its planar simultaneity.

---

[417] Gordon E. Moore, 1965, "Cramming More Components onto Integrated Circuits," *Electronics* 38(8):114–17.

[418] https://jpeg.org/jpeg/index.html   [419] www.cipa.jp/std/documents/e/DC-008-2012_E.pdf

Near-infinite depth of field in digitally processed images also brings three-dimensional reality onto an absolutely two-dimensional plane, again in a way unlike the eyes or the blurring of unfocused backgrounds and foregrounds in film photography. The *trompe l'oeuil* of the digital photograph is in this respect more like painting than film photography. In this way too, digital photographs accentuate the planar nature of visualization in "unrealistic" ways. The more "realistic" they become, the greater the distance of image from the realities of seeing. However, in a sense, this is a late modernity where more is the same – in this case, a culture of visual distortion that creates illusions of realism is as old as linear perspective.§MS2.2c

In digital photography, from the start we have mostly had a lot of numbers do a lot of naming for a lot of things, transpositions from image elements, to alphanumeric names for the qualities of light, to image element. The calculations are of a laboriously cumbersome kind that no human could practicably undertake – this is what Turing was referring to when he spoke of machine intelligence.§MS1.3.2b We could if we wished do this kind of simple calculation manually with a small array of pixels, but without mechanical support, never many.

Then comes the much-hyped "artificial intelligence."[420] Digital imaging is a good place to explore the general nature of these particular processes of transposition via calculation.

Apple tells us that their phones use "machine learning" in a "Neural Engine ... to analyze data from the camera sensor, quickly distinguishing faces in the frame." This, in a revealing mixture of its metaphors, Apple calls "facial landmarking," and "depth mapping."[421]

Before we reach the depths of "neural nets," we must pass by machine learning. There are two kinds of machine learning.[422] The first, supervised machine learning, is where humans train the machine. Lots of human trainers tag this part of an image as a face, and another part as sky. When this combination of pixels comes up again, the computer can "say," this is a "sky," and this a "face." Then, if I tag a particular face with a person's name a few times on social media or in image storage software, after a while the computer will suggest their name if it "thinks" the same person might be in another photograph. This is a second kind of machine learning that is called unsupervised, where the computer notices repeated patterns and asks the user whether there is a label that might be applied.

[420] Nils J. Nilsson, 2009, *The Quest for Artificial Intelligence: A History of Ideas and Achievements*, Cambridge: Cambridge University Press.
[421] www.apple.com/iphone-xr/cameras/
[422] ChengXiang Zhai and Sean Massung, 2016, *Text Data Management and Analysis: A Practical Introduction to Information Retrieval and Text Mining*, Williston, VT: ACM and Morgan & Claypool, pp. 34–36.

So, the machine learns – but not because it ever really knows faces in general or this face in particular. All it knows is zeros and ones, for the purposes of naming and calculating, two vectors of transposition in computing that we discussed earlier.[§MS1.3.2] To this, we now add a third vector, rendering, or in the case of images putting the zeros and ones back together into a picture.

These are the text ⟺ image transpositions, mechanized from: view image > tag text > calculated pixel comparison > view image with suggested text tag. The stuff in the middle is intelligent for the number of calculations and their speed, but crushingly dull in the quality of each calculation. The limits of the meaning in this case are the limits of its transposability.

No two pictures are the same, so our theory of design explains.[§MS0.4.1] This means that the ostensibly intelligent calculations in the middle can never be "correct." They can only be probabilistic – likely this is a person, then likely it is this person. The machine becomes smarter each time a user confirms or denies a suggestion. But the elemental calculations can never become smarter. The intelligence is in the "bigness" of data, and not (so much) the sophistication of the probabilistic statistics.

Neural nets involve multiple layers of pattern recognition, finding patterns in the numbers, then patterns within the patterns, again and again until they become fuzzier, then working their way back from highly abstracted fuzziness to other instances of the pattern which are probabilistically similar.[423] This can't work without a massive amount of data. And it is only neural by analogy, as if the brain can be reductively reduced to 0/1 calculations, which it can't. Its roots are a statistical technique less than inspiringly called "back-propagating errors" in the 1986 paper by its creators.[424]

Soon, we are now told, will come quantum computing, though this may be just another kind of probabilistic statistics, still built on the mechanical capacity of electricity to be on and off.

The only artificiality in artificial intelligence is in the mindless granularity of the datapoints and the scale of the calculations. The rest is human intelligence, transposing the meanings of their images into text, and the computer repeating our own words back to us when a similar array of pixels turns up.

Or, to say this in the more general terms of our three vectors of transposition, in from medium to calculation and back again to medium. **Naming:** the computer decomposes and names mostly miniscule things in unspeakable ways. **Calculation:** the computer counts them in ways that could not sensibly or practicably done by hand. **Rendering:** the computer gives the results of the

[423] Alex Krizhevsky, Ilya Sutskever, and Geoffrey E. Hinton, 2012, "Imagenet Classification with Deep Convolutional Neural Networks," *Advances in Neural Information Processing Systems* 25:1097–105.
[424] David E. Rumelhart, Geoffrey E. Hinton, and Ronald J. Williams, 1986, "Learning Representations by Back-Propagating Errors," *Nature* 323:533–36.

calculations back as image (and its variant, text) and sound (and its variant, speech). This is how AI works, no matter how fancy the statistics. It is a process of functional transposition into and out of quantities, and multimodal transposition, such as the text ⇔ image dependencies that underpin machine learning. AI's power is in the grammar of its transpositions, not its mathematics.

§1.4.7   Text

> **Text.** *Meanings made by combining the elemental, character-level components of writing (graphemes), as documented in Unicode. Graphemes can represent sounds (phonemes), and ideas or things (ideographs).*

Text is a kind of image. In our definition, it is anything that can be written in Unicode[§MS0.2.1a] – not that this makes our definition of text descriptively new, because Unicode is just an exhaustive list of all the characters used across several thousand years of scripting. It is a comprehensive historical retrospective, the character set of all character sets. Text in this definition consists of characters (graphemes) that capture the elemental components of sound (phonemes) or images that represent ideas or things (ideographs).

The materiality of text not only shares features with imaging. It also involves some peculiar multimodal relations with body and object: holding a pen, typing on a keyboard, turning the page, swiping a screen, moving a mouse, clicking a button, drawing a line. Meaning with text is a material process, and as such unavoidably multimodal. In these respects, as a medium text is closer to object and body in our narrow definition of its constituent components, gesticulation and enactment, than sound or speech.

The affordances of text – its capacities to mean in the logistics of its materialization as medium – are, as we have argued at length in these two books, fundamentally different from speech. The meanings are transposable for sure, but the distance traversed in this transposition is deceptively large, at least as large as any other form–form transposition, often more.

It is the length of this distance in text–speech transposition and not their conflation that, it might seem paradoxically, makes some of our contemporary texts so meaningful. Two examples for the moment, video lectures and text messaging.

MOOCs[§1.2.2b] and video lectures for the "flipped classroom" use media that is as accessible nowadays as laptop computers and phones. When scripted in full or summarized in the ubiquitous bullet points of the slide deck, video lectures bring to speech the characteristic grammar of text. Even when extemporaneous, speakers who are habituated to writing speak as if they were dictating for text. They are voices who would otherwise speak with manifest subjectivity, but here they speak with feigned objectivity.

Then, there is the journey the other way, the tele-prompted TED Talks for instance, that speak with the feigned authenticity of orality.* Viewing the video is in some respects more like a reading than listening – the viewers view in their own time; they can skip parts, speed up parts, go back over parts, and read the closed captioning.

And another ubiquitous text–speech transposition, text messages, chat bots, and social media interactions recreate in text the conversational logic that is characteristic of speech as a medium for co-located persons. The chunks of content in these interchanges can just as easily be fragments of recorded speech as typed text. Recorded speech can be transcribed by the device as text.

However, for all the marvels of multimodal transposition, this does not bring the grammars of text and speech closer together. Science becomes more arcane and less speakable in its writerly imaging; while ridesharing an Uber becomes more conversational.§1.4.1d

§1.4.7a *Jack Goody's* Domestication of the Savage Mind

After Ferdinand de Saussure,§MS3d and after Roman Jakobson,§1.4.1a Claude Lévi-Strauss applies his structuralism to the categorical thinking of so-called primitive peoples, peoples whose lives precede writing in the modern understanding of that practice. Here he finds patterns of multimodal meaning as extensively complex, and in their own ways as writerly, as those of so-called "civilized" peoples.

In *The Savage Mind*, Lévi-Strauss refers to Spencer and Gillen's expeditions into Aboriginal Australia at the end of the nineteenth and beginning of the twentieth centuries. The more they and others have explored these systems of thinking, the more complex they have appeared to be. "The greater our knowledge, the more obscure the overall scheme. The dimensions multiply, and the growth of axes of reference beyond a certain point paralyses intuitive methods: it becomes impossible to visualize a system when its representation requires a continuum of more than three or four dimensions." Perhaps they are so complex, Lévi-Strauss muses, that only computers – one day – might be able to figure them out. "[T]he day may come," he said in 1962, "when all the available documentation on Australian tribes is transferred to punched cards and with the help of a computer that their entire techno-economic, social and religious structures can be shown to be like a vast group of transformations."[425] This day has not yet come.

---

* http://meaningpatterns.net/text

[425] Claude Lévi-Strauss, 1962 [1966], *The Savage Mind*, Chicago, IL: University of Chicago Press, p. 88.

Then comes writing, and what Jack Goody[§MS0.2.1a] calls in the title of his book, and with more than a hint of irony, *The Domestication of the Savage Mind.** In the history of the human species, writing arrives at the moment of inequality, and serves that inequality. Before the so-called "Neolithic revolution,"[426] the societies of First Peoples had marked differences but not marked inequalities.[427] Inequality is a cause and consequence of a complex of conjunctions in human relations to nature and each other. Boastfully, we call these innovations civilization. Writing becomes its defining measure.

The first writings were lists of things that the poor owed to the rich. Relationships between persons became extended, depersonalized relationships of text referring to the meanings of owned objects over space. Records of ownership and debt extended demands for the distribution of resources abstractly over time.[428]

V. Gordon Childe is the great and now largely forgotten Australian theorist of the Neolithic revolution – the turning point in human affairs that was the introduction of farming, the domestication of animals, and the invention of metallurgy. Childe adds quantification to the conceptual innovations at this time. "The beginnings of writing and of mathematics and the standardization of weights and measures coincide in time with the revolution."[429] We include mathematics as a form of writing. This is the moment when humans find a need to separate quantity from quality, quantify qualities, and create instantiations more finely specified than "many."[§MS1.3]

Childe also adds to these marks of "civilization" new religions that privilege text. Among the first account books were listings of money owed to the temple and its priests as intermediaries, negotiating the impossible promises of the gods.[§MS0.4a] A priestly class forms an alliance with a ruling class, and a class of scribes is privileged for the work it does, accounting for resources, while also brokering life against death and hope against fate.

And the origins of schooling in the origins of religion: "A large collection of tablets unearthed at Shuruppak (Fara) illustrates the development of Sumerian writing at the beginning of the historical period – alter 3000 B.C. These documents are exclusively temple accounts and sign-lists used as school-texts."[430]

As if to uncivilize the boastfully civilized, Claude Lévi-Strauss concludes: "The only phenomenon with which writing has always been concomitant is the

---

* http://meaningpatterns.net/goody

[426] V. Gordon Childe, 1925, *The Dawn of European Civilization*, New York: Alfred A. Knopf.

[427] Marshall Sahlins, 1972, *Stone Age Economics*, New York: Aldine.

[428] Jack Goody, 1977, *The Domestication of the Savage Mind*, Cambridge: Cambridge University Press; Jack Goody, 1986, *The Logic of Writing and the Organization of Society*, Cambridge: Cambridge University Press; Jack Goody, 1987, *The Interface between the Written and the Oral*, Cambridge: Cambridge University Press.

[429] V. Gordon. 1936 Childe, *Man Makes Himself*, London: Watts, p. 179.   [430] Ibid., p. 182.

creation of cities and empires, that is the integration of large numbers of individuals into a political system, and their grading into castes or classes."[431] He is writing here in an unbearably sad, wistful, semi-autobiographical book about his fieldwork in Brazil, *Tristes Tropiques* – a title that remains on the English edition because it is too beautiful to bear translation from the French.

A "pattern of development observed from Egypt to China," Lévi-Strauss says of writing, "at the time when it first emerged, seems to have favoured the exploitation of human beings rather than their enlightenment. This exploitation ... made it possible to assemble thousands of workers and force them to carry out exhausting tasks." He is referring here to the architecture of ruins, the legacies of these supposed civilizations. "My hypothesis, if correct, would oblige us to recognize the fact that the primary function of written communication is to facilitate slavery."[432]

In this light, the pyramids and other such monumental ruins of past "civilizations" might be re-seen as malicious stupidities, and most of the writings of their times trivial or misleading supports for unconscionable social systems.

Walter Benjamin:[§MS0b] "a historical materialist views ... 'cultural treasures' ... with cautious detachment. For in every case these treasures have a lineage which he cannot contemplate without horror ... There is no document of culture which is not at the same time a document of barbarism."[433]

§1.4.7b Empress Wu Zetian's "Printed Paper"

The first mentions of printed text were woodblocks printed to paper at the command of Chinese Empress Wu Zetian.[*] In 691, she sent a message to a certain subject of her realm, Wang Qingzhi, "If you want to see me, just show this 'printed paper' to the palace gate keeper." The "printed paper" to which she refers would have been stamped from a woodblock, its uniformity a mark of authenticity. This early evidence of woodblock printing is offered by Li Zhizhong, Dean of the Development Research Academy of the National Library of China, and a member of the Chinese People's Political Consultative Conference.[434]

Near the end of her life and her rule in 706, Empress Wu Zetian had a religious message of thirty-one characters printed that she sent out to

---

[*] http://meaningpatterns.net/chinese-printing

[431] Claude Lévi-Strauss, 1955 [1976], *Tristes Tropiques*, Harmondsworth, UK: Penguin, p. 392.
[432] Ibid., pp. 393–94.
[433] Walter Benjamin, 1940 [1999], "On the Concept of History," pp. 389–400 in *Walter Benjamin: Selected Writings, Volume 4: 1938–1940*, edited by M.W. Jennings, H. Eiland, and G. Smith, Cambridge, MA: Harvard University Press, pp. 391–92.
[434] Li Zhizhong, 2010, "On the Invention of Wood Blocks for Printing in China," pp. 35–44 in *The History and Cultural Heritage of Chinese Calligraphy, Printing and Library Work*, edited by S.M. Allen, L. Zuzao, C. Xiaolan, and J. Bos, Berlin: Walter de Gruyter, p. 40.

monasteries around her kingdom, the *Great Spell of Unsullied Pure Light.* "Loving the true way and the long-living holy immortals," she began, in her appeal to immortality and power.[435]

Wu Zetian was a Buddhist, and the first Buddhist texts had been translated into Chinese as early as the second century. Writing the Buddha's words was a path to the forgiveness of sins and immortality. Emperors in the century before her had ordered hundreds of thousands of scrolls to be hand-copied. Printing was a logical extension of this expression of religious and imperial power through the multiplication of text.[436]

Karl Wittfogel calls the type of regime that Wu Zetian ruled, "oriental despotism." First an avid communist forced to flee Nazi Germany for the United States, after the travesties of Stalinism had been revealed he became an equally avid anti-communist who went so far as to testify against his former comrades in the McCarthy hearings. In imperial China and other such states, Wittfogel said, three kinds of power were concentrated into one: an agromanagerial bureaucracy, an army, and religion closely attached to the state – hence "genuinely despotic (total) power."[437] Wu Zetian's armies brutally conquered large swathes of Western China. She ruled her court by murder and fear, cultivating in Buddhist texts a sense of her own supernatural powers.[438]

These were the symptomatic meanings of Wu Zetian's texts – to gain safe passage into her lethally despotic court, and to connect religion to power, distributing those closely associated meanings far and wide across the kingdom. What the texts did was more important than what they said.

In two key technical respects, the media for this message-making were innovations of world-historical importance, paper and printing. The invention of paper is the older of the two, attributed to imperial courtier Tshai Lun in 105 CE. These were refinements, it seems, of even older processes. The second, however, was from Wu Zetian's own time – woodblock printing.[439]

Wu Zetian's "printed paper" exists only in mention, its material manifestation now lost. The oldest extant printed book is a Chinese translation of the

---

[435] T.H. Barrett, 2008, *The Woman Who Discovered Printing*, New Haven, NJ: Yale University Press, pp. 91–103; Denis Twitchett, 1983, *Printing and Publishing in Medieval China*, New York: Frederic C. Beil, p. 13.

[436] T.H. Barrett, 2008, *The Woman Who Discovered Printing*, New Haven, NJ: Yale University Press, pp. 47, 62.

[437] Karl A. Wittfogel, 1957, *Oriental Despotism: A Comparative Study of Total Power*, New Haven, CT: Yale University Press, p. 100.

[438] Jonathan Clements, 2008, *Wu: The Chinese Empress Who Schemed, Seduced and Murdered Her Way to Become a Living God*, Stroud, UK: Sutton Publishing; Nigel Cawthorne, 2007, *Daughter of Heaven: The True Story of the Only Woman to Become Emperor of China*, London: Oneworld Publications.

[439] Tsuen-hsuin Tsien and Joseph Needham, 1985, *Science and Civilisation in China*, Volume 5: *Chemistry and Chemical Technology*, Part 1: *Paper and Printing*, Cambridge: Cambridge University Press, pp. 40–41.

Buddhist *Diamond Sutra* of 868CE. Now in the British Library, it consists of seven sheets of paper, pasted together into a scroll over five meters long. Along with thousands of other scrolls, it was discovered in a monastery cave in Western China by a monk, who in 1907 sold it to Hungarian-British archaeologist, Aurel Stein.[440]

In the third sheet of this *Diamond Sutra*, the Buddha explains that "learning four lines of this text and teaching them to others would bring Subhuti more merit than if he filled three thousand galaxies with treasure and then gave it all away to the poor." Such was the power of mystical text ahead of the iniquities of inequality. Or, this was a way to reconcile oneself to their inevitability by diverting attention. Veneration for sacred text and its reduplication must have been the motive of the printer, who said in a colophon at the end of the scroll, "'Reverently made for universal free distribution by Wang Jie on behalf of his two parents, 11 May 868.'"[441]

Movable type came to China with an invention of Pi Sheng (990–1051). None of his printed texts survive, but a detailed contemporary description of his setting ceramic types convincingly explains the technology and its workings: types kept in cases; formes in which they were arrayed; then printing by impression onto paper.

"If one were to print only two or three copies," says the commentator, "this method would be neither simple nor easy. But for printing hundreds or thousands of copies, it was marvelously quick." This is perhaps the first insight into notions of modularization and economies of scale that were later to drive the industrial revolution. Wooden movable type is credited to Wang Chen (1290–1333), then bronze movable type in the second half of the fifteenth century.[442]

Paper was not introduced into Europe until nearly a thousand years after its invention in China. And as for Gutenberg's famous printing press of 1454, the great sinologist Joseph Needham says, "It has always been extremely hard to believe that Johannes Gutenberg ... knew nothing (even by hearsay) of the Chinese printed books which had been circulating in large numbers in China for five previous centuries."[443] The caves where the *Diamond Sutra* and other printed materials had been kept, at least since the ninth century, were on the "Silk Route" from China to Europe.

If Gutenberg's printed works were in any immediate way a contribution to "enlightenment," it was more of a Buddhist kind than modern or scientific. His 42-line Bible[§1.4.7c] was, after all, in the Latin of a priestly elite, not the German vernacular. Its meaning was in the owning of the text rather than its reading and

---

[440] Ibid., p. 151.   [441] www.bl.uk/onlinegallery/ttp/sutra/accessible/section3.html#content

[442] Tsuen-hsuin Tsien and Joseph Needham, 1985, *Science and Civilisation in China*, Volume 5: *Chemistry and Chemical Technology*, Part 1: *Paper and Printing*, Cambridge: Cambridge University Press, pp. 201, 206–08, 211.

[443] Ibid., p. xii.

learning; it was a talisman before it was a text. This massive compendium of words was sacred for their objectification, their speaking-to more than their speaking.

The money Gutenberg lost in the monumental task of printing his Bible, he later made back by printing and selling indulgences, certificates for the remission of sins. The business he had before printing was where he had learned the metallurgy he later applied to type – the manufacture of mirrors that would transfer miraculous qualities in the relics of dead saints to those within their seeing.[444] Gutenberg was a medieval man as much as he was modern.

§1.4.7c Petrus Ramus' Way to Geometry

The University of Illinois has in its Rare Book and Manuscript Library the first twenty-four pages of Johannes Gutenberg's beautiful 42-line Bible of 1454 – just the pages, text with no image. They point not only to the stark consistency of manufactured modernity, but the radical separation of text and image that came with letterpress printing.

The white space around the text on Gutenberg's pages was not left in order for it to have meaning that supplemented the text – meaning we would now call page layout. With one foot still in the world of medieval manuscripts, the margins were left for laborious hand illumination, beautiful but textually inessential ephemera. As a consequence, no two Gutenberg Bibles are the same.[*]

Letterpress printing brought about a revolution of sorts – about twenty million books had been printed by 1500. However, an estimated 77 per cent were in Latin and so inaccessible to all but an elite, 45 per cent were religious, and only 10 per cent scientific or informational. In Lucien Febvre and Henri-Jean Martin's words, the impact of print may have been as much as anything in "popularising long cherished beliefs, strengthening traditional prejudices and giving authority to seductive fallacies."[445]

In the half century that followed Gutenberg's Bible, visual design began to appear in the layout of letterpress books which did have essential meaning in relation to the text. We're staying with our definition of text here, where the space between the words is a character or grapheme – it's Unicode U+0020. Spacing words had been a feature of writing in European languages since about the seventh century. Everything else in the design of pages is in our definition visual.

What comes to European letterpress book production between 1454 and about 1500 is a number of essentially visual devices for the architecting of

---

[*] http://meaningpatterns.net/ramus

[444] John Man, 2002, *The Gutenberg Revolution*, London: Review.
[445] Lucien Febvre and Henri-Jean Martin, 1958 [1976], *The Coming of the Book*, translated by D. Gerard, London: Verso, pp. 248, 278.

textual meaning: title pages, tables of contents, numbered sections, nested subsections, headings, paragraphs, abstracts, indexes, footnotes, running heads, cross references, concordances, and colophons.[446]

And, that most revolutionary of inventions, the page number, supporting the non-linear readings and affording the reader new scope for agency. This is a radical departure from the role of a listener who remains captive in linear time. None of these visual devices were new to print, but now they became the norm. By visual extension, text became what we might today call hypertext.

Perhaps the most prolific of all early modern authors, Petrus Ramus, comes to prominence in print in the century after Gutenberg. Appointed professor at the University of Paris in 1551, Ramus was a prolific writer of textbooks. Walter Ong, exhaustive chronicler and analyst of Ramus' legacy, has identified 750 separately published editions in 1,100 separate printings between 1550 and 1650.[447]

Also in the University of Illinois Rare Books Library is a 1636 English translation of Ramus' *Way to Geometry*. A table of contents points to a Book IV, "Of A Figure," commencing on page 32. Arriving at this page we find a section numbered and named, "1. A figure is a lineate bounded on all parts." Then, "So the triangle is a e 1 ... " and below that, a drawing of a triangle with its three corners labeled a, e, and 1.

In his textbooks, Ramus relies on the visual in ways Gutenberg in his Bible did not. He creates a spatialized architectonics of decomposition, from one visually compartmentalized cell of knowledge to the next, ordered from the simpler ideas to the more complex, and supplemented by the diagrammed taxonomic relationships of main and subsidiary concepts. There is also the multimodal integration of text with image using labels and figure references. Because this is letterpress, the triangles are abstractions, line drawings in their conceptual and abstract generality, not the triangles of concretely instantiated life that in a later era might also be offered by photolithographic or offset printing.

And more on these pages: the form of the textbook; the didactic relationships of author and teacher to student; the multimodal objectivizations of knowledge in mathematics and science. The meaning functions are creatures of their media.

This is Ong's reading: Ramus leaves us with "simple spatial models" and dichotomies. "Persons, who alone speak (and in whom alone knowledge and science exist), will be eclipsed insofar as the world is thought of as an assemblage of the sort of things which vision apprehends – objects or surfaces." Of teachers, Ong says, "Instead of carrying on a dialogue in the give-and-take Socratic form,

---

446 Elizabeth L. Eisenstein, 1979, *The Printing Press as an Agent of Change: Communications and Cultural Transformation in Early-Modern Europe*, Cambridge: Cambridge University Press, pp. 52–54, 105.
447 Walter J. Ong, 1958 [1983], *Ramus, Method and the Decay of Dialogue*, Cambridge, MA: Harvard University Press, p. 5.

the university don had largely reduced the oral component by converting it into his own classroom monologue, which he produced not as the spirit moved him but on schedule at fixed places and hours. At the same time his interest both in logic and in explicitness, in an 'object' (of knowledge) rather than in a 'subject' (of discourse), had driven him further still toward the visile pole with its typical ideals of 'clarity,' 'precision,' 'distinctness,' and 'explanation' itself – all best conceivable in terms of some analogy with vision and a spatial field." This was an epistemological revolution, spelling the end of the "evanescent world of discourse."[448] Gone are dialectic as to-and-fro interchange, and rhetoric as appeal to persons. Telling replaces dialogue. Fact displaces argument.

Ong does not hold Ramus in terribly high regard. He was "not a great intellectual but a savant," whose work was "superficially revolutionary but at root highly derivative." The geometry was just Euclid, its reconstruction in textbook form in Ong's view intellectually trivial.[449]

Walter Ong, Jesuit priest, does not hide his dislike of Petrus Ramus, a convert to Protestantism in 1561. "The Ramist arts of discourse are monologue arts. They develop the didactic, schoolroom outlook which ... tends finally even to lose the sense of monologue in pure diagrammatics." But the epistemological revolution wrought by the textbook was of enormous significance. Ramism "crowds spatial models into the universe of the mind," a precursor, for better or for worse, of "the Newtonian revolution, with its stress on visually controlled observation of mathematics, and its curiously silent, nonrhetorical universe."[450]

"Diagrammatics" is an apt word because it highlights the peculiarity of Ramus' visual designs of knowledge. Ramus' Protestantism was hostile to realistic images. The purely textual Word of God might, at most, be supplemented by spatially arranged verses and intertextual concordances. If there were to be diagrams of any kind, Christ's cross was an abstraction. In his textbook on religion, Ramus quoted the warning in Deuteronomy not to "corrupt yourselves, and make you a graven image, the similitude of any figure the likeness of male or female."[451] The spiritual revolution of Protestantism would smash Catholic statues and stained glass likenesses across Europe.§MS2.2.1b

For his selective iconoclasm and anti-Catholic apostasy, Ramus was brutally murdered in his rooms at the University during the St Bartholomew's Day Massacre of 1572. His body was thrown from the window, decapitated then cast into the Seine.[452]

---

[448] Ibid., pp. 8, 9, 151, 155.   [449] Ibid., p. ix.   [450] Ibid., pp. 287, 318.

[451] Frances A. Yates, 1966 [1999], *The Art of Memory*, Volume 3, London: Routledge, p. 236.

[452] Walter J. Ong, 1958 [1983], *Ramus, Method and the Decay of Dialogue*, Cambridge, MA: Harvard University Press, p. 29; Frank Pierrepoint Graves, 1912, *Peter Ramus and the Educational Reformation of the Sixteenth Century*, New York: Macmillan, pp. 105–07.

§1.4.7d Charles Goldfarb's Generalized Markup Language

Digitization comes to published text with the Linotron 1010 typesetter,[*] installed in the US Government Printing Office in 1966.[453] Evelyn Berezin, daughter of Jewish Bronx, New York, invented the first word processor for offices, the Redactron of 1971. In a male-dominated industry, she decided to found her own company to manufacture and market her machine. An early advertisment hailed "the death of the dead-end secretary." When asked more than forty years later whether she anticipated that her creation would endanger women's jobs, she said, "I'm embarrassed to tell you that I never thought of it — it never entered my mind."[454]

The first word processor to reach a wide consumer market was WordStar for personal computers, launched in 1978. Word processing also meant that the broad masses of text-creators were required for the first time to learn some of the half-millennium long, arcane technical language of letterpress typesetting: fonts, point sizes, justification, and if they wanted to dig deeper, other obscurities such as leading, the spaces between the lines which had formerly been blocked out with lead in the type formes. These are all concepts related to the visual design that adds meaning in the surrounds of text.[§1.4.7c]

One of the most profound accompanying changes was to take text and its creation in the direction of a less linear architectonics. As material practices, handwriting and typing had until then been constrained by resistant, linear temporality of the line on a page, grapheme after immovable grapheme. Changes and corrections created a mess on the page, and when things got too bad, there was no alternative to the pain of having to rewrite or retype the page.

In this respect, scribing and typing suffered the same disadvantages as speech. Where the linearity of speech required audible self-correction, the linearity of scribed or typewritten text required visible amendment. Typesetting and word processing make changes invisible. The page is always clean, and correction friction-free.

The text you see before you now has gone through many iterations, starting with messy fragments, notes and instructions to selves that have been written over, and over again. Words, phrases, and sentences have been moved around many times, rethought, reframed, and rephrased. The job of text work has changed from one dominated by resistant linearity to infinitely fluid, multi-linear complexity.

---

[*] http://meaningpatterns.net/gml

[453] John F. Cavanaugh, 1978, "Text Handling at the United States Government Printing Office," *Technical Communication* 25(3):12–15.

[454] https://www.nytimes.com/2018/12/10/obituaries/evelyn-berezin-dead.html?action=click&module=Well&pgtype=Homepage&section=Obituarieshttps://en.wikipedia.org/wiki/Evelyn_Berezin

This may not be a good thing in some respects. But perhaps the text you are reading is awkward for the jumping about in its writing, perhaps we were afforded too much scope for revision. The neatness of a draft may deceive. Nobel prize-winning novelist Günter Grass distrusted the illusion of the text looking finished after a first draft, preferring for his own writing the slow, methodical process of scribing and then typing the novel three and sometimes four times.[455] Whatever the disadvantages and no matter how subtle the differences in the final text, the materiality of medium affects its meaning. This multilinear architectonics in digital text work makes it less than ever like the work of speaking.

Digital text adds to naming and counting[§MS1.3.2] a third vector of transposition into quantity: rendering. In writing, this vector runs: text > alphanumeric naming of graphemes (Unicode) + visual design > decomposition into pixels > recomposition for rendering on screens or on paper as digital print.

The fact that this vector of transposition uses the same technologies of naming and calculation as image[§1.4.6c] and sound[§1.4.2d] accounts for the deep multi-modality of contemporary texts. Until photolithographic and then digital printing,[456] realistic image and text were placed for practical purposes on different pages or sections in books. Until digital television, there wasn't much text in video – but now on the business and sports channels, there is a cacophony of text-image overlays because this possibility is so readily available.

Digital video layers sound over moving image with far greater ease than film because, though analogue sound and film were fundamentally different technologies, an electromagnetic sound track is merely stuck beside the film image. Even though the juxtaposition of technologies is awkward, the processes of transposition of sound and image are roughly the same in analogue and digital moving image and not much changes with digitization. But layering text into digital image is very much easier, and so this affordance has pushed moving image into new domains of possibility.

And another hugely significant thing happens in the transition from analogue media to digital. Every rendering is a recalculation. In analogue print, each new page, by dint of economies of setup and scale, was the same as the previous. In digital print, whether that be printed bills sent in the mail or rendering of a video to a screen, every image is recalculated for its rendering. This affords enormous possibilities for variation, including in the case of screens, user interfaces which allow the reader-viewer to co-design the reading-viewing experience.

---

[455] www.theguardian.com/books/2010/aug/24/gunter-grass-last-autobiography;   Matthew   G. Kirschenbaum, 2016, *Track Changes: A Literary History of Word Processing*, Cambridge, MA: Harvard University Press.

[456] Bill Cope, 2001, "New Ways with Words: Print and Etext Convergence," pp. 1–15 in *Print and Electronic Text Convergence, Volume 2.1: Technology Drivers across the Book Production Supply Chain, from the Creator to the Consumer*, edited by B. Cope and D. Kalantzis, Melbourne: Common Ground.

Digital media no longer have lock-step replication built into the processes of their manufacture. Every digital text, image, or sound rendered is a re-manufacture, on-the-fly. Between the source and its rendering are numbers that bear no visible or speakable resemblance either to the source or its rendered destination. This allows space for the re-manufacture to be modified in the using or by the user.

Which brings us to Charles Goldfarb. Trained as a lawyer and confounded by the labor-intensive processes of legal documentation, Goldfarb took a position in the IBM labs in Cambridge, Massachusetts. There in 1969, he and several colleagues created Generalized Markup Language (GML),[457] the first conceptual departure from the five-century-old discourses and practices of typography. They retained the word "markup," the instructions to the typesetter about the visual design of the page written around a handwritten or typed manuscript. But the fundamental principle of markup that Goldfarb and his colleagues established was new.

Using GML, tags would be inserted into the digital text specifying paragraphs, sections, headings, tables, lists, and the like. These tags did not indicate how these meaning functions were to look, or the form they were to take when rendered. Instead, there were to be separate "stylesheets" which rendered text in different ways depending on the end device, whether, for instance, that was a paper printer or a screen. So, re-manufacture was not reproduction. The redesign was not a replicant of the design. Or, to use terminology of this grammar, the tags indicate meaning functions; the stylesheets determine the particularities of meaning form as realized in variable media.

Following these foundational principles were Standard Generalized Markup Language (SGML, 1974),[458] then Hypertext Markup Language (HTML, 1993),[459] Extensible Markup Language (XML, 1996),[§MS3.3b] and Microsoft Word XML (2003).[460] This is how digital texts can today so easily move around from device to device, medium to medium.

A fundamental change in textual practice, this is often described as a change from visual markup established by typography to "structural and semantic markup." In HTML, the tag <title> is semantic, and the tag <p> for paragraph is structural. But these distinctions are not so clear, because as well as naming a document, <title> is in a structural sense located in a particular place in a text

[457] Charles F. Goldfarb, Edward J. Mosher, and Theodore I. Peterson, 1970 [1997], "An Online System for Integrated Text Processing," *Journal of the American Society for Information Science* 48(7):656–61; Charles F. Goldfarb, 1990, "A Brief History of the Development of SGML," SGML Users' Group, retrieved February 5, 2002 (www.oasis-open.org/cover/sgml hist0.html).

[458] Charles F. Goldfarb, 1991, *The SGML Handbook*, Oxford: Oxford University Press.

[459] Tim Berners-Lee, 1990, "Information Management: A Proposal," Geneva: CERN (www.w3 .org/History/1989/proposal.html).

[460] Liam Magee and James A. Thom, 2014, "What's in a WordTM? When One Electronic Document Format Standard Is Not Enough," *Information Technology & People* 27 (4):482–511.

for the purposes of meaningful rendering, and <p> is semantic to the extent that it defines the beginning of a new idea.

Starting with GML, these were systems for specifying text grammatically and using that grammar to manufacture the text. The tags are a meta-text that re-manufacture the text. Each tag is an executable instruction at the same time as it is a description.[461] This is what Goldfarb calls an "Abstraction support – that trait of an information representation (data format, notation, et al.) that allows its users to distinguish what they consider to be the 'abstract' information content of a document from the 'style information' that is used to render it."[462] Here, in another way, the erstwhile linearity of texts is overcome, in markup that describes then renders information hierarchies, nesting, cross-referencing, and co-relational structures such as tables.[463]

Not that the path from SGML to subsequent digital markup has always been straightforward. The function/form distinction made so clearly in SGML became mixed up with textual–visual function, which included in early versions of HTML such horrors as the <blink> tag. It has taken many torturous revisions of HTML to return it to something closer to the founding principles of SGML.

Nor have we escaped typographical markup. Half a century after Goldfarb's insights, we still use widely used back-to-the future formats such as word processor documents and Portable Document Format (PDF). These continue to insist on faithfully reproducing typographic markup in fixed pages, making them hard to render across different devices and resistant to textual intervention on the part of users.

§1.4.7e Larry Page and Sergey Brin's "PageRank" Algorithm

In the digital era, meanings are connected by the peculiar universal protocols for the transposition by calculation of text,[§1.4.7d] image[§1.4.6c] and sound.[§1.4.2d] Not that the idea of explicitly interconnected artifacts of meaning is new. In the case of books, the systematic forms of these interconnection are as old as letterpress typography or even older – as old as the citation of a related or quoted work in a footnote[464] or the listing of a work in a library catalogue.[465]

---

[461] Bill Cope and Mary Kalantzis, 2004, "Text-Made Text," *E-Learning* 1(2):198–282.

[462] www.sgmlsource.com/infaqs.htm

[463] Allen Renear, Elli Mylonas, and David Durand, 1996, "Refining Our Notion of What Text Really Is: The Problem of Overlapping Hierarchies," *Research in Humanities Computing* 4:263–80; Dino Buzzetti and Jerome McGann, 2006, "Electronic Textual Editing: Critical Editing in a Digital Horizon," pp. 53–73 in *Electronic Textual Editing*, edited by L. Burnard, K.O.B. O'Keeffe, and J. Unsworth, New York: Modern Language Association of America.

[464] Anthony Grafton, 1997, *The Footnote: A Curious History*, London: Faber and Faber.

[465] Roger Chartier, 1992 [1994], *The Order of Books: Readers, Authors, and Libraries in Europe between the Fourteenth and Eighteenth Centuries*, translated by L.G. Cochrane, Stanford, CA: Stanford University Press, pp. 77ff.

What is new is the interconnection of just about every piece of text in the world, past and present, by networked computers, by transposition of text via calculation to reproduced text.$^{§1.4.7d}$

The first known plan for a wide-ranging network of computers was the system of "electronic socialism," approved by the Politburo of the USSR in 1963: the "All-State System for the Gathering and Processing of Information for Accounting and Governance of the National Economy."[*] In the Russian acronym, it was known as "OGAS." Its leading architect, Viktor Gluskov, said "cybernetics fits our socialist planned economy like a glove."[466] Today, the map of the planned OGAS system might be called "cloud computing."

Huge investments in Soviet cybernetics followed. However, although a large number of computer centers were created around the Soviet Union, they were never connected. Benjamin Peters tells a painful story of military opposition (they had their own secret network which they wouldn't share), bureaucratic territorialism (enterprises whose autonomy and capacity for number-rigging would be reduced), and a layer of the informal economy (a large unsanctioned market economy and widespread corruption, vested interests that such a system would expose and possibly eliminate).

In the United States, comprehensively networked computing did not come until the Advanced Research Projects Agency Network (ARPANET). This began its life as a military project in 1969. Academic access was allowed in 1981, and the internet protocol TCP/IP$^{§MS1.1.1f}$ established in 1982. Peters calls this the "American military-industrial-academic complex," where he says the actors behaved like socialists. Meanwhile, "the Soviet networked command economy fell apart not because it resisted the superior practices of competitive free markets but because it was consumed by unregulated conflicts among institutional and individual self-interests."[467] The Soviets, ironically, were behaving like capitalists. Or, we would say by way of homage to Deng Xiaoping, this part of the Cold War was won by a socialism that had American characteristics.

As for the distributed logic of the network, system architect and inventor of "packet switching," Polish-born Jewish refugee Paul Baran, had nuclear war in mind. A distributed network was more likely to survive nuclear devastation than a centralized one. He published widely hoping the Soviets would take note, because the best deterrent for nuclear war, it seemed to him at the time, would be the indestructability of the other side.[468]

---

[*] http://meaningpatterns.net/www

[466] Benjamin Peters, 2016, *How Not to Network a Nation: The Uneasy History of the Soviet Internet*, Cambridge, MA: MIT Press, pp. 107–08.
[467] Ibid., pp. 197, 187.   [468] Ibid., pp. 94–97.

Then, "hypertext," to get all the meanings connected that were referenced in computers. Ted Nelson is credited with coining the word. "Ordinary text," he said in 1967, "called by McLuhan and others 'linear,' is a continuing sequence in a fixed order ... Hypertext diverges from ordinary text in that the readers' possible sequences diverge from plain sequence." He predicted "new forms of writing, appearing on computer screens, that will branch to perform at the reader's command. A hypertext is a non-sequential piece of writing; only the computer display makes it practical. Somewhere between a book, a TV show and a penny arcade, the hypertext can be a vast tapestry of information."[469]

In this definition, the origins of hypertext were in the sixteenth century, with the invention of page numbers, indexes, tables of contents, headings, figures cross-referenced in text, and beyond the covers of the book, library catalogues, shelving systems, bibliographies, and citation protocols.[§1.4.7c] All of these were designed for non-linear readings, accommodating the interested and interpreting reader.[§1.2.3a] They also encapsulated the foundational epistemologies of modern science and scholarly knowledge, a social intertextuality acknowledging the sources of quotations, the provenance of ideas.

The integrated network was to depend on precise text-mediated, text-to-text connections in the form of Uniform Record Locators (URLs),[§MS1.1.1f] names for places where copyable sources were to be located, in highly regulated conditions where no two names could ever be the same. When hypertext became a reality in HTML, it was with the <link> tag, though this had not been in Berners-Lee's 1991 version and was only to appear from HTML 2 in 1995.[§1.4.7d] Nelson had defined this in 1973: "link – connection between two points ... which may serve as a jump from one to the other."[470] The innovation here was not the textuality of interconnection. It was the now universal computer protocols of its activation and the speed with which it could operationalize these.

Next came the web browser, by means of which files could be located and viewed. The first widely used web browser, Mosaic, was developed in the National Center for Supercomputing Applications at the University of Illinois and released in 1993.

Then, in 1998, Stanford University students Larry Page and Sergei Brin presented a paper about their doctoral research project at the Seventh International World-Wide Web Conference in Brisbane, Australia, "The Anatomy of a Large-Scale Hypertextual Web Search Engine." In their paper, they described the "full text and hyperlink database of at least 24 million pages" that they had developed, and the "PageRank" algorithm which used "the link structure of the Web to calculate a quality ranking for each web page."

[469] Theodor H. Nelson, 1977, *Selected Papers, 1965–77*, Swarthmore, PA: Swathmore College, pp. 15–16.

[470] Ibid., p. 105.

Keyword search would bring up a huge number of pages in no priority order. But by counting the number of backward links – other pages that had already cited a particular page – they were able to rank pages.[471]

A patent application for Page and Brin's invention had been filed several months before, with ownership assigned to Stanford University according to the practice required of graduate students in the United States.[472] Their research had been supported by a grant from the National Science Foundation under the US Government's Digital Library initiative. The University did a deal in which it took Google shares instead of royalties, then sold its shares for a tiny fraction of their subsequent value. This is how oligarchies are created in the twenty-first century.

Not that was there anything particularly original about the PageRank algorithm. Larry Page was son of a Michigan State University computer science professor, and professors are of course conscious of their citations.[473] In 1955, Eugene Garfield began to develop a database that counted scientific article citations as a measure of their impact – the backward links from later work that acknowledge antecedent works.[474] The Lithuanian-Italian-Jewish Garfield had studied in the same linguistics department at the University of Pennsylvania as Noam Chomsky. Then, in 1960, Garfield created a company to sell these data, the Institute for Scientific Information. Page and Brin did not cite Garfield in their Brisbane paper, ironically demonstrating that the source of ideas is not necessarily explicitly linked to their later impact. But they did cite Garfield in another, lesser known paper dated to that year,[475] and in their patent application. This is how the idea of backward linking slipped into the hands of the company they founded, Google, as private intellectual property.

Actually, it was not the algorithm that proved significant, but the copy of the 24 million pages Page and Brin had copied and indexed to test the algorithm. Nor is the link count a measure of quality, as their Brisbane paper claimed. It's a measure of a quantity: popularity counted by links. Accentuating this, a link from an already well-linked page is ranked above a link from a page less linked.

---

[471] Sergy Brin and Larry Page, 1998, "The Anatomy of a Large-Scale Hypertextual Web Search Engine," paper presented at the Seventh International World-Wide Web Conference, 14–18 April, Brisbane (http://ilpubs.stanford.edu:8090/361/).

[472] Lawrence Page, 2001, "Method for Node Ranking in a Linked Database," edited by U.S. Patent Office. Stanford, CA: The Board of Trustees of the Leland Stanford Junior University.

[473] David A. Vise, 2005, *The Google Story*, New York: Delacorte Press, p. 37.

[474] Eugene Garfield, 1955 [2006], "Citation Indexes for Science: A New Dimension in Documentation through Association of Ideas," *International Journal of Epidemiology* 35 (5):1123–27, doi: 10.1093/ije/dyl189; Eugene Garfield, 2006, "Commentary: Fifty Years of Citation Indexing," ibid.:1127–28; Bill Cope and Mary Kalantzis, 2014, "Changing Knowledge Ecologies and the Transformation of the Scholarly Journal," pp. 9–84 in *The Future of the Academic Journal* (Edn 2), edited by B. Cope and A. Phillips, Oxford: Elsevier.

[475] Lawrence Page, Sergey Brin, Rajeev Motwani, and Terry Winograd, 1998, "The Pagerank Citation Ranking: Bringing Order to the Web," Stanford, CA: Stanford InfoLab.

And the more people searching something, the more the algorithm recommends the same link to others. This is not information quality, but populism on an industrial scale.

Page and Brin founded the web search company Google in 1998. Google has a copy of the whole web – there are several others, including those held by Microsoft and Yahoo, but these pale into insignificance by comparison. Clickstream data independently collected in 2018 showed that Google had 92.96% of market share. The second largest provider is Yahoo, at 1.57% of the market, followed by Microsoft Bing at 1.48%.[476] Google was the first copy and remains the most used. These copies, incidentally, were made without ever asking permission of creators or publishers, so contravening the foundational principles of private ownership of intellectual property. Private property is supposedly inviolate, but some violators the system tolerates more than others. But then, Google, Microsoft, and Yahoo are today megacorporations that are too big to be criminal.

When you search at Google, you are not actually searching the web – that would be impossibly slow. You are searching Google's indexed copy of the web. The logic of web search that Google and the other companies offer is principally a business of counting collocations of letters as proxies for the meanings of words, then using hyperlinks as a measure of popularity. This is what brings you to the first page of a search listing. Hence the junk populism of the internet. Then there is a cultural and epistemic version of corruption, where you can pay to be placed ahead of others, where money can trump popularity. This is Google's business model, and for that matter today, the ailing business model of liberal democracy.

Several decades later, Google has made a copy of everything, not just the whole internet, but every book for Google Book Search, and every journal article for Google Scholar. Google is just as interested in copying your private ephemera – every web search you happen to make, every email you send by GMail or through its hidden proxies, and everything you write in Google Docs or save to Google Drive. Nothing is too trivial for Google to know, for its figuring exactly what each one of us is meaning, in our finely nuanced differences.[§2.2.2] It's a well-targeted advertising business.

Google's transpositions are fundamentally algorithmic. Its main technology is to count the graphemes where statistical similarities might add up to meanings that are never more than latent.[477] Even though its main business is words, it has precious little reliance on linguistics.[§2.2.1a] Instead, it relies on ontologies that make sense of the words by locating them in the universal encyclopedia of human experience.[§MS3.4]

[476] https://sparktoro.com/blog/2018-search-market-share-myths-vs-realities-of-google-bing-ama zon-facebook-duckduckgo-more/

[477] Thomas K. Landauer, Danielle S. McNamara, Simon Dennis, and Walter Kintsch, eds. 2007, *Handbook of Latent Semantic Analysis*, New York, NY: Routledge.

As for the distributed network, the reality is the increasingly opposite. The cloud is a network of highly centralized server farms, not only at Google (for search), but Facebook (for social media), and that cloud of clouds, Amazon Web Services. Google has laid undersea cables around the world, creating its own private internet. The power of these companies comes from their ownership of industrial plant, to even greater monopolistic effect than the industrial robber barons of early modernity.

For all the talk of the free market, there are by now just a handful of digital behemoths,[478] and as a consequence we live our lives in pseudo-public places of the internet, where we consent to certain kinds of control and an imbalance of benefits that guarantees corporate profits on a scale not seen even in the industrial era. Why would a megacorporation give you anything for free? Because the value of what they get back out of you is greater than the cost of their "giving."

Today we have a massively interlinked but also highly centralized, universal infrastructure of meanings. This is held together by an oligarchy of centrally controlled entities who come together when needed to agree on protocols of standardization in this new, stateless regime for the governance of our meanings.

This was what Viktor Gluskov was thinking for his network design of 1963 – and not.

§1.5 Association

> **Association.** *Exophoric meaning connections, meanings within frames that point out to context, and contexts pointing in, filling gaps of ellipsis. Functions of contextual association include seriality, scaling, and expressive causality.*

Texts, images, spaces, objects, bodies, sounds, and speech point out from themselves by virtue of their intrinsic form-to-form transposability: an image transposes with an object in a still life; text transposes with speech in reported dialogue; bodies transpose with architected spaces in shopping. These transpositions occur by means of reference, agency, structure, context, and interest.

Of these functions, context encompasses some specialized ways of pointing out and across meaning forms. We have already seen the materialization of meanings from context via likeness, directedness, or abstraction;[§1.1] the varied functions of participation in meaning in the form of the practices of representation, communication, and interpretation;[§1.2] positioning in time and space;[§1.3]

---

[478] Matteo Pasquinelli, 2009, "Google's Pagerank Algorithm: A Diagram of Cognitive Capitalism and the Rentier of the Common Intellect," pp. 152–62 in *Deep Search*, edited by K. Becker and F. Stalder, London: Transaction Publishers.

and the forms of meaning that are possible given the opportunities and constraints offered by material media, found and reworked.[§1.4]

Now to alternative functions of association in context, be they by way of seriality, scaling, or expressive causality. But before association can be established, we need to define the separations that make association meaningful: the edges, frames,[479] boundaries, or borders that define commonly distinguishable acts and artifacts of meaning. These are conventional and their meanings habituated: the front and back covers of a book; the entry and exit to a building; the frame of a picture; the opening and closing bar of a piece of music; the start and end of a telephone conversation.

Here, we want to make a distinction between endophoric relations, within the frame (structure, Part 3 in the *Making Sense* volume), and exophoric associations, beyond the frame (context, our concern in this Part). Context is how the stuff on the outside of a text, image, space, object, body, sound, or spoken

Forms / Functions	Text	Image	Space	Object	Body	Sound	Speech
Structure: Endophoric Relations	Cross-connection, e.g. pronouns, deictics, ellipsis previously referenced in the text	Content and arrangement within the frame	Inside the space	Workability of the object, the range of its potentials	Physiological sensuous capabilities	Sound structures	Phonemic patterns
Context: Exophoric Association	External connection, e.g. pronouns, deictics, ellipsis not referenced in the text	Positioning of the frame	Outside the space	Usability of the object, the meaning of its use in context	Activities where context co-creates embodied meaning	Hearability as shaped by context	Listenability as shaped by context, from physical context to the predilections of hearers

Fig. 1.5(i): Endophoric relations (structure) and exophoric relations (context)

utterance meaningfully connects with the stuff on the inside. Not that structure and context can be meaningfully separated – decontextualized meaning is at best vastly reduced meaning – indeed, so reduced that much of the time it is almost meaningless. Here are some examples:

The logic of endophoric relations and exophoric associations, we find, often look and sound the same. "This" can refer to something earlier in a spoken utterance (structure: cohesion), or something outside of it (context). Grammatically, however, the two "this"s are profoundly different.

---

[479] Gunther Kress, 2014, "What Is Mode?," pp. 60–75 in *The Routledge Handbook of Multimodal Analysis*, edited by C. Jewitt, London: Routledge, p. 73; Erving Goffman, 1974, *Frame Analysis: An Essay on the Organization of Experience*, Cambridge, MA: Harvard University Press.

We classified structural relations loosely as kind-of, part-of, and causes.[§MS3.3] Halliday and Hasan call these relations synonymy (repetition); antonymy (paired opposites); hyponymy (kind-of); meronomy (part-of); conjunction (an ambiguous range including cause); and ellipsis (meaningful absence). They can look back across time with its sequential unfolding of media and the experiences these media depict. This they do by way of retrospective association (anaphora), or forward by way of anticipatory association (cataphora).[480] These grammatical concepts can be applied, not only to text and speech, but to image, space, object, body, and sound as well.

The same devices that work for endophoric structure within the frame also work to make meaningful exophoric connections beyond the frame.[481] Of course, pushing them out to context profoundly changes the nature of their work of meaning, and this is why for the purposes of this grammar we make the separation between relations in structure and associations in context. If our frame is a book, words, sentences, paragraphs, and chapters sit in part-of relations to each other, but when a book is part-of a library or a bookstore, these are quite different kinds of association. Vectors many establish causal relations in an image, but the potential causal associations in the display of an image are quite different.

Now, to certain kinds of association in context. For a multimodal grammar, we identify three: seriality, scaling, and expressive causality. Seriality is a function of meanings that are associated by juxtaposition, often because they are a kind-of. Scaling is a function of meanings that fit inside each other, because the one is part-of the other. If we can track immediate causality in structure, expressive causality is a function of the wider context, in its multiplicity, where a framed meaning is symptomatic of a social structure, a culture, a way of life, or an historical era.

Fig. 1.5(ii) shows some roughly categorized examples of seriality, scaling, and expressive causality across the canonical meaning forms.

Jean-Paul Sartre[§MS3.1.2b] contrasts three kinds of social collocation, illustrating for us this seriality/scaling/expressive causality distinction.[*] A group of people, he says, are waiting for a bus in front of the church in Place Saint-Germain, Paris. They are together in this moment as a consequence of "the inert effect of separate activities." This, we would term a serial association, the association of bodies in a crowd. "[W]e are concerned here with a plurality of isolations: these people do not care about or speak to each other and, in general,

---

[*] http://meaningpatterns.net/association

[480] M.A.K. Halliday and Ruqaiya Hasan, 1985, *Language, Context, and Text: Aspects of Language in a Social-Semiotic Perspective*, Geelong, Australia: Deakin University Press, pp. 74–95; M.A.K. Halliday and Ruqaiya Hasan, 1976, *Cohesion in English*, London: Longman.

[481] Leonard Talmy, 2017, *The Targeting System of Language*, Cambridge, MA: MIT Press.

Forms / Associations	Text	Image	Space	Object	Body	Sound	Speech
Seriality	Texts beside each other, words in dictionaries, keyword lists, indexes, brochures in stands, books shelved in libraries, and web searches	Incidental contiguity of images, for instance in photo websites	Circumstantial arrays, cityscapes, landscapes, buildings	Juxtaposed objects	Pedestrians, passengers, audiences, classes, crowds	Shuffle playlists, ambient sounds across time or spatial movement	Casual conversation, small talk, rambling
Scaling	Words in sentences, citations expanding on an idea, items in ontologies, chapters in books	Images within images, curated exhibitions	The complementary functions of rooms in buildings, buildings in neighborhoods	Objects nested in curated exhibitions, shop displays	Organizations, sports, social classes	Musical pieces in a performance, album, or playlist	Points in a discussion, lectures in a series
Expressive Causality	Textual genres in socio-cultural context	Visual genres in socio-cultural context	Architectonic and landscape genres	Kinds of object in socio-cultural context	Affection, violence etc. in their varied historical and cultural manifestations	Musical genres, soundscapes in socio-cultural context	Kinds of speech act

Fig. 1.5(ii): Some examples of seriality, scaling, and causality

do not look at one another." Such is "the practico-inert ensemble within which there is a movement towards interchangeability … of the instrumental ensemble." This does not mean lack of association, which Sartre calls "serial unity," even if it is a "provisional negation of their reciprocal obligation to Others."

Contrast this with these people's actual social relations, Sartre suggests. These may well be on their mind at the time, waiting for the bus – their families, their bosses, in other words "social structures in so far as they express the fundamental social order." Such meanings involve scaling, from the embodied person to social structures; and expressive causality where instances of meaning are expressive of what Sartre calls a "totality."

Sartre goes on to speak of collectives as the basis for a mapping of social causes, the social meanings made by soldiers in armies, workers in unions, anti-Semites in racist movements – each is an "organized form of social relations." The collective then associates by expressive causality, as a consequence of which "plurality becomes unity, alterity becomes my own spontaneity, … a human relation of reciprocity."[482] Perhaps even, the serially associated bodies at the bus stop might be inspired to take political action in support of public

---

[482] Jean-Paul Sartre, 1960 [1976], *Critique of Dialectical Reason*, translated by A. Sheridan-Smith, London: Verso, pp. 256–57, 261, 268–69.

transport. In our terms, these are vectors of transposition, the ever-present possibility, immanent as well as imminent, of transposition in contextual association between serial juxtaposition, hierarchical scaling, and collective activation or expressive causality. Critical interpretations of seriality, scaling, and expressive causality may become the bases for alternative design analyses. They may become reasons to (re)design.

And another example of association in context: timescaling.[483] I am walking through a gallery that steps through an artist's development, or a natural history museum that chronicles the evolution of life on earth. I am reading a biography or an historical novel. I experience these things serially. Moments in each timeline are nested within the timeframe. These are parallel scales of time, the one compressed scale (my gallery or museum perambulations, my reading), transposing for another (natural history, life history). These may also be taken as expressive causalities, representing the totalities of natural history, a symptomatic life in the culture, or an historical era. In these ways, associations in context are always and necessarily on the move, between seriality, scaling, and expressive totality.

§1.6 Genre

> **Genre.** *Patterns of similarity between artifacts of meaning across context, according to their form and function.*

In our earlier work on genre in writing, we defined genre as "the relation of the social purpose of text to language structure; . . . the different social purposes that inform patterns of regularity in language – the whys and hows of textual conventionality."[484] Now we would call this the relation of form to function, and the ever-present unique recombination in (re)design. We have also built a schema that will encompass multimodality.

M.M. Bakhtin[§2.1.2b] defines "speech genres" as "relatively stable types of . . . utterances," according to their "thematic content" (we expand this to encompass meaning function), "linguistic style, . . . and compositional structure" (which we expand to meaning form).[485] M.A.K. Halliday and Ruqaiya

---

[483] Ron Scollon and Suzie Wong Scollon, 2014, "Multimodality and Language: A Retrospective and Prospective View," pp. 205–16 in *The Routledge Handbook of Multimodal Analysis*, edited by C. Jewitt, London: Routledge; Jay L. Lemke, 2000, "Across the Scales of Time: Artifacts, Activities, and Meanings in Ecosocial Systems," *Mind, Culture and Activity* 7(4):273–90.

[484] Bill Cope and Mary Kalantzis, eds. 1993, *The Powers of Literacy: Genre Approaches to Teaching Writing*, London, UK: Falmer Press and Pittsburgh, PA: University of Pennsylvania Press, p. 2.

[485] M.M. Bakhtin, 1952 [1986], "The Problem of Speech Genres," pp. 60–102 in *Speech Genres and Other Late Essays*, edited by C. Emerson and M. Holquist, Austin: University of Texas Press, p. 60.

Hasan: "A genre is known by the meanings associated with it"[486] – or the functions of the form. Carolyn Miller, on the function side: "a rhetorically sound definition of genre must be centered not on the substance or the form of discourse but on the action it is used to accomplish."[487] John Bateman, on the form side: "Genres ... define families of artifacts or performances as being similar in some respects of organization and form," while at the same time they do "some specifically recognizable social 'work' "[488] (now, the function side).

We locate genre in the function context because it is not just what happens within the frame (the text, the image, the space, the object, the body, the sound, the act of speaking). Genre is the comparability of the meaning form and meaning function with others, the shared features that transcend the peculiarities of the present artifact of meaning. It points us to wider practices of convention. Genre is parallel patterning in the drawing-down of available resources for meaning. Only across context is one church comparable to others as a genre of building in its form and function, or in genres of text, one novel to others.

Here is a rough map, indicative of the range of genres across meaning forms:

Form / Function	Text	Image	Space	Object	Body	Sound	Speech
Genres	Narrative (e.g. novel, short story, web navigation), argument, (e.g. math, report, software code), information (e.g. encyclopedia, textbook, list, database)	Realistic image (e.g. photograph, painting), abstract image, (e.g. map, diagram, some paintings)	Types of room, building, flow paths, environment	Kinds of object, e.g. domestic/ industrial, for utility/ aesthetics, pedagogical/ pleasurable	Kinds of body, appearance and sexuality ("gendre") by physical makeup and cultural ascription	Musical genres in social context, kinds of ambient sound or alert as markers of natural and artificial context	Dialogue, monologue, inner speech

Fig. 1.6: Some genres

Beside the conventionality of genres, these transposable patterns in meaning that configure similarity across context, there are also endemic patterns of

---

[486] M.A.K. Halliday and Ruqaiya Hasan, 1985, *Language, Context, and Text: Aspects of Language in a Social-Semiotic Perspective*, Geelong, Australia: Deakin University Press, p. 108.

[487] Carolyn R. Miller, 1984, "Genre as Social Action," *Quarterly Journal of Speech* 70(2):151–67, p. 151.

[488] John A. Bateman, 2016, "Methodological and Theoretical Issues in Multimodality," pp. 36–74 in *Handbuch Sprache Im Multimodalen Kontext*, edited by N. Klug and H. Stöckl, Berlin: Walter de Gruyter, p. 60; John A. Bateman, 2008, *Multimodality and Genre: A Foundation for the Systematic Analysis of Multimodal Documents*, London: Palgrave.

differing. One pattern of differing is in the always unique redesign of meaning. Available designs, when reworked in a new context, always create (re)designs that are uniquely (re)configured, no matter how minutely, and context plays a big part in that reconfiguration. The world is repeated, but the world is also always new.

Then there is transgression. "The fact that a work 'disobeys' its genre does not make the latter nonexistent," say Tzvetan Todorov and Richard Berrong. Indeed, to the contrary, "transgression, in order to exist as such, requires a law that will, of course, be transgressed. One could go further: the norm becomes visible – lives – only by its transgressions."[489]

There are also hybrid crossovers and in-between genres. Text messaging is like speech, but not, and a distinctive genre in its own right. So are lectures and poetry, distinctive in their form for the way they capture aspects of the affordances of both text and speech.[§1.4.1]

One measure of the existence of genre might be the discomfort of defying conventionality, sleeping in a kitchen or cooking in a bedroom, for instance. Sometimes the discomforts are warranted: running a marathon along a road instead of driving, or camping instead of staying in a hotel. Homeless sleeping in the doorway of an office building is not really a function of the genre of the office or its built form, nor is it like camping. In any event, discomfort is a helpful metaphor, the price of resisting fit-to-genre, with good reason, or not.

§1.6a Gÿorgy Lukács' Theory of the Novel

"Soul and Form," is how György Lukács[§2.4.2b] spoke to a tension in the work of art, the title of one of his earliest works across a long career in always-vexed contexts. His student, György Márkus,[§2.4.2b] speaks to continuities across these works, from *Soul and Form*,[490] to *The Theory of the Novel*,[491] to *History and Class Consciousness*,[492] written by Lukács while in exile in Vienna after the failure of the 1919 Hungarian Revolution, to *The Historical Novel*,[493] written in Moscow under the strictures Stalinism,

---

[489] Tzvetan Todorov and Richard M. Berrong, 1976, "The Origin of Genres," *New Literary History* 8(1):159–70, p. 160.

[490] György Lukács, 1910 [1974], *Soul and Form*, translated by A. Bostock, Cambridge, MA: MIT Press.

[491] György Lukács, 1920 [1978], *The Theory of the Novel: A Historico-Philosophical Essay on the Forms of Great Epic Literature*, translated by A. Bostock, London: Merlin.

[492] György Lukács, 1923 [1971], *History and Class Consciousness*, Translated by R. Livingstone, London: Merlin Press.

[493] György Lukács, 1937 [1983], *The Historical Novel*, translated by H. Mitchell and S. Mitchell, Lincoln: University of Nebraska Press.

to his late writings on art and literature[494] before and after the suppressed Hungarian uprising of 1956.[*]

From Márkus' paraphrase of Lukács' earliest works: in art the "many facts and elements of life can be arranged and combined into meaningful structures by means of form." Lukács in his own words: "It is the form that prescribes speed, rhythm, fluctuation, density and liquidity, hardness and softness; that accentuates what is deemed important while removing what is deemed unimportant; that places some things at the center, others into the background, structuring each group within itself." This is just what we mean by "form" in this grammar.

As for the other side of Lukács' soul–form antinomy, the "soul" as expressed in art is "the process of rendering life meaningful and conscious, overcoming the vicissitudes of life situations and life contexts . . . Every art work entails a kind of glancing at and through life."[495] For now-anachronistic notion of "soul," we would substitute "meaning function."

In the case of the novel, we want to make a distinction between text as form and novel as genre. Novels are text, and almost purely so compared to information books which rely more heavily on layout and image. The layout of information texts facilitates non-linear readings, with their granular and clearly headed sectioning, tables of contents, indexing, and hypertextual referencing of external sources. They also have image–text relations in captioned pictures, diagrams, tables, mathematical notation, or maps.[§1.4.7c] But novels are minimally multimodal, if at all. To the extent that they are, it is in their restricted capacity to reproduce the sounds and idioms of speech in direct quotation, and their attempts to describe settings in ways that are picture-like in their gratuitous detail.

Nevertheless, from their form as text, novels as a genre inherit some fundamental meaning functions. Their design is premeditated and stylized in a way that is impossible in speech, by meticulous phrasing and repeated working-over. Before word processing this was achieved by slow and repeated drafting. With the digitization of scribing, the recursive multilinearity in fabrication is intensified, if and when the author takes the care.[§1.4.7d]

In the genre of the novel, these intrinsic affordances of text are hidden by a series of figurative tricks. The narrator is a pseudo-speaker. This is the paradox of linear reading, where the text of the novel flows smoothly past as if it were monologue, the narrator it seems merely speaking, streaming word after word, paragraph after paragraph after paragraph, chapter after unyielding chapter. Direct quotes attributed to the characters re-enact speech. But of course, these

---

[*] http://meaningpatterns.net/lukacs

[494] György Lukács, 1947 [2013], *The Culture of People's Democracy*, Chicago, IL: Haymarket Books.
[495] György Márkus, 1977, "The Soul and Life: The Young Lukacs and the Problem of Culture," *Telos* (32):95–115, p. 105.

wordings on the printed page have been carefully premeditated, without necessary redundancy, without irrelevance, without miscues, without slips except the ones that have to be feigned, and without the inaudible overlapping of speakers or time-wasting pauses.

There is also vivid picturing of scenes, as if the reader might be able to see the same thing in their mind's eye, but of course they can't, no matter how graphic the attempt. And unlike a picture, the viewing path through the text is relentlessly linear, descriptive word by descriptive word. Readers are made to see in a way never required in an image. These are just tricks, transpositions from speech and image that either fail to retain their characteristic forms, or do so only by pretense. Such are the affordances of text-as-form, inherited by the novel.

Now, the novel as genre. Texts play through canonically as macro-genres: narrative, argument, or information. Orientation > complication > resolution, we might instruct children writing stories. The novel runs according to a macro-patterning of genre that we call narrative, whose function is to reconstruct a time- and place-delimited event.[496] The novel is a sub-genre. In a further generic subdivision, there are the historical novel, romance, science fiction, the detective story, and a myriad of others. Genre is how we analyze and classify these finer variations in text-form and function.

In terms of their associations, by seriality novels might be collocated alphabetically by author in a bookstore or library. Or, less trivially, subgenres are scaled from specialized to more general: historical novel > novel. However, the most insightful of analyses address the genre of the novel in terms of its expressive causality. In its most general terms, what is the social function of the novel as a genre?

Asks Lukács at the beginning of *The Theory of the Novel*, "what is the task of true philosophy if it is not to draw [an] archetypical map?" That map, in the case of the novel, is a peculiarly modern one. "[T]he novel seeks, by giving form, to uncover and construct the concealed totality of life" through "the problematic individual's journeying ... towards clear self-recognition." It "irradiates the individual's life as immanent meaning; but the conflict between what is and what should be has not been abolished." The novel "raises an individual to the infinite heights of one who must create an entire world through his experience."[497]

---

[496] Mary Macken, Mary Kalantzis, Gunther Kress, Jim Martin, Bill Cope, and Joan Rothery, 1990, *A Genre-Based Approach to Teaching Writing, Years 3–6, Book 3: Writing Stories: A Teaching Unit Based on Narratives About Fairy Tales*, Sydney: Directorate of Studies, N.S.W. Department of Education; Bill Cope and Mary Kalantzis, eds. 1993, *The Powers of Literacy: Genre Approaches to Teaching Writing*, London, UK: Falmer Press and Pittsburgh, PA: University of Pennsylvania Press.

[497] György Lukács, 1920 [1978], *The Theory of the Novel: A Historico-Philosophical Essay on the Forms of Great Epic Literature*, translated by A. Bostock, London: Merlin, pp. 29, 60, 80, 83.

So, to Tolstoy in *War and Peace*. The personal thoughts of Andrey Bolkonsky overlay the horrors of war. The specificities of domestic life and war are generalizable as meanings of love and war – its insubstantiality, its disappointments, its rhythms, its necessities, its solidarities, its lines of visceral conflict. Subjective feelings are writ large as war impacts private lives. "Epochal characteristics" are expressed in the minutiae of speech and location.[498]

In the genre of the novel, the individual is expressive of the social whole, in the talismanic characters, the patterns of their actions, the things they think in their speaking, and the symptomatic micro-events (this particular conversation, this person being wounded in battle at this moment). The modernity of the novel is its transpositions between the introspective self (the narrator, the direct speech of the character) and the generalizable social, the personal standing for the existential.

Then another transposition, as the lone reader puts themselves virtually in the place of the novel's setting. The reader commits to take on, by sympathy or resistant repugnance, the narrator's and the characters' mindsets. And they make a mental shift across time frames, reading in a shorter time a reported sequence of events that, if they were real, would take much longer to unfold – except for wanton genre-transgression, where to read though Leopold Bloom's perambulating thoughts for a day in James Joyce's *Ulysses* will take the reader longer than the single day the novel purports to portray.

For all its quintessentially modern, angsty, personalized emotion, for the narcissism of both narrators and characters – as if they could ever be expressive of society or history in its totality – the novel nevertheless inherits some of its most general features from earlier narrative genres. In Biblical narratives, medieval exegesis identified a four-level system of transposition, a "fourfold differentiation of senses" in the words of mid-thirteenth-century theologian Dom Jean Leclercq: "history, allegory, tropology, and anagogy."[499] These, in more contemporary terms, are four kinds of expressive causality, four transpositions of writing to reading: the literal historical narrative, of Christ's life for instance; allegory, where parts of the Old Testament prefigure the New and these in turn prefigure a prophetic future; moral lessons, repeatable in life; and reasoning towards revelation of essential meanings.[500] The novel does its own version of these old narrative maneuvers, albeit in a modern, quasi-spoken, psyche-centered, voice.

---

[498] Ibid., pp. 149–50; György Lukács, 1937 [1983], *The Historical Novel*, translated by H. Mitchell and S. Mitchell, Lincoln: University of Nebraska Press, pp. 43, 285–87; György Lukács, 1947 [2013], *The Culture of People's Democracy*, Chicago, IL: Haymarket Books, p. 118.

[499] Henri de Lubac, 1959 [1998], *Medieval Exegesis: The Four Senses of Scripture*, Volume 1, Grand Rapids, MI: William B. Eerdmans Publishing Company, p. 73.

[500] Fredric Jameson, 1971, *Marxism and Form: Twentieth Century Dialectical Theories of Literature*, Princeton, NJ: Princeton University Press, pp. 29–31.

Back to *War and Peace*. The novel later transposes its form to film, with the gains as well as losses that accompany any such movement. Hollywood made a version with Audrey Hepburn in the 1950s, seen by large audiences in the Soviet Union. It became a point of communist pride to best it with Sergei Bondarchuk's version of 1965–67, allegedly the most expensive film ever made. Antiques were taken from museums; costumes and weapons were meticulously reconstructed – such are the cinematic devices for transposition, faithful by trope to the historical record.[501]

If the American version is cinematic literature of romance, the Soviet version transposes the experience of Napoleon's invasion of Russia, outside of the living memory of audiences, with Hitler's, then still within the living memory. The extras on the cinematic battlefield really were soldiers from the Red Army, and this really was the Cold War.

---

[501] Denise J. Youngblood, 2014, *Bondarchuk's War and Peace: Literary Classic to Soviet Cinematic Epic*, Lawrence: University Press of Kansas.

Part 2 Interest

§2.0   Overview of Part 2

Interest disrupts the idea that meanings are shared in communication – a common definition of communication as meaning-congruence, as shared understanding between participants, as the meeting of minds. This assumption frequently underlies theories of meaning that prioritize communication over representation and interpretation. However, as soon as representation and interpretation are brought into the picture, productive divergences in interest and conflicts of interest come into view.

Our premise in this grammar is that the interests of participants in meaning are never simply shared. Perhaps the not-sharing is in small ways. Or the differences may be major in the case of fundamental misunderstandings. The non-alignment can at times be gross. Sometimes the differences are mutually beneficial. Other times, the one interest can be at the expense of the other. There is also always more of meaning that could be shared, and the ellisions are symptomatic. The boundaries of sharable and shared meanings might be determined by their apparent relevance, the self-restraint of sociability, or deliberate dissembling.

Whatever the modulations, the interest of participants in meaning is always at play in the dialectical relations of their differences, not anticipated sameness. Indeed, communication as simply-shared, straightforwardly congruent meaning, is impossible. If meanings are shared, it is only in part. Meaning also entails systematic incongruence.

Among the illustrations in this part of the book, we will look at the dynamics of incongruence in the politics of persuasion (rhetoric), and the pragmatics of buying and selling (reification). Here we will find a range of differences in meaning that are integral to participation, some in the activation of complementary interests, others deceptive in subtle or unsubtle ways. On the measure of sociability, some interplays of differential interest are antagonistic; others solidary.

All expressions of meaning and realizations of interest involve transformation, some of which replicate configurations of interest in their essentials, though their design is reactivated in the moment, and so is specific and contingent. In this sense, the interplay of different interests is unrepeated and unrepeatable. All transformations involve change in the relations of interest, some in small ways, others in larger. Parsing the changes can uncover meanings that were not immedictely obvious. To parse the world is to change its meaning. To change the world is to act on that parsing.

The terms of our discussion are as follows:

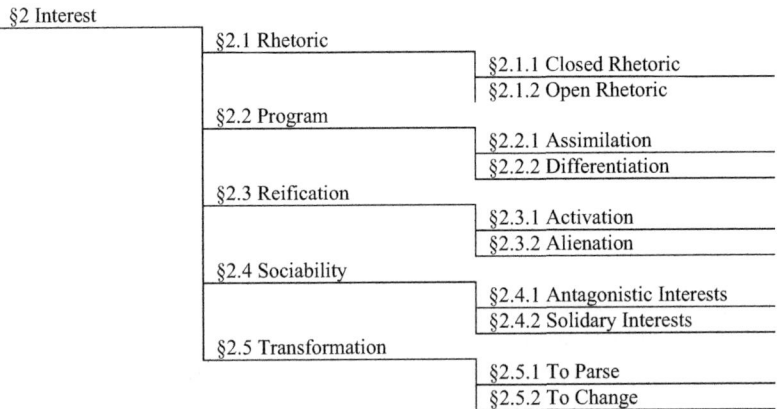

Fig. 2.0: Functions of interest

§2.0a   Jürgen Habermas' Theory of Communicative Action

"At German universities between 1949 and 1954 it was in general only possible to study with professors who had either been Nazis themselves or had conformed. From a political and moral standpoint, German universities were corrupted."[1] So Jürgen Habermas, prolific and widely influential philosopher of communicative competence, describes his experience as a young student after the Second World War.

"[W]e attempted at the time to comprehend the incomprehensible regression into the abyss of fascism. This infected my generation with a deep self-distrust. We began to search for those nagging, anti-Enlightenment genes that had to be hiding in our own traditions . . . Before any preoccupation with philosophy, that was for me the elementary lesson to be learned from the catastrophe: our traditions were under suspicion."[2]

---

[1] Michaël Foessel and Jürgen Habermas, 2008 [2015], "Critique and Communication, Philosophy's Missions: A Conversation with Jürgen Habermas," *Esprit* (8–9): 40–54, p. 40.

[2] Ibid., p. 3.

Among the "corrupted" in post-war West German academe were not only Heidegger, most obviously, but Gadamer, philosopher of "tradition."[§1.2.3b] Habermas wanted to agree with Gadamer about the role of socio-historical context in the process of interpretation, where meanings are not straightforwardly communicated.[3] However, he also wanted to disagree vehemently. Says Habermas in a celebrated scholarly debate, "Gadamer has used hermeneutical insight into the prejudicial structure of understanding to rehabilitate prejudice."[4] Gadamer, he says, describes the communicative-interpretative processes for the active internalization and refinement of tradition, not for its critique. Wittgenstein's "form of life,"[§MS2.3.2a] Habermas also says, is even more restrictive than Gadamer's "tradition," because Wittgenstein doesn't even take into account its cultural peculiarity or historicity.[5] There is no place in Wittgenstein for the critical parsing of a form of life.

The problem that Habermas[*] raises in his critiques of Gadamer and Wittgenstein is the existence of "systematically distorted communication," or communication corrupted by disguised or undisguised interests.[6] "Language is also a medium of domination and social power. It serves to legitimate relationships of organized force."[7] Domination is institutionalized by "structures of distorted communication."[8] Referring both to Gadamer and Wittgenstein, "we have good reason to suspect that the background consensus of established traditions and language games can be a consciousness forged of compulsion, a result of pseudocommunication."[9]

In cases of systematic distortion, the meaning of the communication is not in a meaning that is ostensibly shared; it is in the disjunction between the interests of the participants in that meaning. Habermas goes on to elaborate his theory of

---

* http://meaningpatterns.net/habermas

[3] Jürgen Habermas, 1978, *Knowledge and Human Interests*, London: Heinemann, Chapter 8.
[4] Jürgen Habermas, 1970 [1985], "On Hermeneutics' Claim to Universality," pp. 293–319 in *The Hermeneutics Reader: Texts of the German Tradition from the Enlightenment to the Present*, edited by K. Mueller-Vollmer, New York: Continuum, p. 315.
[5] Jürgen Habermas, 1967 [1988], *On the Logic of the Social Sciences*, translated by S.W. Nicholsen and J.A. Stark, Cambridge, MA: MIT Press, pp. 116–20, 148–49.
[6] Jürgen Habermas, 1970 [1985], "On Hermeneutics' Claim to Universality," pp. 293–319 in *The Hermeneutics Reader: Texts of the German Tradition from the Enlightenment to the Present*, edited by K. Mueller-Vollmer, New York: Continuum, pp. 310, 316.
[7] Jürgen Habermas, 1967 [1988], *On the Logic of the Social Sciences*, translated by S.W. Nicholsen and J.A. Stark, Cambridge, MA: MIT Press, p. 172.
[8] Jürgen Habermas, 1971 [1974], *Theory and Practice*, translated by J. Viertel, London: Heinemann, p. 22.
[9] Jürgen Habermas, 1970 [1985], "On Hermeneutics' Claim to Universality," pp. 293–319 in *The Hermeneutics Reader: Texts of the German Tradition from the Enlightenment to the Present*, edited by K. Mueller-Vollmer, New York: Continuum, p. 317; Jürgen Habermas, 1970 [1990], "A Review of Gadamer's 'Truth and Method'," pp. 213–44 in *The Hermeneutic Tradition: From Ast to Ricoeur*, edited by G.L. Ormiston and A.D. Schrift, Albany: State University of New York Press.

an ideal communicative situation where it is possible to argue through interests and so to resolve problems of human life – in the political discourse of social democracy, for instance. This points us towards "the transcending force of reflection."[10]

One of the key vectors of distortion in Habermas' account is the rise of "instrumental reason"[11] in modernity, an institutional-technocratic discourse of ends and means that obscures human interests in the everyday, subjective, communicative experience of "the lifeworld."[12] To restore a self- and social understanding of interest – this becomes Habermas' philosophical and political project.[13]

"I term as 'communicative reason' the capacity of social actors to operate in this space of reasons with a critical probe instead of fumbling blind. This ability manifests itself in saying 'no,' in loudly protesting or in quietly annulling an assumed consensus."[14] Habermas' project was to create ideal situations for critical communicative action.

Habermas held great hope for social democracy and the creation of conditions where arguments about interest could be fairly had, and just resolutions reached. He thought that, after the horrors of the twentieth century, the European Union might evolve into a new model of cosmopolitan constitutionalism, escaping the narrowness of nationalism and Europe's authoritarian past. He held out hope for the United Nations as a site of democratic governance in an era of globalization.

But by the turn of the twenty-first century, he had arrived at pessimistic conclusions. In a 1998 paper "Learning by Disaster," he chronicled persistent failures to communicate and to learn – social, economic, and environmental.[15]

The world cannot be changed by communication alone, in part because the context of communication is one where interests are unbalanced by inequalities, where those with power are able to dominate processes of participation in meaning – and beyond communication, our interpretations and representations too. Not only is communication distorted; so are our meanings, both in the institutions of social life and the lifeworld of everyday experience.

The question, then, is what is to be done?

[10] Jürgen Habermas, 1967 [1988], *On the Logic of the Social Sciences*, translated by S.W. Nicholsen and J.A. Stark, Cambridge, MA: MIT Press, p. 172.

[11] Jürgen Habermas, 1981 [1984], *The Theory of Communicative Action*, Volume 1: *Reason and the Rationalization of Society*, translated by T. McCarthy, London: Heinemann, p. 366.

[12] Jürgen Habermas, 1981 [1987], *The Theory of Communicative Action*, Volume 2: *Lifeworld and System, a Critique of Functionalist Reason*, translated by T. McCarthy, Boston, MA: Beacon Press, pp. 117–19.

[13] Jürgen Habermas, 1978, *Knowledge and Human Interests*, London: Heinemann, pp. 306–11.

[14] Michaël Foessel and Jürgen Habermas, 2008 [2015], "Critique and Communication, Philosophy's Missions: A Conversation with Jürgen Habermas," *Esprit* (8–9): 40–54, p. 49.

[15] Jürgen Habermas, 1998, "Learning by Disaster: A Diagnostic Look Back on the Short Twentieth Century," *Constellations* 5(3):307–20.

§2 INTEREST

> ***Interest.*** *The purposes that participants in meaning bring from their context of meaning to each situation of meaning; and the meaning-work participants do to negotiate their inevitable differences.*

One of the tasks for a functional grammar is to trace the dynamics of participation in meaning when interests diverge, as always they must. Elsewhere, we have created a classification scheme for the kinds of differences with which modern societies are riven, differences entailing inequalities which over the past several thousand years have manifested themselves both in the vicious controls of formal institutions and in informal but nevertheless durable lifeworld traditions. These we have catalogued as: material conditions (social class, locale, and family); corporeal attributes (age, "race," sex and sexuality, physical and mental abilities); and cultural forms (language, ethnos, and communities of commitment). Or deeper still, and more variegated, lifeworld differences of affinity, persona, agency, and experiential narrative. Interests are always uniquely configured in a matrix of history and experience.[16]

We are going to classify the negotiation of these interests in the processes of meaning into several kinds of appeal: rhetorical, programmatic, reifying, sociable, and transformative. These are different kinds of activity for the expression of interest. They may be simultaneous, and in the incessant fluidity the one may readily transpose into the other.

In rhetoric, different interests are explicitly built in, relatively undisguised and so, for better or for worse, experienced by communicators and interpreters as one-sided. The effects may be to assimilate or differentiate, to create antagonistic or solidary interests, to parse the world or to change the world.

Programs create frames of reference for meaning, either by assimilating, oriented to thinking and being alike, or differentiating, dividing at times to establish autonomy, at times in order to rule. Such frames are bounded by notions of "us" and "them."

In reified meanings, interests are embedded; they can disappear from view because they are "naturalized" in the apparently inexorable presence of things and states of affairs; or they can be brought to light for the interests that they embody. Reified meanings can be activated in ways which realize our interests; or they can work contrary to our interests, in which case the effect may be alienation.

---

[16] Mary Kalantzis and Bill Cope, 2016b, "Learner Differences in Theory and Practice," *Open Review of Educational Research* 3(1):85–132; Mary Kalantzis and Bill Cope, 2012, *New Learning: Elements of a Science of Education* (Edn 2), Cambridge: Cambridge University Press, Chapter 5.

There is also an invariably sociable aspect to interests, where differences are put to generative use. These may be antagonistic, where interests conflict, or solidary, where they are mutually beneficial. In transpositions that cross alternative programs, antagonistic interests can attempt to force sameness by assimilation, or divide and rule by differentiation. Solidary interests can also work on assimilations of sorts (inclusion, access, equity, equality); or modes of differentiation that are solidary in their intent and effect, functions of participation in meaning that we have elsewhere termed "productive diversity"[17] or "civic pluralism."[18]

Then transformation: we can parse the world and we can change the world. And the parsing may demand of us the changing.

§2a   Sophia's Praying Mantis

> "PRAYING MANTIS"   "PAPOU LOVES INSECTS."
> BY SOPHIA 1.31.12

On the paper below these words, there is a large expanse of black, in broad brushstrokes. Sophia, aged two and a half, wanted to make a present for her Papou (Greek for grandfather).[*] Her teacher helped her make an artwork, there in My Little Village, Sophia's preschool on Avenue A, "Alphabet City," in New York's East Village. "A" is for assault, "B" is for battery, "C" is for crime, "D" for death, they used to say for each of these Avenues, before the East Village became fashionable. Sophia said what the picture meant and her teacher wrote it for her. This was for Papou's birthday.

Later her Papou had the picture framed, in pink because he knew it was at the time her favorite color. (By five, she was in partial gender revolt; blue had become her favorite color, and she couldn't understand why Papou had framed it because by then, she had learned to do "better" pictures.)

What is this picture? To cycle back over some ideas we have been developing in this grammar, Sophia is representing something she and Papou had seen together, though not in New York City, at Papou's place in the country. Papou's gender game is not to be scared of these beautiful, delicate things – you can take one gently without hurting it, and it will walk up your arm, funny feeling, but be brave! Look at these creatures with love and care. Be a scientist!

---

* http://meaningpatterns.net/sophia

[17] Bill Cope and Mary Kalantzis, 1997b, *Productive Diversity*, Sydney: Pluto Press; Mary Kalantzis and Bill Cope, 2016a, "New Media and Productive Diversity in Learning," pp. 310–25 in *Diversity in Der Lehrerinnenbildung*, edited by S. Barsch and N. Glutsch, Münster: Waxmann.
[18] Mary Kalantzis, 2000, "Multicultural Citizenship," pp. 99–110 in *Rethinking Australian Citizenship*, edited by W. Hudson and J. Kane, Melbourne: Cambridge University Press.

From representation to communication, there is a transposition of form to form: from the embodied meaning in the feeling of a praying mantis on the skin of your arm, to a painting; from Sophia's experience to her speech; from Sophia's speaking to her teacher's listening and writing; from art as communication to the interpretative aids of title, date, and descriptive gloss following the conventions of art and galleries, with an explanatory gloss after the title, all pointing to the artist's intent; from the gesture of the gift to birthday rituals and "papous" of Greek, a language whose presence in New York is at once exotic for the polis and normal for the cosmopolis. Sophia must have told the teacher what a "Papou" was, and the teacher must have liked that, not to have translated it into English. These are just a few vectors of interest in a polyphony of multimodal transpositions.

Here we have the complex warp and weft of shared, but also critically different interests in meaning – where love, science, and teacherly support come together in the social project that is participation in meaning. "Praying Mantis" is to be located in a community of parties to some very special pleadings. Papou loves insects, and Sophia is trying to love them too, for him. Both parties' participation is born of their difference: Papou wishing Sophia to love science but Sophia's anxieties about the crawly materiality of its creatures; Sophia's living in the city and Papou's living in the country; Papou's grandfatherhood and Sophia's granddaughterhood; Sophia's studentliness and her teacher's teacherliness. The interests in this context differ in these and so many other ways.

So there is the meaning, but not the false hope of isomorphism that accompanies the word "communication." Communication in this sense cannot be more or less effective by virtue of its faithful transmission of meaning, because there can be no such thing. But the meanings-in-difference can be parsed and understood.

The practice of meaning is multimodal, and the meaning happens in the work of transposition. Any account of meaning must extend way beyond the making and the seeing of the picture and the reading of its text. Then, on a functional vector, this is not just an act of communication because the meanings integrally depend upon and anticipate acts of representation and interpretation.

And another vector of functional transposition: Sophia starts with abstraction – in Peirce's terms, the symbolic – and later learns to value "better paintings" because they offer a more realistic likeness – Peirce's iconic.[§1.0b] The form of this communication is just a function of Sophia's capacities at age two and a half, and painting as her chosen form of visualization.

Michael Halliday[§MS0.3a] studied his Nigel, where the linguist found his son meaning before he had language. "Before he can *talk about* meaning, a child is engaging in *acts of* meaning." When babbling comes, that is meaningful too, even for the habituated linguist: "before he has a mother tongue, he is using his own child tongue to organise his view of the world (and of himself), and to interact with the people around him."[19] This is representation without (so much) communication.

Gunther Kress[§2c] studied his Michael, where he traced one small step in learning to conceptualize using image, moving from the abstract to the concrete.

"Do you want to watch me? I'll make a car ... got two wheels ... and two wheels at the back ... and two wheels here ... This is a car."

This, Kress says, is double sign, where each of the circles means "wheel," and more than one wheel means "car."[20] In the terms we have been developing in this grammar, Michael is at once instantiating wheels and conceptualizing cars.[§MS1.1]

Kress uses Saussure's sign terminology,[§MS3d] but he will also argue against Saussure. Not merely, as Saussure would have it, arbitrary, for Kress these are "motivated signs; ... it is the interest of the sign-maker at the moment of making the sign that leads to the selection of the criteria for representing ... 'wheel-ness' and 'car-ness'." Michael's "interest arises out of his (physical, affective, cultural, social) position in the world at that moment, vis-à-vis the object to be represented. His sign reflects his 'position.' Generalising, we can say that interest at the moment of sign-making arises out of the sign-maker's position in the world; it shapes attention; that frames a part of the world and acts as a principle for the selection of apt signifiers."[21]

§2b   Plato's Sophist

VISITOR [A SOPHIST]: I'll produce some speech by putting a thing together with an action by means of a name and a verb. You have to tell me what it is about.
THEAETETUS: I'll do it as well as I can.
VISITOR: "Theaetetus sits." ... Your job is to tell me what it's about, what it's of.
THEAETETUS: Clearly, it's about me, of me ...
VISITOR: Wherever there is speech it has to be about something ... [The speaker] accomplishes something, by weaving verbs with names. That's why we said he speaks and doesn't just name. In fact, it is this weaving that we use the word "speech" for.[22]

---

[19] M.A.K. Halliday, 1977 [2003], "Ideas About Language," pp. 92–115 in *On Language and Linguistics*, The Collected Works of M.A.K. Halliday, Volume 3, edited by J.J. Webster, London: Continuum, p. 115; M.A.K. Halliday, 1975, *Learning How to Mean: Explorations in the Development of Language*, London: Edward Arnold.

[20] Gunther Kress, 2003, *Literacy in the New Media Age*, London: Routledge, pp. 42–43.

[21] Gunther Kress, 2009, *Multimodality: A Social Semiotic Approach to Contemporary Communication*, London: Routledge, pp. 70–71.

[22] Plato, c.399–347 BCE [1997], "Sophist," in *Complete Works*, edited by J.M. Cooper, Indianapolis, IN: Hackett, 263a, 262e, 262d.

In his inaugural lecture at the University of Sydney in 1976, Michael Halliday used Plato's *Sophist* to highlight an old tension in the study of language, between what he characterized as formalism on the one hand, and the orientation of his linguistics toward a "functional grammar of rhetoric."[23]

Plato's student, Aristotle, was the formalist par excellence – language for him expressed generalizable logico-syntactic reasoning. He "subordinated language to the structure of logic," with his "image of language . . . [as] a set of constituent structure rules," focusing on the structure of sentences as propositions. For the Sophists, however, "a unit of discourse is considered as something that is arguable, something that can be maintained, denied, disputed, contradicted, doubted and urged . . . The sophists saw language as a resource; as a mode of action and a means of putting things across to others." Their "basic view of language is a rhetorical one. A sentence has . . . the potential for being stated, refuted, queried and so on. And stating, refuting, querying – all these are forms of action."[24]

Reaching far back into the history of thinking about language and meaning as he started this new phase of his career in Sydney, the difference Halliday wanted to highlight was between his functional orientation to linguistics, and the structuralists, who in the tradition of Aristotle analyzed language as a formal logico-syntactic system.[*] Rather than a "prescriptive, normative" view, Halliday's was a "descriptive-ethnographic" one, "concerned with meaning in relation to rhetorical function."[25]

With Chomsky's *Syntactic Structures*,[§MS3.1.2f] rhetoric had been thrown out of linguistics. Halliday puts this down to Chomsky's "violent polemic . . . [N]ever before in the history of ideas about language have the two views, of language as resource and language as rule, been made to seem so incompatible. The difference between the two was presented as an opposition between a concern with language as system and a concern with language as behaviour . . . It gradually became clear that the price to be paid for the Chomskyan type of formalism was too high; it required a degree of idealization so great as to reduce natural language back to the status of an artificial syntax."[26] "Instrumental rationality," Habermas might have called this kind of thinking,[§2.0a] blind to variable lifeworld interests, we would add.

In his Sydney years, Halliday went on to elaborate a linguistics that conceived language as a "functional grammar of rhetoric" where language is

---

[*] http://meaningpatterns.net/sophists

[23] M.A.K. Halliday, 1977 [2003], "Ideas About Language," pp. 92–115 in *On Language and Linguistics*, The Collected Works of M.A.K. Halliday, Volume 3, edited by J.J. Webster, London: Continuum, p. 95.
[24] Ibid., pp. 96–98.   [25] Ibid., pp. 99–100.   [26] Ibid., p. 110.

deployed as a "resource for meaning."[27] His was an ethnographic view of language in the context of culture.[§1.1.3b]

"It's about me, of me," Theaetetus had replied to the Sophist-Visitor's question. Not only is this an old discussion in the West, but also in Indian[§MS3.3d] and Arabic[§MS3c] philosophies of meaning.

In the context of culture, language strives to mean – as do images, objects, spaces, gestures, and soundings. Meaning is an appeal from person to person via things or media. It is a negotiation of interests. Rhetoric is the appeal of interest, to interest.

However, even when the words and the syntax seem formally the same, the interests of persons always differ. Participation in meaning occurs at the intersection of interests. Complementary differences meet in the moment of participation or, as it may transpire, interests that prove conflicting and perhaps irresolvably so.

Whatever the nature of agreement or the extent of disagreement, interest is uniquely configured in every situation. Meanings are situation-specific, and situations are endlessly varied.

§2c   *Gunther Kress on Interest and Rhetoric*

Gunther Kress extends Halliday's notions of interest and rhetoric into a grammar of multimodality.[*]

In the work of meaning-making, "the rhetor as maker of a message . . . makes an assessment of all aspects of the communicational situation: of her or his interest; of the characteristics of the audience; the semiotic requirements of the issue at stake and the resources available for making an apt representation." This encompasses not just speaking and writing, but image-making, embodied gesture, spatial and object representations, and communication, perhaps in "YouTube, Facebook, but also non-legitimated sites such as those created by graffito artists."[28]

Agency is established between socially-sourced conventions of meaning and the expressed interest of the meaning-maker, between system-structure and rhetoric-function. In drawing upon available designs for meaning, then in redesigning meanings to express their own representational, communicative, and interpretative interests, rhetors find themselves "uneasily hovering between regularity and repeatability on the one hand – the effect of social

---

* http://meaningpatterns.net/kress-interest

[27] Ibid., p. 95.
[28] Gunther Kress, 2009, *Multimodality: A Social Semiotic Approach to Contemporary Communication*, London: Routledge, pp. 26–27.

stabilities and of regulations erected around text to keep them close to 'convention' – and the dynamic for constant flux and change on the other."[29]

Even the most ordinary social encounter is never entirely predictable; it is always new in some way, however slight, so that the "accommodations" produced in any encounter are always new in some way. They project social possibilities and potentials which differ, even if slightly, from what there had been before the encounter. As a consequence, the semiotic work of interaction is always socially productive, projecting and proposing possibilities of social and semiotic forms, entities and processes which reorient, refocus, and "go beyond," by extending and transforming what there was before the interaction ...

[E]very event of communication is in principle unpredictable in its form, structure and in its "unfolding." The absence of secure frames requires of each participant in an interaction that they assess, on each occasion, the social environment, the social relations which obtain in it and the resources available for shaping the communicational encounter. This demands a rhetorical approach to communication.[30]

In 1994, we had some funds left over from the research we had been doing on workplace literacies. We felt that although we had made progress in an earlier conversation about language conventions clustered around the term "genre,"[31] our thinking had become overly formalized in its emphasis on structure and convention. So, we brought together three of the former Sydney genre group (Gunther Kress and us) with seven others who had shown interest in this work,[§MS0.0] but who had nevertheless expressed ambivalences – divergent interests of a potentially productive kind: Courtney Cazden,[§1.4.1c] Norman Fairclough, Jim Gee,[§1.4.3f] Allan Luke, Carmen Luke, Sarah Michaels and Martin Nakata.

New London, New Hampshire, is a quaint New England town. It was far enough away for us to have an uninterrupted week of discussions, roughly at a mid-point between our geographically disparate locations. By this time Gunther had moved to take up a position at the Institute of Education, London University – old London, old England – and we had moved to James Cook University in North Queensland.

GK I would like now to see the subject at the centre of the theory of representation, the subject is socially constructed, socially located in social and cultural interactions ... I mean, here is a human being ... and that's for me the centre of it ... I think the theory of ... representation needs to have a human agentive social subject at the centre ... The individual makes his or her own subjectivity in the context of available resources, which is a sort of paradox between subjectivity [and

[29] Gunther Kress, 2003, *Literacy in the New Media Age*, London: Routledge, p. 102.
[30] Gunther Kress, 2009, *Multimodality: A Social Semiotic Approach to Contemporary Communication*, London: Routledge, pp. 34, 26.
[31] Bill Cope and Mary Kalantzis, eds. 1993, *The Powers of Literacy: Genre Approaches to Teaching Writing*, London, UK: Falmer Press and Pittsburgh, PA: University of Pennsylvania Press.

conventionality] ... [M]y reading happens from the point of a particular social interest so that the reading of the semiotic world is already an act of transformation, that is, in the reading of this world through my particular interests and my available resources I transform [that world] ...

MK I still like the notion we used to talk about, lifeworlds, and I think they're important ...

GK You used to say, a long time ago in Australia, and I picked it up and have used it, the term "sociality." ... [Y]ou talked about schools in Australia, in Sydney, where there is no commonality in terms of cultural contents; ... all there is, I think you said, are ways of being together, pleasantly, humanly, I mean that's a sort of a brilliant form of being, forms of social living.[32]

By the end of that week, the conversation had been summed up in a word, "Multiliteracies." Then came an article in the *Harvard Educational Review*, and a book, then more,[33] and now this.

§2.1   Rhetoric

> **Rhetoric.** Appeals to differential interests in negotiation among participants through representation, communication, and interpretation.

With its roots in the Latin *communicare*, Raymond Williams points out in his etymology of keywords in social theory, "communicate" means "to make common to many, to impart." This, he says, "has remained its main range of use." However, it is also "useful to recall the unresolved range of the original noun of action, represented in its extremes by 'transmit,' a one-way process, and share, (cf. 'communion' and especially 'communicant'), a common or mutual process."[34]

Either way, whether the idea is "transmit" or "share," the assumption is that a meaning is something that becomes more or less the same for both parties, a

---

[32] Mary Kalantzis and Bill Cope, 2013, "On Transformations: Reflections on the Work of, and Working with, Gunther Kress," pp. 16–32 in *Multimodality and Social Semiosis: Communication, Meaning-Making and Learning in the Work of Gunther Kress*, edited by M. Böck and N. Pachler, London: Routledge.

[33] New London Group, 1996, "A Pedagogy of Multiliteracies: Designing Social Futures," *Harvard Educational Review* 66(1):60–92; Bill Cope and Mary Kalantzis, eds. 2000, *Multiliteracies: Literacy Learning and the Design of Social Futures*, London: Routledge; Bill Cope and Mary Kalantzis, 2009, "'Multiliteracies': New Literacies, New Learning," *Pedagogies: An International Journal* 4:164–95; Mary Kalantzis, Bill Cope, Eveline Chan, and Leanne Dalley-Trim, 2016, *Literacies* (Edn 2), Cambridge: Cambridge University Press; James Paul Gee, 2017, "A Personal Retrospective on the New London Group and Its Formation," pp. 32–45 in *Remixing Multiliteracies: Theory and Practice from New London to New Times*, edited by F. Serfini and E. Gee, New York: Teachers College Press.

[34] Raymond Williams, 1976, *Keywords: A Vocabulary of Culture and Society*, Glasgow: Fontana/ Croom Helm, pp. 62–63.

communion achieved in the convergence of interests. These meanings may be aspirational, idealized, for good reasons as well as at times not-so-good, but they do not capture effectively the more complex realities of communication as rhetoric.

We find this orientation to communication as shared meanings in the work of Umberto Eco, the twentieth century's best-known follower of Charles Sanders Peirce.[§1.0b] In Eco's model of semiosis, there is a message sender, a message expression containing information, and an addressee who receives the message.[*]

Of course, Eco is not so naïve as to consider semiosis to be straightforwardly a process of transmission. His system is full of wise qualifications. There may be ambiguities in the message. The sender may have ideological biases that they do not acknowledge, dooming the message to failure even before it has been received. But these are deviations from the ideal from the sender's perspective, failures to achieve congruence of meaning on the part of the addressee.

Eco's further qualifications: on the receiving end of the message, there is "unpredictable decoding" resulting in "interpretative failures" on the part of the addressee, some of which, perhaps, "the sender would never have foreseen." These may result in "aberrations" that are a "betrayal of the sender's intentions." And even though we are participants in a "vast . . . probabilistic matrix" of meaning, the messages are not indeterminate.[35]

Notwithstanding the complexities and the hazards, if the message-sending proves successful, it must be because something remains of the message that is transmitted and shared. Barring these aberrations, the "normal" state of communication remains sender → message → addressee.

We want to reverse these fundamental presuppositions about the intersection of interests in meaning. In our rhetorical view of communication, these are not failures, betrayals, or unfortunate circumstances of unpredictability. They are the rhetorical norm. They are not system failures; they are the system. The crux of the matter is not about what can be the same; it is about the differences. The ground of meaning is a not a place of architected, in-common sameness. It is a common ground where differences meet – innocently or benevolently at some times, not so innocently and even maliciously at others. Messaging purports, impossibly, to be transmission and communion. Rhetoric, in contrast, is an appeal based, for better and sometimes for worse, in differential interest.

Kinds of rhetoric might be found in evidence in information that one person has but another doesn't; an explanation that a person seeks; or an arguable

---

[*] http://meaningpatterns.net/eco

[35] Umberto Eco, 1976, *A Theory of Semiotics*, Bloomington: Indiana University Press, pp. 140–42.

orientation to some matter. In each case, the reason for participation is the difference. We don't have communion; we have common ground premised on the negotiation of difference.

On the common ground of meaning, we find teachers with students, parents with children, artists with audiences, writers with readers, drivers with passengers, doctors with patients, priests with congregations, builders with inhabitants, sellers with buyers, men with women, bosses with workers, rulers with ruled. In every case, the meaning of participation is the difference. In every case, rhetoric takes form in multimodal transposition, moving across most or all of text, image, space, object, body, sound, and speech. And functional transpositions: the embedded meanings of reification are always ready to be brought to more explicit meanings of rhetoric; rhetoric's programmatic appeal can be assimilative or differentiating; it can be an appeal to the meaning of meaning (to parse), or an appeal to action (to change); some rhetorics may be antagonistic, others solidary. Any moment, each of these expressions of interest can lapse into any other.

Some of the differences that rhetoric brings together may prove to be unconscionable, when for instance the forms of rhetoric reflect and reproduce inequalities, authoritarianism, or prejudice. Other rhetorics may be conscionable, representing necessary or transitory inequalities – parents and children, teachers and learners, experts and lay people, for instance. But even these momentarily conscionable rhetorics of inequality are fraught in a world where all-too-often they align with or refract unconscionable rhetorics designed to perpetuate inequality.

The result is that, in their rhetorical play, some differences of interest may be complementary and generative – we will call this "productive diversity."[36] But equally, the result may in other moments of rhetorical interaction be what Habermas calls "distorted communication."[§2.0a] This may be deliberately so, an appeal to interests that is deceptive to the extent that its consequence is to serve one interest at the expense of the other, while purporting to share. Whether more or less obvious, rhetoric has the capacity to wish away differential interests, as much as to put them to productive use. Rhetoric has the capacity to occlude as much as it has to reveal. Functionally, rhetoric is a shifty thing.

§2.1.1   Closed Rhetoric

> **Closed Rhetoric.** Sets out to limit the scope for meaning of interpreters, to enforce a narrow range of meaning in interpretation.

[36] Bill Cope and Mary Kalantzis, 1997b, *Productive Diversity*, Sydney: Pluto Press; Mary Kalantzis and Bill Cope, 2016a, "New Media and Productive Diversity in Learning," pp. 310–25 in *Diversity in Der Lehrerinnenbildung*, edited by S. Barsch and N. Glutsch, Münster: Waxmann.

Notwithstanding his underlying assumptions about an ideal congruence of meanings-in-participation,[§1.2.3a] Umberto Eco nevertheless makes a useful distinction between closed and open rhetorics. Take, for instance, a process of writing in which the "author has to assume that the ensemble of codes he relies upon is the same as that shared by his possible reader . . . (hereafter Model Reader)."

Closed texts have a fixed view of the Model Reader. They attempt to force a certain kind of interpretation. Open texts, on the other hand, allow more scope for readers to interpret.

But herein lies a paradox: "closed texts, even though aimed at 'obedient' co-operation, are in the last analysis randomly open to every pragmatic accident." The attempt at closure prompts resistance. Meanwhile, the open text, "however 'open' it be, cannot afford whatever interpretation. An open text outlines a closed project of its Model Reader." It may anticipate alternative interpretations and direct the reader, subtly perhaps, towards a model reading. In this way, an open text may, despite appearances, reduce indeterminacy. In both cases, "the 'author' is nothing else but a textual strategy establishing semantic correlations and activating the Model Reader." In both cases, referring now to J.L. Austin,[§MS2.3.1a] "the Model Reader is a textually established felicity condition."[37]

We want to use the idea of open and closed texts, not to point in the direction of interpretative outcome, a model reader or reading, because this is always open. Rather, open and closed texts are rhetorical orientations, different ways in which communicators may attempt to realize their interests in moments of participation.

Closed rhetoric tells or orders. It sets out to erase differences by edict. This may to some degree succeed or fail, but no rhetoric works perfectly to align interests. Even when closed by design, the effect of closed rhetoric can never be completely that. In cases of relative failure, the interpretative effect of closed rhetoric may be to indicate or precipitate dissonance and conflict.

§2.1.2   Open Rhetoric

> ***Open Rhetoric.*** Anticipates the possibility of differences in interpretation, making space for alternatives.

Open rhetoric offers space for negotiation. It accommodates differences, often not for mutual benefit (we call this the "productive diversity" of solidary

---

[37] Umberto Eco, 1979, *The Role of the Reader: Explorations in the Semiotics of Texts*, Bloomington: Indiana University Press, pp. 7, 10, 11.

interests[§2.4.2]), but to assimilate them. If closed rhetoric is an expression of hard power, open rhetoric is soft power.

This is not to say that the purveyors of open rhetoric are always good at what they do. They may think they have anticipated differences, but they may have anticipated wrongly. They may come off as obsequious, or patronizing, or smarmy.

Notwithstanding their contrasting rhetorical orientations, both open and closed rhetoric are premised on perceived or actual disjunctions of meaning. Nor is open rhetoric any more likely to "succeed," because at least somewhat different interests will always remain. It's just that interests are expressed in quite different ways in closed and open rhetoric.

Here are some expressions of interest in open and closed rhetoric:

Form Function: Rhetoric	Text	Image	Space	Object	Body	Sound	Speech
Closed Rhetoric	Information, explanation, argument	Realistic	Strict architectonic programs that channel flows and determine uses	Restricted use	Pointing, beckoning, directing	Alerts	Telling
Open Rhetoric	Narrative, activity streams, feeds, forms	Abstract	Architectonic programs that allow alternative flows and uses	Wide range of uses	Expressions of sentiment, turn-taking	Ambient sounds	Dialogue

Fig. 2.1.2: Closed and open rhetoric

§2.1.2a *Eloise Murphy's* Love Wheels

When we were in Calcutta and met Mother Teresa,[§MS3.3d] we also visited the Indian Museum down the road. Founded in 1814, it is the oldest museum in South Asia. The current building was opened in 1875, in the heyday of the British Raj. Then, it was the Imperial Museum at Calcutta, and Calcutta was the capital of British India.[38]

A room full of stuffed birds, every bird of the subcontinent, we imagined, all in glass cases. Then a room full of minerals, a room full of fossils, a room full of Buddhas. Today there are 102,646 items, Wikipedia says. It seemed to us that one of every kind of thing of national significance must be on display as a matter of empirically exhaustive principle. There was also "a fine series of human skulls representing various Indian races."

[38] Shakunt Pandey, 2014, "The Indian Museum Completes 200 Years," *Science Reporter*, October: 38–41.

Now to another national museum, the National Museum of Australia in Canberra.[*] "The National Museum brings to life the rich and diverse stories of Australia through compelling objects, ideas and events," says its website. Instead of showing everything, the museum offers a sampling of what it considers "compelling." And of all the things that could be shown, "[w]e focus on Indigenous histories and cultures, European settlement and our interaction with the environment."[39] In the museum, long stretches of "interpretative" text belabor "compelling" narrative. Interpretation here means that "we," the curators, are here to help you to understand.

"Love Wheels" went on display at the Museum in 2018, the year after Australians voted in a referendum to support marriage equality. Although the museum said it was documenting both sides of the debate, on display was just one "compelling" object, representing just one side.

"Eloise Murphy," the curator explained, is a "yarn bomber" and member of the guerrilla crochet movement, "bringing unexpected bursts of colour to cities, and covering ordinary objects – such as street signs, trees and bicycles, with extraordinary crocheted decorations." She had placed the bicycle, crocheted in rainbow colors, outside Prime Minister Malcolm Turnbull's house – his decision to put the issue to a referendum had been controversial. But later he with his wife came to the opening of the display at the museum.

"Artist's motivation: I wanted to be able to say how lovely it would be if everyone could have the same feelings Malcolm did all those years ago by being free to marry the person they love as well."[40] It's not clear whether "Malcolm's" feelings had been quite so straightforwardly lovely during this contentious political process.

Here we encounter the paradox of closed and open texts that Umberto Eco addresses.[§2.1.1] The Indian Museum is a closed text for its empirical exhaustiveness but it leaves a lot of space for the visitor to find things that interest them, or to resist them when they reach the glass case of skulls. The Australian National Museum is open for its "inclusiveness,"[41] welcoming of cosmopolitan diversity. But its rhetorical strategy is closed. We might want to agree (or not) with its directly expressed sentiments, but it feels didactic, a "politically correct"[42] plea to conform with the curator, while the Indian museum does not.

---

* http://meaningpatterns.net/museum

[39] www.nma.gov.au/about_us
[40] www.nma.gov.au/about_us/news/articles/love-wheels-canberra
[41] Amareswar Galla, ed. 2012, *World Heritage: Benefits Beyond Borders*, Cambridge: Cambridge University Press.
[42] Bill Cope and Mary Kalantzis, 1997a, "White Noise: The Attack on Political Correctness and the Struggle for the Western Canon," *Interchange* 28(4):283–329.

§2.1.2b M.M. Bakhtin's "Heteroglossia"

Mikhail Bakhtin[0.1a] was a man of multiple lives. He started his intellectual life in the first years of the Russian Revolution living in a vibrant community of artists including Marc Chagall and Kazemir Malevich. Here, he explored "the architectonics of answerability." Then he became a writer of literary and linguistic theory; was tried and exiled to Kazakhstan for speech crimes; became a professor of literature in a small regional university; and finally, in the last years of his life, a celebrated Soviet intellectual. His multiple lives were also lived in parallel, publishing under the names M.M. Bakhtin, V.N. Vološinov, and P.N. Medvedev. Bakhtin's theory, just as much as his life, speaks to multiple sources and contingent meanings.[*]

For his thinking, the counterpoint Bakhtin chose was Ferdinand de Saussure's[MS3d] "abstract objectivism." Saussure, he says, focuses "language as a system of normatively identical forms" at the expense of the "individuality and randomness" of utterances. This he tracks back to an occupational hazard for linguists whose starting point was the "ancient written monument," texts that can only now be "defunct, monological utterance . . . European linguistic thought formed and matured over concern with the cadavers of written languages." Having in mind, surely, that Saussure was a Sanskrit scholar, Bakhtin says, "Despite the vast differences in cultural and historical lineaments from the ancient Hindu priests to the modern European scholar of language, the philologist has always been a decipherer of alien, 'secret' scripts . . . foreign and incomprehensible to the profane. To decipher the mystery of sacred words was a task meant to be carried by the priest-philologists."[43]

Bakhtin was interested in the profane, the ordinary, the everyday, where meaning-system is always in play with the infinite variability of contexts, "the uniqueness and irreplaceability of my place in the world."[44] So, the meaning of a word "is inseparable from the concrete situation of its implementation. This meaning is different each time, just as the situation is different each time." Language is not a "stable and always self-equivalent signal, but . . . always changeable and adaptable sign." As it is "a ceaseless flow of becoming, . . . there is no real moment in time when a synchronic system of language could be constructed." This fluid reality of meaning in language Bakhtin calls "heteroglossia."[45]

---

[*] http://meaningpatterns.net/heteroglossia

[43] V.N. Vološinov, 1929 [1973], *Marxism and the Philosophy of Language*, translated by L. Matejka and I.R. Titunik, Cambridge, MA: Harvard University Press, pp. 58, 60, 61, 71, 74.

[44] M.M. Bakhtin, 1919–24 [1990], *Art and Answerability*, translated by V. Liapunov, Austin: University of Texas Press, p. 23.

[45] V.N. Vološinov, 1929 [1973], *Marxism and the Philosophy of Language*, translated by L. Matejka and I.R. Titunik, Cambridge, MA: Harvard University Press, pp. 101, 68, 66.

Nor is this just a matter of speech. No social meanings are wholly expressible in words, hence image, music, ritual, gesture, and action.[46] Embodied feelings may cross between a suffering person and a person empathizing, though of course there is a huge difference between suffering and empathizing; each is motivated by fundamentally different interests, albeit always, we would say, sociable.[§2.5b] Ethical actions "such as assistance, rescue, consolation" may be motivated by "the emotional and volitional tones which pervade this world of objects," and bodies.[47]

Here Bakhtin is considering embodied meanings "at the borderline ... between the organism and the outside world." Or hunger: "even the cry of a nursing infant is 'oriented' towards its mother." A person "can apprehend one's hunger apologetically, irritably, angrily, indignantly." Or a collective can experience hunger, and protest, in which case their "experience [is] to achieve ideological clarity ... [T]here is an extremely subtle and complex set of possibilities for intoning an experience."[48]

Bakhtin's life was dominated by the closed rhetoric of Soviet Communism. He nevertheless managed to maintain his own remarkably polyvalent voice. He was arrested in January 1929 for speech crimes, including association with a Russian Orthodox Christian sect and "corrupting the young with his ideas." He was sentenced to six years' exile in Kazakhstan. By then, he had written a number of major books, one on Dostoevesky[49] under his own name, but also, most probably written by him, books on Freudian theory[50] and language[51] that appeared under the name of V.N. Vološinov, a friend who taught at Leningrad University, and a book on *The Formal Method of Literary Scholarship*[52] by P.N. Medvedev, who worked at the State Publishing House.

Perhaps it was easier to get the books published under the names of people more closely connected with the government. Or perhaps Vološinov and Medvedev contributed some to the final texts, though that now seems unlikely, or at least their contributions were minimal. Either way, Bakhtin was safely exiled during the most vicious of Stalin's purges. His only publication in this period was an article in the journal *Soviet Trade*, management lessons from his

---

[46] Ibid., pp. 15, 19.

[47] M.M. Bakhtin, 1919–24 [1990], *Art and Answerability*, translated by V. Liapunov, Austin: University of Texas Press, p. 25.

[48] V.N. Vološinov, 1929 [1973], *Marxism and the Philosophy of Language*, translated by L. Matejka and I.R. Titunik, Cambridge, MA: Harvard University Press, pp. 26, 87, 89, 87.

[49] M.M. Bakhtin, 1963 [1984], *Problems of Dostoyevsky's Poetics*, translated by C. Emerson, Minneapolis: University of Minnesota Press.

[50] V.N. Vološinov, 1927 [1976], *Freudianism: A Marxist Critique*, translated by I.R. Titunik, New York: Academic Press.

[51] V.N. Vološinov, 1929 [1973], *Marxism and the Philosophy of Language*, translated by L. Matejka and I.R. Titunik, Cambridge, MA: Harvard University Press.

[52] P.N. Medvedev, 1928 [1985], *The Formal Method in Literary Scholarship: A Critical Introduction to Sociological Poetics*, Cambridge, MA: Harvard University Press.

experiences now working as a bookkeeper on a collectivized farm. Vološinov died young. In March 1938, Medvedev, then a professor at the Tolmachev Military Academy, was arrested and shot.[53]

In 1936, Bakhtin moved back to Russia, though safely out of the way, as a one-man world literature department at the newly created Mordovian Pedagogical Institute in Saransk. The people of the region, known also for its prison camps, spoke the Finno-Ugric language, Mordovian. When asked by the Saransk City Party Committee, he gave a public lecture on "Lenin and Stalin on Party-Mindedness in Literature and Art."[54]

Only in the last decade of his life did Bakhtin's work gain recognition in the Soviet Union. Old manuscripts were republished. Fragmentary texts were reconstructed, including remnants of a manuscript of a book on the novel – one copy had been lost when the publisher's offices burned in the Nazi siege of Leningrad; Bakhtin had used his other copy to make cigarette paper.[55]

In the 1960s, linguist Roman Jakobson[§1.4.1a] drew Bakhtin's work to the attention of intellectuals in the West. In Russia, the daughter of the head of the KGB, Yuri Andropov, learned of his work in a seminar at Moscow University and arranged for Bakhtin and his wife to move to Moscow for medical treatment and a comfortable apartment.[56] Andropov later became the General Secretary of the Communist Party, where he promoted Mikhail Gorbachev and designated him his successor. Gorbachev was to be the Communist Party of the Soviet Union's last General Secretary.

§2.2   Program

> **Program.** Orientations to difference in communication, whether to assimilate or to differentiate.

From M.M. Bakhtin's perspective,[§2.1.2b] the universe of meaning is a place of proliferating differences, of heteroglossia. This is what we are saying about communication, too, which is not a meeting of minds but an encounter of complementary or conflicting interests. Difference is the meaning function.

Now, we want to use the concept "program" to refer to alternative orientations to differences in the negotiation of meaning. One orientation is to

---

[53] Katerina Clark and Michael Holquist, 1984, *Mikhail Bakhtin*, Cambridge, MA: Harvard University Press, pp. 141–42, 110–11, 144–66, 257, 264.

[54] Ibid., pp. 259–60.

[55] M.M. Bakhtin, 1979 [1986], *Speech Genres and Other Late Essays*, translated by V.W. McGee, Austin: University of Texas Press, p. xiii.

[56] Katerina Clark and Michael Holquist, 1984, *Mikhail Bakhtin*, Cambridge, MA: Harvard University Press, pp. 331, 336.

assimilate, a program to achieve sameness. Hear what I say! Think as I think! These are typical appeals in a program of assimilation. Some assimilative programs may insist on conformity to the detriment of established lifeworlds; others may be to demand equality and rights.

An alternative orientation is to differentiate, recognizing and at times accentuating differences in meaning, for better perhaps in a culture of civic pluralism, or for worse in a state of divide and rule.

Heteroglossia is intrinsic, inevitable. Programs – assimilating, differentiating – present alternative ways of making sense of differences. Though of course, this is not a dichotomy of distinctly counterposed agendas. By transposition, the one means for pursuit of interest is always ready to become the other. Like all transpositions, the relationship is one of tension and torsion with many intermediate places by way of ambivalence, pretense, dissembling, self-delusion, and a myriad of other scandals. Rhetors are forever working to cover their tracks.

§2.2a   Noam Chomsky's Logical Structures of Linguistic Theory

Noam Chomsky managed to get a fellowship at Harvard despite only having a master's degree on morphophonetics in Modern Hebrew. Beyond the fellowship, he had no expectation of getting a job there. "Jewish intellectuals could not get jobs" in many universities, and at Harvard, he said, "you could cut the anti-Semitism with a knife."[57]

Nevertheless, Chomsky's program[§MS3.1.2f] was an assimilating one, an inheritor of Saussure's[§MS3d] and the Sanskritists'[§MS0.4a] focus on universal structures, overwriting heteroglossia with a syntactic formalism so universal that differences in human meaning could be disregarded – indeed, specific meanings of any kind. Had he engaged, M.M. Bakhtin, creator of the term "heteroglossia,"[§2.1.2b] would surely have taken issue with Chomsky, as have a whole host of other linguists over the years on these or related grounds.[58]

While a junior fellow at Harvard from 1951 to 1955, Chomsky wrote *The Logical Structure of Linguistic Theory*, one chapter of which he submitted for his Ph.D. at the University of Pennsylvania.[59] Densely logico-mathematical,

---

[57] Chris Knight, 2016, *Decoding Chomsky: Science and Revolutionary Politics*, New Haven, CT: Yale University Press, p. 30.

[58] Ian Robinson, 1975, *The New Grammarian's Funeral: A Critique of Noam Chomsky's Linguistics*, Cambridge: Cambridge University Press; G.P. Baker and P.M.S. Hacker, 1984, *Language, Sense and Nonsense: A Critical Investigation of Modern Theories of Language*, Oxford: Basil Blackwell; Rudolf P. Botha, 1989, *Challenging Chomsky: The Generative Garden Game*, Oxford: Basil Blackwell; Geoffrey Sampson, 2005, *The "Language Instinct" Debate*, London: Continuum.

[59] Robert F. Barsky, 1997, *Noam Chomsky: A Life of Dissent*, Cambridge, MA: MIT Press, p. 83.

Chomsky's adviser, Zellig Harris, considered it "crazy." But Yehoshua Bar-Hillel, an Israeli logician and enthusiast of machine translation who had met Harris in Palestine four years earlier, was intrigued. He read the thesis and made comments that Chomsky took on board.[60]

Logical Structure was not published until 1975, and then in a greatly abridged version.* The full version finally came to light in about 2014 when Robert Berwick, with Chomsky a fellow MIT professor and co-author of their book on language evolution,[61] posted to his blog a 919-page PDF copy made from hazy microfiche.[62] (The link to the page where we found the PDF now generates an error message.) Computational linguist and lapsed follower of Chomskyan linguistics, George Ramsay, says of the 1975 published version that it is, in retrospect, "full of algebraic notation which may look impressive to the mathematically naïve, but when carefully examined turns out to be mathematically semi-literate."[63]

In *Logical Structure,* Chomsky announces some principles from which he never deviates. "[N]o reliance is placed on the meaning of linguistic expressions in this study ... because semantic notions, if taken seriously, appear to be quite irrelevant to the problems being investigated here." Having abandoned meaning, "I think there is hope of developing ... linguistic theory ... on the basis of a small number of operational primitives."[64]

Here for the first time we find the oft to-be-repeated, made-up examples, including the perfectly grammatical "colorless green ideas sleep furiously."[65] It doesn't matter this would normally be considered meaningless, because it illustrates the correct application of the operational primitives that are in play. With these, an infinity of sentences can be generated, and it is irrelevant to the grammar whether they are meaningful or not.

Eventually, 247 pages into the manuscript, we get to some of the specifics of these primitives, starting with phrase structure, "the next larger unit after the word." After these we more toward sentences with their recursive rules. So, "a sentence ... [is] a sequence of operations ... derived from a kernel. Each such sequence of operations, is interpreted as a string in a concatenation algebra and

---

* http://meaningpatterns.net/chomsky-theory

[60] Chris Knight, 2016, *Decoding Chomsky: Science and Revolutionary Politics*, New Haven, CT: Yale University Press, p. 60.
[61] Robert C. Berwick and Noam Chomsky, 2016, *Why Only Us: Language and Evolution*, Cambridge, MA: MIT Press.
[62] Noam Chomsky, 1955, "Logical Structure of Linguistic Theory," Cambridge, MA: MIT.
[63] Chris Knight, 2016, *Decoding Chomsky: Science and Revolutionary Politics*, New Haven, CT: Yale University Press, p. 58.
[64] Noam Chomsky, 1955, "Logical Structure of Linguistic Theory," Cambridge, MA: MIT, pp. 6, 24–25.
[65] Ibid., pp. 41, 60, 171, 889.

originating ultimately from a fixed sequence of kernel sentences." For instance, a sentence combining a noun phrase and verb phrase may take the form "NP VP" – say, "The person runs fast." Even in these most elemental of formulations, the page is covered in Chomsky's scratchings-out.[66] Things that came to sound clear and definitive on the printed page were fraught in their formulation.

In 1955, linguist and friend Roman Jakobson[§1.4.1a] arranged for Chomsky to get a job at MIT, in the Research Laboratory of Electronics where Bar-Hillel had been working on machine translation.[67]

Chomsky's work did not gain widespread attention until a paper he presented at an MIT symposium on information theory in 1956, "Three Models for the Description of Language*." The asterisked reference at the foot of the page acknowledged, "*This work is supported by the army (Signal Corps), the Air Force (Office of Scientific Research, Air Research and Development Command), [and] the Navy (Office of Naval Research)."[68]

"We have, on the one hand, a kernel of basic sentences that are derived from the terminal strings of the phrase structure grammar by application of only obligatory transformations," Chomsky said in the "Three Models" paper. "We then have a set of derived sentences that are generated by applying optional transformations to the strings underlying kernel sentences."[69]

People got excited about the paper, and not just because it promised to reveal an elementary structure of language across the infinite variability of actual sentences. Crucially, this structure promised to be computable. In funding the Research Laboratory of Electronics, the military was focusing its investment on one aspect of computability, machine translation, and Chomsky had promised "a cross-cultural valid account."[70]

§2.2b   Yehoshua Bar-Hillel's "Mechanical Translation"

Yehoshua Bar-Hillel was in 1952 working on machine translation in the MIT Research Laboratory of Electronics when he began a collaboration with leading light of the former Vienna Circle,[§MS1.1.3i] Rudolf Carnap.* Together, they wrote a paper, "An Outline of a Theory of Semantic Information." This paper suggested the computability of linguistic meaning. Sentences had a handful

---

* http://meaningpatterns.net/bar-hillel

[66] Ibid., pp. 247, 906–07, 247.
[67] Robert F. Barsky, 1997, *Noam Chomsky: A Life of Dissent*, Cambridge, MA: MIT Press, p. 86.
[68] Noam Chomsky, 1956, "Three Models for the Description of Language," *IRE Transactions on Information Theory* 2(3):113–24.
[69] Ibid., p. 123.
[70] Noam Chomsky, 1955, "Logical Structure of Linguistic Theory," Cambridge, MA: MIT, p. 881.

of kinds of "atomic" logic.[71] Syntax is logical, which is why "in practice, every logician since Aristotle, in laying down rules, has dealt mainly with sentences."[72]

Carnap and Bar-Hillel's thesis was unlike Chomsky's to the extent that Carnap and Bar-Hillel did not dismiss semantics outright. "The semantic information carried by a sentence . . . may well be regarded as the 'ideal' pragmatic information which this sentence would carry for an 'ideal' receiver whose only empirical knowledge is formulated in exactly this class of sentences. By an 'ideal' receiver we understand, for the purposes of this illustration, a receiver with a perfect memory who 'knows' all of logic and mathematics, and together with any class of empirical sentences, all of their logical consequences."[73]

As we have been arguing, such an ideal sender-to-receiver relation never exists. The logic of communication in practice always is the opposite – differentials without end, or what Bakhtin would call "heteroglossia."[§2.1.2b] So, we must turn our analysis to patterns in the differentials. However, this critique of basic assumptions is not our point for the moment, which is to trace foundational thinking about mechanisms for the computability of sentences and their meanings.

Carnap and Bar-Hillel mention two fundamental components, "empirical knowledge," and "logic." During the years of the Vienna Circle, the years when Wittgenstein was building his sister's house and when the Circle was so interested in his *Tractatus*,[§MS2.1.1a] Carnap had set an agenda for defining "the logical structure of the world." Its assumption: that a synthesis was possible between the work of empiricists and rationalists, and where "[t]he senses provide the material of cognition, [and] reason synthesizes the material so as to produce an organized system of knowledge." These two halves, the sensible and the rational, Carnap and others fused into an amalgam that he and others in the Circle called "Logical Positivism."[74]

Otto Neurath[§MS1.1.3h] called the program "empirical rationalism," and set up a committee to guide the development of the *International Encyclopedia of Unified Science* which would lay out a full agenda. As well as Neurath this included Carnap, John Dewey,[§1.1] C.K. Ogden,[§1a] and Bertrand Russell.[§MS1a] Neurath also planned to create an Isotype Thesaurus to support the project, with system of "unified visual aids."[75]

---

[71] Rudolf Carnap and Yehoshua Bar-Hillel, 1952, "An Outline of a Theory of Semantic Information," Cambridge, MA: Research Laboratory of Electronics, p. 4.

[72] Rudolf Carnap, 1934 [1937], *The Logical Syntax of Language*, translated by A. Smeaton, London: Routledge and Kegan Paul, pp. 1–2.

[73] Rudolf Carnap and Yehoshua Bar-Hillel, 1952, "An Outline of a Theory of Semantic Information," Cambridge, MA: Research Laboratory of Electronics, p. 3.

[74] Rudolf Carnap, 1922–25 [1967], *The Logical Structure of the World*, translated by R.A. George, Berkeley, CA: University of California Press, p. vi.

[75] Otto Neurath, Rudolf Carnap, and Charles Morris, 1938 [1955], *International Encyclopedia of Unified Science*, Volume 1, Chicago, IL: University of Chicago Press, pp. 24–25.

Setting aside the empirical half of the program, Carnap focused on "pure syntax," something that is "wholly analytic, and is nothing more than a combinatorial analysis."[76] Reduced to their logical essence, a robot even might be able to operationalize such mechanisms.[77]

Bar-Hillel for a time also focused on the analytic side of the Vienna Circle's agenda, "a real challenge for structural linguists" because of "their thesis that language can be exhaustively described in non-referential terms" – that is, stripped of empirical or semantic specifics.

Though Carnap's work on the logical syntax of language seemed to point in the right direction, it was not yet the right grammar for machine translation. "To my knowledge, no sufficiently complete operational syntax of any language has thus far been produced, mainly because the importance of such a syntax has not been recognized."[78] What was needed, Bar-Hillel said, was a "quasi-mathematical notation for syntactic description" capable of implementation in "a completely mechanical procedure" such as "mechanical translation."[79] This is why he had been so excited to read Chomsky's dissertation.

§2.2c   The Automatic Language Processing Advisory Committee

"A \$500,000 super calculator, the most versatile electronic brain known, translates Russian into English," says the commentator in a 1954 newsreel.[*] The man they interviewed in the research lab said that within five years, "We would be able to do . . . about one to two million words an hour, and this would be quite an adequate speed to cope with the whole output of the Soviet Union in just a few hours of computer time a week."[80]

Yehoshua Bar-Hillel organized the first conference on machine translation at MIT in September 1952, and military sponsorship of the research was in the air. In his introductory chapter to the published volume of papers, Warren Weaver drew connections between wartime cryptography and machine translation.[81] Weaver was famous for his work with Claude Shannon[§MS1.3.2b] in *The*

---

[*] http://meaningpatterns.net/machine-translation

[76] Rudolf Carnap, 1934 [1937], *The Logical Syntax of Language*, translated by A. Smeaton, London: Routledge and Kegan Paul, p. 7.

[77] Rudolf Carnap, 1956, *Meaning and Necessity: A Study in Semantics and Modal Logic*, Chicago, IL: University of Chicago Press, p. 244.

[78] Yehoshua Bar-Hillel, 1953a, "Some Linguistic Problems Connected with Machine Translation," *Philosophy of Science* 20:217–25, pp. 217, 218–19.

[79] Yehoshua Bar-Hillel, 1953b, "A Quasi-Arithmetical Notation for Syntactic Description," *Language* 29(1):47–58, p. 47.

[80] www.youtube.com/watch?v=K-HfpsHPmvw

[81] Warren Weaver, 1949 [1955], "Translation," pp. 15–23 in *Machine Translation of Languages*, edited by W.N. Locke and A.D. Booth, Cambridge, MA: The Technology Press of MIT, pp. 16–17, 22–23.

Mathematical Theory of Communication.[82] Papers addressing specific language translation issues were mostly about translation from Russian.[83] The US Government and military poured many millions of dollars into machine translation in the 1950s. The Soviets responded with substantial investment for their researchers.[84]

Then came doubts. Bar-Hillel returned to Israel, where he took up a position at Hebrew University. His successor in the MIT Research Laboratory of Electronics, Victor Yngve, started off equally convinced that Chomsky's approach was worth pursuing. But try as they may, he and others in the lab couldn't make it work. Chomsky's program was "based on logical arguments and a priori assumptions about requirements of an abstract grammar, [and] ignored the fact that sentences are produced by people using a finite processor [with] ... limited temporary memory." And although Chomsky's grammar was "meant to be generative in the mathematical sense, [it] did not actually construct sentences one at a time to order in real time."[85]

Then Bar-Hillel expressed his doubts about the whole project. Writing now in 1959, "A few years ago, I proposed what I called a quasi-arithmetical notation for syntactic description ... whose employment should allow, after some refinements, for a mechanical determination of the constituent structure of any given sentence. I am now quite convinced that this hope will not come true."[86]

In a "Demonstration of the Nonfeasibility of Fully Automatic High Quality Translation," Bar-Hillel offered the sentence, "The box was in the pen." The pen in this case was not the writing instrument, but the enclosure in which small children play, the playpen. "I now claim that no existing or imaginable program will enable an electronic computer to determine that the word 'pen'" has this meaning. However, a human with knowledge of the relative sizes of different kinds of pens, will. "This knowledge is not at the disposal of the electronic computer."[87] Here, Bar-Hillel returns to the empirical, observable, semantic world that he (in a former life) and Carnap had all-but abandoned in their quest to develop a mechanical analytics, as Chomsky also did in his generative theory.

[82] Claude E. Shannon and Warren Weaver, 1949, *The Mathematical Theory of Communication*, Urbana: University of Illinois Press.

[83] William N. Locke and A. Donald Booth, eds. 1955, *The Machine Translation of Languages*, Cambridge, MA: The Technology Press of MIT.

[84] W. John Hutchins, ed. 2000a, *Early Years in Machine Translation: Memoirs and Biographies of Pioneers*, Amsterdam: John Benjamins, pp. 197ff.

[85] Victor H. Yngve, 2000, "Early Research at M.I.T.," pp. 39–72 in *Early Years in Machine Translation: Memoirs and Biographies of Pioneers*, edited by W.J. Hutchins, Amsterdam: John Benjamins, pp. 64–65.

[86] Yehoshua Bar-Hillel, 1959, "Report of the State of Machine Translation in the United States and Great Britain," Jerusalem: Hebrew University, Appendix II, p. 1.

[87] Yehoshua Bar-Hillel, 1960, "The Present Status of Automatic Translation of Languages," *Advances in Computers* 1:91–163, pp. 158–60.

Finally came abandonment of the project by the US military-scientific establishment. In 1965, the Department of Defense, the Central Intelligence Agency, and the National Science Foundation formed a committee to review progress "on research and development in the general field of mechanical translation of foreign languages." An awful lot of money had been spent, the report concluded, and even with human post-editing the result was "machine translations [that] are slow, expensive, of poor graphic arts quality, and not very good translations." Chomsky's work had not been successfully applied to computers and, said the committee, "[t]here can be no doubt that the disappointingly slender computer results realized on the basis of [linguistic] theory must have been important in shaking at least some inquisitive linguists out of their contentment."

Besides, there was plenty of capacity for human translation of Russian. "There is no emergency in the field of translation. The problem is not to meet some nonexistent need through nonexistent machine translation."[88]

§2.2d   Noam Chomsky's Theory of Interest

With the failure of the project which had initially funded his work, Chomsky embarked on a new line of thinking. By sleight of hand, we're calling this a "theory of interest" – our terminology, because Chomsky would neither call this work "theory," nor its focus "interest."[*]

We're referring here to Chomsky's writings on politics. Wikipedia needs a separate page to list his works, divided into linguistics and politics, and the politics list is about twice the length of linguistics, including, on our count, ninety-two books, some jointly authored, others book-length interviews, but mostly singly authored.[89]

The first of Chomsky's political works was not published until 1967. By that time there was no more military funding for linguistics. Nor were there prospects for the application of his kind of linguistics in computing generally; or for that matter, to other practical areas of social life such as education.

The cause with which his politicking began was the Vietnam War, though the war was already years old when he began to write about it. In his first foray, a manifesto for the next phase of his career, he asks, what is the responsibility of intellectuals?

---

[*] http://meaningpatterns.net/chomsky-interest

[88] Automatic Language Processing Advisory Committee, 1966, "Language and Machines: Computers in Translation and Linguistics," Washington, DC: National Research Council, pp. 44, 123, 16.
[89] https://en.wikipedia.org/wiki/Noam_Chomsky_bibliography_and_filmography

Intellectuals are in a position to expose the lies of governments, to analyze actions according to their causes and motives and often hidden intentions. In the Western world, at least, they have the power that comes from political liberty, from access to information and freedom of expression. For a privileged minority, Western democracy provides the leisure, the facilities, and the training to seek the truth lying hidden behind the veil of distortion and misrepresentation, ideology and class interest, through which the events of current history are presented to us.[90]

By then a tenured professorship at MIT afforded him this kind of leisure and freedom from the constraints of funding agencies. Not that he considered social analysis legitimate academic work – "Is there anything in the social sciences that even merits the term 'theory?'" he asks. "That is, some explanatory system involving hidden structures with non-trivial principles that provide understanding of phenomena? If so, I have missed it."[91] Linguistics, by comparison, was for him properly rigorous in the manner of natural sciences such as mathematical physics. His linguistics was purely theoretical, deducing things about the brain through formalized analysis of logic in syntax. He kept doing that in his day job, never allowing the politics to cross over into his research and teaching.

Chomsky's political works are of interest to us because, though they don't fall within the scope of his understanding of grammar, or linguistics, or legitimate academic work, they are within the scope of ours. His political writings address aspects of what we term the function of "interest," and in particular the closed rhetorics[§2.1.1] that he calls "propaganda." Programmatically, the orientation of propaganda is to assimilate, to bring a message receiver over to the message sender's point of view. This is appropriate territory for social theory, we would say, and something that cannot be separated either from linguistics, narrowly conceived, nor the more expansive transpositional grammar we have been developing.

In the terms of the theory we have been outlining in this book, Chomsky's grammar does not extend beyond structure, and, more narrowly still, the form of a sentence in text. But when we arrive at interests in our grammar, these may be as wide as the world and as varied in their forms as our human capacities for synesthesia. Interests are also to be found in sentences, starting with the elementary configurations of agency,[§MS2] though even there, Chomsky ignores interests.

Writing with Edward Herman, Chomsky advances the "propaganda model" of media, an "analytical framework that attempts to explain the performance of the US media" where "the media serve, and propagandize on behalf of, the powerful societal interests that control and finance them." The "essential

[90] Noam Chomsky, 1967, "The Responsibility of Intellectuals," *New York Review of Books* 8 (3): 23.

[91] Alison Edgley, 2000, *The Social and Political Thought of Noam Chomsky*, London: Routledge, p. 154.

ingredients" of the model, say Herman and Chomsky, are "the concentrated ownership, owner wealth and profit orientation of the dominant mass-media firms," the influence of advertisers as their primary revenue source, "the reliance of media on information provided by government, business, and 'experts' funded and approved by these primary sources, and 'anticommunism' as a national religion and control mechanism."[92]

The result is "necessary illusions," created in a system of "thought control." Even if this is not always "conscious deceit . . ., [i]n the democratic system, the necessary illusions cannot be imposed by force. Rather, they must be installed in the public mind by more subtle means."[93] This is why in democratic societies "you have to turn to the techniques of propaganda. The logic is clear. Propaganda is to a democracy what the bludgeon is to a totalitarian state."[94]

The sources of inspiration for Chomsky's theory are conservative. He frequently harks back to the founders of the practice of "public relations," Walter Lippmann and Edward Bernays. His phrase "manufacture of consent" is directly from Lippmann. Democracy cannot be left to the ill-informed masses, says Lippmann, living as they do in an environment that is for them "altogether too big, too complex and too fleeting for direct acquaintance." Hence the need to propagandize "a simpler model." For "the generation now in control of affairs, persuasion has become a self-conscious art and a regular organ of popular government."[95]

And here is Bernays describing the systems-necessity of what he called "the engineering of consent: . . . The conscious and intelligent manipulation of the organized habits and opinions of the masses is an important element in demo-cratic society . . . Our invisible governors . . . govern us by . . . their ability to supply needed ideas and by their key position in the social structure." Born into Jewish Vienna, Bernays was Sigmund Freud's nephew. He stayed in close, admiring contact with Freud throughout his life.

Democratic societies, Bernays continued, are "dominated by the relatively small number of persons . . . who understand the mental processes of the masses. It is they who pull the wires which control the public mind, who harness old social forces and contrive new ways to bind and guide the world."[96]

---

[92] Edward S. Herman and Noam Chomsky, 1988 [2002], *Manufacturing Consent: The Political Economy of Mass Media*, New York: Pantheon Books, pp. xi, 2–31.

[93] Noam Chomsky, 1989, *Necessary Illusions: Thought Control in Democratic Societies*, Boston, MA: South End Press, pp. 19, 48.

[94] Noam Chomsky, 1991, *Media Control: The Spectacular Achievements of Propaganda*, New York: Seven Stories Press, pp. 20–21.

[95] Walter Lippmann, 1922 [1997], *Public Opinion*, New York: Free Press, pp. 11, 158.

[96] Edward Bernays, 1928 [2005], *Propaganda*, Brooklyn, NY: IG Publishing, pp. 9–10; Edward L. Bernays, 1923, *Crystalizing Public Opinion*, New York: Liveright Publishing; Edward L. Bernays, 1971, "Emergence of the Public Relations Counsel: Principles and Recollections," *The Business History Review* 45(3):296–316.

Neither Lippmann nor Bernays would say it, but to the extent that their analysis holds true, liberal democracy is a sham.

Chomsky did not disagree with Lippmann's or Bernays' analysis of propaganda.[97] He just disagreed with the moral intent of its narrative and its social effects. His relentless unmasking of propaganda started with the Vietnam War. Why did the US propaganda machine never call it an "invasion?" he asks. Over the decades of his activism and across his massive published output it seems there is no travesty of US imperialism that Chomsky has left unexamined.

Some of his causes his friends as well as critics considered problematic. One was his signing of a petition supporting the right to free speech of Robert Faurisson, a professor at the University of Lyon in France, and a holocaust denier.[98] Another was his apparent diminution of the atrocities of Pol Pot in Cambodia by comparison with the Indonesians in East Timor, the latter being "far more important for the simple and sufficient reason that something could be done to terminate them."[99]

§2.2e   Herbert Schiller's Mass Communications

Chomsky is at least right about his own political books[§2.2d] – they do not reach the standards one would expect for social science. From a scholarly point of view, they are widely considered to be sloppy rhetoric. Their sources are mostly newspaper articles, and their theoretical referencing and conceptual architecture does not go beyond ideas he has taken from Bernays and Lippmann.

Among Chomsky's contemporaries, Herbert Schiller offers a properly social-scientific account in much the same interpretative frame of reference.[*] In *Mass Communications and American Empire* and a body of related writings produced across a long career, Schiller spoke of the relations of the mass media system of radio, television, and newspapers to its audience. He analyzed the structure of the "communications-military-industrial coalition," dominated by a handful of companies whose ownership was becoming more and more concentrated. "If monolithic corporate enterprises command the informational apparatus, this is in keeping with the distribution of power in the economy at large."[100]

---

[*] http://meaningpatterns.net/schiller

[97] Noam Chomsky, 2003, *Hegemony or Survival: America's Quest for Global Dominance*, New York: Metropolitan Books, pp. 6–8.

[98] Robert F. Barsky, 2007, *The Chomsky Effect: A Radical Works Beyond the Ivory Tower*, Cambridge, MA: MIT Press, pp. 72–77.

[99] Noam Chomsky, 1989, *Necessary Illusions: Thought Control in Democratic Societies*, Boston, MA: South End Press, p. 157.

[100] Herbert I. Schiller, 1971, *Mass Communications and American Empire*, Boston, MA: Beacon Press, pp. 54, 149.

Says Schiller, "The industries that serve as the sites for the creation, packaging, and transmission of cultural messages – corporate ones especially – have grown greatly as their importance and centrality to the corporate economy increases." They also have evolved to "require gargantuan capital requirements for entry."[101]

From their position of power, the "mass media . . . instruct their audiences . . . governed confidently by a propertied-managerial corps . . . organized by an extremely concentrated group of commercial commanders." Their ideological messages are dominated by the interests of the capitalist class, aligned with the administrative-military state.[102] The outcome is "powerful, social conditioning machinery – the outpourings of the 'leisure-entertainment' conglomerates."[103]

In the second half of the twentieth century, Schiller goes on to argue, the communications-media complex aggressively extended its sway across the whole world. If geographical colonialism was no longer feasible in the postcolonial world, global domination of mass communications had to become the standard bearer of a new colonialism, that of free-market capitalism. Its neoimperial mission was to proselytize. This was in a context where one-quarter of the world's population had already fallen to communism, Vietnam was still slowly falling, and other parts of the "third world" were aflame with communist-aligned insurgencies.[104]

§2.2.1 Assimilation

> **Assimilation.** *Negotiation of differential interests in programs where it is anticipated that the message receiver will come over to the message sender's expression of interest.*

The programmatic function of mass media and propaganda as described by Herbert Schiller[§2.2e] and Noam Chomsky[§2.2d] we would characterize as assimilation. The mass media promulgates a broadly homogenous message consistent with the class interests of its owners, and the masses, it is hoped and anticipated, will buy into that message. The message is what Habermas would call "systematically distorted communication."[§2.0a] It is also monolithic, variations at most on otherwise relentlessly common themes. Chomsky unmasks the distortions. Schiller analyzes their socio-economic ground.

---

[101] Herbert I. Schiller, 1989, *Culture Inc.: The Corporate Takeover of Public Expression*, New York: Oxford University Press, pp. 130, 36.

[102] Herbert I. Schiller, 1971, *Mass Communications and American Empire*, Boston, MA: Beacon Press, p. 2.

[103] Herbert I. Schiller, 1981, *Who Knows: Information in the Age of the Fortune 500*, Norwood, NJ: Ablex Publishing, p. 176.

[104] Herbert I. Schiller, 2000a, *Living in the Number One Country: Reflections from a Critic of American Empire*, New York: Seven Stories Press.

The social reality that Chomsky and Schiller analyze is a particular phase in modernity, and things are different now. However, even for the phase in which they lived, this analysis is inadequate, as we will argue when we get to the question of reification and the alternatives for sociability.[§2.3]

But we are now in a new phase, where even their programmatic analysis of rhetoric, part true for a time, no longer holds. There has been a change in the means of production of meaning, and this, circumstantially, has changed the global frame for the negotiation of meanings.

In the twenty-first century, the logic of digital media is driven by rhetorics, not of assimilation, but differentiation.[§2.2.2] While the differences of interest integral to participation in meaning remain, the social program with which these are managed has changed. From a program that attempts to force different interests into sameness, differentiation is now used to accentuate social division. Today, this is how powerful interests serve their rhetorical purposes. Communication is still distorted, powerful interests are still served, inequalities persist, but the rhetorical means have fundamentally changed.

To reach this point in our argument, we need to return to our story of the changes brought about in the means of production of meaning. These will take us into a digital modernity of differentiated rhetorics.

§2.2.1a   Statistical Machine Translation at IBM

Robert Mercer graduated from the University of Illinois in 1972, with a Ph.D. in computer science.[*] After that, he went to work for IBM, where he joined a team developing a purely statistical approach to machine translation.[105] Instead of trying to figure out how language worked, all they had to do now was to dump already translated texts into the computer and do statistical analysis – "bags of words," the doyens of natural language processing would call these.[106] (Ironically, this phrase was first coined in 1954 by Chomsky's adviser, Zellig Harris, although then he was trying to say that language is not just that.[107])

---

[*]   http://meaningpatterns.net/ibm

[105]   Peter F. Brown, John Cocke, Stephen A. Della Pietra, Vincent J. Della Pietra, Fredrick Jelinek, John D. Lafferty, Robert L. Mercer, and Paul S. Roossin, 1990, "A Statistical Approach to Machine Translation," *Computational Linguistics* 16(2):79–85; Peter F. Brown, Stephen A. Della Pietra, Vincent J. Della Pietra, and Robert L. Mercer, 1991, "Word Sense Disambiguation Using Statistical Methods," pp. 264–70 in *ACL '91 Proceedings of the 29th Annual Meeting of the Association for Computational Linguistics*, Berkeley, CA.

[106]   Helmut Schmid, 2010, "Decision Trees," pp. 181–96 in *The Handbook of Computational Linguistics and Natural Language Processing*, edited by A. Clark, C. Fox, and S. Lappin, Chichester: Wiley-Blackwell, pp. 188–91.

[107]   Zellig S. Harris, 1954, "Distributional Structure," *Word* 10(2–3):146–62, p. 156.

"Regrettably," said Mercer, with co-author Church, "interest in empiricism faded in the late 1950s and early 1960s with a number of significant events including Chomsky's criticism ... in *Syntactic Structures*." Now they were advocating a return to empiricism, in the form of a "data-intensive" approach to language that they called "Text Analysis ... a pragmatic approach that is well suited to meet the recent emphasis on numerical evaluations and concrete deliverables. Text Analysis focuses on broad (though possibly superficial) coverage of unrestricted text, rather than deep analysis of (artificially) restricted domains."[108] Mercer's boss was pleased with the results of their work, Mercer recalled in his 2014 acceptance speech for a Lifetime Achievement Award from the Association of Computational Linguistics. "Whenever I fire a linguist," the boss said, "the system gets better."[109]

Statistical machine translation is what would make Google Translate work when it was launched in 2006 (at least in its first iterations[§2.2.1d]), and work quite well. Its power was not so much the algorithms that drove it, but the size of the bilingual corpus that Google had managed to copy from the web. When a word, phrase, or sentence needs to be translated something similar can be found, and the larger the corpus, the better it works. Where theoretical structuralist linguistics had failed, Statistical Machine Translation would be a triumph of US empiricism.

§2.2.1b Petr Petrovich Troyanskii's "Intermediate Logical Symbols"

"[M]ore should be known about this Babbage of MT," said Yehoshua Bar-Hillel in his 1960 overview, "The Present Status of Automatic Translation of Languages."[110] He was referring to the pioneering work of Petr Petrovich Troyanskii.[*] "MT" is machine translation, and Charles Babbage was the person who with Ada Lovelace[§MS1.3.2a] prefigured in the nineteenth century the principles and mechanics of computing.

After the October Revolution, Troyanskii entered the Institute of Red Professors, taught at a number of institutions of higher education, and contributed to the Great Soviet Encyclopedia. From the early 1930s until his death in 1950, his life was devoted to the development of the theory and practice of machine translation. For his first efforts, he was awarded in 1933 an "author's

---

[*] http://meaningpatterns.net/troyanskii

[108] Kenneth W. Church and Robert L. Mercer, 1993, "Introduction to the Special Issue on Computational Linguistics Using Large Corpora," *Computational Linguistics* 19(1):1–24, p. 1.

[109] www.bloomberg.com/news/features/2016-01-20/what-kind-of-man-spends-millions-to-elected-cruz-

[110] Yehoshua Bar-Hillel, 1960, "The Present Status of Automatic Translation of Languages," *Advances in Computers* 1:91–163, p. 126.

certificate," number 40995. This was the equivalent of a patent in the USSR, where intellectual property could not become private property.[111]

Digital computing was unimaginable at the time, but photographic film was readily available. So Troyanskii developed a mechanism not unlike the photo-typesetting systems that were to come into widespread use in the 1970s. In his own words from the 1933 application, "The proposed machine is designed for selecting and typing words when translating from one language to another or several others simultaneously and essentially consists of a belt moving on a desk with words in different languages upon it and provided with perforations for positioning the belt in front of a photographic camera, adjacent to which is located a typewriter with additional keys for typing conventional signs along-side the photographed word."[112]

Over the years, Troyanskii developed his idea, and by 1947, this was no mere word-for-word process. Between any pair of languages to be translated was an intermediate language of "logical symbols," which Troyanskii initially borrowed from Esperanto. At the Sixteenth Party Congress of the Communist Party of the Soviet Union held in Moscow in 1930, Joseph Stalin had said that "in the period of the victory of socialism on a world scale, when socialism is consolidated and becomes part of every-day life, national languages will inevitably merge into one common language which, of course, will be neither Great Russian nor German, but something new."[113] This was in line with a version of the Marxist theory of base and superstructure, where the social, political, and cultural infrastructures reflected and served the interests of the ruling class who controlled the economic base. According to this theory, language was in the superstructure. When the base changed, culture and language would inevitably change too, by virtue of their economic determination.

Later, Stalin came to consider this kind of internationalism, the very notion that one day there might be a world language, a sign of collaboration with the "internationalist" enemies of the Soviet Union, and its proponents were impri-soned or executed.[§2.2.1e] The possibility of worldwide revolution Stalin replaced with the idea "socialism in one country."

In a series of articles and exchanges with linguists in *Pravda* in the last years of his life and later published as a book, Stalin now said that language transcended epochs and class interests, and so its basis would not change with the arrival of socialism.[§2.2.1e] "Grammar is the outcome of a process of abstraction performed by the human mind over a long period of time; it is an indication of the tremendous achievement of thought. In this respect grammar resembles

---

[111] W. John Hutchins, 2000b, "Petr Petrovich Troyanskii (1894–1950): A Forgotten Pioneer of Mechanical Translation," *Machine Translation* 15(3):187–221.

[112] Ibid.

[113] J.V. Stalin, 1950 [1972], *Marxism and Problems of Linguistics*, Beijing: Foreign Languages Press.

geometry, which in giving its laws abstracts itself from concrete objects, regarding objects as bodies devoid of concreteness, and defining the relations between them not as the concrete relations of concrete objects but as the relations of bodies in general."[114] These were odd things for a dictator to care about.

So, with Stalin's change of heart about language, Troyanskii dropped the Esperanto, but kept the intermediate logical symbolism. "[U]niversality of logical make-up brings languages together despite the diversity of their structures, grammars, and lexicons, and that makes the differences surmountable ... It is on the basis of this universality that I created the so-called form of logical parsing common for all languages, as a text form intermediate in the translation process."[115]

Despite numerous publications and discussions with the USSR Academy of Sciences, Troyanskii did not manage to garner support to translate his theories into mechanized practice. However, the significance of his thinking came to be realized after his death. In 1957 the Academy of Sciences set up a committee of its Presidium to investigate Troyanskii's work, and to publish his unpublished manuscripts.[116] Stalin had died, and the Khrushchev era was a time of comparative openness in the USSR and scientific triumphalism too. It was time to return to Troyanskii's ideas.

By the time Bar-Hillel undertook his international survey in 1959, he found ten research groups working on machine translation in the USSR. At the first All-Union Conference on Machine Translation in Moscow in 1958, seventy-nine institutions were represented, with seventy-one presentations on the program. "If anything," he concluded, "Russian scientists may be somewhat ahead in the linguistic analysis, whereas they are probably somewhat behind in actual machine-testing."[117]

A number of these research groups were working with versions of Troyanskii's idea of a formal, intermediating language, or interlingua. One of the most advanced of the groups was the Leningrad State University Experimental Laboratory of Machine Translation, led by N.D. Andreyev.[118] Igor Mel'chuk and others were working on a different version of this idea at the

---

[114] Ibid.

[115] W. John Hutchins, 2000b, "Petr Petrovich Troyanskii (1894–1950): A Forgotten Pioneer of Mechanical Translation," *Machine Translation* 15(3):187–221, pp. 191–92.

[116] Ibid.

[117] Yehoshua Bar-Hillel, 1960, "The Present Status of Automatic Translation of Languages," *Advances in Computers* 1:91–163, pp. 125–28.

[118] N.D. Andreev, 1967, "The Intermediary Language and the Focal Point of Machine Translation," pp. 1–27 in *Machine Translation*, edited by A.D. Booth, Amsterdam: North-Holland Publishing; W. John Hutchins, 1995, "Machine Translation: A Brief History," pp. 431–45 in *Concise History of the Language Sciences: From the Sumerians to the Cognitivists*, edited by E.F.K. Koerner and R.E. Asher, Oxford: Pergamon Press; Raimund J. Piotrovskij, 2000, "MT in the Former USSR and the Newly Independent States (NIS): Prehistory, Romantic Era, Prosaic Time," pp. 232–51 in *Early Years in Machine Translation: Memoirs and*

Institute of Linguistics in Moscow.[119] So was D.Yu. Panov at the Institute of Scientific Information of the USSR Academy of Sciences.[120]

§2.2.1c Margaret Masterman's "Mechanical Thesaurus"

Margaret Masterman[§1.4.1b] had been a student of Wittgenstein's at Cambridge. With some fellow students, she wrote up notes from his 1933–34 lectures in *The Blue Book*[121] – reflecting Wittgenstein's thinking in transition, between the *Tractatus*[§MS2.1.1a] and *Philosophical Investigations.*[§MS2.3.2a]

Masterman worked at Cambridge after she graduated, founding the Cambridge Language Research Unit in 1955, which she directed until her death in 1986.[*] The Unit's focus for these decades was computational work that had a rigorous philosophical basis. For this, she worked on the development of a thesaurus based on semantic principles, in the form of a computerized lexical database. The challenge, she believed, was not just to develop single-level dictionaries or ontologies that classified lexical sets, but to develop a view of the relations between sets. Lexicographers never got beyond single-level naming.

The thesaurus Masterman proposed would offer a more sophisticated, multi-layered account of meaning, as well as connecting its constituent parts with semantic primitives. It would also function as an interlingua for machine translation and other applications of computers to information and meaning.[122] But importantly, unlike the Chomskyans, her work was grounded in the empirical messiness of language and the meanings to which language referred. The thesaurus would emerge from the analysis of the practice of language.[123] Today, this idea would be called "machine learning,"[§1.4.6c] and her thesaurus would be called an "ontology."[§MS3.3a]

---

* http://meaningpatterns.net/masterman-thesaurus

    Biographies of Pioneers, edited by W.J. Hutchins, Amsterdam: John Benjamins; Jurij N. Marčuk, 2000, "Machine Translation: Early Years in the USSR," pp. 243–52 in ibid.

[119] F. Papp, 1966, *Mathematical Linguistics in the Soviet Union*, The Hague: Mouton, pp. 121–22.

[120] D. Yu. Panov, 1960, *Automatic Translation*, London: Pergamon Press, pp. 54–64.

[121] Ludwig Wittgenstein, 1933–34 [1958], *Preliminary Studies for the "Philosophical Investigations," Generally Known as the Blue and Brown Books*, New York: Harper and Row.

[122] Margaret Masterman, 1967, "Mechanical Pidgin Translation," pp. 195–227 in *Machine Translation*, edited by A.D. Booth, Amsterdam: North-Holland Publishing; Margaret Masterman, 2005, *Language, Cohesion and Form*, Cambridge: Cambridge University Press, pp. 83–145.

[123] Yorick Wilks, 2000, "Margaret Masterman," pp. 279–97 in *Early Years in Machine Translation: Memoirs and Biographies of Pioneers*, edited by W.J. Hutchins, Amsterdam: John Benjamins; Frank Knowles, 1987, "Margaret Masterman: Her Life and Work," *Computers and Translation* 2(4):198–203.

An early collaborator in this endeavor was Richard Richens. In his regular job, he was Director of the Commonwealth Bureau of Plant Breeding and Genetics at Cambridge University, where his main claim to fame was to create an exhaustive taxonomy of the elm tree. As a taxonomist, he was interested not just in the definitions of terms, but their systematic inter-relations.

In 1958, Richens wrote a paper, "Interlingual Machine Translation." Here, he said, "Linguistic and translation problems are, to one way of thinking, more clearly and usefully formulated in terms of a standard language, devised, as Wittgenstein once suggested, to mirror the logical multiplicity of the state of affairs which is being represented. Thus the twelve English terms *stallion, bull, ram, mare, cow, ewe, colt, calf, lamb, horse, ox, sheep* can obviously be replaced by three terms for the animal species and terms, respectively, for sex, masculine, youth and contrariety. It is redundant to allocate a term for female, which can be defined in terms of *sex, male* and *contrariety.*" Margaret Masterman was a vocal champion of women's rights, so perhaps it is with her in mind that he added, "If preferred, feminists could define *male* in terms of *sex, female* and *contrariety,* but it is not possible to dispense with both *male* and *female.* Natural languages recede from formal simplicity in using homonyms. These have no place in an efficient interlingua."[124] An interlingua, Richens concluded, would need to be minimalist and non-redundant.

With these principles in mind, Richens embarked on the NUDE project, ("naked ideas for the bare essentials of language"), a notational interlingua which he first created for plant biology.[125] In later developments, NUDE adopted some ideas from Charles Fillmore's[§MS2.1.2a] case grammar.[126]

Also closely associated with the Unit at the time was Michael Halliday,[§MS0.3a] then University Lecturer in Chinese at Cambridge University. Masterman took from Halliday the idea that grammar was fundamentally semantic and pragmatic, or about meaning in the play of social purposes or interests. Working with Halliday, she also became interested in the Chinese ideograph, seeing in it something with which Wittgenstein had been wrestling in his picture theory.[§MS2.1.1d] An arrow could represent movement; objects could be arranged to express facts; an utterance can point to a situation.[127] The interlanguage she was proposing would be ideographic, or in our terms, multimodal and transpositional.

---

[124] R.H. Richens, 1958, "Interlingual Machine Translation," *Computer Journal* 1(3):144–47, p. 144.
[125] Karen Sparck Jones, 2000, "R.H. Richens: Translation in the Nude," pp. 263–78 in *Early Years in Machine Translation: Memoirs and Biographies of Pioneers*, edited by W.J. Hutchins, Amsterdam: John Benjamins.
[126] Yorick Wilks, 2000, "Margaret Masterman," pp. 279–97 in ibid., pp. 287–88.
[127] Ibid., p. 285.

In the context of his work with Masterman's Unit, Halliday had also been thinking of a "mechanical thesaurus" taking an "interlingual form" capable of, among other things, supporting machine translation. Because "the present writer happens to be interested in railways," he said, he took a number of sentences about train travel and looked at what it would take to disambiguate the terminology of "station," "stop," "platform," "track," "train," "line," "rail," and "coach" in English, French, Italian, and Chinese. The thesaurus would leverage "contextual determination within the language ... The principle on which it rests, that of 'make the language do the work,' can only be fully applied after the linguists have done the work on the language."[128]

Halliday also published with Richens on "Word Decomposition for Machine Translation," articulating principles of "stemming," or reducing words to semantic elements – "jumps," "jumping," and "jumped" can all be stemmed to "jump." This technique was to become an integral part of the discipline now called Natural Language Processing.[129]

When Masterman died, the Research Unit's offices were cleared out, and its trove of research papers thrown into a dumpster. Today, she is credited as having been a foundational thinker in the development of artificial intelligence.[130]

§2.2.1d Google Rediscovers "Interlingua"

"The Mind-blowing AI Announcement from Google that You Probably Missed" was the 2017 headline of an article on the social journalism site, *Medium*.[131] Since its launch in 2006, Google Translate had used statistical machine translation[§2.2.1a] for matching words and phrases.[132] (Arabic and Chinese had by now displaced Russian as languages of potential enemy interest.) A scholarly article describing the breakthrough was authored by members of the "Google Brain" artificial intelligence research team. Though the citations in most AI papers are

---

[128] M.A.K. Halliday, 1956 [2005], "The Linguistic Basis of a Mechanical Thesaurus," pp. 6–19 in *Computational and Quantitative Studies: The Collected Works of M.A.K. Halliday, Volume 6*, edited by J.J. Webster, London: Continuum, pp. 12–14, 19.

[129] R.H. Richens and M.A.K. Halliday, 1957, "Word Decomposition for Machine Translation," paper presented at the Eighth Annual Round Table Meeting on Linguistics and Language Studies, Georgetown University, Washington, DC (mt-archive.info/GURT-1957-Richens.pdf).

[130] Yorick Wilks, 2000, "Margaret Masterman," pp. 279–97 in *Early Years in Machine Translation: Memoirs and Biographies of Pioneers*, edited by W.J. Hutchins, Amsterdam: John Benjamins.

[131] https://medium.freecodecamp.org/the-mind-blowing-ai-announcement-from-google-that-yo u-probably-missed-2ffd31334805#.dytec365b

[132] https://research.googleblog.com/2006/04/statistical-machine-translation-live.html

rarely more than a few years old, Mercer and co-researchers were given due credit as progenitors of this idea in the 1990s.[133]

Now, in 2017 Google was announcing its new Google Neural Machine Translation system.[134] The problem: "so far there has not been a sufficiently simple and efficient way to handle multiple language pairs" in order to "cut down the total number of models necessary when dealing with multiple languages."[*] The solution Google was proposing: "shared semantic representations (interlingua) between languages ... , a universal interlingua." Of the thirty-two citations in this paper,[135] most were recent – except, standing out oddly in the references, there was "Richens (1958)."[§2.2.1c] Interlingua was back, now in hybrid relation to statistical methods.[136]

The mechanism for generating the interlingua was to be algorithmic – consistent with Margaret Masterman's insistence that the interlingua be generated empirically, and Halliday's that language would have to do the work.[§2.2.1c] But by 2017, the process was called "neural nets,"[§1.4.6c] where the input and output might be a word or phrase, but the connecting "neuron" is a number representing an intermediate meaning.[137] In our grammar, numbers can reference instances and concepts, so an intermediate number might as well be a word.[§MS1.1.1d]

Inspired by Halliday, we had been working for some time on the logic and processes for what we termed an "interlanguage."[138] We had applied for a patent which, despite all the difficulties related to software as intellectual property, made it through the U.S. Patent Office.[139] Our focus was not machine translation, but the interoperability of partially overlapping ontologies. However, the underlying principle of creating an interlanguage, which we called Common Ground Markup Language, was the same. Whether it is

---

[*] http://meaningpatterns.net/interlingua

[133] Yonghui Wu, Mike Schuster, Zhifeng Chen, Quoc V. Le, and Mohammad Norouzi, 2016, "Google's Neural Machine Translation System: Bridging the Gap between Human and Machine Translation," arXiv: 1609.08144v2.

[134] https://research.googleblog.com/2016/09/a-neural-network-for-machine.html

[135] Melvin Johnson, Mike Schuster, Quoc V. Le, Maxim Krikun, Yonghui Wu, Zhifeng Chen, Nikhil Thorat, Fernanda Viégas, Martin Wattenberg, Greg Corrado, Macduff Hughes, and Jeffrey Dean, 2017, "Google's Multilingual Neural Machine Translation System: Enabling Zero-Shot Translation," arXiv.org: 1611.04558 [cs.CL], pp. 1–2, 15.

[136] Marta R. Costa-jussà and José A.R. Fonollosa, 2015, "Latest Trends in Hybrid Machine Translation and Its Applications," *Computer Speech and Language* 32:3–10.

[137] Kyunghyun Cho, Bart van Merrienboer, Caglar Gulcehre, Dzmitry Bahdanau, Fethi Bougares, Holger Schwenk, and Yoshua Bengio, 2014, "Learning Phrase Representations Using Rnn Encoder-Decoder for Statistical Machine Translation," arXiv: 1406.1078v3 [cs.CL].

[138] Bill Cope and Mary Kalantzis, 2011, "Creating an Interlanguage of the Social Web," pp. 371–428 in *Towards a Semantic Web: Connecting Knowledge in Academic Research*, edited by B. Cope, M. Kalantzis, and L. Magee, Cambridge: Elsevier.

[139] Bill Cope, 2011, "Method for the Creation, Location and Formatting of Digital Content," edited by U.S. Patent Office.

machine translation or ontology alignment, the most practical way to achieve many-to-many mappings is to use a middle term which is a semantic abstraction. As soon as you do that, it suggests there could be a parallel term in any/all other possible languages or ontologies.

We wrote to Google Brain, noting the similarities with our work. One of the authors of the articles wrote back saying we should take this up with the patent department at Google, so we sent an email and never received a reply. Such is the futility of patents in practice for all but rich corporations, aside from their problems in principle.

§2.2.1e *Joseph Stalin's* Problems of Linguistics

Late in his life, Joseph Stalin[§2.2.1b] changed his mind, coming to the new conclusion that language was independent of class and political interests.[*] The Russian language of feudalism and capitalism was the same language as the Russian of communism, he said. The economic base had changed as a consequence of revolution, and with it the cultural and political infrastructure had changed too. But in its essentials, language had not changed and would not change.

Nicholas Marr then became an object for Stalin's vilification. Marr was a widely published linguist from the University of Baku, famous for having theorized the existence in the distant past of shared protolanguages. The obverse of this argument had been that as society moved in the direction of internationalist communism, languages would move back in the direction of a shared, world language. This had originally been Stalin's view, but now he had changed his mind.

Stalin said that Marr "introduced into linguistics the incorrect, non-Marxist formula that language is a superstructure." As a consequence, he also "introduced into linguistics another and also incorrect and non-Marxist formula, regarding the 'class character' of language . . . Soviet linguistics cannot be advanced on the basis of an incorrect formula." And more: "N.Y. Marr introduced into linguistics an immodest, boastful, arrogant tone alien to Marxism and tending towards a bald and off-hand negation of everything done in linguistics prior to N.Y. Marr . . . I think that the sooner our linguistics rids itself of N.Y. Marr's errors, the sooner will it be possible to extricate it from its present crisis."[140]

Language is intrinsically neutral, Stalin was saying, without bias towards any particularistic interest of one social or political bent or another. Nor was it integral to the productive forces, either in capitalist or socialist societies.

---

[*] http://meaningpatterns.net/stalin

[140] J.V. Stalin, 1950 [1972], *Marxism and Problems of Linguistics*, Beijing: Foreign Languages Press.

"[W]ere language capable of producing material wealth, wind-bags would be the richest men on earth," he said.[141]

In the twenty-first century it seems that the windbags have inherited the earth. Nearing the end of the first quarter of this century, high in the list of the richest companies in the world are Apple, Google, Amazon, Microsoft, and Facebook. Mostly they peddle language (or in our twenty-first-century reconception, multimodal meanings), or they have made multimodal meanings integral to the means of production and distribution of material things. Multimodal meanings are central to the twenty-first-century global economy. And they are loaded with interests. These interests have come to be arrayed in a program we will call "differentiation."

§2.2.2   Differentiation

> **Differentiation.** *Negotiation of differential interests in programs where the message receiver's particular interest is recognized, and the message is differentiated.*

Media do not determine messages. Technology does not determine social outcomes. But media and technologies offer affordances, meaningful things that can be done. They are not necessarily done, so if they are, the reasons are social. All media and technology do is offer scope in the form of social possibility.

We will briefly sketch two maps, the first of the dominant media in Noam Chomsky's[§2.2d] and Herbert Schiller's[§2.2e] media-communications era and the second today. In their past, the dominating program was to channel the invariably differential interests of the world towards social homogeneity through a program of assimilation.

In Chomsky and Schiller's day, there were the big newspaper companies, the big radio-television companies, the big book publishers, together dominating the production and transmission of information, knowledge, and culture. Their infrastructures, as Schiller rightly says, were "gargantuan" in their scale and capital-intensive: huge printing presses, sophisticated radio or television studios and transmission towers, mainframe computers. Even in a large city, there was no more than a handful of newspapers, television channels, and not so many more radio stations.

The dominant US corporate media players in Schiller's analyses were CBS, NBC, Time, the Hearst Corporation, the big city newspapers, and the Hollywood Studios. Owned by the rich, the business models of the mass

---

[141] Ibid.

media were driven mostly by advertising. The underlying ideological purposes of owners and advertisers shaped the content of mass communications.

The workers in these corporations, their message producers, were professionals always more or less bound as employees to the corporate ideology. They were also positioned as a cultural–intellectual elite, incorporated by proxy into its values and, as Hermann and Chomsky point out, maintaining a high degree of conformity to conventional social and political wisdoms.

The program for the expression of ruling interests was monological. The letter to the editor, or the caller on talkback radio were no more than token representatives of largely silent audiences and reading publics. The message was assimilating – an elite of writers, image makers, and speakers communicated, and according to the logic of "mass" the audience would set aside its differences. The cultural program was to create homogeneity in the shape of mass consumerism, nationalism, and the generic family.

The balance of rhetorical agency was in Chomsky and Hermann's heyday weighted in favor of the few who had the privilege to think and communicate, at the expense of the many whose responsibility it was to listen and conform. And if this was the model of mass media in the making of mass culture, there was a convenient isomorphism between this and a type of consumerism where mass production anticipated mass consumption. "Any color you like as long as it is black," said Henry Ford, famously.[142]

Now here's a revised map, a brief outline of the world of digital media several decades into the twentieth century, and with them, a newly dominant program of differentiation. Today, the big corporate players are Apple, Google, Amazon, Microsoft, and Facebook. The old mass media players have disappeared or faded to positions of relative insignificance. Such are the dynamics that Joseph Schumpeter called "creative destruction,"[143] endemic to capitalism.

This new generation of corporate behemoths peddles its information and culture in the digital media. Here, the function of interest plays according to a completely new rhetorical program, that of differentiation.

Where there were just a few TV channels in the second half of the twentieth century, there are now countless cable channels and social media feeds. A web search as we type this sentence tells us there are seven billion videos on YouTube, any of which can be seen on-demand.

---

[142] Henry Ford, 1922, *My Life and Work*, Sydney, Australia: Angus & Robertson, p. 72.
[143] Joseph A. Schumpeter, 1950 [1976], *Capitalism, Socialism and Democracy*, New York: Harper and Row, p. 81.

Where there were a couple of local or regional papers on the old newsstand, there are countless newsfeeds in the internet, including every single Facebook, Instagram, or Twitter user, where a meal has become as much news as a war. If the old news media were expensively capital-intensive, the new news media are cheap and accessible to all users. (We are all "users" now.)

Where radio stations used to play the "top forty hits" on rotation, people now curate and share their quirky tastes in their music playlists. With its suggestion algorithms, Spotify and Apple Music try to second-guess the finer nuances of personal taste, often with startling prescience.

Where Walmart hit a limit with 75,000 items,[144] a point at which it became counterproductive to make its "big box" stores any bigger, Amazon's virtual box is limitless, including not only all the stuff in its warehouse, but anything in anyone else's little store as well, if they care to sign up as a seller.$^{\S MS2.1.1c}$

Even printed books, those quintessentially "old" media, have been transformed by digitization. Now most titles are manufactured with "variable print" or "print-on-demand" using the digital Xerographic technologies that have largely replaced photolithographic offset or before that letterpress. Requiring the manufacture of expensive plates, offset or letterpress made no economic sense for print runs of less than about a thousand. Books had to sell well to be viable; "best sellers" were the publishing industry's ideal. With variable print, it is possible to print one book at a time, and there are no economies of scale. Today, there is no need to push for best sellers when printing a thousand different books costs the same per unit as printing a thousand of the same.[145] Amazon doesn't care how many different books or products are in its online store. All that matters is to sell in quantity. The business theorists call this new production regime "mass customization."[146]

In these ways, where the analogue media assimilated to "mass," digital media differentiate.

Across the forms of meaning, here then are some examples of programs where interest is assimilated or differentiated. Of course, both programs are as old as modernity and both programs persist; it's just that the dominant program has changed from assimilation to differentiation.

---

[144] Barney Warf and Thomas Champman, 2006, "Cathedrals of Consumption: A Political Phenomenology of Wal-Mart," pp. 163–78 in *Wal-Mart World: The World's Biggest Corporation in the Global Economy*, edited by S.D. Brunn, New York: Routledge, p. 169.

[145] Bill Cope and Robert Black, 2001, "Print Technology in Transition," pp. 151–71 in *Creator to Consumer in a Digital Age: Book Production in Transition*, Volume 1, edited by B. Cope and D. Mason, Melbourne: Common Ground.

[146] B. Joseph Pine, 1999, *Mass Customization: The New Frontier in Business Competition*. Brighton, MA: Harvard Business School Press.

Form Function: Program	Text	Image	Space	Object	Body	Sound	Speech
Assimilation	Propaganda (e.g. mass media)	Mass distributed images (e.g. posters)	Singularly programmed spaces (e.g. lecture theaters, prisons)	Mass consumption objects	Regulated embodiment, (e.g. marching, queuing, uniforms, conventionally gendered families)	Collective listening (e.g. spaces filled with shared sound)	For mass or repetitive hearing (e.g. lyrics)
Differentiation	Heteroglossia (e.g. customized news feeds and activity streams)	Customized image selection (e.g. digital image feeds)	Variable uses (e.g. parks, lounges)	Bespoke or user-customizable objects	Personalized demeanors (e.g. quirky styles, varied family forms)	Customizable sound experiences, (e.g. earphones, personalized playlists)	Uniquely in the moment, (e.g. spontaneous speech)

Fig. 2.2.2(i): Program

In differentiating programs of interest, the balance of agency also changes. Social media involve as much writing as they do reading, as much image making and sharing as image viewing, as much navigation and selection of music, ideas, or consumable objects as they do their reception and use.

With digital media and its changed balance of agency, some celebrate the coming, at last, of cultural democracy. The masses can speak, instead of just being spoken-to.[147] Economically, they say, freely shared social production may portend the end of the old, hierarchy-bound capitalism.[148] The creative commons may displace private ownership of culture and knowledge.[149] A thousand identities might flourish, instead of being overwritten and oppressed by programs of assimilation. And as soon as the masses are granted agency they no longer that; their differences of lifeworld and historical experience start to come to light, then proliferate in a kaleidoscope of ceaseless fracturing. This is the structural basis for optimistic talk of multiculturalism and cosmopolitanism.[150]

[147] Lawrence Lessig, 2008, *Remix: Making Art and Commerce Thrive in the Hybrid Economy*, New York: Penguin Press.

[148] Yochai Benkler, 2006, *The Wealth of Networks: How Social Production Transforms Markets and Freedom*, New Haven, CT: Yale University Press; Lawrence Lessig, 2004, *Free Culture*, New York: Penguin Press.

[149] Lawrence Lessig, 2001, *The Future of Ideas: The Fate of the Commons in a Connected World*, New York: Random House; Phillip Kalantzis-Cope, 2017, *The Work and Play of the Mind in the Information Age: Whose Property?*, Cham, Switzerland: Palgrave/Springer.

[150] Charles Taylor, 1994, *Multiculturalism: Examining the Politics of Recognition*, Princeton, NJ: Princeton University Press; Bill Cope and Mary Kalantzis, 1997b, *Productive Diversity*, Sydney: Pluto Press.

Notwithstanding the liberal enthusiasm for the politics of difference, these new media are not so innocent, because a lot of money is being made on the free labor of "users."[151] In the old model, media workers were paid, but in the new model only the likes of real estate developers and purveyors of hydrocarbons get to be paid. So much for the "knowledge economy." Knowledge is becoming an anti-economy, except for the massive corporations who own the platforms for unpaid and underpaid work. Unpaid: nearly all users work without remuneration, and almost all content is user-generated. Underpaid: mostly for a pittance, you can create "apps" for Apple or Google, or music for Spotify, or videos for YouTube, or write fake reviews of Amazon products. McKenzie Wark calls these digital media, not the much-vaunted "culture industries," but the "vulture industries."[152]

Nor are the digital media entirely new in their programmatic effects, because alongside differentiating programs, assimilating programs persist. Recent literature on digital media are inclined to notice the assimilation more than the differentiation.[153]

This, then, is the shape of programs that differentiate interests in the era of digital media. The social effect of such programs is to fracture, fragment, factionalize. It means that differentiating programs have become powerfully effective forms of politics.[§2.2.2a] Instead of mass, we have a million communication bubbles, whose members can be ruled by division. When we come to analyze these frames of interest in terms of their sociability, their scope is narrow.

Fig. 2.2.2(ii) is a rough map of where we stand, a matrix of rhetorics and programs designed to advance interests, with some media examples.

What makes this shift in the dominant modes of the expression of interest from massifying to differentiating programs possible?[*] It is the emergence, we would argue, of a new mode of production of meaning, driven by a mix of interlingua in the form of ontologies like Margaret Masterman's[§2.2.1c] and technologies of multimodal computational analysis like Robert Mercer's.[§2.2.1a]

The interlingua part is the collection of structured data – in social media or smartphone apps, for instance,[§2.2.2a] or online shopping data, or cookies that record web movements. It takes the form of markup and tagging whose semantics is now universal and interoperable across platforms – linking to words and images

---

* http://meaningpatterns.net/big-data

[151] Phillip Kalantzis-Cope, 2016a, "Whose Data? Problematizing the 'Gift' of Social Labour," *Global Media and Communication* 12(3):295–309.

[152] McKenzie Wark, 2012, *Telesthesia: Communication, Culture and Class*, Cambridge: Polity, p. 208.

[153] John Naughton, 2018, "The New Surveillance Capitalism," *Prospect*, January 19; Mary Aiken, 2016, *The Cyber Effect*, New York: Speigel & Crau; Alexander Klimburg, 2017, *The Darkening Web: The War for Cyberspace*, New York: Penguin Press; Cathy O'Neil, 2016, *Weapons of Math Destruction: How Big Data Increases Inequality and Threatens Democracy*, New York: Broadway Books.

Program Rhetoric	Assimilating	Differentiating
Open Rhetoric	"Balanced" reporting (but within a range whose narrowness is unstated), comprehensive empirical presentations (but where the empirical selection is constrained)	Ambiguous messages, nuanced suggestions, "nudges,"[a] induced "inattentional blindness"[b]
Closed Rhetoric	Opinion, mass media editorializing, overt propaganda	Inclusionary/exclusionary memes

[a] Richard H. Thaler and Cass R. Sunstein, 2008, *Nudge: Improving Decisions About Health, Wealth, and Happiness*, New Haven, CT: Yale University Press; Cathy N. Davidson, 2011, *Now You See It: How the Brain Science of Attention Will Transform the Way We Live, Work and Learn*, New York: Viking.
[b] Arien Mack and Irven Rick, 1998, *Inattentional Blindness*, Cambridge, MA: MIT Press; Siemon Scammell-Katz, 2012, *The Art of Shopping: How We Shop and Why We Buy*, London: LID Publishing, pp. 85–7.

Fig. 2.2.2(ii): Rhetorics and programs

concepts of person, place, purchase, life status, or personality trait. This is captured as a myriad of instances tagged by concepts, and together these add up to finely grained "intersectional" demographics. This interlingua part, we contend, is the most powerful aspect of these technologies.

Together, this makes for a new kind of universal, multimodal meaning schema structured by underlying semantics, where the surface forms of different natural languages have become for the practical purposes of meaning exchange, surmountable, and so merely circumstantial. Underlying an ATM which offers alternative language options, for instance, is the translingual ontology of banking.[§MS3.3b] When everything that comes up on the screen of a digital device is machine-translatable, its language becomes less important than its semantics, and if the text has structural and semantic markup, the translation works better.[§2.2.1d]

Then, on top of this, and in close relation to the structured data, is machine reading of unstructured data, running over natural language with computational linguistics, and pictures with image-recognition software. The ontologies or interlingua train the machine to see patterns in the unstructured data. The algorithms can't mean much unless they are connected to semantics, the most important part of which is to tie instances to concepts whose meanings have been standardized on the web.[§MS3.4b]

Yehoshua Bar-Hillel gave up on computational linguistics when he came to the realization that "the box was in the pen"[§2.2b] would need more than a kernel of syntax plus vocabularies for computer applications to human meaning to work. It would, he said, need a "universal encyclopedia." For practical purposes, given the capacities of computers at the turn of the 1960s, he considered this impossible, at least in his foreseeable future.[154]

[154] Yehoshua Bar-Hillel, 1960, "The Present Status of Automatic Translation of Languages," *Advances in Computers* 1:91–163, p. 160.

Today we spend our lives incrementally adding data to just such a universal encyclopedia, governed by a ramshackle and overlapping interlingua of ontologies, but where nevertheless there is also a great deal of singular and now mostly universal conceptual agreement about meanings and their structures.[§MS3.4a]

Facebook, Google, Amazon, Apple, and the other big companies maintain the encyclopedia. They talk to each other about overall meanings of their conceptualizations in not-for-profit, meaning-mediating entities that create the standard frameworks for digital meaning. The interlingua they create hold the whole thing together. This is the way in which the sociability of the web, and our meanings, are governed today.

Every little instantiation we make – a post, a purchase, a geotagged move, an affinity-connection to an online group, a tagged person, or a connection with an object in the internet of things, goes into this great encyclopedia, this record of meaningful human experience. Everything we do involves a play of the theoretical (ontological/conceptual/the database fields/the markup tags) and the empirical (the material/the instance/the entries in the fields/the digital objects of markup).

So, the world of ephemeral experience is now incidentally entered into the historical record and chronicled in this universal encyclopedia, including things so trivial that we have barely paid any attention to their recording: text messages and emails that might have in the past been unrecorded phone calls; web navigation paths tracked with cookies and clickstreams leading to purchases that might have in the past been untracked trips to a mall; social media likes and friend networks. These record moments of multimodal meaning that in past ages would have disappeared without trace into the ether of private forgetfulness.

The encyclopedia of digital modernity, although structured around universal ontologies and connected via interlingua, captures configurations of instances that are infinitely varied. What springs to view in any analysis of the recordings is that no two people have the same shopping habits, web-defined interests, or conversational flows in texts and emails.

The paradoxical consequence of this universal encyclopedic record is the knowability of our interests in finely differentiated detail. This was not possible in the past. With this resource, the most effective rhetorics of digital meaning will now be based in programs of differentiation. Meanings that anticipate assimilation to a singular meaning have become clumsy, heavy-handed, and anachronistic.

§2.2.2a Robert Mercer's "Psychographics"

On the subject of differentiating programs of interest, here is the rest of Robert Mercer's story.[§2.2.1a] He has never been involved in material production in a sense that Joseph Stalin[§2.2.1e] might have been able to understand, nor for that matter Henry Ford.[§1.4.3e] His is a story of putting language and multimodal meanings to work in a way that serves material interests, just like the other megacorporations of twenty-first-century, digital capitalism.* Stalin would have classified him a windbag, not a producer.

Mercer left IBM in 1993 to join a hedge fund, Renaissance Technologies, and later became its CEO. Here, with others, some of whom had previously worked with him on language processing at IBM, he developed elaborate algorithms to detect market fluctuations. Renaissance became one of the most profitable of all investment funds.[155] A third of the 200 employees had Ph.D.s, but "PhDs in finance need not apply," nor "anyone with even the slightest whiff of Wall Street bona fides."[156]

At 1.07 on April 23, 2013 the Syrian Electronic Army hacked the AP News Agency in Washington with the tweet, "Breaking: Two Explosions in the White House and Barack Obama is injured." Within minutes, the computers scanning the news for events relevant to autotrading on Wall Street brought the Dow Jones index down 140 points, wiping out $200 billion in capital.[157] Renaissance's edge is its algorithms, tracking the psychology of markets, not human understanding of companies or their productive work.

Then, the 2016 US presidential election. Mercer decided to devote some of his enormous fortune and prodigious talents to getting a Republican elected. First, he supported Ted Cruz, who did surprisingly well in the primaries despite his extreme right-wing views. Then, when Cruz dropped out, Mercer switched his support to Donald Trump.

"Steve Bannon's psychological warfare mindfuck tool."[158] This is how Christopher Wylie, a programmer at the company Cambridge Analytica, described the work they did for the Trump campaign. Bannon was the director of Breitbart.com, an alt-right news channel, then vice president of Cambridge Analytica, and after that Trump's campaign manager. Mercer had bought shares in Breitbart and was a founding investor in Cambridge Analytica.

Wylie, a self-described "gay Canadian vegan," said of Bannon, "He's the only straight man I've ever talked to about intersectional feminist theory. He saw its relevance straightaway to the oppressions that conservative, young white men feel." And of Mercer, "In politics, the money man is usually the dumbest person in the room. Whereas it's the opposite way around with Mercer ... He really listened. He wanted to understand the science."[159]

---

* http://meaningpatterns.net/mercer

[155] Scott Patterson, 2010, *The Quants: How a New Breed of Math Quizzes Conquered Wall Street and Nearly Destroyed It*, New York: Crown Business, pp. 106–17.

[156] James Owen Weatherall, 2013, *The Physics of Finance: How Science Has Taken over Wall Street*, New York: Houghton Mifflin, p. xii.

[157] www.telegraph.co.uk/finance/10188335/Quants-the-maths-geniuses-running-Wall-Street.html

[158] www.theguardian.com/news/2018/mar/17/data-war-whistleblower-christopher-wylie-faceook-nix-bannon-trump

[159] Ibid.

The science was "differential psychology" based on a "lexical hypothesis." People's personalities are different, and their psychological makeup can be determined by analysis of the words they use.[160] The immediate science and the "Cambridge" of Cambridge Analytica came from the work of researchers in the Psychometrics Centre in the Judge Business School at Cambridge University.

A 2013 paper by Kosinski, Stillwell, and Graepel showed how "Private traits and attributes are predictable from digital records of human behavior." Some 58,000 research subjects had "volunteered" their Facebook profiles by signing up to an app, myPersonality. It was possible to "predict individual psychodemographic profiles," not just in terms of self-classified profile characteristics, but in terms of the personality profile captured in the myPersonality survey, including such dimensions as agreeableness, extraversion, conscientiousness, openness, and other psychometrically-defined "traits."[161]

Then, in a 2015 paper using an even bigger dataset, Youyou, Kosinski, and Stillwell announced that "computer-based personality judgments are more accurate than those made by humans." This was in the fine print: "Conflict of interest statement: D.S. received revenue as the owner of the myPersonality Facebook application."[162] David Stillwell was deputy director of the Psychometric Center and co-author of another article, "Money Buys Happiness When Spending Fits Our Personality."[163] His page on the Cambridge Judge Business School website says, "Today myPersonality has collected data from more than 6 million people, and the resulting database has become a priceless academic resource used by numerous researchers all over the world."[164]

Stillwell, along with a lecturer in psychology at Cambridge, Aleksandr Kogan, were approached by Chris Wylie. They came together in what they called in their diaries the "Panopticon Meeting," a reference to Michel Foucault's theory of modern social surveillance and Jeremy Bentham's incarcereal practice.[§2.5a] Kogan went on to create his own Facebook app on the same principles, thisisyourdigitallife. 270,000 people offered their personality data there, which when linked to Facebook profiles yielded 57 billion friendships. Born in the USSR, Kogan also worked at St Petersburg University and had been granted Russian research funds.[165]

[160] Gerald Matthews, Ian Deary, and Martha Whiteman, 2003, *Personality Traits*, Cambridge: Cambridge University Press.
[161] Michal Kosinski, David Stillwell, and Thore Graepel, 2013, "Private Traits and Attributes Are Predictable from Digital Records of Human Behavior," *Proceedings of the National Academy of Sciences* 110(15):5802–05.
[162] Wu Youyou, Michal Kosinski, and David Stillwell, 2015, "Computer-Based Personality Judgments Are More Accurate Than Those Made by Humans," *Proceedings of the National Academy of Sciences* 112(2):1036–40.
[163] Sandra C. Matz, Joe J. Gladstone, and David Stillwell, 2016, "Money Buys Happiness When Spending Fits Our Personality," *Psychological Science* 27(5):715–25.
[164] www.psychometrics.cam.ac.uk/about-us/directory/david-stillwell
[165] www.motherjones.com/politics/2018/03/cloak-and-data-cambridge-analytica-robert-mercer

Priceless indeed, because associated companies, including Cambridge Analytica, were soon pitching, for a price, the data and its associated analytics – to the State Department, the Pentagon, Steve Bannon, and then Robert Mercer.[166]

The history of this particular science – where differential psychology meets statistical text-mining – takes us back to Mercer's intellectual roots. While Mercer was studying for his Ph.D. in computer science at the University of Illinois, one of the University's most famous scholars, Raymond B. Cattell, was undertaking foundational work on personality traits using computational, lexically-oriented psychometrics. Catell had moved from Harvard to Illinois in 1945 because the Illinois Automatic Computer was being built there, the first such machine in a US University,[§MS1.3.2c] and heavy-duty computation work was going to be a key to his work in the area of psychological testing.

In a discipline where this kind of thing seems particularly to matter, Cattell is the seventh most cited psychologist of the past century.[167] If Cattell and Mercer did not work together (and we may never know, because Mercer is notoriously secretive), the intellectual direction of both their work must at the very least have been in the air within the statistical text analytics circles at the University of Illinois.

In 1997, the American Psychological Association withdrew its nomination of Cattell for a lifetime achievement award after a flurry of protests. Dr. Barry Mehler, director of the Institute for the Study of Academic Racism at Ferris State University, was one of the protesters. Mehler had also earned his doctorate at the University of Illinois. He posted a statement to the web saying "the potential awardee has a lifetime commitment to fascist and eugenics causes."[168] In a lengthy scholarly analysis, Mehler noted that Cattell had been a Nazi supporter before the Second World War, and that he had not substantially changed his views after the war. Cattell's writing, Mehler concluded, was "striking for its extremism, racism, and virulent bias against the poor." Opposed both to immigration and foreign aid, Catell said in 1972, "What is called for here is not genocide, the killing off of the populations of incompetent cultures. But we do need to think realistically in terms of phasing out of such peoples."[169]

In any event, Cambridge Analytica became an inheritor of the Facebook app data and a purveyor of Cattell's science. Director Alexander Nix said, "Your behavior is driven by your personality and actually the more you can understand about people's personality as psychological drivers, the more you can

[166] Tamsin Shaw, 2018, "The New Military-Industrial Complex of Big Data Psy-Ops," *New York Review of Books.*

[167] https://en.wikipedia.org/wiki/Raymond_Cattell

[168] www.nytimes.com/1997/08/15/us/racism-accusations-and-award-is-delayed.html

[169] Barry Mehler, 1997, "Beyondism: Raymond B. Cattell and the New Eugenics," *Genetica* 99:153–63, pp. 154, 155.

actually start to really tap in to why and how they make their decisions. We call this behavioral microtargeting and this is really our secret sauce, if you like. This is what we're bringing to America."[170] And not long after, "We are thrilled that our revolutionary approach to data-driven communication has played such an integral part in President-elect Trump's extraordinary win."[171]

As Cambridge Analytica employees Harris MacLeod and Tim Gilster explain, "if you are an 'Individualistic and Imaginative Type,' and we were marketing Ted Cruz to you, we would emphasize the fact that he's in a new generation of Republican leaders . . . He's got new ideas, fresh ideas, innovative ideas – you'll be able to file your taxes on a postcard, whatever, abolish the IRS . . . [I]f you are low-conscientiousness . . . it's about being the Washington outsider, blowing through the received way of doing things . . . It would be 'everything is bigger in Texas' – it would be bold visuals, bold statements."

The word Cambridge Analytica began to use for its approach was "psychographics." Until now, Nix explained, election campaigns had differentiated their targets with old-school demographics. "A really ridiculous idea," he said. "The idea that all women should receive the same message because of their gender – or all African Americans because of their race."[172] Messages needed to be much more finely tuned to differentials, and now social media technologies made this possible. "We can address villages or apartment blocks in a targeted way. Even individuals." In the "little Haiti" district of Miami, the Trump campaign sent a message about Clinton Foundation failures after the Haiti earthquake, doubtless not enough to get Haitians to vote Republican, but enough at least to discourage them from voting for Hillary Clinton.[173]

Trump campaign's Digital Director explained the process in a television interview:

BRAD PARSCALE: I understood early that Facebook was how Donald Trump was going to win. Twitter is how he talked to the people. Facebook was going to be how he won . . .

LESLEY STAHL: And Facebook IS how he won.

BRAD PARSCALE: . . . Facebook was the method – it was the highway . . . which his car drove on . . . Yeah. Facebook now lets you get to places and places possibly that you would never go with TV ads . . . We took opportunities that I think the other side didn't.

LESLEY STAHL: Like what?

BRAD PARSCALE: Well, we had our – their staff embedded inside our offices.

LESLEY STAHL: What?

---

[170] www.bloomberg.com/news/features/2015-11-12/is-the-republican-party-s-killer-data-app-for-real-

[171] https://motherboard.vice.com/en_us/article/mg9vvn/how-our-likes-helped-trump-win

[172] Ibid.   [173] Ibid.

BRAD PARSCALE: Yeah, Facebook employees would show up for work every day in our offices [in the Trump Tower, to make ads]. We were making hundreds of thousands of 'em.

LESLEY STAHL: You make 100,000 ads.

BRAD PARSCALE: Programmatically. In one day. In one day.

LESLEY STAHL: So 100,000 different ads every day?

BRAD PARSCALE: Average day 50–60 thousand ads . . . This was all automated.

BRAD PARSCALE: Changing language, words, colors, changing things because certain people like a green button better than a blue button. Some people like the word "donate" or "contribute."

LESLEY STAHL: This one is tax, this one is childcare, this one is energy.

BRAD PARSCALE: They were all targeted to different users . . . Sent out to different people. And it could be each other's next-door neighbors . . . all in Ohio.

LESLEY STAHL: This one person at 11 Elm Street gets this one and 13 Elm Street gets that one.

BRAD PARSCALE: Yup, yup.[174]

§2.3   Reification

> *Reification. Processes of transposition by means of which social meanings are presented (activation) and distorted or concealed (alienation) by their objectification, thereby serving interests differentially.*

In the closing pages of Volume One of *Capital*, Karl Marx's monumental analysis of the capitalist mode of production, the hapless Mr Peel makes an appearance. Cousin of Sir Robert Peel, Secretary of State and later Prime Minister of England,[§MS1.3.2a] Thomas Peel was founder of an English colony on the Swan River, Western Australia. Mr Peel took with him all the tools and farming implements he thought would be needed to build the settlement.* Marx says, tongue-in-cheek, Mr Peel also "had the foresight to bring with him, besides, 3,000 persons of the working class, men, women, and children."

But when they arrived, the workers ran off, hoping to start their own farms, and "Mr. Peel was left without a servant to make his bed or fetch him water from the river." With no compulsion for the workers to sell themselves as wage laborers, the colony foundered and then almost failed. "Unhappy Mr. Peel who provided for everything except the export of English modes of production to Swan River!"

---

* http://meaningpatterns.net/peel

[174] www.cbsnews.com/news/facebook-embeds-russia-and-the-trump-campaigns-secret-weapon

How could Mr Peel have made such a fundamental mistake? Mr Peel's belated discovery, says Marx, was something that had not been immediately evident in England because it was so deeply written into the everyday practices of capitalism, "that capital is not a thing, but a social relation between persons, which is mediated through things."[175] Mr Peel brought all the instruments of productive life, but failed to see the social conditions of compulsion required for workers to use them. The subsequent process of distortion of meanings, focusing on things to the neglect of their social meanings, we call "reification."

By reification, we do not mean "thinginess" in the narrow sense of making three-dimensional objects, one of our forms of meaning in this grammar. We mean reification as a kind of fixing, of objectifying and hypostasizing states of human affairs in multimodal configurations of text, image, space, object, body, sound, and speech.

Reification is a process of making things to seem inevitably so, ineluctably so, always-obviously so. Then, paradoxically, for their overwhelming self-evidence their underlying meanings become hard to see or disappear from view. As a consequence, such states of affairs seem impervious to redesign, less obviously designs in the sense of having been made to serve one interest or another and so, not obviously contingent and changeable. Mostly, this works in favor of the status quo, and so the differential interests of the powers-that-be.

If rhetoric makes interests explicit, reification is implicit meaning. And if rhetoric is obvious in ways that are at times heavy handed, reification can be pervasive and subtle. Then there is always a possibility for functional transposition, where reification can be rearticulated as rhetoric, or rhetoric rendered redundant or buried by reification. When the rhetoric rings hollow, the fatalism of reification may do the same job. Such is the shiftiness of transpositions in the meanings of interest.

Ostensibly objective realities, however, have ever been designed. And their having-been-designed can be recovered in a transpositional grammar. Then, their historicity springs back into view. History is never inevitable. Things could have been different, which means they could still be, again. Objectivity is unmasked as circumstantial, social, and interest-laden.

It is through these processes of reification that the "freedom" of the market comes to seem inevitable, inarguable, natural. What you seem to see in front of your eyes is a "free contract between buyer and seller, between equally independent owners of commodities, the owner of the commodity of capital on one side, the owner of the commodity of labour

---

[175] Karl Marx, 1867 [1976], *Capital: A Critique of Political Economy*, Volume 1, translated by B. Fowkes, Harmondsworth, UK: Penguin, pp. 932–33.

on the other." Left at this, we have a useful fiction, encapsulated in Marx's irony in the person of the "wage-labourer, . . . compelled to sell himself of his own free will." So, in the case of Mr Peel, "In the colonies where no such seemingly natural compulsion exists, the beautiful illusion of freedom is torn aside."[176]

We need a transpositional grammar to disentangle the systematic distortions of meaning that may occur in the objectification of meanings. We need such a grammar to disentangle the social designs of reality, and so also to raise the possibility of their redesign.

Here now is a rough map of some rhetorical compared to reifying means for the expression of interest:

Form Function	Text	Image	Space	Object	Body	Sound	Speech
Rhetoric	Explicit statements and commands	Immediately, didactically visible	Self-evident paths, uses	Manifest thinginess	Explicit gesture, bodily positioning	Sounds clearly projected and heard	Things said directly
Reification	Implicit meanings, symptomatic absences, textual displacements, that become noticeable with parsing	The meaningful but invisible, at least at first glance	Manipulations not visible without uncovering	Provenance, underlying social meanings	Implicit gesture, circumstantial bodily positioning	Unconsciously absorbed sounds, in soundscapes whose meanings require special attention	Symptomatic silences

Fig. 2.3: Rhetoric and reification

§2.3a   Karl Marx's "Commodity Fetishism"

"Mediated through things"[§2.3] was an idea that Karl Marx had begun to explore in the first chapter of his masterwork, *Capital*. If interests are articulated in rhetorics, they are frequently concealed in things – not just object-things, but things as generalized states of affairs. Objectification is overwhelmingly pervasive, seemingly ineluctable, a state of apparent inevitability.

We are going to work through Marx's analysis of the commodity as an example of the processes of recovery of meanings-in-interests with a transpositional grammar, analyzing the role of reification in the maintenance of differential interests that favor some parties at the expense of others. The commodity, for us, is just one example of the processes of parsing of differential interests when meanings have been reified, albeit a particularly interesting one and profoundly important in our modern lives.

Marx's analysis begins with this elemental unit of social and economic life in capitalism. The commodity, he says, is "an extremely obvious, trivial thing," or

---

[176] Ibid., p. 935.

so it seems at first glance. But on closer analysis it is also a "a very strange thing, abounding in metaphysical subtleties and theological niceties."[*]

There are two aspects to the commodity, says Marx. One is obvious, its "use value," an object that "by its properties . . . satisfies human needs." The other, its exchange value, is more mysterious because it embodies a whole lot of social designs which are not so obvious when experiencing an object in its use value, or even its price as a sign of its exchange value.

Take the table in front of your eyes, says Marx. "It is absolutely clear, that by his activity, man changes the forms of the materials of nature, in such a way as to make them useful to him. The form of wood, for instance, is altered if a table is made out of it. Nevertheless, the table continues to be wood, an ordinary, sensuous thing." Its meaning is in its use, and its usefulness has been rendered in its making.

But then there is the second aspect to the table. It has been sold and bought, and so has the spoon lying on the table – and on the same measure, money. This is its exchange value. However, if the use value of a table stares you in the face, the social processes for the determination of its exchange value are more elusive. There is more to money than meets the eye. Tables are dearer than spoons because tables take more labor to be made. Labor is a "physiological fact . . . of the human organism . . . essentially the expenditure of human brain, nerves, muscles, and sense organs."[177] More such embodied effort is required to make a table than a spoon.

In the capitalist modernity of Marx's analysis, both tables and spoons are made in factories, where the capitalist class owns the infrastructure and tools of production. The table is not sold simply for the value of its labor because the capitalist also extracts surplus value, a bounty for having control of the means of production. In this way, the laborer makes the capitalist richer, more able to expand the owner's means of production. The laborer earns just enough to consume and so never acquires means of production. The capitalist reinvests their surplus. Hence, expanding inequality.

This everyday thing, the wooden table, "as soon as it emerges as a commodity, . . . changes into a thing which transcends sensuousness. It not only stands with its feet on the ground, but, in relation to all other commodities, it stands on its head, and evolves out of its wooden brain grotesque ideas, far more wonderful than if it were to begin dancing of its own free will."

Now the mystery can be revealed, a mystery that Marx famously terms "the fetishism of the commodity."

---

[*] http://meaningpatterns.net/marx

[177] Ibid., pp. 163–64.

[T]he socially useful character of private labour [such as when a person makes a table] is reflected in the form that the product of labour has to be useful to others, and the social character of the equality of various kinds of labour is reflected in the form of the common character, as values, possessed by these materially different things, the products of labour [exchange values, where tables and spoons can be traded on the same terms] ... It is however precisely this finished form of the world of commodities – the money form – which conceals the social character of private labour and the social relations between the individual workers ... Value, therefore, does not have its description branded on its forehead; it rather transforms every product into a social hieroglyphic. Later on, men try to decipher the hieroglyphic, to get behind the secret of their own social products; for the characteristic which objects of utility have as being values, is as much a social product as is their language.[178]

Or even, perhaps, more social than language: "Table" in text mainly refers to its mundane use value, conceptually replicated for all the tables in the world. Tables in wood require multimodal parsing if their multifaceted social meanings are adequately to be revealed for what they are.

Back now to Mr Peel and the mistake he made in Western Australia.[§2.3] When they got there, his laborers considered themselves "free" to take land, means of production capable of supporting their own subsistence. Of course, this was a perverse colonial freedom because it treated the ancestral lands of First Peoples as simply free and for the taking, *terra nullius* or "empty lands" in the legal theory of colonial appropriation. Notoriously, Mr Peel was a perpetrator in the Pinjarra Massacre of 1834, when more than thirty Bindjareb men, women, and children were killed by a militia in which he participated.

However, among his own people, in his attempt to transplant capitalism Mr Peel had failed to understand that capitalism talks freedom but requires unfreedom, the unfreedom that comes with having no means of production. This is how workers have to become, by dint of sheer material necessity, wage laborers in the employ of capitalists, making tables, spoons, or whatever. The so-called "freedom" of the labor market Marx renamed, in the interest of unconcealment, "wage slavery."

Reframed in the terms of our grammar, there is a transposition between rhetoric and reification, where the rhetoric aligns with the immediate appearances of objective reality (freedom, of sorts), but belies its underlying designs (slavery, of sorts). And more: text lets you get away with reification a little more easily ("table," in passing), while the object form may suggest a deeper parsing.

The meaning of table-as-use is not the same as its meaning-for-exchange, says Marx, and in the case of exchange, price hides a multitude of evils. No comprehensive sense can be made of the table's meaning-for-exchange without

---

[178] Ibid., pp. 166, 168, 167.

an analysis of the whole social context of the commodity form, including the structures of inequality that drive the capitalist system of production and markets, its purported freedoms and underlying unfreedoms.

To reframe in the terms of our grammar, the distortion that occurs is a consequence of the incomplete transposition of meanings when we don't get past the immediate objectivities of the world. We live our everyday lives in the phenomenal world of things and their exchange values on the market, the superficialities of their prices, but don't as a matter of habit go further into their meanings. The immediate presence of things and the market for their exchange seems insurmountable. We don't get past their reified meanings. As a consequence, interests are concealed.

We could, however, parse the system that underlies trade in tools, and spoons, and everything else. In another layer of grammatical analysis, we could analyze the interests embodied in those same meanings, and the messy transpositions between immediate speaking-to (rhetoric) and deeper meanings-in (by parsing reification).

When we analyze these ordinary things for their immanent social grammar, interests are revealed, and the implications are political. But mostly we don't do this. We just keep going about our everyday lives, without interrogating the wider and deeper meanings in differential interests. So, society in its current form goes on, meaning what it does, as it does, one commodity transaction at a time.

If Mr Peel's beautiful illusions were shattered in Western Australia, we may ask: what then, are the general conditions for tearing aside all such illusions? How do we overcome their seeming "objectivities," the reifications in the status quo?

§2.3b   The Architecture of "Red Vienna"

In the post-war turmoil of 1919, the Social Democratic Party took over the municipal government of Vienna, where it remained in control until 1934. "Red Vienna" was governed by a set of social theories of political principles called "Austro-Marxism," with a determination to make revolution democratically, not the Bolshevik way. Factory councils were created in 1919 as a first step towards eventual public ownership of the means of production. Rent controls were imposed in a step towards public ownership of housing.

Between 1919 and 1934, the city government built 63,924 new residences, mostly apartments in buildings that were monumental in scale. In the spirit of socialism, said party leader and theorist, Otto Bauer, apartment blocks included "central kitchens and laundries, central heating, play and classrooms for children, common dining rooms, reading and game rooms for adults, and the cooks, laundresses and child-care specialists required for the functioning of these communal facilities." These comprehensively designed social spaces would configure a "new person." The architect was a social engineer; the urban reformer was a pedagogue.[179] By changing the objective conditions of life, people would change.[*]

Otto Neurath[§MS1.1.3h] was a founder of the Settlement, Housing, and Construction Guild of Austria, an alliance of the construction workers' union and the tenants' union. This was a cooperative organized according to guild socialist lines. Later he became General Secretary of a successor organization, where settlement theory and design was taught by Neurath, architect Adolf Loos,[§MS2.1.1b] and others.[180]

"Dissemination of knowledge about housing and the organization and equipment of dwelling space is becoming an increasingly significant component of worker education," said Neurath. "We are in an activist frame of mind here, because the worker administration of our city is building and decorating so much! . . . [W]e are convinced that the realization of the new art will fall to the proletariat."[181]

The new public housing was a theme regularly addressed by Neurath and Marie Reidemeister in their Social and Economic Museum.[§MS1.1.3h] Its displays presented their innovative pictorial statistics, photographs, plans, and models. Neurath stressed "the need to regard the building as a kind of machine . . . One can only judge if a machine is well-designed if one understands its inner workings, . . . [and if one is] able to judge the effectiveness of a design." To make it accessible to the workers, the museum also opened at night.[182]

Not that, for all their novelty and modernist rationalism, the new socialist housing machines were without historical reference. With its huge arched gateways, Karl-Marx-Hof referenced the old city walls of Vienna. Its garden courts spoke to landscaped spaces hitherto only accessible to lords and kings in their palaces, but now made possible by the small footprint of apartment blocks whose balconies looked out over the vista. These were expressions of the workers' interests, the public spirit of socialism. If pictorial statistics, photographs, and plans spoke to socialist interests visually in two-dimensional miniature, the architecture of public housing spoke to them spatially, life-sized and in three dimensions.

This was more than "constructivism," said Neurath, doyen of the Vienna Circle,[§MS1.1.3i] which "seems satisfied to make a spectacle of rationalism rather than to strive for a deeper engagement with its principle."[183]

---

[*] http://meaningpatterns.net/red-vienna

[179] Helmut Gruber, 1991, *Red Vienna: Experiment in Working Class Culture*, Oxford: Oxford University Press, pp. 39–50.

[180] Eve Blau, 1999, *The Architecture of Red Vienna*, Cambridge, MA: MIT Press, pp. 97–98.

[181] Ibid., pp. 395, 390.   [182] Ibid., pp. 393–94.   [183] Ibid., p. 394.

§2.3c   *Victor Gruen's* Shopping Towns USA

Victor Grünbaum studied architecture at Vienna Academy of Fine Arts in the 1920s, where he was much influenced by the modernism of Adolf Loos. This was the same modernism that had influenced Ludwig Wittgenstein when he was building his sister's house in Vienna.§MS2.1.1b After he graduated, he worked by day in an architectural and construction firm whose activities included the great public housing projects, the "people's palaces" which would eventually house one-tenth of Vienna's population.§2.3b By night Grünbaum, a committed socialist, played in the Politisches Kabarett. "I was in the thick of the revolutionary movement – acting and writing social commentaries for the little theaters."

When the fascists came to power in 1934, though atheist by persuasion, Grünbaum was classified Jew by race. The only commissions he was able to come by were Vienna storefronts. Then, on March 12, 1938, Hitler annexed Austria, and Grünbaum spent a long night feeding the stove with his plays and writings – "my past goes up in flames," he lamented.[184] Many of the leaders of Austrian socialism had been Jews, and for the fascists, the socialist danger was a Jewish danger. Grünbaum was briefly jailed and his design firm seized. He fled to New York, where he became Victor Gruen.[185]

Gruen's first architectural jobs in the USA were to work on designs for the 1939 New York World's Fair, then storefronts in the city. Soon after that, he started to work on architectural theory.* Just as the highly elaborated theories of Austro-Marxism had driven its political practice, in 1952 Gruen co-wrote an article "Shopping Centers: The New Building Type." Then the most widely circulating architecture magazine in the United States, *Progressive Architecture* devoted almost a whole issue to the article. It was more like a manifesto, because no examples yet existed of the building type he announced. As in Red Vienna, practice was to follow theory.

Gruen's starting point was critique: "the anarchistic wilderness of our cities," where "millions of gasoline driven 'spirits' get into each other's way and choke the highways, roads and parking areas," and, with suburbanization, "the ring of blighted slum areas which surrounds so many of the downtown districts." Beyond the city, there was a "vacuum created by the absence of social, cultural and civic crystallization points in our vast suburban areas."[186]

---

* http://meaningpatterns.net/gruen

[184] Victor Gruen, 1979 [2017], *Shopping Town: Designing the City in Suburban America*, translated by A. Bauldauf, Minneapolis: University of Minnesota Press, p. 5.

[185] M. Jeffrey Hardwick, 2004, *Mall Maker: Victor Gruen, Architect of an American Dream*, Pittsburgh: University of Pennsylvania Press, pp. 8–17.

[186] Victor Gruen and Laurence P. Smith, 1952, "Shopping Centers: The New Building Type," *Progressive Architecture* (June):67–109, pp. 70, 67–68.

The solution was planning. The regional shopping center, "[t]his new architectural design concept, is ... neither publicly owned nor completely controlled by one institution, ... a conscious and conscientious co-operative effort."[187] Gruen's vision for the shopping center sounded rather like Viennese socialism.

With the advent of the large shopping center there will be a new outlet for that primary human instinct to mingle with other humans – to have social meetings, to relax together, to enjoy art, music, civic activities, the theater, films, good food, and entertainment in the company of others. What are the requisites to the fulfillment of this function of a social and cultural center?

First of all, to include, from the inception of the general plan, attributes which go beyond the commercial needs: auditoriums, lecture rooms, exhibit rooms, reading rooms, theaters, restaurants of many types, club rooms, community centers, libraries, children's day nurseries, boy and girl scout dens.

Second, to take advantage of the existence of public areas – such as garden courts, malls, arcades, terraces, covered walkways – for relaxation and amusement. There will be greenhouses, play areas, band shells, outdoor theaters, outdoor fashion shows, miniature zoos, outdoor shows of painting and sculpture, flower shows, picnic grounds.

Third, to realize an architectural concept and treatment which offer variety without confusion, colorful appearance without garishness, gaiety without vulgarity; ... an architectural treatment which, by the application of scientific design, eliminates what appears as an ugly rash on the body of our cities – the countless smoke stacks, telephone poles, power poles, dangling wires, air conditioning and ventilating ducts ... The myriad warning signs, lamp posts, bus-stop signs, directional signs, hydrants, waste baskets, letter boxes – all must be redesigned, coordinated and brought into a disciplined pattern. Here, at last, is an opportunity for contemporary art to find a place as part of a new architectural concept. Here is space for sculptures, murals, fountains, mosaics on floors, and mosaics on walls.[188]

Victor Gruen's manifesto became a reality, at least in part, with his Northland Center outside of Detroit, opened in 1954, and after that the first fully indoor shopping center, Southdale Center in Edina, Minnesota, opened in 1956. Gruen went on to design many more, and today there are enclosed shopping malls in almost every city in the world.[189]

Gruen was proposing a new spatial grammar, an historic compromise between the interests of the real estate developers, retailers, and the public. Cars would be quarantined on the outside. Walking one's way along the arcades to the heart of the shopping center, an introverted multifunction urban square was to be found. Around this, arcades were stacked several stories high, indoor pedestrian streets with a range of stores reminiscent of the old main street. Open storefronts blurred the seemingly public outside spaces from the private commercial spaces of the stores. Escalators prompted people to ascend, then the

---

[187] Ibid., p. 70. [188] Ibid., pp. 68–69.
[189] Alex Wall, 2005, *Victor Gruen: From Urban Shop to New City*, Barcelona: Actar.

necessity to circulate past other store fronts before descending – a maze-like perambulatory experience.[190]

The mall is a quintessentially modern site for the forms of its engagement of differential interests – in this case, the interests of retailers and the interests of consumers. In the ultra-localized and effervescently short life of the commodity, this is the site of a defining moment in the complex interplay of use values and exchange values. Here, the social processes of production and distribution meet the imagined potentialities of use value to ignite the spark of exchange value. The mall is a place for the entanglement of differential meanings, a carefully designed amalgam of text, image, space, object, body, sound, and speech. "Metaphysical subtleties and theological niceties," Karl Marx would say. We would say, the mysteries of transposition.[§2.3a]

The roots of the mall are not as old as humanity, for First Peoples had no such things. But they are at least as old as the fairs and markets of slave and feudal societies. Though another market of sorts, the post-Gruen mall has its own, distinctively nuanced grammar. "Shopping," we might write glibly on this page, reifying the experience as if it were objective, a concept forever. But if we parse the mall itself as an experience of multimodal meaning, we will uncover some of its depths, some of its historically-specific manifestations.

Here are just a few parts of this experience.

Text: carefully sized and placed signs, written in what Ron Scollon calls the "visual holophrastic language"[191] of typography for the brands of stores, where the unit of meaning is as ideographic as a Chinese character. Gruen was fastidious about the regularity of signage in the mall. But there was not much text: Gruen advised how much was too much, what would become a distraction.

Image: posters in storefronts put fashions onto pictured models; places are portrayed where commodities can be put to use in life; directional icons; and navigation maps – mall owners feel they need to have these in deference to retailers, but they are mostly confusing, because the space is confusing by design, so purchasers can become lost in a trance of consumerism.[192]

Space: This is a meticulously planned, holistically ordered space, a designerly escape from the chaos of the car-oriented cityscape, a sanctuary

[190] David Smiley, 2013, *Pedestrian Modern: Shopping and American Architecture, 1925–1956*, Minneapolis: University of Minnesota Press.

[191] Ron Scollon, 1999, "Multilingualism and Intellectual Property: Visual Holophrastic Discourse and the Commodity/Sign," pp. 404–17 in *Georgetown University Round Table on Languages and Linguistics*, edited by J.E. Alatis and A.-H. Tan, Washington, DC: Georgetown University Press.

[192] Paco Underhill, 2004, *The Call of the Mall*, New York: Simon and Schuster, p. 43.

from fragmented ugliness of the capitalist city, an artificial utopia, hermetically sealed even from the natural vagaries of weather. People go there just to be there, and they shop more because they are there.[193] Wide open doors, or entirely open storefronts, blur the boundary between the notional street and the store, beckoning people across the threshold of the pseudo-public.

Object: the aromas wafting out of stores; the stuff you can handle at the entry to the store; or the typically high-touch stuff on the little stalls that emulate traditional markets, taking retail labor back to the medieval market-place, except now, the latter-day feudal landlord extracts rent for the space of the stall.

Body: Shoppers see many stores at a glance across multiple levels in atriums, and their bodily perambulations across levels are at once easy (esca-lators) and circuitous (how the escalators are placed in relation to each other). "I don't like to go to malls because I always get lost," a woman told William Kowinski while he was documenting the mall experience, "and that's embar-rassing. I feel stupid. It makes me mad."[194] But if there is stupidity, if she is bodily disoriented, this woman should not blame herself; her stupidity is by design. If she were to parse the processes of reification, she might come to realize that it is not her.

Sound: the barely noticeable piped music of an ideal moodscape; the audio of an event in the atrium drawing you to stop and watch.

Speech: As a mall worker checks the coats of customers for drops of forecast rain, they ask, "has it started yet?" With the absence of weather, says Kowinski wryly, comes an absence of civil liberties. The companies who own the mall not only have control over the weather; they also exercise control over speech. Private security guards regulate acceptable presence, and the mall owners determine who can speak publicly in the courtyards or set up tables for petitioning.[195] Some kinds of activism and politics are not good for shopping, and the mall owners determine which these are.[196] Non-commercial talk of a possible world outside of the mall rarely gets beyond the weather.

In these ways, the shopping mall is a space of total design, the result of fastidiously integrated social planning of Austro-Marxist proportions. But the interests at play are not the same. In Red Vienna the differentials were between the socialist theorists and the educable masses. In the shopping mall, the differences are between mall owners as proxies for tenant retailers, and

---

[193] William Severini Kowinski, 1985, *The Malling of America: An inside Look at the Great Consumer Paradise*, New York: William Morrow and Company, pp. 120–21.

[194] Ibid., p. 338.   [195] Ibid., pp. 344, 338, 356–57, 362.

[196] Paco Underhill, 2004, *The Call of the Mall*, New York: Simon and Schuster, p. 32; William H. Whyte, 1988, *City: Rediscovering the Center*, New York: Doubleday, pp. 208–10.

shoppers. The mall owner's program is to reify social experience in the immediate material practices of text, image, space, object, body, sound, and speech.

These reifications frame a social architecture of meaning, orchestrating the interplay of mall owner and shopper where deeper interests are more obvious to mall owner than to shopper, where meanings are obscured for shoppers in a pseudo-public space. The effect of the design is to regulate and control. The bottom line for the mall owner is profit, but the reifying game they play is social. The mall is a museum of nicely arranged use values. Prices are a nod to exchange value, but in the immediate experience of shopping, the deeper interplay of interests is mostly inscrutable.

In this play of differential interests, mall owners control the program. After all, their capital constructs the place; they determine its multimodal designs. There is never a question that a democracy of consumers might be involved in the design of a mall. In the negotiation of differential social interests, the mall becomes at best an appropriation, at worst a travesty of the principles of Red Vienna.

By these means, consumer agency is channeled by seemingly objective realities, as if this is all there is, and there can be no other way to be.

Gruen kept theorizing as he built. In 1960, a book, *Shopping Towns USA: The Planning of Shopping Centers* – "shopping centers have taken the characteristics of urban organisms serving a multitude of human needs and activities, thus justifying the designation: 'shopping towns.'"[197] The subtitle of this book indicates that its focus is social planning in order to mitigate the worst excesses of freewheeling markets.

Then in 1973 another book, a plea to return to the values of urbanism in the context of environmental disaster and car-induced urban blight: *Centers for the Urban Environment: Survival of the Cities:* "In order to be meaningful, concern regarding any specific part of the human environment must be related to the wider horizons of settlements for human beings. It must be based on an awareness that environmental planning is the key to human survival on this planet."[198] In this book, he created a notation for the design of a multifunctional center, where human functions in space met supporting structural and mechanical forms.

And finally, in 1978, just two years before he died, an article, "The Sad Story of Shopping Centers," reprinting a speech he gave at the Conference of the International Council of Shopping Centres in London. There, he described them as "huge, specialized ghettos, ... disastrous expressions of mono-

[197] Victor Gruen, 1960, *Shopping Towns USA: The Planning of Shopping Centers*, New York: Reinhold Publishing, p. 11.
[198] Victor Gruen, 1973, *Centers for the Urban Environment: Survival of the Cities*, New York: Van Norstrand Reinhold, p. 3.

function, . . . [built by] anonymous real-estate . . . speculators who just wanted to make a fast buck . . . ruinous for American cities . . . The environmental and humane ideas underlying . . . in the original centres . . . were completely forgotten. Only those features which had proved profitable were copied."[199] This is probably not what the conference participants expected or wanted to hear.

And of the America where he started this trend, Gruen said it had become a place where "everybody is persuaded to buy what he doesn't need with money he doesn't own in order to impress people he actually can't stand."

At the end of his life, Gruen returned to live in Vienna, only to find to his dismay, a new wave of shopping malls stripping life from the city of his birth.[200]

§2.3d   Hermann Henselmann's Karl-Marx-Allee

Aldo Rossi, Italian architect and theorist, called it "Europe's last great street."[*] American Architect Philip Johnson called it "true city planning on a great scale."[201] Until the Second Word War, it had been named Frankfurter Allee, passing through the working class district of Friedrichshain, Berlin. The area was reduced to a ruin by Allied bombing, then the Red Army created further damage as they fought their way down this street until they reached the center of the city. As part of the Soviet Sector of the divided city, it was named Stalinallee on the dictator's seventieth birthday in 1949. Then, after Khrushchev's admission of Stalin's crimes, without ceremony in the middle of one night in August 1961 it was renamed Karl-Marx-Allee.[202]

If Victor Gruen's notion of planning was thwarted in the capitalist west, in East Berlin the planners were left to design with reference only to the public interest. The ruins of the war were razed, and a vast boulevard created, 90 meters wide, symbol of the newborn socialist society.

Hermann Henselmann was of part Jewish ancestry, and though he had survived the Nazis, his opportunities to practice as an architect had been few.[203]

---

* http://meaningpatterns.net/karl-marx-allee

[199] Victor Gruen, 1978, "The Sad Story of Shopping Centers," *Town and Country Planning* 46(7–8):350–53, pp. 351–52.

[200] M. Jeffrey Hardwick, 2004, *Mall Maker: Victor Gruen, Architect of an American Dream*, Pittsburgh: University of Pennsylvania Press, p. 218.

[201] Brian Ladd, 1997, *The Ghosts of Berlin: Confronting German History in the Urban Landscape*, Chicago, IL: University of Chicago Press, p. 187; Aldo Rossi, 1982, *The Architecture of the City*, translated by D. Ghirardo and J. Ockman, Cambridge, MA: MIT Press.

[202] Owen Hatherley, 2015, *Landscapes of Communism*, London: Allen Lane, pp. 49–50.

[203] www.archinform.net/arch/281.htm

Henselmann worked on Stalinallee, then in 1953 was appointed head architect for the city of Berlin, capital of the new German Democratic Republic.

Henselmann's style had originally been Bauhaus-Modernism, but after a delegation of architects and planners traveled to Moscow in 1949, his and his colleagues' style changed. Moscow State University and the other "seven sisters" were under construction.$^{§MS1.1.3g}$ So, when the work started on Stalinallee from around Frankfurter Tor, it was in the same monumental, neoclassical style they had seen in Moscow. The Russians called the style "formalism," as opposed to the "cosmopolitanism" of the Bauhaus style. Or in another reading, Bauhaus modernism was what a party newspaper called cheap "egg carton" construction, expressing "the greed for profit and contempt for humanity of the dying capitalist system."[204]

Walking towards the city center from Frankfurter Tor in 1981 and then again in the 2000s, we came to a stretch of construction that began in 1961. This reflected a switch to socialist modernism that also came with the change in the name of the street to Karl-Marx-Allee, and a change at that time in the architectural sentiment of the General Secretary in Moscow – Khrushchev favored modernist functionalism.

Carefully restored and maintained in its original form since the fall of the German Democratic Republic, in a now hyper-commercialized world, Karl-Marx-Allee was eerily strange for its absence of commercial pleading, and remains so today. The trees have grown large, so the broad street is parklike and traffic barely noticeable. Apartment blocks are spaced widely apart. There's the Kino International Cinema where the premieres of GDR films used to be screened, the former Mocha Milk Ice Bar, and Café Moskau with its Sputnik replica floating above a mural depicting abstractly idealized Soviet life. The artist was Bert Heller, Rector of the Fine Arts Academy. Alongside were schools, daycare centers, doctors' surgeries, pharmacies – the stuff of everyday material needs for the inhabitants of the Allee. Several stores displayed, museum-like, the latest socialist consumer goods. The shops and cafés, and of course the doctor's surgeries and daycares, were all publicly owned – suitably enough, suitably spaced, suitably sized to accommodate the people whose right it was to use them, freely.

Further down the street there was Henselmann's House of Teachers, skirted by its wide mosaic, then his concert Hall, then the Berlin TV tower surmounted by a massive Sputnik look-alike viewing level, for which Henselmann provided the initial designs.

For all its unfreedoms, the GDR was also a country of peculiar freedoms, expressed in the now-strange space of Karl-Marx-Allee: free, universal

---

[204] Brian Ladd, 1997, *The Ghosts of Berlin: Confronting German History in the Urban Landscape,* Chicago, IL: University of Chicago Press, p. 183.

childcare with public mothers-milk banks; free education; free healthcare. And freedom from the culture of the commodity.

Stranger still, "free body culture." In this case, freedom was from woolen, pre-lycra swimsuits that were both expensive to purchase in commodity-sparse GDR and uncomfortable when wet. A 1966 survey found that 81 percent of young workers and 87 percent of students bathed or sunbathed nude in public places. Naked and clothed bathers mingled freely. Said one of the interviewees, "Here the woman is not an object of desire, she is a comrade, there is no bikini to excite you." And another: "The view of another person's body allows decent people no room for erotic feelings." And a third: "It is of great value to socialism that nudism prevents any unclean erotic fantasies."[205]

Now, we turn from Karl-Marx-Allee onto Karl-Liebknecht-Strasse, named after the Communist leader murdered along with his co-leader Rosa Luxemburg by right-wing militias in January 1919. As we cross onto Museum Island on the River Spree, on one side of the street is the pseudo-Baroque cathedral, church and mausoleum for the Hohenzollern Emperors, completed in 1905. Opposite there had been the Palace of the Emperors, just as pseudo-Baroque and not that much older. After the abdication of the last emperor in 1918, Karl Liebknecht stood at one of its balconies to announce the short-lived Free Socialist Republic.

Badly damaged during the Second World War, the Emperor's palace was demolished by the GDR. In 1976, a new gold-tinted, glass, steel, and marble palace was opened on the site, the Palace of the Republic. Not just a parliament for the party congresses, it was also a gallery and concert hall, with discos, bars, cafés, even a bowling alley, all in one uncommercial building. From the perspective of our near-universal twenty-first-century experience of pervasive markets, this people's palace seems strangely configured. A permanent gallery included works commissioned to address the theme, "Are Communists allowed to dream?" On entering, visitors were greeted by a huge canvas, *People on the Beach* by Hans Vent, with naked and clothed people pictured together in the same scene as if there were no noticeable difference.[206]

The German Democratic Republic fell in 1990, and in 2006, the socialists' palace was demolished.[207] In its place a replica of the Emperor's palace was rebuilt, or at least the façade speaks to that, because façadism is all it is. "No

---

[205] Josie McLellan, 2007, "State Socialist Bodies: East German Nudism from Ban to Boom," *The Journal of Modern History* 79(1):48–79, pp. 65, 73, 67.

[206] Barbara Wolbert, 2001, "De-Arranged Spaces: East German Art in the Museums of Unified Germany," *The Anthropology of East Europe Review* 19(1):57–64.

[207] Christian von Steffelin, 2011, *Palast Der Republik, 1994–2010*, Ostfildern, Germany: Hatje Cantz Verlag.

palace without an emperor!" somebody wrote in a comment book for an exhibition showing off the new-old designs.

Protesting the demolition, one man said, "They want to get rid of everything from the GDR ... to tear down every symbol, principally out of simple revenge, nothing more." And a woman: "This was like a second home to me. This is where I came to meet people, to experience culture and beauty. It was part of my life."[208]

§2.3e   *Germaine Krull's Shops of Paris*

Walter Benjamin included Germaine Krull in the pantheon of great modern photographers in his "Little History of Photography," which he illustrated with two of her pictures.* He had selected thirteen of her photographs and placed them in the archive for his *Arcades* project.[§MS0b] No merely textual philosophy of modernity and theory of history, he had intended the book to be richly visual.

Germaine Krull had been a contributor to Paris-based *Vu* magazine since its inception, an early example of the photo news magazine, notable for its innovative modernist imagery. *Vu*'s photographers captured evocative abstracted moments with small hand-held cameras, rather than the descriptive, front-on pictorialism of large cameras on tripods. Krull contributed articles on many of the things that interested Benjamin in his *Arcades* project: the Paris arcades themselves; iron and steel in architecture and industry; shopping; and street life. Perhaps Benjamin was thinking of a format like *Vu* for the *Arcades* book. True to this vision, when an exposé of the project[209] and then the full version of his convolutes was finally published,[210] they were full of images.

Krull had been in the crowd of "women, children, soldiers, intellectuals, workers, all together" who marched on the royal palace in Munich in November 1918, bringing to an end the Bavarian Monarchy. She was close friends with Kurt Eisner, leader of the Bavarian Independent Socialist Republic, the first parliamentary republic in Germany, murdered by a right wing militia in January 1919. When that government fell, she became closely involved with the Bavarian Soviet Republic,[§MS1.1.3h] also short-lived. Escaping the conservative reaction, she spent nearly two years in Moscow working for a Soviet photographic press service. She was there in person for Lenin's five-

---

* http://meaningpatterns.net/krull

[208] https://archive.org/details/Brokedown_Palast
[209] Susan Buck-Morss, 1989, *The Dialectics of Seeing: Walter Benjamin and the Arcades Project*, Cambridge, MA: MIT Press.
[210] Walter Benjamin, 1999b, *The Arcades Project*, translated by H. Eidland and K. McLaughlin, Cambridge, MA: Harvard University Press.

hour-long speech at the Third World Congress of the Communist International in 1921.[211]

During those revolutionary days in Munich she had met and developed a lasting friendship with Max Horkheimer, later a founder of the School for Social Research in Frankfurt, and after that the New School for Social Research in New York, another friend of Walter Benjamin. Krull met Benjamin in 1926, and the two remained friends, staying in regular communication until 1938. There were, said Benjamin referring to Krull and other photographic innovators, "lessons inherent in the authenticity of the photograph ... The camera is getting smaller and smaller, ever ready to capture fleeting and secret images." Photography is an "act of unmasking."[212]

When she comes to picture them, Krull's Paris arcades are dark, melancholy places. Once marvels of architectural novelty, pedestrian streets enclosed and covered with steel and glass roofs, by the time she was photographing them and Benjamin was writing about them, they were old, relics of the previous century's modernity. Of their past allure, Benjamin said, in the arcades "art enters the service of the merchant." "The Phalanstery" – a group of people living in a shared utopian community – "is a city composed of arcades ... street galleries ... The arcade is a street of lascivious commerce ... wholly adapted to arousing desires ... [T]he commodity proliferates along the margins and enters into fantastic combinations ... In this *ville en passages*," this city of passage-ways, "the engineer's construction takes on a phantasmagorical character."[213] With their glass and steel roofs and pedestrian-only, shop-lined passages, nineteenth-century Paris arcades prefigure certain motifs for Victor Gruen's considerably larger, suburban "shopping towns" in the second half of the twentieth century.§2.3c

As for the people of the arcades and the city, in 1928 Krull contributed a series of images to a story in *Vu* on "Tramps in the Lower Depths of Paris."[214] She and Benjamin were both interested in the marginal, street-strolling denizens of the commercial city, capturing a critical relation to the commod-ity in its urban presentation. Benjamin's emblematic street person was the flâneur, a person who is at once anonymous – "The flâneur seeks refuge in the

[211] Kim Sichel, 1999, *Germaine Krull: Photographer of Modernity*, Cambridge, MA: MIT Press, pp. 18–25; Michel Frizot, 2015, *Germaine Krull*, Paris: Editions Hazan, pp. 17–19.

[212] Walter Benjamin, 1931 [1999], "Little History of Photography," pp. 507–30 in *Walter Benjamin: Selected Writings,* Volume 2: *1927–1934*, edited by M.W. Jennings, H. Eiland, and G. Smith, Cambridge, MA: Harvard University Press, pp. 526–27.

[213] Walter Benjamin, 1939 [1999], "Paris, Capital of the Nineteenth Century," pp. 14–26 in *The Arcades Project*, edited by H. Eidland and K. McLaughlin, Cambridge, MA: Harvard University Press, pp. 15, 17; Walter Benjamin, 1999b, *The Arcades Project*, translated by H. Eidland and K. McLaughlin, Cambridge, MA: Harvard University Press, p. 42.

[214] Michel Frizot, 2015, *Germaine Krull*, Paris: Editions Hazan, p. 96.

crowd"[215] – but at the same time one in a collective, a representative of the mass. "Streets are the dwelling place of the collective. The collective is an eternally unquiet, eternally agitated being that – in the space between the building fronts – experiences, learns, understands, and invents."[216] Sartre spoke in similar terms of the transitory modulations of the collective in the streets of Paris.[§1.5]

The flâneur has a way of seeing, where the "city appears now as landscape, now as room," and this "seems later to have inspired the décor of department stores, which has thus put flânerie to work for profit."[217] Or beyond reach, the "commodity whispers to a poor wretch who passes a shop window containing beautiful and expensive things."[218] "[T]he flâneur becomes attuned to the commodity. ... he takes the abstract concept of 'For Sale'-ness on a stroll through the streets."[219] "The flâneur is the observer of the marketplace. His knowledge is akin to the occult science of industrial fluctuations."[220]

No mere flunky of commercialism, the flâneur is equally capable of seeing into and seeing through the commodities on display: "The more conscious he becomes of his mode of existence, the mode imposed on him by the system of production ... the less he will feel like empathizing with commodities."[221]

Germaine Krull photographed scenes of Paris shopping: in the shop windows, reflected images of the street overlaying the fashions on display; some mannequins woodenly re-enacting life; and other mannequins stripped-naked, commodity-less, starkly waiting to be dressed. These are images taken at the intersection of use value (wish images, embodied aesthetics, culture) and exchange value (the imminent possibility of sale, the reduction of material things to an abstract monetary equivalence).[§2.3a] But they are not sales images. They are reflections of a transformative

[215] Walter Benjamin, 1939 [1999], "Paris, Capital of the Nineteenth Century," pp. 14–26 in *The Arcades Project*, edited by H. Eidland and K. McLaughlin, Cambridge, MA: Harvard University Press, p. 21.

[216] Walter Benjamin, 1999b, *The Arcades Project*, translated by H. Eidland and K. McLaughlin, Cambridge, MA: Harvard University Press, p. 422.

[217] Walter Benjamin, 1939 [1999], "Paris, Capital of the Nineteenth Century," pp. 14–26 in *The Arcades Project*, edited by H. Eidland and K. McLaughlin, Cambridge, MA: Harvard University Press, p. 21.

[218] Walter Benjamin, 1938 [1999], "The Paris of the Second Empire in Baudelaire," pp. 3–94 in *Walter Benjamin: Selected Writings, Volume 4: 1938–1940*, edited by M.W. Jennings, H. Eiland, and G. Smith, Cambridge, MA: Harvard University Press, p. 32.

[219] Walter Benjamin, 2003, *Selected Writings, Volume 4: 1938–1940*, Cambridge, MA: Harvard University Press, p. 208.

[220] Walter Benjamin, 1999b, *The Arcades Project*, translated by H. Eidland and K. McLaughlin, Cambridge, MA: Harvard University Press, p. 427.

[221] Walter Benjamin, 1938 [1999], "The Paris of the Second Empire in Baudelaire," pp. 3–94 in *Walter Benjamin: Selected Writings, Volume 4: 1938–1940*, edited by M.W. Jennings, H. Eiland, and G. Smith, Cambridge, MA: Harvard University Press, p. 33.

moment in the life of a commodity where these things, awkwardly, uneasily, coincide.

Even in his most polished and coherent moments, Benjamin is elusive, which makes a selective reading more than convenient; it is necessary. So this is what we would say for his reading of what Germaine Krull was showing us in the shop windows of Paris: if we perform an act of historical recovery, behind each commodity exchange we might trace a history of laboring, a division of labor and a bringing to market which involves conflicting interests, as between seller and purchaser, capitalist and worker.

Every commodity has a material and social genesis; as do commodities in general, in a broader historical frame. But in the narrowed experience of shopping, the object takes precedence, its allure and the imagination of its imminent use – hence "reification." Its immediate quantification is price, the most immediate calculator in the lowest common denominator of monetary equivalence.

Now, push the wish-images in commodity aesthetics and we test the constraints of the market, the pragmatics of inequality. The implications, for Benjamin, are revolutionary – a desire for utopia, where the material temptations of the commodity stretch to a breaking point the social structures of inequality. Utopian imagination involves uncovering meanings obscured by reification and commodity fetishism. This he calls "profane illumination, a materialistic, anthropological inspiration."[222]

For our grammar of transpositions, we find Benjamin exploring the social history and potential destiny in commodities that are only mundanely material in a first, superficial and reifying glance. We also find him exploring the movement of bodies, laboring to produce, streetwalking to purchase or not to purchase, and mental prefigurations of consumability, the conjunction of (or unaffordable inability to conjoin) use value and exchange value.

§2.3f   Siemon Scamell-Katz's Art of Shopping

Leaving the street now, or the arcade, or the quasi-streetscape of the mall,[§2.3c] let's go into the shop.[*]

In commercial architecture and store design, the "Gruen effect" or "Gruen transfer" refers to the seemingly magical capacity of the design of shopping

---

[*] http://meaningpatterns.net/shopping

[222] Walter Benjamin, 1929 [1999], "Surrealism: The Last Snapshot of the European Intelligentsia," pp. 207–21 in *Walter Benjamin: Selected Writings,* Volume 2: *1927–1934,* edited by M.W. Jennings, H. Eidland, and G. Smith, Cambridge, MA: Harvard University Press, p. 209.

spaces to lure customers to purchase things that they had not necessarily intended to buy.[223] According to Siemon Scamell-Katz's theory of shopping, people enter a store on a "mission." The design of the space transforms them from mission-driven walkers into flâneurs of sorts, wanderers partly lost in a commercial spectacle, where the smallest and easiest of moves, pulling an item off the shelf and putting it into a trolley, can materialize a commodity relation that may not have been part of their original intention.

Walter Benjamin parsed two of the foundational innovations in Paris of the nineteenth century: the arcade and the department store.[§2.3e] In the twentieth century, some more radical innovations were to come. Piggly Wiggly was the first self-service store, opened in Memphis in 1916.[224] Its inventor, Clarence Saunders, took out a patent on its apparatus. "The object of my said invention is to provide a store equipment by which the customer will be enabled to serve himself and, in so doing, will be required to review the entire assortment of goods carried in stock, conveniently and attractively displayed ... [T]he goods may be selected and taken by the customers themselves while making a circuitous path through the store."[225] For this new moment in the history of the market, the invention is strikingly clear-sighted about the effects of spatial framing and the micro-dynamics directing the interests of shoppers in the interests of the retailer.

Then, the first supermarket, "King Kullen" store in Queens, New York City, opened in 1930 by Michael J. Cullen, in a large, vacant garage with plenty of nearby parking. It was the beginning of the Great Depression, and the key to rapid success was high sales volume and heavy discounting. "Why pay more?" was the store's slogan, though with an array of one thousand items within reach, it was designed for customers to spend more.

By 1934, there were 94 supermarkets in the United States, and two years after that, 1200. Then after the Second World War came the shopping center, where the self-service store and the supermarket were combined with the shopping arcade and "anchor" department store: 2,900 by 1959, 13,000 in 1970, then in 16,000 new centers built in the 1980s, a peak decade of mall construction, bringing the total to 45,721 by 2001.[226]

The architecture – the multimodal grammar – of self-service stores and supermarkets were different from Benjamin's arcades, where the flâneur's relation to commodities was separated by glass and price, so raising the

---

[223] Victor Gruen, 1979 [2017], *Shopping Town: Designing the City in Suburban America*, translated by A. Bauldauf, Minneapolis: University of Minnesota Press, p. x.

[224] Siemon Scammell-Katz, 2012, *The Art of Shopping: How We Shop and Why We Buy*, London: LID Publishing, p. 28.

[225] Clarence Saunders, 1917, "Self Serving Store," edited by U.S. Patent Office.

[226] Peter Coleman, 2006, *Shopping Environments: Evolution, Planning and Design*, Oxford: Architectural Press, pp. 40, 43.

possibility of critical detachment. Now, Saunders' "circuitous path" took shoppers past products they could pick up, feel as if they might become theirs, and with a simple gesture drop into a trolley, large enough to take more than you need, and with ease.

Concludes Siemon Scamell-Katz: "All of this was followed by a long, slow demise of the practice of selling in shops, which was replaced by the art of presenting product in space."[227] Here, products speak for themselves, and a new pattern for the meeting of differential interest is established, a new kind of flânerie. The old relationship of human salesperson to consumer – "Can I help you?" followed by suggestive patter, the conversational wiles of an effective salesperson – is replaced by the active, strolling, seeing, feeling, selecting consumer. Speech is displaced by spatial, object-oriented, and embodied meanings. Reification replaces rhetoric.

Scamell-Katz is a leader in a field of business consultants selling the psychology and physiology of shopping to retailers. So is Paco Underhill, a theorist of the "science of shopping," and owner of the consultancy, Envirosell.[228] Their theories are tested and refined in a research practice of fastidious observation, including analyses of body- and eye-tracking video recordings.

For Scamell-Katz, advertising is an old-school, "linear" model of persuasion: attract attention > stimulate interest > create desire > attain purchase. Instead, he analyzes the spatial and bodily dynamics of shopping, where advertising- or needs-induced missions can be diverted.

"Destination items," the things like milk that you must buy, are located in the back corner, so you have to pass a myriad of "impulse items" to get there, things you didn't think you needed until there. They stare you in the face at "buy level," between waist and chest level, because we look slightly down while walking. Space at the end of aisles (the "endcap" or "gondola end", grammatically speaking) is purchased by "signpost brands," even though this creates redundancy for the supermarket order[§MS0d] according to which the library of possible purchases is otherwise catalogued, some things now appearing at two places, one expected, the other not. The ordering itself is a mnemonic, a reminder of things that replaces the pre-formulated list, while also supplementing it with things too-easily overlooked or forgotten in purely textual remembering. Then there is the "grab zone" near the checkout where, while waiting in the queue, you are confronted by chocolates and trashy magazines with sensational headlines.[229]

These are just a few of the elements of the spatial-object grammar in these tightly controlled spaces. There are also consultancies that can offer finely

---

[227] Siemon Scamell-Katz, 2012, *The Art of Shopping: How We Shop and Why We Buy*, London: LID Publishing, p. 28.

[228] Paco Underhill, 1999, *Why We Buy: The Science of Shopping*, New York: Simon and Schuster.

[229] Siemon Scamell-Katz, 2012, *The Art of Shopping: How We Shop and Why We Buy*, London: LID Publishing, pp. 30, 46, 65, 70.

specified advice on the design and devices for the delivery of ambient sound (such as Muzak[230]) and smell (such as Scentair[231]).

At their fringes, shopping theories start to smack of voodoo, such as Weishar's "invariable right," based on evidence he provides that people always look right when first entering a space, followed by a right–left "bounce pattern" where it is possible to predict patterns of lateral looking and so the most effective places to display items for sale.[232]

Charles Fillmore parses what he calls the "commercial event"[233] in his frame semantics,[§MS2.1.2a] by which he means "framing the appeal, in perceiving, thinking, and communicating, to structured ways of interpreting experiences." These are "cognitive and interactional frames," "knowledge prototypes," "schemas," "scenarios," or "internal models of the world: . . . [T]he idea is that people have in memory an inventory of schemata for structuring, classifying, and interpreting experiences, and that they have various ways of accessing these schemata and various procedures for performing operations on them . . . A frame is a kind of outline figure with not necessarily all of the details filled in."[234]

As between the participants, between seller and purchaser, radically differential interests are expressed in an event whose experience is shared: sell ⇔ buy; charge ⇔ pay. Different aspects of the shared meaning event are foregrounded depending on the participant's role. The event would not even occur without the differences. These are deeply embedded in transpositional experience. Every re-enactment replicates the experience such that each becomes habitual. But each event is unique, in time and space, and in the configuration of need or desire and anticipated use of specific commodities. The use values vary, and circumstantially their exchange values (their prices), but the frame remains the same.

Interrogating these differential interests, in the shop the retailer appropriates the humane promise of use for the mercenary purposes of exchange. The bottom line for their framing of the event is not the qualities of use, because their self-interest in the market is to ensure that the act of exchange is not left unconsummated. The shopper on the other hand prefigures use in their mindsight,[§MS3.1.2b] interpolating the commodity into the ideal of a life redesigned by its presence – a self re-embodied by a fashion item, a life enhanced by a nice or useful thing, a food product that will satiate a craving. This is what pulls the shopper across the line into the social relation that is exchange.

---

[230] Joseph Lanza, 1994, *Elevator Music: A Surreal History of Muzak, Easy Listening, and Other Moodsong*, New York: St Martin's Press.

[231] www.scentair.com/whos-scenting/retail-scent-marketing-enhances-customer-experience.html

[232] Joseph Weishar, 1992, *Design for Effective Selling Space*, New York: McGraw-Hill, p. 47.

[233] Charles J. Fillmore, 1977, "The Case for Case Reopened," *Syntax and Semantics* 8:59–82, pp. 72–74.

[234] Charles J. Fillmore, 1976, "Frame Semantics and the Nature of Language," *Annals of the New York Academy of Sciences* 280(1):20–32, pp. 20, 23, 14, 13, 23, 29.

In a commercialized age, such transpositions of meaning draw us as near as possible to moments that would once have been considered spiritual, reminiscent of a time when saintly images or sacred objects could perform miracles, and when the bread and wine of the eucharist could be the body and blood of Christ.[§1.1.2a] Shopping is the transubstantiation of our time.

Or, in a more modern parsing: "I shop therefore I am." So says Barbara Kruger,[235] for her late twentieth-century update of Descartes.

§2.3.1   Activation

> **Activation.** *Processes of transposition by means of which social meanings are presented as states of affairs, differentially serving interests.*

Reification happens through the interest that people take in things, not narrowly conceived as objects (one of the forms of meaning in this grammar), but as multimodal states-of-affairs.

We want to draw a distinction, however, between two forms of reification: activation and alienation. Activation is the immediate expression of interest, when human needs translate into a quest for use values, for instance, or the superficial translation of exchange value into price. In activation, the object world represents a realization of interests that are in one sense complementary: your product ⟺ my need or desire; your price ⟺ my capacity and willingness to pay.

However, with activation, there may also come alienation, where differential interests are at the same time not-so-complementary, in fact where they may to some degree be in conflict. Such conflicts may be explicit or implicit, conscious or unconscious, interpreted as such or misinterpreted, understood or misunderstood.

The tricky thing is that activation and alienation often come together, two layers in the same meaning, the one ever-ready to be transposed for the other. As we put the best construction on the activation, we may overlook the alienation.

§2.3.1a deadmalls.com

By the mid 2010s, malls everywhere were closing, and outside of the mall, "big box" stores were being shuttered.[*] A *Time* magazine story reported 8,600 major store closings in the US in 2017, and the future of one out of four malls was in doubt. Analysts were calling it a "retail apocalypse" on a scale not seen since

---

* http://meaningpatterns.net/dead-malls

[235] Alexander Alberro, Martha Gever, Miwon Kwon, and Carol Squiers, eds. 2010, *Barbara Kruger*, New York: Rizzoli.

the Great Depression; 448,000 retail jobs lost in the United States over the previous fifteen years, a 25 percent decline.[236]

In the brief moment of their efflorescence, the mall and the big box store emptied out the old "main street," in some towns and cities reducing it to a near-empty ruin. Now malls and big box stores are suffering the same fate.

The website deadmalls.com wistfully, regretfully, nostalgically documents this decline. Dan Bell produces videos of abandoned and dying malls that draw millions of views to the site's YouTube channel. "When you go into a dead mall, it's like shock and awe at the same time," he says. "I think that's really appealing for a lot of young people. It's like watching the Titanic sink."[237]

It's not the decline of the mall or the store that captures our attention so much as the profound reconfigurations of interest of which these changes are a symptom. Nor even this, so much as to develop a grammar with which to read changes of this enormity.

The mall and the supermarket are paradigmatic sites where, in the material life of commodities, the pressure in the relation of the differential interests of seller and buyer is towards assimilation. The experience of the shopper was more or less the same, perambulating through the shared arcades or supermarket aisles, following much the same path prefigured in the ordering of products, with the same images for all to see, the same piped music, the same aromas. The missions of individual shoppers may be somewhat different, but the distractions are the same. Such are the affordances of space. There is limited scope for difference.

To the extent that there is demographic variation, in the mall it is crudely configured. A mall may have scores of stores, but there is less space for men, as stereotypically conceived by the mall, than for women.[238] Men have to go elsewhere for the hardware store or the auto parts store. Nor is there space for the meagerly consuming poor, a difference marked often by race – not having a car can keep them away.

Going to the physical store, the 75,000 items in a Walmart would, you might think, allow plenty of scope for differentiation.[§2.2.2] But, in its attempt to be comprehensive, a Walmart can only have a few of each kind of thing, mostly cheap and Chinese-made. Meanwhile a data service provider called ScrapeHero reported that on January 4, 2017 Amazon had a total of 398,040,250 products, an 8% increase on the previous month.[239] In that year, its total sales were up 30% from the year before, and in 2018 it reached 49.1% of all online retail sales in the United States, followed by eBay and Apple, leaving Walmart in fourth place for e-commerce sales at a meager 3.7%.[240]

[236] Josh Sanburn, 2017, "Why the Death of Malls Is About More Than Shopping," *Time*, July 20.
[237] Ibid.
[238] Paco Underhill, 2004, *The Call of the Mall*, New York: Simon and Schuster. pp. 97ff, 126ff.
[239] www.scrapehero.com/how-many-products-are-sold-on-amazon-com-january-2017-report
[240] https://medium.com/futuresin/amazon-owns-half-of-ecommerce-in-the-u-s-904523f7aea2

Nobody could browse through all these items in the Amazon store, so instead of the singular and synergistic juxtaposition of items in a physical store, we find them by searching a database. This is a fundamentally different way of representing and communicating purchasable products.[§MS2.1.1c]

Relational databases are neither two-dimensional (as is the store map); nor three (as is perambulating the store in architectural space). By comparison, they are non-dimensional. Each of the tables that sits behind a relational database may in the first instance be two-dimensional,[§1.4.6a] but when tables are layered over tables and ontologies map semantic relations over tables, what we then have is an infinitely varied relationality that transcends the essential contiguities of two-dimensional maps and three-dimensional spaces.

Shopping, so transformed, is still shopping, but the affordances are different. This is a radical transposition, from in-store shopping to online. There is both a profound continuity (the commodity form as an essentially modern social frame for interest) and profound change (a shift in the program of interest from assimilation to differentiation).

Where physical stores dealt with differences in the crudest and often most frustratingly ineffective of ways, Amazon's unit of social difference is reduced to a handful of "people like you," and only in this miniscule respect: they are people who happen to have directed their interest for a moment to one of those four hundred million-odd use values. The database has a record of the billions of such instances of shopping, information lost to a physical store. By committing these instances to the historical record, by documenting their excruciating detail in the universal encyclopedia of shopping, online stores can switch at whim and in an instant their program for the management of market interests. If in the dynamic of the physical store, by dint of the affordances of its forms of multimodal meaning "to shop" was to assimilate, then the dynamic of the online store is to differentiate.

§2.3.1b Takahashi Taiyou's Unboxing of Big Thomas & Friends Pocket Fantasy Station

Not that the physical allure of objects as use values and the consumer's sensuousness of embodied connection to them has gone from the virtual store. Rather, the modes of their activation take new forms.

Here is one example that bears parsing: beside the shift to online retailing has emerged a new genre of "unboxing" videos.[241] The first was in 2006, for a Nokia phone.[242] Just before we wrote this sentence, a search for "unboxing" on YouTube returned "about 86,900,000 results."[*]

---

[*] http://meaningpatterns.net/unboxing

[241] James Bridle, 2018, *The New Dark Age: Technology and the End of the Future*, London: Verso, pp. 216–17.

[242] https://finance.yahoo.com/news/why-unboxing-videos-are-so-satisfying-99561095209.html

It takes 15.56 minutes to unbox the Thomas the Big Thomas & Friends Pocket Fantasy Station – we were the 9,175,478th viewer of Takahashi Taiyou's YouTube video. The reference is arcane, lost to most consumers, buried in the depths of industrial history. Thomas was modeled on the E2 class locomotives, built for the London, Brighton and South Coast Railway. Only ten of these were built between 1913 and 1916 and all of them were cut up for scrap between 1961 and 1963.[243]

There have been many reincarnations of Thomas. One was a locomotive, Jessie, who had lived her life as a shunter in a Welsh steel mill. When she was retired in 1965, she was placed in a children's playground in Cardiff. Taken from the park in 1980 and restored to working order, in 2011 she underwent a rebuild and gender reassignment so she could look like Thomas.[244]

And, another layer of reference, almost as arcane: Thomas' first literary appearance was in 1946, in the second of twenty-six "Railway Series" children's books written or co-written by an Anglican priest, Rev. W. Awdry.[245] Then a television series first screened in 1984 with ex-Beatle Ringo Starr's narrative voiceover. Then a myriad of products, even Thomas theme parks in the US, England, and Japan. And now about 762,000 "Thomas the Tank Engine unboxing" videos, according to our YouTube search on these words.

The creator of our Thomas unboxing video is Japanese, so it is in wordless gesture language, transcending the limitations of speech in the era of pervasively accessible digital media. The video replaces the immediate time- and space-bound presence of objects in physical shopping with their recorded representation, by this means also transcending time and space for the purposes of online shopping. The unboxing video is to shopping what writing once was to speech, and the transposition just as radically transformative.

The viewer hears no speech and sees no person except for the hands of the anonymous unboxer. The camera is exactly where the viewer would be if they were themselves the unboxer. The vicarious hands are virtually the viewer's. Third person is transposed into second, then first.[§MS2.2] "Hand of God[§MS2.2a] shots," these are called.

A relation of use values is thus established but in ways that are very different from physical stores. As much as retailers tried to activate bodily interaction with objects, the customer couldn't unbox like this in the store without damaging the package. Nor would they normally be allowed to take 15.56 minutes to do it. Viscerally, multimodally, this beats in-store shopping, or at least its affordances are fundamentally different. Again, here we encounter another of the transubstantiations[§1.1.2a] of

[243] Brian Sibley, 1995, *The Thomas the Tank Engine Man: The Story of the Reverend W. Awdry and His Really Useful Engines*, London: Heinemann, p. 123.

[244] www.walesonline.co.uk/lifestyle/nostalgia/search-jessie-graffiti-covered-old-14584850

[245] The Rev. W. Awdry, 1946 [2015], *Thomas the Tank Engine*, London: Egmont.

our time, where the image is experienced spiritually as object, and where by mysterious fiat, another's body – the unboxer's – might as well be our own.

Nor is the unboxer caught in the inauthentic wiles of salesperson or the manipulations of shop and mall designs. Beyond the rhetorical seller–purchaser pleadings of advertising, this is authentic user-to-user talk. The amateurishness of the videos is integral to their "truthiness"[§2.5.1] – though these are unmasked to some degree once we find that manufacturers give their products for free to unboxers who they can trust will say complimentary things, and the unboxers earn advertising revenues from Google. This information is not publicized, but unboxers report that they get between $2 and $4 per thousand views.[246] This is the new, no-wage, take-your-own-risk advertising industry. The advertisements are uncannily well-targeted by virtue of Google's detailed knowing of you from your search histories, YouTube viewing habits, and the texts of your emails in Gmail and Google Docs that its bots have read.

People have been leaving the malls and the big box stores because of their assimilating, homogenizing tendencies, unavoidable consequences of their affordance as sites of multimodal meaning. Compared to the endless use values to be found in the non-dimensional spaces of online stores,[§2.3.1a] physical stores have become bland, boring, generic. Their technologies of activation are becoming anachronistic. You never seem to be able to find just what you want. But you can online, with the help of strangers finely calibrated to be weirdly "like you." People like you will likely be more interested in the same peculiar variant of Thomas the Tank Engine products as you. You can hear their authentic voices in reviews, that is, as long as they are not fake reviews, paid for by sellers.

To achieve even a crude level of differentiation, surveillance cameras had been set up in physical stores in the service of the generic, homogenizing "science of shopping." In online shopping, these have been replaced by the ever-present "big data" recording of clickstreams, cookie triggers, and screen navigation heat maps – all designed to find new ways to draw the duly differentiated consumer into "the ecommerce funnel."[247]

Some things stay the same, principally the absolute singularity of the social relations of the commodity, where the differential interests of retailer and consumer are activated in the mystical transposition between the use value of an object and the social process of its exchange. This is a paradoxically universal differential, for market societies at least, though not of course for other configurations of human life. The meanings of First Peoples that we have attempted to parse elsewhere in

---

[246] www.cnn.com/2014/02/13/tech/web/youtube-unboxing-videos/index.html
[247] Matt Isherwood, 2017, *Designing Ecommerce Websites*, Kindle Edition: Transmitter Press, Location 72.

this book show that, in a human-wide frame of reference, this apparent universal is historically peculiar. In their time, there were no commodities or markets.

The infinite differentiability of these digital means of production of meaning tends to obscure a universal character that transcends the digital itself, and perhaps even to a greater degree than in the era when assimilation was the primary program. So, we have another kind of reification at work. Immersing ourselves in the endless array of use values, we forget the social generalities, albeit now with the aid of a new technology of forgetting.

After the debased urbanity and corrupted sociability of the shopping mall, against which even Victor Gruen eventually recoiled,[§2.3c] in online shopping we now have the isolating relation of one person to one screen. Though underpaid and bored, in the store we did at least meet the checkout person, and there was some inkling of the social relations of paid worker and paying consumer. There was also a utopian aesthetic to the mall, even if, for its disingenuousness, this at times wore thin. By comparison, Amazon's warehouses are factories of the most utilitarian kind, with dreadful working conditions, out of sight and so out of mind, except for the postings of the anti-Amazon activists.[248]

Meanwhile, the shift to managing reified interests from assimilation to differentiation within the logic of the market is to be witnessed in the shuttered stores and ruined malls. "All that is solid melts into air," said Marshall Berman in his evocative recall of Marx and Engels; "all that is sacred is profaned."[249]

For the last little while in this part of the book we've been shopping. But now we've reached the same place shopping that Robert Mercer did on his excursion into politics.[§2.2.2a] In our latest shade of modernity, some things have stayed the same, such as the commodity form, but this much has changed: in the activation of the commodity human interests are now being pushed towards infinite differentiation and asocial fracturing.

§2.3.2 Alienation

> **Alienation.** *Interaction of differential social interests that entails dissonance or conflict, explicitly or implicitly, understood or misunderstood.*

Things and states of affairs are more or less repeated (available designs become the redesigned), and so their meanings appear settled by habituation.

---

[248] www.pastemagazine.com/articles/2017/12/7-examples-how-amazon-treats-their-90000-warehouse.html

[249] Marshall Berman, 1988, *All That Is Solid Melts into Air: The Experience of Modernity*, New York: Penguin Books.

Some of the time, an activation may be innocent, smelling the roses, so to speak. It may be what it is. Activation is an almost-innocent function of reification, and the innocence may be warranted. We will come to this idea when we discuss solidary interests later in this part of the book.[§2.4.2]

However, activation can also realize conflicts of interest as between the participants in meaning. At the activation of a purchase, use values satisfy needs and desires, and prices represent a point of agreement about exchange value.

But at another level, the level of alienation, reification may not be so innocent. This is the case when there are systematic conflicts of interest. These may not be immediately visible. Then, participation in alienated meanings may be unknowing rather than knowing, unconscious rather than conscious, misconstrued rather than accurately construed, misunderstood rather than understood, unsettling rather than making one feel settled. We may participate in the activation but might miss the alienation.[*] Indeed, the enveloping experience of activation may distract from the alienation, casually in a moment of "inattentional blindness" to the proverbial elephant in the room,[250] or by design in the case of systematic deceptions.[§2.4b]

For these reasons, the meanings of activations in the form of states of affairs are not necessarily to be trusted. In the case of unknowing, unconscious, misconstrued, misunderstood, and unsettling meanings, the task of a transpositional grammar is to know, make conscious, construe, understand, and settle. And when we do, we may want to call for a new state of affairs, in our own interest and the interest of our fellows.

§2.3.2a Adam Smith's "Hidden Hand"

Frequently, the interplay of interests in meaning proves hard to parse because such meanings come in deceptively multiple layers. Things seem to mean something at one level, but mean something else at another. Nor do the interests at one level neatly and congruently transpose into interests at another. Human interests at one level may occlude interests at another, and do so by design.

Scottish philosopher and economist Adam Smith was one of the first great theorists of such disjunctions in interest.[†] At various times he was a professor of moral philosophy at the University of Glasgow, then a well-paid tutor to the Duke of Buccleuch, and finally Commissioner of Customs for Scotland.[251] Today he is best known as author of the seminal *Inquiry into the Nature and*

---

[*] http://meaningpatterns.net/inattention   [†] http://meaningpatterns.net/smith

[250] Arien Mack and Irven Rick, 1998, *Inattentional Blindness*, Cambridge: MIT Press.
[251] Nicholas Phillipson, 2010, *Adam Smith: An Enlightened Life*, New Haven, CT: Yale University Press.

Causes of the Wealth of Nations, published in 1776. With this book, he is considered founder of the discipline of economics.

Before *The Wealth of Nations*, Smith had achieved fame for his 1759 *Theory of Moral Sentiments*. Here he argued that although "our senses ... never can carry us beyond our own person ... By the imagination we place ourselves in [another's] situation, ... conceiving what we ourselves should feel in the like situation ... It is the impressions of our senses only, not those of his, which our imaginations copy." This process he calls "sympathy or correspondence of sentiments." Its trigger might be the "grief or joy" in the "look and gestures" of another. Or it may simply be a reading of the other's situation as if it could be one's own. It is this "imaginary change of situation upon which ... sympathy is founded."[252]

Moral sentiments, for Smith, are neither intrinsic to a human spirit, nor are they a spirit commandeered by God. They are grounded in the ordinary materiality of embodied feelings, and meanings made through sympathy.

Or to rephrase this in the terms of our grammar of transposition, the ideal is grounded in the experience of the material, but by transposition in the sentiment of sympathy, it necessarily exceeds the material.[§MS3.1] The second or third person becomes, in our imaginations, a virtual first person.[§MS2.2] And, in our counterpoint to a conventional theory of communication as meaning-transmission, there is a difference between the immediate, multimodal experiences of sympathizer and sympathized, a transposition of meaning that is connected by signs of sentiment and social meanings that can never be experienced in the same way.[§2.5b] These are several of the transpositions of differential interest that Smith would have called "sympathy."

In *The Wealth of Nations*, Smith adapts his moral philosophy to the market. "The word value ... has two different meanings, and sometimes expresses the utility of some particular object, sometimes the power of purchasing other goods which the possession of that object conveys. The one may be called 'value in use'; the other, 'value in exchange.'"[253]

As for sympathy, as for moral sentiments, use and exchange each prompts its own kinds of reflexive sociability in the meeting of differential interests. Use value: the butcher, baker, and brewer need each other's commodities, for the eating and the drinking. Exchange value: these are reduced to the "common stock" of calculable monetary equivalence. These are the means by which, in a "sympathy" of sorts, it is possible to share qualitatively different things for the purposes of living together sociably, each able to enjoy the fruits of the other's labor.

---

[252] Adam Smith, 1790 [1817], *The Theory of Moral Sentiments*, Boston, MA: Wells and Lilly, pp. 2, 14, 5, 4, 20.

[253] Adam Smith, 1776 [1937], *An Inquiry into the Nature and Causes of the Wealth of Nations*, New York: The Modern Library, p. 28.

But now, famously, his theory of market sentiments becomes less sympathetic:

It is not from the benevolence of the butcher, the brewer or the baker that we expect our dinner, but from regard to their own self-interest ... [M]an has almost constant occasion for the help of his brethren, and it is in vain for him to expect it from their benevolence only. He will be more likely to prevail if he can influence their self-love in his favour ... [G]enerally, indeed, [he] neither intends to promote the publick interest, nor knows how much he is promoting it ... [B]y directing that industry in such a manner as its produce may be of the greatest value, he intends only his own gain, and he is in this, as in many other cases, led by an invisible hand to promote an end that was no part of his intention ... By promoting his own interest he frequently promotes that of society more effectually than when he really intends to promote it.[254]

Here, in the interplay of differential interests, we have some aspects that are immediate and obvious, others that are not so obvious and for this reason, not generally noticed. While focusing on the exchange of their wares – the multimodal meanings of meat, bread, and beer as use values – butchers, bakers, and brewers tend not to notice the social system in which they participate. Or to the extent that they venture into the realm of exchange, it is the "deal"[255] around price rather than the value of labour. Bread and prices are explicitly communicated, but the social system they create, the patterns of human agency, the underlying structures of meaning, are not so obvious. We have been calling this process reification, a process of just noticing things in their immediate materiality and the superficiality of their sticker price, but not noticing larger patterns of social interest.

Interdependency based on differential interests becomes greater with the intensification of the division of labor integral to modern societies. Smith takes us into a pin factory to see this happening.

One man draws out the wire, another straights it, a third cuts it, a fourth points it, a fifth grinds it at the top for receiving the head; to make the head requires two or three distinct operations; to put it on is a peculiar business, to whiten the pins is another; it is even a trade by itself to put them onto the [packing] paper; and the important business of making a pin is, in this manner, divided into about eighteen distinct operations ... I have seen a small manufactory of this kind where ten men only were employed ... Those ten persons ... could make among them upwards of forty-eight thousand pins in a day.

Without such a division of labor, a single worker "could scarce, perhaps, with his utmost industry, make one pin in a day, and certainly could not make twenty."[256]

It was hard for Smith not to uncover here another vector of reification, one that might also, by way of sympathy, be judged to be a form of alienation.

---

[254] Ibid., pp. 14, 423.

[255] Donald J. Trump and Tony Schwartz, 1987, *Trump: The Art of the Deal*, New York: Random House.

[256] Adam Smith, 1776 [1937], *An Inquiry into the Nature and Causes of the Wealth of Nations*, New York: The Modern Library, pp. 4–5.

The man whose whole life is spent in performing a few simple operations . . . has no occasion to exert his understanding . . . He naturally loses, therefore, the habit of such exertion, and generally becomes . . . stupid and ignorant . . . [T]he mind is . . . suffered to fall into that drowsy stupidity which, in civilised society, seems to benumb the understanding of almost all the inferior ranks of people.[257]

Nor did Smith fail to notice that while the workers were being numbed into stupidity, the owners of the factories where getting richer and their tastes more refined. This brought imminent social dangers should the workers resist their benumbment or choose to rise above their induced stupidity:

Wherever there is great property there is great inequality. For one very rich man there must be at least five hundred poor, and the affluence of the few supposes the indigence of the many. The affluence of the rich excites the indignation of the poor, who are often both driven by want, and prompted by envy, to invade his possessions. [The rich person] is at all times surrounded by unknown enemies, whom . . . he can never appease, and from whose injustice he can be protected only by the powerful arm of the civil magistrate continually held up to chastise it . . . Civil government, so far as it is instituted for the security of property, is in reality instituted for the defense of the rich against the poor, or of those who have some property against those who have none at all.[258]

By this stage in the argument, Smith has accumulated this many layers of differential interest: genuine "sympathy," complimentary use values, superficial prices, underlying labor values, social relations of inequality, and a state that manages interests in favor of property owners. Smith starts off nicely with sympathy and use values, but after that, his parsing of differential interests starts to look less than nice. In his travels, he has passed the invisible hand of the market, but now he has arrived at the visible hand of the state.

§2.3.2b Margaret Fay Unfolds Karl Marx to Rediscover Adam Smith

Margaret Fay died before she could graduate her Ph.D., so the degree was awarded posthumously in 1980 by the University of California, Berkeley. In her thesis, she had left folding instructions for the pages of Karl Marx's 1844 *Economic and Philosophical Manuscripts*,* and with these, a reinterpretation of their meaning and significance.[259]

---

* http://meaningpatterns.net/fay

[257] Ibid., pp. 734–35.   [258] Ibid., pp. 670, 674.
[259] Margaret Fay, 1980, "The 1844 Economic and Philosophical Manuscripts of Karl Marx: A Critical Commentary and Interpretation," Ph.D., Department of Sociology, University of California, Berkeley; Margaret Fay, Johannes Hengstenberg, and Barbara Stuckey, 1983, "The Influence of Adam Smith on Marx's Theory of Alienation," *Science and Society* 47 (2):129–51.

Marx completed his philosophy doctorate in 1841, regarded by teachers and peers as one of the most brilliant of the "Young Hegelians." His project: to extend G.W.F. Hegel's philosophy of the dialectic, a philosophy of tension and movement in reality and ideas of that reality.[260] For his radical political views, Marx had been forced to leave Germany for Paris in the spring of 1844.[261] There he started to read the writings of economists, principally Adam Smith.[§2.3.2a] He also had his first extended meeting with Friedrich Engels,[§1.1.3c] who had recently written a book on the shocking conditions of life of the working class in industrial England.[262]

Marx's 1844 *Manuscripts* are yet another of those elusively fragmentary texts that have led bewitching afterlives. Seventy-six pages of handwritten notes, the *Manuscripts* were first published in German in 1932, and English in 1959. More than a century after they had been written, commentators seized upon them to see Marx afresh: Marx the humanist philosopher rather than Marx the political economist; Marx the philosophical follower of Hegel rather than Marx the social scientist who had unequivocally superseded him; Marx the would-be critic of actually-existing socialism rather than the Marx cast retrospectively as its apologist.[263]

In the published versions, four fragmentary manuscripts are presented, one after the other – a linear text. But like Walter Benjamin's convolutes,[§MS0b] the secret to their meaning lies much more in the form of their construction than the text laid out on a page. This is what Margaret Fay concluded after she went to see them for the first time. The Social Democratic Party of Germany had sold the manuscripts to the International Institute of Social History in Amsterdam in 1938. Banned by the Nazis when they came to power, the party was then in exile and needed the money.

Because of their fragile condition, Margaret Fay was able only to view photocopies when she visited the Institute, but today we can see full colour digital images of the pages, made in 2015.[264] Fay noticed that Marx had written across the page, turned to landscape orientation, which he had divided into three columns, and later,

[260] G.F.W. Hegel, 1807 [1977], *Phenomenology of Spirit*, Oxford: Oxford University Press.
[261] Marcello Musto, 2009, "Marx in Paris: Manuscripts and Notebooks of 1844," *Science and Society* 73(3):386–402.
[262] Friedrich Engels, 1845 [1973], *The Condition of the Working Class in England: From Personal Observation and Authentic Sources*, Moscow: Progress Publishers.
[263] Louis Althusser, Etienne Balibar, Roger Establet, Pierre Macherey, and Jacques Rancière, 1965 [2016], *Reading Capital: The Complete Edition*, translated by B. Brewster and D. Fernbach, London: Verso; György Márkus, 1966 [2014], *Marxism and Anthropology: The Concept of "Human Essence" in the Philosophy of Marx*, Sydney: Modem-Verlag; Herbert Marcuse, 1941 [1960], *Reason and Revolution: Hegel and the Rise of Social Theory*, Boston, MA: Beacon Press; Mihailo Marković, 1974b, *The Contemporary Marx: Essays on Humanist Communism*, Nottingham, UK: Spokesman Books; Lucio Colletti, 1969 [1973], *Marxism and Hegel*, London: Verso; Jean Hyppolite, 1955 [1969], *Studies on Marx and Hegel*, translated by J. O'Neill, New York: Basic Books.
[264] https://search.socialhistory.org/Record/ARCH00860

as the manuscript progressed, just two. He had hand-sewn the pages so the binding was at the top of the page (the long edge) rather than the side.

Fay came to the conclusion that the *Manuscripts* were no linear work of writing, as the published versions would lead the reader to think. They were a complex, multidimensional text. They needed to be read multimodally, as image as well as text, horizontally as well as vertically. The sections of text laid out in the columns were juxtaposed, and when seen this way, a series of horizontal connections and contrasts sprang into view. She provided folding instructions to show how the pages should be reconstructed and read, multidimensionally.[265] Gary Tedman later turned her instructions into a Flash animation, and created a hypertext version of the *Manuscripts* in English.[266]

Fay's reinterpretation of the meaning of the *Manuscripts* is as follows. Marx started the core text of the manuscripts in three columns, headed with Smith's elemental categories of economic life: "Wages of Labor," "Profit of Capital," and "Rent of Land." At first, he was just taking notes, but after a while he started to add thoughts of his own. Juxtaposing the three categories across the columns, he began to see tensions in Smith, contradictions even. After a number of pages, he changes to a two-column format, merging land and capital under the head "Profit of Capital," leaving the other head, "Wages of Labor."

Working his way through Smith, Marx created a more fundamental, overarching category for land and capital, "private property." So, concludes Fay, Marx's theory of private property and alienated labor arises from his systematic reading of Smith, not Hegel.[267]

As his notes in the *Manuscripts* come to an end, Marx begins to draw his own conclusions:

Finally, the distinction between the capitalist and landlord, between the agricultural worker and the industrial worker, disappears and the whole of society must split into the two classes of property owners and propertyless workers ... The worker can create nothing without nature, without the sensuous external world ..., [but with private ownership of capital and land,] the sensuous world becomes less and less an object beginning to his labour; ... the worker becomes a slave to his object ... [T]he more values he creates, the more worthless he becomes; the more his product is shaped, the more misshapen the worker; ... the more powerful the work, the more powerless the

---

[265] Margaret Fay, 1980, "The 1844 Economic and Philosophical Manuscripts of Karl Marx: A Critical Commentary and Interpretation," Ph.D., Department of Sociology, University of California, Berkeley, pp. 368–71.

[266] Gary Tedman, 2004, "Marx's 1844 Manuscripts as a Work of Art: A Hypertextual Reinterpretation," *Rethinking Marxism* 16(4):427–41; http://gary.tedman.pagesperso-orange .fr/navigate.htm

[267] Margaret Fay, 1980, "The 1844 Economic and Philosophical Manuscripts of Karl Marx: A Critical Commentary and Interpretation," Ph.D., Department of Sociology, University of California, Berkeley, pp. 7, 26; Margaret Fay, Johannes Hengstenberg, and Barbara Stuckey, 1983, "The Influence of Adam Smith on Marx's Theory of Alienation," *Science and Society* 47(2):129–51, p. 145.

worker; the more intelligent the work, the duller the worker and the more he becomes a slave to nature ... [I]t also produces him as a mentally and physically dehumanized being. [It] mortifies his flesh and ruins his mind ... [T]herefore it tears away from him his species-life, his true species-objectivity ... [It] estranges man from his own body, from nature as it exists outside of him, his human essence.[268]

It may well be that Smith's three categories have now been transformed into two, but Marx's conclusions about the baleful effects of modern work are not so different from Smith's.

Marx signed a contract with a German publisher in 1844 for a book to be entitled "A Critique of Politics and of Political Economy," which he never delivered. But he kept coming back to these notes in all of his later works. The fruits of these labors in 1844 did not reach the reading public until the publication of *Capital* in 1867.

Smith is the hero of pro-market economics. Margaret Fay shows that Marx amends Smith, though in some respects, barely at all. From Smith, Marx takes the distinction between use and exchange value, and the idea that all economic value is a product of human labour, not money or precious metals as the mercantilist economists before him had thought. Marx also concurred with Smith's view that growing inequality would need to be policed by the state; either that, or what Smith considered to be the context-induced stupidity of workers would be needed to keep them in their place.

To the extent that both Smith and Marx analyze market societies, and in such similar terms, their different conclusions are inconsequential – Smith that market societies are primordial and for better or for worse, unavoidably enduring; Marx that they are historical and changeable.

§2.4   Sociability

> **Sociability.** *The interaction of differential interests, solidary or antagonistic.*

In the meeting of differential interests, sociability is the measure of our participation. Sociability can be innocently complementary, or antagonistic, and when antagonistic, explicitly or implicitly so.

Rhetoric and reification are each, in their own ways, sociable.

Rhetoric is explicit appeal to interest.[§2.1] The forms of its sociability can involve alignment of complementary interests, or an attempt to enforce realignment of interests that are antagonistic. Or a bit of both, in disingenuous appeal to alignment ("surely, we agree?"). Or the disingenuousness might just be a

---

[268] Karl Marx, 1844 [1975], "Economic and Philosophical Manuscripts," pp. 279–400 in *Marx: Early Writing*, edited by Q. Hoare, Harmondsworth, UK: Penguin, pp. 322, 325, 336, 329.

distractor for what proves in fact to be a rhetorical demand to realign (in the final analysis meaning, "and if you don't seem to agree of your own accord, you must!"). These are slippery transpositions, always on the move.

Reification[§2.3] may be a matter of activation of meanings in things and states of affairs, habitually, unreflectively, customarily perhaps. And innocently perhaps, to smell the proverbial roses. Or it can involve alienation, in the case of a conflict of interests where one set of interests is, by design, at the expense of the other. Or a bit of both, in disingenuous activation, only seemingly innocent because it distracts from another perhaps less obvious level where there is a conflict of more fundamental interests.

Expression of Interest Measure of Sociability	Rhetoric	Reification
Solidary Interests	Alignment	Activation
Antagonistic Interests	Realignment	Alienation

Fig. 2.4(i): Measures of sociability in the expression of interest

The disjunctions of interest are always there. However, some disjunctions are complementary, others antagonistic. Some are explicit (rhetorics, denotations), others implicit in things and states of affairs (reifications, connotations). What seems or is made to seem solidary (rhetorical alignments and activations in states of affairs) can be antagonistic in fact (rhetorical realignments and reifications that alienate).

Such functional transpositions of meaning are always ready to happen, juxtaposed as they are in the metaphorical supermarket[§MS0d] of meaning functions. They are imminent because they are immanent. Their immanence makes them imminent.

It follows also that any momentary occlusions are always ready to be revealed for what they are. Meanings that are hidden, surreptitiously or not-so surreptitiously favoring some interests at the expense of others, can always be exposed. In a transpositional grammar, so can the manner of their hiding.

Here now is a rough map of some indicators of solidary and antagonistic interests across the various forms of meaning:

Form Function	Text	Image	Space	Object	Body	Sound	Speech
Solidary Interests	Information	Aesthetic, attractive	Comfortable	It works nicely	Sensuousness	Moodsong	Agreeable talk
Antagonistic Interests	Injunctions, laws, warning signs	Jarring, ugly	Uncomfortable	It doesn't work nicely	Aggression	Warning sounds	Disputatious talk, verbal abuse

Fig. 2.4(ii): Solidary and antagonistic interests

In the preceding sections of this book we have looked at shopping and commodities. The ones that now follow are on money and markets. However, we could have taken for our examples any number of other equally expansive and fraught meanings – "race," "gender," "environment," or such like. Each of these examples may have yielded meanings just as complex, just as significant in our lives, and at times just as misleading. The commodity is just one site of sociability around states of affairs and their meanings, albeit a centrally important one in modernity given its elemental meaning in the market, and its relations to the meanings of waged work, shopping, and a panoply of other "economic" as well as social things. Insofar as it is just one of a number of possible examples, the commodity merely serves us as an illustration, allowing us to demonstrate a method with which to parse the multimodal relations of differential interests.

§2.4a   Milton Friedman's "Island of Stone Money"

Milton Friedman was born in Brooklyn, New York, into a Jewish immigrant family of modest means. He rose to become a leading light of the Chicago School of Economics, won the Nobel Prize for Economics in 1976 for his work on the theory of money, and eventually became an influential adviser to Republican President Ronald Reagan and Conservative Prime Minister Margaret Thatcher.[269] He is credited as having been one of the masterminds in the construction of the post-communist global economic order, an order that has frequently been termed "neoliberal."[270]

After he retired, Friedman wrote a paper, "The Island of Stone Money."[271] He had found an obscure book of the same name written by William Henry Furness, published in 1910.* This book had become somewhat visible to economists because it was followed by an extract in the *Economic Journal* in 1915.

Furness wrote about the people of Yap, several thousand inhabitants living on a small island in the Pacific Ocean, about halfway between Papua New Guinea and China. An ocean and an economic paradigm away, Cambridge University economist John Maynard Keynes had already discovered Furness' writing because he discussed the same stone money in his *Treatise on Money*[272] – though

---

* http://meaningpatterns.net/friedman

[269] Milton Friedman and Rose D. Friedman, 1998, *Two Lucky People: Memoirs*, Chicago, IL: University of Chicago Press; Lanny Ebenstein, 2007, *Milton Friedman: A Biography*, New York: Palgrave Macmillan.

[270] David Harvey, 2005, *A Brief History of Neoliberalism*, Oxford: Oxford University Press.

[271] Milton Friedman, 1992, "The Island of Stone Money," Vol. E-91-3, *Working Papers in Economics*, Stanford, CA: The Hoover Institution.

[272] John Maynard Keynes, 1930 [1950], *A Treatise on Money*, Volume 2, London: Macmillan, p. 292.

Friedman never mentioned that. Like Keynes before him, Friedman thought the story of the Yap was nicely allegorical.

The people of Yap did not produce solely for their own needs, as First Peoples did. They also produced to exchange, Furness explained, buying and selling fish, pigs, and labor to build each other's houses. Also unlike First Peoples, the Yap had systematic differences in wealth and social status, even a slave class.

The Yap system of exchange had produced differences in accumulated wealth represented by stone coins, called *fei*. These were made from limestone quarried on the island of Babelthuap, some 400 miles away. They were of different sizes, between one and twelve feet in diameter, and when they were this big, a hole was cut in the middle so they could be carried on a pole, slung shoulder to shoulder between two people. The value of a *fei* was measured in spans from the index finger to the thumb – the larger, the more valuable. If too large, they were stored outside the house.[273]

Concludes Furness, "the simple-hearted natives of Uap [Yap], who never heard of Adam Smith, have solved the ultimate problem of Political Economy, and found that labour is the true medium of exchange and the true standard of value."[274] The Yap had discovered money as a way to represent exchange value.

When a *fei* was too large and difficult to move, the person who had exchanged his product did not necessarily need to take physical possession (and it was only men who engaged in exchange). After a sale, "its new owner is quite content to accept the bare acknowledgment of ownership and without so much as a mark to indicate the exchange, the coin remains undisturbed on the former owner's premises." In this way, Furness goes on, "[t]he purchasing power of that stone remains, therefore, as valid as if it were leaning visibly against the side of the owner's house, and represents wealth as potentially as the hoarded inactive gold of a miser of the middle ages, or as our silver dollars stacked in the treasury at Washington, which we never see nor touch, but trade with on the strength of a printed certificate that they are there."[275]

Having told his version of the Yap story, Friedman asks, "how many of us have literal personal direct assurance of the existence of most of the items we regard as constituting our wealth? Entries in a bank account, property certified

---

[273] William Henry Furness, III, 1910, *The Island of Stone Money: Uap of the Carolines*, Philadelphia, PA: J.B. Lippincott, pp. 57, 93–95; Cora Lee C. Gillilland, 1974, "The Stone Money of Yap: A Numismatic Survey," Vol. 23, *Smithsonian Studies in History and Technology*, Washington, DC: Smithsonian Institution Press.

[274] William Henry Furness, III, 1910, *The Island of Stone Money: Uap of the Carolines*, Philadelphia, PA: J.B. Lippincott, pp. 92–93.

[275] Ibid., pp. 96, 98.

by pieces of paper called shares of stocks, and so on and on, illustrate how important 'myth,' unquestioned belief, is in monetary matters."[276]

The meaning of the thing we call "money" was not just in the *fei* stones on Yap. Nor is it in our modern experience of markets (just) in the pieces of paper that are banknotes, or the plastic of credit cards, or an invoice or receipt, or the information we can today pull up on screens about our account transactions or balances – some of the multimodal media and transpositional practices by which we mean "money" today.

These texts, and objects, and images transpose for each other because they are not meanings by themselves. Rather they subsist in a social system of value transactions where these objects and actions only make sense as meaning transpositions, never just meanings-of because there are also meanings-in.[§MS2.2c] The meaning of each transposition is within a system of credit and clearance, the decentralized negotiability of value.[277] Such meaning is generated in the meeting of differential interests, and these interests are both solidary and antagonistic – obviously, deceptively, contradictorily, fluidly, unstably so.

Friedman could agree with Keynes on only a few things. One was the role of money in establishing certain kinds of elementary bonds of sociability in the process of exchange. The Yap were a salutary example for both of them. But beyond this, there was very little agreement.

Keynes' larger conclusions about the politics of money, and the tension between solidary and antagonistic interests, was offered as a solution to the Great Depression in his magnum opus, *The General Theory of Employment, Interest and Money.* Here he argued that markets could not be trusted to support human interests and that sociability needed to be underwritten by governments. Intrinsically antagonistic interests in markets needed to be resolved by the state in the humane interests of civil society.

Indeed, with its monopoly over the creation and regulation of money, this was an essential social responsibility of governments – hence the necessity of deficit spending in times of economic contraction, and financing the welfare state to guarantee humane levels of access to material goods, as well as in purely economic terms to buttress aggregate demand during downswings in the business cycle.[278]

Friedman disagreed vehemently, and eventually Ronald Reagan, Margaret Thatcher, and their successors came to follow Friedman's line of thinking

---

[276] Milton Friedman, 1992, "The Island of Stone Money," Vol. E-91-3, *Working Papers in Economics,* Stanford, CA: The Hoover Institution, pp. 4–5.

[277] Dror Goldberg, 2005, "Famous Myths of 'Fiat Money'," *Journal of Money, Credit and Banking* 37(5):957–67, pp. 14, 61; Felix Martin, 2014, *Money: The Unauthorized Biography,* New York: Alfred A. Knopf.

[278] John Maynard Keynes, 1936, *The General Theory of Employment, Interest and Money,* London: Macmillan.

rather than Keynes'. At root was a fundamental disagreement about the underlying configuration of human interests, expressed through money and markets in all their multimodal transpositions.

Returning to the rosier side of Adam Smith, Friedman said that capitalism guaranteed freedom as a consequence of its "proposition that both parties to an economic transaction benefit from it, provided the transaction is bilaterally voluntary and informed. Exchange can therefore bring about co-ordination without coercion ... Since the household always has the alternative of producing for itself, it need not enter any exchange unless both parties benefit from it."[279]

Because the sociability of markets is inherently solidary, argued Friedman – though here we are using our terminology – governments should be as small as possible, and they had no business spending in deficit or supporting a welfare state.[280] "No such thing as a free lunch," he titled one of his best-selling books,[281] a paean to markets and their arguable freedoms. Besides, he claimed controversially, government didn't solve the Great Depression; it had created it.[282]

Sociable markets certainly are, but the matter for dispute between Keynes and Friedman was whether that sociability is to interpreted to be intrinsically solidary (Friedman) or antagonistic (Keynes).

A more nuanced version of the analysis is that they are solidary to a degree, but also at the same time antagonistic, albeit sometimes deceptively so. The antagonistic part is in the inequalities that effectively make some bilateral transactions to some extent involuntary, for instance when, as between buyer and seller, boss and worker, there are power differentials. It is also hard to imagine how a modern household could produce for itself, a "freedom" Friedman proposes. Without inherited wealth it is difficult to see how it is possible to avoid the labor market.

So, it matters which parsing of the meaning of sociability you choose in the configuration of differential interests in the market. When we explore the interests expressed in multimodal transpositions mediated by money we find meanings which seem solidary in one moment but that are in conflict in another.

§2.4b   George Akerlof and Robert Schiller's Phishing for Phools

"Phishing" is the attempt to defraud people through deceptive emails or text messages – fishing, baiting, and catching an unsuspecting user with an email,

---

[279] Milton Friedman, 1962, *Capitalism and Freedom*, Chicago, IL: University of Chicago Press, p. 13.

[280] Milton Friedman and Walter W. Heller, 1969, *Monetary Vs. Fiscal Policy*, New York: W.W. Norton.

[281] Milton Friedman, 1975, *There's No Such Thing as a Free Lunch*, LaSalle, IL: Open Court.

[282] Milton Friedman, 1962, *Capitalism and Freedom*, Chicago, IL: University of Chicago Press, p. 45.

for instance, that appears to be from a trusted seller or business, but that directs the user to hand over money or account information to a thief.* Etymologically, the word tracks back to "phreaking," a term from the 1970s used to describe the theft of free international calls from phone companies by emulating the tone system then used for dial-up. The "ph" is for phone, and "phreak," short for "free call."[283] "Phish" enters the lexicon in the 1990s.[284]

The Anti-Phishing Working Group is another entity in the distributed and democratically unaccountable structures of global governance which, in the era of digital meaning, have replaced the state. In the absence of global governance of a democratic variety, this is a quasi-private, self-appointed global police force for the internet.[285] The Working Group received reports of 268,126 phishes in 2006, and 1,380,432 in 2016.[286]

In their book, *Phishing for Phools,* George Akerlof and Robert Schiller use the idea of phishing as a metaphor for the imperfection of markets – not just the deliberate deceptions of thieves, but also the intrinsic deceptions of their normal working.[287]

Akerlof won the Nobel Prize for Economics in 2001 for his work on the asymmetric information that participants have in markets. It is impossible, for instance, to know whether a second-hand car is a "lemon," because although sellers are going to know, they are not going to disclose this to buyers. The expectation that cars might be lemons affects sellers of good used cars, because uncertainty and lack of trust is built into the relationship. This is one of the reasons why even the best of second-hand cars is so much cheaper than a new car of the same model.[288]

In terms of our transpositional grammar, we have cars, drivers, and speech, perhaps also a written description in an advertisement. Underlying all these meanings is a sociable interest in the sale, a differential interest between buyer and seller that is solidary in one meaning function but antagonistic in another. This is intrinsic to exchange and the market, their function as sociable meanings.

Co-author Robert Schiller also won the Nobel Prize, in 2013, for his analyses of antagonistic interests leading to market failure, in his case the "irrational exuberance" that inflates asset prices.[289]

Akerlof and Schiller show in their book how "the free market system tends to spawn manipulation and deception." They go on to document a multitude of

---

* http://meaningpatterns.net/phishing

[283] https://en.wikipedia.org/wiki/Phreaking
[284] https://en.oxforddictionaries.com/definition/phishing
[285] https://antiphishing.org/about-APWG/APWG/   [286] https://en.wikipedia.org/wiki/Phishing
[287] George A. Akerlof and Robert J. Schiller, 2015, *Phishing for Phools: The Economics of Manipulation and Deception*, Princeton, NJ: Princeton University Press.
[288] George A. Akerlof, 1970, "The Market for 'Lemons': Quality Uncertainty and the Market Mechanism," *The Quarterly Journal of Economics* 84(3):488–500.
[289] Robert J. Schiller, 2000b, *Irrational Exuberance*, Princeton, NJ: Princeton University Press.

antagonistic interests in the market. Advertising, for instance, contains systematic rhetorical exaggerations and omissions. In every sale, buyer and seller know that as well as producing a situation of "good-for-me/good-for-you," markets also "produce good-for-me/bad-for-you's. They do both, so long as a profit can be made."[290]

Nor is it just the little person who has to deal with trickery intrinsic to the market relation, mediated by money and price. The high flyers in the system play the same game of deception, hence the savings and loans crisis of 1986–95, the junk bond crisis of the early 2000s, and the worthless mortgage-based securities and derivatives that without government bailouts in 2008–9 would have brought down the global system of money.[291]

With the Friedmanites in mind, Akerlof and Schiller conclude, "economists ... systematically ignore or downplay the role of trickery and deception in the working of markets ... [C]ompetitive markets by their very nature spawn deception and trickery."[292] This, in the words of another great theorist of the late capitalist market and aspirant to the Nobel Prize, is "the art of the deal."[293]

The solution, say these two good neo-Keynesians, is regulation of markets by democratic governments. This is not to abolish the intrinsic antagonism that drives interests in markets – they wouldn't have got their Nobel Prizes if they had gone that far. Regulatory measures are necessary if the antagonisms intrinsic to the market are not to follow their inevitable tendency to self-destruction. So, the market lives to see another day. According to the normal logic of the market, the banks should have been bankrupted in the 2008 collapse of the financial system, but they were saved by government, an unsurprising irony.

§2.4.1   Antagonistic Interests

> **Antagonistic Interests.** *The meeting of differential interests, frequently enacted by compulsion, explicitly or by means of deception.*

Anthropologist David Graeber says that "all social systems, even economic systems like capitalism, have always been built on top of a bedrock of actually-existing communism."[294] For a transpositional grammar, we rephrase this: all

---

[290] George A. Akerlof and Robert J. Schiller, 2015, *Phishing for Phools: The Economics of Manipulation and Deception*, Princeton, NJ: Princeton University Press, pp. vii, 150.

[291] Ibid., pp. 117ff, 124ff, 23ff.; George A. Akerlof and Paul M. Romer, 1993, "Looting: The Economic Underworld of Bankruptcy for Profit," *Brookings Papers on Economic Activity* (2):1–73. doi: 10.2307/2534564.

[292] George A. Akerlof and Robert J. Schiller, 2015, *Phishing for Phools: The Economics of Manipulation and Deception*, Princeton, NJ: Princeton University Press, pp. 6, 165.

[293] Donald J. Trump and Tony Schwartz, 1987, *Trump: The Art of the Deal*, New York: Random House.

[294] David Graeber, 2011, *Debt: The First 5,000 Years*, Brooklyn, NY: Melville House, p. 95.

meaningful human affairs are by their nature sociable, however in some moments solidary, other moments antagonistic. At still other times solidary and antagonistic interests subsist in uneasy tension within a single event. Money and markets, for instance, both entail social trust, but also in their nature engender mistrust.

Here is a rough taxonomy of antagonistic and solidary interests, a range of qualities of sociability, from purely solidary to purely antagonistic.

At one end of the continuum, we have interests that are simply solidary, what Graeber calls "baseline communism."[295] The factory may be a rotten place to work, but "pass me the spanner" is an enactment of differential interests that is unproblematically solidary. Your having a spanner, and my need for one, are expressed in words, objects, space, and body. The effect is the enactment of solidary interests.

The market establishes patterns for the negotiation of differential interests that are in some respects solidary and at the same time and in other respects antagonistic. "Can I help you?" says the shop assistant, ready to lead you to a product whose whereabouts and qualities they know. But in the moment when the help leads to a sale, the personal element in human relations is removed, and the earlier human relation of help, perhaps in connection with your potential use of the product, is reduced to the reified abstraction that is money.[296] Cold-blooded calculation kicks in, and the differential interests have become intrinsically antagonistic. The initial friendliness, in retrospect, has been simulated, an uneasy transposition between the solidary and the antagonistic.

Moving towards the antagonistic end of the spectrum, we have actions that go beyond the bounds of systematically acceptable antagonism. Theft, phishing, and false advertising fall within the logic of markets; they make sense in terms of the logic of money. But they go beyond the bounds of civility and ethics, taking things too far, to a point where they may become system-threatening. Often, however, this is a fine line, and some of the most "successful" parts of the market operate in a conveniently gray ethical zone.

Finally, interests often meet in relationships of pure compulsion, unmitigated antagonism. The boss's orders are an example of this. Raymond Chandler's *The Visible Hand*, a classic of management theory, is one of the most devastating critiques of the one-sided version of Smith urged by Milton Friedman and his followers.[297] Modern organizations are hierarchical institutional forms, so they need to be "managed." Inside organizations, neither is there freedom in the sense of liberal-democratic freedom (voting for the bosses?), nor is there freedom in the

---

[295] Ibid., p. 99.
[296] Georg Simmel, 1907 [1978], *The Philosophy of Money*, translated by T. Bottomore and D. Frisby, London: Routledge and Kegan Paul, pp. 128–29, 297, 400, 443.
[297] Alfred D. Chandler Jr, 1977, *The Visible Hand: The Managerial Revolution in American Business*, Cambridge, MA: Harvard University Press.

sense of Friedman's freedom of the market. The historical origins of this form of organization are the slave household and the feudal estate.

Organizations may attempt to hide the antagonism with the fictions of "teams" and voluntaristic "workplace cultures."[298] But the reality, Graeber argues, is that within the confines of the organization and the working day, interests are configured in ways that are not in essence different from slavery.[299] Intransigence leads to dismissal, and the only way to escape the compulsion is to resign. Then you have to join another hierarchical organization to survive, and this is not really freedom at all.[§2.3a]

Some societies – First Peoples, for instance – didn't have money or markets, nor hierarchical work organization. These are recent inventions, no more than a few thousand years old across the span of species existence of perhaps a hundred thousand years. They are new to a majority of the world's people only in the nineteenth and twentieth centuries.

Furtive attempts were made in these centuries to abolish markets and organizational hierarchies, leading to the creation of another kind of "actually existing communism." The agenda: to create societies of freely "associated producers," where purely solidary interests were established – "from each according to his abilities; to each according to his needs."[300] But over the course of the twentieth century these communisms themselves succumbed to hierarchy of vicious proportions.

In its early years, the Soviet Union set about abolishing money entirely, though unsuccessfully.[301] By the end of the third quarter of the twentieth century and for a third of the world's population, the countries whose states and economies were managed on the Soviet model managed to all-but eliminate the market. They replaced productive organizations based on private property with state-owned bureaucracies. This shows that dramatic change is possible in the fundamental relations of human interest, although not necessarily for the better.

In the first commercial societies, market relations were limited, mostly restricted to trade in luxury commodities for the rich, while the majority mostly subsisted. On a world scale, this remained the case until the twentieth century, when by century's end and after the Cold War, few of the human species remained unaffected by the social meanings of money and markets.

---

[298] Bill Cope and Mary Kalantzis, 1997b, *Productive Diversity*, Sydney: Pluto Press.

[299] David Graeber, 2007, *Possibilities: Essays on Hierarchy, Rebellion, and Desire*, Oakland, CA: AK Press, pp. 86ff.

[300] Karl Marx, 1875 [2010], "Critique of the Gotha Program," pp. 75–99 in *Marx and Engels: Collected Works*, Volume 24, London: Lawrence and Wishart, p. 87.

[301] Arthur Z. Arnold, 1937, *Banks, Credit, and Money in Soviet Russia*, New York: Columbia University Press, pp. 72ff.

However, even in high capitalism, where much of life has now been commodified, we still have home cooking, domestic child and elder care, private parties, sometimes even old-fashioned selflessness. This tells us that solidary interests of an ordinary kind, uncompromised by antagonism, might still be possible on a wider scale.

§2.4.1a Francesco Datini's Bills of Exchange

When Francesco di Marco Datini died in the Tuscan city Prato in 1410, he left his great fortune, 70,000 gold florins, to the poor of the city.[*] Datini had made his money as a merchant whose trade extended from England in the West to the Caspian Sea in the east.[302] He also left his house to the city, *Palazzo Datini*, today an archive and museum.

Workers restoring Datini's house in 1870 discovered a hidden storeroom under the stairs containing more than 150,000 letters, 500 account books and ledgers, 300 deeds of partnership, 400 insurance policies, as well as countless other documents including bills of exchange and checks.[303] These have proved a rich trove for historians analyzing the origins of merchant capitalism in late medieval Europe.

Datini represents a turning point in the long history of the market. He was a great textual innovator, applying new forms of meaning to realize fundamentally new relations of sociable interest, new meanings of exchange and in the market. Datini may not always have been the first to use each of these textual forms, but he was certainly the first to use them in such a systematic way to create a widely dispersed commercial empire.

Historians characterize this time of transition as the moment of emergence of the "sedentary merchant."[304] Before Datini's time, medieval merchants had traveled to the fair, selling their wares in person, in an immediately present configuration of object, body, and speech. Datini, however, created an expansive trading system transposing the textual and object forms at a distance. Meaning across space and time, this was a new play of the virtual and the real,

---

[*] http://meaningpatterns.net/datini

[302] Giampiero Nigro, 2010a, "Francesco and the Datini Company of Florence in the Trading System," pp. 229–48 in *Francesco Di Marco Datini: The Man and the Merchant*, edited by G. Nigro, Florence: Firenze University Press, p. 241.

[303] Iris Origo, 1957, *The Merchant of Prato: Francesco Di Marco Datini*, New York: Alfred A. Knopf, p. xii.

[304] N.S.B. Gras, 1939, *Business and Capitalism: An Introduction to Business History*, New York: F.S. Crofts and Company, pp. 67–92; Robert S. Lopez, 1976, *The Commercial Revolution of the Middle Ages, 950–1350*, Cambridge: Cambridge University Press, pp. 106–11; Sophus A. Reinert and Robert Fredona, 2017, "Merchants and the Origins of Capitalism," Working Paper 18–021, Cambridge, MA: Harvard Business School.

using text as a transpositional mediator for the extension of the virtual and the real into each other. In so doing, he also extended the transpositional function of alienation, creating another step where the abstractions of exchange were further detached from the immediate, useable physicality of objects and the embodied personages of their owners.

The objects with which Datini dealt were wool, silk, dye, spices, dinnerware. He also traded in bodies in the form of slaves, as well as essentially ideational items such as maps and religious pictures.[305] These various products were created and then traded just for the rich, the privileged few who could at that time participate in the market. These were people who, in feudal society, could extract rents from agricultural serfs whose lands they owned, and so had money to spend. Meanwhile, the mass of society lived largely outside of the market, subject to the hierarchical compulsions of feudalism, the direct rule of the lord over his "domain."[306]

In order to maintain a virtual exchange relation over space-time, a new textual artifact was used, the bill of exchange. Here is one, from the Datini Archive:

In the name of God, 5th February 1410.

Pay by this first letter . . . to Guircardo Catani, four hundred and eighty three lire, twelve soldi, five denari . . . equivalent to 617 francs . . . Make good a payment and pay into the account of Barolino de Nicolao Bartolini of Paris . . .
Antonio di Neve di Montpelier, greetings.

This particular bill is of enormous historical significance because it is the first to include an endorsement on the back: "I, Gherado Cattani, agreed that the aforementioned money is to be paid to Iacopo Aceptanti."[307] The exchange value, in other words, was passed on to a third party in another trade. In this way, the distance of the exchange abstraction had been further attenuated.

It was another small step to issue checks and to become a bank, which Datini also established beside his trading enterprise. The Medicis of Florence went on to do this on a much larger scale over the course of the fifteenth century.[308] In

[305] Michele Cassandro, 2010, "Aspects of the Life and Character of Francesco Di Marco Datini," pp. 3–52 in *Francesco Di Marco Datini: The Man and the Merchant*, edited by G. Nigro, Florence: Firenze University Press, pp. 12, 15; Iris Origo, 1957, *The Merchant of Prato: Francesco Di Marco Datini*, New York: Alfred A. Knopf, pp. 53–57, 87–91.

[306] Marc Bloch, 1939 [1962], *Feudal Society*, London: Routledge and Kegan Paul; Perry Anderson, 1974a, *Passages from Antiquity to Feudalism*, London: New Left Books; Perry Anderson, 1974b, *Lineages of the Absolutist State*, London: New Left Books.

[307] Giampiero Nigro, 2010b, "The Banking Company," pp. 515–28 in *Francesco Di Marco Datini: The Man and the Merchant*, edited by G. Nigro, Florence: Firenze University Press, p. 520.

[308] Raymone de Roover, 1963, *The Rise and Decline of the Medici Bank: 1397–1494*, Cambridge, MA: Harvard University Press.

the monetization of trade debts in the later part of the fourteenth century, concludes Gardiner, lie the origins of the modern market economy.[309]

In order to map people and objects across time and space into new configurations of interest, the "sedentary merchant" required new textual architectures. The bill of exchange was just one. Another was the partnership agreement, establishing parameters of trust for the managers of the holding companies that Datini established, and the branch offices in Genoa, Catalonia, Majorca, and Valencia.[310] Still another was the ledger, a record of accounts taking its most rigorous analytical form in double-entry bookkeeping.[311]

These elaborate textual forms were designed to maintain a balance of solidary and antagonistic interests. In one moment of their meaning, they expressed solidary interests of a kind that are a minimal basis for sociality, a level of trust between partners and traders in the complementary mesh of their differential interests.

But the system of differential interest worked in apprehensive expectation of mistrust and antagonism, and anticipating assault from every direction. We learn a lot about the emotional economy of the trader from Datini's prodigious letter writing. He was a man who was always "scolding his employees."[312] He was perpetually "intolerant, discontented, dissatisfied." His letters were full of orders, disappointments, "accusations of incompetence" and "angry tirades."[313] He was ever worried about risk: theft, piracy, highway robbery, fraud. He was plagued by "constant anxieties and guilt."[314] Such tensions are intrinsic to the conflicted sociability that is the exchange relationship. Datini was discovering them for the first time, becoming in the process a new kind of person, the commercial man.

Datini's guilt came with good reason, because he was always treading a fine line when it came to the sin of usury, charging "interest" on credit, making money out of money itself. "Interest" is a symptomatic word. The way in which

---

[309] Geoffrey W. Gardiner, 2004, "The Primacy of Trade Debts in the Development of Money," pp. 128–72 in *Credit and State Theories of Money: The Contributions of A. Mitchell Innes*, edited by L.R. Wray, Cheltenham: Edward Elgar, pp. 140–41.

[310] Giampiero Nigro, 2010a, "Francesco and the Datini Company of Florence in the Trading System," pp. 229–48 in *Francesco Di Marco Datini: The Man and the Merchant*, edited by G. Nigro, Florence: Firenze University Press, pp. 231, 238–39.

[311] N.S.B. Gras, 1939, *Business and Capitalism: An Introduction to Business History*, New York: F.S. Crofts and Company, pp. 114–19; Giampiero Nigro, 2010b, "The Banking Company," pp. 515–28 in *Francesco Di Marco Datini: The Man and the Merchant*, edited by G. Nigro, Florence: Firenze University Press. p. 523.

[312] Giampiero Nigro, 2010a, "Francesco and the Datini Company of Florence in the Trading System," pp. 229–48 in *Francesco Di Marco Datini: The Man and the Merchant*, edited by G. Nigro, Florence: Firenze University Press, p. 426.

[313] Michele Cassandro, 2010, "Aspects of the Life and Character of Francesco Di Marco Datini," pp. 3–52 in ibid., pp. 12–13.

[314] Iris Origo, 1957, *The Merchant of Prato: Francesco Di Marco Datini*, New York: Alfred A. Knopf, p. xvii.

bills of exchange avoided such a sin was through a fiction for the faithful –
differential exchange rates, profit hidden in the pretense of equivalence.

"In the name of God and profit," the accounts writer was required to head each
new page in the ledger, as if to reassure the parties of their compatibility.[315] The
final extirpation of Datini's possible sins, should they prove on judgment day to
have been ill-gotten, was to bequest his gains to the poor of Prato.

§2.4.1b Satoshi Nakamoto's Blockchain

On March 6, 2014, investigative journalist Leah Goodman announced in
Newsweek that she had managed to track down a man the world had been
looking for, Satoshi Nakamoto. He was living in an ordinary-looking house in
Temple City, California.[316]

On October 31, 2008, a person or persons writing under the name of Satoshi
Nakamoto published a paper online, "Bitcoin: A Peer-to-Peer Electronic Cash
System."* In this paper, Nakamoto described in general terms how a "purely
peer-to-peer version of electronic cash would allow online payments to be sent
directly from one party to another without going through a financial institution." Such a system would be "based on cryptographic proof instead of trust,
allowing any two willing parties to transact directly with each other without the
need for a trusted third party."[317]

In January 2009, Nakamoto posted the first version of the Bitcoin code to
SourceForge, the open source software repository. He also created a website,
bitcoin.org, and participated in code development and online discussions until
late 2010,[318] when he handed control of the source code and the website to the
Bitcoin community. Then he disappeared.

The technology underlying Bitcoin is called "blockchain." This is a digital
version of Datini's bills of exchange,[§2.4.1a] no less and not much more. The "no
less" part is that it is a system where each block in the chain (Datini bill), is
endorsed in every transaction (the transfer of ownership written on the back of
the bill), and the record of the endorsement is kept in a ledger. The "not much
more" is the duplication of the ledger across many computers, and the cryptographic techniques that are used to verify across all these computers that the
record has been faithfully kept. The process of verification is called "mining."[319]

---

* http://meaningpatterns.net/blockchain

[315] Ibid., p. 52.
[316] Leah McGrath Goodman, 2014, "The Face Behind Bitcoin," *Newsweek*, 6 March.
[317] https://nakamotoinstitute.org/bitcoin/#selection-7.4–9.38
[318] https://satoshi.nakamotoinstitute.org/emails/
[319] https://en.bitcoin.it/wiki/Main_Page; John Lanchester, 2016, "When Bitcoin Grows Up,"
London Review of Books 38(8):3–12; Roland Berger, 2017, "Enabling Decentralized, Digital

The people of Yap simply remembered who was the owner of a stone *fei*, trusting each other's memories.[§2.4a] Datini committed to writing the trust that was between trading partners whose acts of exchange were distanced by space and time, so establishing newly attenuated multimodal relations between text, objects, and persons. Late in his life, he institutionalized these textual forms in his nascent banking activities. Soon after, with these same instruments of meaning, the Medicis launched the modern world of finance capitalism.

Consider blockchain just to be writing, huge amounts of text, inerasable, never-to-be-spoken, written over and over again, not practically readable, only to be "read" by other computers for the purposes of multiple verification. Trust in the truthfulness of the chain is established by its exhaustive redundancy (recording over and over again every transaction ever), its multiple distributed recordings, and the fact that the historical record is always read and checked by any miner who chooses to join the chain.

There are some peculiarities in the Satoshi code. There can only be just under 21 million coins, so currencies using the code – Bitcoin is just one – are subject to inflation. And there is so much redundancy in the reading and writing, with the amount of text processed growing all the time, that mining uses environmentally calamitous amounts of electricity.[320] All this energy just for prodigious amounts of practically unreadable writing, over and over again.

Blockchain is a return to the unmediated trust Datini had between partners in the exchange relation, before the establishment of banks and government-regulated finance. For this, it has won the breathless enthusiasm of libertarians who love the market but hate governments and mediating middle people in the form of bureaucratic, institutionalized banks.

Blockchain "disintermediates," the enthusiasts say. "The simple genius of this technology is that it cuts away the middleman . . . It does this by taking the all-important role of ledger-keeping away from centralized financial institutions and handing it to a network of autonomous computers, creating a decentralized system of trust that operates outside the control of any one institution."[321]

It also dispenses with the need for government-regulated currencies and central banks. So say two authors in their book on the "cryptocurrencies" that have been built on Satoshi's blockchain code. They were working at the time of writing at the *Wall Street Journal*. Blockchain is a "truth machine." In what is perhaps an unconscious riff on Adam Smith, they say, blockchain is "a group of otherwise independent actors, each acting in pure self-interest, coming together

and Trusted Transactions: Why Blockchain Will Transform the Financial Services Industry," Munich: Roland Berger GMBE.

[320] Alex de Vries, 2018, "Bitcoin's Growing Energy Problem," *Joule* 2(5):801–05.

[321] Paul Vigna and Michael J. Casey, 2015, *The Age of Cryptocurrency: How Bitcoin and Digital Money Are Challenging the Global Economic Order*, New York: St Martin's Press, p. 5.

to produce something for the good of all."[322] Or at least, this is repeating the bit of Adam Smith that is selectively quoted by advocates of the unrestrained market.[§2.3.2a]

And more, blockchain is a "powerful technology that has the potential to make many things in the economy and society more inclusive, secure, efficient, trustworthy and free."[323] Cryptocurrency has the potential to "bring billions of people from the emerging markets into a modern, digitized, globalized economy."[324]

Grammatically speaking, when we parse blockchain as a kind of writing, when we analyze the ways in which it mediates differential interests, we find the same tension between solidary trust and antagonistic mistrust that has ever structured exchange relations. The trust is the faith held in the documentary record, in the establishment of roughly equivalent values at the point of exchange and monetization. But exchange also invariably involves antagonism; mistrust is built into its meanings.[§2.4b]

For all of blockchain's documentary trust – in ledgers, and cryptography, and expensive redundancy – every one of these artifacts is grounded in the same mistrust always to be found in the world of money. If anything, the greater security of blockchain is grounded in intensified mistrust. Blockchain is writing in the service of limitless mistrust. For this reason, Datini's psychoses, the psychoses of merchant man, remain essentially unchanged, the same in quality if a lot more in quantity, caught again in the nexus of solidary and antagonistic interests. Says a blogger, Kai Stinchcombe, blockchain is for a "lawless and mistrustful world where self-interest is the only principle and paranoia is the only source of safety."[325]

Now, as always, in the nether regions of the antagonisms of money and markets, inevitably there are to be found people taking the logic too far, where too far is systems-destructive. Phishing[§2.4b] and scams abound. In the case of Bitcoin, the first was the "Mt Gox" con of 2011, where a very large tranche of bitcoins went missing.[326]

In the "dark web," drug dealers, money launderers, extortionists, arms dealers, assassins, and their ilk have liked the way Bitcoin is outside the jurisdiction of governments. The FBI was trying to track down the drug trade, not the money

---

[322] Michael J. Casey and Paul Vigna, 2018, *The Truth Machine: The Blockchain and the Future of Everything*, London: HarperCollins, pp. 5, 12.

[323] Roland Berger, 2017, "Enabling Decentralized, Digital and Trusted Transactions: Why Blockchain Will Transform the Financial Services Industry," Munich: Roland Berger GMBE.

[324] Paul Vigna and Michael J. Casey, 2015, *The Age of Cryptocurrency: How Bitcoin and Digital Money Are Challenging the Global Economic Order*, New York: St Martin's Press, p. 4.

[325] https://medium.com/@kaistinchcombe/decentralized-and-trustless-crypto-paradise-is-actu ally-a-medieval-hellhole-c1ca122efdec

[326] Michael J. Casey and Paul Vigna, 2018, *The Truth Machine: The Blockchain and the Future of Everything*, London: HarperCollins, pp. 87–88.

trade, when it busted Ross Ulbricht, mastermind of "The Silk Road," in 2013.[327] A sign of recognition of the reality of currency, though immaterial, was that the FBI sold 144,336 Bitcoins it confiscated from Ulbricht for over $48 million.[328]

Unless the whole thing is, in a sense, fraudulent. No less an authority than Jamie Dimon, head of the bank, JPMorgan Chase, declared that Bitcoin was a "fraud", and that he would fire any employee found trading the cryptocurrency for being "stupid."[329] Not that the ledgers of the big banks were any less than fraudulent in the lead-up to the 2008–9 financial crisis.

Sataoshi Nakamoto left a few tantalizing clues about his social agenda, his interest. The so-called "genesis block," the first block of Bitcoin, was mined by Nakamoto himself on January 3, 2009, and includes the headline of the *Times* of London for that day, "Chancellor on brink of second bailout for banks."[330] Before he went silent, he said in a Bitcoin discussion forum, "It's very attractive to the libertarian viewpoint if we can explain it properly." If it is, "we can gain a new territory of freedom."[331]

This is how the Satoshi Nakamoto of Temple City, California got swept into the conflicting swirl of interests around Bitcoin, and with this, the psychoses of exchange and markets that have plagued merchants and money movers since Datini.

Eleven days after publication, *Newsweek* published online at the foot of its article, the following statement:

My name is Dorian Satoshi Nakamoto. I am the subject of the *Newsweek* story on Bitcoin. I am writing this statement to clear my name.

I did not create, invent or otherwise work on Bitcoin . . .

My background is in engineering. I also have the ability to program. My most recent job was as an electrical engineer troubleshooting air traffic control equipment for the FAA . . .

I have not been able to find steady work as an engineer or programmer for ten years. I have worked as a laborer, polltaker, and substitute teacher. I discontinued my internet service in 2013 due to severe financial distress . . .

My prospects for gainful employment has [*sic*] been harmed because of Newsweek's article . . .

Temple City, California
March 17, 2014[332]

[327] Nathaniel Popper, 2015, *Digital Gold: Bitcoin and the inside Story of the Misfits and Millionaires Trying to Reinvent Money*, New York: HarperCollins, pp. 73ff.; www.wired.com/2013/11/silk-road/; www.wired.com/2015/04/silk-road-1/

[328] http://fortune.com/2017/10/02/bitcoin-sale-silk-road/

[329] www.economist.com/blogs/graphicdetail/2017/11/daily-chart-23?cid1=cust/ddnew/email/n/n/20171129n/owned/n/n/ddnew/n/n/n/nNA/Daily_Dispatch/email&etear=dailydispatch

[330] https://en.bitcoin.it/wiki/Genesis_block   [331] https://en.bitcoin.it/wiki/Satoshi_Nakamoto

[332] Leah McGrath Goodman, 2014, "The Face Behind Bitcoin," *Newsweek*, 6 March.

When Nakamoto asked a reporter for Milton Friedman's proverbial "free lunch,"[§2.4a] he was offered one, and accepted.

Meanwhile, Bitcoin's public log showed that some Satoshi Nakamoto, somewhere, had retained almost one million Bitcoins, valued in December 2017 at US$19 billion.[333]

§2.4.2 Solidary Interests

> ***Solidary Interests.*** *The meeting of differential interests as between equals where meanings are achieved voluntarily and where transparency would not change the meaning.*

Participation in meaning – in representation, communication, and interpretation – happens because between differential interests, there is perhaps a need to know, a need for help, a need to share, and any number of other complementary interests that are the stuff of sociability.

These differentials can present themselves explicitly as rhetoric, or implicitly in states of affairs as reification. Their program may be assimilation, to bring the other over to the meaning-maker's way of thinking and being, or differentiation, to accentuate the differences.

Thus far in this short recap of the dynamics of interest, there need not be antagonism, though often there is. And even when there is antagonism, there is always simultaneously at least some element of solidary interest as between the parties of meaning – the lure of propaganda, the pleasures of shopping, the aesthetics of use in a product of exchange. Such are the wiles of transposition.

But what of interests that are purely solidary? Can we have meanings that do no harm? Could we have a world without antagonism, without the fundamental conflicts of interest that are riven through societies of inequality? Today, these are part feudal in their origins, the antagonisms intrinsic to hierarchical organizations, and part the antagonisms of the "free" market.[§2.4.1] On the scale of human history, hierarchical organizations and markets are both quite new inventions, no more than several thousand years old and only reaching most of the world's population in the past century.

Among our other antagonisms, we have many that have come to be labeled as ideologies and practices of differential interest of a damnable kind, the contemporary "ism"s of racism, sexism, homophobia, ablism,

---

[333] https://medium.com/@altcoininvestor/will-the-real-satoshi-nakamoto-please-stand-up-897189c4bdfb

authoritarianism, to name a few now oft-remarked evils. We also have pervasive cultures of antagonism that are considered more acceptable in their theory and practice: competition, nationalism, self-serving acquisitiveness, profiteering. Not that any of these antagonisms are unproductive or anti-sociable – they are sociable to the extent that they are ways to get things done through social relation, even when those things may be undesirable, either in their effects or in some measures for some participants.

The alternative to these antagonisms is solidary interest: love, mutuality, sharing, kindness, respect. For all the badnesses of our present human condition, these things are ordinary things about our species-being that none of the "isms" can take away. They are an obverse, an essential compensation. They are a balance in sociality when too much antagonism is always about to become counterproductive, and when the transposition from solidary to antagonistic interests is going too far.

How then to optimize solidary interests, how to minimize antagonistic interests? When we attempt to address this question in a later part of this book, we will come to the idea of transformation in meaning.

§2.4.2a Noam Chomsky's Yugoslavia

"Dear Marshal Tito," begins a letter written by Noam Chomsky and some fellow academics in December 1974.[*] Josip Broz Tito had been General Secretary of the League of Communists of Yugoslavia since 1939, then led and won a civil war against the fascist collaborators with the Nazis during the Second World War. After the war, he became Prime Minister and President for Life of the Socialist Federal Republic of Yugoslavia and supreme commander of the Yugoslav people's army – hence the military honorific, "Marshal."

Dear Marshal Tito,

The international community of scholars and scientists feels increasingly concerned about the news of repressive measures against intellectuals and attempts to curtail academic freedom in Yugoslavia. Particularly shocking is the recently introduced law for the Republic of Serbia, abridging self-management of universities … It is understood that the introduction of the law is part of a concerted attack on a number of internationally known and respected Marxist philosophers …

We are friends of the country, who admire Marshal Tito's achievements for the liberation of the Yugoslav peoples and the building of a new, democratic,

* http://meaningpatterns.net/yugoslavia

and humanist socialism. We should hate to see these achievements ruined by a return to authoritarian and reactionary forms of political management.[334]

The first signatory was A.J. Ayer, professor of philosophy at the University of Oxford. A grandson of the Dutch-Jewish Citroën[§MS1.2.2d] automobile family, Ayer had gone to Vienna to study with the Vienna Circle[§MS1.1.3i] in the mid 1930s, just before the Circle was scattered asunder by the Nazis. Ayer brought their Logical Positivism back to England.[335] One of his best and brightest students in the 1950s was a young Yugoslav who had served bravely in Tito's army of liberation, Mihailo Marković. Also signing the letter were Jürgen Habermas[§2.0a] and Ludwig Wittgenstein's[§MS2.1.1a] friend and translator, Georg Henrik von Wright.

The members of the group to which the letter referred were mainly based at the Universities of Belgrade and Zagreb. Marković, by then a professor of Philosophy in Belgrade, was to become their most widely published and best-known representative. They came to be known as the "Praxis Group,"[336] named after the academic journal that they had created in 1964. Published in Serbo-Croat and English editions, *Praxis* attracted considerable international interest.[337] Its annual summer schools were attended by leading thinkers from around the world.

We attended the last of these schools at the University of Zagreb's Inter-University Center for Postgraduate Studies in Dubrovnik, in April 1981, a full eighteen days. The theme for the seminar was "Philosophy and Social Science Theories of Modernity: Normative and Empirical Perspectives." Marković was there, a prominent and captivating speaker and persistent discussant. At this meeting, the journal was relaunched under the banner *Praxis International*, co-edited by US philosopher, Richard Bernstein. This was a new beginning.

We walked each morning to the Center from the state-owned, sharply modernist Hotel Lero. Catching in our eyes the blue glint of the Adriatic, it would have been hard to believe that this was an end, not a beginning. Nor could anyone have had an inkling that things would end as badly as they did, for the Praxis Group, for Yugoslavia, and perhaps still for modernity.

---

[334] Alfred J. Ayer, Noam Chomsky et al. 1975, "Letter to Tito," *New York Review of Books*, February 6.

[335] A.J. Ayer, ed. 1959, *Logical Positivism*, Glencoe, IL: The Free Press.

[336] Mihailo Marković and Robert S. Cohen, 1975, *Yugoslavia: The Rise and Fall of Socialist Humanism, a History of the Praxis Group*, London: Spokesman Books; Gerson S. Sher, 1977, *Praxis: Marxist Criticism and Dissent in Socialist Yugoslavia*, Bloomington: Indiana University Press; Oskar Gruenwald, 1983, *The Yugoslav Search for Man: Marxist Humanism in Contemporary Yugoslavia*, South Hadley, MA: J.F. Bergin; Christian Fuchs, 2017, "The Praxis School's Marxist Humanism and Mihailo Marković's Theory of Communication," *Critique: Journal of Socialist Theory* 45(1–2):159–82.

[337] Mihailo Marković and Gajo Petrović, eds. 1979, *Praxis: Yugoslav Essays in the Philosophy and Methodology of the Social Sciences*, Dortrecht: D. Reidel Publishing.

This was a turning point, a time of intellectual responsibility, Bernstein and Marković said in the editorial of the first issue of *Praxis International*. It was the immediate aftermath of "the defeat of the leading military superpower in Vietnam, the Prague Spring, and the military invasion of Czechoslovakia by the Soviet Union, workers' demands for participation and self-government, the growth of the women's liberation movement, and the recognition of the rights of ethnic minorities. All of these events and movements shared in common a demand for human emancipation, and a refusal to accept unjust, oppressive and authoritarian forms of social life whether labeled 'capitalist' or 'socialist'." So, the philosophical questions to be discussed in the journal were to include "the crises of post-industrial society, the global consequences of the ecological crisis, alternative technologies and the humanization of work, ... and the analysis of new social movements."[338] These were the things we talked about for those eighteen days. We have continued to talk about them since.

Chomsky's reason for writing to President Tito came as much as anything from his sense of affinity to Yugoslavia. Flawed though they were, he pointed to "the experiments with workers' councils in Yugoslavia" and "the effort to awaken popular consciousness and create a new involvement in the social process which is a fundamental element of Third World revolutions, coexisting uneasily with indefensible authoritarian practice."[339]

After the break with Stalin, Yugoslavia vowed to take a different path from the Soviet Union. One of the pillars of the Yugoslav difference was self-managing public enterprise.[340] In his introduction to Chomsky's 2018 book on Yugoslavia, the editor quotes Milovan Đilas, one of the architects of Yugoslav self-management. On re-reading Marx, Đilas had "discovered many new ideas, most interesting of all, ideas about a future society in which the immediate producers, through free association, would themselves make decisions about production and distribution."[341]

Another Yugoslav achievement was its leadership of the Non-Aligned Movement, initiated jointly by Tito and India's Jawaharlal Nehru at a meeting in Yugoslavia in 1956. The movement consisted of postcolonial states which did not want to align with either the United States or the Soviet Union.[342] Its

[338] Richard J. Bernstein and Mihailo Marković, 1981, "Why Praxis International?". *Praxis International* 1(1):1–5, pp. 1–2, 4.

[339] Noam Chomsky, 2018, *Yugoslavia: Peace, War, and Dissolution*, Oakland, CA: PM Press, p. 152.

[340] Branko Horvat, Mihailo Marković, and Rudi Supek, 1975, *Self-Governing Socialism: Volume 2*, White Plains, NY: International Arts and Sciences Press; Hans Dieter Seibel and Ukandi G. Damachi, 1982, *Self-Management in Yugoslavia and the Developing World*, New York: St Martin's Press.

[341] Noam Chomsky, 2018, *Yugoslavia: Peace, War, and Dissolution*, Oakland, CA: PM Press, p. 23.

[342] Slobodan Lukić, 1979. *The Nonaligned Movement and National Emancipation*, Belgrade: Socialist Thought and Practice.

first meeting of heads of state was held in Belgrade in 1961. Today it has 120 member-states.

In a rare connection between his social views and his linguistics, Chomsky invokes linguist Wilhelm von Humboldt and his "concept of human nature: … Language is a process of free creation; its laws and principles are fixed, but the manner in which the principles of generation are used is free and infinitely varied." So, to society, "We have, perhaps, reached a point in history when it is possible to think seriously about a society in which freely constituted social bonds replace the fetters of autocratic institutions."[343]

Chomsky's letter to Tito came from a disappointed sympathizer. Whether the letter had any effect on Tito or not, Marković and his Praxis colleagues never lost their jobs. In the scale of academic travesties, their fate was no cause for excessive concern. They were allowed to remain as fully paid internal critics of Yugoslav socialism.[344]

From intellectual roots that might be traced via Ayer back to the Vienna Circle, Marković embarked on a prolific and eloquent career as world-renowned social philosopher. His magnum opus, *Dialectical Theory of Meaning*,[345] is similar in scope to the pair of volumes we are writing here. However, the way we frame our argument is quite different – our transpositional grammar can be traced more to Halliday than to Marković's roots in Logical Positivism and Analytical Philosophy.

Then there was the Marx side of Marković's thinking.[346] Key here was the rediscovery of the 1844 *Economic and Philosophical Manuscripts*,[§2.3.2b] "a rediscovery of a profound and sophisticated humanist philosophy … It became clear that the problems the young Marx was dealing with – praxis, the conflict of human existence and essence, the question of what constitute the true needs and basic human capacities, alienation, labour and production … underlay all his mature work, and furthermore, even now the living, crucial issues of our time."[347]

Or, in Marković's words, the main question for contemporary philosophy was "How can man realize himself and create himself in a world which he accepts as his own?" Or the question, what are the conditions for "the

---

[343] Noam Chomsky, 2018, *Yugoslavia: Peace, War, and Dissolution*, Oakland, CA: PM Press, pp. 152–53.

[344] Mira Bogdanović, 2015, "The Rift in the Praxis Group: Between Nationalism and Liberalism," *Critique: Journal of Socialist Theory* 43(3–4):461–83, p. 462.

[345] Mihailo Marković, 1961 [1984], *Dialectical Theory of Meaning*, translated by D. Rougé and J. Coddington, Dordrecht: D. Reidl Publishing.

[346] Mihailo Marković, 1974b, *The Contemporary Marx: Essays on Humanist Communism*, Nottingham, UK: Spokesman Books; Mihailo Marković, 1981, "New Forms of Democracy in Socialism," *Praxis International* 1(1):23–38; Mihailo Marković, 1982, *Democratic Socialism: Theory and Practice*, Brighton: Harvester Press.

[347] Mihailo Marković and Robert S. Cohen, 1975, *Yugoslavia: The Rise and Fall of Socialist Humanism, a History of the Praxis Group*, London: Spokesman Books, p. 18.

transformation of an alien, reified world into a humane one?" For instance, in relation to work, how does one go from alienated labor, working under the compulsions of hierarchy, to praxis, where work is self-initiated, self-realizing activity, fulfilling and pleasurable for its own sake, in collegial association with co-workers?

This had been the hope for worker self-management in Yugoslavia, realized only in part. In the new "era of cybernetics," he forecast, the "clashing of particular interests – of various enterprises and economic branches, various regions and nationalities," a "technological revolution" would lead to the "dissolution of all artificial barriers and the integration of small, relatively autonomous economic systems into big ones."[348] This was how it might be possible to bring to a close an era, not only of the hierarchical enterprise, but the bureaucratic socialist state.

Marković calls his *Dialectical Theory of Meaning* an ontology, a term we also use to describe our transpositional grammar. "The starting point for this ontology is neither being nor conceptual thought ... – it is praxis. We immediately and with full certainty aware that we act, make efforts to realize certain purposes, meet resistance from external reality and, as a result of our action, experience changes both in the objective situation and ourselves ... establishing the link between subject and object, mind and matter." Against the "humanization of nature by the attribution of symbolic meanings," there is "the opposing tendency to alienation of symbols from man ... Instead of informing, transmitting a clear message evoking a definite feeling; instead of uniting people, symbols often misinform, divide, activate an emotive resistance, become barriers and agents of disunity. Instead of being instruments of freedom and of control over natural and social forces, symbols become hostile forces controlling man and preventing him from seeing clearly himself and others."[349]

Then, the fall. Tito died in 1980, and the IMF, the World Bank, and Western lenders imposed their insistence on the market in the guise of "structural readjustment."[350] Yugoslavia fell into disunity and ethnonationalist war in which 140,000 people were killed and four million refugees were displaced. One country dissolved into separate countries, uneasily, impossibly, ethnically-defined.

Marković chose Serbia as his country. In 1986, he co-authored a memorandum from the Serbian Academy of Sciences and Arts complaining that Serbs had been discriminated against in the Yugoslav Constitution. "In the spring of

---

[348] Mihailo Marković, 1974a, *From Affluence to Praxis: Philosophy and Social Criticism*, Ann Arbor: University of Michigan Press, pp. 21, 63–65, 227.

[349] Mihailo Marković, 1961 [1984], *Dialectical Theory of Meaning*, translated by D. Rougé and J. Coddington, Dordrecht: D. Reidl Publishing, pp. xiv, 6.

[350] Naomi Klein, 2007, *The Shock Doctrine: The Rise of Disaster Capitalism*, New York: Alfred A. Knopf.

1981, open and total war was declared on the Serbian people," it said. The memorandum was referring to the first volley of the war, "the physical, political, legal, and cultural genocide of the Serbian population in Kosovo."[351] This was the subject of Marković's last article in *Praxis International*, in 1989.[352]

In 1990, Marković joined the successor in Serbia to the Yugoslav League of Communists, the Socialist Party of Serbia. From 1990–2 he was vice-president to Slobodan Milošević, and wrote the party's program. He remained active in the party during some of the most vicious years of the war, until 1995.[353] Milošević was extradited to the Hague in 2001, put on trial for war crimes, and died in prison without a conviction.

Kosovo had been the site of the beginning of the end, and in 1999 it was where the war entered its last stages. This was also when Chomsky rejoined the Yugoslav fray. In numerous interviews, articles, and two books, Chomsky opposed the NATO bombing of Serbia and Serbian forces in Kosovo as illegal causes of the humanitarian crisis, and not the solution that they purported to be.[354] The "humanitarian" case made by the US in justification of its aggression, was, for Chomsky, pure "propaganda."[355] Marković would not have disagreed. Nor did Habermas, who called the Western military intervention in Yugoslavia "bestiality."[356]

Writes Marković of the overthrow of Milošević, "What happened on 5 October 2000 ... threw Serbia six decades back into weak, greatly stagnant liberal capitalism ... It was also a road to unprecedented plunder of wealth of the nation created in the course of the past six decades ... [I]t was the first step in the process of losing national sovereignty and in becoming a protectorate of neocolonial global powers."[357]

> Once upon a time,
> there was a country ...
> and its capital was Belgrade.

---

[351] www.trepca.net/english/2006/serbian_memorandum_1986/serbia_memorandum_1986.html
[352] Mihailo Marković, 1989, "Tragedy of National Conflicts in 'Real Socialism': The Case of Kosovo," *Praxis International* 9(4):408–24.
[353] Mira Bogdanović, 2015, "The Rift in the Praxis Group: Between Nationalism and Liberalism," *Critique: Journal of Socialist Theory* 43(3–4):461–83, pp. 464–66.
[354] Noam Chomsky, 1999, *The New Military Humanism: Lessons from Kosovo*, Monroe, ME: Common Courage Press.
[355] Noam Chomsky, 2018, *Yugoslavia: Peace, War, and Dissolution*, Oakland, CA: PM Press, pp. 145–46, 177–81, 191–92.
[356] Jürgen Habermas, 1999, "Bestiality and Humanity: A War on the Border between Legality and Morality," *Constellations* 6(3):263–72.
[357] Mira Bogdanović, 2015, "The Rift in the Praxis Group: Between Nationalism and Liberalism," *Critique: Journal of Socialist Theory* 43(3–4):461–83, p. 467; Božidar Jakšić, 2010, "Praxis – Critical Thinking and Acting, 2009 Interview with Mihailo Marković," *Filozofskom Društvu* 2010(1):1–16.

April 6, 1941 . . .
I'll kill them, my friend!

These are the opening lines of *Underground*, winner in 1995 of the Cannes Film Festival's *Palme d'Or*. The film begins with the Nazi invasion of Yugoslavia, then enjoins a civil war on economic principles, traces the surreal history of the coming of the League of Communists, and comes to a close with the country's dissolution in another civil war in the 1990s, this time fought on the recessive principles of ethnonationalism. The film ends:

> Here we built new houses
> with red roofs
> and chimneys where storks will nest.
> With wide-open doors
> for dear guests.
> We'll thank the soil for feeding us
> and the sun for warming us.
> And the fields for reminding us
> of the green grass of home.
> With pain, sorrow and joy,
> we shall remember our country,
> as we tell our children
> stories that start like fairytales:
> Once upon a time,
> there was a country . . .[358]

When we attended the Praxis seminar in Dubrovnik, we were living in Greece. The day after it ended, we started the long drive home, through the endless mountains of Croatia, Montenegro, Kosovo, Macedonia, then Northern Greece. Nearing Pristina, capital of Kosovo, we were stopped by the police; the road was closed. This was the beginning of the end, the April 1981 Kosovo riots.

In December 1991, the Inter-University Center in Dubrovnik, where this last Praxis seminar had been held, was destroyed in shelling by Milošević's – and Marković's – "Yugoslav Army."

§2.4.2b   György Márkus' Language and Production

We had found out about the Praxis seminar[§2.4.2a] from György Márkus, whose lectures on Kant and Husserl we were attending at the University of Sydney.[*] Márkus' office was in the Department of General Philosophy, not so far from M.A.K. Halliday's[§MS0.3a] in Linguistics. We don't know whether they ever

---

[*] http://meaningpatterns.net/markus

[358] www.springfieldspringfield.co.uk/movie_script.php?movie=underground

met, but surely they knew of each other's work – language work, they both did, and more.

Márkus had been doing his Ph.D. in philosophy in Moscow when Stalin died. But, he told us, Sydney felt colder than Moscow in winter – nothing was properly heated because nobody believed it got cold there, a peculiarly Australian denial of reality as a consequence of which moderately cold days felt bitterly cold. He had come to Australia from Hungary in 1977, a political refugee of a rigidly Stalinist regime, exiled along with other members of the "Budapest School": Maria Márkus, Agnes Heller, and Ferenc Fehér. They were sometime students and colleagues of the Hungarian social and literary philosopher, György Lukács.[359]

Lukács' story as prelude:[§1.6a] after the failure of the Hungarian Soviet Republic of 1919 in which he had been Director of the People's Commissariat for Education, Lukács narrowly escaped execution. He fled to Vienna – Wittgenstein's,[§MS2.1.1b] and Neurath's,[§MS2.1.1d] and Grünbaum's[§2.3c] Vienna – where over the next several years he wrote the book for which he is most famed, *History and Class Consciousness*.[360]

Here is the thesis of *History and Class Consciousness*, not in its own terminology, but paraphrased in the terms we have been developing for this grammar. In a context of antagonistic interests, participants in meaning are often unable or unwilling to see what is in their own, truer interests. They live in the narrowness of a world that seems unchangeable – reification – where they gloss over or try to ignore the alienation. The processes of reification and alienation can only be seen from the perspective of sociability in general, disentangling the consequences of social differentiation whose antagonisms favor some kinds of people, some groups, at the expense of others. If and when participants come to realize this, they might be prompted to act, to do something to change the conditions of their living – to change fundamental patterns of meanings in the inseparable world of bodies, and objects, and spaces, and images, and texts, and sound, and speech. The commodity form and the late feudal, authority-dominated hierarchical administrative organization might be two of the things that can be changed. It is the oppressed who are in the best position to come to this realization and advocate for change.

For his time, Lukács' terminology was "imputed class consciousness," the consciousness that the proletariat would have if it were aware of its own

---

[359] György Lukács, 1920 [1978], *The Theory of the Novel: A Historico-Philosophical Essay on the Forms of Great Epic Literature*, translated by A. Bostock, London: Merlin; György Lukács, 1957 [1963], *The Meaning of Contemporary Realism*, translated by J. and N. Mander, London: Merlin Press; György Lukács, 1978b, *Writer and Critic, and Other Essays*, translated by A. Kahn, London: Merlin; György Márkus, 1977, "The Soul and Life: The Young Lukacs and the Problem of Culture," *Telos* (32):95–115.

[360] György Lukács, 1923 [1971], *History and Class Consciousness*, Translated by R. Livingstone, London: Merlin Press.

interests, instead of being trapped in the seemingly inevitable, "reifying" realities of commodities and waged labor. The broader social perspective that would illuminate these iniquities, he called "the totality," the system as a whole and its "dialectic" – its tension-ridden antagonisms creating contradictions that trended towards periodic crisis. Such illumination was only possible from the perspective of this working class, when it had risen to "class consciousness."[361]

As the twenties moved on, Lukács felt compelled to renounce his earlier views. He wrote a hagiography of Lenin.[362] He moved to Moscow, where he worked as a researcher in the Marx-Engels Institute and was one of the first to read Marx's 1844 *Economic and Philosophical Manuscripts* once their existence had come to light.[§2.3.2b] He later described this reading as a moment of revelation.[363]

A 92-page manuscript in defense of *History and Class Consciousness*, written in response to his critics, was found by researchers in the Soviet archives in 1996. Across the front was scrawled the Soviet archivist's note, "Destroy maybe? Incomprehensible script from a whinger who does not express his point of view clearly and straightforwardly."[364]

Returning to Hungary after the Second World War, Lukács joined the political fray again. During the Hungarian uprising of 1956 – a whinger again – he joined the government of Imre Nagy as Minister for Culture. In the aftermath of the Soviet invasion, Nagy and other ministers were executed, but Lukács once again narrowly escaped with his life.

Returning to Budapest from his studies in Moscow, György Márkus started to teach philosophy and work with Lukács. His first book was on Wittgenstein. He translated the *Tractatus* into Hungarian.[365] Márkus began to write *Language and Production* while he was still in Hungary and finished it in Sydney.

The counterpoint for Márkus' case in *Language and Production* is "the linguistic turn" in twentieth-century philosophy – "argument from, or on the analogy of, language."[366] Analytical Philosophy[§MS1a] and Logical

---

[361] Ibid.; György Lukács, 1978a, *The Ontology of Social Being*, Volume 1: *Hegel's False and His Genuine Ontology*, translated by D. Fernbach, London: Merlin Press; György Lukács, 1978d, *The Ontology of Social Being*, Volume 2: *Marx's Basic Ontological Principles*, translated by D. Fernbach, London: Merlin Press; György Lukács, 1978c, *The Ontology of Social Being*, Volume 3: *Labour*, translated by D. Fernbach, London: Merlin Press.

[362] György Lukács, 1924 [1977], *Lenin: A Study in the Unity of His Thought*, translated by N. Jacobs, London: Verso.

[363] György Lukács, 1923 [1971], *History and Class Consciousness*, Translated by R. Livingstone, London: Merlin Press, p. xxxvi.

[364] György Lukács, 1925 [2000], *A Defence of "History and Class Consciousness": Tailism and the Dialectic*, translated by E. Leslie, London: Verso, p. 41.

[365] John Grumley, Paul Crittenden, and Pauline Johnson, eds. 2002, *Culture and Enlightenment: Essays for György Márkus*, Aldershot: Ashgate, p. 331.

[366] György Márkus, 1975–79 [1986], *Language and Production: A Critique of the Paradigms*, Dordrecht: D. Reidel, p. 2.

Positivism[§MS2.1.1d] were symptoms of this turn. So were Saussure,[§MS3d] the early Wittgenstein of the *Tractatus*,[§MS2.1.1a] and Gadamer,[§1.2.3b] each with their own focus on the circumstantial, self-referential, internal logic of language. This conception of language as a formal system of meaning reflected a turn away from Descartes, formerly the hero of egocentrically human-centered understandings of self-actualizing meaning, a tradition of philosophy which was to be extended by Kant and Hegel.

The achievement of the late Wittgenstein in *Philosophical Investigations*, says Márkus, was to "identify 'meaning' with 'use' ... in the 'language games' of particular 'forms of life'."[§MS2.3.2a] "The acquisition of a language game is ... an eminently practical process ('the mastering of a technique'), guaranteed only by participation in the appropriate form of life."[367] This much, Márkus agrees. The meaning of language is its meaning embedded in life, not a meaning formally analyzable in isolation in terms of its own internal logic, its grammar.

But Márkus fundamentally disagrees with Wittgenstein's implication that to participate, one must of necessity "play the game." In Wittgenstein, "[w]hat is not possible ... , at all, is the critique of a language game, (i.e. a form of life) as a totality ... [O]ne can never have as a meaningful goal the conscious ... transformation of a form of life." Wittgenstein, says Márkus, would have us trapped inside our language games, leaving them "radically impenetrable to conscious reflection." Not only in Wittgenstein, but in Saussure and Gadamer as well, "the 'paradigm of language' offers no possibility for uncovering the causal mechanism of historical change."[368] Nor to act upon the consequences of such uncovering.

The canvas for Márkus' philosophy was wider than language and its logic. It was no less than, "how to create and maintain effective forms of human solidarity across, and in, all the non-accidental diversity of our beliefs, interests and aspirations." This raises the problem of "'unintended' social control and compulsion," not explicitly articulated in language and "embodying the domination of certain social interests."[369] To address this problem, Márkus returns to the Marx of the 1844 manuscripts. These were also Lukács' moment of revelation.[370]

Instead of language, Márkus' focus is on "productive activity," in which language, bodies, things, and spaces are inseparable in a meaningful whole, the one form of meaning ever-ready to transpose for the other – now we are using the phraseology of our forms of meaning to gloss this idea.

The frame of reference for Márkus' is consciousness, or in our terms, the play of material and ideal structures of meaning.[§MS3.1] In contrast to the

---

[367] Ibid., pp. 16–17. [368] Ibid., pp. 17–18, 38. [369] Ibid., pp. xv, 8, 11.
[370] György Márkus, 1966 [2014], *Marxism and Anthropology: The Concept of "Human Essence" in the Philosophy of Marx*, Sydney: Modem-Verlag, pp. 7–11.

passivity of language-bound philosophy, "human beings are not merely observers or suffering participants of the historical process as a fated flux of events but are, rather, active and conscious co-creators of their own history."[371]

Against the grain of prevailing forms of life and their language games, Márkus' (and before him Lukács', and Marx's) agenda is "practical, namely to articulate the possibility, and thereby to promote the emergence, of a radical social praxis, here and now, able to overcome those concrete historical limits that have turned under contemporary conditions into the barriers, both to 'life' and the 'consciousness' of concrete, living individuals."[372] Our word for this is "transformation."[§2.5]

György and Maria Márkus, Ágnes Heller, and Ferenc Fehér were forced to leave Hungary for Australia in 1977 because the leading faction in the Moscow-aligned ruling party, the Hungarian Socialist Workers' Party, had reached a point where the expression of any such hopes for social transformation had become intolerable.

Márkus wrote in an article about "really existing socialism" in the first volume of *Praxis International*, which later became a chapter in a book co-written with Heller and Fehér.[373] Fundamentally different from the market, these societies had their own forms of domination and tissues of deception, bred of peculiar social antagonisms. These were quite different from those of the commodity and the "free" labour market.

At the heart of the system was "central bureaucratic planning" from which flowed "an integrated system of binding orders that aims to determine the essential characteristics of the economic behaviour of all subordinated units." In this respect, the whole society was organized like a contemporary capitalist enterprise, driven by a logic of hierarchy that we would trace to essentially feudal roots.[§2.4.1] "This economy certainly functions through an uninterrupted process of conscious political decision-making taking the form of central plan-commands ... , institutional requirements dictated by the existing system of social domination."[374]

The logic of communication in "really existing socialism" was driven by the rhetoric of propaganda more than reification. Meanwhile, social antagonisms were articulated, notwithstanding the implausibly solidary rhetoric of the "general interest," but in a three-layered tissue of deception.

At a first, legally sanctioned level, enterprise managers competed for state-dispensed resources "by simultaneously over- and underestimating their

---

[371] György Márkus, 1975–79 [1986], *Language and Production: A Critique of the Paradigms*, Dordrecht: D. Reidel, p. 39.

[372] Ibid., p. 43.

[373] Ferenc Fehér, Agnes Heller, and György Márkus, 1983, *Dictatorship over Needs*, Oxford: Basil Blackwell.

[374] György Márkus, 1981, "Planning the Crisis: Remarks on the Economic System of Soviet-Type Societies," *Praxis International* 1(3):240–57, pp. 247, 246.

claims," a form of "cheating" based "on what they can get away with, that is, on the power position of the concerned bureaucracy." Behind this was another layer of deception, a "second economy" of informal or illegal trading, profiteering and corruption. And a "third economy" of unremunerated mutuality despite the system, when, for instance in times of shortage, people gave each other things and helped each other.[375] The end came to most Soviet-style economies in the 1990s. With the implosion of "actually existing socialism," the apparatchiks and operators in the first and second economies were perfectly positioned to steal the state.

Agnes Heller was the only one of the Budapest School to return to Hungary. After Australia, she had moved to New York to work in the New School for Social Research. Back in Hungary in the late 2010s, she encountered what she termed "the refeudalization of society," this time in the form of corrupt relationships between ostensibly liberal democracy and the post-communist kleptocrats. "Take ... Lorinc Meszaros. He was a nobody but in a few years he amassed enormous wealth and now is one of the richest people in the world. He basically has half of Hungary under his control ... Of course, everybody knows that this is [Prime Minister] Orbán's money, not Meszaros' ... [T]he oligarchy depends on politics, and not politics on oligarchy."[376] Nationalism, anti-immigrant sentiment, and racism became their ideologies of choice, their propaganda of mass distraction.

"Hungary is removing statue of philosopher György Lukács: He was Marxist and Jewish." So read a 2017 headline in the Hungarian Free Press.[377] Márkus, Heller, and Fehér were also Jewish – that had been another dimension of their exile.

At dawn on March 31, 2017, the statue of Hungary's most famous philosopher was removed from the park where it had stood for over four decades. The Lukács archive was closed on May 24, 2018, its books and manuscripts removed from public access.[378] Such are the ignominies and agonies of history.

§2.5   Transformation

> **Transformation.** *The changes that occur in the world as a consequence of meaning, where the configuration of interests may in some circumstances remain essentially the same (replication), where they are changed in small ways (hacks of recognition or redistribution), or where fundamental changes are effected in patterns of meaning (paradigmatic or revolutionary change).*

[375] Ibid., pp. 248, 254–57.
[376] http://politicalcritique.org/cee/hungary/2018/agnes-heller-orban-is-a-tyrant/
[377] http://hungarianfreepress.com/2017/02/16/hungary-is-removing-statue-of-philosopher-gyorg y-georg-lukacs-he-was-marxist-and-jewish/
[378] https://jacobinmag.com/2018/02/lukacs-hungary-archives-marxism

Meaning, invariably, is a matter of design. We are always (re)making the world, materially or in the ideal.[§MS3.1] And, for their remaking, redesigns can never quite be the same.[§MS3.2] To mean is to transform.

But there is design and design. Some designs replicate the world in this sense: their transformations do nothing to change the configuration of interests. We buy a product, an event that is unique in the history of exchange and use even if in the tiniest of ways, and transformative of our lives; but the patterning of interests in terms of the logic of the commodity remains unchanged.

Other transformations change the world in small ways; they are "hacks." We might gift something that is normally sold; or we might bend gender identity by wearing a new or different item of clothing. A "hack" may occur in a moment of recognition of identity or redistribution of resources – but without systems change.

Still other transformations change the world in substantial, perhaps revolutionary, ways. Among the more revolutionary changes, some might be personal – sex transitioning, religious enlightenment, or intellectual awakenings, for instance. Others might involve groups, creating a new kind of organization or a predictable kind of organization with a new kind of focus. Others might be called social: the revolution in Yugoslavia after the defeat of the Germans in 1945, then the nationalist, pro-market revolution there half a century later;[§2.4.2a] or the moment of colonization in Australia, as a consequence of which the ways of life of its First Peoples were upturned.[§MS2.1.2e] These were fundamental transformations in the grammar of interests, systems change where there was a fundamental reconfiguration of social and natural designs.

Sometimes agents of transformation may be unaware or only partly aware of the meanings they are making. They may be acting out of habit, or tradition, or convention, or custom – in which cases the transformations tend to replication. Other times they might be well aware of deeper and wider meanings, and so more directly implicated in the replication of meaning. Or they may just be swept along in the tide of revolutionary change.

No matter what its transformative scope, from replicating the world to changing the world in substantial ways, and no matter what the degree of self-awareness, the agency required for design is irreducible. Agency is always equivalent. Responsibility is shared amongst participants, even when the balance is uneven.

Meaning is in its nature ephemeral, whether participants are fully conscious of its implications or not. It doesn't happen unless it is made, and as soon as it is made it has to be remade in order to mean again. All that is left are material traces – in buildings and architected spaces, in food and garments, in written texts and remembered speech. But these do not mean again until they are remade, by representation, communication, or interpretation, and then the meanings are never quite the same.

Meaning designers can become more aware. They can parse meanings for their depths and breadths. This is a process of "doing grammar," so to speak. The effect of such revelations might simply be to become more self-aware, and for that perhaps self-satisfied. Or the effect of revelation may be to uncover the roots of unbalanced interests, deeply rooted patterns of antagonism, and so to heighten dissatisfaction.

Keith Richards and Mick Jagger:[*]

> When I'm watchin' my TV and a man comes on and tells me
> How white my shirts can be
> But, he can't be a man 'cause he doesn't smoke
> The same cigarettes as me
> I can't get no, oh, no, no, no, hey, hey, hey
> That's what I say
> I can't get no satisfaction

And following dissatisfaction, possibly disruption, actions that upset established patterns of unbalance. Agency, always equal in its effect, can be configured in different ways in relation to patterns of unbalanced interest – to replicate or to change.

§2.5a   Michel Foucault Debates Noam Chomsky on Human Nature

ELDERS: ... You have already refused to speak about your own creativity and
    freedom, haven't you? Well, I am wondering what are the psychological reasons
    for this?
FOUCAULT: [*Protesting.*] Well, you can wonder about it, but I can't help that.[379]

Fons Elders was hosting for Dutch Television a discussion between Michel Foucault, historian and philosopher of "discourses of modernity," and Noam Chomsky, linguist.[§MS3.1.2e]

We've already heard Chomsky speak a good deal in this book and its companion volume. Here he is again, this time in the television debate: "There is something biologically given, unchangeable, ... for whatever it is that we do with our mental capacities." To the extent that there is scope for human agency, it is to realize otherwise hard-wired bio-grammar in unique sentences. The task Chomsky leaves for himself is to develop a "mathematical theory of mind; by that I simply mean a precisely articulated, clearly formulated, abstract theory."[380]

---

[*] http://meaningpatterns.net/transformation

[379] Noam Chomsky and Michel Foucault, 1971 [2006], *The Chomsky–Foucault Debate: On Human Nature*, New York: The New Press, p. 30.
[380] Ibid., pp. 7, 13.

Then, from a bio-determinism that offers such narrow scope of agency,[§MS3.1.2j] a huge leap into politics.[§2.2d] "There is no longer any social necessity for human beings to be treated as mechanical elements in the productive process. . . . [P]rivate capitalism or state totalitarianism" – communism or "actually-existing socialism" – "[t]hey are all vestiges to be overthrown, eliminated in favor of direct participation in the form of workers' councils or other free associations that individuals will constitute for themselves for the purpose of their social existence and productive labor." And this, in a move "towards the true, humanly valuable concepts of justice and decency and love and kindness and sympathy, which I think are real." Looking to the future, "the technology of data-processing, or communication . . . can be liberating . . . [though it can also be] converted . . . into an instrument of oppression because power is badly distributed."[381]

Now Foucault, historian of power, for whom a science like Chomsky's is never more than an "epistemological indicator,"[382] a figment of discourse, itself another momentary configuration of power. Power takes its characteristically modern forms by the end of the eighteenth century, as exemplified in asylums,[383] prisons,[384] and hospitals,[385] and their practices of confinement, rationalized by the new sciences of medicine and social regulation. So, "in the historical studies that I have been able to make, I have without doubt given very little room to what you might call the creativity of individuals."[386]

As for politics, "I admit to not being able to define, nor for even stronger reasons to propose, an ideal social model."[*] And antagonisms based on economic inequalities: if "[t]he proletariat makes war with the ruling class, [it is] . . . because it wants to take power . . . One makes war to win, not because it is just." This is why, following Nietzsche, Foucault "doesn't speak in terms of justice but in terms of power."[387] No sides in the perennial struggle for power are to be privileged; no justice is to be attributed to any particular cause; all interests are as power-directed as each other.

If the essentials of meaning in Chomsky are to be found in language as bio-expression, in Foucault they are to be located in "discourse." This is "not [just]

---

* http://meaningpatterns.net/foucault

[381] Ibid., pp. 38, 55, 64.   [382] Ibid., p. 6.
[383] Michel Foucault, 1961 [1988], *Madness and Civilization: A History of Insanity in the Age of Reason*, translated by R. Howard, New York: Vintage Books.
[384] Michel Foucault, 1975 [1977], *Discipline and Punish: The Birth of the Prison*, translated by A. Sheridan, New York: Vintage Books.
[385] Michel Foucault, 1963 [1973], *The Birth of the Clinic: An Archaeology of Medical Perception*, translated by A.M. Sheridan, London: Taylor and Francis.
[386] Noam Chomsky and Michel Foucault, 1971 [2006], *The Chomsky–Foucault Debate: On Human Nature*, New York: The New Press, p. 15.
[387] Ibid., pp. 40, 51, 54.

the language used by discourse ... but discourse itself as a practice," where "the unity of discourse [is] in the objects themselves, in their distribution, in the interplay of their differences, in their proximity or distance ... a group of rules that are immanent in the practice."[388]

Take the famous sentence, "Colorless green ideas sleep furiously," says Foucault in his *Archaeology of Knowledge*, assuming his reader will know that Chomsky its author.[§MS3.1.2f] "In fact, to say that a sentence like this is meaningless presupposes that one has already excluded a number of possibilities – that it describes a dream, that it is part of a poetic text, that it is a coded message, that it is spoken by a drug addict – and that one assumes it must be a certain type of statement that must refer, in a very definite way, to some visible reality."[389]

So what does Chomsky mean by this sentence? He was not dreaming, or being poetic, or speaking in code, or on drugs – this sentence is meaningfully famous as an example of meaninglessness but only within a frame of discursive practice that has eliminated dreams, poetry, code, or drugs as normal speech or text. Chomsky has defined as meaningful only those sentences that refer in a congruent way to empirical things. This is what he means, this is the nature of his science.

For Foucault, it is not enough "for a sequence of linguistic elements to be regarded and analysed as a statement." It must also be analyzed in terms of its "material existence ... Even if a sentence is composed of the same words, bears exactly the same meaning, and preserves the same syntactical and semantic identity, it does not constitute the same statement if it is spoken by some one in the course of a conversation, or printed in a novel; if it was written one day centuries ago, and if it now reappears in an oral formulation. The coordinates and the material status of the statement are part of its intrinsic characteristics."[390]

The task of "enunciative analysis ... reveals ... what men 'really meant' not only in their words and texts, their discourses and their writings, but also in the institutions, practices, techniques, and objects that they produced, ... this implicit, sovereign, communal 'meaning.'" As a consequence, "statements (however numerous they may be) are always in deficit; on the basis of the grammar and of the wealth of vocabulary available at a given period, there are, in total, relatively few things that are said."[391]

---

[388] Michel Foucault, 1969 [1972]; *The Archaeology of Knowledge*, translated by A.M.S. Smith, New York: Pantheon, pp. 46, 48; Michel Foucault, 1966 [1970], *The Order of Things: An Archaeology of the Human Sciences*, London: Tavistock, p. xiv.

[389] Michel Foucault, 1969 [1972]; *The Archaeology of Knowledge*, translated by A.M.S. Smith, New York: Pantheon, p. 90.

[390] Ibid., p. 100.   [391] Ibid., pp. 118–19.

But does "discursive practice" in Foucault include institutions, objects, actions? This is unclear. Mostly it seems that it doesn't – discourse is text or reported speech in context, and his method in linguists' terms a kind of pragmatics.§MS0.3a So even though at times his method appears to capture multimodal meaning, in the end we have another reduction of meaning to language. Though, as if to equivocate, Foucault admits that "[t]his rarity of statements, the incomplete, fragmented form of the enunciative field, the fact that few things, in all, can be said, explain that statements are not, like the air we breathe, an infinite transparency."[392]

Foucault also, but secondarily, directs attention to the visual, and its realization in the form of the "gaze" of power. His allegory of modern power is Jeremy Bentham's hypothetical design for a prison, the Panopticon, a circular building with a guardhouse in the middle, guards able to see into every cell but the inmates unable to see each other. "Each individual, in his place, is securely confined to a cell from which he is seen from the front by the supervisor; but the side walls prevent him from coming into contact with his companions."[393]

This architecture creates a "permanent visibility that assures the automatic functioning of power." The outcome is an "axial visibility; but the divisions of the ring, those separated cells, imply a lateral invisibility." Such is the prototypical design of modern institutions of power. "If the inmates are convicts, there is no danger of a plot, an attempt at collective escape, the planning of new crimes for the future, bad reciprocal influences; if they are patients, there is no danger of contagion; if they are madmen there is no risk of their committing violence upon one another; if they are schoolchildren, there is no copying, no noise, no chatter, no waste of time."[394]

But from the gaze, Foucault returns us to discourse, where in the hospital, for instance, "clinical experience represents a moment of balance between speech and spectacle. A precarious balance, for it rests on a formidable postulate: that all that is visible is expressible, and that it is wholly visible because it is wholly expressible." The visible symptoms are reduced to linguistic diagnosis and medical taxonomy, "the organization of objectivity on the basis of sign values, the secretly linguistic structure of the datum."[395] So too, the gaze of the Panopticon is reducible to the classifications of criminality and the social discourse of law. The gaze of the teacher is reducible to the discourse of curriculum and testing.

---

[392] Ibid., pp. 119–20.
[393] Michel Foucault, 1975 [1977], *Discipline and Punish: The Birth of the Prison*, translated by A. Sheridan, New York: Vintage Books, p. 200.
[394] Ibid., pp. 200–01.
[395] Michel Foucault, 1963 [1973], *The Birth of the Clinic: An Archaeology of Medical Perception*, translated by A.M. Sheridan, London: Taylor and Francis, pp. 115, 199.

Discursive power is for Foucault pervasive, so thoroughly internalized by participants that it becomes virtually unassailable. It is "not an institution, and not a structure. . . . Power is not something that is acquired, seized, or shared, something that one holds on to or allows to slip away; power is exercised from innumerable points. . . . Power comes from below; that is, there is no binary and all-encompassing opposition between rulers and ruled at the root of power relations, and serving as a general matrix."[396] It is as if, for Foucault, prisoners and warders, patients and doctors, students and teachers, were equally complicit in the replication of structures of power, as if there were no centers of power, as if power were so inevitable as to be impervious to change.

To return now to the frame of reference of our grammar of multimodality, the forms of expression of this power are broader than discourse and gaze. Power is realized in the spatial arrangement of buildings, the positioning of bodies, the imagery, the sounds and silences, and perhaps least directly in speech and text – the one transposable into the other. Their practical power arises from their transposability.

Not only are differential interests unbalanced, their relations are antagonistic, and as such they are always ready to be changed. They systematically favor one social group at the expense of another, and so contain intrinsic conflicts of interest which always beg resolution. However compliant the powerless, for the moment at least, the power they experience has been imposed. More than an undifferentiated matrix, in unequal societies there are centers of power and power is imposed on the many by the few. The antagonisms always beg reconfiguration, small or large. Power relations are not unassailable. Replication is not the only option. Hacks that make incremental changes the patterning of interests are possible; so are revolutionary changes that create fundamental transformations.

Foucault started visiting the United States from 1970, initially on lecture tours, spending more time there as the years went on. At one point, he contemplated moving to the US. One of his American revelations was a vibrant gay "subculture of sado-masochism" – his terminology.[397] He spent a sabbatical at the University of California, Berkeley in 1975. There he was drawn, in the words of one of his biographers, to "the unusual array of pleasures to be found on Folsom Street – the hub of San Francisco's 'leather' scene . . . [where d]epending on the club, one could savor the illusion of bondage – or experience the most directly physical sorts of self-chosen 'torture.'" Foucault told an interviewer from the gay journal *Body Politic,* "The S/M culture is interesting," because "there are roles and everybody knows very well that the roles can be

---

[396] Michel Foucault, 1976 [1978], *The History of Sexuality,* Volume 1: *An Introduction,* translated by R. Hurley, New York: Pantheon, pp. 93–94.
[397] Didier Eribon, 1991, *Michel Foucault,* translated by B. Wing, Cambridge, MA: Harvard University Press, p. 315.

reversed. Sometimes the scene begins with the master and the slave, and at the end the slave has become the master."[398]

While Chomsky's politics led him to sympathize with the worker-controlled enterprises and non-aligned globalism of Yugoslavia,[§2.4.2a] Foucault's politics was heading somewhere else. He visited Iran several times in 1978 during the social ferment that lead to the Islamic revolution. Here, he found what he thought to be the possibility of "a political spirituality." He was impressed to see women wearing the veil as a political gesture. Religion in Iran had become, he said, "a real force ... the force that can make a whole people rise up."[399] When the still-exiled Ayatollah Khomeini came to live in Paris shortly before his triumphal return to Tehran, Foucault was among the first to meet him. No mere politician, no figure of conventional governmental power, Foucault said, "Khomeini is the point of fixation for a collective will."[400]

Or to retreat from politics, from any possible agenda for social change: "the historical ontology of ourselves must turn away from all projects that claim to be global or radical. In fact we know from experience that the claim to escape from the system of contemporary reality so as to produce the overall programs of another society, of another way of thinking, another culture, another vision of the world, has led only to the return of the most dangerous traditions."[401] There's no way out of here, Foucault's insane joker might have said to his incarcerated thief. Looking back to his version of modernity, we see a scene of sado-masochistic compliance.

Foucault's orientation to change now seems strangely dated. The institutions he chose for his talismans were always peculiar – not the mainstream of the market, not the enterprises where most adults spent their working days, not the family except for his late work on ancient Greece and Rome. The institutions he analyzed were in their genesis and still were in his time instruments of state power, places of peculiarly intense confinement outside the everyday sociabilities and diffuse power antagonisms of work, consumption, and family.

Since the time when Foucault wrote, asylums have been emptied, prisons and hospitals privatized, and, in the reconfiguration of global interests in the post-Cold War era, the modern state has been withered away in favor of markets. The first decades of the twenty-first century have been halcyon years for Milton Friedman's capitalist idealism,[§2.4a] with its peculiar dynamics

[398] James Miller, 1993, *The Passion of Michel Foucault*, New York: Simon & Schuster, pp. 259–60, 263.

[399] David Macey, 1993, *The Lives of Michel Foucault*, New York: Pantheon Books, p. 410.

[400] Didier Eribon, 1991, *Michel Foucault*, translated by B. Wing, Cambridge, MA: Harvard University Press, pp. 285–87.

[401] Michel Foucault, 1984, "What Is Enlightenment?," pp. 32–50 in *The Foucault Reader*, edited by P. Rabinow, New York: Pantheon, p. 46.

of "freedom."[§2.3a] With few exceptions, the centralized power of authoritarian and welfare states has given way to the dispersed logic of the market.

In social media, the radial gaze of the Panopticon has been displaced by the "multisynopticon,"[402] with everyone's seeing each other and narcissistically exhibiting themselves for the seeing. Deprivation of agency in centralized institutions and mass media has given way to social media where users become agents of their own meanings, whether these are felt to be oppressive or liberating and even if the platform owners appropriate these freely given meanings for private profit. In the negotiation of differential and antagonistic interests, the dominance of an all-encompassing, assimilating logic of power has given way to logics of differentiation.[§2.2.2] There are still today profound asymmetries of power, but their dynamics are quite different from Foucault's modernity.

Had he lived to experience these days, Foucault might well have been pleased to see that we are today governed less, at least in terms of the old-fashioned expressions of power via state or state-sanctioned institutional control that he described. Our being governed now happens in other ways.

Foucault died of AIDS in 1984, at that time an incurable disease. His last words in his last lecture at the Collège de France on 28 March of that year: "There you are, listen, I had things to say to you about the general framework. But well, it's too late. So thank you."[403]

And earlier, of that framework he had said, "[t]o all those who wish to talk about man, his reign or his liberation, to all those who still ask themselves questions about what man is in his essence, to all those who want to take him as a starting-point in their attempts to reach the truth ... to all these warped and twisted forms of reflection we can only answer with a philosophical laugh – which means, to a certain extent, a silent one."[404]

§2.5b   Edith Stein's On the Problem of Empathy

Michel Foucault[§2.5a] was dismissive of all-encompassing intellectual projects like Edmund Husserl's.[§MS0.4c] Any such projects were in his view misguided quests to find origins, causes, "cultural totalities," moves that were typical of

---

[402] Petrilson Pinheiro, 2019, "The Age of Multisynopticon: What Does It Mean to Be (Critically) Literate Nowadays?," pp. 237–60 in *Linguística Aplicada Para Além Das Fronteiras*, edited by R.F. Maciel, R. Tilio, D.M. de Jesus, and A.L. d'E.C. de Barros, Campinas, Brazil: Pontes; Thomas Mathiesen, 1997, "The Viewer Society: Michel Foucault's 'Panopticon' Revisited," *Theoretical Criminology: An International Journal* 1(2):215–32.

[403] Michel Foucault, 1984 [2011], *The Courage of Truth (the Government of the Self and Others II): Lectures at the Collège De France, 1983–1984*, translated by G. Burchell, London: Palgrave, p. 338.

[404] Michel Foucault, 1966 [1970], *The Order of Things: An Archaeology of the Human Sciences*, London: Tavistock, pp. 342–43.

the "transcendental reflexion" in "all humanist ideologies." In his "archaeology of knowledge," he would not deign to trace anything wider than "thresholds, ruptures, ... differences, changes and mutations," a "whole play of displacements."[405] In the same spirit, Jacques Derrida spent his career arguing with Husserl[406] – though always reverentially – on the basis of the endless, irreducible chains of difference in meaning.§MS0.4d

Between 1915 and his death in 1938, Husserl worked on successive drafts of a second volume of *Ideas*, not published until after his death. Initially, the manuscript was assembled and revised by Edith Stein, his doctoral student and research assistant.[407] Stein's dissertation was published in 1917, *On the Problem of Empathy.*[*] Husserl's work and Stein's became closely intertwined. We are going to quote from the two books separately, but they are hardly that.

Stein: "A friend tells me that he has lost his brother . . . I become aware of his pain . . . [because] his face is pale and disturbed, his voice toneless and strained. Perhaps he also expresses the pain in words." This is not my pain, but I become pained, for him. Stein asks, "What kind of awareness is this?" Her answer: "the act of empathy."[408] Or, to rephrase, empathy is a solidary meaning, a transposition between other and self, expressed multimodally.

Husserl: The "intersubjective" self "stand[s] in a relation of empathy to the other cognizing subjects, and for that he must have Corporeality and belong to the same world."[409] Subjects stand in relation to subjects, separate bodies, connected by shared corporeality.

Stein: "The subject of the empathized experience ... is not the subject empathizing, but another. And this is what is fundamentally new in contrast with the memory, expectation, or the fantasy of our own experiences." As I remember my own pain, I can anticipate pain, I can fantasize pain, and each of these meaning transpositions (to rephrase in the terms of our grammar) is a transposition over time within the first person-self. Empathy, by contrast, is

---

* http://meaningpatterns.net/stein

[405] Michel Foucault, 1969 [1972]; *The Archaeology of Knowledge*, translated by A.M.S. Smith, New York: Pantheon, pp. 202–03.

[406] Jacques Derrida, 1962 [1989], *Edmund Husserl's Origin of Geometry: An Introduction*, Lincoln: University of Nebraska Press; Jacques Derrida, 1967 [1973], *Speech and Phenomena, and Other Essays on Husserl's Theory of Signs*, translated by D.B. Allison, Evanston, IL: Northwestern University Press.

[407] Alisdair MacIntyre, 2006, *Edith Stein: A Philosophical Prologue, 1913–1922*, Lanham, MD: Rowman and Littlefield, pp. 99–108; Marianne Sawicki, 1997, *Body, Text, and Science: The Literacy of Investigative Practices and the Phenomenology of Edith Stein*, Dordrecht: Springer Science, pp. 153–65.

[408] Edith Stein, 1917 [1989], *On the Problem of Empathy*, translated by W. Stein, Washington, DC: ICS Publications, p. 6.

[409] Edmund Husserl, 1952 [1989], *Ideas Pertaining to a Pure Phenomenology and a Phenomenological Philosophy, Second Book: Studies in the Phenomenology of Constitution*, translated by R. Rojcewicz and A. Schuwer, Dordrecht: Kluwer, p. 87.

"reflexive sympathy, where my original experience returns to me as an empathized one," a transposition of other-to-self-to-other across bodies and space.[§MS2.2] Stein references Adam Smith's notion of "sympathy" here.[§2.3.2a] Empathy is a "particular case of reiteration" of meaning.[410]

Husserl: "[A]ll that is thingly-real in the surrounding world ... has its relation to the Body," including the "possibility of 'other' Bodies, understood in the sense of an apprehension of the human."[411] Instances of the self and other, these come together in the form of solidary interests in the human-in-general.

Stein: "How is my body constituted within consciousness?" The body is "a real thing, a physical body," where the "tactile and visual senses ... call each other as witnesses, though do not shift the responsibility on one another."[412] Our gloss: consciousness is grounded in multimodal meaning.

Husserl: "Such an intersubjective experienceability ... is thinkable only through 'empathy,' which for its part presupposes an intersubjectively experienceable Body." In this way, "reciprocal empathy" is "unified into a nexus which constitutes intersubjective objectivities," – the objectivities of society and history, "when we live with one another, talk to one another, shake hands with one another in greeting, or are related to one another in love and aversion, in disposition and action, in discourse and discussion."[413]

Stein: "By empathy with differently composed personal structures we become clear on what we are not ... Thus, together with self-knowledge, we also have an important aid to self-evaluation ... [A]t the same time as new values are acquired by empathy, our own unfamiliar values become visible ... Every comprehension of different persons can become the basis of understanding."[414]

Husserl never goes as far as Stein, because his empathizing self establishes a connection with the other by an idealized identity in abstract meaning. But now, in Stein, there comes a recognition that empathetic meanings are meanings as much in the materiality of bodies. Empathy is no merely textual or discursive meaning. It can at times become a viscerally full-bodied experience. You may cry during a movie, empathizing with the fate of a character. You might laugh

---

[410] Edith Stein, 1917 [1989], *On the Problem of Empathy*, translated by W. Stein, Washington, DC: ICS Publications, pp. 10, 14, 18.

[411] Edmund Husserl, 1952 [1989], *Ideas Pertaining to a Pure Phenomenology and a Phenomenological Philosophy, Second Book: Studies in the Phenomenology of Constitution*, translated by R. Rojcewicz and A. Schuwer, Dordrecht: Kluwer, pp. 61, 86.

[412] Edith Stein, 1917 [1989], *On the Problem of Empathy*, translated by W. Stein, Washington, DC: ICS Publications, p. 41.

[413] Edmund Husserl, 1952 [1989], *Ideas Pertaining to a Pure Phenomenology and a Phenomenological Philosophy, Second Book: Studies in the Phenomenology of Constitution*, translated by R. Rojcewicz and A. Schuwer, Dordrecht: Kluwer, pp. 101, 118, 192.

[414] Edith Stein, 1917 [1989], *On the Problem of Empathy*, translated by W. Stein, Washington, DC: ICS Publications, p. 116.

with a conversational partner, recognizing the absurdity of their situation. You might fear for another person's danger. Simply, and ordinarily, "to feel for" is a transposition of self and other. In these moments of empathy, you virtually become other, a functional transposition. Identities that have moved apart by differentiation draw towards assimilation by empathy, another functional transposition.

Because she was a woman, Husserl didn't support examination of Stein's habilitation thesis which would have allowed her appointment to the university as a professor.[415] The second volume of *Ideas* was not published until after his death. Husserl must have thought highly of Stein's dissertation because he published it in his *Yearbook* in 1922.[416] Edith Stein never became a professor but nevertheless went on to become one of Germany's most significant twentieth-century philosophers and feminists.[417]

Husserl: "The historian asks what the members of the society in their communal life represented, thought, valued, desired, etc. How have these people 'determined' themselves reciprocally, how have they allowed themselves to be determined by the surrounding world of things, how have they, for their part, shaped the world in turn, etc.? ... Phenomenology ... investigates the total system of possible acts of consciousness, of possible appearances and meanings related to precisely those objects."[418]

Stein: "[T]he goal of phenomenology" – the science of sciences – "is to clarify and thereby to find the ultimate basis of all knowledge."[419]

In his late works, Husserl gave a new name to what he and Stein had previously called the "surrounding world": the "lifeworld." This is the world of everyday experience, contrasted with the depth and breadths of science and phenomenology. "The lifeworld is a realm of original self-evidences. That which is self-evidently given is, in perception, experienced as 'the thing itself,' in immediate presence, or, in memory ... lies in these intuitions themselves as that which is actually, intersubjectively experienceable."[420]

In the lifeworld, we "are constantly active on the basis of our passive having of the world ... ; it is to this or that object that we pay attention, according to our

[415] Edith Stein, 1987 [1993], *Self Portrait in Letters, 1916–1942*, translated by J. Koeppel, Washington, DC: ICS Publications, p. 35.

[416] Edith Stein, 1922 [2000], *Philosophy of Psychology and the Humanities*, translated by M.C. Baseheart and M. Sawicki, Washington, DC: ICS Publications.

[417] Edith Stein, 1959 [1987], *Essays on Woman*, translated by F.M. Oben, Washington, DC: ICS Publications.

[418] Edmund Husserl, 1952 [1989], *Ideas Pertaining to a Pure Phenomenology and a Phenomenological Philosophy, Second Book: Studies in the Phenomenology of Constitution*, translated by R. Rojcewicz and A. Schuwer, Dordrecht: Kluwer, pp. 241, 325.

[419] Edith Stein, 1917 [1989], *On the Problem of Empathy*, translated by W. Stein, Washington, DC: ICS Publications, p. 3.

[420] Edmund Husserl, 1954 [1970]; *The Crisis of European Sciences and Transcendental Phenomenology*, Evanston, IL: Northwestern University Press, pp. 127–28.

interests; with them we deal actively in different ways; through our acts they are 'thematic' objects." In these ways, the lifeworld is a place of "naïve experiential self-evidence, the certainty of coming to know, through seeing, touching, feeling, hearing etc., the same thing through its properties, through 'repetition' of the experiences."[421]

However, there are "two sorts of truth: on the one hand, everyday practical situational truths, relative, to be sure, . . . exactly what praxis, in its particular projects, seeks and needs." This is the truth of the lifeworld. But "on the other side are scientific truths, and their grounding leads back precisely to the situational truths."[422] Science or the phenomenological method are processes of "uncovering . . . intentional horizons, . . . a radical clarification of the sense and origin (or of the sense in consequence of the origin) of the concepts: world, Nature, space, time, psychophysical being, man, psyche, animate organism, social community, culture, and so forth."[423] In our grammar, we will call this the parsing of interests.

In science and phenomenology "[w]e find ourselves with the self-evident capacity to reflect – to turn to the horizon and to penetrate it in an expository way. But we also have, and know that we have, the capacity of complete freedom to transform, in thought [at least], our human historical experience and what is there exposed as its lifeworld."[424]

Stein: "In the 'exchange of thoughts' a thinking together arises . . . as our common thinking. All scientific activity is executed in this form . . . on the basis of the already accumulated repertoire that I take over . . . And with this mental doing of mine, I find myself inserted into the great network of motivation, the knowledge-process of humanity."[425]

Moved by the atrocities of the First World War, Stein volunteered as a Red Cross nurse, later studying and working under Husserl.[426] One of his sons had died in the war, and the other was severely wounded. A Jew by birth and an atheist while working with Husserl, she converted to Catholicism in 1921, taught in several religious colleges, then joined the Carmelite Order in 1933, assuming the monastic name of Teresa Benedicta of the Cross. When the Nazis came to power, for safety's sake the Carmelites transferred her to a monastery in the Netherlands. After the invasion of the Netherlands she was

---

[421] Ibid., pp. 108, 343.   [422] Ibid., p. 132.

[423] Edmund Husserl, 1931 [1960], *Cartesian Meditations: An Introduction to Phenomenology*, translated by D. Cairns, The Hague: Martinus Nijhoff Publishers, pp. 153–54.

[424] Edmund Husserl, 1954 [1970]; *The Crisis of European Sciences and Transcendental Phenomenology*, Evanston, IL: Northwestern University Press, pp. 374–75.

[425] Edith Stein, 1922 [2000], *Philosophy of Psychology and the Humanities*, translated by M.C. Baseheart and M. Sawicki, Washington, DC: ICS Publications, p. 170.

[426] Edith Stein, 1933 [1986], *Life in a Jewish Family, 1891–1916: An Autobiography*, translated by J. Koeppel, Washington, DC: ICS Publications, pp. 318–67.

arrested by the SS and sent to Auschwitz. She died in the gas chambers in August 1942.[427]

Edith Stein was made a saint by the Catholic Church in 1998, controversially for some Catholics, because they said she had not been martyred as a co-religionist, but murdered for her Jewish "race."[428] Stein's entry to sainthood was on the basis of a miracle in which the father of Benedicta, a little girl who had swallowed enough Tylenol to kill her sixteen times over, prayed to her namesake, and the child miraculously recovered – a transposition by empathy, it might seem, of which only saints are capable.

Dr. Ronald Kleinman, who had treated the young Benedicta at Massachusetts General Hospital, attended Edith Stein's canonization by Pope John Paul II at St Peters, Rome in October 1998.

"I'm not saying it was a miracle," said Dr. Kleinman, "I'm saying it was miraculous. I'm Jewish. I don't believe per se in miracles, but I can say I didn't expect her to recover."[429]

§2.5.1 To Parse

> **To Parse.** To account for patterns of meaning and to bring to account the unequal play of differential interests.

Both Michel Foucault[§2.5a] and Jacques Derrida[§MS0.4d] might have counseled against the kind of intellectual project that we have been attempting in this grammar.

We explained earlier how, notwithstanding our admiration for Edmund Husserl,[§MS0.4c] we wanted some of Derrida too, the part that is able to trace the microdynamics of always-designed, ever-changing meanings. Now we want some of Foucault as well, and for the same reasons. We want the historian in Foucault, with his archaeologist's eye for the configuration of interests in the dynamics of power in their vividly granular specificity. But we fear the consequences of Foucault's anti-humanist side, and his unconscionable tendency to explain away our tolerance for pain and our readiness to suffer the indignities of unequal power. We worry at his refusal to find a critical measure outside of historical contingencies, and his pessimism about possibilities for change.

---

[427] Waltraud Herbsrith, 1971 [1985], *Edith Stein: A Biography*, San Francisco, CA: Harper and Row.

[428] Harry James Cargas, ed. 1994, *The Unnecessary Problem of Edith Stein*, Lanham, MD: University Press of America.

[429] www.nytimes.com/1998/10/11/world/child-s-close-call-aided-nun-s-way-to-sainthood.html

Our program is to trace, not just circumstantial contingencies, the never-having-been and never-to-be repeated moments of transformation in the process of meaning design, but also the wider and deeper patterns of continuity and conventionality in meanings. The patterns of meaning in their generality may be epochal – the commodity form and the relations of the market, for instance. Or they may go to the essence of our human natures in every epoch – empathy, for instance, as a dimension of our sociability, notwithstanding our at times willful and systematic failures to empathize.

So, we want to have our Foucault-Derrida, and our Husserl-Stein too. We want our contextual relativity and human universality as well. We want our historical contingency and our humanism. The purpose of this grammar has been to show how we might be able to have both.

To design is to transform. The effect of the transformations can be to replicate configurations of difference, or to hack them into something somewhat different. Or, within the parameters of our natural life as species, it may be to make fundamental changes to our being.

"To parse" is to account for patterns of meaning, one aspect of which is to bring to account unequal configurations of interest. This is to uncover the grammar of interests, to make sense of the play of solidary and antagonistic interests. It is to see that meanings-in are also meanings-for.[§MS0.3.3] The outcome is revelation. Sometimes this suggests action, failing which, at the very least, inaction that is not unthinking. "To change" is to act upon the parsing.

Though of course, one person's parsing may be another person's bullshit.[*] Or one person's change may be another person's travesty. Philosopher of bullshit, Harry Frankfurt, despairs that his subject is a "phenomenon … so vast and amorphous that no crisp and perspicuous analysis of its concept can avoid being procrustean."[430]

We put bullshit, and truth as well, down to the transpositions of interest in a dialectic where, between representation and communication, meanings can never be completely shared. Bullshit is when the not-sharing involves bad faith. Less than outright lies, it may be (mere) exaggertion, affectation, pretense, deliberate ellision, feigned sincerity, or faked knowing. This is just the beginning of a potentially endless catalogue of intentional or unintentional failures to communicate interest. In each case, the untruth is the rhetorical truth. The comedian Stephen Colbert has a nice word for this, "truthiness." Bullshit is never only that.

Rhetoric may result in more or less congruent meaning, but meanings always will remain incongruent to some degree. Communication can never complete representation becase the representable truth is inexhaustible. In solidary

---

[*] http://meaningpatterns.net/bullshit

[430] Harry G. Frankfurt, 2005, *On Bullshit*, Princeton, NJ: Princeton University Press, p. 3.

interests the not-sharing is benign. In antagonistic interests, the lies and the bullshit are in the gap between sharing and not-sharing. Rhetorics are always ready to descend into bullshit. But some things are more bullshit than others, and our parsing may unmask this.

Reification often works to the same effect, where immediate objectifications obscure underlying patterns of agency and interest. Localized truth may serve as a cover for generalized lies.

As for the project of parsing the truth, we like the distinction Husserl makes between lifeworld and science.[§2.5b] The lifeworld sustains vernacular truths as well as everyday bullshit. Science is a kind of parsing that tries to cut through the bullshit and get closer to the truth. Sometimes, however, the bullshit masquerades as science, and when it does, this too demands our parsing.

§2.5.1a Nancy Fraser's "Parity of Participation"

Nancy Fraser didn't attend the last Praxis meeting in Dubrovnik in 1981,[§2.4.2a] but that year she did contribute a paper discussing the work of Michel Foucault[§2.5a] to the *Praxis International* journal.[*]

Of course, Fraser said, Foucault had provided "a rich empirical account of the early stages in the emergence of some distinctively modern modalities of power." In Foucault, she said, "modern power is 'capillary'; ... [it] operates at the lowest extremities of the social body in everyday social practices; ... such power touches people's lives more fundamentally through their social practices than through their beliefs." But for all his empirical insights, Fraser argued, Foucault's work was riven with "normative confusions ... I find no clues in Foucault's writings as to what his alternative norms might be. I see no hints as to how concretely to interpret 'domination,' 'subjugation,' 'subjection,' etc., in some completely new 'post-liberal' fashion." Or worse, in Nietzschean bleakness: "Power is productive, ineliminable, and, therefore, normatively neutral."[431]

Axel Honneth, then a student of Jürgen Habermas,[§2.0a] was at the Praxis meeting in Dubrovnik. He would later be appointed a director of the Institute for Social Research, the famed Frankfurt School.[§MS0b] Fraser and Honneth were to become comradely protagonists, debating the tangle of antagonistic interests that is modernity.

Honneth's argument was that social theory and political practice in the twentieth century had become overly focused on economic inequalities, prioritizing the working class over other social classifications such as gender or

---

* http://meaningpatterns.net/fraser

431 Nancy Fraser, 1981, "Foucault on Modern Power: Empirical Insights and Normative Confusions," *Praxis International* 1(3):272–87, pp. 272, 283, 285.

ethnic identities, and class antagonisms over other social fault lines. In order to rectify the consequent omissions and blind spots, he proposed that any social analysis begin with "recognition" as an elemental form of intersubjective activity, an original empathy first learned by small children in their developmental phase.

On this measure, we can analyze and critique the subsequent objectification of others. "Misrecognition" in the form of sexism, says Honneth, turns women into objects. The misrecognition that is slavery turns bodies into objects according to race.[432] He pointed to the rise of a politics of recognition in the social movements of the late twentieth century. These ground their programs in "identity claims," including feminist, anti-racist, anti-colonialist, and a panoply of other agendas.[433]

Nancy Fraser, in response, argued that "[f]ar from comprehending the totality of moral life, recognition for me is one crucial but limited dimension of social justice." In a chapter for a book honoring the work of György Márkus,[§2.4.2b] she argued that recognition was not merely a matter of identity; it was also a matter of practically lived status, and the swing to identity politics in the late twentieth century had gone too far, to the neglect of economic injustices.[434]

So, Fraser proposed "two analytically distinct orders of subordination: class stratification, rooted primarily in economic system mechanisms, and status hierarchy, based largely in institutionalized patterns of cultural value ... Whereas class stratification corresponds to maldistribution, status hierarchy corresponds to misrecognition." Her conclusion, and her measure: "both orders of subordination violate a single overarching principle of justice, the principle of participatory parity."[435]

If Fraser retains misrecognition but adds back maldistribution, we want to suggest that there are three great fissures of inequality and social antagonism in our latest modernity: material conditions (social class, locale, and family); corporeal attributes (age, race, sex and sexuality, physical and mental abilities); and cultural forms (language, ethnos, and communities of commitment).[436]

---

[432] Axel Honneth, 2008, *Reification: A New Look at an Old Idea*, Oxford: Oxford University Press.

[433] Axel Honneth, 2003, "Redistribution as Recognition: A Reply to Nancy Fraser," pp. 110–97 in *Redistribution or Recognition? A Political-Philosophical Exchange*, edited by N. Fraser and A. Honneth, London: Verso.

[434] Nancy Fraser, 2002, "Integrating Redistribution and Recognition: On Class and Status in Contemporary Society," pp. 149–65 in *Culture and Enlightenment: Essays for György Márkus*, edited by J. Grumley, P. Crittenden, and P. Johnson, Aldershot: Ashgate.

[435] Nancy Fraser, 2003, "Distorted Beyond All Recognition: A Rejoinder to Axel Honneth," pp. 198–236 in *Redistribution or Recognition? A Political-Philosophical Exchange*, edited by N. Fraser and A. Honneth, London: Verso, p. 218; Nancy Fraser, 2008, "From Redistribution to Recognition? Dilemmas of Justice in a 'Postsocialist' Age," pp. 11–41 in *Adding Insult to Injury: Nancy Fraser Debates Her Critics*, edited by K. Olson, London: Verso; Nancy Fraser, 2009, "Feminism, Capitalism and the Cunning of History," *New Left Review* (56):97–117.

[436] Mary Kalantzis and Bill Cope, 2016b, "Learner Differences in Theory and Practice," *Open Review of Educational Research* 3(1):85–132; Mary Kalantzis and Bill Cope, 2012, *New*

As for our multimodal grammar, in modern times, every text, every image, every space, every embodied gesture, every verbal utterance, is riddled with these antagonisms. Every such meaning can be parsed for the differential interests of the parties to participation in meaning. And when we parse, we may want to act to achieve at least greater, or ideally balanced, parity of participation – in other words, to change.

§2.5.1b Banksy's "Dismaland"

Disneyland opened in Anaheim California on July 17, 1955.[*] The day began with Walt Disney driving his steam train into "Main Street" station. The Republican Governor of California and the President of the Santa Fe Railroad were with him in the cab of the locomotive. There to greet the train were Ronald Reagan and two other celebrities who covered the day on television, watched by an estimated audience of 70 million.[437]

"Here age relives fond memories of the past. And youth may savor the challenge and promise of the future. Disneyland is dedicated to the ideals, the dreams, and the hard facts that have created America," Disney said in the town square outside of the station.

"The happiest place on earth," promised the big sign on the highway; 3.6 million people visited Disneyland in its first year.[438]

"Fond memories of the past" – Main Street begins with the railroad station. The station and the buildings along the street recreate the imagined commercial heart of small town America, the little stores selling things to passers-by. Disney had grown up in Marcelene, Missouri, a town that had developed around the railroad station, and some of his family had been railroad workers. The "fond memories" were idealized from his own past.

"Promise of the future" – in 1959, Disney added a monorail to Disneyland, and Vice President Richard Nixon came to the ribbon cutting with his wife and daughters. Disney, said the Monorail's designer Bob Gurr, thought that the electric monorail was the solution to the urban problems created by the motor car, able to carry more people than cars, cleanly and quietly gliding through the city of the future.[439]

---

[*] http://meaningpatterns.net/disney

   Learning: Elements of a Science of Education (Edn 2), Cambridge: Cambridge University Press, Chapter 5.

[437] Neal Gabler, 2006, *Walt Disney: The Triumph of the American Imagination*, New York: Alfred A. Knopf, pp. 532–33.

[438] Ibid., p. 537.

[439] Christian Moran, 2015, *Great Big Beautiful Tomorrow: Walt Disney and Technology*, New York: Theme Park Press, pp. 90–93.

The railroad is part illusion, at 3 ft gauge scaled down to 5:8 of the standard gauge of 4 ft 8½ in. Its design was based on a model railroad Disney had built to run around his house.[440] The Disneyland station as well as the buildings on Main Street were figments of forced perspective, with the ground floors at 9:10 scale, the second floors 8:10 and the third 7:10.[441] At first, linear perspective had only been on a horizontal plane, but with the arrival of skyscraping modernity, artists came to apply the same principles to the vertical plane.[§MS2.2c] Now Disney was employing these principles to an architected recreation of the past.

Disneyland was an idealized spatial extension of the innovations Disney had created two-dimensionally of the cinematic image. Of Disney's animated films, Walter Benjamin[§MS0b] said, "So the explanation for the huge popularity of these films . . . is simply the fact that the public recognizes its own life in them." But then also, "These films disavow experience more radically than ever before." And enigmatically, "In these films, mankind makes preparations to survive civilization."[442]

Benjamin revered pioneering Russian film maker Sergei Eisenstein,[§MS1.1.3f] and Eisenstein also revered Disney, whose methods he called "animism," or "the momentary endowment of life and soul of an inanimate object, . . . for example, when we bump into a chair and swear at it as if it were a living thing, or the prolonged endowment with life that primitive man confers upon inanimate nature."[443]

So too in Disneyland, where on Main Street, the animism is undergirded by the idea of capitalist community. Disney parses the historical main street, then redesigns it. This transformation happens not just by special visual effects. It also replicates fundamental patterns of differential interest while fudging them in the redesign.

For all its meticulously stylized historical references, Disney's Main Street is not true. There are none of the ordinary things that would have been the objects of use and exchange on the main street of Disney's childhood; all that the shops sell on Disneyland's Main Street are sugary foods, trademarked trinkets, and Mickey Mouse ears.

Not true also was the ideal of the small shopkeeper. Disney, always going broke, and always working his way out of trouble by clever innovation, lit upon

---

[440] Steve DeGaetano, 2015, *The Disneyland Railroad: A Complete History in Words and Pictures,* New York: Theme Park Press, p. 11.

[441] Neal Gabler, 2006, *Walt Disney: The Triumph of the American Imagination,* New York: Alfred A. Knopf, p. 533.

[442] Walter Benjamin, 1999a, *Selected Writings,* Volume 2: *1927–1934,* translated by R. Livingstone, Cambridge, MA: Harvard University Press, p. 535.

[443] Oksana Bulgakowa, 2010, "Disney as a Utopian Dreamer," pp. 116–25 in *Animism,* edited by A. Franke, Berlin: Sternberg Press, p. 119; Sergei Eisenstein, 1986, *On Disney,* London: Seagull Books.

the idea of corporate sponsorship. The Atchison, Topeka and Santa Fe Railway sponsored the railroad, and for that, it was officially branded the Santa Fe & Disneyland Railroad.[444] Coca Cola, improbably, had its own store on Main Street. It was as if corporate America could retrospectively colonize main street in order to spin its own genesis myth.

Far from the idealized small businesses of the historical main street, the workers in every store were wage workers for a single corporation – Disney. There was nothing of the market in this Main Street, and the control of the corporation was feudal in its proportions. The overwrought niceness of the "cast" was tutored at the "Disney University." Alert to the slightest disturbance, the street was subject to the rigorous order of private security police. Its excessive cleanliness was maintained by a vigilant cast, costumed as period street cleaners. Dirt and social antagonism were edited out of the retrospective narrative, and so were class and race – the Congress for Racial Equality in 1963 called out Disney for its dearth of Black employees.[445]

As for capitalist community, guests (not citizens) found themselves wandering down Main Street, passing anonymous strangers they'd never seen before and never would again. This was a far cry from the imagined community of small town shopkeepers who might have known their customers and where passers-by in the street might have known each other. On the street, solidary interests extended little beyond the nuclear family. If Main Street was untrue to the past, it was in certain senses true to the configuration of alienated interests in the present.

Though in certain respects, Main Street was untrue to its present as well. In the fifties and sixties, suburban malls and big box stores were destroying main streets. In any event, Disneyland's Main Street was more like a mall than a street, with its rigorously controlled, tightly planned structures – so in this way, in another moment of untruth Main Street paradoxically becomes true again. Just like Victor Gruen,[§2.3c] Disney quarantined his meticulously designed utopia from the enormous, ugly parking lots that surrounded them. There is walking and there are trains, new and old, to get around Disneyland, but car ugliness is excluded, a forbidden reality.

Disney, the great parser of capitalism's past and future, told fibs to reach some of its inner truths. Richard Nixon acknowledged the depth of his feeling for Disney, and his genius, with a commemorative medal. "I once asked Walt Disney how I should describe him when we went out and dedicated the monorail at Disneyland. He said that he was an 'imagineer,' which means he was an engineer with imagination."[446]

[444] Neal Gabler, 2006, *Walt Disney: The Triumph of the American Imagination*, New York: Alfred A. Knopf, p. 527.
[445] Ibid., pp. 528–29; Marc Eliot, 1993, *Walt Disney: Hollywood's Dark Prince*, New York: Birch Lane Press.
[446] www.presidency.ucsb.edu/ws/index.php?pid=1973

Disney got some things wrong – there was to be no cleanly, sleekly, mono-railed future. And on November 17, 1973, Richard Nixon was in the auditorium of Disney World's futuristic Contemporary Resort Hotel, through which a monorail whisked visitors to attractions, when he gave his famous "I'm not a crook" speech.

Then, in August–September 2015, another theme park, this time parsing Disney's parsing of the world: an art installation by the street artist Banksy, created in the ruins of the abandoned Tropicana – once the largest outdoor swimming pool in Europe – in the seaside town of Weston-super-Mare, Somerset, England.

"Dismaland" was billed as a "bemusement park," with works by Banksy and fifty-eight other artists, a "family theme park unsuitable for children." "The UK's most disappointing new visitor attraction!" said the brochure.

Are you looking for an alternative to the soulless sugar-coated banality of the average family day out? Or just somewhere cheaper. Then this is the place for you – a chaotic new world where you can escape from mindless escapism . . . A theme park whose big theme is: theme parks should have bigger themes.[447]

Six million people crashed the park's website in their effort to get tickets, and 200,000 visited in the thirty-six days it was open.[448]

Dismaland revealed things about modernity that had been wantonly edited out of Disneyland. Visitors entered through a fake screening area, with morose guards and a long list of forbidden things in red-crossed warning signs. Inside: a "hook-a-duck-from the muck" sideshow; a merry-go-round from "occupy the reality studios" ridden by a mannequin with a gas mask; a police truck sinking in the lake: a refugee boat crossing the moat in front of a ruined Cinderella's castle; a bevy of paparazzi photographing the crash of Cinderella's pumpkin coach; glum security guards selling black balloons emblazoned "I am an imbecile."

"The shittest, most depressing theme park in the world," one critic dubbed it. Or perhaps also a "gross send-up of Weston-super-Mare, . . . cruel mockery, art as clickbait."[449]

Alongside Satoshi Nakamoto,[§2.4.1b] Banksy is another of late modernity's famously missing people.[450] Perhaps a woman? Perhaps a collective? So commentators have mused.[451] Some geospatial researchers found a numerical

---

[447] www.thisiscolossal.com/2015/08/dismaland/

[448] www.dazeddigital.com/artsandculture/article/26020/1/welcome-to-banksy-s-dismaland

[449] www.dazeddigital.com/art-photography/article/41049/1/three-years-legacy-of-banksy-dismaland-weston-super-mare-england-tropicana

[450] Will Ellsworth-Jones, 2012, *Banksy: The Man Behind the Wall*, New York: St Martin's Press; Robert Clarke, 2012, *Seven Years with Banksy*, London: Michael O'Mara Books.

[451] www.citylab.com/design/2014/11/why-banksy-is-probably-a-woman/382202/

answer that added up for them, publishing their results without hint of irony in the *Journal of Spatial Science.*

Here, we use a Dirichlet process mixture (DPM) model of geographic profiling, a mathematical technique developed in criminology ... to analyse the spatial patterns of Banksy artworks in Bristol and London ... Our analysis highlights areas associated with one prominent candidate (e.g., his home), supporting his identification as Banksy. More broadly, these results support previous suggestions that analysis of minor terrorism-related acts (e.g., graffiti) could be used to help locate terrorist bases before more serious incidents occur.[452]

Meanwhile, the Disney Corporation's income in 2014 was \$48.8 billion, making it larger than the economies of two-thirds of the world's countries.[453] And in Disney World, guests wearing MagicBands – rubber wristbands with RFID chips[§MS1.1.1g] – use them to schedule their rides and pre-order food. At all times their movement is tracked, so channeling the obsessively controlling corporate spirit of Walt Disney, but on a scale not even he could have imagined.

"Welcome Mr/s (Your Name)," the host says as you cross the drawbridge into Cinderella's castle, to eat a meal that knows the name of its consumer even before you arrive.[454]

§2.5.2   To Change

> **To Change.** *To transform not only by recognition of meanings (to parse) but in material media and tangible experience. Change comes in several intensities: replication, where conventions are repeated notwithstanding the inevitably unique reconfigurations of (re)design; the "hack" or incremental change; and paradigmatic or revolutionary change.*

Parsing is a kind of revelation, an unconcealment of meaning. Changing is the doing that may or may not come with the revelation.

But there is changing and changing. One paradoxical kind of change is the change that leaves things the same in their abstract meaning, new by instance but the same by concept. This is replication by design. Or perhaps at times this is a kind of undesign, to the extent that agents are unaware of the designs. This is how, often unbeknown to themselves, meaning-makers become complicit, perhaps by way of fatalism or seemingly insurmountable common sense.

---

[452] Michelle V. Hauge, Mark D. Stevenson, D. Kim Rossmo, and Steven C. Le Comber, 2016, "Tagging Banksy: Using Geographic Profiling to Investigate a Modern Art Mystery," *Journal of Spatial Science* 61(1):185–90.

[453] https://medium.com/matter/burning-down-the-mouse-7113c261a8a5

[454] www.wired.com/2015/03/disney-magicband/

Then there is incremental change, things that are different by small degrees. A concept may evolve. A material practice may be improved, or it may deteriorate. A "hack" may indicate a slight shift in a wider frame of reference.

Finally there is paradigmatic change, fundamental change in the order of things, be this change in conceptual frameworks or change in the material relations of people in nature. Change of this order includes those wrought by the arrival of unequal societies in some parts of the world as long as several thousand years ago, and upon some First Peoples only recently. Change again, and of this order, is possible still. If we have been so different in our other human natures, we can be different again.

Here are some examples, working across Nancy Fraser's recognition/redistribution distinction:[§2.5.1a]

Function: To Parse / Function: To Change	Recognition (for example, gender)	Redistribution (for example, differential interests in the market)
Replication	To be as one is already, conventionally, and as seen to be	Buying and selling things
Incremental change	Gender edginess, revising the self	Theft, generosity, sharing, co-operative work
Paradigmatic change	Gender transitioning, becoming another self	Changing social relations of inequality and destructive relations in nature

Fig. 2.5.2: To change

These aspects of transformation are never straightforward, the one function ever begging the other. Parsing may prompt change. Replications can become hacks. Hacks can turn into paradigmatic or revolutionary change.

Now that we have nearly reached the end of these two volumes, perhaps it is time to ask ourselves, what is the nature of the change we have made in our little world of multimodal grammar? We hope it has been more than to replicate well-worn ideas, though in frequent moments of self-doubt we have wondered. If this is to be a change that is wider than replication, we might plead the following.

First, we have created a generalized grammar that works across all forms of meaning.

Underlying our proposal is a claim that it is possible to mean the same things across the forms of text, image, space, object, body, sound, and speech. These same things we may identify as reference, agency, structure, context, and interest. However, the same things meant in one form then another are never quite the same, as the particular shape of different forms of meaning is determined by the material affordances of their media, their openings to and contraints upon meaning. Forms do not mean in the same way, and as a consequence meanings that would be the same come out slightly differently.

This is why we have multimodality – to supplement one form of meaning with another and to extend or deepen meaning even when this is at the cost of some amount of redundancy. The multimodality that unfolds is not just in the juxtaposition of forms. It is in the across-ness, the between-ness, and the ever-readiness for reiteration in a different form. The meanings are in the urgencies, insistences, and necessities of transposition across forms.

Second, after the "language turn" of the twentieth century (Analytical Philosophy, poststructuralism, and all that), we advocate an "ontological turn" for the twenty-first.

Here our claim is at once philosophical and technological. Philosophically, ontology is the living of our meanings materially manifest in media: text, image, space, object, body, sound, and speech. Technologically, the power of digital media and artificial intelligence is more in the ontologies or meaning schemas that drive them than the relatively trivial elementary algorithmic calculations of mechanical reason.

Having made our ontological turn, we conclude that "language" has become an unhelpful category, so unhelpful in fact that we have suggested we should abandon it. This is because, as we have tried to argue, text and speech are so radically different. The transpositions between them are no less in their distance than any of the other form-form transpositions we have analyzed in this grammar. If anything, text is more closely aligned with image and space, and speech is more closely aligned with sound and body – hence the way we have arrayed these forms across the metaphorical shelf in our "supermarket" of meanings.

Today, the separation of digital text from speech is becoming greater than ever, in part because so much text has become practically unspeakable. Many meanings are impossible to recall in spontaneous conversation without the digital devices that have become necessary extensions of our minds, our cognitive prostheses. This is paradoxically despite (but perhaps also because of) the ease with which both text and speech can be recorded and rendered on the same devices.

Third, we have described the dynamics of what we have called functional transposition.

One aspect of this is a function of our attentions. All of reference, agency, structure, context, and interest are present in every meaning, in every form and any combination of forms. So at this macro level, transposition is a change of focus, a question of whether we are parsing a meaning by one function or another.

Then, within each function there is incessant movement and impatient expectation of movement. Instances can be re-meant as concepts. Others can by empathy be re-meant as selves. Entities can be re-meant as actions. Possibilities can be re-meant as assertions. Representations can be re-meant as communication. Rhetorically expressed interests can be re-meant in reification, and a myriad of other such imminent functional transpositions.

Structuralisms of the ilk of Saussure's or Chomsky's attempt to classify each meaning-function as a thing, and arrange them into a system of repetitions. Poststructuralisms of the Derridean kind find in the same world of speech and text unrepeatable differences and constant change.

Beyond structuralism and poststructuralism, we make the case that the meaning of the elements of the system is in their dynamic tensions, their tortured torsions. The meaning of a function is in its readiness to change, the impending possibility of it becoming something different. It is a false hope to stabilize elements because their meaning is as much as anything in their uneasy urge towards transposition into something else. Then, by design, meanings show traces of repetition as a result of their provenance in available resources for meaning; while they have also always been uniquely (re)designed at least to some degree.

This interminable complexity does not mean we should give up on finding patterns. The meaning is in the vectors of transposability of elements in the system, not their momentary conceptual freezing as elements. It is always possible to account for the unique bending of meaning in a design, as well as its provenance in conventionalities. So, beyond poststructuralism, there is method in the otherwise maddening instability, and this is the pattern in the vectors of movability. Among the endless possibilities, some functional transpositions are more impatient to happen than others.

Fourth, we have reframed one of the great tensions in modern Western philosophy – between antinomies that are loosely called materialism and idealism. In this struggle, Locke and Skinner prioritize the material, while Descartes, Kant, and Chomsky prioritize the ideal. Though of course, in moments of reasonableness, all parties to the discussion invoke the other side of the antinomy.

We have also found refractions of this struggle in the lives and thinking of First Peoples, as well as Arabic and Indian philosophies of meaning. We could have searched other places and times as well, but we hope these perspectives have been enough to make our case.

Our reframing is this: that there is no possibility of meaning-in the material without there also being the possibility of meaning-of the ideal, though at times the material can exceed the ideal (the discoverable) and the ideal can exceed the material (the imaginable). This is perhaps the most fundamental of all transpositions in a grammar of multimodality. Now, ontology can replace metaphysics.

These then are our suggestions for changes in the paradigm of the meaning of meaning. Whether these amount to replication, a hack or a paradigm change – that is up to you, dear reader, to decide.

§2.5.2a   The Tech Model Railroad Club at MIT and the "Hack"

In the jargon of railway modeling, to "hack" is to take a commercially produced model – of a particular class of locomotive on a particular line, for instance – and to make changes to its design and livery so that the model represents another class or line, not commercially available as a model. The commodity is the starting point, and the modification is the hack.[*]

Just down the way from Chomsky's office at Massachusetts Institute of Technology was the Tech Model Railroad Club or TMRC. This was where the word "hack" jumped from model railways to computers. Founded in 1946, by the late 1950s the club members had built an enormous and complex 1:87 scale model.

Over time, the membership bifurcated into two complementary factions, differential interests if you like. One was emotionally connected to the historical aesthetic of the railroad. This group worked above the baseboard, hacking rolling stock and making scenery. The other group, the Signals and Power Subcommittee, worked in the tangle of wires and relays under the baseboard. The Subcommittee's elaborate ARRC, Automated Railroad Running Computer, "The System" for short, was at first made from telephone system components, later computer parts.[455]

Just as Disney's Railroad and Monorail[§2.5.1b] spoke moral agendas to the world, the TMRC railroad also spoke in anticipatory transposition. There was a real world visible to viewers, faithfully represented in historical detail, and below there was an abstract world of electronic control – The System literally and metaphorically underneath the baseboard.

The process of The System's evolution was via a series of innovations called "hacks." The Signals and Power people called themselves "hackers."

HACK: . . . an unconventional or unorthodox application of technology.

HACKER: one who hacks, or makes them. A hacker avoids the standard solution. The hack is the basic concept; the hacker is defined in terms of it.[456]

Signals and Power Subcommittee member Peter Samson documented the proliferating acronyms and invented jargon in 1959 in the TMRC Dictionary, including this definition of "hack."

Here is Walter Benjamin[§MS0b] on model trains: "the adult, who finds himself threatened by the real world and can find no escape, removes its sting by

---

[*]   http://meaningpatterns.net/hack

[455]   Steven Levy, 1984 [1994], *Hackers: Heroes of the Computer Revolution*, London: Penguin, pp. 17–25; Joseph Onorato and Mark Schupack, 2002, *Tech Model Railroad Club of MIT: The First Fifty Years*, Cambridge, MA: TRMC, pp. 42–47, 66–68.

[456]   www.gricer.com/tmrc/tmrc-dictionary-intro.html

playing with the image in reduced form." The modeler reverts to the inventiveness of childhood. "[T]he most enduring modifications in toys are never the work of adults ... but are the results of children at play." The process: "Children's play is everywhere permeated by mimetic modes of behavior." But this is not just copying: "Here it is not enough to think of what we understand today by the concept of similarity, ... [of] microcosm and macrocosm." Rather, we encounter "mimetic powers ... residues of the magical correspondences and analogies that were familiar to ancient peoples."[457]

Or, in the terms we have been developing for this grammar, the transposition of meaning across scale is an act of design and thus transformation, where the lessons learned at one scale are transferred to another, though the meaning is never quite the same. And insights gained at one scale find their way back into the other. This repurposing and reimagining, this animism of mutual transformation of connected objects, we might call a "hack."

By 1984, hacking had become a computer ethic, inspired by the title of Steven Levy's book *Hackers*, whose narrative starts with the TMRC.[458] The first Hackers Conference was held in that year, organized by Stuart Brand, founder of the Whole Earth Catalog. Famously, at the conference he coined the expression, "information wants to be free," though the full quote captures the tension and complexity of hacking – more than mere replication, but hardly revolutionary transformation.

On the one hand information wants to be expensive, because it's so valuable ... On the other hand, information wants to be free, because the cost of getting it out is getting lower and lower all the time. So you have these two fighting against each other.[459]

To which, Apple co-founder Steve Wozniak replied, "Information should be free but your time should not."[460]

The work of hackers has ranged from just-for-the-fun-of-it to the clandestine and illegal, striking at the heart of the global system of digital media. At the illegal end of the spectrum are leakers and whistleblowers like Chelsea Manning and Edward Snowden, copyright avoidance systems such as BitTorrent and Pirate Bay, and "hactivist" groups such as Anonymous. Tactics include computer break-ins, website defacement, and Distributed Denial of Service attacks that shut down websites.[461]

---

[457] Walter Benjamin, 2003, *Selected Writings,* Volume 4: *1938–1940,* Cambridge, MA: Harvard University Press, pp. 100–01, 720–21.
[458] Steven Levy, 1984 [1994], *Hackers: Heroes of the Computer Revolution,* London: Penguin.
[459] Stewart Brand, 1987, *The Media Lab: Inventing the Future at MIT,* New York: Viking.
[460] https://medium.com/backchannel/the-definitive-story-of-information-wants-to-be-free-a8d95427641c#.y7d0amvr3
[461] Gabriella Coleman, 2017, "From Internet Farming to Weapons of the Geek," *Current Anthropology* 58(Supplement 15):S91–101; Gabriella Coleman, 2014, *Hacker, Hoaxer, Whistleblower, Spy: The Many Faces of Anonymous,* London: Verso; Harry Halpin, 2012,

When he was arrested in 1986, a hacker known by the pseudonym The Mentor wrote the now-famous *Hacker Manifesto:*

This is our world now ... the world of the electron and the switch, the beauty of the baud. We make use of a service already existing without paying for what could be dirt-cheap if it wasn't run by profiteering gluttons, and you call us criminals. We explore ... and you call us criminals. We seek after knowledge ... and you call us criminals ... You build atomic bombs, you wage wars, you murder, cheat, and lie to us and try to make us believe it's for our own good, yet we're the criminals ...

Yes, I am a criminal. My crime is that of curiosity ... My crime is that of outsmarting you ...

I am a hacker, and this is my manifesto. You may stop this individual, but you can't stop us all.[462]

The practice of the hack also found its way into the heart of the system. At MIT, computer scientist and self-professed hacker Richard Stallman was incensed that key software code created in the university was being enclosed by copyright restrictions and finding its way into corporate hands as marketable private intellectual property. In response, he resigned his job, remaining at MIT as unpaid visiting scientist to create the free GNU operating system.[463]

Stallman's system came with another hacker's manifesto, the GNU Manifesto:

Many programmers are unhappy about the commercialization of system software. It may enable them to make more money, but it requires them to feel in conflict with other programmers in general rather than feel as comrades. The fundamental act of friendship among programmers is the sharing of programs; marketing arrangements now typically used essentially forbid programmers to treat others as friends ... Once GNU is written, everyone will be able to obtain good system software free, just like air.[464]

Solidary interests in the writing and sharing of code could not, however, be left to goodwill – they would have to be enforced via the GNU General Public License that locks derivative software designs into communal ownership. Stallman was quick to say that people should not be paid for the products of their labor, but they could still be paid for the labor itself. "Don't think free as in beer; think free as in speech."[465]

Linus Torvalds followed with the Linux operating system. Less politically motivated, the "open source" software movement that it spawned was driven

"The Philosophy of Anonymous: Ontological Politics without Identity," *Radical Philosophy* 176(November/December):19–28.

[462] www.phrack.org/issues/7/3.html

[463] Richard Stallman, 2002, *Free Software, Free Society*, Boston, MA: GNU Press; Richard Stallman, 2018, "Talking to the Mailman: Interview with Rob Lucas," *New Left Review* (113):69–93.

[464] www.gnu.org/gnu/manifesto.html

[465] Sam Williams, 2002, *Free as in Freedom: Richard Stallman's Crusade for Free Software*, Sebastapol, CA: O'Reilly.

by the idea that open collaboration is a better way to build better software than closed and proprietary systems.[466]

Then for intellectual and cultural work generally came the Creative Commons licenses, and the promise of new, post-capitalist social relations. Here is Laurence Lessig, leading legal light behind the cc licenses: "If communism versus capitalism was the struggle of the twentieth century, then control versus freedom will be the debate of the twenty-first century."[467]

In his play on Adam Smith's *Wealth of Nations*,[§2.3.2a] Yochai Benkler spoke to the new "wealth of networks" and "the rise of effective, large-scale cooperative efforts – peer production of information, knowledge and culture; ... new and important cooperative and coordinate action carried out through radically distributed, nonmarket mechanisms."[468]

And McKenzie Wark in the *Hacker Manifesto:* "In liberating information from its objectification as a commodity, it liberates also the subjective force of statement ... Expressive politics ... seeks to permeate existing states with a new state of existence, spreading the seeds of an alternative practice of everyday life."[469]

However, the irony of the free software, open source, and creative commons licenses is that the public law of copyright, in which the right to intellectual property rights is by default private, is overwritten by individual copyright contracts and requiring that individuals cede their rights to the collective one contract at a time. This is just one of their many cascading contradictions.[470]

Some of the richest companies in the world today use open source software for their private profit – Google's search engine[§1.4.7e] was written in Linux, and the derivative Android operating system is open source, as by dint of contract it must be.

Open source software and free culture is a hack on capitalism, an incremental change and no more, because in their essentials the system of commodities and labor, and the authoritarian feudalism of the corporation, remain unchanged.

---

[466] Gabriella Coleman, 2013, *Coding Freedom: The Ethics and Aesthetics of Hacking*, Princeton, NJ: Princeton University Press, pp. 74–78; Johan Soderberg, 2008, *Hacking Capitalism: The Free and Open Source Software Movement*, London: Routledge.

[467] Lawrence Lessig, 2002, "The Architecture of Innovation," *Duke Law Journal* 51(6):1783–802, p. 1785; Lawrence Lessig, 2001, *The Future of Ideas: The Fate of the Commons in a Connected World*, New York: Random House; Lawrence Lessig, 2004, *Free Culture*, New York: Penguin Press; Lawrence Lessig, 2008, *Remix: Making Art and Commerce Thrive in the Hybrid Economy*, New York: Penguin Press.

[468] Yochai Benkler, 2006, *The Wealth of Networks: How Social Production Transforms Markets and Freedom*, New Haven, CT: Yale University Press, pp. 5, 3.

[469] McKenzie Wark, 2004, *A Hacker Manifesto*, Cambridge, MA: Harvard University Press, §257.

[470] Phillip Kalantzis-Cope, 2016b, "Geopolitical Structuring in the Age of Information: Imagining Order, Understanding Change," *Alternatives: Global, Local, Political* 41(4):179–93; Phillip Kalantzis-Cope, 2017, *The Work and Play of the Mind in the Information Age: Whose Property?*, Cham, Switzerland: Palgrave/Springer.

Or, in Gabriella Coleman's nice formulation, hacks turn out to be mere "micro-gestures within broader, deterministic forces."[471]

Software genius Robert Mercer[§2.2.1a] was never a hacker. In railroad modeling, he was only ever a member of the faithful-to-historical-reality, above-the-baseboard, commercial-rolling-stock-and-scenery faction. His vision was realized in a meticulously accurate 1:87 scale model of an idealized capitalist past when the New York Central Railroad dominated the spaces and flows of the US northeast. When it comes to transformations, Mercer is a replication man.

And even then, Mercer is the kind of person who would rather pay others to realize his vision than replicate for himself. When RailDreams Custom Model Railroad Design billed him $2,694,833 for the model railroad it had constructed in the basement of his Long Island, NY mansion, he took them to court, arguing unsuccessfully that the bill should have been no more than $704,669.[472] "He is a hedge fund guy, part of the reason why the country is in the situation it's in," said RailDreams' president, Richard Taylor.[473]

§2.5.2b Raymattja Marika-Mununggiritj's "Yolngu Metaphors for Learning"

Raymattja Marika – the name we knew her by – has now been gone from this earth long enough for us to be able to speak her name once more.[*] She died in 2008. We got to know Raymattja during our research visits to Yirrkala, land of the Yolŋu peoples in remote North East Arnhemland, Australia. There, she made our presence comprehensible by assigning us tribal names.

Four words, Raymattja said, the elders use to speak about learning. First, _dhin'thun_, "identifying the tracks of animals and following the tracks to find the animal. As we learn, we learn to recognize what we see in the environment." This speaks to investigation, history, and deliberative decision-making. Then _lundu-nhäma_, "to see," "footsteps or gait," to journey and to see patterns in the journeying. Next _dhudakthun_, where past meets present, "more than just copying what the ancestors have done." Rather, it is "the effect of bringing our spiritual past to life again through our modern behavior . . . putting us 'in tune with' our spiritual past, shaping us like our ancestors." And finally _galtha_, "a connecting spot," which might be a place, a sacred ceremony, people coming

---

* http://meaningpatterns.net/marika

[471] Gabriella Coleman, 2017, "From Internet Farming to Weapons of the Geek," _Current Anthropology_ 58(Supplement 15):S91–101.

[472] www.courtlistener.com/opinion/2342560/mercer-v-raildreams-inc/

[473] www.nydailynews.com/news/hedge-fund-hotshot-robert-mercer-files-lawsuit-2m-model-train-accusing-builder-overcharge-article-1.368624

together for the preparation of bread from cycad nuts, or sitting on the ground to negotiate collective purpose.

Galtha is the name the elders gave the Aboriginal curriculum in the community school. *Galtha* is the possibility of people acting properly. "*Galtha* is everywhere."[474]

Michael Christie was a school teacher in Yolŋu country who became a long-time co-worker with Raymattja Marika. Later he was to become a professor in The Northern Institute at Charles Darwin University, where Raymattja was awarded an honorary doctorate. Christie compares *galtha* to modern thinking in the following terms. Instead of atomizing things and persons into neatly separated discontinuities as is our wont in modern thinking, fixing and counting these as components into structures of meaning, *galtha* establishes deeply interconnected, fluid and negotiable meanings.

And instead of separating the subjects and objects of history and living experience, *galtha* is the embedded truth of a unified subject-object, the material-ideal. "The objective world attains reality only through the received meanings through which, in negotiation, we choose to foreground the pattern of our relatedness." Then, "freedom is no more nor less than the freedom to explore one's environment, regulate one's own behaviour and to negotiate with all others the construction of one's self, and one's individually distinctive and creative vantage point in the web of negotiated meaning."[475]

Trying to make sense of Yolŋu ontology, anthropologist Ian Keen came to realize that the intricate structures of Aboriginal meaning confounded the categories that he, as an anthropologist, had been trained to use. "Concepts such as lineage, clan, descent group, and corporate group depend on images of segmentary structure, external boundaries, and taxonomic hierarchy. These constructs go hand in hand with concepts of land and country, which also entail spatial metaphors of enclosure and boundaries which imply hierarchies of small bounded places contained in larger ones of a different type." He concludes, "none of these tropes fit Yolŋu modes of 'group' identity and relations."[476]

Galtha describes a layered connectedness that defies neatly bounded spatiality. It denies the possibility of signifiers that speak with persistence to their signifieds. Instead, says Keen, in Yolŋu language "[t]erms for two similar body parts, the elbow (*likan*) and knee (*bon*), connote connections among ancestors,

---

[474] Raymattja Marika-Mununggiritj and Michael J. Christie, 1995, "Yolngu Metaphors for Learning," *International Journal of the Sociology of Language* 113(1):59–62.

[475] Michael J. Christie, 1994, "Grounded and Ex-Centric Knowledges: Exploring Aboriginal Alternatives to Western Thinking," pp. 24–34 in *Thinking: International Interdisciplinary Perspectives*, edited by J. Edwards, Highlett, Australia: Hawker Brownlow Education, pp. 32–33.

[476] Ian Keen, 1995, "Metaphor and the Metalanguage: 'Groups' in Northeast Arnhem Land," *American Ethnologist* 22(3):502–27, p. 502.

persons, places, and ceremonies."[477] *Galtha* is a point of negotiation, and no two points of negotiation are the same.[478]

Keen and Christie say that the differences between Aboriginal and Western ontologies can be traced to the metaphors they use. But we want to use the word "transposition," because we think metaphor is too associated with language and the idea of similarity.[§1.4.4a] In Yolŋu epistemology, transposed meanings are not similar to each other; they are each other in their manifest identity and difference. A person is a totem, is a sacred object, is a place is an animal or plant is an ancestor, is another same-named and kin-located person. "Is" means immanent; immanent bodes imminent.

The connection is not the word, but the meaning. By transposition, meanings take quantum leaps[§1.4.4b] that are at once the self-same meaning, and for the transposition, an always-new meaning. The designs of meaning are in their redesigning. Meaning always and necessarily requires the recreation of the world. When a Yolŋu person dies, the world does not only have to be renamed. It has to be changed.

On one of our visits to Yirrkala, we'd brought Courtney Cazden,[§1.4.1c] researching indigenous literacy and bilingual education in the community school, and the learning resources that had been created in the Bilingual Literature Production Centre.

A funeral was happening at the time. All day and most of the night for several weeks, the relentless beat of clap sticks and the singing of Yolŋu voices threaded apprehension through the tropical air. The funeral was happening in *galtha*, an open air ceremony ground, a meeting place of tribal groups, of past and present, of life and death.

For the cover of this book, we have used an image created by Yolŋu artist Rerrkirrwaŋa Mununɡurr.[479] The center of the image is the ceremonial ground used for funerals, a time and place where people meet to make sense of life and death. The crosshatching encloses what would be, without it, a barely comprehensible black space. The ceremonial space is within the image, but also ambiguously it is constituted as such by its frame. The crosshatching marks an outside as well. It is there to add sense to the black. Among its many references: the shimmering surfaces of the freshwater lagoons that surround the ceremonial site, providing food and life. Across this threshold, the deceased soul returns to the sacred waters. And less abstractly, the spears with which fish are caught, and in the crosshatching, the patterns of the fish nets. Then more

---

[477] Ibid., p. 511.

[478] Raymattja Marika, Daynawa Ngurruwutthun, and Leon White, 1990, *Always Together, Yaka Gana: Participatory Research at Yirrkala as Part of the Development of a Yolgnu Education*, Yirrkala, Australia: Yirrkala Literature Production Centre, p. 17.

[479] Elina Spilia, 2007, "Shark People: Djapu Painting and the Miny'tji Buku Larrŋgay Collection," *Art Bulletin of Victoria* (47):7–16.

abstractly, meanings where a person is a place is a sacred totem, and where a place is a song is a ceremonial dance and now also a bark painting.

The day after the funeral, the Yirrkala band Yothu Yindi flew to Darwin, capital of the Northern Territory. As it happens, so did we. Yothu Yindi was going to Darwin to play at the Darwin Showgrounds, the same singers who had participated with their kin in the funeral, and we joined them there. The band's lead singer was the school principal, Mandawuy Yunupingu, and the band's members were his former students. For nearly a decade, the Yothu Yindi had traveled the globe, a dazzling exemplar of "world music."

Introducing the song "Tribal Voice," Yunupingu says, "The thing that we always believe, as Aboriginal People, Indigenous People of Australia, is that ... we don't own mother earth, the earth owns us." Another transposition.

> All the people in the world are dreaming (get up, stand up)
> Some of us cry for the rights of survival now (get up, stand up)
> Say c'mon c'mon, stand up for your rights
> While others don't give a damn
> They are all waiting for a perfect day
> You better get up and fight for your rights
> Don't be afraid of the move that you make

References

Adorno, Theodor W. 1949 [2006]. *Philosophy of New Music*. Translated by R. Hullot-Kentor. Minneapolis, MN: University of Minnesota Press.

Adorno, Theodor W. 2002. *Essays on Music*. Translated by S.H. Gillespie. Berkeley, CA: University of California Press.

Adorno, Theodor W. and Max Horkheimer. 1944 [2002]. *Dialectic of Enlightenment*. Translated by E. Jephcott. Stanford, CA: Stanford University Press.

Agamben, Giorgio. 2011 [2013]. *The Highest Poverty: Monastic Rules and Form-of-Life*. Translated by A. Kotsko. Stanford, CA: Stanford University Press.

Aiken, Mary. 2016. *The Cyber Effect*. New York, NY: Speigel & Crau.

Akerlof, George A. 1970. "The Market for 'Lemons': Quality Uncertainty and the Market Mechanism." *The Quarterly Journal of Economics* 84(3):488–500.

Akerlof, George A. and Paul M. Romer. 1993. "Looting: The Economic Underworld of Bankruptcy for Profit." *Brookings Papers on Economic Activity* (2):1–73. doi:10.2307/2534564.

Akerlof, George A. and Robert J. Schiller. 2015. *Phishing for Phools: The Economics of Manipulation and Deception*. Princeton, NJ: Princeton University Press.

Alberro, Alexander, Martha Gever, Miwon Kwon and Carol Squiers, eds. 2010. *Barbara Kruger*. New York, NY: Rizzoli.

Alexander, Christopher. 1979. *The Timeless Way of Building*. New York, NY: Oxford University Press.

Alexander, Christopher, Sara Ishikawa, and Murray Silverstein. 1977. *A Pattern Language: Towns, Buildings, Construction*. New York, NY: Oxford University Press.

Allen, Jonathan, M. Sharon Hunnicutt and Dennis Klatt. 1987. *From Text to Speech: The Mitalk System*. Cambridge, UK: Cambridge University Press.

Althusser, Louis, Etienne Balibar, Roger Establet, Pierre Macherey, and Jacques Rancière. 1965 [2016]. *Reading Capital: The Complete Edition*. Translated by B. Brewster and D. Fernbach. London, UK: Verso.

Anderson, Perry. 1974a. *Passages from Antiquity to Feudalism*. London, UK: New Left Books.

Anderson, Perry. 1974b. *Lineages of the Absolutist State*. London, UK: New Left Books.

Andreev, N.D. 1967. "The Intermediary Language and the Focal Point of Machine Translation," pp. 1–27 in *Machine Translation*, edited by A.D. Booth. Amsterdam, NL: North-Holland Publishing.

Arnold, Arthur Z. 1937. *Banks, Credit, and Money in Soviet Russia*. New York, NY: Columbia University Press.

Aurnague, Michel, Maya Hickmann and Laure Vieu, eds. 2007. *The Categorization of Spatial Entities in Language and Cognition.* Amsterdam, NL: John Benjamins.

Automatic Language Processing Advisory Committee. 1966. "Language and Machines: Computers in Translation and Linguistics." Washington, DC: National Research Council.

Awdry, The Rev. W. 1946 [2015]. *Thomas the Tank Engine.* London, UK: Egmont.

Ayer, A.J., ed. 1959. *Logical Positivism.* Glencoe, IL: The Free Press.

Ayer, Alfred J., Noam Chomsky et al. 1975. "Letter to Tito." *New York Review of Books,* February 6.

Baker, G.P. and P.M.S. Hacker. 1984. *Language, Sense and Nonsense: A Critical Investigation of Modern Theories of Language.* Oxford, UK: Basil Blackwell.

Bakhtin, M.M. 1919–24 [1990]. *Art and Answerability.* Translated by V. Liapunov. Austin, TX: University of Texas Press.

Bakhtin, M.M. 1952 [1986]. "The Problem of Speech Genres," pp. 60–102 in *Speech Genres and Other Late Essays,* edited by C. Emerson and M. Holquist. Austin, TX: University of Texas Press.

Bakhtin, M.M. 1963 [1984]. *Problems of Dostoyevsky's Poetics.* Translated by C. Emerson. Minneapolis, MN: University of Minnesota Press.

Bakhtin, M.M. 1979 [1986]. *Speech Genres and Other Late Essays.* Translated by V.W. McGee. Austin, TX: University of Texas Press.

Ball, Philip. 2017. "Quantum Teleportation Is Even Weirder Than You Think." *Nature.* doi:10.1038/nature.2017.22321.

Bar-Hillel, Yehoshua. 1953a. "Some Linguistic Problems Connected with Machine Translation." *Philosophy of Science* 20:217–25.

Bar-Hillel, Yehoshua. 1953b. "A Quasi-Arithmetical Notation for Syntactic Description." *Language* 29(1):47–58.

Bar-Hillel, Yehoshua. 1959. "Report of the State of Machine Translation in the United States and Great Britain." Jerusalem: Hebrew University.

Bar-Hillel, Yehoshua. 1960. "The Present Status of Automatic Translation of Languages." *Advances in Computers* 1:91–163.

Barad, Karen. 2003. "Posthumanist Performativity: Toward an Understanding of How Matter Comes to Matter." *Signs: Journal of Women in Culture and Society* 28(3):801–31.

Barad, Karen. 2007. *Meeting the Universe Halfway: Quantum Physics and the Entanglement of Matter and Meaning.* Durham, NC: Duke University Press.

Barad, Karen. 2012. "Nature's Queer Performativity." *Kvinder, Køn og forskning/ Women, Gender and Research* 12(1–2):25–53.

Barrett, T.H. 2008. *The Woman Who Discovered Printing.* New Haven, NJ: Yale University Press.

Barsky, Robert F. 1997. *Noam Chomsky: A Life of Dissent.* Cambridge, MA: MIT Press.

Barsky, Robert F. 2007. *The Chomsky Effect: A Radical Works Beyond the Ivory Tower.* Cambridge, MA: MIT Press.

Barthes, Roland. 1964 [1977]. *Elements of Semiology.* New York, NY: Hill and Wang.

Barthes, Roland. 1976. *Image-Music-Text.* Translated by S. Heath. London, UK: Fontana.

Bateman, John A. 2008. *Multimodality and Genre: A Foundation for the Systematic Analysis of Multimodal Documents.* London, UK: Palgrave.

Bateman, John A. 2011. "The Decomposability of Semiotic Modes," pp. 17–38 in *Multimodal Studies: Exploring Issues and Domains,* edited by K. O'Halloran and B.A. Smith. London, UK: Routledge.

Bateman, John A. 2016. "Methodological and Theoretical Issues in Multimodality," pp. 36–74 in *Handbuch Sprache Im Multimodalen Kontext*, edited by N. Klug and H. Stöckl. Berlin, Germany: Walter de Gruyter.

Bauman, H-Dirksen L. 2008. "Listening to Phonocentrism with Deaf Eyes: Derrida's Mute Philosophy of (Sign) Language." *Essays in Philosophy* 9(1):1–14.

Bean, Robert Bennett. 1932. *The Races of Man: Differentiation and Dispersal of Man.* New York, NY: The University Society.

Beissinger, Mark R. 1988. *Scientific Management, Socialist Discipline, and Soviet Power.* Cambridge, MA: Harvard University Press.

Beldoch, Michael. 1964. "Sensitivity to Expression of Emotional Meaning in Three Modes of Communication," pp. 31–42 in *The Communication of Emotional Meaning*, edited by J.R. Davitz. New York, NY: McGraw-Hill.

Beleza, Sandra, et al. 2012. "The Timing of Pigmentation Lightening in Europeans." *Molecular Biology and Evolution* 30(1):24–35.

Benjamin, Walter. 1929 [1999]. "Surrealism: The Last Snapshot of the European Intelligentsia," pp. 207–21 in *Walter Benjamin: Selected Writings*, Volume 2: *1927–1934*, edited by M.W. Jennings, H. Eidland, and G. Smith. Cambridge, MA: Harvard University Press.

Benjamin, Walter. 1931 [1999]. "Little History of Photography," pp. 507–30 in *Walter Benjamin: Selected Writings*, Volume 2: *1927–1934*, edited by M.W. Jennings, H. Eiland, and G. Smith. Cambridge, MA: Harvard University Press.

Benjamin, Walter. 1936 [2008]. "The Work of Art in the Age of Its Technological Reproducibility," in *The Work of Art in the Age of Its Technological Reproducibility and Other Writings on Media*, edited by M.W. Jennings, B. Doherty, and T.Y. Levin. Cambridge, MA: Harvard University Press.

Benjamin, Walter. 1938 [1999]. "The Paris of the Second Empire in Baudelaire," pp. 3–94 in *Walter Benjamin: Selected Writings*, Volume 4: *1938–1940*, edited by M.W. Jennings, H. Eiland, and G. Smith. Cambridge, MA: Harvard University Press.

Benjamin, Walter. 1939 [1999]. "Paris, Capital of the Nineteenth Century," pp. 14–26 in *The Arcades Project*, edited by H. Eidland and K. McLaughlin. Cambridge, MA: Harvard University Press.

Benjamin, Walter. 1940 [1999]. "On the Concept of History," pp. 389–400 in *Walter Benjamin: Selected Writings*, Volume 4: *1938–1940*, edited by M.W. Jennings, H. Eiland, and G. Smith. Cambridge, MA: Harvard University Press.

Benjamin, Walter. 1999a. *Selected Writings*, Volume 2: *1927–1934*. Translated by R. Livingstone. Cambridge, MA: Harvard University Press.

Benjamin, Walter. 1999b. *The Arcades Project.* Translated by H. Eidland and K. McLaughlin. Cambridge, MA: Harvard University Press.

Benjamin, Walter. 2003. *Selected Writings*, Volume 4: *1938–1940*. Cambridge, MA: Harvard University Press.

Benkler, Yochai. 2006. *The Wealth of Networks: How Social Production Transforms Markets and Freedom.* New Haven, CT: Yale University Press.

Berger, Roland. 2017. "Enabling Decentralized, Digital and Trusted Transactions: Why Blockchain Will Transform the Financial Services Industry." Munich, Germany: Roland Berger GMBE.

Bergson, Henri. 1922 [1965]. *Duration and Simultaneity, with Reference to Einstein's Theory.* Translated by L. Jacobson. Indianapolis, IN: Bobbs-Merrill.

Bergson, Henri. 1934 [1946]. *The Creative Mind*. Translated by M.L. Andison. New York, NY: The Philosophical Library.

Berman, Marshall. 1988. *All That Is Solid Melts into Air: The Experience of Modernity*. New York, NY: Penguin Books.

Bernays, Edward. 1923. *Crystalizing Public Opinion*. New York, NY: Liveright Publishing.

Bernays, Edward. 1928 [2005]. *Propaganda*. Brooklyn, NY: IG Publishing.

Bernays, Edward. 1971. "Emergence of the Public Relations Counsel: Principles and Recollections." *The Business History Review* 45(3):296–316.

Berners-Lee, Tim. 1990, "Information Management: A Proposal." Geneva: CERN. (www.w3.org/History/1989/proposal.html).

Bernstein, Richard J. and Mihailo Marković. 1981. "Why Praxis International?" *Praxis International* 1(1):1–5.

Berwick, Robert C. and Noam Chomsky. 2016. *Why Only Us: Language and Evolution*. Cambridge MA: MIT Press.

Bishop, Jacob and Matthew Verleger. 2013. "The Flipped Classroom: A Survey of the Research." Paper presented at the American Society for Engineering Education, 23–26 June, Atlanta, GA.

Blau, Eve. 1999. *The Architecture of Red Vienna*. Cambridge, MA: MIT Press.

Blelock, Weston and Julia Blelock, eds. 2009. *Roots of the 1969 Woodstock Festival: The Backstory of Woodstock*. Woodstock NY: Woodstock Arts.

Bloch, Marc. 1939 [1962]. *Feudal Society*. London, UK: Routledge and Kegan Paul.

Bogdanović, Mira. 2015. "The Rift in the Praxis Group: Between Nationalism and Liberalism." *Critique: Journal of Socialist Theory* 43(3–4):461–83.

Bogost, Ian. 2006. *Unit Operations: An Approach to Videogame Criticism*. Cambridge, MA: MIT Press.

Bolter, Jay David and Richard Grusin. 1999. *Remediation: Understanding New Media*. Cambridge, MA: MIT Press.

Bosi, Marina and Richard E. Goldberg. 2003. *Introduction to Digital Audio Coding and Standards*. New York, NY: Springer Science.

Botha, Rudolf P. 1989. *Challenging Chomsky: The Generative Garden Game*. Oxford, UK: Basil Blackwell.

Boyle, W.S. and G.E. Smith. 1970. "Charge Coupled Semiconductor Devices." *The Bell System Technical Journal* 49(4):587–93.

Bradford, Richard. 1994. *Roman Jakobson: Life, Language, Art*. London, UK: Routledge.

Brand, Stewart, ed. 1986. *The Whole Earth Software Catalog*. Garden City, NY: Quantum Press.

Brand, Stewart. 1987. *The Media Lab: Inventing the Future at MIT*. New York, NY: Viking.

Brent, Joseph. 1993. *Charles Sanders Peirce: A Life*. Bloomington, IN: Indiana University Press.

Bridle, James. 2018. *The New Dark Age: Technology and the End of the Future*. London, UK: Verso.

Brin, Sergy and Larry Page. 1998. "The Anatomy of a Large-Scale Hypertextual Web Search Engine." Paper presented at the Seventh International World-Wide Web Conference, 14–18 April, Brisbane, Australia (http://ilpubs.stanford.edu:8090/361/).

Brown, Peter F., John Cocke, Stephen A. Della Pietra, Vincent J. Della Pietra, Fredrick Jelinek, John D. Lafferty, Robert L. Mercer, and Paul S. Roossin. 1990. "A Statistical Approach to Machine Translation." *Computational Linguistics* 16 (2):79–85.

Brown, Peter F., Stephen A. Della Pietra, Vincent J. Della Pietra, and Robert L. Mercer. 1991. "Word Sense Disambiguation Using Statistical Methods," pp. 264–70 in *ACL '91 Proceedings of the 29th Annual Meeting of the Association for Computational Linguistics*. Berkeley, CA.

Buck-Morss, Susan. 1989. *The Dialectics of Seeing: Walter Benjamin and the Arcades Project*. Cambridge, MA: MIT Press.

Buck-Morss, Susan. 2000. *Dreamworld and Catastrophe: The Passing of Mass Utopia in East and West*. Cambridge, MA: MIT Press.

Bulgakowa, Oksana. 2010. "Disney as a Utopian Dreamer," pp. 116–25 in *Animism*, edited by A. Franke. Berlin, Germany: Sternberg Press.

Butt, David and Rebekah Wegener. 2008. "The Work of Concepts: Context and Metafunction in the Systemic Functional Model," pp. 590–618 in *Continuing Discourse on Language: A Functional Perspective*, Volume 2, edited by R. Hasan, C.M.I.M. Matthiessen, and J.J. Webster. London, UK: Equinox.

Butt, David G. 2008. "The Robustness of Realizational Systems," pp. 59–83 in *Meaning in Context: Strategies for Implementing Intelligent Applications of Language Studies*, edited by J.A. Webster. London, UK: Continuum.

Buzzetti, Dino and Jerome McGann. 2006. "Electronic Textual Editing: Critical Editing in a Digital Horizon," pp. 53–73 in *Electronic Textual Editing*, edited by L. Burnard, K.O.B. O'Keeffe, and J. Unsworth. New York, NY: Modern Language Association of America.

Calderon, Margarita and Jim Cummins. 1982. "Communicative Competence in Bilingual Education, Theory and Research, Packet I: Language Proficiency Acquisition, Assessment, and Communicative Behavior, Series B, Teacher Edition." Bilingual Education Teacher Training Packets. Dallas, TX: Evaluation, Dissemination and Assessment Center, Dallas Independent School District.

Canale, Michael and Merrill Swain. 1980. "Theoretical Bases of Communicative Approaches to Second Language Teaching and Testing." *Applied Linguistics* 1:1–47.

Canales, Jimena. 2015. *The Physicist and the Philosopher: Einstein, Bergson, and the Debate That Changed Our Understanding of Time*. Princeton, NJ: Princeton University Press.

Cann, Ronnie. 1993. *Formal Semantics*. Cambridge, UK: Cambridge University Press.

Cargas, Harry James, ed. 1994. *The Unnecessary Problem of Edith Stein*. Lanham MD: University Press of America.

Carnap, Rudolf. 1922–25 [1967]. *The Logical Structure of the World*. Translated by R.A. George. Berkeley, CA: University of California Press.

Carnap, Rudolf. 1934 [1937]. *The Logical Syntax of Language*. Translated by A. Smeaton. London, UK: Routledge and Kegan Paul.

Carnap, Rudolf. 1956. *Meaning and Necessity: A Study in Semantics and Modal Logic*. Chicago, IL: University of Chicago Press.

Carnap, Rudolf and Yehoshua Bar-Hillel. 1952. "An Outline of a Theory of Semantic Information." Cambridge, MA: Research Laboratory of Electronics.

Carroll, Lewis. 1876 [1981]. *The Hunting of the Snark*. Los Altos, CA: William Kaufmann.

Casey, Michael J. and Paul Vigna. 2018. *The Truth Machine: The Blockchain and the Future of Everything*. London, UK: HarperCollins.

Cassandro, Michele. 2010. "Aspects of the Life and Character of Francesco Di Marco Datini," pp. 3–52 in *Francesco Di Marco Datini: The Man and the Merchant*, edited by G. Nigro. Florence, Italy: Firenze University Press.

Cavanaugh, John F. 1978. "Text Handling at the United States Government Printing Office." *Technical Communication* 25(3):12–5.

Cawthorne, Nigel. 2007. *Daughter of Heaven: The True Story of the Only Woman to Become Emperor of China*. London, UK: Oneworld Publications.

Cazden, Courtney B. 2001. *Classroom Discourse: The Language of Teaching and Learning*. Portsmouth, NH: Heinemann.

Cazden, Courtney B. 2018. *Communicative Competence, Classroom Interaction, and Educational Equity: The Selected Works of Courtney B. Cazden*. New York, NY: Routledge.

Cazden, Norman. 1951. "Towards a Theory of Realism in Music." *The Journal of Aesthetics and Art Criticism* 10(2):135–51.

Cazden, Norman. 1962. "Sensory Theories of Musical Consonance." *The Journal of Aesthetics and Art Criticism* 20(3):301–19.

Cazden, Norman. 1979. "Can Verbal Meanings Inhere in Fragments of Melody?" *Psychology of Music* 7(1):34–38.

Cazden, Norman. 1980. "The Definition of Consonance and Dissonance." *International Review of the Aesthetics and Sociology of Music* 11(2):123–68.

Cazden, Norman, Herbert Haufrechet, and Norman Studer. 1982. *Folk Songs of the Catskills*. Albany, NY: State University of New York Press.

Chanan, Michael. 1995. *Repeated Takes: A Short History of Recording and Its Effects on Music*. London, UK: Verso.

Chandler Jr, Alfred D. 1977. *The Visible Hand: The Managerial Revolution in American Business*. Cambridge, MA: Harvard University Press.

Chartier, Roger. 1992 [1994]. *The Order of Books: Readers, Authors, and Libraries in Europe between the Fourteenth and Eighteenth Centuries*. Translated by L.G. Cochrane. Stanford, CA: Stanford University Press.

Childe, V. Gordon. 1925. *The Dawn of European Civilization*. New York, NY: Alfred A. Knopf.

Childe, V. Gordon. 1936. *Man Makes Himself*. London, UK: Watts.

Cho, Kyunghyun, Bart van Merrienboer, Caglar Gulcehre, Dzmitry Bahdanau, Fethi Bougares, Holger Schwenk, and Yoshua Bengio. 2014. "Learning Phrase Representations Using Rnn Encoder-Decoder for Statistical Machine Translation." arXiv: 1406.1078v3 [cs.CL].

Chomsky, Noam. 1955. "Logical Structure of Linguistic Theory." Cambridge, MA: MIT.

Chomsky, Noam. 1956. "Three Models for the Description of Language." *IRE Transactions on Information Theory* 2(3):113–24.

Chomsky, Noam. 1967. "The Responsibility of Intellectuals." *New York Review of Books* 8(3): 23.

Chomsky, Noam. 1989. *Necessary Illusions: Thought Control in Democratic Societies*. Boston, MA: South End Press.

Chomsky, Noam. 1991. *Media Control: The Spectacular Achievements of Propaganda.* New York, NY: Seven Stories Press.

Chomsky, Noam. 1999. *The New Military Humanism: Lessons from Kosovo.* Monroe, ME: Common Courage Press.

Chomsky, Noam. 2002. "Chomsky's Revolution: An Exchange." *New York Review of Books*, 18 July, pp. 64–65.

Chomsky, Noam. 2003. *Hegemony or Survival: America's Quest for Global Dominance.* New York, NY: Metropolitan Books.

Chomsky, Noam. 2018. *Yugoslavia: Peace, War, and Dissolution.* Oakland, CA: PM Press.

Chomsky, Noam and Michel Foucault. 1971 [2006]. *The Chomsky–Foucault Debate: On Human Nature.* New York, NY: The New Press.

Christian, David. 2004. *Maps of Time: An Introduction to Big History.* Berkeley, CA: University of California Press.

Christie, Michael J. 1994. "Grounded and Ex-Centric Knowledges: Exploring Aboriginal Alternatives to Western Thinking," pp. 24–34 in *Thinking: International Interdisciplinary Perspectives*, edited by J. Edwards. Highlett, Australia: Hawker Brownlow Education.

Church, Kenneth W. and Robert L. Mercer. 1993. "Introduction to the Special Issue on Computational Linguistics Using Large Corpora." *Computational Linguistics* 19 (1):1–24.

Clark, Katerina and Michael Holquist. 1984. *Mikhail Bakhtin.* Cambridge, MA: Harvard University Press.

Clarke, Robert. 2012. *Seven Years with Banksy.* London, UK: Michael O'Mara Books.

Clements, Jonathan. 2008. *Wu: The Chinese Empress Who Schemed, Seduced and Murdered Her Way to Become a Living God.* Stroud, UK: Sutton Publishing.

Codd, E.F. 1970. "Relational Model of Data for Large Shared Data Banks." *Communications of the ACM* 13(6):377–87.

Cohen, Jean-Louis and Tim Benton. 2014. *Le Corbusier Le Grand.* New York, NY: Phaidon.

Coleman, Gabriella. 2013. *Coding Freedom: The Ethics and Aesthetics of Hacking.* Princeton, NJ: Princeton University Press.

Coleman, Gabriella. 2014. *Hacker, Hoaxer, Whisteblower, Spy: The Many Faces of Anonymous.* London, UK: Verso.

Coleman, Gabriella. 2017. "From Internet Farming to Weapons of the Geek." *Current Anthropology* 58(Supplement 15):S91–101.

Coleman, Peter. 2006. *Shopping Environments: Evolution, Planning and Design.* Oxford, UK: Architectural Press.

Colletti, Lucio. 1969 [1973]. *Marxism and Hegel.* London, UK: Verso.

Connor, Steven. 2014. *Beyond Words: Sobs, Hums, Stutters and Other Vocalizations.* London, UK: Reaktion Books.

Cope, Bill. 1998. "The Language of Forgetting: A Short History of the Word," pp. 192–223 in *Seams of Light: Best Antipodean Essays*, edited by M. Fraser. Sydney, Australia: Allen and Unwin.

Cope, Bill. 2001. "New Ways with Words: Print and Etext Convergence," pp. 1–15 in *Print and Electronic Text Convergence*, Volume 2.1: *Technology Drivers across the Book Production Supply Chain, from the Creator to the Consumer*, edited by B. Cope and D. Kalantzis. Melbourne, Australia: Common Ground.

Cope, Bill. 2011. "Method for the Creation, Location and Formatting of Digital Content." Edited by U.S. Patent Office.

Cope, Bill and Robert Black. 2001. "Print Technology in Transition," pp. 151–71 in *Creator to Consumer in a Digital Age: Book Production in Transition*, Volume 1, edited by B. Cope and D. Mason. Melbourne, Australia: Common Ground.

Cope, Bill and Mary Kalantzis, eds. 1993. *The Powers of Literacy: Genre Approaches to Teaching Writing*. London, UK: Falmer Press and Pittsburgh, PA: University of Pennsylvania Press.

Cope, Bill and Mary Kalantzis. 1997a. "White Noise: The Attack on Political Correctness and the Struggle for the Western Canon." *Interchange* 28(4):283–329.

Cope, Bill and Mary Kalantzis. 1997b. *Productive Diversity*. Sydney, Australia: Pluto Press.

Cope, Bill and Mary Kalantzis, eds. 2000. *Multiliteracies: Literacy Learning and the Design of Social Futures*. London, UK: Routledge.

Cope, Bill and Mary Kalantzis. 2004. "Text-Made Text." *E-Learning* 1(2):198–282.

Cope, Bill and Mary Kalantzis. 2009. "'Multiliteracies': New Literacies, New Learning." *Pedagogies: An International Journal* 4:164–95.

Cope, Bill and Mary Kalantzis. 2011. "Creating an Interlanguage of the Social Web," pp. 371–428 in *Towards a Semantic Web: Connecting Knowledge in Academic Research*, edited by B. Cope, M. Kalantzis, and L. Magee. Cambridge, UK: Elsevier.

Cope, Bill and Mary Kalantzis. 2014. "Changing Knowledge Ecologies and the Transformation of the Scholarly Journal," pp. 9–84 in *The Future of the Academic Journal* (Edn 2), edited by B. Cope and A. Phillips. Oxford, UK: Elsevier.

Cope, Bill and Mary Kalantzis. 2015. "Assessment and Pedagogy in the Era of Machine-Mediated Learning," pp. 350–74 in *Education as Social Construction: Contributions to Theory, Research, and Practice*, edited by T. Dragonas, K.J. Gergen, S. McNamee, and E. Tseliou. Chagrin Falls, OH: Worldshare Books.

Cope, Bill and Mary Kalantzis. 2017. "Conceptualizing E-Learning," pp. 1–45 in *E-Learning Ecologies*, edited by B. Cope and M. Kalantzis. New York, NY: Routledge.

Cope, Bill, Mary Kalantzis and Liam Magee. 2011. *Towards a Semantic Web: Connecting Knowledge in Academic Research*. Cambridge, UK: Elsevier.

Costa-jussà, Marta R. and José A.R. Fonollosa. 2015. "Latest Trends in Hybrid Machine Translation and Its Applications." *Computer Speech and Language* 32:3–10.

Cowan, Katharine and Gunther Kress. 2019. "Documenting and Transferring Meaning in the Multimodal World: Reconsidering 'Transcription'," pp. 66–77 in *Remixing Multiliteracies: Theory and Practice from New London to New Times*, edited by F. Serfini and E. Gee. New York. NY: Teachers College Press.

Cox, Brian and Jeff Forshaw. 2011. *The Quantum Universe: Everything That Can Happen Does Happen*. London, UK: Allen Lane.

Crawford, Nicholas G. et al. 2017. "Loci Associated with Skin Pigmentation Identified in African Populations." *Science* 235(8433):1–14.

Crystal, David. 2008. *Txting: The Gr8 Db8*. Oxford, UK: Oxford University Press.

Cust, Mrs Henry. 1931. *Other Dimensions: A Selection from the Later Correspondence of Victoria Lady Welby, Edited by Her Daughter*. London, UK: Jonathan Cape.

D'Eramo, Marco. 2017. "Maps of Ignorance." *New Left Review* (108):43–45.

Dacey, Michael F. and Duane F. Marble. 1965. "Some Comments on Certain Technical Aspects of Geographic Information Systems." Office of Naval Research.

Damasio, Antonio. 1994. *Descartes' Error: Emotion, Reason and the Human Brain.* New York, NY: Penguin Putnam.

Damasio, Antonio. 2010. *Self Comes to Mind: Constructing the Conscious Brain.* New York, NY: Pantheon.

Davidson, Cathy N. 2011. *Now You See It: How the Brain Science of Attention Will Transform the Way We Live, Work and Learn.* New York, NY: Viking.

de Beauvoir, Simone. 1949 [2011]. *The Second Sex.* Translated by C. Borde and S. Malovany-Chevallier. New York, NY: Vintage Books.

de Lubac, Henri. 1959 [1998]. *Medieval Exegesis: The Four Senses of Scripture*, Volume 1. Grand Rapids, MI: William B. Eerdmans Publishing Company.

de Roover, Raymone. 1963. *The Rise and Decline of the Medici Bank: 1397–1494.* Cambridge, MA: Harvard University Press.

de Vries, Alex. 2018. "Bitcoin's Growing Energy Problem." *Joule* 2(5):801–05.

Deacon, Terrence W. 1997. *The Symbolic Species: The Co-Evolution of Language and the Brain.* New York, NY: W.W. Norton.

Dear, Brian. 2017. *The Friendly Orange Glow: The Untold Story of the Plato System and the Dawn of Cyberculture.* New York, NY: Pantheon Books.

DeGaetano, Steve. 2015. *The Disneyland Railroad: A Complete History in Words and Pictures.* New York, NY: Theme Park Press.

Deleuze, Gilles. 1969 [1990]. *The Logic of Sense.* Translated by M. Lester. New York, NY: Columbia University Press.

Derrida, Jacques. 1962 [1989]. *Edmund Husserl's Origin of Geometry: An Introduction.* Lincoln, NE: University of Nebraska Press.

Derrida, Jacques. 1967 [1973]. *Speech and Phenomena, and Other Essays on Husserl's Theory of Signs.* Translated by D.B. Allison. Evanston, IL: Northwestern University Press.

Derrida, Jacques, Hans-Georg Gadamer, and Philippe Lacque-Labarthe. 1988 [2016]. *Heidegger, Philosophy, and Politics: The Heidelberg Conference.* Translated by J. Fort. New York, NY: Fordham University Press.

Dewey, John. 1925. *Experience and Nature.* Chicago, IL: Open Court.

Dinwoodie, David W. 2006. "Time and the Individual in Native North America," pp. 327–48 in *New Perspectives on Native North America*, edited by S.A. Kan and P.T. Strong. Lincoln, NE: University of Nebraska Press.

Dixon, R.M.W. 1980. *The Languages of Australia.* Cambridge, UK: Cambridge University Press.

Donald, Merlin. 1991. *Origins of the Modern Mind.* Cambridge, MA: Harvard University Press.

Donald, Merlin. 2001. *A Mind So Rare: The Evolution of Human Consciousness.* New York, NY: W.W. Norton.

Du Bois, W.E.B. 1897. "Strivings of the Negro People." *The Atlantic* (August).

Du Bois, W.E.B. 1903. *The Souls of Black Folk: Essays and Sketches.* Chicago, IL: A.A. McClurg & Co.

Du Bois, W.E.B. 1906. *The Health and Physique of the Negro American: Report of a Social Study Made under the Direction of Atlanta University.* Atlanta, GA: Atlanta University Press.

Durkheim, Emile and Marcel Mauss. 1903 [1963]. *Primitive Classification.* Translated by R. Needham. Chicago, IL: University of Chicago Press.

Ebenstein, Lanny. 2007. *Milton Friedman: A Biography*. New York, NY: Palgrave Macmillan.

Eco, Umberto. 1976. *A Theory of Semiotics*. Bloomington, IN: Indiana University Press.

Eco, Umberto. 1979. *The Role of the Reader: Explorations in the Semiotics of Texts*. Bloomington, IN: Indiana University Press.

Eco, Umberto. 1984. *Semiotics and the Philosophy of Language*. Bloomington, IN: Indiana University Press.

Edgley, Alison. 2000. *The Social and Political Thought of Noam Chomsky*. London, UK: Routledge.

Eggins, Suzanne and Diana Slade. 1997. *Analysing Casual Conversation*. London, UK: Cassell.

Eisenstein, Elizabeth L. 1979. *The Printing Press as an Agent of Change: Communications and Cultural Transformation in Early-Modern Europe*. Cambridge, UK: Cambridge University Press.

Eisenstein, Sergei. 1986. *On Disney*. London, UK: Seagull Books.

Elias, Norbert. 1987 [1992]. *Time: An Essay*. Translated by E. Jephcott. Oxford, UK: Blackwell.

Eliot, Marc. 1993. *Walt Disney: Hollywood's Dark Prince*. New York, NY: Birch Lane Press.

Elleström, Lars. 2010. "The Modalities of Media: A Model for Understanding Intermedial Relations," pp. 11–50 in *Media Borders, Multimodality and Intermediality*, edited by L. Elleström. London, UK: Palgrave Macmillan.

Ellsworth-Jones, Will. 2012. *Banksy: The Man Behind the Wall*. New York, NY: St Martin's Press.

Engels, Freidrich. 1845 [1973]. *The Condition of the Working Class in England: From Personal Observation and Authentic Sources*. Moscow, USSR: Progress Publishers.

Engels, Friedrich. 1892. *The Origin of the Family, Private Property and the State*. New York, NY: International Publishers.

Erdely, Stephen. 1981. "Norman Cazden (1914–1980)." *Ethnomusicology* 25(3):493–6.

Eribon, Didier. 1991. *Michel Foucault*. Translated by B. Wing. Cambridge, MA: Harvard University Press.

Escuder, Jesús Adrián. 2015. "Heidegger's 'Black Notebooks' and the Question of Anti-Semitism." *Gatherings: The Heidegger Circle Annual* 5:21–49.

Farmer, F. Randall and Bryce Glass. 2010. *Web Reputation Systems*. Sebastopol, CA: O'Reilly.

Fay, Margaret. 1980. "The 1844 Economic and Philosophical Manuscripts of Karl Marx: A Critical Commentary and Interpretation." Ph.D., Department of Sociology, University of California, Berkeley.

Fay, Margaret, Johannes Hengstenberg, and Barbara Stuckey. 1983. "The Influence of Adam Smith on Marx's Theory of Alienation." *Science and Society* 47(2):129–51.

Febvre, Lucien and Henri-Jean Martin. 1958 [1976]. *The Coming of the Book*. Translated by D. Gerard. London, UK: Verso.

Fehér, Ferenc, Agnes Heller, and György Márkus. 1983. *Dictatorship over Needs*. Oxford, UK: Basil Blackwell.

Feinberg, Walter. 2019. *Educational Thought at the University of Illinois at Urbana-Champaign, 1867 to 2017: A Philosophical History*. Unpublished manuscript.

Feynman, Richard P. 1985. *QED: The Strange Theory of Light and Matter*. Princeton, NJ: Princeton University Press.

Filippas, Apostolos, John J. Horton, and Joseph M. Golden. 2018. "Reputation Inflation," in *EC '18: Proceedings of the 2018 ACM Conference on Economics and Computation*. Ithaca, NY.

Fillmore, Charles J. 1976. "Frame Semantics and the Nature of Language." *Annals of the New York Academy of Sciences* 280(1):20–32.

Fillmore, Charles J. 1977. "The Case for Case Reopened." *Syntax and Semantics* 8:59–82.

Fine, Gary Alan and Philip Manning. 2000. "Erving Goffman," pp. 457–85 in *The Blackwell Companion to Major Contemporary Social Theorists*, edited by G. Ritzer. Oxford, UK: Blackwell.

Fine, Thomas. 2008. "The Dawn of Commercial Digital Recording." *ARSC Journal* 39 (1):1–17.

Firth, J.R. 1937 [1986]. *The Tongues of Men*. Westport, CT: Greenwood Press.

Firth, J.R. 1968. *Selected Papers of J.R. Firth, 1952–1959*. Bloomington, IN: Indiana University Press.

Fitzgerald, Percy. 1890. *The Story of "Bradshaw's Guide"*. London, UK: The Leadenhall Press.

Flusser, Vilém. 1991 [2014]. *Gestures*. Translated by N.A. Roth. Minneapolis, MN: University of Minnesota Press.

Foessel, Michaël and Jürgen Habermas. 2008 [2015]. "Critique and Communication, Philosophy's Missions: A Conversation with Jürgen Habermas." *Esprit* (8–9): 40–54.

Forbes, F.A. 1921. *Saint Benedict*. New York, NY: P.J. Kennedy and Sons.

Ford, Henry. 1922. *My Life and Work*. Sydney, Australia: Angus & Robertson.

Foster, Hal, ed. 1983. *Postmodern Culture*. London, UK: Pluto Press.

Foucault, Michel. 1961 [1988]. *Madness and Civilization: A History of Insanity in the Age of Reason*. Translated by R. Howard. New York, NY: Vintage Books.

Foucault, Michel. 1963 [1973]. *The Birth of the Clinic: An Archaeology of Medical Perception*. Translated by A.M. Sheridan. London, UK: Taylor and Francis.

Foucault, Michel. 1966 [1970]. *The Order of Things: An Archaeology of the Human Sciences*. London, UK: Tavistock.

Foucault, Michel. 1969 [1972]. *The Archaeology of Knowledge*. Translated by A.M.S. Smith. New York, NY: Pantheon.

Foucault, Michel. 1975 [1977]. *Discipline and Punish: The Birth of the Prison*. Translated by A. Sheridan. New York, NY: Vintage Books.

Foucault, Michel. 1976 [1978]. *The History of Sexuality*, Volume 1: *An Introduction*. Translated by R. Hurley. New York, NY: Pantheon.

Foucault, Michel. 1984. "What Is Enlightenment?," pp. 32–50 in *The Foucault Reader*, edited by P. Rabinow. New York, NY: Pantheon.

Foucault, Michel. 1984 [2011]. *The Courage of Truth (the Government of the Self and Others II): Lectures at the Collège De France, 1983–1984*. Translated by G. Burchell. London, UK: Palgrave.

Frank, Gelya. 1997. "Jews, Multiculturalism, and Boasian Anthropology." *American Anthropologist* 99(4):731–45.

Frankfurt, Harry G. 2005. *On Bullshit*. Princeton, NJ: Princeton University Press.

Fraser, Nancy. 1981. "Foucault on Modern Power: Empirical Insights and Normative Confusions." *Praxis International* 1(3):272–87.

Fraser, Nancy. 2002. "Integrating Redistribution and Recognition: On Class and Status in Contemporary Society," pp. 149–65 in *Culture and Enlightenment: Essays for György Márkus*, edited by J. Grumley, P. Crittenden, and P. Johnson. Aldershot, UK: Ashgate.

Fraser, Nancy. 2003. "Distorted Beyond All Recognition: A Rejoinder to Axel Honneth," pp. 198–236 in *Redistribution or Recognition? A Political-Philosophical Exchange*, edited by N. Fraser and A. Honneth. London, UK: Verso.

Fraser, Nancy. 2008. "From Redistribution to Recognition? Dilemmas of Justice in a 'Postsocialist' Age," pp. 11–41 in *Adding Insult to Injury: Nancy Fraser Debates Her Critics*, edited by K. Olson. London, UK: Verso.

Fraser, Nancy. 2009. "Feminism, Capitalism and the Cunning of History." *New Left Review* (56):97–117.

Freud, Sigmund. 1930 [2005]. *Civilization and Its Discontents*. Translated by J. Strachey. New York, NY: W.W. Norton.

Fricke, Ellen. 2013. "Towards a Unified Grammar of Gesture and Speech: A Multimodal Approach," pp. 733–54 in *Body-Language-Communication: An International Handbook on Multimodality in Human Interaction*, edited by C. Müller, A. Cienki, E. Fricke, S.H. Ladewig, D. McNeill, and J. Bressem. Berlin, Germany: De Gruyter Mouton.

Friedman, Milton. 1962. *Capitalism and Freedom*. Chicago, IL: University of Chicago Press.

Friedman, Milton. 1975. *There's No Such Thing as a Free Lunch*. LaSalle IL: Open Court.

Friedman, Milton. 1992. "The Island of Stone Money." Vol. E-91-3. *Working Papers in Economics*. Stanford CA: The Hoover Institution.

Friedman, Milton and Rose D. Friedman. 1998. *Two Lucky People: Memoirs*. Chicago, IL: University of Chicago Press.

Friedman, Milton and Walter W. Heller. 1969. *Monetary Vs. Fiscal Policy*. New York, NY: W.W. Norton.

Frizot, Michel. 2015. *Germaine Krull*. Paris, France: Editions Hazan.

Fuchs, Christian. 2017. "The Praxis School's Marxist Humanism and Mihailo Marković's Theory of Communication." *Critique: Journal of Socialist Theory* 45 (1–2):159–82.

Furness, William Henry III. 1910. *The Island of Stone Money: Uap of the Carolines*. Philadelphia, PA: J.B. Lippincott.

Gabler, Neal. 2006. *Walt Disney: The Triumph of the American Imagination*. New York, NY: Alfred A. Knopf.

Gadamer, Hans-Georg. 1960 [2004]. *Truth and Method*. Translated by J. Weinsheimer and D.G. Marshall. London, UK: Continuum.

Galan, F.W. 1985. *Historic Structures: The Prague School Project, 1928–1946*. Austin, TX: University of Texas Press.

Galla, Amareswar, ed. 2012. *World Heritage: Benefits Beyond Borders*. Cambridge, UK: Cambridge University Press.

Galloway, Alexander R. 2006. *Gaming: Essays on Algorithmic Culture*. Minneapolis, MN: University of Minnesota Press.

Galloway, Alexander R., Eugene Thacker, and McKenzie Wark. 2014. *Excommunication: Three Inquiries in Media and Mediation*. Chicago, IL: University of Chicago Press.

Gärdenfors, Peter. 2014. *Geometry of Meaning: Semantics Based on Conceptual Spaces*. Cambridge, MA: MIT Press.

Gardiner, Geoffrey W. 2004. "The Primacy of Trade Debts in the Development of Money," pp. 128–72 in *Credit and State Theories of Money: The Contributions of A. Mitchell Innes*, edited by L.R. Wray. Cheltenham, UK: Edward Elgar.

Garfield, Eugene. 1955 [2006]. "Citation Indexes for Science: A New Dimension in Documentation through Association of Ideas." *International Journal of Epidemiology* 35(5):1123–27. doi:10.1093/ije/dyl189.

Garfield, Eugene. 2006. "Commentary: Fifty Years of Citation Indexing." *International Journal of Epidemiology* 35:1127–28.

Gee, James Paul. 1992 [2013]. *The Social Mind: Language, Ideology, and Social Practice*. Champaign, IL: Common Ground.

Gee, James Paul. 2003. *What Video Games Have to Teach Us About Learning and Literacy*. New York, NY: Palgrave Macmillan.

Gee, James Paul. 2004. *Situated Language and Learning: A Critique of Traditional Schooling*. London, UK: Routledge.

Gee, James Paul. 2005. *Why Video Games Are Good for Your Soul: Pleasure and Learning*. Melbourne, Australia: Common Ground.

Gee, James Paul. 2007. *Good Video Games + Good Learning: Collected Essays on Video Games, Learning and Literacy*. New York, NY: Peter Lang.

Gee, James Paul. 2013. *The Anti-Education Era: Creating Smarter Students through Digital Learning*. New York, NY: Palgrave Macmillan.

Gee, James Paul. 2015. *Unified Discourse Analysis: Language, Virtual Worlds, and Video Games*. London, UK: Routledge.

Gee, James Paul. 2017. "A Personal Retrospective on the New London Group and Its Formation," pp. 32–45 in *Remixing Multiliteracies: Theory and Practice from New London to New Times*, edited by F. Serfini and E. Gee. New York, NY: Teachers College Press.

Genosko, Gary. 2008. "A-Signifying Semiotics." *Public Journal of Semiotics* 11 (1):11–21.

Gernsheim, Helmut and Alison Gernsheim. 1969. *The History of Photography, from the Camera Obscura to the Beginning of the Modern Era*. New York, NY: McGraw-Hill.

Gibson, James J. 1966. *The Senses Considered as Perceptual Systems*. Boston, MA: Houghton Mifflin.

Gibson, James J. 1977. "The Theory of Affordances," pp. 67–82 in *Perceiving, Acting, and Knowing: Toward an Ecological Psychology*, edited by R. Shaw and J. Bransford. London: Routledge.

Gibson, James J. 1979 [2015]. *The Ecological Approach to Visual Perception*. New York, NY: Psychology Press.

Gillilland, Cora Lee C. 1974. "The Stone Money of Yap: A Numismatic Survey." Vol. 23. *Smithsonian Studies in History and Technology*. Washington, DC: Smithsonian Institution Press.

Glazer, Nathan. 1961. *The Social Basis of American Communism*. New York, NY: Harcourt, Brace & World.

Glinsky, Albert. 2000. *Theremin: Ether Music and Espionage*. Urbana, IL: University of Illinois Press.

Goffman, Erving. 1959. *The Presentation of Self in Everyday Life*. New York, NY: Doubleday Anchor.

Goffman, Erving. 1974. *Frame Analysis: An Essay on the Organization of Experience*. Cambridge, MA: Harvard University Press.

Goldberg, Dror. 2005. "Famous Myths of 'Fiat Money'." *Journal of Money, Credit and Banking* 37(5):957–67.

Goldfarb, Charles F. 1990. "A Brief History of the Development of SGML." SGML Users' Group. Retrieved February 5, 2002 (www.oasis-open.org/cover/sgmlhist0 .html).

Goldfarb, Charles F. 1991. *The SGML Handbook*. Oxford, UK: Oxford University Press.

Goldfarb, Charles F., Edward J. Mosher, and Theodore I. Peterson. 1970 [1997]. "An Online System for Integrated Text Processing." *Journal of the American Society for Information Science* 48(7):656–61.

Gombrich, E.H. 1964. "Moment and Movement in Art." *Journal of the Warburg and Courtauld Institutes* 27:293–306.

Goodman, Leah McGrath. 2014. "The Face Behind Bitcoin." *Newsweek*, 6 March.

Goody, Jack. 1977. *The Domestication of the Savage Mind*. Cambridge, UK: Cambridge University Press.

Goody, Jack. 1986. *The Logic of Writing and the Organization of Society*. Cambridge, UK: Cambridge University Press.

Goody, Jack. 1987. *The Interface between the Written and the Oral*. Cambridge, UK: Cambridge University Press.

Gordon, Mel. 1992. "Songs from the Museum of the Future: Russian Sound Creation, 1910–30," pp. 197–243 in *Wireless Imagination: Sound, Radio and the Avant-Garde*, edited by D. Kahn and G. Whitehead. Cambridge, MA: MIT Press.

Gordon, W. Terrence. 1990. "Significs and C.K. Ogden: The Influence of Lady Welby," pp. 179–96 in *Essays on Significs: Papers Presented on the Occasion of the 150th Anniversary of the Birth of Lady Victoria Welby, 1837–1912*, edited by H.W. Schmitz. Amsterdam, NL: John Benjamins.

Grad, Burton. 2007. "The Creation and the Demise of Visicalc." *IEEE Annals of the History of Computing* 29(3):20–31.

Graeber, David. 2007. *Possibilities: Essays on Hierarchy, Rebellion, and Desire*. Oakland, CA: AK Press.

Graeber, David. 2011. *Debt: The First 5,000 Years*. Brooklyn, NY: Melville House.

Grafton, Anthony. 1997. *The Footnote: A Curious History*. London, UK: Faber and Faber.

Gras, N.S.B. 1939. *Business and Capitalism: An Introduction to Business History*. New York, NY: F.S. Crofts and Company.

Graves, Frank Pierrepoint. 1912. *Peter Ramus and the Educational Reformation of the Sixteenth Century*. New York, NY: Macmillan.

Grondin, Jean. 2003. *Hans-Georg Gadamer: A Biography*. Translated by J. Weinsheimer. New Haven, CT: Yale University Press.

Grosz, Elizabeth. 2004. *The Nick of Time: Politics, Evolution, and the Untimely*. Durham, NC: Duke University Press.

Gruber, Helmut. 1991. *Red Vienna: Experiment in Working Class Culture*. Oxford, UK: Oxford University Press.

Gruen, Victor. 1960. *Shopping Towns USA: The Planning of Shopping Centers.* New York, NY: Reinhold Publishing.

Gruen, Victor. 1973. *Centers for the Urban Environment: Survival of the Cities.* New York, NY: Van Norstrand Reinhold.

Gruen, Victor. 1978. "The Sad Story of Shopping Centers." *Town and Country Planning* 46(7–8):350–53.

Gruen, Victor. 1979 [2017]. *Shopping Town: Designing the City in Suburban America.* Translated by A. Bauldauf. Minneapolis, MN: University of Minnesota Press.

Gruen, Victor and Laurence P. Smith. 1952. "Shopping Centers: The New Building Type." *Progressive Architecture* (June):67–109.

Gruenwald, Oskar. 1983. *The Yugoslav Search for Man: Marxist Humanism in Contemporary Yugoslavia.* South Hadley, MA: J.F. Bergin.

Grumley, John, Paul Crittenden, and Pauline Johnson, eds. 2002. *Culture and Enlightenment: Essays for György Márkus.* Aldershot, UK: Ashgate.

Guattari, Félix. 1979 [2001]. *The Machinic Unconscious: Essays in Schizoanalysis.* Translated by T. Adkins. Los Angeles, CA: Semiotext(e).

Guberina, Petar. 1964 [1971]. "Studies in the Verbo-Tonal System." Columbus, OH: Department of Speech, Ohio State University.

Gumperz, John J. and Stephen C. Levinson. 1991. "Rethinking Linguistic Relativity." *Current Anthropology* 32(5):613–23.

Habermas, Jürgen. 1967 [1988]. *On the Logic of the Social Sciences.* Translated by S.W. Nicholsen and J.A. Stark. Cambridge, MA: MIT Press.

Habermas, Jürgen. 1970 [1985]. "On Hermeneutics' Claim to Universality," pp. 293–319 in *The Hermeneutics Reader: Texts of the German Tradition from the Enlightenment to the Present,* edited by K. Mueller-Vollmer. New York, NY: Continuum.

Habermas, Jürgen. 1970 [1990]. "A Review of Gadamer's 'Truth and Method'," pp. 213–44 in *The Hermeneutic Tradition: From Ast to Ricoeur,* edited by G.L. Ormiston and A.D. Schrift. Albany, NY: State University of New York Press.

Habermas, Jürgen. 1971 [1974]. *Theory and Practice.* Translated by J. Viertel. London, UK: Heinemann.

Habermas, Jürgen. 1978. *Knowledge and Human Interests.* London, UK: Heinemann.

Habermas, Jürgen. 1981 [1984]. *The Theory of Communicative Action,* Volume 1: *Reason and the Rationalization of Society.* Translated by T. McCarthy. London, UK: Heinemann.

Habermas, Jürgen 1981 [1987]. *The Theory of Communicative Action,* Volume 2: *Lifeworld and System, a Critique of Functionalist Reason.* Translated by T. McCarthy. Boston, MA: Beacon Press.

Habermas, Jürgen. 1998. "Learning by Disaster: A Diagnostic Look Back on the Short Twentieth Century." *Constellations* 5(3):307–20.

Habermas, Jürgen. 1999. "Bestiality and Humanity: A War on the Border between Legality and Morality." *Constellations* 6(3):263–72.

Hall, Stuart, Jessica Evans, and Sean Nixon. 2013. *Representation.* London, UK: Sage.

Halliday, M.A.K. 1956 [2005]. "The Linguistic Basis of a Mechanical Thesaurus," pp. 6–19 in *Computational and Quantitative Studies: The Collected Works of M.A.K. Halliday, Volume 6,* edited by J.J. Webster. London, UK: Continuum.

Halliday, M.A.K. 1975. *Learning How to Mean: Explorations in the Development of Language.* London, UK: Edward Arnold.

Halliday, M.A.K. 1977 [2003]. "Ideas About Language," pp. 92–115 in *On Language and Linguistics*, The Collected Works of M.A.K. Halliday, Volume 3, edited by J.J. Webster. London, UK: Continuum.

Halliday, M.A.K. 1999. "The Notion of 'Context' in Language Education," pp. 1–24 in *Text and Context in Functional Linguistics*, edited by M. Ghadessy. Amsterdam, NL: John Benjamins.

Halliday, M.A.K. 2000 [2002]. "Grammar and Daily Life: Concurrence and Complementarity," pp. 369–83 in *On Grammar*, The Collected Works of M.A.K. Halliday, Volume 1, edited by J.J. Webster. London, UK: Continuum.

Halliday, M.A.K. and Ruqaiya Hasan. 1976. *Cohesion in English*. London, UK: Longman.

Halliday, M.A.K. and Ruqaiya Hasan. 1985. *Language, Context, and Text: Aspects of Language in a Social-Semiotic Perspective*. Geelong, Australia: Deakin University Press.

Halliday, M.A.K. and Christian Matthiessen. 2004. *An Introduction to Functional Grammar*. London, UK: Routledge.

Halliday, M.A.K. and Christian M.I.M. Matthiessen. 2014. *Halliday's Introduction to Functional Grammar* (Edn 4). Milton Park, UK: Routledge.

Halpin, Harry. 2012. "The Philosophy of Anonymous: Ontological Politics without Identity." *Radical Philosophy* 176(November/December):19–28.

Haraway, Donna. 1985 [2016]. *A Manifesto for Cyborgs: Science, Technology, and Socialist Feminism in the 1980s*. Minneapolis, MN: University of Minnesota Press.

Hardwick, Charles S., ed. 1977. *Semiotics and Significs: The Correspondence between Charles S. Peirce and Victoria Lady Welby*. Bloomington, IN: Indiana University Press.

Hardwick, M. Jeffrey. 2004. *Mall Maker: Victor Gruen, Architect of an American Dream*. Pittsburgh, PA: University of Pennsylvania Press.

Harris, Zellig S. 1954. "Distributional Structure." *Word* 10(2–3):146–62.

Harvey, David. 2005. *A Brief History of Neoliberalism*. Oxford, UK: Oxford University Press.

Hatherley, Owen. 2015. *Landscapes of Communism*. London, UK: Allen Lane.

Hauge, Michelle V., Mark D. Stevenson, D. Kim Rossmo, and Steven C. Le Comber. 2016. "Tagging Banksy: Using Geographic Profiling to Investigate a Modern Art Mystery." *Journal of Spatial Science* 61(1):185–90.

Haviland, John B. 1985. "The Life History of a Speech Community: Guugu Yimidhirr at Hopevale." *Aboriginal History* 9(1/2):170–204.

Haviland, John B. 1993. "Anchoring, Iconicity, and Orientation in Guugu Yimithirr Pointing Gestures." *Journal of Linguistic Anthropology* 3(1):3–45.

Haviland, John B. 1996a. "Projections, Transpositions, and Relativity," pp. 271–323 in *Rethinking Linguistic Relativity*, edited by J.J. Gumperz and S.C. Levinson. Cambridge, UK: Cambridge University Press.

Haviland, John B. 1996b. "Owners Versus Bubu Gujin: Land Rights and Getting the Language Right in Guugu Yimithirr Country." *Journal of Linguistic Anthropology* 6 (2):145–60.

Haviland, John B. 1998. "Guugu Yimithirr Cardinal Directions." *Ethos* 26(1):25–47.

Haviland, John B. 2000. "Pointing, Gesture Spaces, and Mental Maps," pp. 13–46 in *Language and Gesture*, edited by D. McNeil. Cambridge, UK: Cambridge University Press.

Hayes, R.M. 1989. *3-D Movies: A History and Filmography of Stereoscopic Cinema.* Jefferson, NC: McFarland and Company.

Hegel, G.F.W. 1807 [1977]. *Phenomenology of Spirit.* Oxford, UK: Oxford University Press.

Heilig, Morton L. 1962. "Sensorama Simulator." Edited by U.S. Patent Office.

Herbsrith, Waltraud. 1971 [1985]. *Edith Stein: A Biography.* San Francisco, CA: Harper and Row.

Herman, Edward S. and Noam Chomsky. 1988 [2002]. *Manufacturing Consent: The Political Economy of Mass Media.* New York, NY: Pantheon Books.

Heynick, Frank. 1983. "From Einstein to Whorf: Space, Time, Matter, and Reference Frames in Physical and Linguistic Relativity." *Semiotica* 45(1/2):35–64.

Hickmann, Maya and Stéphane Robert, eds. 2006. *Space in Languages: Linguistic Systems and Cognitive Categories.* Amsterdam, NL: John Benjamins.

Hjelmslev, Louis. 1943 [1961]. *Prolegomena to a Theory of Language.* Translated by F.J. Whitfield. Madison, WI: University of Wisconsin Press.

Hjelmslev, Louis. 1963 [1970]. *Language: An Introduction.* Translated by F.J. Whitfield. Madison, WI: University of Wisconsin Press.

Hobsbawm, Eric. 1988. *Uncommon People: Resistance, Rebellion, and Jazz.* New York, NY: The New Press.

Hobsbawm, Eric. 1989 [1993]. *The Jazz Scene.* New York, NY: Pantheon Books.

Honneth, Axel. 2003. "Redistribution as Recognition: A Reply to Nancy Fraser," pp. 110–97 in *Redistribution or Recognition? A Political-Philosophical Exchange,* edited by N. Fraser and A. Honneth. London, UK: Verso.

Honneth, Axel. 2008. *Reification: A New Look at an Old Idea.* Oxford, UK: Oxford University Press.

Horvat, Branko, Mihailo Marković, and Rudi Supek. 1975. *Self-Governing Socialism: Volume 2.* White Plains, NY: International Arts and Sciences Press.

Hossenfelder, Sabine. 2018. *Lost in Math: How Beauty Leads Physics Astray.* New York, NY: Basic Books.

Huang, Yan. 2014. *Pragmatics.* Oxford, UK: Oxford University Press.

Husserl, Edmund. 1931 [1960]. *Cartesian Meditations: An Introduction to Phenomenology.* Translated by D. Cairns. The Hague, NL: Martinus Nijhoff Publishers.

Husserl, Edmund. 1952 [1989]. *Ideas Pertaining to a Pure Phenomenology and a Phenomenological Philosophy, Second Book: Studies in the Phenomenology of Constitution.* Translated by R. Rojcewicz and A. Schuwer. Dordrecht, NL: Kluwer.

Husserl, Edmund. 1954 [1970]. *The Crisis of European Sciences and Transcendental Phenomenology.* Evanston, IL: Northwestern University Press.

Hutchins, W. John. 1995. "Machine Translation: A Brief History," pp. 431–45 in *Concise History of the Language Sciences: From the Sumerians to the Cognitivists,* edited by E.F.K. Koerner and R.E. Asher. Oxford, UK: Pergamon Press.

Hutchins, W. John, ed. 2000a. *Early Years in Machine Translation: Memoirs and Biographies of Pioneers.* Amsterdam, NL: John Benjamins.

Hutchins, W. John. 2000b. "Petr Petrovich Troyanskii (1894–1950): A Forgotten Pioneer of Mechanical Translation." *Machine Translation* 15(3):187–221.

Hyppolite, Jean. 1955 [1969]. *Studies on Marx and Hegel.* Translated by J. O'Neill. New York, NY: Basic Books.

International Phonetic Association. 1999. *Handbook of the International Phonetic Association*. Cambridge, UK: Cambridge University Press.

Isherwood, Matt. 2017. *Designing Ecommerce Websites*. Kindle Edition: Transmitter Press.

Izvolov, Nikolai. 1998. "The History of Drawn Sound in the USSR." *Animation Journal*:54–59.

Jackendoff, Ray and Steven Pinker. 2005. "The Nature of the Language Faculty and Its Implications for Evolution of Language (Reply to Fitch, Hauser, and Chomsky)." *Cognition* 97(2):211–25.

Jagara (pseudonym). 1946(?). *Frederick Engels, Lewis Morgan and the Australian Aborigine*. Sydney, Australia: Current Book Distributors.

Jakobson, Roman. 1960. "Closing Statement: Linguistics and Poetics," pp. 350–77 in *Style in Language*, edited by T.A. Sebeok. Cambridge, MA: MIT Press.

Jakobson, Roman. 1970. *Main Trends in the Science of Language*. New York, NY: Harper and Row.

Jakobson, Roman. 1971. *Selected Writings*, Volume 2: *Word and Language*. The Hague, NL: Mouton.

Jakobson, Roman. 1972. "Verbal Communication." *Scientific American* 227(3):72–81.

Jakobson, Roman. 1976 [1978]. *Six Lectures on Sound and Meaning*. Translated by J. Mepham. Cambridge, MA: MIT Press.

Jakobson, Roman. 1980 [1985]. *Verbal Art, Verbal Sign, Verbal Time*. Minneapolis, MN: University of Minnesota Press.

Jakobson, Roman. 1992 [1997]. *My Futurist Years*. Translated by S. Rudy. New York, NY: Marsilio Publishers.

Jakobson, Roman and Morris Halle. 1956. *Fundamentals of Language*. The Hague, NL: Mouton.

Jakobson, Roman and Linda R. Waugh. 1979 [2002]. *The Sound Shape of Language*. Berlin, Germany: Mouton de Gruyter.

Jakšić, Božidar. 2010. "Praxis – Critical Thinking and Acting, 2009 Interview with Mihailo Marković." *Filozofskom Društvu* 2010(1):1–16.

Jameson, Fredric. 1971. *Marxism and Form: Twentieth Century Dialectical Theories of Literature*. Princeton, NJ: Princeton University Press.

Jameson, Fredric. 1991. *Postmodernism, or, the Cultural Logic of Late Capitalism*. Durham, NC: Duke University Press.

Johnson, Mark. 2007. *The Meaning of the Body: Aesthetics of Human Understanding*. Chicago, IL: University of Chicago Press.

Johnson, Melvin, Mike Schuster, Quoc V. Le, Maxim Krikun, Yonghui Wu, Zhifeng Chen, Nikhil Thorat, Fernanda Viégas, Martin Wattenberg, Greg Corrado, Macduff Hughes and Jeffrey Dean. 2017. "Google's Multilingual Neural Machine Translation System: Enabling Zero-Shot Translation." arXiv.org: 1611.04558 [cs.CL].

Jolly, A.T.H. and Frederick G.G. Rose. 1943. "The Place of the Australian Aboriginal in the Evolution of Society." *Annals of Eugenics* 12:44–87.

Kalantzis, Mary. 2000. "Multicultural Citizenship," pp. 99–110 in *Rethinking Australian Citizenship*, edited by W. Hudson and J. Kane. Melbourne, Australia: Cambridge University Press.

Kalantzis, Mary and Bill Cope. 2012. *New Learning: Elements of a Science of Education* (Edn 2). Cambridge, UK: Cambridge University Press.

Kalantzis, Mary and Bill Cope. 2013. "On Transformations: Reflections on the Work of, and Working with, Gunther Kress," pp. 16–32 in *Multimodality and Social Semiosis: Communication, Meaning-Making and Learning in the Work of Gunther Kress*, edited by M. Böck and N. Pachler. London, UK: Routledge.

Kalantzis, Mary and Bill Cope. 2015. "Learning and New Media," pp. 373–87 in *The Sage Handbook of Learning*, edited by D. Scott and E. Hargreaves. Thousand Oaks CA: Sage.

Kalantzis, Mary and Bill Cope. 2016a. "New Media and Productive Diversity in Learning," pp. 310–25 in *Diversity in Der Lehrerinnenbildung*, edited by S. Barsch and N. Glutsch. Münster, Germany: Waxmann.

Kalantzis, Mary and Bill Cope. 2016b. "Learner Differences in Theory and Practice." *Open Review of Educational Research* 3(1):85–132.

Kalantzis, Mary, Bill Cope, Eveline Chan, and Leanne Dalley-Trim. 2016. *Literacies* (Edn 2). Cambridge, UK: Cambridge University Press.

Kalantzis-Cope, Phillip. 2016a. "Whose Data? Problematizing the 'Gift' of Social Labour." *Global Media and Communication* 12(3):295–309.

Kalantzis-Cope, Phillip. 2016b. "Geopolitical Structuring in the Age of Information: Imagining Order, Understanding Change." *Alternatives: Global, Local, Political* 41 (4):179–93.

Kalantzis-Cope, Phillip. 2017. *The Work and Play of the Mind in the Information Age: Whose Property?* Cham, Switzerland: Palgrave/Springer.

Kant, Immanuel. 1770 [1894]. *Kant's Inaugural Dissertation*. Translated by W.J. Eckoff. New York, NY: Columbia College.

Kant, Immanuel. 1787 [1933]. *Critique of Pure Reason*. Translated by N.K. Smith. London, UK: Macmillan.

Keen, Ian. 1995. "Metaphor and the Metalanguage: 'Groups' in Northeast Arnhem Land." *American Ethnologist* 22(3):502–27.

Keen, Maurice. 1986. "Wyclif, the Bible, and Transubstantiation," pp. 1–16 in *Wyclif in His Times*, edited by A. Kenny. Oxford, UK: Oxford University Press.

Kendon, Adam. 1989. *Sign Languages of Aboriginal Australia: Cultural, Semiotic and Communicative Perspectives*. Cambridge, UK: Cambridge University Press.

Kendon, Adam. 2004. *Gesture: Visible Action as Utterance*. Cambridge, UK: Cambridge University Press.

Kenny, Anthony. 1985. *Wyclif*. Oxford, UK: Oxford University Press.

Kern, Richard. 2015. *Language, Literacy, and Technology*. Cambridge, UK: Cambridge University Press.

Keynes, John Maynard. 1930 [1950]. *A Treatise on Money*, Volume 2. London, UK: Macmillan.

Keynes, John Maynard. 1936. *The General Theory of Employment, Interest and Money*. London, UK: Macmillan.

Kirschenbaum, Matthew G. 2016. *Track Changes: A Literary History of Word Processing*. Cambridge, MA: Harvard University Press.

Kittler, Friedrich A. 1999 [2010]. *Optical Media*. Translated by A. Enns. Cambridge, UK: Polity.

Kittler, Friedrich A. 2009. "Towards an Ontology of Media." *Theory, Culture & Society* 26(2–3):23–31. doi:10.1177/0263276409103106.

Klein, Naomi. 2007. *The Shock Doctrine: The Rise of Disaster Capitalism*. New York, NY: Alfred A. Knopf.

Klimburg, Alexander. 2017. *The Darkening Web: The War for Cyberspace*. New York, NY: Penguin Press.

Klotz, Heinrich. 1984 [1988]. *The History of Postmodern Architecture*. Cambridge, MA: MIT Press.

Knight, Chris. 2008. "Early Human Kinship Was Matrilineal," pp. 61–82 in *Early Human Kinship*, edited by N.J. Allen, H. Callan, R. Dunbar, and W. James. Oxford, UK: Blackwell.

Knight, Chris. 2016. *Decoding Chomsky: Science and Revolutionary Politics*. New Haven, CT: Yale University Press.

Knowles, Frank. 1987. "Margaret Masterman: Her Life and Work." *Computers and Translation* 2(4):198–203.

Koch, Christof. 2004. *The Quest for Consciousness: A Neurobiological Approach*. Engelwood, CO: Roberts and Company.

Konstan, Joseph A. and John Riedl. 2012. "Recommender Systems: From Algorithms to User Experience." *User Modeling and User-Adapted Interaction* 22(1–2):101–23. doi:10.1007/s11257-011-9112-x.

Kosinski, Michal, David Stillwell, and Thore Graepel. 2013. "Private Traits and Attributes Are Predictable from Digital Records of Human Behavior." *Proceedings of the National Academy of Sciences* 110(15):5802–05.

Kövecses, Zoltán. 2002. *Metaphor: A Practical Introduction*. Oxford, UK: Oxford University Press.

Kowinski, William Severini. 1985. *The Malling of America: An inside Look at the Great Consumer Paradise*. New York, NY: William Morrow and Company.

Krause, Bernie. 2015. *Voices of the Wild: Animal Songs, Human Din, and the Call to Save Natural Soundscapes*. New Haven, CT: Yale University Press.

Kress, Gunther. 2003. *Literacy in the New Media Age*. London, UK: Routledge.

Kress, Gunther. 2009. *Multimodality: A Social Semiotic Approach to Contemporary Communication*. London, UK: Routledge.

Kress, Gunther. 2014. "What Is Mode?" pp. 60–75 in *The Routledge Handbook of Multimodal Analysis*, edited by C. Jewitt. London, UK: Routledge.

Krizhevsky, Alex, Ilya Sutskever, and Geoffrey E. Hinton. 2012. "Imagenet Classification with Deep Convolutional Neural Networks." *Advances in Neural Information Processing Systems* 25:1097–105.

Ladd, Brian. 1997. *The Ghosts of Berlin: Confronting German History in the Urban Landscape*. Chicago, IL: University of Chicago Press.

Lakoff, George and Mark Johnson. 1980 [2003]. *Metaphors We Live By*. Chicago, IL: University of Chicago Press.

Lakoff, George and Mark Johnson. 1999. *Philosophy in the Flesh: The Embodied Mind and Its Challenge to Western Thought*. New York, NY: Basic Books.

Lanchester, John. 2016. "When Bitcoin Grows Up." *London Review of Books* 38 (8):3–12.

Landauer, Thomas K., Danielle S. McNamara, Simon Dennis, and Walter Kintsch, eds. 2007. *Handbook of Latent Semantic Analysis*. New York, NY: Routledge.

Lanza, Joseph. 1994. *Elevator Music: A Surreal History of Muzak, Easy Listening, and Other Moodsong*. New York, NY: St Martin's Press.

Latour, Bruno and Steve Woolgar. 1986. *Laboratory Life: The Construction of Scientific Facts*. Princeton, NJ: Princeton University Press.

Le Corbusier. 1928 [2007]. *Toward an Architecture*. Translated by J. Goodman. Los Angeles, CA: Getty Publications.

Le Poidevin, Robin. 2007. *The Images of Time: An Essay on Temporal Representation*. Oxford, UK: Oxford University Press.

Leeding, Velma J. 1996. "Body Parts and Possession in Anindilyakwa," pp. 193–249 in *The Grammar of Inalienability: A Typological Perspective on Body Part Terms and the Part–Whole Relation*, edited by H. Chappel and W. McGregor. Berlin, Germany: Mouton de Gruyter.

Lemke, Jay. 2000. "Across the Scales of Time: Artifacts, Activities, and Meanings in Ecosocial Systems." *Mind, Culture and Activity* 7(4):273–90.

Lemke, Jay. 2009. "Multimodal Genres and Transmedia Traversals: Social Semiotics and the Political Economy of the Sign." *Semiotica* 173(1):283–97.

Lemke, Jay. 2014. "Multimodality, Identity, Time," pp. 165–75 in *The Routledge Handbook of Multimodal Analysis*, edited by C. Jewitt. London, UK: Routledge.

Leontiev, L.A. 1944. "Political Economy in the Soviet Union." *Science & Society* 8 (2):115–25.

Lessig, Lawrence. 2001. *The Future of Ideas: The Fate of the Commons in a Connected World*. New York, NY: Random House.

Lessig, Lawrence. 2002. "The Architecture of Innovation." *Duke Law Journal* 51 (6):1783–802.

Lessig, Lawrence. 2004. *Free Culture*. New York, NY: Penguin Press.

Lessig, Lawrence. 2008. *Remix: Making Art and Commerce Thrive in the Hybrid Economy*. New York, NY: Penguin Press.

Lévi-Strauss, Claude. 1955 [1976]. *Tristes Tropiques*. Harmondsworth, UK: Penguin.

Lévi-Strauss, Claude. 1962 [1966]. *The Savage Mind*. Chicago, IL: University of Chicago Press.

Levinson, Stephen C. 1983. *Pragmatics*. Cambridge, UK: Cambridge University Press.

Levinson, Stephen C. 1996a. "Relativity in Spatial Conception and Description," pp. 177–202 in *Rethinking Linguistic Relativity*, edited by J.J. Gumperz and S.C. Levinson. Cambridge, UK: Cambridge University Press.

Levinson, Stephen C. 1996b. "Language and Space." *Annual Review of Anthropology* 25:353–82.

Levinson, Stephen C. 1997. "Language and Cognition: The Cognitive Consequences of Spatial Description in Guugu Yimithirr." *Journal of Linguistic Anthropology* 7 (1):98–131.

Levinson, Stephen C. 2003. *Space in Language and Cognition: Explorations in Cognitive Diversity*. Cambridge, UK: Cambridge University Press.

Levinson, Stephen C., Sotaro Kita, Daniel B.M. Haun, and Björn H. Rasch. 2002. "Returning the Tables: Language Affects Spatial Reasoning." *Cognition* 84(2):155–88.

Levinson, Stephen, Sérgio Meira, and the Language and Cognition Group. 2003. "'Natural Concepts' in the Spatial Topological Domain–Adpositional Meanings in Crosslinguistic Perspective: An Exercise in Semantic Typology." *Language* 79 (3):485–516.

Levy, Steven. 1984 [1994]. *Hackers: Heroes of the Computer Revolution*. London, UK: Penguin.

Lévy-Bruhl, Lucien. 1910 [1985]. *How Natives Think*. Translated by L.A. Clare. Princeton, NJ: Princeton University Press.

Lévy-Bruhl, Lucien. 1921 [1923]. *Primitive Mentality*. Translated by L.A. Clare. New York, NY: Macmillan.

Li Zhizhong. 2010. "On the Invention of Wood Blocks for Printing in China," pp. 35–44 in *The History and Cultural Heritage of Chinese Calligraphy, Printing and Library Work*, edited by S.M. Allen, L. Zuzao, C. Xiaolan, and J. Bos. Berlin, Germany: Walter de Gruyter.

Lippmann, Walter. 1922 [1997]. *Public Opinion*. New York, NY: Free Press.

Liskov, Barbara. 1993. "Practical Uses of Synchronized Clocks in Distributed Systems." *Distributed Computing* 6(4):211–19.

Lloyd, Dan. 2012. "Neural Correlates of Temporality: Default Mode Variability and Temporal Awareness." *Consciousness and Cognition* 21:695–703.

Locke, William N. and A. Donald Booth, eds. 1955. *The Machine Translation of Languages*. Cambridge, MA: The Technology Press of MIT.

Lopez, Robert S. 1976. *The Commercial Revolution of the Middle Ages, 950–1350*. Cambridge, UK: Cambridge University Press.

Lucy, John A. 1992. *Language Diversity and Thought: A Reformulation of the Linguistic Relativity Hypothesis*. Cambridge, UK: Cambridge University Press.

Lucy, John A. 1997. "Linguistic Relativity." *Annual Review of Anthropology* 26:291–312.

Lucy, John A. 1998. "Space in Language and Thought: Commentary and Discussion." *Ethos* 26(1):105–11.

Ludlow, Peter. 1999. *Semantics, Tense, and Time: An Essay on the Metaphysics of Natural Language*. Cambridge, MA: MIT Press.

Lukács, György. 1910 [1974]. *Soul and Form*. Translated by A. Bostock. Cambridge, MA: MIT Press.

Lukács, György. 1920 [1978]. *The Theory of the Novel: A Historico-Philosophical Essay on the Forms of Great Epic Literature*. Translated by A. Bostock. London, UK: Merlin.

Lukács, György. 1923 [1971]. *History and Class Consciousness*. Translated by R. Livingstone. London, UK: Merlin Press.

Lukács, György. 1924 [1977]. *Lenin: A Study in the Unity of His Thought*. Translated by N. Jacobs. London, UK: Verso.

Lukács, György. 1925 [2000]. *A Defence of "History and Class Consciousness": Tailism and the Dialectic*. Translated by E. Leslie. London, UK: Verso.

Lukács, György. 1937 [1983]. *The Historical Novel*. Translated by H. Mitchell and S. Mitchell. Lincoln, NE: University of Nebraska Press.

Lukács, György. 1947 [2013]. *The Culture of People's Democracy*. Chicago, IL: Haymarket Books.

Lukács, György. 1957 [1963]. *The Meaning of Contemporary Realism*. Translated by J. and N. Mander. London, UK: Merlin.

Lukács, György. 1978a. *The Ontology of Social Being*, Volume 1: *Hegel's False and His Genuine Ontology*. Translated by D. Fernbach. London, UK: Merlin Press.

Lukács, György. 1978b. *Writer and Critic, and Other Essays*. Translated by A. Kahn. London, UK: Merlin Press.

Lukács, György. 1978c. *The Ontology of Social Being*, Volume 3: *Labour*. Translated by D. Fernbach. London, UK: Merlin Press.

Lukács, György. 1978d. *The Ontology of Social Being*, Volume 2: *Marx's Basic Ontological Principles*. Translated by D. Fernbach. London, UK: Merlin Press.

Lukić, Slobodan. 1979. *The Nonaligned Movement and National Emancipation.* Belgrade, Yugoslavia: Socialist Thought and Practice.

Lukin, Annabelle, Alison Moore, Maria Herke, Rebekah Wegener, and Canzhong Wu. 2008. "Halliday's Model of Register Revisited and Explored." *Linguistics and the Human Sciences* 4(2):187–213.

Luria, Aleksandr Romanovich. 1981. *Language and Cognition.* New York, NY: John Wiley and Sons.

Lyotard, Jean-François. 1979. *The Postmodern Condition: A Report on Knowledge.* Manchester, UK: Manchester University Press.

MacCannell, Dean. 2000. "Erving Goffman (1922–1982)," pp. 8–36 in *Sage Masters of Modern Social Thought: Erving Goffman,* edited by G.A. Fine and G.W.H. Smith. London, UK: Sage.

Macey, David. 1993. *The Lives of Michel Foucault.* New York, NY: Pantheon Books.

MacIntyre, Alisdair. 2006. *Edith Stein: A Philosophical Prologue, 1913–1922.* Lanham, MD: Rowman and Littlefield.

Mack, Arien and Irven Rick. 1998. *Inattentional Blindness.* Cambridge MA: MIT Press.

Macken, Mary, Mary Kalantzis, Gunther Kress, Jim Martin, Bill Cope, and Joan Rothery. 1990. *A Genre-Based Approach to Teaching Writing, Years 3–6, Book 3: Writing Stories: A Teaching Unit Based on Narratives About Fairy Tales.* Sydney, Australia: Directorate of Studies, N.S.W. Department of Education.

Magee, Liam and James A. Thom. 2014. "What's in a WordTM? When One Electronic Document Format Standard Is Not Enough." *Information Technology & People* 27 (4):482–511.

Maguire, Eleanor A., David G. Gadian, Ingrid S. Johnsrude, Catriona D. Good, John Ashburner, Richard S.J. Frackowiak, and Christopher D. Frith. 2000. "Navigation-Related Structural Change in the Hippocampi of Taxi Drivers." *Proceedings of the National Academy of Sciences* 97(8):4398–403.

Majid, Asifa, Melissa Bowerman, Sotaro Kita, Daniel B.M. Haun, and Stephen C. Levinson. 2004. "Can Language Restructure Cognition? The Case for Space." *Trends in Cognitive Sciences* 8(3):108–14.

Makdisi, George. 1981. *The Rise of Colleges: Institutions of Learning in Islam and the West.* Edinburgh, UK: Edinburgh University Press.

Malinowski, Bronislaw. 1913 [1963]. *The Family among the Aborigines.* New York, NY: Schocken Books.

Malinowski, Bronislaw. 1922 [1984]. *Argonauts of the Western Pacific.* Prospect Heights, IL: Waveland Press.

Malinowski, Bronislaw. 1948. *Magic, Science and Religion, and Other Essays.* Glencoe, IL: The Free Press.

Malinowski, Bronislaw. 1962. *Sex, Culture, and Myth.* New York, NY: Harcourt, Brace & World.

Malotki, Ekkehart. 1983. *Hopi Time: A Linguistic Analysis of the Temporal Categories in the Hopi Language.* Berlin, Germany: Mouton.

Man, John. 2002. *The Gutenberg Revolution.* London, UK: Review.

Manovich, Lev. 2001. *The Language of New Media.* Cambridge, MA: MIT Press.

Marčuk, Jurij N. 2000. "Machine Translation: Early Years in the USSR," pp. 243–52 in *Early Years in Machine Translation: Memoirs and Biographies of Pioneers,* edited by W.J. Hutchins. Amsterdam, NL: John Benjamins.

Marcuse, Herbert. 1941 [1960]. *Reason and Revolution: Hegel and the Rise of Social Theory.* Boston, MA: Beacon Press.

Marika, Raymattja, Daynawa Ngurruwutthun, and Leon White. 1990. *Always Together, Yaka Gana: Participatory Research at Yirrkala as Part of the Development of a Yolgnu Education.* Yirrkala, Australia: Yirrkala Literature Production Centre.

Marika-Mununggiritj, Raymattja and Michael J. Christie. 1995. "Yolngu Metaphors for Learning." *International Journal of the Sociology of Language* 113(1):59–62.

Marković, Mihailo. 1961 [1984]. *Dialectical Theory of Meaning.* Translated by D. Rougé and J. Coddington. Dordrecht, NL: D. Reidl Publishing.

Marković, Mihailo. 1974a. *From Affluence to Praxis: Philosophy and Social Criticism.* Ann Arbor, MI: University of Michigan Press.

Marković, Mihailo. 1974b. *The Contemporary Marx: Essays on Humanist Communism.* Nottingham, UK: Spokesman Books.

Marković, Mihailo. 1981. "New Forms of Democracy in Socialism." *Praxis International* 1(1):23–38.

Marković, Mihailo. 1982. *Democratic Socialism: Theory and Practice.* Brighton, UK: Harvester Press.

Marković, Mihailo. 1989. "Tragedy of National Conflicts in 'Real Socialism': The Case of Kosovo." *Praxis International* 9(4):408–24.

Marković, Mihailo and Robert S. Cohen. 1975. *Yugoslavia: The Rise and Fall of Socialist Humanism, a History of the Praxis Group.* London, UK: Spokesman Books.

Marković, Mihailo and Gajo Petrović, eds. 1979. *Praxis: Yugoslav Essays in the Philosophy and Methodology of the Social Sciences.* Dortrecht, NL: D. Reidel Publishing.

Márkus, György. 1966 [2014]. *Marxism and Anthropology: The Concept of "Human Essence" in the Philosophy of Marx.* Sydney, Australia: Modem-Verlag.

Márkus, György. 1975–79 [1986]. *Language and Production: A Critique of the Paradigms.* Dordrecht, NL: D. Reidel.

Márkus, György. 1977. "The Soul and Life: The Young Lukacs and the Problem of Culture." *Telos* (32):95–115.

Márkus, György. 1981. "Planning the Crisis: Remarks on the Economic System of Soviet-Type Societies." *Praxis International* 1(3):240–57.

Martin, Felix. 2014. *Money: The Unauthorized Biography.* New York, NY: Alfred A. Knopf.

Martin, J.R. 1992. *English Text: System and Structure.* Philadelphia, PA: John Benjamins.

Martin, J.R. 1999. "Modelling Context: A Crooked Path of Progress in Contextual Linguistics," pp. 25–62 in *Text and Context in Functional Linguistics*, edited by M. Ghadessy. Amsterdam, NL: John Benjamins.

Martin, J.R., ed. 2013. *Interviews with M.A.K. Halliday: Language Turned Back on Himself.* London, UK: Bloomsbury.

Marx, Karl. 1844 [1975]. "Economic and Philosophical Manuscripts," pp. 279–400 in *Marx: Early Writing*, edited by Q. Hoare. Harmondsworth, UK: Penguin.

Marx, Karl. 1867 [1976]. *Capital: A Critique of Political Economy*, Volume 1. Translated by B. Fowkes. Harmondsworth, UK: Penguin.

Marx, Karl. 1875 [2010]. "Critique of the Gotha Program," pp. 75–99 in *Marx and Engels: Collected Works*, Volume 24. London, UK: Lawrence and Wishart.

Massumi, Brian. 2002. *Parables for the Virtual: Movement, Affect, Sensation*. Durham, NC: Duke University Press.

Masterman, Margaret. 1957. "Metaphysical and Ideographic Language," pp. 283–360 in *British Philosophy in the Mid-Century*, edited by C.A. Mace. London, UK: George Allen and Unwin.

Masterman, Margaret. 1967. "Mechanical Pidgin Translation," pp. 195–227 in *Machine Translation*, edited by A.D. Booth. Amsterdam, NL: North-Holland Publishing.

Masterman, Margaret. 2005. *Language, Cohesion and Form*. Cambridge, UK: Cambridge University Press.

Mathiesen, Thomas. 1997. "The Viewer Society: Michel Foucault's 'Panopticon' Revisited." *Theoretical Criminology: An International Journal* 1(2):215–32.

Matthews, Gerald, Ian Deary, and Martha Whiteman. 2003. *Personality Traits*. Cambridge, UK: Cambridge University Press.

Matz, Sandra C., Joe J. Gladstone, and David Stillwell. 2016. "Money Buys Happiness When Spending Fits Our Personality." *Psychological Science* 27(5):715–25.

McEvoy, Brian, Sandra Beleza, and Mark D. Shriver. 2006. "The Genetic Architecture of Normal Variation in Human Pigmentation: An Evolutionary Perspective and Model." *Human Molecular Genetics* 15(2): R176–81.

McLellan, Josie. 2007. "State Socialist Bodies: East German Nudism from Ban to Boom." *The Journal of Modern History* 79(1):48–79.

McLuhan, Marshall. 1964 [2001]. *Understanding Media: The Extensions of Man*. London, UK: Routledge.

McLuhan, Marshall and Quentin Fiore. 1967 [1996]. *The Medium Is the Massage: An Inventory of Effects*. Berkeley, CA: Gingko Press.

McNeill, Daniel. 1998. *The Face*. Boston, MA: Little, Brown and Company.

McNeill, David. 1992. *Hand and Mind: What Gestures Reveal About Thought*. Chicago, IL: University of Chicago Press.

McNeill, David. 2012. *How Language Began: Gesture and Speech in Human Evolution*. Cambridge, UK: Cambridge University Press.

Medvedev, P.N. 1928 [1985]. *The Formal Method in Literary Scholarship: A Critical Introduction to Sociological Poetics*. Cambridge, MA: Harvard University Press.

Mehler, Barry. 1997. "Beyondism: Raymond B. Cattell and the New Eugenics." *Genetica* 99:153–63.

Merleau-Ponty, Maurice. 1945 [2002]. *Phenomenology of Perception*. Translated by C. Smith. London, UK: Routledge.

Mey, Jacob L. 2001. *Pragmatics: An Introduction*. Oxford, UK: Blackwell Publishing.

Mieczkowski, Yanek. 2013. *Eisenhower's Sputnik Moment: The Race for Space and World Prestige*. Ithaca, NY: Cornell University Press.

Miles, Robert. 1989. *Racism*. London, UK: Routledge.

Miller, Carolyn R. 1984. "Genre as Social Action." *Quarterly Journal of Speech* 70 (2):151–67.

Miller, Daniel. 2010. *Stuff*. Cambridge, UK: Polity.

Miller, James. 1993. *The Passion of Michel Foucault*. New York, NY: Simon & Schuster.

Milner, Greg. 2016. *Pinpoint: How GPS Is Changing Technology, Culture, and Our Minds*. New York, NY: W.W. Norton.

Mischler, Paul C. 1999. *Raising Reds: The Young Pioneers, Radical Summer Camps, and Communist Political Culture in the United States*. New York, NY: Columbia University Press.

Mocnik, Franz-Benjamin. 2018. "The Polynomial Volume Law of Complex Networks in the Context of Local and Global Optimization." *Scientific Reports* 8(11274):1–10.

Mocnik, Franz-Benjamin, Amin Mobasheri, Luisa Griesbaum, Melanie Eckle, Clemens Jacobs and Carolin Klonner. 2018. "A Grounding-Based Ontology of Data Quality Measures." *Journal of Spatial Information Science* (16):1–25.

Monteath, Peter and Valerie Munt. 2015. *Red Professor: The Cold War Life of Fred Rose*. Mile End, Australia: Wakefield Press.

Moore, Gordon E. 1965. "Cramming More Components onto Integrated Circuits." *Electronics* 38(8):114–17.

Moran, Christian. 2015. *Great Big Beautiful Tomorrow: Walt Disney and Technology*. New York, NY: Theme Park Press.

Morrison, Toni. 2015. *God Help the Child*. New York, NY: Knopf Doubleday.

Musmann, Hans Georg. 2006. "Genesis of the Mp3 Audio Coding Standard." *IEEE Transactions on Consumer Electronics* 52(3):1043–9.

Musto, Marcello. 2009. "Marx in Paris: Manuscripts and Notebooks of 1844." *Science and Society* 73(3):386–402.

Myers, William Andrew. 1995. "Victoria, Lady Welby (1837–1912)," pp. 1–24 in *A History of Women Philosophers*, Volume 4, edited by M.E. Waithe. Dordrecht, NL: Kluwer Academic Publishers.

Nakamura, Eita and Kunihiko Kaneko. 2018. "Statistical Evolutionary Laws in Music Styles." arXiv:1809.05832 [physics.soc-ph].

Naughton, John. 2018. "The New Surveillance Capitalism." *Prospect*, January 19.

Navasky, Victor. 1980. *Naming Names*. New York, NY: Viking Press.

Nelson, Theodor H. 1977. *Selected Papers, 1965–77*. Swarthmore, PA: Swathmore College.

Nerlich, Brigitte. 1990. *Change in Language: Whitney, Bréal, and Wegener*. London, UK: Routledge.

Neurath, Otto, Rudolf Carnap, and Charles Morris. 1938 [1955]. *International Encyclopedia of Unified Science*, Volume 1. Chicago, IL: University of Chicago Press.

New London Group. 1996. "A Pedagogy of Multiliteracies: Designing Social Futures." *Harvard Educational Review* 66(1):60–92.

Newfield, Denise. 2014. "Transformation, Transduction and the Transmodal Moment," pp. 100–13 in *The Routledge Handbook of Multimodal Analysis*, edited by C. Jewitt. London, UK: Routledge.

Nielsen, Rasmus, Joshua M. Akey, Mattias Jakobsson, Jonathan K. Pritchard, Sarah Tishkoff, and Eske Willerslev. 2017. "Tracing the Peopling of the World through Genomics." *Nature* 541:302–10.

Nigro, Giampiero. 2010a. "Francesco and the Datini Company of Florence in the Trading System," pp. 229–48 in *Francesco Di Marco Datini: The Man and the Merchant*, edited by G. Nigro. Florence, Italy: Firenze University Press.

Nigro, Giampiero. 2010b. "The Banking Company," pp. 515–28 in *Francesco Di Marco Datini: The Man and the Merchant*, edited by G. Nigro. Florence, Italy: Firenze University Press.

Nilsson, Nils J. 2009. *The Quest for Artificial Intelligence: A History of Ideas and Achievements*. Cambridge, UK: Cambridge University Press.

O'Neil, Cathy. 2016. *Weapons of Math Destruction: How Big Data Increases Inequality and Threatens Democracy*. New York, NY: Broadway Books.

Ogden, C.K. and I.A. Richards. 1923 [1989]. *The Meaning of Meaning*. San Diego, CA: Harcourt Brace Jovanovich.

Ong, Walter J. 1958 [1983]. *Ramus, Method and the Decay of Dialogue*. Cambridge, MA: Harvard University Press.

Onorato, Joseph and Mark Schupack. 2002. *Tech Model Railroad Club of MIT: The First Fifty Years*. Cambridge, MA: TMRC.

Origo, Iris. 1957. *The Merchant of Prato: Francesco Di Marco Datini*. New York, NY: Alfred A. Knopf.

Page, Lawrence. 2001. "Method for Node Ranking in a Linked Database." Edited by U.S. Patent Office. Stanford, CA: The Board of Trustees of the Leland Stanford Junior University.

Page, Lawrence, Sergey Brin, Rajeev Motwani, and Terry Winograd. 1998. "The Pagerank Citation Ranking: Bringing Order to the Web." Stanford, CA: Stanford InfoLab.

Palmer, Bill. 2015. "Topography in Language: Absolute Frame of Reference and the Topographic Correspondence Hypothesis," pp. 179–226 in *Language Structure and Environment: Social, Cultural, and Natural Factors*, edited by R.J. LaPolla and Rik De Busser. London, UK: John Benjamins.

Palmer, Richard E. 2002. "A Response to Richard Wolin on Gadamer and the Nazis." *International Journal of Philosophical Studies* 10(4):467–82.

Pandey, Shakunt. 2014. "The Indian Museum Completes 200 Years." *Science Reporter*, October: 38–41.

Panov, D. Yu. 1960. *Automatic Translation*. London, UK: Pergamon Press.

Papp, F. 1966. *Mathematical Linguistics in the Soviet Union*. The Hague, NL: Mouton.

Park, Jaram, Vladimir Barash, Clay Fink and Meeyoung Cha. 2013. "Emoticon Style: Interpreting Differences in Emoticons across Cultures." Paper presented at the Proceedings of the Seventh International AAAI Conference on Weblogs and Social Media.

Pasquinelli, Matteo. 2009. "Google's Pagerank Algorithm: A Diagram of Cognitive Capitalism and the Rentier of the Common Intellect," pp. 152–62 in *Deep Search*, edited by K. Becker and F. Stalder. London, UK: Transaction Publishers.

Patterson, Scott. 2010. *The Quants: How a New Breed of Math Quizzes Conquered Wall Street and Nearly Destroyed It*. New York, NY: Crown Business.

Pearson, Noel. 1993. "A Troubling Inheritance." *Race and Class* 35(4):1–9.

Peirce, Charles Sanders. 1992. *The Essential Peirce: Selected Philosophical Writings*, Volume 1: *1867–1893*. Bloomington, IN: Indiana University Press.

Peirce, Charles Sanders. 1998. *The Essential Peirce: Selected Philosophical Writings*, Volume 2: *1893–1913*. Bloomington, IN: Indiana University Press.

Peters, Benjamin. 2016. *How Not to Network a Nation: The Uneasy History of the Soviet Internet*. Cambridge, MA: MIT Press.

Peters, John Durham. 1999. *Speaking into the Air: A History of the Idea of Communication*. Chicago, IL: University of Chicago Press.

Peters, John Durham. 2015. *The Marvelous Clouds: Toward a Philosophy of Elemental Media*. Chicago, IL: University of Chicago Press.

Petrilli, Susan. 2015. "Sign, Meaning, and Understanding in Victoria Welby and Charles S. Peirce." *Signs and Society* 3(1):71–102.

Phillipson, Nicholas. 2010. *Adam Smith: An Enlightened Life*. New Haven CT: Yale University Press.

Piaget, Jean. 1923 [2002]. *Language and Thought of the Child*. London, UK: Routledge.

Pine, B. Joseph. 1999. *Mass Customization: The New Frontier in Business Competition*. Brighton, MA: Harvard Business School Press.

Pinheiro, Petrilson. 2019. "The Age of Multisynopticon: What Does It Mean to Be (Critically) Literate Nowadays?," pp. 237–60 in *Linguística Aplicada Para Além Das Fronteiras*, edited by R.F. Maciel, R. Tilio, D.M. de Jesus, and A.L. d'E.C. de Barros. Campinas, Brazil: Pontes.

Piotrovskij, Raimund J. 2000. "MT in the Former USSR and the Newly Independent States (NIS): Prehistory, Romantic Era, Prosaic Time," pp. 232–51 in *Early Years in Machine Translation: Memoirs and Biographies of Pioneers*, edited by W.J. Hutchins. Amsterdam, NL: John Benjamins.

Plato. *c*.399–347 BCE [1997]. "Phaedo," in *Complete Works*, edited by J.M. Cooper. Indianapolis, IN: Hackett.

Plato. *c*.399–347 BCE [1997]. "Sophist," in *Complete Works*, edited by J.M. Cooper. Indianapolis, IN: Hackett.

Popper, Nathaniel. 2015. *Digital Gold: Bitcoin and the inside Story of the Misfits and Millionaires Trying to Reinvent Money*. New York, NY: HarperCollins.

Raboy, Marc. 2016. *Marconi: The Man Who Networked the World*. Oxford, UK: Oxford University Press.

Reichenbach, Hans. 1920 [1965]. *The Theory of Relativity and a Priori Knowledge*. Translated by M. Reichenbach. Berkeley, CA: University of California Press.

Reichenbach, Hans. 1927 [1957]. *The Philosophy of Space and Time*. Translated by M. Reichenbach and J. Freund. New York, NY: Dover Publications.

Reichenbach, Hans. 1930 [1957]. *Atom and Cosmos: The World of Modern Physics*. Translated by E.S. Allen. New York, NY: George Braziller Inc.

Reichenbach, Hans. 1942. *From Copernicus to Einstein*. New York, NY: Philosophical Library.

Reichenbach, Hans. 1944. *Philosophic Foundations of Quantum Mechanics*. Berkeley, CA: University of California Press.

Reichenbach, Hans. 1947. *Elements of Symbolic Logic*. New York, NY: Macmillan.

Reichenbach, Hans. 1953. *The Rise of Scientific Philosophy*. Berkeley, CA: University of California Press.

Reichenbach, Hans. 1957. *The Direction of Time*. Berkeley, CA: University of California Press.

Reinert, Sophus A. and Robert Fredona. 2017. "Merchants and the Origins of Capitalism." Working Paper 18–021. Cambridge, MA: Harvard Business School.

Renear, Allen, Elli Mylonas, and David Durand. 1996. "Refining Our Notion of What Text Really Is: The Problem of Overlapping Hierarchies." *Research in Humanities Computing* 4:263–80.

Rheingold, Howard. 1991. *Virtual Reality*. New York NY: Summit Books.

Richens, R.H. 1958. "Interlingual Machine Translation." *Computer Journal* 1 (3):144–47.

Richens, R.H. and M.A.K. Halliday. 1957. "Word Decomposition for Machine Translation." Paper presented at the Eighth Annual Round Table Meeting on Linguistics and Language Studies, Georgetown University, Washington, DC (mt-archive.info/GURT-1957-Richens.pdf).

Roberts, Dorothy. 2011. *Fatal Invention: How Science, Politics, and Big Business Re-Create Race in the Twenty-First Century*. New York, NY: Free Press.

Robinson, Ian. 1975. *The New Grammarian's Funeral: A Critique of Noam Chomsky's Linguistics*. Cambridge, UK: Cambridge University Press.

Rose, Frederick G.G. 1960. *Classification of Kin, Age Structure and Marriage Amongst the Groote Eylandt Aborigines: A Study in Method and a Theory of Australian Kinship*. Berlin, Germany: Academie-Verlag.

Rose, Frederick G.G. 1965. *The Winds of Change in Central Australia: The Aborigines at Angus Downs, 1962*. Berlin, Germany: Academie-Verlag.

Rose, Frederick G.G. 1968. *Australia Revisited: The Aborigine Story from the Stone Age to the Space Age*. Berlin, Germany: Seven Seas Publishers.

Rose, Frederick G.G. 1987. *The Traditional Mode of Production of the Australian Aborigines*. Sydney, Australia: Angus and Robertson.

Rose, Frederick G.G. and A.T.H. Jolly. 1942. "An Interpretation of the Taboo between Mother-in-Law and Son-in-Law." *Man* 42:15–16.

Rossi, Aldo. 1982. *The Architecture of the City*. Translated by D. Ghirardo and J. Ockman. Cambridge, MA: MIT Press.

Rumbaugh, Duane M., ed. 1977. *Language Learning by a Chimpanzee: The Lana Project*. New York, NY: Academic Press.

Rumelhart, David E., Geoffrey E. Hinton, and Ronald J. Williams. 1986. "Learning Representations by Back-Propagating Errors." *Nature* 323:533–36.

Sahlins, Marshall. 1972. *Stone Age Economics*. New York, NY: Aldine.

Sampson, Geoffrey. 2005. *The "Language Instinct" Debate*. London, UK: Continuum.

Sanburn, Josh. 2017. "Why the Death of Malls Is About More Than Shopping." *Time*, July 20.

Sapir, Edward. 1921. *Language: An Introduction to the Study of Speech*. New York, NY: Harcourt Brace.

Sartre, Jean-Paul. 1960 [1976]. *Critique of Dialectical Reason*. Translated by A. Sheridan-Smith. London, UK: Verso.

Saunders, Clarence. 1917. "Self Serving Store." Edited by U.S. Patent Office.

Sawicki, Marianne. 1997. *Body, Text, and Science: The Literacy of Investigative Practices and the Phenomenology of Edith Stein*. Dordrecht, NL: Springer Science.

Scammell-Katz, Siemon. 2012. *The Art of Shopping: How We Shop and Why We Buy*. London, UK: LID Publishing.

Schiller, Herbert I. 1971. *Mass Communications and American Empire*. Boston, MA: Beacon Press.

Schiller, Herbert I. 1981. *Who Knows: Information in the Age of the Fortune 500*. Norwood, NJ: Ablex Publishing.

Schiller, Herbert I. 1989. *Culture Inc.: The Corporate Takeover of Public Expression*. New York, NY: Oxford University Press.

Schiller, Herbert I. 2000a. *Living in the Number One Country: Reflections from a Critic of American Empire*. New York, NY: Seven Stories Press.

Schiller, Robert J. 2000b. *Irrational Exuberance*. Princeton NJ: Princeton University Press.

Schivelbusch, Wolfgang. 1977 [2014]. *The Railway Journey: The Industrialization of Time and Space in the Nineteenth Century*. Berkeley, CA: University of California Press.

Schmid, Helmut. 2010. "Decision Trees," pp. 181–96 in *The Handbook of Computational Linguistics and Natural Language Processing*, edited by A. Clark, C. Fox, and S. Lappin. Chichester, UK: Wiley-Blackwell.

Schumpeter, Joseph A. 1950 [1976]. *Capitalism, Socialism and Democracy*. New York, NY: Harper and Row.

Scollon, Ron. 1999. "Multilingualism and Intellectual Property: Visual Holophrastic Discourse and the Commodity/Sign," pp. 404–17 in *Georgetown University Round Table on Languages and Linguistics*, edited by J.E. Alatis and A.-H. Tan. Washington, DC: Georgetown University Press.

Scollon, Ron and Suzie Wong Scollon. 2014. "Multimodality and Language: A Retrospective and Prospective View," pp. 205–16 in *The Routledge Handbook of Multimodal Analysis*, edited by C. Jewitt. London, UK: Routledge.

Scott-Brown, Denise. 1989 [2015]. "Room at the Top? Sexism and the Star System in Architecture." *MAS Context* 27:25–39.

Segerdahl, Pär, William Fields and Sue Savage-Rumbaugh. 2005. *Kanzi's Primal Language: The Cultural Initiation of Primates into Language*. London, UK: Palgrave Macmillan.

Seibel, Hans Dieter and Ukandi G. Damachi. 1982. *Self-Management in Yugoslavia and the Developing World*. New York, NY: St Martin's Press.

Shannon, Claude E. and Warren Weaver. 1949. *The Mathematical Theory of Communication*. Urbana, IL: University of Illinois Press.

Shaw, Tamsin. 2018. "The New Military-Industrial Complex of Big Data Psy-Ops." *New York Review of Books*, 21 March.

Sher, Gerson S. 1977. *Praxis: Marxist Criticism and Dissent in Socialist Yugoslavia*. Bloomington, IN: Indiana University Press.

Sibley, Brian. 1995. *The Thomas the Tank Engine Man: The Story of the Reverend W. Awdry and His Really Useful Engines*. London, UK: Heinemann.

Sichel, Kim. 1999. *Germaine Krull: Photographer of Modernity*. Cambridge MA: MIT Press.

Simmel, Georg. 1907 [1978]. *The Philosophy of Money*. Translated by T. Bottomore and D. Frisby. London, UK: Routledge and Kegan Paul.

Slobin, Dan I. 1996. "From "Thought and Language" to "Thinking for Speaking"," pp. 70–96 in *Rethinking Linguistic Relativity*, edited by J.J. Gumperz and S.C. Levinson. Cambridge, UK: Cambridge University Press.

Smiley, David. 2013. *Pedestrian Modern: Shopping and American Architecture, 1925–1956*. Minneapolis, MN: University of Minnesota Press.

Smirnov, Andrey. 2013. *Sound in Z: Experiments in Sound and Electronic Music in Early 20th Century Russia*. London, UK: Koenig Books.

Smith, Adam. 1776 [1937]. *An Inquiry into the Nature and Causes of the Wealth of Nations*. New York, NY: The Modern Library.

Smith, Adam. 1790 [1817]. *The Theory of Moral Sentiments*. Boston, MA: Wells and Lilly.

Soderberg, Johan. 2008. *Hacking Capitalism: The Free and Open Source Software Movement*. London, UK: Routledge.

Sontag, Susan. 1977. *Illness as Metaphor*. New York, NY: Farrar, Straus and Giroux.

Sontag, Susan. 2003. *Regarding the Pain of Others*. London, UK: Hamish Hamilton.

Sparck Jones, Karen. 2000. "R.H. Richens: Translation in the Nude," pp. 263–78 in *Early Years in Machine Translation: Memoirs and Biographies of Pioneers*, edited by W.J. Hutchins. Amsterdam, NL: John Benjamins.

Spilia, Elina. 2007. "Shark People: Djapu Painting and the Miny'tji Buku Larrŋgay Collection." *Art Bulletin of Victoria* 47:7–16.

St Benedict. *c.*530 [1949]. *The Holy Rule of St. Benedict*. Translated by Rev. Boniface Verheyen. Grand Rapids, MI: Christian Classics Ethereal Library.

Stalin, J.V. 1950 [1972]. *Marxism and Problems of Linguistics*. Beijing, China: Foreign Languages Press.

Stallman, Richard. 2002. *Free Software, Free Society*. Boston, MA: GNU Press.

Stallman, Richard. 2018. "Talking to the Mailman: Interview with Rob Lucas." *New Left Review* (113):69–93.

Stein, Edith. 1917 [1989]. *On the Problem of Empathy*. Translated by W. Stein. Washington, DC: ICS Publications.

Stein, Edith. 1922 [2000]. *Philosophy of Psychology and the Humanities*. Translated by M.C. Baseheart and M. Sawicki. Washington, DC: ICS Publications.

Stein, Edith. 1933 [1986]. *Life in a Jewish Family, 1891–1916: An Autobiography*. Translated by J. Koeppel. Washington, DC: ICS Publications.

Stein, Edith. 1959 [1987]. *Essays on Woman*. Translated by F.M. Oben. Washington, DC: ICS Publications.

Stein, Edith. 1987 [1993]. *Self Portrait in Letters, 1916–1942*. Translated by J. Koeppel. Washington, DC: ICS Publications.

Stern, Daniel L. 1985. *The Interpersonal World of the Infant: A View from Psychoanalysis and Developmental Psychology*. New York, NY: Basic Books.

Stöckl, Hartmut. 2009. "The Language-Image-Text: Theoretical and Analytical Inroads into Semiotic Complexity." *Arbeiten aus Anglistik und Amerikanistik* 34 (2):203–26.

Stöckl, Hartmut. 2014. "Semiotic Paradigms and Multimodality," pp. 274–86 in *The Routledge Handbook of Multimodal Analysis*, edited by C. Jewitt. London, UK: Routledge.

Straus, Erwin W. 1966. *Phenomenological Psychology: The Selected Papers of Erwin W. Straus*. New York, NY: Basic Books.

Talmy, Leonard. 2017. *The Targeting System of Language*. Cambridge MA: MIT Press.

Tanner, Norman P., ed. 1990. *Decrees of the Ecumenical Councils*, Volume 1: *Nicea I to Lateran V*. London, UK: Sheed and Ward.

Taylor, Charles. 1994. *Multiculturalism: Examining the Politics of Recognition*. Princeton, NJ: Princeton University Press.

Taylor, Frederick Winslow. 1911. *The Principles of Scientific Management*. New York, NY: Harper & Brothers.

Tedman, Gary. 2004. "Marx's 1844 Manuscripts as a Work of Art: A Hypertextual Reinterpretation." *Rethinking Marxism* 16(4):427–41.

Thaler, Richard H. and Cass R. Sunstein. 2008. *Nudge: Improving Decisions About Health, Wealth, and Happiness*. New Haven, CT: Yale University Press.

Theremin, Leo Sergejewitsch. 1928. "Method of and Apparatus for the Generation of Sounds." Edited by U.S. Patent Office.

Thompson, E.P. 1976. "Time, Work-Discipline, and Industrial Capitalism." *Past & Present* 38:56–97.

Thompson, Emily. 2002. *The Soundscape of Modernity: Architectural Acoustics and the Culture of Listening in America, 1900–1933*. Cambridge, MA: MIT Press.

Tobler, W.R. 1970. "A Computer Movie Simulating Urban Growth in the Detroit Region." *Economic Geography* 46(Supplement: Proceedings of the International Geographical Union, Commission on Quantitative Methods):234–40.

Tobler, W.R. 2004. "On the First Law of Geography: A Reply." *Annals of the Association of American Geographers* 94(2):304–10.

Todorov, Tzvetan and Richard M. Berrong. 1976. "The Origin of Genres." *New Literary History* 8(1):159–70.

Trump, Donald J. and Tony Schwartz. 1987. *Trump: The Art of the Deal*. New York, NY: Random House.

Tsien, Tsuen-hsuin and Joseph Needham. 1985. *Science and Civilisation in China*, Volume 5: *Chemistry and Chemical Technology*, Part 1: *Paper and Printing*. Cambridge, UK: Cambridge University Press.

Twitchett, Denis. 1983. *Printing and Publishing in Medieval China*. New York NY: Frederic C. Beil.

Underhill, Paco. 1999. *Why We Buy: The Science of Shopping*. New York, NY: Simon and Schuster.

Underhill, Paco. 2004. *The Call of the Mall*. New York, NY: Simon and Schuster.

Venturi, Robert, Denise Scott Brown, and Steven Izenour. 1977. *Learning from Las Vegas: The Forgotten Symbolism of Architectural Form*. Cambridge, MA: MIT Press.

Vigna, Paul and Michael J. Casey. 2015. *The Age of Cryptocurrency: How Bitcoin and Digital Money Are Challenging the Global Economic Order*. New York, NY: St Martin's Press.

Vise, David A. 2005. *The Google Story*. New York, NY: Delacorte Press.

Vološinov, V.N. 1927 [1976]. *Freudianism: A Marxist Critique*. Translated by I.R. Titunik. New York, NY: Academic Press.

Vološinov, V.N. 1929 [1973]. *Marxism and the Philosophy of Language*. Translated by L. Matejka and I.R. Titunik. Cambridge, MA: Harvard University Press.

von Steffelin, Christian. 2011. *Palast Der Republik, 1994–2010*. Ostfildern, Germany: Hatje Cantz Verlag.

Vygostky, Lev Semyonovich. 1934 [1986]. *Thought and Language*. Cambridge, MA: MIT Press.

Wajcman, Judy. 2015. *Pressed for Time: The Acceleration of Life in Digital Capitalism*. Chicago, IL: University of Chicago Press.

Wall, Alex. 2005. *Victor Gruen: From Urban Shop to New City*. Barcelona, Spain: Actar.

Wallach, Hans, Edwin B. Newman, and Mark R. Rosenzweig. 1949. "The Precedence Effect in Sound Localization." *The American Journal of Psychology* 62:315–36.

Warf, Barney and Thomas Champman. 2006. "Cathedrals of Consumption: A Political Phenomenology of Wal-Mart," pp. 163–78 in *Wal-Mart World: The World's Biggest*

Corporation in the Global Economy, edited by S.D. Brunn. New York, NY: Routledge.

Wark, McKenzie. 2004. *A Hacker Manifesto*. Cambridge, MA: Harvard University Press.

Wark, McKenzie. 2007. *Gamer Theory*. Cambridge, MA: Harvard University Press.

Wark, McKenzie. 2012. *Telesthesia: Communication, Culture and Class*. Cambridge, UK: Polity.

Weatherall, James Owen. 2013. *The Physics of Finance: How Science Has Taken Over Wall Street*. New York, NY: Houghton Mifflin.

Weaver, Warren. 1949 [1955]. "Translation," pp. 15–23 in *Machine Translation of Languages*, edited by W.N. Locke and A.D. Booth. Cambridge, MA: The Technology Press of MIT.

Wegener, Philipp. 1885 [1971]. "The Life of Speech," pp. 111–294 in *Speech and Reason: Language Disorder and Mental Disease*, edited by D.W. Abse. Charlottesville, VA: University Press of Virgina.

Wegener, Rebekah. 2016. "Studying Language in Society and Society through Language: Context and Multimodal Communication," pp. 227–48 in *Society in Language, Language in Society: Essays in Honour of Ruqaiya Hasan*, edited by W.L. Bowcher and J.Y. Liang. Berlin, Germany: Springer.

Weiffenbach, George and William Guier. 1998. "Genesis of Satellite Navigation." *Johns Hopkins APL Technical Digest* 19(1):14–7.

Weishar, Joseph. 1992. *Design for Effective Selling Space*. New York, NY: McGraw-Hill.

Welby, V. 1897. "A Royal Slave."*Fortnightly Review* 62:432–34.

Welby, V. 1903. *What Is Meaning? Studies in the Development of Meaning*. London, UK: Macmillan.

Welby, V. 1911. *Significs and Language: The Articulate Form of Our Expressive and Interpretative Resources*. London, UK: Macmillan.

Wendel, Delia Duong Ba. 2012. "The 1922 'Symphony of Sirens' in Baku, Azerbaijan." *Journal of Urban Design* 17(4):549–72.

Wertsch, James V. 1991. *Voices of the Mind*. Cambridge, MA: Harvard University Press.

West, Gladys B. 1986. *Data Processing System Specifications for the Geosat Satellite Radar Altimeter*. Report NSWC TR 86-149. Dahlgren, VA: Naval Surface Weapons Center.

Whorf, Benjamin Lee. 1936. "The Punctual and Segmentative Aspects of Verbs in Hopi." *Language* 12(2):127–31.

Whorf, Benjamin Lee. 1938. "Some Verbal Categories of Hopi." *Language* 14 (4):275–86.

Whorf, Benjamin Lee. 1950. "An American Indian Model of the Universe." *International Journal of American Linguistics* 16(2):67–72.

Whorf, Benjamin Lee. 1956. *Language, Thought and Reality: Selected Writings of Benjamin Lee Whorf*. Cambridge, MA: MIT Press.

Whyte, William H. 1988. *City: Rediscovering the Center*. New York, NY: Doubleday.

Wilks, Yorick. 2000. "Margaret Masterman," pp. 279–97 in *Early Years in Machine Translation: Memoirs and Biographies of Pioneers*, edited by W.J. Hutchins. Amsterdam, NL: John Benjamins.

Williams, Raymond. 1976. *Keywords: A Vocabulary of Culture and Society*. Glasgow, UK: Fontana/Croom Helm.

Williams, Sam. 2002. *Free as in Freedom: Richard Stallman's Crusade for Free Software*. Sebastapol, CA: O'Reilly.

Windley, Phillip J. and Devlin Daley. 2006, "A Framework for Building Reputation Systems." (www.windley.com/essays/2006/dim2006/framework_for_building_re putation_systems).

Wittenberg, David. 2013. *Time Travel: The Popular Philosophy of Narrative*. New York, NY: Fordham University Press.

Wittfogel, Karl A. 1957. *Oriental Despotism: A Comparative Study of Total Power*. New Haven, CT: Yale University Press.

Wittgenstein, Ludwig. 1933–34 [1958]. *Preliminary Studies for the "Philosophical Investigations," Generally Known as the Blue and Brown Books*. New York, NY: Harper and Row.

Wittgenstein, Ludwig. 1973. *Letters to C.K. Ogden*. Oxford, UK: Basil Blackwell.

Wolbert, Barbara. 2001. "De-Arranged Spaces: East German Art in the Museums of Unified Germany." *The Anthropology of East Europe Review* 19(1):57–64.

Wolin, Richard. 2000. "Untruth and Method: Nazism and the Complicities of Hans-Georg Gadamer." *New Republic* (May 15):36–45.

Wrege, Charles D. and Ronald G. Greenwood. 1991. *Frederick W. Taylor, the Father of Scientific Management: Myth and Reality*. Homewood, IL: Business One Irwin.

Wu, Yonghui, Mike Schuster, Zhifeng Chen, Quoc V. Le and Mohammad Norouzi. 2016. "Google's Neural Machine Translation System: Bridging the Gap between Human and Machine Translation." arXiv: 1609.08144v2.

Wyclif, John. c.1382 [1892]. *De Eucharista Tractatus*, edited by I. Loserth. London, UK: Trubner & Co.

Yates, Frances A. 1966 [1999]. *The Art of Memory*, Volume 3. London, UK: Routledge.

Yngve, Victor H. 2000. "Early Research at M.I.T.," pp. 39–72 in *Early Years in Machine Translation: Memoirs and Biographies of Pioneers*, edited by W.J. Hutchins. Amsterdam, NL: John Benjamins.

Young, Iris Marion. 1980. "Throwing Like a Girl: A Phenomenology of Feminine Body Comportment, Motility, and Spatiality." *Human Studies* 3(1):137–56.

Youngblood, Denise J. 2014. *Bondarchuk's War and Peace: Literary Classic to Soviet Cinematic Epic*. Lawrence, KS: University Press of Kansas.

Youyou, Wu, Michal Kosinski, and David Stillwell. 2015. "Computer-Based Personality Judgments Are More Accurate Than Those Made by Humans." *Proceedings of the National Academy of Sciences* 112(2):1036–40.

Yudell, Michael. 2014. *Race Unmasked: Biology and Race in the Twentieth Century*. New York, NY: Columbia University Press.

Yudell, Michael, Dorothy Roberts, Rob DeSalle, and Sarah Tishkoff. 2016. "Taking Race out of Human Genetics: Engaging a Century-Long Debate About the Role of Race in Science." *Science* 351(6273):564–65.

Zhai, ChengXiang and Sean Massung. 2016. *Text Data Management and Analysis: A Practical Introduction to Information Retrieval and Text Mining*. Williston, VT: ACM and Morgan & Claypool.

Index